COMMERCIAL REMEDIES: RESOLVING CONTROVERSIES

The law of commercial remedies gives rise to a number of important doctrinal, theoretical and practical controversies which deserve sustained and rigorous examination. This volume explores such controversies and suggests solutions directed at ensuring that the law is defensible, clear and just. With contributions from twenty-three leading academic and practitioner experts, this book addresses significant issues in the law which, taken together, range across the entire remedial jurisdiction as it applies to commercial disputes. The book focuses primarily on the resolution of controversies in the English law of commercial remedies, but recent developments elsewhere are also considered, especially in other common law jurisdictions. The result is a remarkably comprehensive coverage of the field which will be of relevance to academics, students, judges and practitioners. The aim has been to deal with the law as at 1 November 2016.

The chapters in this volume are the product of a conference held in Cambridge under the auspices of the Cambridge Private Law Centre, co-directed by Graham Virgo and Sarah Worthington.

COMMERCIAL REMEDIES: RESOLVING CONTROVERSIES

Edited by

GRAHAM VIRGO QC (HON)
University of Cambridge

SARAH WORTHINGTON QC (HON), FBA
University of Cambridge

CAMBRIDGE
UNIVERSITY PRESS

CAMBRIDGE
UNIVERSITY PRESS

University Printing House, Cambridge CB2 8BS, United Kingdom

One Liberty Plaza, 20th Floor, New York, NY 10006, USA

477 Williamstown Road, Port Melbourne, VIC 3207, Australia

4843/24, 2nd Floor, Ansari Road, Daryaganj, Delhi – 110002, India

79 Anson Road, #06–04/06, Singapore 079906

Cambridge University Press is part of the University of Cambridge.

It furthers the University's mission by disseminating knowledge in the pursuit of
education, learning, and research at the highest international levels of excellence.

www.cambridge.org
Information on this title: www.cambridge.org/9781107171329
DOI: 10.1017/9781316759905

First published 2017

Printed in the United Kingdom by Clays, St Ives plc

A catalogue record for this publication is available from the British Library.

Library of Congress Cataloging-in-Publication Data
Names: Virgo, Graham, editor. | Worthington, Sarah, editor
Title: Commercial remedies : resolving controversies / edited by Graham Virgo,
Sarah Worthington.
Description: Cambridge [UK] ; New York : Cambridge University Press, 2017.
Identifiers: LCCN 2017003192 | ISBN 9781107171329 (hardback)
Subjects: LCSH: Commercial law – England. | Remedies (Law) – England. |
BISAC: LAW / Corporate.
Classification: LCC KD1629 .C667 2017 | DDC 346.4207–dc23
LC record available at https://lccn.loc.gov/2017003192

ISBN 978-1-107-17132-9 Hardback

CONTENTS

CONTRIBUTORS

NEIL ANDREWS is Professor of Civil Justice and Private Law at the University of Cambridge

ANDREW BURROWS QC is Professor of the Law of England at the University of Oxford

MINDY CHEN-WISHART is Professor of the Law of Contract at the University of Oxford

CARMINE CONTE is formerly a Fellow at Homerton College, Cambridge

PAUL S DAVIES is Associate Professor of Law at the University of Oxford

MATTHEW DYSON is Associate Professor of Law at the University of Oxford

JAMES GOUDKAMP is Associate Professor of Law at the University of Oxford

AMY GOYMOUR is University Lecturer in Law at the University of Cambridge

SARAH GREEN is Associate Professor of Law at the University of Oxford

LOUISE GULLIFER is Professor of Commercial Law at the University of Oxford

RICHARD HOOLEY is University Lecturer in Law at the University of Cambridge

PAUL JARVIS is a Barrister at 6 King's Bench Walk, London

ADAM KRAMER is a Barrister at 3 Verulam Buildings, London

NICHOLAS J MCBRIDE is College Lecturer in Law at Pembroke College, Cambridge

LOUISE MERRETT is Reader in International Commercial Law at the University of Cambridge

JONATHAN MORGAN is University Senior Lecturer in Law at the University of Cambridge

JANET O'SULLIVAN is University Senior Lecturer in Law at the University of Cambridge

ANDREW SUMMERS is Associate Professor of Law at the London School of Economics

P G TURNER is University Lecturer in Law at the University of Cambridge

GRAHAM VIRGO QC is Professor of English Private Law at the University of Cambridge

STEPHEN WATTERSON is University Lecturer in Law at the University of Cambridge

CHARLIE WEBB is Lecturer in Law at the London School of Economics

SARAH WORTHINGTON QC is Downing Professor of the Laws of England at the University of Cambridge

ACKNOWLEDGEMENTS

The editors wish to note their gratitude for the financial support and encouragement from Clifford Chance, which funded the symposium on commercial remedies in July 2015. We also wish to thank Christopher Jenkins, Rachel Leow and Liron Shmilovits for their editorial assistance in the preparation of this volume.

TABLE OF CASES

PART I

Introduction

1

Commercial Remedies: Identifying Themes and Controversies

GRAHAM VIRGO AND SARAH WORTHINGTON

1.1 Remedies and their Importance

This is a volume on commercial remedies. Much of the genius of English commercial law rests on the success of its courts in delivering appropriate remedies. But success has never equated with complacency, and many of the issues underpinning the remedial framework are contested. This volume focuses on the controversies, with the goal of contributing to the debate which is essential to ensuring that the law is in the best possible state for commercial parties.

Common law jurisdictions are often caricatured as remedial rather than rights-based.[1] As with many caricatures, there is an essential truth here which makes the study of remedies in these jurisdictions vitally important. The necessary examination is not easy, however. The task is harder still for the judges who have, historically, borne the primary responsibility for building the common law legal regime from the ground up. This explains the focus of this collection of essays on unravelling some of the more challenging controversies.

What makes the task difficult is not simply the exacting process of building any coherent regime in a bottom-up way, somehow always balancing the pressure to deliver a regime which is certain and stable against the pressure to deliver one which is fair and flexible. There are other still greater difficulties. For a start, it is surprisingly difficult to explain exactly what is meant at law by a 'remedy'. That task is not made easier by confining the examination to commercial contexts, as this volume does. Even if this can be settled, once a regime takes a bottom-up remedial

---

[1] See William Blackstone, *Commentaries on the Laws of England*, VI, p 23, 1 Co Inst 95b, advancing the notion also expressed in legal maxims that 'where there is no remedy, there is no right': i.e. our rights are essentially measured by our remedies.

starting point, it seems nigh on impossible to hold to some clear and overarching useful meta-principles, and shake loose from an irresistible urge towards the pragmatic response. And if such a change in approach were managed, too many of the foundational principles underpinning commercial contractual engagements are still deeply contested. A coherent and stable regime cannot be built on shaky foundations. Finally, even assuming these foundational principles were settled, they would still necessarily come into conflict with each other, requiring difficult balancing exercises from the judges. All these various difficulties – the nature of a remedy, the drive to pragmatism, the challenge of conflicting foundational principles, and the inescapable need to balance competing goals – run as persistent threads through all the chapters in this volume. In this introductory chapter, however, something should be said to help draw out the difficulties which are in the sightlines.

1.2   The Nature of a Remedy

Put at its simplest, a remedy is 'a cure for something nasty';[2] it is a means of righting an undesirable situation. Legal maxims reinforce the notion that where there is no remedy, there is no right: our rights are measured by our remedies. Some rights merit better protection than others, we often say, suggesting that all depends on the nature of the right itself. But the common law has grown up from responses to facts before the court; it has grown up thinking first about appropriate remedies. Articulating the quality of rights is a descriptive exercise which necessarily comes later. True, however, once the description has stabilised, it aids analysis to start from the right and its appropriate categorisation, and move from there to the remedy which will arise on its infringement.

This later notion of rights generating remedies is implicit in the description of contract given by Lord Diplock in *Photo Production Ltd v Securicor Transport Ltd*:

> [A] contract is a source of primary legal obligations upon each party to it to procure that whatever he has promised will be done is done . . . Every failure to perform a primary obligation is a breach of contract. The secondary obligation on the part of the contract breaker to which it gives rise by implication of the common law is to pay monetary compensation to the other party for the loss sustained by him in consequence of the breach.[3]

[2] Peter Birks, 'Rights, Wrongs, and Remedies' (2000) 20 OJLS 1, 9.
[3] [1980] AC 827 (HL) 848–49.

This notion of primary and secondary obligations, with the secondary obligations being remedial, has dominated much of the scholarship in contract and tort in the recent past.[4] Yet even on its own terms this falls far short of describing the rich breadth of the remedial landscape. Moreover, even the mechanics may be flawed. Later scholars have pointed out, with some merit, that the remedy is hardly an obligation, at least as we normally think of obligations, and might be better described as a liability.[5]

But this too does not seem to quite capture the breadth of the issues in play. Peter Birks came far closer to our shared understanding. He noted that the word could be used in many contexts and with quite different meanings, but at root every remedy had one thing in common: as noted earlier, it provided 'a cure for something nasty'.[6] This headline notion of remedies is preferable, because it leaves open the source of the remedy (the courts, statute, the parties' own agreement), and whether the remedy is put in place before or after the nasty event.

It is this broadest possible conception of remedies that is adopted here. The chapters in this volume range across remedies delivered via the default rules of the law of contract, torts and unjust enrichment; it also includes those provided for by the parties themselves; and there is even a chapter on the remedies arising under criminal law, as well as certain other private law statutes. These various remedies may themselves be personal or proprietary, monetary or by way of specific relief, and they may be ordered by the court or obtainable through self-help. They may arise as a result of statute, common law default rules, or contractual provisions adopted by the parties themselves. All contribute to the landscape of commercial remedies.

A proper understanding of all these remedial responses is enormously illuminating. It often reveals the nuances of previously imperfectly understood rights and obligations. This volume aims to contribute to that endeavour. The focus is exclusively on remedies in the commercial sphere, where disputes involve commercial parties, not consumers. Commercial parties receive less paternalistic protection from statute; they appear to be given greater leeway in settling the terms of their engagements; and, finally, assessments of remedies can generally take place without concern for the

---

[4] One of its most vocal advocates was Peter Birks. This taxonomy underpinned much of his thinking about private law. See in particular Birks (n 2).

[5] See various writings of Stephen A Smith, especially 'Duties, Liabilities, and Damages' (2011–12) 125 *Harvard LR* 1727.

[6] Birks (n 2) 9, with the various meanings of the word 'remedy' considered at 9–17.

reality of consent to the engagement itself or for the potential domestic fallout when remedies are ordered. Of course, commercial parties differ widely in their sophistication. We have not concerned ourselves directly with that issue, although occasionally its ramifications emerge in discussions of particular types of remedies.

In pursuing our examination of all this detail, what becomes clear remarkably quickly is that, despite the enormous number of commercial deals which take place, and the years of effort in refining the rules on remedies, so much still remains contested. It was for this reason that a symposium on commercial remedies was organised by the Cambridge Private Law Centre in July 2015 to encourage rigorous doctrinal and theoretical analysis of the issues. This volume is the result of that endeavour.

The goal was not to write a textbook on legal remedies. It was to focus on current controversies, and do so across the full range of remedies in commercial law. The idea was for each author to subject a particular issue to penetrating and critical examination, and then for those early assessments to be shared in discussion amongst the authors themselves, with the assistance of a number of practitioners and judges. All the chapters presented here have been revised in the light of that useful and challenging discussion, and occasionally also in light of new input from the courts. Although the focus of attention was exclusively on areas of controversy, the result is a remarkably comprehensive coverage of the field of commercial remedies. That in itself merits comment. It may at first seem a damning indictment of the state of the law, but if remedies are as important as we believe them to be, then it is not surprising that they are contested, nor is it surprising that they must evolve to meet changing commercial demands. The true test of the success of the English jurisdiction is not so much that its remedial rules are clear and settled, but that they are clear and sufficiently flexible to meet the developing needs of the parties relying on them. But clarity is key, and here there is undoubtedly work to be done.

Nevertheless, something more is clearly at stake in this area. The controversies discussed here have not arisen because the law is struggling to contend with fast-moving commercial needs. Indeed, the foundational principles of commerce have been remarkably immutable. What does change is the subject matter of the dealings, the nature of the counterparties, the process of engagement, and the global reach of the endeavour. But commercial parties still make much the same demands of the legal regime which supports their endeavour as they always have: clear rules of engagement to determine when promises become binding; efficient and effective rules on interpretation where there are disputes over what was agreed; sensible rules on variation, waiver and dispute resolution; and finally, and perhaps most importantly, default rules, including default rules on remedies, to address the practicalities when the contract is silent. Given these rather stable requirements, why, it might be asked, is the remedial landscape still so beset by uncertainties and controversies? As noted earlier, it is suggested in this chapter that the instability is driven primarily by the drive to pragmatism, the challenge of conflicting foundational principles, and the practical difficulty of balancing competing but equally important goals in a compelling and satisfactory manner. Each of these sources of uncertainty and contention continue to infect and unsettle all aspects of remedies. The result is a landscape shot through with instances where it seems that pragmatism overrides doctrine and principle, discretion weakens rights, and muddled analysis risks weakening all.

1.3   The Drive to Pragmatism

Pragmatism is unavoidable. In the arena of commercial remedies it comes in various guises. Perhaps the first pragmatic driver in developing an attractive legal regime and providing individual remedies is an understanding that the law exists to support and serve society, here the commercial community, and must necessarily mould itself to meet their needs and expectations.[7] Obviously such needs and expectations do not necessarily all pull in the same direction. Tugging in one direction is the demand from commercial parties for a legal regime which is clear, simple and predictable. If the law responds pragmatically, then in this instance it will be well aligned with the approach advocated by those preferring to focus on headline principles underpinned by rigorous doctrinal theory, and with clear rules of operation. True, the particular principles in issue might well be shaped in different ways by each group, but the structural outcome is one which ought to suit both pragmatists and theorists. Morgan in his chapter argues for developments in the field of commercial remedies to be in this direction, in particular starting with commercial expectations and only then reasoning from these to appropriate legal rules and principles, not the other way around. Merrett, too, makes the

---

[7] David Campbell, 'Contract Law and Contract Practice: Bridging the Gap between Legal Reasoning and Commercial Expectation' (2014) 130 LQR 526.

important point that an increasing number of commercial transactions are now global, and if the law is to be intelligible across national boundaries then it is essential to have clear and stable rules which can be articulated intelligibly to those outside the common law legal castle.

This particular seam of pragmatism would thus seem to be perfectly aligned with the aspirations of the camp preferring to adopt stable and unambiguous overarching principles underpinned by clear-cut rules. However, although this described alignment is accurate in theory, the practice is judicial reluctance – and perhaps quite properly so – to do anything which smacks of radical change to existing rules, sometimes seemingly regardless of how compelling are the arguments from both principle and pragmatism.[8] No doubt this approach renders the law more stable, but it also renders it more hidebound. Which is worse is sometimes debatable.

But pragmatism can also work in other ways. If remedies are truly to provide a cure for something nasty, then the particularities of the situation must be brought into play. These realities include consideration not only of what remedy is available, but also how it can best be obtained. This can sometimes lead to counter-productive or counterintuitive outcomes. Most obviously, if the potential benefits of litigating are outweighed by the risk of a failed claim and its associated legal costs, then parties are likely to be left without a practical remedy, no matter what their legal rights might suggest to the contrary. This is pragmatism writ large, and is not discussed in this volume. However, the search for alternative and better means of protection of rights and recovery of remedies is a constant one, and Dyson and Jarvis's chapter reminds us that assistance can come from unexpected quarters. Their chapter highlights the potential personal advantages to commercial parties of various remedies which are sought and obtained through the criminal courts at the instigation of public officials rather than the parties themselves. This of course has advantages and disadvantages, and their chapter discusses the pragmatic use of such opportunities to best effect.

In the same vein, pragmatic assessments of the likely success in litigation will also need to pay regard to matters of proof, both proof of causation and proof of quantification. Much of the remedial framework

---

[8] Lord Robert Walker, 'Developing the Common Law: How Far Is Too Far?' (2013) 37 *Melbourne ULR* 232. See, e.g., the approaches in *Prest v Petrodel Resources Ltd* [2013] UKSC 34, [2013] 2 AC 415 (not discussed in this volume, but illustrative in this context); and *Cavendish Square Holding BV v Talal El Makdessi; ParkingEye Ltd v Beavis* [2015] UKSC 67, [2016] AC 1172.

of commercial law (and perhaps all law) is built on the need to prove actual facts and probable facts, and actual causation and probable causation. It is on such matters that compensatory and other varieties of damages claims are built. This creates enormous practical problems. A number of these are highlighted in Kramer's chapter on proving contract damages and the significance of presumptions. He suggests that in practice the most important legal principles in this area are not those concerning remoteness, mitigation or causation, but what he calls the 'messy and largely unappealable' business of proving the 'what if' question: i.e. what would have happened had there not been a breach of contract? This crystal ball gazing is given pragmatic assistance by the law's recognition of certain presumptions. But this in itself raises another issue for the remedial landscape: what is the reasonable and proper boundary between proof and presumption? Where should the line be drawn in order to provide reasonable legal rules for the protection of both parties to the commercial deal?

In this area of proof, not every problem is a practical one. There are occasions where the law has tied itself in knots over issues which might have been better resolved by a clear eye to exactly what facts (or causes or consequences) require proof, and why. If this is not done, then terrible muddles are likely. Green's chapter on lost chances makes the point that loss of a chance is a legitimate form of damage, but a lost chance of a successful legal action is not. In drawing that clear distinction and then pursuing its logical consequences to their inevitable ends, Green manages to cut through a confusing body of existing case law to extract clear and defensible principles. Even when pragmatic choices must be made, they are invariably best made against a backdrop of clear legal principle. The rule of law would be set at naught if this were not so.

All this talk of pragmatism would seem to lend support to the intuition of Oliver Wendell Holmes, that '[t]he life of the law has not been logic; it has been experience',[9] an idea perhaps put more elegantly and forcibly by David Ibbetson, at least so far as it applies to the issues of concern in this volume:

> Law cannot be treated purely as an intellectual system, a game to be played by scholars whose aim is to produce a perfectly harmonious structure of rules. It is something which operates at a practical level in society, and has to be understood as such.[10]

---

[9] Oliver Wendell Holmes Jr, *The Common Law* (Little & Brown 1881 or Macmillan 1882) 1.

[10] David Ibbetson, 'Comparative Legal History: A Methodology' in Anthony Musson and Chantal Stebbings (eds), *Making Legal History: Approaches and Methodologies*

But that 'something which operates at a practical level in society' also has to define a legal regime which will operate according to the rule of law. In particular, like cases must be treated alike. The challenge is obvious. Meeting the challenge requires a clear, robust and rigorous understanding of the relevant legal principles so as to ensure that their core underpinnings are adhered to, yet an understanding which is sufficiently nuanced to enable appropriate application in a variety of contexts. Many of the modern controversies surrounding commercial remedies reflect shortcomings on this front, and most chapters devote at least some pages to the issues.

All of this begins to sound as though the landscape of commercial remedies is enormously complex, and the terrain exceptionally rocky. In the face of that, a good map is much to be desired. But what sort of map will best serve the needs of the various stakeholders? High-level principles are all very well – and indeed essential – but as in so many areas of life, the devil really is in the detail. Nevertheless, that detail can be constructed far more thoughtfully and effectively if a clear overview of the issues to be dealt with is to hand. Civilian jurisdictions provide this map by way of civil codes. American lawyers have their restatements. And across European and international boundaries there are model laws, perhaps rather more effective in alerting us to our differences and enriching our understandings than in providing a model code designed to govern real commercial practice, but useful nevertheless. In England, we have little to match any of this.[11] Some universities still teach Roman law precisely to provide novice lawyers with an intelligible overview of a complete legal system. Designing an equivalent means of overview for the legal regime of a complex modern society is difficult, but in this volume Andrews' chapter addresses the possibility of a code governing commercial remedies, and proposes a range of essential elements.

Perhaps from all of this it is obvious that a healthy degree of pragmatism is essential in framing a workable legal regime, especially in the commercial arena, but that there is also a deep-seated practical and

---

(Cambridge University Press 2012) 131, 135, and cited in Mark Leeming, 'Theories and Principles Underlying the Development of the Common Law: The Statutory Elephant in the Room' (2013) 36 UNSWLJ 1002, 1002.

[11] Of course there are statutes, but none to match the approach taken in civilian codes. And analogies to the US Restatements are now provided by Andrew Burrows, *A Restatement of the English Law of Unjust Enrichment* (Oxford University Press 2012) and Andrew Burrows, *A Restatement of the English Law of Contract* (Oxford University Press 2016).

theoretical need for clear foundational principles if the pragmatically conceived regime is to function according to the rule of law. It is to these foundational principles that we turn next.

1.4   The Challenge of Conflicting Foundational Principles

Moving from pragmatism to principle, it might be thought that any debate would be short. Legal principles are surely the foundation of any legal regime; they define and shape its structure. Without them it is difficult to apply even the simplest of rules to anything but the most straightforward of contexts.[12] Despite this, a number of foundational principles underpinning the commercial remedies regime remain deeply contested, and vigorously so. Several of the most significant are noted here.

1.4.1   Party Autonomy vs Judicial Control

Contracts are private arrangements. The promises made by one party to the other are entered into voluntarily. It is not difficult to see why a developed society would give legal recognition to these arrangements, and provide either judicial remedies or statutory remedies for breach. But even with this supplementary court-ordered input, the very context suggests that party autonomy should be sovereign. In particular, it might be assumed that the parties themselves would be able to decide which obligations they are prepared to undertake, and the conditions and contingencies surrounding them. Yet many of the most controversial areas of commercial remedies are those which address the issues arising when just these sorts of private arrangements are put in place. Notwithstanding the fully informed agreement by both sides, nor the inability of the courts to articulate the particular problem they seek to redress, many of these arrangements risk court bans or restrictions on their operation. This looks all the more odd when the same courts are at pains to stress that the parties remain free to settle their primary obligations; the concern is only with obligations which are remedial.[13] It seems doubtful that the line between 'right' and 'remedy' can be defined with the necessary clarity to invoke such a discriminatory rule,[14] but without

---

[12] *Makdessi* (n 8) [3].

[13] See Mark P Gergen, 'A Theory of Self-Help Remedies in Contract' (2009) 89 *Boston University Law Review* 1397.

[14] Birks (n 2).

any supporting rationale it is not at all clear why it is necessary to trouble over the distinctions in any event.

At its root, this opens up the general question of when the courts should be able to step in to curtail the freedom of the parties to determine the terms of their engagement, including specific remedial consequences. For Morgan, the courts' common law scheme of remedies should be regarded as a default regime, and one which (with limited exceptions) should be capable of modification by the parties themselves. Many other authors in this volume take the same line, favouring party autonomy and freedom of contract over judicial intervention and constraint. The issues emerge predictably with a vengeance in Part IV, dealing with agreed and party-specific remedies. Those authors coming down clearly on the side of party autonomy include Gullifer, Hooley and Worthington.

But not all authors are persuaded, and certainly not in all contexts. On the side of freedom of contract and party autonomy, Morgan speculates that the remedy of specific performance should be enforced whenever it is agreed by the parties, whether or not it would otherwise be available. This puts party autonomy centre stage as the principle having primacy in the area of commercial contracts. But Chen-Wishart provides a nuanced defence of the current rules, where specific performance is the exception even when ordered by the court, and the parties themselves would have no claim to including it as an enforceable term of their agreed engagement. Moreover, she does this by resort to a more subtle understanding of party autonomy itself, and not by resort to some superior overriding principle. There are lessons for everyone from the careful and detailed analyses in all these chapters.

1.4.2 The Importance of Promises

Commercial contracts involve promises. But where one party has failed to keep her promise, the default remedy is not that she should be compelled to perform her promise, but rather that she should compensate the other party for the failure to perform. From this it might be assumed that keeping promises is not one of the key objectives of commercial remedies. A number of authors take issue with this, at least without serious qualification. Webb, for example, in his chapter on performance damages, is at pains to distinguish between a party's interest in performance and the various specific or monetary remedies which might be awarded. He concludes that the legal duty on the defendant to perform does not necessarily disappear because the counterparty cannot enforce performance. What is needed is a principled description of how and why the particular remedial choices are being made. This is not what is generally done. The courts typically take entitlement to compensatory damages not only as the most common default remedy, but also as the mandatory default remedy unless proof is advanced that it is inappropriate in the circumstances; only then will the alternatives – specific performance, damages reflecting the performance interest, disgorgement damages, etc – be granted. Some explanation of this is necessary. The idea is taken up again in the next subsection.

A party's interest in performance, rather than compensatory damages, emerges on the remedial landscape in other contexts. O'Sullivan and Summers both deal in different ways with the problem of remedies following repudiation, where one party has indicated to the other that it will not proceed with the promised performance. Both criticise the current law, and confront directly the question of whether the innocent party can simply reject the repudiatory breach and continue with its own performance, so as to claim in full the payments which then become due, and can do this notwithstanding that the counterparty no longer desires performance. The right to behave in this way is at one level a further test of the value placed on the performance interest; at another level it also tests judicial reaction to the balancing exercise necessary when rights to terminate and rights to perform clash head on. Perhaps predictably, it is the 'remedial rights' which are constrained – the right to perform is not an unqualified right – but the careful analysis in these chapters provides for a deeper and more subtle understanding of the scope of the performance interest and the importance of promising.

If these chapters and others touching the same theme show anything, it is that our legal regime has not yet settled on an answer to the importance of promising. The most telling illustration of this is the common law's preference for compensatory damages rather than performance, especially where these compensatory damages can so easily fail to provide the equivalent of actual performance, leaving parties instead to damages measured by equivalences in economic position. This is hardly the same thing. The distinction is most telling in all those contracts where the primary objective is something other than attaining a market position. The failure to nail these foundational principles is reflected in difficulties identified in almost every chapter in this volume, but see especially the chapters by Webb on the performance interest, Chen-Wishart on specific performance, Davies on injunctions and Worthington on penalties.

1.4.3   The Legitimate Objectives of Contracts

The problems just highlighted in relation to the importance of promises flow over into a tension across the remedial regime about the permissible objectives which can be pursued by commercial parties in their contracts. Comment has already been made on the approach taken by the common law default rules on remedies. If the default rule typically only protects market measures, there is an implicit message about the contracting purposes which will be supported by the legal regime.[15] But recent years have seen rather dramatic changes on this front. Reformulated judicial approaches to express termination clauses and penalty clauses together reflect a sea change in approach, explicitly recognising as legitimate parties' interests which go well beyond compensatory damages. Now that the genie is out of the bottle, albeit in the context of these narrow doctrines, there may be no putting it back, and the ideas could flow out into the general rules on damages: see the chapters by Hooley and Worthington.

But the tensions range far more widely. Despite frequent nods to the value of party autonomy, there are a good number of circumstances where party autonomy and agreed commercial objectives are subordinated to judicially mandated goals. Sometimes that subordination is completely proper, as when contracting goals conflict with the general laws of the land. In those circumstances, proper pursuit of social goals and the protection of non-contracting parties require interference in the agreed arrangements between contracting parties. Gullifer provides an illustration of this type of conflict in her consideration of whether flawed assets should be governed according to their terms, or should be regarded as arrangements in breach of the insolvency-triggered anti-deprivation rule (and, consequently, unravelled, with benefits then flowing to unsecured creditors).

But in other instances the conflict between agreed contractual objectives made plain by the parties and contradictory judicially mandated goals seems impossible to explain. Historically this has been most obvious in the broad cluster of cases concerning party-agreed provision of self-help remedies. The judicial starting point in all these cases, historically, has been that the latitude shown to agreements on primary obligations disappears in the context of agreements on secondary or remedial obligations (despite the difficulty in drawing the line between

---

[15] Ralph M Cunnington, 'The Inadequacy of Damages as a Remedy for Breach of Contract' in Charles EF Rickett (ed), *Justifying Private Law Remedies* (Hart Publishing 2008).

these two categories). It was then difficult to avoid the conclusion that the courts were effectively insisting that not only were common law contractual remedies the default rules in the absence of party provision, they were in large measure also the mandatory rules in defiance of party provision. There has been a good deal of rolling back from that position, especially in the last decade. All of the chapters in Part IV address this particular tension, assessing the important and common commercial contractual provisions relating to express termination clauses (Hooley), penalty clauses (Worthington), deposit clauses (Conte) and flawed assets clauses (Gullifer). There is much to be learnt from these chapters on the difficult tension between freedom of contract and permitting the parties to control their own relationship, and court review of any arrangements which smack of remedial intention. In this area, too, detailed and critical analysis of legal principle is rendered well-nigh impossible given a general failure to pin down the principles which are working in conflict with the principle of freedom of contract.

1.4.4   The Role of Doctrinal Analysis: Principle and Policy in Practice

This final challenge is of a different order, but nevertheless is a challenge of sufficient significance to put it in this foundational category. The conflict here is between the pragmatic approach (see the earlier discussion) and the theoretical approach. The reality of course is that these are not pitted against each other; in an ideal world they work in complementary ways. It is obviously self-serving for academics, in a volume written largely by academics, to suggest that theoretical analyses are important. But practitioners and judges are equally committed in the same endeavour. Theoretical analyses enable defensible principles and sensible rules to be drawn out of what would otherwise be an ill-classified mass of case law. They assist in identifying the reasons and rationales behind various doctrines, and inconsistencies and gaps in the law. They enable not only a better understanding of the current state of the law, but also provide advice for the resolution of controversies and suggested direction for the future development of the law.

Every chapter in this volume reflects that ambition and its execution. This exercise is especially useful in areas where decades of case law have been subjected to a variety of possible analyses, none of which has successfully commanded overwhelming support. The outcome is then often a growing muddle as advocates latch onto whichever approaches best serve their current needs and modern cases pick up diverging themes. At some stage a higher court will then have to cut through the swathes of competing arguments and settle on a preferred approach, preferably one which is defensible because it is obviously right rather than one which is accepted merely because it is authoritative. Academic analyses can provide useful guidance in this endeavour. Chapters which are particularly illustrative of just such guidance are those on the controversial topics of subrogation (Watterson), rescission (McBride), exemplary damages (Goudkamp), gain-based remedies (Virgo), set-off (Turner) and flawed assets (Gullifer).

But the added advantage of presenting all these different analyses in one volume is that very often the sum is greater than any of the parts. The views expressed in this volume are not all consistent, but the challenge of considering and assimilating opposing approaches is typically an essential route towards the best possible outcome. To that end, there are clear differences in views, or at least in the subtleties underpinning those views, expressed by Virgo and Watterson (on the role of the proprietary interest in unjust enrichment), Conte and Worthington (on deposits), and Chen-Wishart and Davies (on court orders for performance). Those disputes merely add to the richness of the arguments which inform these debates on issues which are undoubtedly controversial.

But the 'sum is greater than the parts' applies more broadly. The practical impetus to a better understanding of our law is often greatly enhanced by the challenge of dealing with competing remedies available on the same facts. There is little else which is quite so useful in ensuring that doctrine, policy and outcomes across the remedial landscape remain coherent. Just these types of conflicts are evident where there is remedial competition between compensation and performance, compensation and disgorgement, or personal and proprietary remedies, etc. Similar challenges also come from the competition between private law and public law approaches (Dyson and Jarvis on the criminal law; Gullifer on insolvency law), and between general law and party-agreed approaches (as in the various chapters noted earlier), or even between private law statutes and general common law rules (see Burrows on the rules on interest payments).

Finally, an understanding of our own jurisdiction is inevitably enhanced by raising our heads above the parapet and looking at what is done elsewhere. Very little academic scholarship and few judicial analyses pay sufficient attention to this. But in one area it is unavoidable – conflict of laws. Moreover, since commerce is often transnational, private international lawyers are often superbly well placed to point out the oddities in our own jurisdiction (see Merrett on private international law conflicts).

However, in considering all this high theory, its practical purposes must not be forgotten. As Chris Patten famously said (speaking of politicians, but the advice is equally apt for academic lawyers), most people can do vision at the drop of a hat; practical implementation is far more difficult. Put another way, it is often easier to get from A to Z than from A to B. In all these theoretical analyses it is important to cover both options.

1.5   Balancing Competing Goals

Beyond the important foundational uncertainties just noted, there are also a number of more specific legal, practical and policy themes which operate across the remedial landscape. All of these present problems and difficulties which might be resolved more easily by looking across the various instances where difficulties arise, and seeking coherent responses which meet the underlying general concerns.

1.5.1   The Interaction between the Parties' Own Arrangements, the Common Law and Statute

As lawyers, we are used to the idea that a particular set of facts may be amenable to analysis in different ways: the same facts can give rise to different claims, and different remedies, depending on the rights and remedies being pursued. We are also used to the fact that, typically, it is the claimant's right to elect the remedy which operates most favourably for her. But across the remedial terrain the courts' own approach can have a profound impact, effectively barring certain party-preferred approaches and channelling adoption of others. Some sense of this tension has already emerged in discussion in the earlier sections. Illustrations are not difficult to find.

To be clear, the issue here is not the possibility of parties pursuing inconsistent claims[16] or asserting rights which deliver double recovery. It is the far more important issue that alternative claims can be closed off because the courts impose their own remedial hierarchy, insisting that certain avenues are not open unless, for other reasons, the court-favoured option is itself closed off.

---

[16] In those circumstances the proper approach is described in *Tang Man Sit v Capacious Investments Ltd* [1996] AC 514 (PC).

Perhaps the easiest and most familiar cases are those where the remedial competition is between different statutory remedies (see Goymour
discussing the remedies for vindicating ownership rights in real property), or between common law and statutory remedies[17] (see Burrows
discussing claims for interest payments). Very often these problems can
be resolved by the rules and priorities expressed or implicit in the
statutory provisions themselves. The answers are then particular to the
statute in issue, and do not provide general guidance on the debate on
conflicting goals under discussion here.

The question is more difficult where the competition is between
different common law options. For example, Summers' chapter looks at
the interaction between debt claims (claims for an agreed sum), which
can obviously only be made when the contract creating them is kept alive,
and the conflicting claims of the counterparty seeking to repudiate the
contract. Faced with this competition, what should the courts do?
The answer cannot depend on who gets to court first, but requires
a seriously nuanced understanding of the objectives of contract law and
its remedial framework.

The same difficulty underpins the common problem that specific
performance, injunctions and all the different varieties of damages claims
other than compensatory damages are all said to be available only where
compensatory damages are considered to be an inadequate remedy. This
expresses a very strong judicially imposed hierarchy of remedies, without, it must be said, much by way of explanation or justification. Chen-
Wishart's chapter goes some way to explaining the preference. But given
that contracting is all about voluntary promises between the parties, it is
a serious question whether the courts should be imposing remedial
constraints of the form just described. Of course, this rule would itself
lose all its practical force if it were routinely recognised that contracts can
be entered into in pursuit of interests beyond market measures of gain.
That, in turn, plays into various issues addressed in the earlier sections.
But even without such a move, Virgo's chapter on gain-based remedies
considers this limiting principle and finds it wanting, noting in any event
that the division between compensation for loss suffered and restitution
of a gain made is not as clear as is often thought. By way of illustration he
suggests that remedies granted by way of the 'hypothetical bargain'
measure, or 'negotiation damages', indicate a more flexible approach
from the courts.

---

[17] See the discussion of this conflict in Leeming (n 10).

More difficult still are those cases where the question before the court –
even if not put to them by either of the parties to the contract – is whether
the court should afford protection to third parties who are not before it in
any guise. This issue emerges in Davies' discussion of damages in lieu of
injunctions, especially when nuisance is claimed: damages may satisfy the
party before the court; but an injunction might well serve a more general
public interest. Similarly, Gullifer's chapter on flawed assets considers the
interests of third-party unsecured creditors who are potentially disadvantaged by the agreed arrangements between contracting parties.

All these issues can be presented as instances of conflict between
different goals of contract law, where the courts must settle a priority.
But that cannot be done in a convincing or coherent way across all these
instances unless it is underpinned by a compelling rationale. At some
stage it will become essential to be clearer about the role of party
autonomy and the importance of promising, both as between the parties
to the deal and as between strangers affected by the deal.

1.5.2   Judicial Discretion

At one level, all the issues discussed in the previous section raise matters
which could lay claim to being a result of the exercise of judicial discretion.
However, the suggestion advanced there was that what is really needed is
a clear set of principles and a rationale for action. If that were the case, then
all that would be required of the courts would be the usual application of
principle to facts – not necessarily an easy exercise in itself, but not one
which raises the spectre of judicial discretion in the sense intended here.

Across the remedial landscape, however, the issue of potential palm
tree justice and the role of judicial discretion in the control over remedies
is widely discussed by commentators. That detail has not been repeated
in this volume, although that is not to undervalue its significance.
Consider by way of illustration the hotly contested debate over discretionary remedialism in the context of proprietary remedies ordered by
way of constructive trust. In this regard the approach in England is often
pitted against the approach taken in the rest of the common law world[18]
(see Virgo's analysis of the remedial constructive trust).

[18] Simon Evans, 'Defending Discretionary Remedialism' (2001) 23 *Sydney L Rev* 463; Lord
Neuberger, 'The Remedial Constructive Trust – Fact or Fiction' (Banking Services and
Finance Law Association Conference, Queenstown, New Zealand, August 2014) <www
.supremecourt.uk/docs/speech-140810.pdf>; JD Heydon, 'Commentary on Lord
Neuberger's "The Remedial Constructive Trust – Fact or Fiction" Queenstown, New

What is of more concern in this volume is the crucial discretion exercised by judges in reconfiguring and restating the general common law remedial rules themselves, and, of only marginally lesser importance, the discretion exercised by judges in awarding or declining to award specific remedies to particular claimants.

Taking the first of these, the judges themselves show great reluctance to reformulate overarching common law rules.[19] In the modern context, this is perhaps seen most dramatically in the penalties jurisdiction (Worthington), and perhaps also in relation to subrogation (Watterson). And yet respected commentators have often made the point that if the law is to be set on stable but commercially useful foundations then restatements based on more compelling principles may sometimes be necessary, and complete revisions and new inventions may also be demanded. All of these areas raise potential conflicts between the role of the courts and the role of the legislature, and problems of democratic deficit. Taken too far, however, this principled caution could condemn the common law itself. Its underpinnings are judicial, not legislative, and so far we have not decided that this approach should be completely abolished in favour of legislation by elected representatives.

Moving from those grand themes to simpler issues, judicial discretion is also crucially important in remedies which are roundly recognised as essentially discretionary. All the performance remedies are in this category, and the difficulties faced by the court and the concerns which should motivate their decisions need careful articulation. In that context see especially the chapters by Chen-Wishart (noting that orders for specific performance need to take into account the individual human dynamic, protecting a more nuanced understanding of party autonomy and engaging with substantive and procedural fairness) and by Summers (noting the distinctions between injunctions which might simply work as economic bargaining tools, and those in respect of personal services, especially where there is loss of confidence between the parties).

The point to note in all these areas is that convincing, robust and compelling exercises of judicial discretion are made very difficult when the goals of private law in general and commercial remedies in particular

Zealand 10 August 2014' (2015) <www.eiseverywhere.com/file_uploads/118066829 b9658bdab9146d9c3cb1f30_P1-HonDysonHeydonAC.pdf> accessed 12 July 2016; Paul Finn, 'Equitable Doctrine and Discretion in Remedies' in WR Cornish and others (eds), *Restitution Past, Present and Future* (Hart Publishing 1998); Justice William Gummow, 'Equity: Too Successful?' (2003) 77 *Australian Law Journal* 30, 41.
[19] Walker (n 8).

are unclear. This is especially so where it is not only the parties' interests which are in play, but also a public interest concerning parties not before the court (as in nuisance cases or insolvency cases).

1.5.3   Practical Matters

Finally, it is necessary to return to and repeat the importance of practical issues in delivering commercial remedies. Whatever the relevant principles might mandate as theoretically possible, when the parties come before the courts to assert their claims, they are inevitably constrained by matters of proof, whether proof of the facts generating the claim itself, or proof of causation, or proof of quantification. Remedies will be unavailable, whatever the theoretical claims, unless the factual realities can be presented in a robust way to the court.

But practical matters are not limited to proof of facts or probabilities. There is a broad consensus that the legal regime for commercial remedies should be clear, simple and predictable. In practice, and as a matter of practicality, laws outside this class are less useful than those within it (see the chapters by Morgan and Andrews).

1.6   Conclusion

Returning to where we started, our rights are defined by our remedies. In this volume the discussion of remedies is broadly conceived to encompass judicial, statutory and party-agreed responses to problems arising between contracting commercial parties.

The common law regime is built from the ground up. This is the source of the notion that our rights are defined by our remedies. But for such a system to be described as a legal regime, and under equally telling pressures from commercial parties themselves, there is inevitably a fast retreat to certainty in the courts. This is amply evident from the modern report card for 'UK commercial law': its central proposition is, to be sure, that the common law provides flexibility, party autonomy, and freedom of contract, but, above all, it provides certainty, enabling commercial parties to predict the limits that the law places on individual and institutional behaviour, and providing precise guidelines for personal and corporate behaviour.

But in all this certainty there is surely a downside. The advantages come at a price, possibly a high price. The capacity to innovate and move with the times is likely to disappear at exactly the same rate that certainty and predictability and all the other advantages just noted are being delivered. The parliamentary mechanism cannot possibly cope with the gap that is left, and this is happening at a time where the need for the law to innovate is patently greater than it has ever been. Could common law courts now deliver a *Donoghue v Stevenson*,[20] or the trust, or different forms of security, or equitable property rules, or performance-based remedies, or proprietary-based remedies supported by tracing?

If the answer to those questions is no, then where does that leave us? We cannot solve these problems by pragmatic response, notwithstanding that this is commonly said to be the English genius. Instead, we need detailed, rigorous, robust focus on principle and policy and hard doctrinal analysis. If we do not know the purposes behind the provision of particular rights, then we are hardly in a position to propose appropriate remedies. To that end, the courts, too, need to be clear about their own responses to contractual rights and what counts as a breach, and to commercial wrongs and what counts as an appropriate remedy. If we do not know how important party autonomy is, or how important promises are, or whether contracts are intended to deliver performance or something else, then we are hardly in a position to construct a rational regime of commercial remedies.

The chapters which follow address the various difficulties and controversies encountered in building the remedial regime for commercial contracts from the ground up, and in undertaking any necessary repairs and reshaping of the foundations under the existing edifice without causing the entire structure to collapse.

---

[20] [1932] AC 562 (HL).

On the Nature and Function of Remedies for Breach of Contract

JONATHAN MORGAN

2.1 Introduction

Contract law's function is to give effect to the preferences of its clients. The choices made by contracting parties are just as central for the question of remedies (the means for enforcing their agreements) as to 'substance'. It is anyway doubtful that a distinction between 'content' and 'remedies' is feasible since agreeing to do *X* cannot ultimately be divorced from the degree of *X*'s enforceability. Freedom of contract should apply as fully to party-agreed remedies as to any other contract term. The remedies supplied by law should govern breach only in default of agreed remedy terms.

Of course, freedom of contract is not absolute. Enforcement is subject to countervailing reasons of public policy; parties are not permitted to contract out of rules such as *ex turpi causa non oritur actio*. But apart from the illegality doctrine, most of the 'immutable' (or 'mandatory') rules in the law of contract regulate structural power imbalances – such as those between businesses and consumers. Many of these rules are plainly inapplicable to commercial contracts.[1] Limits on freedom of commercial contracting require strong public interest justifications.[2]

This might seem an implausible account of contract remedies – one incomplete to the point of distortion. After all, while the content of an agreement is (everybody accepts) basically a matter for each pair of

---

[1] Not *all*: for example, the narrow common law doctrines of force (physical duress) and fraud are mandatory across the board.

[2] See Michael Bridge and Jo Braithwaite, 'Private Law and Financial Crises' (2013) 13 Jo Corp LS 361, 363: 'The role of private law in the financial markets is first and foremost a facilitative one . . . English law, in particular, is not heavy handed when it comes to public policy. Instead, what private law can offer in an uncertain world boils down essentially to two things: contractual certainty and dependable property rights.'

contractors to decide, the law has developed an extensive and elaborate body of remedies applicable to all breaches of contract. True enough. But remedy 'doctrines' are no less terms 'implied' (really *imposed*) by law as those inserted by, for example, the Sale of Goods Act 1979. Remedies are certainly extensive and elaborate. But it is hard to imagine a functional law of contract lacking remedies for breach. Whenever parties enter into a legally binding agreement it is scarcely contestable that there must be *some* legal consequences if it is breached (or it would not, in fact, be 'legally binding'). If lawyers do not normally think of remedies as 'terms implied by law' it may be that remedies' existence (if not their precise form) is so obviously essential as to be genuinely uncontroversial. We cannot conceive of a contract without remedies for breach. That cannot be said for other implied terms (it is *not* impossible to envisage a law of sale which leaves all risks and losses where they fall – *caveat emptor et venditor*). So while the very existence of many legally supplied terms is contestable, whatever 'minimum decencies' the law of contract must cover to be worthy of the name,[3] they surely must include some remedies for breach.

Yet this indispensability leads lawyers into error. The status of remedies as (mere?) terms implied by law tends to be overlooked. No teacher of the law of contract would deny the rich and satisfying complexity of the law of remedies. It is not surprising that remedies exert a powerful fascination for the contract scholar – of which this book is merely the latest evidence. Stephen Smith has noted that amid the burgeoning debates on contract theory, remedies attract the most attention of all.[4]

Remedies do indeed help illuminate the law's underlying theory of contractual obligation.[5] Hence the intellectual interest in the field. But it must be emphasised that remedies reveal *the law's* conception of contract – i.e. that of courts and lawyers as developed through common law doctrine. Ultimately, however, this is no more than a *default* regime. According to any liberal notion of contracting, parties should be free to modify the law's remedies (along with other legally supplied rules), subject only to

---

[3] Karl Llewellyn's formula to determine those terms 'which a court will insist upon as essential to an enforceable bargain of a given type': KN Llewellyn, 'The Standardization of Commercial Contracts in English and Continental Law by O Prausnitz' (1939) 52 Harvard LR 700, 703.

[4] Stephen A Smith, *Contract Theory* (Clarendon Press 2004) 387.

[5] E.g. E Allan Farnsworth, 'Damages and Specific Relief' (1979) 27 Am Jo Comparative Law 247, 247: 'No aspect of a system of contract law is more revealing of its underlying assumptions than is the law that prescribes the relief available for breach.'

overriding mandatory rules of public policy. Standard forms commonly do include such a customised remedial regime.[6] Many other parties do not contract out, of course[7] – but whether through enthusiastic concurrence with the common law's remedial approach, or through indifference, ignorance, or inertia, it is regrettably difficult to say. But whatever the ambiguities of silence,[8] when the express terms of a contract are inconsistent with the law's default regime, the latter has to give way on basic principle.

This conception of contract remedies downgrades their importance. Far from being the shining star in the firmament of contract theory, they exist only *faute de mieux* – the 'better' here being party agreement. Indeed, excepting the public policy exceptions noted above, *all* contractual 'doctrines' are merely contingent place-fillers of secondary importance. The law's rules apply only in default of party agreement covering the point. The centre of attention properly shifts from legal doctrine to how contracts are negotiated and drafted. Contracting parties themselves focus on transactional lawyers, employed to design legal instruments to give effect to their intentions, rather than courts and litigation lawyers (which come into play only rarely, in pathological situations).[9] Given the '[v]ast amounts of intellectual effort' devoted to 'understanding, predicting or assisting judges', such a shift of perspective is bound to meet resistance.[10] But painful though it is, not least in legal academia, the intellectual change should be made.[11]

The sections below explain why contract remedies should be understood as default rules. We then suggest how the content of those rules is

---

[6] Hugh Collins, *The Law of Contract* (4th edn, Cambridge University Press 2003) 365; Richard Hooley, ch 15 below (widespread inclusion of express termination clauses).

[7] LL Fuller and William R Perdue Jr, 'The Reliance Interest in Contract Damages: 1' (1936) 46 Yale LJ 52, 58: 'If a contract represents a kind of private law, it is a law which usually says nothing at all about what shall be done when it is violated.'

[8] E.g. *Allied Marine Transport Ltd v Vale do Rio Doce Navegacao SA (The Leonidas D)* [1985] 1 WLR 925, 937 (Robert Goff LJ).

[9] David Howarth, *Law as Engineering: Thinking About What Lawyers Do* (Edward Elgar 2013) 190: 'Law-as-engineering shifts attention away from judges and those who argue in front of them, to those who make law and those who apply it to themselves.'

[10] Ibid.

[11] It raises various issues that cannot be pursued in detail here – such as the extent to which default rules may alter parties' underlying preferences (Alan Schwartz, 'The Default Rule Paradigm and the Limits of Contract Law' (1993) 3 S Cal Interdisc LJ 389, 413–15; Ben Depoorter and Stephan Tontrup, 'How Law Frames Moral Intuitions: The Expressive Effect of Specific Performance' (2012) 54 Arizona LR 673); and the many practical obstacles to optimal contract drafting (text to n 23).

to be established. The result is a cautious pragmatism. That might seem theoretically unsophisticated – indeed atheoretical. But it is no worse for that. Commercial parties prefer settled rules that aim, above all, to give effect to their contracts as drafted. Doubtless to the disappointment of philosophers everywhere there is little commercial attraction towards a system marked by fluidity, πάντα ῥεῖ, as it strives for theoretical perfection ('works itself pure' as common lawyers like to put it). It would take an even more hard-boiled jurist than the present author to deny that law can sometimes be imbued with beauty, truth and justice. But it is not true of the law of contract. A morally uplifting contract law is all very well in a monograph or series of lectures, but would commercial actors choose to bind themselves by its rules? It seems most unlikely. As Kirby P wisely observed:

> The wellsprings of the conduct of commercial people are self-evidently important for the efficient operation of the economy. Their actions typically depend on self-interest and profit-making not conscience or fairness ... [C]ourts should ... be wary lest they distort the relationships of substantial, well-advised corporations in commercial transactions by subjecting them to the overly tender consciences of judges.[12]

A legal system that failed to heed such warnings might find itself with a law of contract (remedies – and everything else) that did not apply to any actual contracts. The customers would look elsewhere, as they are entirely free to do. Or at minimum, devote time and money to circumventing the 'fair and just results' at which the rule aimed.[13] What would be the point of such a system?

2.2   Default Rules: Taking Choice Seriously

Contract law is based on freedom of choice. This freedom is much broader than that permitting contracting-out from unsuitable default rules. Nobody is obliged to enter into an agreement in the first place; if an agreement is made, nobody is forced to make it legally enforceable; and if a legally enforceable contract is formed, nobody is required to use English contract law to govern it. These are fundamental facts central to any discussion of the function of contract law. Their implication is clear. Other things being equal, the less attractive a given system of contract law, the more likely (advertent) parties are to contract out of its

---

[12] *Austotel Pty Ltd v Franklins Selfserve Pty Ltd* (1989) 16 NSWLR 582 (CA) 586.
[13] Schwartz (n 11).

unpalatable rules on a case-by-case basis; or contract out of that system wholesale (using a choice of law clause); or even contract out of legal enforcement altogether (through a 'gentlemen's agreement' clause, or opting for non-judicial dispute resolution or enforcement mechanisms).[14] Of course, this raises the big question of what contracting parties *do* want. Before addressing that, it is worth reflecting on the reality of choice, to underline the inescapable necessity of satisfying commercial preferences.

Freedom of choice of law is especially important for sophisticated commercial actors. A global 'market for laws' is now generally acknowledged, in which conscious choice is made between national legal systems through choice of law clauses. No doubt the choice depends on numerous factors, which certainly include procedural matters (speed, cost and reliability of the system) and indeed entirely non-legal questions, as well as the law's substantive 'quality'.[15] However, at least *ceteris paribus*, the latter surely matters too. A system unconcerned with, or hostile to, commercial contractors' needs would not be likely to attract substantial offshore business as the law chosen to govern widely used standard forms in international shipping, financial transactions (such as derivatives and swaps), or commodity trading.

It is no doubt implausible to attribute to typical contracting parties detailed knowledge about different jurisdictions' laws of contract.[16] It may be financially prohibitive for individual firms to attempt a reasonably well-educated choice. But that does not discredit the 'choice using substantive quality' argument. The institutional experience, resources and economy of scale for such bodies as the Baltic and International Maritime Council, International Swaps and Derivatives Association, or Grain and Feed Trade Association, means that sophisticated choice when drafting trade-standard contracts is entirely plausible. It would in fact be surprising if such contract-standardising bodies did *not* take careful account of the way in which the contracts are interpreted and given effect in a given legal system before deciding to include (or retain) it as the standard governing law.[17]

---

[14] See generally Thomas Dietz, *Global Order Beyond Law: How Information and Communication Technologies Facilitate Relational Contracting in International Trade* (Hart 2014) pt III.

[15] Stefan Vogenauer, 'Regulatory Competition Through Choice of Contract Law and Choice of Forum in Europe: Theory and Evidence' (2013) 21 Eur Rev Private L 13.

[16] Or indeed their *own* jurisdiction's contract law: Andrew Robertson, 'The Limits of Voluntariness in Contract' (2005) 29 Melbourne Univ LR 179, 202–16.

[17] Such bodies' knowledge of the background rules of contract law might answer the criticism of Robertson ibid (but cf his views on standard forms, ibid 187–202).

Thus our hypothesis is: the more exactly a given law of contract satisfies commercial needs and expectations, the greater the number of parties that will choose to have their relations governed by it; and vice versa. Some might ask: why does it matter how popular a given law of contract is in the global market for laws? While popularity should not be the sole criterion of 'successful contract law',[18] its total absence would suggest failure. What would be the point of a pure system of contract law that instantiated distributive equality and upright promissory morality were no contracts actually governed by it? It would be utopian theory, not an extant system of law. Of course, in practice, even if sophisticated commercial parties invariably contracted out of such an 'uncommercial' law of contract, others who failed to exercise any positive choice of law would still be governed by it, by default. But setting up contract law as a snare for the unwary seems questionable.

Therefore, if the law of contract is to facilitate commercial parties entering into legally binding agreements, preference-satisfaction is desirable. Indeed it is to a great degree inevitable, to avoid the threat of practical irrelevance. What then do contracting parties want?

The core desideratum is freedom of choice. When parties enter an agreement containing express rules they expect those to govern their relations. The plainest way to defeat that expectation is through immutable rules – those from which the law prohibits contracting-out, for reasons of public policy. Accordingly, these should be imposed with caution. So the first, negative, precept is to curb the range of immutable rules. In excess they will discourage contracting altogether (or at least contracting using the *dirigiste* system's law).

Most of contract law's rules are accepted to be defeasible by contrary party intention. Such 'default' rules do not directly challenge freedom of choice. But their indirect influence may. For example, courts routinely presume that parties 'cannot have intended' to vary a given legally supplied rule, and accordingly construe terms against their plain meaning to preserve the law's 'default' position.[19] The strength of such presumptions varies between and within legal systems. The distinction between 'immutable' and 'default' rules thus seems more a spectrum than a dichotomy. The 'stickier' the default rule, the closer it approaches

---

[18] Successive UK governments have stressed the importance of London's global legal services market for the national economy.

[19] E.g. *Bank of Credit and Commerce International SA v Ali* [2001] UKHL 8, [2002] 1 AC 251; *HIH Casualty and General Insurance Ltd v Chase Manhattan Bank* [2003] UKHL 6, [2003] 2 Lloyd's Rep 61. Hooley, ch 15 below, documents this problem well.

de facto immutability.[20] Whether the best drafter in the world could force a court to accept a meaning of which it strongly disapproves is a good question. But defaults should be readily defeasible – as far as possible 'frictionless' rather than sticky.

To this end a permissive set of 'altering rules' should be recognised, to enable a clear answer to the third of Ian Ayres's central questions for transactional lawyers: 'What is the presumptive legal rule?', 'Can it be changed?' and, 'How can I change it?'[21] Sometimes 'safe harbour' provisions ordain precisely how this is to be done. But frequently courts seem reluctant to provide clear guidance on how contracting parties (and drafters) might rebut the default position. Ayres finds this 'see-mingly intentional fuzziness' of rules for contracting around to be an 'important ... puzzle'; it may be telling that his examples are leading US cases where courts refused to award the 'cost of cure' measure of damages.[22] The sense that remedies are peculiarly in the province of the courts seems widespread. But it is regrettable. It should be sufficient to exclude a default remedy simply for the parties to state an inconsistent term. This approach maximises their freedom.

Furthermore, 'friction' will be minimised by a less extensive, less complex body of default rules. It is easier to contract out of clear rules than broad principles. It has sometimes been suggested that the main consequence of introducing new heads of liability will be to lengthen commercial contracts as parties attempt routinely to exclude them (if only *ex abundanti cautela*).[23] So default rules are not costless. A vital preliminary question is whether to have any default rule ('doctrine') to govern a given problem. The more terms the law 'implies' into contracts, and the 'stickier' those rules are, and the less harmonious they are with commercial expectations, the greater the costs. Parties will have to draft longer, more complex contracts to insist on their own preferences (itself a significant cost), with the cost of drafting failure being the imposition of an uncommercial rule. Of course, ill-conceived default rules are

---

[20] Omri Ben-Shahar and John AE Pottow, 'On the Stickiness of Default Rules' (2006) 33 Florida State Univ LR 651.

[21] Ian Ayres, 'Regulating Opt-Out: An Economic Theory of Altering Rules' (2012) 121 Yale LJ 2032.

[22] Ian Ayres, 'Empire or Residue: Competing Visions of the Contractual Canon' (1999) 26 Florida State Univ LR 897, 906.

[23] Eric A Posner, *Law and Social Norms* (Harvard UP 2000) 163 (criticising pre-contractual liability after *Hoffman v Red Owl Stores Inc* 133 NW 2d 267 (1965)); Edward Granger, 'Sweating Over an Implied Duty of Good Faith' [2013] LMCLQ 418, 424 (considering *Yam Seng Pte Ltd v International Trade Corp Ltd* [2013] EWHC 111 (QB)).

inevitably a trap for unsophisticated parties (who will make no attempt to contract out of them).

These precepts could be summed up as a minimalist conception of contract.[24] But how far does this 'minimalism' go? Would it be bold logic, or a *reductio ad absurdum*, to call for the exclusion of default rules altogether?[25] While total elimination could indeed be desirable in some areas,[26] there is a necessity for rules supplied by law to answer certain questions. First, without some rules governing when a contract has been formed,[27] the enterprise of giving effect to the parties' agreement could not even get off the ground. Secondly, as already conceded, it is inconceivable that there could be a *contract* (legally enforceable agreement) without some remedies for its non-performance. So there does need to be a legally supplied remedial regime, applicable in default of express agreement. In accordance with the desiderata outlined above, these default remedies should be as clear as possible, should readily give way to the parties' alternative regime (to minimise 'stickiness'), and should eschew immutable rules (those that overtly trump party choice).

2.3   Designing Default Remedies for Breach of Contract

The notion that terms agreed in contracts might supplant general rules of law is age-old. The debate about 'default rules' has been said to contribute little except a new name.[28] The terminology is no longer particularly novel – Lord Steyn used it when describing terms implied by law as 'standardised ... default rules'.[29] But it usefully underscores the central point. Such rules apply only *by default*, in the absence of a term governing the point in the contract.

This then is the *nature* of the law's remedies for breach of contract. In very broad terms, the *function* of this default regime is to supply some enforcement mechanism for contracts duly formed. But would not *any* recognisable remedial regime serve that broad purpose equally

[24] Jonathan Morgan, *Contract Law Minimalism: A Formalist Restatement of Commercial Contract Law* (Cambridge University Press 2013).
[25] Schwartz (n 11).
[26] Jonathan Morgan, *Great Debates in Contract Law* (2nd edn, Palgrave 2015) ch 5 (doctrine of frustration).
[27] On the extent of their modifiability consider *RTS Flexible Systems Ltd v Molkerei Alois Müller GmbH & Co KG (UK Production)* [2010] UKSC 14, [2010] 1 WLR 753.
[28] W David Slawson, 'The Futile Search for Principles for Default Rules' (1993) 3 S Cal Interdiscip LJ 29.
[29] *Equitable Life Assurance Society v Hyman* [2002] 1 AC 408, 458.

well? This section suggests more precisely the content of successful default remedies.

First, remedies should be *acknowledged* as mere default rules – capable of modification by the parties, and subject always to a contrary intention. Secondly, they should be as clear and simple as possible. Thirdly, they should be relatively settled. These last points are tritely familiar to the commercial lawyer, but they have additional importance in the default rule analysis. For parties wishing to replace the law's default rules with their own preferred regime, their task is eased by a static and well-defined target, rather than a moving, elusive one.

Fourthly, the rules should reflect commercial expectations. This also seems trite. But oft-cited as the aspiration is, putting it into practice faces great difficulties. It is questionable whether any unified set of reasonable expectations, shared by all commercial contractors, actually exists to be satisfied.[30] The contexts of contracts are endlessly variable. If the ambition is merely to satisfy the *majority* of contractors (to limit the amount of contracting-out from the default rule),[31] the problem remains of how the court, or legislature, is to identify the majority preference.[32]

Legislation is not infallible in this respect. The level of hard empirical evidence behind much law reform is regrettably scanty. Conversely, the existence of political lobbying by economically powerful groups can hardly be denied. Parliamentary laws may have democratic legitimacy but we may doubt whether they genuinely satisfy the preference of a majority of contractors (rather than suiting those that enjoy the greatest political influence).

The picture for the courts is also mixed. Judges sometimes remind themselves of their limited competence to second-guess commercial imperatives.[33] Others have the point made for them.[34] Yet for all these

---

[30] CA Riley, 'Designing Default Rules in Contract Law: Consent, Conventionalism, and Efficiency' (2000) 20 OJLS 367, 376.

[31] A goal not universally shared. For 'penalty defaults' (deliberately unattractive ones, designed to stimulate contracting-out) see Ian Ayres and Robert Gertner, 'Filling Gaps in Incomplete Contracts: An Economic Theory of Default Rules' (1989) 99 Yale LJ 87.

[32] Schwartz (n 11) argues that given incomplete information it is impossible to formulate 'acceptable' default rules as a matter of general contract law (i.e. rules which 'solve a problem that a reasonable portion of contractors will face in a way that is acceptable to those contractors': 392).

[33] E.g. *Skanska Rashleigh Weatherfoil Ltd v Somerfield Stores Ltd* [2006] EWCA Civ 1732 [22] (Neuberger LJ).

[34] E.g. John Gava, 'The Perils of Judicial Activism: The Contracts Jurisprudence of Justice Michael Kirby' (1999) 15 Jo Contract L 156.

well-known problems, some mileage remains in the notion that common law adjudication can devise satisfactory practical solutions to individual disputes, and that the accumulation of experience eventually coalesces into a body of rules. Lord Diplock issued a classical statement of this process.[35]

Professor Collins has argued that the common law has certain advantages as a form of 'reflexive' regulation.[36] Rules laid down by the courts can be revised in the light of experience. Problems return to court and if an earlier judicial solution was unsatisfactory, this will tend to come to light. While there are some problems with this model, for example the fact that litigated cases are not a random sample but may be presented in furtherance of a deliberate litigation strategy, the idea of a 'feedback loop' has some plausibility in frequently litigated areas of commercial law. (According to Lord Diplock, one of the main purposes of standard form charterparties is to permit 'exegesis by the courts so that the way in which they will apply . . . will be understood in the same sense by both the parties'.[37]) The courts have long recognised that should 'inconvenience' result from their interpretation, the terms of future contracts can be amended ('It is, no doubt, not an easy thing to introduce a new form of contract into mercantile use, but it can be done.').[38]

Against this, it has been argued (of litigation in the wake of the catastrophic collapse of Lehman Brothers bank) that 'The judicial arts needed to deal with transactional wreckage do not always provide comfort and assurance to those planning future transactions.'[39] Judicial shortcomings are compounded by inertia among those drafting standard form contracts. A striking example is the ongoing failure of law firms negotiating sovereign debt contracts to amend the standard forms

[35] *EL Oldendorff & Co GmbH v Tradax Export SA (The Johanna Oldendorff)* [1974] AC 479, 554.
[36] Hugh Collins, *Regulating Contracts* (Oxford University Press 1999) ch 4.
[37] *Federal Commerce & Navigation Co Ltd v Tradax Export SA (The Maratha Envoy)* [1978] AC 1, 8. cf Howarth (n 9) 3: 'Contracts . . . are often drafted not as instructions to judges about enforcement but as plans for those affected by them to apply directly to themselves. Court enforcement is often seen not as a benefit the document might bring but as a disaster to be avoided.'
[38] *Postlethwaite v Freeland* (1880) 5 App Cas 599, 622 (Lord Blackburn).
[39] Bridge and Braithwaite (n 2) 366. Unfortunate, since the Lehman cases have attracted 'very keen attention' (concerning rarely litigated clauses of the ISDA Master Agreement): Jo Braithwaite, 'Law after Lehmans' (2014) Law, Society and Economy Working Paper 11/2014 (LSE) <http://eprints.lse.ac.uk/55834/> accessed 18 December 2015.

following a commercially unacceptable judicial construction.[40] There are strong pressures towards conformity (and against innovation – even when the new contract would demonstrably be superior). It may take an external shock to produce a new (superior) status quo.[41] A more familiar problem is that the best-drafted contract may contain slips or omissions.[42] Omniscience is impossible, rationality bounded. So each side of the regulatory 'feedback loop' is prone to failure.

Even if we remain guardedly optimistic about the common law's potential to accommodate commercial expectations, some of its other characteristic features are less beneficial. In particular, common law development produces ever-more elaborate rules over time. This runs against the clarity, simplicity, and certainty that are so important for commercial planning. However, elaboration is an inherent feature of the case-law method, in which courts have to address 'More and more fact situations, each new one not being startlingly different from the others, but each nonetheless unique', driving a continual increase in 'scale and intricacy'.[43] The process is tangible and visible in the middle-aged spread (and geriatric corpulence) of venerable textbooks. Some judges are aware of the complexity problem in commercial law. Lord Diplock argued that since 'a considerable degree of certainty as to the meaning and application of standard [charterparty] forms and clauses has been achieved by costly litigation over the years', the courts should be very slow to depart from earlier decisions on those clauses' meaning.[44] Nevertheless there are many examples of accelerating judicial elaboration of contract doctrine, not least (since 1998) over the elementary question of how contracts should be interpreted.[45]

Few would subscribe to a strongly Darwinian theory of the common law – i.e. that its rules grow inexorably towards optimality by the 'survival

---

[40] Mitu Gulati and Robert E Scott, *The 3½ Minute Transaction: Boilerplate and the Limits of Contract Design* (University of Chicago Press 2013).

[41] James Davey and Cliona Kelly, '*Romalpa* and Contractual Innovation' (2015) 42 JL & S 358.

[42] E.g. *Beaufort Developments (NI) Ltd v Gilbert-Ash NI Ltd* [1999] 1 AC 266, 273–74 (Lord Hoffmann): 'In the case [of the JCT] contract which has been periodically renegotiated, amended and added to over many years, it is unreasonable to expect that there will be no redundancies or loose ends.'

[43] Steve Hedley, 'How Has the Common Law Survived the 20th Century?' (1999) 50 NILQ 283, 287.

[44] *The Maratha Envoy* (n 37) 14.

[45] Since *Investors Compensation Scheme Ltd v West Bromwich Building Society* [1998] 1 WLR 896; PS Davies, 'Interpreting Commercial Contracts: Back to the Top' (2011) 127 LQR 185 (frequent interpretation appeals to Supreme Court harming commercial certainty).

of the fittest'. However, a weaker version has greater plausibility. To the extent that settled rules of a system seem to meet commercial approval (i.e. firms choose to use the system, and there is no pressure from commercial parties and their legal representatives to reform its rules), it could be said to succeed in meeting commercial expectations. English contract remedies have characteristic features that 'puzzle' many theorists.[46] The default regime's tolerance for breach of contract perplexes them. Common law remedies have not traditionally sought to prevent breach (whether directly by injunctions, or deterring it through exemplary damages or accounts of profits), nor to enforce contractual obligations (specific performance), nor otherwise to vindicate the right to performance. Yet English law has nevertheless enjoyed significant international commercial popularity.[47] That suggests that its distinctive remedial structure is not incompatible with commercial needs and expectations. Such evidence is indirect and inconclusive (as noted above, English law's commercial appeal could depend on procedural factors as much as the substance of its remedy rules). But against the background of its longstanding and widespread commercial acceptance, anybody proposing a radical reform of English contract remedies would need to demonstrate clearly how that would satisfy commercial requirements better than the existing law.

2.4   False Moves

Characterisation of contract remedies as default rules could be dismissed as a statement of the obvious. However, it is incompatible with various familiar approaches.

2.4.1   *Morality*

Many have sought (and found) the theoretical basis for the law of contract in promissory morality. An emphasis on the immorality of breaking promises has clear implications for remedies (or so it appears).[48] Breach should not be tolerated, as it so flagrantly is in English contract law, but

---

[46] Smith (n 4) 417–18 and ch 11 *passim*.

[47] See large-scale empirical study by Gilles Cuniberti, 'The International Market for Contracts: The Most Attractive Contract Laws' (2014) 34 Northwestern Jo Int L & Bus 455.

[48] Cf Richard Craswell, 'Contract Law, Default Rules, and the Philosophy of Promising' (1989) 88 Michigan LR 489.

instead prevented and (where irreversible) condemned.[49] The focus would be protecting, enforcing, and vindicating the right to performance. This would require a radical reform of English law: the general availability of positive and negative orders to perform (specific performance and injunctions) and of punitive, vindicatory, and profit-stripping monetary remedies. These remedies are currently exceptional (or unavailable – as with exemplary damages). But were the promissory stance adopted, and its implications worked through, a revolution in remedies for breach of contract would seem the natural consequence.

Accepting for now that, according to the logic of promissory morality, the current basic structure of English remedies is seriously defective, an anterior question arises: why should contract law adopt the moral stance in the first place? Given that the practice of contracting (making legally enforceable agreements) is optional all the way down, it would seem odd to freight its rules with such ethical splendours. What is the point of *optional morality*? The promissory theorist of contract must either recognise that the theory's breach-intolerant remedies would be freely modifiable (i.e. that they are default rules), or insist on their immutability. The first answer suggests a rather weak degree of moral commitment.[50] The second seems to flow naturally from the remedies' *moral* inspiration. But would commercial parties tolerate (let alone actively seek out) a system in which performance was enforced and breach of contract punished, whether the parties liked it or not – even when they had expressly contracted for a breach-tolerant alternative?

It seems unlikely. True, promissory theorists have not sought to argue otherwise: their prospectus for reform derives, after all, from abstract deontic propositions rather than sordid evidence about what actual contracting parties expect from the law. But for the reasons already explained, this noble approach risks creating a law of contract that no well-advised commercial parties would willingly use. The practical value

---

[49] E.g. TM Scanlon, *What We Owe to Each Other* (Harvard UP 1999) 301–02: 'The obligation to fulfill a promise [is not] neutral between warning, fulfillment and compensation ... the obligation one undertakes when one makes a promise is an obligation to do the thing promised, not simply to do it or to compensate the promisee accordingly.' But cf Craswell ibid.

[50] Cf Barbara H Fried, 'The Holmesian Bad Man Flubs his Entrance' (2012) 45 Suffolk Univ LR 627, 641–42: 'Given that the parties to a contract generally have no moral duty to assume *any* contractual obligations to each other, if they voluntarily choose to do so, why should they not be free, morally speaking, to limit the scope of those obligations by providing one or both sides with alternatives to performance?'

of a morally pure law of contract which governed few contracts is not apparent.

Might not a performance-focused law of contract remedies be commercially appealing? The financial crash of 2008 has fuelled widespread interest in the role of ethics in well-functioning markets.[51] The common law's tolerance for deliberate breach of contract has been singled out for undermining social morality.[52] Deterring such breach, in order to protect 'the stability of [the institution of] contract itself', is the rationale for broad disgorgement remedies in US contract law.[53] Were these arguments correct,[54] sophisticated commercial actors (at least those capable of taking the long view) might indeed prefer ethically inspired remedies. But needless to say, there has been firm opposition.

Defenders of the common law status quo praise the flexibility that breach affords. If costs of performance (unexpectedly) rise such that it is cheaper to breach and compensate on the 'expectation' measure than to perform, is it really unethical (let alone uncommercial) to breach deliberately?[55] Is not forgiveness an important rival ethical principle, mandating adjustment and release rather than stringent enforcement by promisees?[56] Insisting on uneconomic performance overreaches the 'sanctity' of contract, degenerating into 'contractual sadism'.[57] So breach is ethically defensible. Professor Campbell also underlines its economic importance. Breach is 'central to the efficiency of the market economy' (Campbell contrasts the rigidity of specifically enforceable adherence to the Central Plan in communist economies); those who rail against it on ethical grounds 'simply have no inkling of the economic difficulties involved in their pursuit of general literal enforcement'.[58] Admittedly, the empirical evidence is lacking for a final determination of the economically optimal regime of contract remedies – as seen in stalemate

---

[51] E.g. Paul J Zak (ed), *Moral Markets: The Critical Role of Values in the Economy* (Princeton UP 2008).

[52] Seana Valentine Shiffrin, 'The Divergence of Contract and Promise' (2007) 120 Harvard LR 708.

[53] American Law Institute, *Third Restatement of Restitution*, §39, Comment b.

[54] Cf Hanoch Dagan, 'Restitutionary Damages for Breach of Contract: An Exercise in Private Law Theory' (2000) 1 Theoretical Inq L 115, 121–25.

[55] Steven Shavell, 'Why Breach of Contract May Not Be Immoral Given the Incompleteness of Contracts' (2009) 107 Michigan LR 1569.

[56] Jean Braucher, 'The Sacred and Profane Contracts Machine: The Complex Morality of Contract Law in Action' (2012) 45 Suffolk Univ LR 667.

[57] David Howarth, 'Against *Lumley v Gye*' (2005) 68 MLR 195, 218.

[58] David Campbell, 'A Relational Critique of the Third Restatement of Restitution §39' (2011) 68 Washington & Lee LR 1063, 1100–01.

over 'efficient breach'.[59] But longstanding commercial acceptance of the common law approach would be surprising if it were seriously defective.

In short, using commercial expectations to defend performance-focused remedies (the literal enforcement of unqualified, unconditional promises) would be questionable. And mostly this has not been attempted. The approach depends instead on the morality of promising. We have already questioned whether formulating contract law according to exemplary moral standards, on a take-it-or-leave-it basis, is a worthwhile enterprise. This casts doubt on the deontological reasoning (and unconcealed indifference, or even hostility, to party expectations) that characterises much theoretical writing about contract remedies.

2.4.2 Doctrinal Fundamentalism

While nobody today would assert straight-faced that the common law is 'the perfection of reason', most lawyers still believe that it develops according to distinctive internal logic – following 'some ethereal and timeless *principles* that are above mere politics' as Professor Hedley puts it, unconvinced.[60] But there are dangers in carrying the common law's deep-felt distinctiveness too far, in the sphere of contract. As argued above, the rules in this area are merely a provisional regime, place-holders against the absence of express remedial terms in the contract. 'Doctrine' should always give way to the parties' contrary intentions. But this central truth about the nature of contract remedies, their *optional* nature, is more likely to be overlooked the more emphasis is placed on common law rules as the result, and repository, of a long and glorious legal tradition.[61] This tendency (which comes very naturally to any common lawyer) must nonetheless be resisted. Doctrine for doctrine's sake is a rather peculiar idea – is private law really 'just like love',[62] a beautiful and transcendent end in itself? Rather, we maintain, an instrumental perspective is inevitable in a world where well-advised, mobile commercial parties can and do exercise freedom of choice. They are unlikely to share romantic notions of the common law's intrinsic

---

[59] Ian R Macneil, 'Efficient Breach of Contract: Circles in the Sky' (1982) 68 Virginia LR 947.

[60] Hedley (n 43) 293 (emphasis in original).

[61] E.g. John Gava, 'How Should Judges Decide Commercial Contract Cases?' (2013) 30 Jo Contract L 133, 149–55.

[62] Ernest J Weinrib, *The Idea of Private Law* (Oxford University Press 2012) 6.

value.[63] From this perspective, contract 'doctrines' are valuable only to the extent that they give proper effect to the agreements that parties want to make.

Some judges have expressly recognised the 'default' nature of contract remedies. *The Achilleas* is a prominent example.[64] Lord Hoffmann characterised the venerable remoteness rules derived from *Hadley v Baxendale* as the common law's *presumption* of the extent of consequential loss that the parties *intended* to be recoverable (i.e. what they can usually be taken to have intended).[65] It followed that the presumption could be rebutted by evidence that the contractors actually intended liability on a more, or less, extensive basis than *Hadley v Baxendale* lays down. For Lord Hoffmann, this restatement of the basis of remoteness flowed from a more general point about contractual obligation. Ultimately it is rooted in the agreement of the parties, including what they have agreed about the consequences of non-performance. Lord Hoffmann dismissed a rival conception of *Hadley v Baxendale* as pure doctrine, imposed by law on the parties, and external to their actual intentions. His Lordship's speech is then clear support for the default rule approach. But it shows the dangers of an unmediated appeal to implicit party expectations and (therefore) the prudential value of traditionally conceived doctrinal rules.

First, it has to be accepted that Lord Hoffmann's approach has not established itself as new orthodoxy. Only Lord Hope clearly supported it in *The Achilleas* itself, with Lord Rodger taking a different approach, Lord Walker agreeing with all three conflicting speeches, and Baroness Hale distinctly *dubitante*. Doctrinal fundamentalism is no Aunt Sally. As Professor Coote writes, the Hoffmann approach has, predictably, been 'strongly resisted [because] it runs counter to that very widely held perception that, as in tort, liability in contract is something imposed by law *ab extra* on parties who, in the case of contract, have fulfilled the technical requirements for formation'.[66] Coote himself has long been a critic of that approach, arguing that all contractual obligations (primary

---

[63] Or a vision of its judges as 'distant God-like defenders of abstract rights based on a timeless morality': Howarth (n 9) 191.

[64] *Transfield Shipping Inc v Mercator Shipping Inc (The Achilleas)* [2008] UKHL 48, [2009] 1 AC 61.

[65] *Hadley v Baxendale* (1854) 9 Ex 341, 156 ER 145.

[66] Brian Coote, 'Contract as Assumption and Remoteness of Damage' (2010) 26 Jo Contract L 211, 216.

and secondary) are ultimately assumed by the parties. This has practical importance. If viewed as rules imposed by law:

> it could be expected there would be at least some bias towards applying the imposed rule or rules, in full force and with a minimum of exceptions. On the other hand, any bias could well be the other way if the rules as to remoteness gave rise to no more than indications, assumptions, or rebuttable presumptions [of what the parties intended].[67]

Lord Hoffmann's restatement is compelling as an exercise in contract theory. Remedies should be acknowledged to depend on the liability that the parties intended to assume.[68] Any intention inconsistent with those rules should be enforced automatically. 'The operative rules should be chosen by the parties for their own purposes, not by the law for its purposes.'[69] For critics of the Hoffmann approach such as Catherine Mitchell (who questions the 'turn' by which all questions of contractual obligation increasingly depend on the court's interpretation of what the parties intended),[70] the question is – on what else should contractual liability depend?[71] In addition to the theoretical grounding of contract in party intention, we have already suggested that a system of contract law which diminishes the role of party choice, in favour of 'bias towards applying the [law's] imposed rules', is not likely to attract sophisticated commercial parties (dismissing the fantasy by which those rules manage to meet the expectations of all contracting parties perfectly).

Despite its impeccable rationalisation, Lord Hoffmann's *Achilleas* approach threatens (or rather, threatened) to cause great uncertainty. Doctrine has a valuable role – perhaps more than Lord Hoffmann allowed – in supplying predictable rules. To decide what the parties

---

[67] Ibid 214. Compare discussion of 'stickiness' section 2.2 above.

[68] Adam Kramer, 'An Agreement-Centred Approach to Remoteness and Contract Damages' in Nili Cohen and Ewan McKendrick (eds), *Comparative Remedies for Breach of Contract* (Hart 2004).

[69] Richard A Epstein, 'Beyond Foreseeability: Consequential Damages in the Law of Contract' (1989) 18 JLS 105, 108.

[70] Catherine Mitchell, 'Obligations in Commercial Contracts: A Matter of Law or Interpretation?' (2012) 65 CLP 455.

[71] Cf Fried (n 50) 634: 'The right position for a will theorist or any other liberal contract theorist to hold with respect to the [remedies] available to the promisor in lieu of performance is, in the first instance, no position at all – or more precisely, that the promisor has available whatever alternatives the parties agreed he should have. If the promisee has agreed to give the promisor a free option to walk away from the contemplated exchange ... why should a liberal contract theorist want to substitute his own preferred alternative (payment of expectation damages or an order of specific performance)? Whose contract is this, anyway?'

implicitly intended on every question of contractual obligation – an inevitably uncertain inquiry – would bring the law to the point of collapse. Despite its theoretical attractions, such an intractable approach must be resisted. This suggests that provision of clear default rules may be superior to sole reliance on party intentions (which are frequently not made explicit). A set of rigid doctrines might well be artificial, but as so often pointed out, it is more important for commercial law to be certain than correct.

The two approaches are not mutually exclusive. It is possible to confine the unsettling mischief of *The Achilleas* while retaining Lord Hoffmann's insight, by insisting that although *Hadley v Baxendale* is only a presumption of the parties' intentions (and not an 'external' rule), the *Hadley* approach will apply in every case except where the parties *expressly* say it should not.[72] This could be justified as a salutary incentive for contract draftsmen to say what they mean clearly, when they want to be relieved from the usual (default) liabilities. Insistence on express contracting-out would have been fatal in *The Achilleas* itself, where Lord Hoffmann relied on evidence of commercial expectations (rather than inconsistent terms in the charter-party). It might seem hard to hold the charterers liable when (as one of the arbitrators accepted) the whole shipping industry believed they would not be liable for the loss of follow-on charters (even though such losses were reasonably foreseeable). But requiring an alteration to industry-standard forms could be seen as the price for the convenience of applying *Hadley v Baxendale* mechanically (unless expressly excluded). Later judges have not gone quite so far as to require express contracting-out, although Hamblen J has sought to confine *The Achilleas* exception to cases where 'clear evidence' establishes that 'unquantifiable, unpredictable, uncontrollable or disproportionate liability ... would be contrary to market understanding and expectations'.[73] The existence of such clear evidence on the facts of *The Achilleas* might well be exceptional. In which case, *Hadley v Baxendale* will apply as before in virtually every future case.

Application and refinement of common law doctrine is what the courts do best. They are not well equipped to engage in active regulation of the contracting process.[74] Nor are they well placed to revolutionise the law by

---

[72] Hugh Beale, *Mistake and Non-Disclosure of Facts: Models for English Contract Law* (Oxford University Press 2012) 110.

[73] *Sylvia Shipping Co Ltd v Progress Bulk Carriers Ltd (The Sylvia)* [2010] EWHC 542 (Comm), [2010] 2 Lloyd's Rep 81 [40].

[74] E.g. John Gava and Janey Greene, 'Do We Need a Hybrid Law of Contract? Why Hugh Collins is Wrong and Why it Matters' (2004) 63 CLJ 605; Riley (n 30).

rejecting traditional doctrinal reasoning in favour of a 'contextual' approach where the attitudes and expectations of contracting parties become the primary source of legal rules.[75] Such an approach would likely be unacceptably unpredictable. The relatively clear and determinate doctrines of traditional common law are superior – as long as it is always borne in mind that they are defeasible by contrary party intention. Thus, the traditional conception of *Hadley v Baxendale* as a hard *rule* that applies unless the parties clearly say otherwise is superior to Lord Hoffmann's approach. The Hoffmann restatement is correct to recognise that remedy doctrines, being defaults, are always subject to variation by contracting parties. The application of those rules is contingent on a gap in the contract. But 'gaps' should be given a wider meaning than Lord Hoffmann was willing to allow. Only an express contract term should exclude the default rule (by filling the 'gap'). Otherwise, there is considerable tactical value in traditional doctrinal reasoning. Ironically, a system of rules may satisfy the key imperative of certainty better than an overtly instrumental approach to the development of default rules.[76]

2.5 Some Implications

Our approach is basically a conservative one. It endorses Lord Diplock's method: courts should develop contract law by reflecting on what the parties must be taken to have intended, as reasonable commercial actors.[77] It follows, of course, that when a contract spells out the parties' desired remedies, there is no need to construct such *hypothetical* intentions. Indeed, it would be illegitimate to do so. Thus common law remedies, however long-established, and however just they seem, should be recognised as merely the law's provisional solution to the problem of the incomplete contract (i.e. one that fails to stipulate remedies) – and nothing more significant. The main doctrinal reform recommended is the abolition of all immutable rules: most obviously on penalty clauses. Otherwise, the default approach cautions against grand schemes for the

---

[75] *Pace* Catherine Mitchell, *Contract Law and Contract Practice: Bridging the Gap Between Legal Reasoning and Commercial Expectation* (Hart 2013).

[76] Gava, 'How Should Judges Decide Commercial Contract Cases?' (n 61) 155 concedes that traditional contract law might best be understood as providing 'rough and ready predictability' as a 'proxy for a truly formalist system' (although still insists that it should 'not aspire to becoming a pure and instrumentalist system of law designed to enhance business transacting in the market').

[77] *The Johanna Oldendorff* (n 35).

reorientation of remedies – particularly where presented as the logical product of deontological reasoning. Only where a radical shift would produce a demonstrably superior default rule is it worth the uncertainty that is bound to follow from the change. Deductions from moral premises make satisfying theories but poor commercial law.

2.5.1   The Penalty Doctrine: The Compensation Dogma

This doctrine hardly wants for critics so we can be brief.[78] English law has long distinguished liquidated damages (designed as genuine compensation of loss) and unenforceable 'penalties' (intended to be supra-compensatory). In other words, the common law insists that agreed monetary remedies *must* be compensatory. This is 'a blatant interference with freedom of contract'.[79] There seems to be no pressing reason of public policy to justify it. The doctrine is particularly misguided because one important justification for the common law's traditional refusal to award exemplary damages, or an account of profits, could be to recognise party freedom to contract out of the law's *compensatory* default position.[80] The penalty doctrine serves to harden this default into unchallengable dogma. It wrongly elevates compensatory default rules to compulsory status. This mistakes the nature of contract remedies.

The Supreme Court recently handed down a landmark decision on penalty clauses in which their Lordships, only too predictably, unanimously dismissed a direct invitation from counsel to abolish the penalty doctrine altogether (or at least in commercial cases).[81] There was, at least, a welcome recognition that a supra-compensatory clause inserted as a deterrent against breach is not necessarily an unenforceable 'penalty' (provided the promisee's interest in the contract being performed is thought by the court 'legitimate', and the detriment imposed on the promisor to achieve that end thought 'proportionate'). But the previous category error – elevating the compensatory approach to immutable status – is not confined to the penalty doctrine. A *sub*-compensatory

---

[78] See further Sarah Worthington, ch 16 below.
[79] *Makdessi v Cavendish Square Holdings BV* [2013] EWCA Civ 1539, [2014] 2 All ER (Comm) 125 [44] (Christopher Clarke LJ).
[80] Solene Rowan, 'For the Recognition of Remedial Terms Agreed *Inter Partes*' (2010) 126 LQR 448.
[81] *Cavendish Square Holding v El Makdessi, ParkingEye Ltd v Beavis* [2015] UKSC 67, [2015] 3 WLR 1373. See Jonathan Morgan, 'The Penalty Clause Doctrine: Unlovable but Untouchable' [2016] 75 CLJ 11.

agreed sum still seems prone to artificially narrow judicial construction because of the alleged 'inherent improbability' that parties could intend to release each other from liabilities that the law would otherwise, by default, impose.[82] More dangerous still, a clause stipulating damages on a less generous basis than the default measure apparently increases the prospect of an intrusive order for specific relief. This proceeds from the highly questionable premise that the sum agreed between the parties would be 'inadequate' compensation, thereby 'open[ing] the door to the exercise of the court's discretion' over equitable relief (in casu an injunction).[83] But equity is supposed to address the inadequacies of the common law. Equity does not exist to override the parties' allocation of risk through a limitation (or agreed damages) clause. Worse still if such intervention rests upon the assumption that deviations from common law damages, agreed by the contracting parties, are (thereby) 'inadequate' remedies. This is preposterous.

2.5.2 Agreement and Specific Remedies

It has been forcefully argued that the common law's toleration of breach is commercially optimal.[84] That would explain notorious subordination of specific performance. But even assuming the argument to be correct, it would be a great mistake to elevate the primacy of damages into an immutable rule. Parties should be free to contract out of the default breach-permissive common law regime, and stipulate for enforcement of the contract (just as they should be free to stipulate for penal remedies to deter breach).[85] Even the staunchest defender of 'efficient breach' should recognise that it can only be a default rule, and when the parties contract for a stronger regime of enforcement that must be presumed optimal for them and enforced. It is therefore to be hoped that English law will learn from the proposal to amend the US Uniform Commercial Code to award specific performance when agreed to by the parties.[86] There should be a strong presumption in favour of granting specific performance when the parties have agreed to it in their

---

[82] *Ailsa Craig Fishing Co Ltd v Malvern Fishing Co Ltd* [1983] 1 WLR 964, 970 (Lord Fraser).

[83] *AB v CD* [2014] EWCA Civ 229, [2015] 1 WLR 771 [30] (Underhill LJ); discussed by Davies, ch 6 below.

[84] E.g. David Campbell and Donald Harris, 'In Defence of Breach: A Critique of Restitution and the Performance Interest' (2002) 22 *Legal Studies* 208.

[85] Rowan (n 80) 449–55.

[86] Uniform Commercial Code (2003 Proposed Revision) § 2–716(1).

contract.[87] The presumption should be rebuttable only by strong public interest reasons (e.g. the concern to avoid forced labour, or exceptional hardship on the promisor – although neither of these has much apparent scope in commercial law – or to avoid wasteful court supervision of an ongoing hostile relationship).[88]

It is suggested that believers in the superiority of performance-oriented remedies ought to champion the modifiability thesis of this chapter. It confers freedom on parties who want such remedies. The common law's primacy of compensation may be the efficient default, but it certainly should not be compulsory. Freedom to stipulate for penal or disgorgement remedies,[89] or specific relief, must be recognised. Unfortunately, few advocates of the performance interest have taken this route,[90] preferring instead to attack the default rules themselves.

2.5.3   *Vindicating the Right to Performance*

The common law tradition of breach-tolerant remedies has increasingly been challenged. The critique tends to travel along similar lines, beginning from the premise that a contract creates obligations to perform, with correlative rights to the performance. From this it follows that the current remedies are defective. To remedy the common law's remedies a number of complementary reforms are envisaged. These include specific performance as the primary remedy; exemplary and profit-stripping remedies to punish and deter deliberate breach of contract; and transforming the basis of damages from compensation of loss to vindication of the right to performance.

These critiques can be questioned on their own terms – by inquiring whether every creation of a contractual duty *must of itself* necessitate strong enforcement remedies.[91] If parties do not necessarily intend this, a key assumption in the critics' argument is falsified. There is then no deontological, or doctrinal, *necessity* for performance-oriented remedies. However, the transformation could still be justified by its superiority as an attractive set of (preference-respecting and clear) default rules. Such an argument would, of course, be alien to much of the scholarly writing in this area. It could be said not to take that scholarship seriously, or anyway not to engage with it in its own terms. But we have already argued that

---

[87] Robyn Carroll, 'Agreements to Specifically Perform Contractual Obligations' (2012) 29 Jo Contract L 155.

[88] M Chen-Wishart, ch 5 below.   [89] Rowan (n 80) 457–60.

[90] An exception is Rowan ibid.   [91] Cf Craswell (n 48).

moral or doctrinal-fundamentalist scholarship does not deserve to be taken seriously in commercial law. It misses the point. This area of law needs to be understood instrumentally (which hardly resolves the controversy, but indicates the lines along which the battles need to be fought). That is how its commercial clients understand it.

However, there is good reason to believe that the current regime, tolerant of breach, is much closer to commercial expectations[92] – certain throwaway aphorisms notwithstanding.[93] Rules that seem inexplicably kind to contract breakers – wicked creatures deserving only of condemnation from the moralist perspective – are in fact appealing to both promisors *and* promisees (*ex ante*). The promisor is permitted to cut its losses when performance becomes uneconomic (i.e. given the option of paying compensation instead).[94] In an uncertain world this is sometimes bound to happen (and the common law's strict liability and narrow frustration doctrine admit of few exceptions). Both parties recognise that permitting breach reduces the cost of performance and that means lower prices paid by promisees. It is obvious that (and obvious why) a promisor would charge a premium for binding itself to perform come hell or high water, rather than according to the common law's default breach-or-pay regime. (Of course, performance might be so important to a given promisee that he will stipulate for specific performance and/or breach-deterring remedies; the price charged for such an onerous obligation will rise to reflect the promisor's greater level of commitment and higher costs.) Payment of damages instead of performing may not be immoral after all.[95]

Similar points may be made about mitigation. It seems extraordinary to the promissory ethicist that the victim of deliberate breach is not only powerless to compel performance, but must take active steps to limit his loss (a requirement which apparently benefits only the breaching promisor). But again, *both* parties actually benefit. By limiting the extent of losses mitigation lowers the cost of performance, which translates into the promisor charging lower prices for the same service. It is therefore in

---

[92] Campbell (n 58).

[93] WW Buckland, 'The Nature of Contractual Obligation' (1944) 8 *CLJ* 247, 247: 'One does not buy a right to damages, one buys a horse.'

[94] Accordingly it may be argued that the better construction of contractual obligations is an option to perform *or* pay (and so it is a *non sequitur* to see enforcement as the natural remedy for breach): Alan Schwartz and Daniel Markovits, 'The Myth of Efficient Breach: New Defenses of the Expectation Interest' (2011) 97 Virginia LR 1939.

[95] Shavell (n 55).

the parties' mutual interest to cooperate after breach. Campbell is accordingly critical of 'vindicatory' approaches to breach of contract for undermining this crucial, cost-reducing spirit of cooperation in the face of breach.[96] There is evidence that a default rule of specific performance 'increases a promisee's sense of entitlement and resentment against breach'.[97]

Of course, again, the parties should be free to stipulate for remedies that make mitigation irrelevant (e.g. liquidated damages or specific performance). They know their business best. But doctrines from which mitigation has been excluded as a matter of law are controversial.[98] To add to the number of such rules would be questionable. Yet supporters of performance-vindicating remedies are clear and unrepentant about vindication's incompatibility with mitigation.[99] They do not ask whether the run of contracting parties would prefer a system of rights-vindication; that question appears quite irrelevant. But it should not be. What would be the point of a systemic re-ordering of English remedies if (at best) it inspired mass contracting-out from those rules by sophisticated parties and trade-standard forms or (at worst) spurred an exodus to rival jurisdictions like New York, as a superior framework for international trade? To reform commercial law insulated from the needs of its customers really would be to 'stand aloof on [the] chill and distant heights'.[100] It would misunderstand the optional nature of contract remedies in any liberal, intention-based system of contract. It would be damaging and futile.

2.6 Conclusion

Contract remedies are by their nature a system of default rules. Their function, albeit only a provisional place-holding one – in the absence of party intention – must be to satisfy commercial expectations. A number of consequences follow. Some appear negative but we should not shrink from them. First, the default rule approach downgrades the importance of 'doctrine' in the law of contract. Instead the intentions, needs and practices of the parties (or of those who draft contracts) should have primary

---

[96] Campbell (n 58).   [97] Depoorter and Tontrup (n 11).

[98] See especially *White and Carter (Councils) Ltd v McGregor* [1962] AC 413. Cf J O'Sullivan, ch 3 below, and Jonathan Morgan, 'Smuggling Mitigation into *White & Carter v McGregor*: Time to Come Clean?' [2015] LMCLQ 575.

[99] E.g. Charlie Webb, 'Performance and Compensation: An Analysis of Contract Damages and Contractual Obligation' (2006) 26 OJLS 41, 64–68.

[100] Benjamin N Cardozo, *The Nature of the Judicial Process* (Yale University Press 1921) 168.

emphasis. This accords with the orientation of legal practice (most lawyers are transactional lawyers, and not involved in litigation).[101] Perhaps contract law scholarship needs to catch up with reality.

Secondly, what *are* the expectations of commercial parties, and how is the law to go about satisfying them? These are extremely difficult questions to which no final answers are offered here. But the method for addressing them has been indicated. By reflecting on the likely preferences of reasonable contractors the common law process might be able to produce commercially acceptable bodies of law.[102] That this is an uncertain process affords even greater importance to the *default* nature of the legally supplied remedies. It would be astonishingly arrogant to suggest that the common law could provide the optimal remedy in every case, such that no parties should be permitted to contract out of them. So any tendency to elevate the law's rules to near-immutable status through interpretive presumptions must be checked. Defaults must be 'frictionless' where possible, and legal mechanisms sufficient to alter them given clear recognition.

Because of the great importance of clarity and predictability, we should be cautious about basing default rules on unmediated commercial practice (the fashionable 'contextual' approach). Nor should every question be reduced to one of the parties' implicit intentions. There is much to be said for clear doctrinal rules as a prudential simplifying strategy, despite all contractual obligations being ultimately rooted in party intent. At least traditional, hard-edged doctrines provide certainty; if they are suboptimal the parties can more easily contract out of them.

But this pragmatic acceptance of the value of doctrine should not be carried too far. In particular, it should not lead back to the worship of common law rules for their own sake, which tends to obscure their default nature. Still less should scholars attempt to satisfy commercial needs by reasoning deductively from axioms of promissory morality. Of course, the satisfaction of commercial expectations plays no part in such reasoning. That is why it is misconceived.

---

[101] Howarth (n 9) ch 2.   [102] Cf Schwartz (n 11).

PART II

Specific Remedies

3

Repudiation: Keeping the Contract Alive

JANET O'SULLIVAN

3.1 Introduction

This chapter explores and takes issue with Lord Reid's famous *obiter* qualification in *White & Carter (Councils) Ltd v McGregor*[1] that the innocent party,[2] faced with a repudiation by the other contracting party,[3] does not have an unfettered right to elect to keep the contract alive, perform and claim the price:

> It may well be that, if it can be shown that a person has no legitimate interest, financial or otherwise, in performing the contract rather than claiming damages, he ought not to be allowed to saddle the other party with an additional burden with no benefit to himself. If a party has no interest to enforce a stipulation, he cannot in general enforce it: so it might be said that, if a party has no interest to insist on a particular remedy, he ought not to be allowed to insist on it. And, just as a party is not allowed to enforce a penalty, so he ought not to be allowed to penalise the other party by taking one course when another is equally advantageous to him. If I may revert to the example which I gave of a company engaging an expert to prepare an elaborate report and then repudiating before anything was done, it might be that the company could show that the expert had no substantial or legitimate interest in carrying out the work rather than accepting damages: I would think that the *de minimis* principle would apply in determining whether his interest was substantial, and that he might have a legitimate interest other than an immediate financial interest. But if the expert had no such interest then that might be regarded as a proper case for the exercise of the general equitable jurisdiction of the court.[4]

In accordance with our theme, this chapter will deal with commercial transactions only: it may be that different considerations would apply

I am grateful to Jia Wei Lee and Oriyan Prizant for research assistance in the preparation of this chapter; all errors and omissions that remain are entirely my own.
[1] [1962] AC 413 (HL).   [2] Referred to throughout as the claimant.
[3] Referred to throughout as the defendant.   [4] *White & Carter* (n 1) 431.

where a consumer is in repudiatory breach of contract with a commercial entity.[5] Likewise it will focus solely on the innocent party's *financial* interest, leaving out of account matters such as enhancement of reputation that may well be legitimate contractual expectations.

3.2   What is Meant by a 'Legitimate Financial Interest'?

This question is inherently puzzling.[6] When considering the claimant's legitimate financial interest in performance, as opposed to damages, the starting point ought to be the trite proposition that expectation damages for breach of contract are meant to put the claimant into the same position as if the contract had been performed.[7] This suggests that the question of whether the claimant has a financial interest in performance (i.e. rejecting the repudiation, keeping the contract alive, then performing, then claiming the price) must be tied up with the question of the measure of damages that would be recoverable if the claimant had instead accepted the repudiation.

But this leads to an odd result. Two alternative conclusions seem to be available, as a matter of logic:

- Either a claimant will *never* have a financial interest in performance (as opposed to damages), because the court does not recognise inadequacies in its measure of damages, which should *ex hypothesi* always be the precise equivalent of performance. (Or, to qualify slightly, a claimant will only have such an interest in those rare cases where specific performance is available because the court acknowledges that damages are not an adequate remedy.)
- Or a claimant will *always* have a financial interest in performance (as opposed to damages), because claiming damages (instead of an action for the price) invariably involves being subject to the burden of pleading and proving loss, the requirement of mitigation, the rules of remoteness of damage, and problems of quantum.[8]

---

[5] The repudiating party in *White & Carter* itself, Mr McGregor, appears to have been trading as a small business, not incorporated, but certainly contracting for business purposes.

[6] Lord Reid's language is described as 'uncharacteristically vague' by JW Carter, '*White and Carter v McGregor* – how unreasonable' (2012) 128 LQR 490, 491.

[7] *Robinson v Harman* (1848) 1 Ex 850, 154 ER 363 (Court of Exchequer).

[8] And, as Carter (n 6) above points out, at 492, 'Given the ever-present risk of insolvency in the commercial world, it is difficult to envisage any situation in which it could seriously be argued that a plaintiff has no legitimate interest to prefer a claim in debt over a claim in damages.'

Yet the consensus about the meaning of the 'no legitimate interest' concept in case law and commentary seems to be that the claimant will have a legitimate financial interest in *virtually all* cases, *other than* in exceptional circumstances where it would be utterly unreasonable for the claimant to insist on keeping the contract alive. For example, Cooke J in *Isabella Shipowner SA v Shagang Shipping Co Ltd (The Aquafaith)*[9] said:

> The effect of the authorities is that an innocent party will have no legitimate interest in maintaining the contract if damages are an adequate remedy and his insistence on maintaining the contract can be described as 'wholly unreasonable', 'extremely unreasonable' or, perhaps, in my words, 'perverse'.[10]

Furthermore, when the courts identify what those 'exceptional circumstances' are – why precisely it would be wholly unreasonable or perverse for the claimant to keep the contract alive and claim the price – they rarely consider in detail what the hypothetical measure of damages would be if the repudiation had been accepted. Instead there is a tendency to focus on the extent of the burden imposed on the *defendant* (by the claimant's decision to reject the repudiation) in having to perform/pay the price, rather than pay damages, adopting language such as the 'commercial absurdity' of 'imposing unwanted performance on an unwilling recipient'. This has little to do with the claimant's financial interest in performance, more a concern to respect the defendant's lack of interest in performance, a desire to minimise waste by not requiring the defendant to pay for an unwanted performance. Yet this burden is imposed by the contract, not by the claimant's actions or choices in response to the repudiation, and it is hard to defend a principle that allows the court, in effect, to relieve a repudiating defendant of a bad bargain, where no such jurisdiction exists in the absence of a repudiation.

3.3 The Case Law: How is 'Legitimate Financial Interest' Interpreted?

It is helpful to start by exploring a selection of authorities in detail, dividing them into two categories. First we will consider cases where Lord Reid's qualification was not applied, so the claimant was permitted to claim the price, exploring what reasoning was adopted to determine that there was a legitimate financial interest and what the hypothetical

---

[9] [2012] EWHC 1077 (Comm), [2012] 2 All ER (Comm) 461.   [10] Ibid [44].

measure of damages would have been if the claimant had instead accepted the repudiation. Secondly, we will consider authorities where Lord Reid's qualification was applied and the claimant was not permitted to claim the price, this time asking why the court held there was no legitimate financial interest in performance, and what measure of damages was awarded instead. In doing so, it will be suggested that there is a narrower but more principled explanation of those cases where the qualification has been applied.

3.3.1 Authorities Where the Claimant was Held to Have a Legitimate Financial Interest

3.3.1.1 *White & Carter (Councils) Ltd* v *McGregor*

Like many seminal cases, the facts of *White & Carter* are at one and the same time very well known, but often misremembered or over-simplified, so it is worth setting them out in detail. White & Carter ('W&C') supplied bins to local authorities and charged customers to display advertising plates on the bins; McGregor ran a small garage business in Clydebank. The parties originally had a contract for three years from November 1954; in June 1957, when it was nearing the end of the initial term, McGregor's sales manager renewed the contract for three more years (156 weeks), on the same terms. However, the sales manager lacked authority to do this, and McGregor wrote to W&C purporting to cancel the renewed contract on the same day. This amounted to a repudiation, which W&C did not accept, but continued to display the adverts: the first display under the new contract began at the start of November 1957, when the old contract came to an end. Sums due from McGregor under the contract (2s per week per plate together with 5s per annum per plate) were payable annually in advance, the first payment being due seven days after the first display. Unsurprisingly, McGregor did not make any payment after November 1957.

Crucially, the contract contained a price acceleration clause in clause 8, as follows:

> In the event of an instalment or part thereof being due for payment, and remaining unpaid for a period of *four weeks* or in the event of the advertiser being in any way in breach of this contract then the whole amount due for the 156 weeks or such part of the said 156 weeks as the advertiser shall not yet have paid shall immediately become due and payable.

W&C relied on clause 8 and commenced proceedings in October 1958 in the Sherriff's Court for the full three years' price (£196 4s), whilst continuing to display the plates for the full three years of the renewed contract.

The unusual features of the case combined to make it something of a 'perfect storm': the sales manager's error which meant the contract was made and cancelled on the same day; the fact that it was a renewal of an existing contract which meant that W&C already had the advertising material so could perform without the co-operation of McGregor; and the price acceleration clause which allowed proceedings for three years' price to be brought after just one month.

When this perfect storm reached the House of Lords, a majority (Lord Tucker, Lord Hodson and Lord Reid) held that W&C was entitled to elect to reject McGregor's repudiation, perform and claim the price, while Lords Morton and Keith dissented on the basis that W&C could not indirectly compel performance by McGregor in circumstances where specific performance would not be available: 'In my opinion, my Lords, the appellants' only remedy was damages, and they were bound to take steps to minimise their loss, according to a well-established rule of law.'[11]

It is noteworthy that Lord Reid was the only member of the House to mention the 'no legitimate financial interest' qualification and it was not the subject of argument. Unsurprisingly then, there was no attempt to consider what W&C's measure of damages would have been if it had accepted McGregor's repudiation at the outset, nor what would have been required by way of mitigation. And this is not a simple issue. If W&C had accepted McGregor's repudiation immediately, its own primary obligations would have come to an end and, with them, its opportunity to earn any part of the instalments of price and thus to trigger the price acceleration clause. How then would mitigation operate? We do not know anything about the market conditions in 1950s Clydebank, whether or not the demand for bin advertising exceeded W&C's stock of bins[12] or what W&C's negotiating stance would have been concerning clause 8. There is at least a chance that W&C might not have been able to replace McGregor's business immediately, or might only have been able to do so if the new customer's contract did not include a price acceleration clause, terms which the requirement of

---

[11] *White & Carter* (n 1) 433 (Lord Morton).

[12] By analogy with the supply/demand issue under s 50(2) of the Sale of Goods Act 1979, exemplified in *Thompson (WL) Ltd v Robinson (Gunmakers) Ltd* [1955] Ch 177 (Ch), compared with *Charter v Sullivan* [1957] 2 QB 117 (CA).

mitigation would suggest W&C should accept, rather than hold out for
an identical contract. This would suggest that quantification of W&C's
damages, if it had accepted the repudiation at the outset, would have
included some compensation for the lost chance of expedited receipt of
the price. If so, it becomes impossible to argue that W&C had no
legitimate financial interest in keeping the contract alive.

3.3.1.2 *Gator Shipping Corporation* v *Trans-Asiatic Oil Ltd and Occidental Shipping Establishment (The Odenfeld)*[13]

In May 1973 the charterers chartered a ship from the owners, Occidental
(a one-ship shell company) on a basic ten-year charterparty, with hire
fixed for the first two years, thereafter with provision for review.
The difficulty was that the charterers wanted the contract to provide for
hire to fluctuate with market movements, whereas Occidental and its
parent company (MFC) wanted upwards-only review, as this was
a requirement of funding institutions and MFC wanted to borrow
money secured on the charter. So a deal was stitched up: on its face the
charterparty set an upwards-only review of the hire based on market
value (to be determined by an expert panel) subject to a minimum
$3.49 per dead weight ton. But a side letter was also signed at the time
of the charterparty, to be kept secret from potential funders, whereby the
parties agreed that if the panel assessed the market value as less than
the $3.49 minimum, Occidental promised to pay the difference back to
the charterers. Occidental's obligations under the side letter were
guaranteed by its parent, MFC.

In June 1973, MFC approached the plaintiffs for a loan, disclosing the
charterparty but not the side letter, and the loan agreement was executed;
the benefit of the charterparty was assigned to the plaintiffs, whereupon
the charterers were obliged to pay all money due under the contract to the
plaintiffs. By April 1975 the charter market had collapsed and the panel
fixed the market rate at $1.50, although the minimum of $3.49 continued
to be payable under charter. This triggered the terms of the side letter:
MFC paid the difference back to the charterers for a few months then
stopped, purportedly invoking rights of set-off under other transactions.

Until January 1976 the charterers continued to pay the full contractual
hire to the plaintiffs, but then ceased, alleging that Occidental had
repudiated the charter by not honouring the side letter. This was the
first time the plaintiffs learnt of the side letter deal. In February the

[13] [1978] 2 Lloyd's Rep 357 (Com Ct).

plaintiffs declared the loan in default and called it in, but received nothing; the charterers refused to do anything with the ship, asserting that the charterparty was already at an end. In July, the ship was laid up with consent of the plaintiffs and at their expense. Finally in September 1976, the plaintiffs reached a compromise with MFC: the ship was transferred to the plaintiffs and at this point they conceded that the charter was at an end. They then claimed the full hire from the charterers for the period from January–September 1976; the charterers joined Occidental as a defendant and counterclaimed for a declaration that the contract had come to an end in January.

Kerr J first rejected the charterers' argument that they were entitled to terminate the contract in January because of Occidental's breach of the side letter: as a matter of construction, he concluded that the transaction was:

> [A] carefully formulated scheme designed to ensure that the defendants would pay the hire fee due under the charter in any event, but that they were to be secured in many different ways against the possibility of their payments exceeding the market rate. The charter-party and the side letter were carefully designed to be capable of operating independently of each other.[14]

On the contrary, it was the charterers' conduct in refusing to proceed with the contract that itself amounted to a repudiation. Kerr J then considered whether Occidental had been entitled to reject that repudiation and keep the contract alive, opining that '[T]he real question is simply whether, as the result of their assumed repudiation, the defendants are to be relieved from their undertaking to the plaintiffs to pay them the hire due under the charter.'[15] In concluding that Occidental were indeed entitled to keep the contract alive,[16] he explicitly recognised (unusually) that the key to 'legitimate financial interest' is to compare the claimant's position in a hypothetical claim for damages if it had accepted the repudiation:

> In practice it is an extremely difficult and lengthy process to assess damages in a situation such as this. How are they to be fairly assessed, when at the time of the repudiation the charter still had about 6½ years to

---

[14] Ibid 371.   [15] Ibid 375.

[16] Although he went on to hold (ibid 379) that Occidental accepted the charterers' repudiation in July, when the ship was laid up, since 'laying up a vessel is so inconsistent with the continuing existence of the time charter that Occidental and the plaintiffs cannot be heard to say in the same breath that the charter was still on foot'.

run with many possible variables in the market rate and the performance of the vessel? Of course the law provides some answer, but having to establish a claim for damages puts a shipowner into a very different position from that of being entitled to hire under a subsisting charter.[17]

It is suggested that Kerr J's reasoning is of general application, once it is accepted that the focus should be on the claimant's interest in performance rather than damages, since having to establish a claim for damages (with the attendant issues of remoteness, mitigation and quantum) invariably puts the claimant into a 'very different' and less favourable position than performing and claiming the price.

Nonetheless, Kerr J recognised that a claimant's freedom to keep the contract alive is not entirely untrammelled, qualifying his conclusion as follows:

> However, in saying this I must not be thought to be implying that Occidental and the plaintiffs could necessarily have maintained the same position for a further six years ... Moreover the passage of time might in itself alter the legal position of the parties, because an insistence to treat the contract as still in being might in time become quite unrealistic, unreasonable and untenable.[18]

This caveat is not principally concerned with the claimant's interest in performance or lack thereof, but arguably reflects the law's broader policy concern not to endorse stalemate between the parties or, in other circumstances, perpetual obligations. It will be suggested that this issue represents a more principled, but considerably narrower, qualification than Lord Reid's dictum, which will be examined further in due course.

3.3.1.3   *Isabella Shipowner SA* v *Shagang Shipping Co Ltd (The Aquafaith)*[19]

This case involved a five-year[20] time charter: with ninety-four days left to run the charterers redelivered the ship, saying they had no further use for it and would not pay the hire for the remainder of the term. The owners refused to accept this repudiation and went to arbitration. The arbitrator found that the owners had no legitimate interest in insisting that the charter remained alive; they were thus required to take redelivery of the vessel, trade it on the spot market by way of mitigation and claim damages in respect of their loss. This decision was overturned on appeal to Cooke J, who regarded the arbitrator's approach as unsupportable:

[17] Ibid 374.   [18] Ibid 375.   [19] *The Aquafaith* (n 9).
[20] Strictly, for fifty-nine to sixty-one months.

The arbitrator found in terms that there was 'nothing extraordinary or indeed unusual in respect of this case' ... [and the rule about] the exception only operating in extreme cases, was ignored. It appears that the arbitrator thought that it was necessary for the owners to show that it was an extreme case to justify maintaining the charter in existence, thus reversing the burden of proof and confusing the general principle with the exception. He misunderstood what was meant by 'no legitimate interest' in *White and Carter* and ignored all the succeeding authorities in relation to it.[21]

On the contrary, with the appropriate focus on the claimant's position, this was a clear case of a legitimate financial interest in performance, when compared with claiming damages. For Cooke J, '[T]he contract breaker was ... seeking to be shot of the difficulties in trading the vessel by imposing that burden on the innocent party, as well as depriving him of the assured income of advance hire.'[22] The arbitrator should have asked himself:

whether the charterers had discharged the burden of showing that the owners had no legitimate interest in maintaining the charter and had done so by showing that this was an extreme case where damages would be an adequate remedy and where an election to keep the contract alive would be so unreasonable that the owners should not be allowed to do so. He should have explored whether there was *any benefit* to the owners, whether or not small in comparison to the loss to the charterers.[23]

Applying this approach to the facts yielded a straightforward answer:

With only 94 days left of a 5 year time charter in a difficult market where a substitute time charter was impossible, and trading on the spot market very difficult, it would be impossible to characterise the owners' stance in wishing to maintain the charter and a right to hire as unreasonable, let alone beyond all reason, wholly unreasonable or perverse. As the arbitrator said, this is not an extreme or unusual case and in such circumstances the exception to the *White and Carter* principle cannot apply.[24]

So for Cooke J, Lord Reid's qualification can be rephrased in the language of 'utter unreasonableness' or 'perversity', but this is being judged by reference to the claimant's position, and not the impact on the defendant of being held to the contract. The implication is that a claimant is allowed to ignore even a large downside for the defendant, as long as there is some small benefit to himself in obtaining performance rather than claiming damages. This is close to the view propounded in this chapter that

---

[21] *The Aquafaith* (n 9) [45].   [22] Ibid [48].   [23] Ibid [42] (emphasis added).
[24] Ibid [56].

a claimant will *always* have a legitimate financial interest in performance because it is invariably advantageous not to have to mitigate and worry about quantum and remoteness. Cooke J gives an example where a claimant would not be entitled to keep the contract alive, citing a case[25] where the charterer was obliged to repair a badly damaged ship but declined to do so: the owner's refusal to accept this repudiation was 'plainly' perverse:

> [S]ince the cost of repair was double the value of the ship when repaired and four times as much as its scrap value. To refuse to accept a premature re-delivery of the vessel in order for such repairs to be done would therefore be truly perverse. Repair in such circumstances would be an exercise in futility.[26]

This supports the suggestion that another, more restrictive, principle occasionally operates to trump the claimant's interest in performance, namely the policy concern to avoid futility and stalemate in a contractual setting. This will be explored further in the next section, dealing with three authorities in which the claimant was *not* permitted to keep the contract alive. It will be suggested that the first is indefensible, whereas the second and third are explicable on a basis other than Lord Reid's qualification.

3.3.2   Authorities Where the Claimant was Held Not to Have a Legitimate Financial Interest

3.3.2.1   Clea Shipping Corp v Bulk Oil International Ltd (The Alaskan Trader) (No 2)[27]

Here, a twenty-four-month time charter was made in October 1979, for the period December 1979–December 1981. The contract obliged the owners to repair the ship. In October 1980, the ship suffered serious engine failure, for which repairs would take several months, so the charterers repudiated the contract. The owners did not accept the repudiation, undertook expensive repairs to the ship at a cost of approximately £800,000, which were completed in April 1981. The charterers were not interested in taking the ship back for the remainder of the term, so between April and December 1981 the owners kept the ship fully

---

[25] *Attica Sea Carriers Corp v Ferrostaal Poseidon Bulk Reederei GmbH (The Puerto Buitrago)* [1976] 1 Lloyd's Rep 250 (CA), see below.
[26] *The Aquafaith* (n 9) [44].   [27] [1984] 1 All ER 129 (Com Ct).

crewed and ready, then claimed the hire for that period. The charterers paid without prejudice, then brought proceedings to reclaim the hire.

The arbitrator held that the owners were obliged to mitigate their loss – which meant accept the repudiation – in April 1981,[28] so could only claim damages thereafter. The owners' conduct was regarded as a 'commercial absurdity' since they knew the charterers no longer wanted the ship. Lloyd J dismissed the owners' appeal,[29] holding that the arbitrator had applied the right test and declining to interfere with the arbitrator's decision.

It is noteworthy that no attempt was made by Lloyd J to assess the owners' financial interest in performance in the sense of comparing the quantum of damages with the hire fee, merely asserting that the arbitrator reached a view that he was entitled to take. This is somewhat puzzling, since the arbitrator was confining the owners to their award of damages, presumably reasoning that damages would therefore be less than the remaining hire, yet this is surely an argument that the owners *did* have a financial interest in performance? Presumably the owners were expected to mitigate by finding someone else to hire the ship, and claim the difference in rates from the original charterers, yet the hassle and expense of mitigating demonstrates their financial interest in keeping the contract alive.

This suggests that, despite lip service to the language of the claimant's legitimate interest, the court is principally concerned with the burden on the defendant of being saddled with an unwanted contract, a common interpretation of Lord Reid's qualification to which we will return. But there is a more problematic aspect of the reasoning in *The Alaskan Trader*, revealed if we ask what substantive difference there is between the eight months remaining on the charter term here and the ninety-four days left at the end of the *Aquafaith* term. The answer is that there is no difference, apart from the £800,000-worth of repairs here and the fact that the ship was kept fully crewed. Crucially, though, these were at the *owners'* expense, costs which the owners were of course not seeking to pass on to the charterers. This is why *The Alaskan Trader* is wrongly decided – the owners did nothing more 'unreasonable' than to take seriously the bilateral aspect of their election to keep the contract alive and perform in full their own onerous obligations under it. The court's decision penalises them for honouring their side of the bargain.

---

[28] Not in October 1980 when the repairs became necessary.

[29] Albeit somewhat half-heartedly, granting leave to appeal to the Court of Appeal.

The next two cases are more problematic, as the finding for the defendant in each case was indeed justified on the merits. On careful reading, however, neither actually involves a claimant rejecting a repudiation, performing and claiming the price; thus the outcomes could have been achieved without engaging the *White & Carter* qualification:

3.3.2.2   *Attica Sea Carriers Corporation v Ferrostaal Poseidon Bulk Reederei GmbH (The Puerto Buitrago)*[30]

This case involved a bareboat charter by demise for seventeen months from January 1974 to May 1975. The contract obliged the charterers to keep the ship manned and repaired; there was also an express obligation on the charterers to repair and put the ship into good condition before redelivery at the end of the term. At some point during the term (it is unclear from the law report exactly when), the ship developed engine trouble. The cargo was unloaded and the ship was towed to Kiel in September 1975 (four months after the end of the basic charter period). The cost of repairs would have been $2 million, whereas the value of the ship if repaired would only have been $1 million, so the charterers declined to repair. The owners refused to accept this repudiation, arguing that the charterers were bound to repair and to pay hire until the repairs were done, even though the basic charter period was already at an end. Mocatta J found for the owners, but the Court of Appeal allowed the charterers' appeal, holding that the owners could not specifically enforce the charterers' obligations to repair and to pay the hire in the meantime.

Lord Denning MR gave the principal judgment, which reveals his dislike of the general principle and result in *White & Carter*, a decision he calls 'grotesque': he would prefer to confine it to its particular facts and impose a general requirement of mitigation on claimants faced with a repudiation. Unsurprisingly then he did not explicitly explore the notion that 'legitimate financial interest' must involve a comparison between the claimant's financial position on performance versus the applicable measure of damages, simply holding that damages were an adequate remedy:

> [T]he shipowners seek to compel specific performance of one or other of the provisions of the charter – with most unjust and unreasonable consequences – when damages would be an adequate remedy. I do not think the law allows them to do this. I think they should accept redelivery and sue for damages. The charterers are, we are told, good for the money. That should suffice.[31]

---

[30] See n 25.   [31] Ibid 255.

Similarly, the owner's measure of damages on acceptance of the repudiation was not explored, but it is instructive to do so. The owner would be required to mitigate, which presumably means write off the ship, as the repairs would cost more ($2 million) than its value when repaired ($1 million), and recover the difference between the $1 million value of the repaired ship and its scrap value ($0.5 million) without the repair; the 'cost of cure' measure would be ruled out as 'wholly disproportionate'.[32] Of course the charterers' obligation to repair at the end of the term is not specifically enforceable, but the same applies to most contractual repair obligations. All this is relevant to is the owners' interest in performance rather than damages (bearing in mind that the contract explicitly put the risk of disrepair on the charterers), since the measure of damages transfers the risk of having to repair or write off the ship from the charterers to the owners.

Nonetheless, the result in *The Puerto Buitrago*, is explicable in orthodox terms. Despite always being cited as such, it is not squarely within the *White & Carter* fact pattern. First, it is not about repudiation: the charterers were not purporting to cancel the demise charter during its term, and the owners were not seeking to claim hire for the remainder of the term. The basic term was already at an end, and the dispute was instead about an 'ordinary' breach of a contractual promise to repair the ship; this promise was not specifically enforceable and was also not a condition,[33] thus its breach could be remedied in damages only.

Secondly, given that the contract appeared to make the hire payable indefinitely until the repairs were carried out, the result was driven by the policy imperative to avoid stalemate and perpetual obligations. Orr LJ's judgment points out that the case differs from *White & Carter* because 'here it cannot be said that the owners could fulfil the contract without any co-operation from the charterers'.[34] In other words, the only way to break the deadlock and avoid a perpetual obligation to pay the hire is for the charterers to perform their repair obligation, but that is precisely what will not be ordered by way of specific performance. The law's abhorrence of stalemate again trumps the claimant's performance interest. A similar concern can explain the most recent authority purporting to apply Lord Reid's qualification.

---

[32] *Tito v Waddell (No 2)* [1977] Ch 106 (Ch); *Ruxley Electronics and Construction Ltd v Forsyth* [1996] AC 344 (HL).
[33] *The Puerto Buitrago* (n 25) 253.   [34] Ibid 256.

3.3.2.3 *MSC Mediterranean Shipping Company SA v Cottonex Anstalt*[35]

In a complex dispute, the claimant was a carrier which carried on container shipping; the defendant was a shipper trading in raw cotton. In 2011 the parties contracted for the carrier to carry thirty-five containers of raw cotton by sea to Bangladesh, which was shipped in three lots under five bills of lading. The cotton was sold to a consignee, with payment by confirmed letter of credit; all sorts of disputes and court proceedings arose, but it seems the shipper was paid in full by the consignee. Nonetheless the consignee never collected the cotton, which remained in the Bangladeshi port, still packed inside the containers (the Bangladesh Customs Authority would not allow the containers to be released without a court order). The question for the English High Court was whether the shipper was 'liable to pay the Carrier a daily charge, described as "demurrage", for each day that the containers remain unavailable to the Carrier because they are still being used to hold the goods'.[36] Leggatt J held that daily rate demurrage started to accrue, pursuant to an express term in the contract,[37] once the containers were discharged in July 2011. The carrier was therefore claiming over $1 million in demurrage by the date of the trial, which amounted to almost ten times the value of the containers, while the shipper argued that its obligation had long since ceased.

The judge dealt first with the question of whether the shipper was in repudiatory breach, holding that this occurred on 27 September 2011 when 'the Shipper informed the Carrier that it did not have legal title to the goods as they had been paid for . . . I in any event consider that by this time the delay in collecting the goods had become so prolonged as to frustrate the commercial purpose of the venture'.[38]

The judge then turned to the question of whether the carrier could keep the contract alive and claim demurrage thereafter, or whether it was obliged to accept the repudiatory breach and claim damages, concluding:

---

[35] [2015] EWHC 283 (Comm), [2015] 1 Lloyd's Rep 359. This decision has since been partly reversed by the Court of Appeal [2016] EWCA Civ 789 on other grounds, with the court expressing the view that it was not a case to which the *White & Carter* principle applies.

[36] Ibid [6].

[37] Leggatt J held the provision for daily demurrage was a liquidated damages clause, a conclusion which, as Jonathan Morgan, 'Smuggling Mitigation into *White & Carter*: Time to Come Clean' (2015) 4 LMCLQ 575, 588 points out, is not uncontroversial.

[38] *MSC Mediterranean* (n 35) [87].

I have no doubt that the Carrier had a legitimate interest in keeping the contracts of carriage in force for as long as there was a realistic prospect that the Shipper would perform its remaining primary obligations under the contracts by procuring the collection of the goods and the redelivery of the containers. Once it was quite clear, however, that the Shipper was in repudiatory breach of these obligations and that there was no such prospect, the Carrier no longer had any reason to keep the contracts open in the hope of future performance.[39]

Leggatt J's conclusion is hard to justify as a straightforward application of a test of the carrier's financial interest in performance, as opposed to mitigating and claiming damages immediately. Explained in context, it is justifiable, although the two reasons offered by Leggatt J are controversial. First, he was of the view that if the demurrage obligation did indeed give the carrier an unfettered right to ignore the shipper's repudiation and carry on claiming demurrage indefinitely, it would be unenforceable as a penalty clause.[40] This would distinguish it from the various primary payment obligations in other *White & Carter* authorities,[41] on the basis that the carrier's obvious financial interest in continued performance could not be treated as a *legitimate* one, but is hard to reconcile with the Supreme Court's reversal of *Makdessi*.[42] Secondly, Leggatt J applied a growing body of case law imposing an obligation of good faith where a contractual discretion is exercised,[43] an analogous issue which he regarded as restricting a claimant's freedom to ignore the interests of the repudiating defendant when responding to the repudiation. This suggestion is of more general application to our topic, and we will return to it in the next section.

There is arguably a better justification of the result in *MSC Mediterranean*, despite the claimant's financial interest in performance. This is because, like *The Puerto Buitrago*, it is not really about repudiation in the sense of the wrongful cancellation of a contract before the end of its

---

[39] Ibid [104].

[40] Applying *Makdessi v Cavendish Square Holdings BV* [2013] EWCA Civ 1539, [2014] 2 All ER (Comm) 125, subsequently reversed on appeal to the Supreme Court [2015] UKSC 67, [2015] 3 WLR 1373.

[41] The price acceleration clause in *White & Carter* itself was not regarded as a liquidated damages clause and thus not susceptible to the penalty jurisdiction.

[42] Morgan (n 37) suggests that a demurrage provision has never before been struck down as a penalty, a point made by Moore-Bick LJ in the Court of Appeal in *MSC* [2016] EWCA Civ 789 at para [46].

[43] These included *Paragon Finance plc v Nash* [2001] EWCA Civ 1466, [2002] 1 WLR 685; and *British Telecommunications plc v Telefónica O2 UK Ltd* [2014] UKSC 42, [2014] Bus LR 765. Moore-Bick LJ in the Court of Appeal doubted this explanation of the *White & Carter* qualification, see para [45].

term; nor is it about an innocent party seeking to keep the contract alive, perform its side of the bargain, and claim the finite agreed price. Instead, it can be seen as another example of the law's abhorrence of stalemate and the policy of not endorsing perpetual obligations.

This is seen in other private law contexts. The rule against perpetuities in the law of real property, put in statutory form in the Perpetuities and Accumulations Act 1964, is well known. In the law of contract, where a contractual stipulation is expressly unlimited as to time or phrased to last 'in perpetuity', the courts are reluctant to interpret that wording so as to rule out the possibility of termination.[44] In *Staffordshire Area Health Authority v South Staffordshire Waterworks Co*[45] the Court of Appeal construed[46] a provision in a 1929 contract that the water company would provide the health authority with water 'at all times hereafter' as meaning 'until terminated on reasonable notice'. Similarly, in *Harbinger UK Ltd v GE Information Services Ltd*[47] Evans LJ held that, although the phrase 'in perpetuity' in an obligation to provide computer support was 'inconsistent with a time limit',[48] nonetheless:

> [17] This does not mean literally 'for ever' or 'until the crack of doom'. The contract itself – meaning the unilateral contract under which the obligation to provide support and maintenance arises – will not live forever. The time will come when the technology is superseded and the software is outdated. As a result, customers will require a change in the software (and no doubt in the hardware) which they use and they will no longer make the annual payments in return for which the services are provided.

It is not surprising that the same reluctance to endorse perpetual obligations and stalemate is found in the courts' remedial response to repudiation. This policy concern pervades the *MSC Mediterranean* case and explains the result better than an orthodox application of Lord Reid's qualification, as seen in the following two paragraphs:

> It follows that the goods shipped under the first four bills of lading ceased to be the property of the Shipper when it received payment for those goods on 23 May 2011. The Consignee never sought to reject the goods. Indeed, there is no evidence that the Consignee has ever alleged any breach of the contract of sale. Any right to reject the goods, if it existed

---

[44] See for example *BMS Computer Solutions Ltd v AB Agri Ltd* [2010] EWHC 464 (Ch).
[45] [1978] 1 WLR 1387 (CA).
[46] Applying the modern contextual approach to construction pioneered by Lord Wilberforce in the House of Lords in *Reardon Smith Line Ltd v Yngvar Hansen-Tangen* [1976] 1 WLR 989 (HL).
[47] [2000] 1 All ER (Comm) 166 (CA).   [48] Ibid [16].

and had not already been lost by the time that payment was made, must have been lost shortly thereafter. *Nor is there any legal basis, so far as I can see or that has been suggested, on which the Shipper could have compelled the Consignee to collect the goods and return the containers to the Carrier in circumstances where the Shipper no longer had title or any right to possession of the goods.* I therefore conclude that by some time in June 2011 the Shipper was wholly and finally disabled from further performance of the first four bill of lading contracts.

. . .

I accordingly find that the Carrier had no basis for claiming on 27 September 2011 that it was suffering any loss as a result of the Shipper's breach of contract. In these circumstances I conclude that the Carrier had no legitimate interest in keeping the contracts of carriage in force after that date in order to continue claiming demurrage. Its election to do so, and to go on doing so ever since, can in my view properly be described as wholly unreasonable. It is wholly unreasonable because the Carrier has not been keeping the contracts alive in order to invoke the demurrage clause for a proper purpose but in order, in effect, to *seek to generate an unending stream of free income.*[49]

3.4 Explaining the 'No Legitimate Interest' Qualification in Terms of Protecting the Defendant from Economic Waste?

If we put to one side the alternative explanation of some of the cases based on an abhorrence of stalemate and perpetual obligations, where does that leave Lord Reid's qualification? As has been seen, there is no one accepted approach in the authorities to exploring the claimant's 'financial interest' in performance. Some judges do focus, as Lord Reid anticipated, on the difference between the claimant's position if the price can be claimed, compared with the measure of damages that would be awarded if the repudiation was accepted. Others focus instead on the defendant's position, emphasising the need for the claimant, post repudiation, to consider the position of the defendant and to avoid burdening the defendant with unwanted performance, referred to as 'economic waste'. Although this approach is often seen as an aspect of mitigation, we should note that this is an unusual form of mitigation, which generally requires the claimant to keep his *own* loss to a minimum, not the defendant's.

Many academic commentators rely on this version of mitigation to support a version of Lord Reid's qualification that requires the claimant to protect the defendant from unwanted, wasteful performance. For

[49] Ibid [86] and [121] (emphasis added).

some, the claimant's freedom to keep the contract alive should be constrained by such concerns only in exceptional circumstances. For example, noting the *White & Carter* decision at the time, Nienaber concludes that, 'where the overall waste inherent in the performance is completely out of proportion to the innocent party's interest in performing, a sound case for the general restriction of the principle underlying the doctrine of election may well exist'.[50] Likewise, Liu expresses the view that:

> Since the main countervailing factor for the victim's performance interest in earning the contract price is the wastefulness of its continuing performance, regard must be had not only to the victim's interests, but also to the contract-breaker's interests. It is not sufficient for the contract breaker to show the mere fact of wastefulness, namely, that the benefits of the victim's continuing performance are small in comparison with its costs. The benefit-cost gap must be 'completely out of proportion'. The excessiveness of the wastefulness is necessary for the victim's claim for the contract price to be resisted ...[51]

Others advocate a more general principle akin to mitigation, requiring the claimant to act reasonably to minimise loss to the defendant, in all cases of response to repudiation. This position is adopted in The Principles of European Contract Law 2002, which provide:

(2) Where the creditor has not yet performed its obligation and it is clear that the debtor will be unwilling to receive performance, the creditor may nonetheless proceed with its performance and may recover any sum due under the contract unless:
    (a) it could have made a reasonable substitute transaction without significant effort or expense; or
    (b) performance would be unreasonable in the circumstances.[52]

Recently, Morgan has offered a coherent and detailed argument in favour of a general mitigation qualification of the claimant's right to elect to keep the contract alive, arguing that to minimise unwanted, wasteful costs benefits both parties and that rational contracting parties would choose a default regime incorporating such a principle.[53] Space does not permit a detailed exploration of these economic arguments, other than to note that – unusually – we do know what the (presumably rational) claimant would choose in a *White & Carter* situation, because the argument concerns

---

[50] PM Nienaber, 'The Effect of Anticipatory Repudiation: Principle and Policy' [1962] CLJ 213, 232.

[51] Qiao Liu, 'The White & Carter Principle: A Restatement' (2011) 74 MLR 171, 193.

[52] Article 9:101 (ex art 4.101) – Monetary Obligations.　　[53] Morgan (n 37).

whether or not to prohibit that choice. Undeniably a requirement of mere 'reasonableness' and a regime which encourages the avoidance of 'economic waste', may seem uncontroversial, indeed intuitively attractive. Yet this chapter argues that, on closer inspection, the position is different: a claimant who, when faced with a repudiation, chooses to honour and perform the contractual regime to obtain contractual performance should be permitted to do so,[54] regardless of the impact on the defendant. Indeed, whether articulated by reference to the claimant's interest in performance, or the defendant's protection from economic waste, it is suggested that Lord Reid's qualification should be abandoned.

3.5 Why the 'No Legitimate Interest' Qualification should be Abandoned

A number of arguments can be offered in support of this position. First, the law on repudiatory breach is already skewed against upholding the parties' bargain and the claimant's performance interest, in favour of encouraging acceptance of the repudiation and termination of the contractual regime with an accelerated right to claim damages. A claimant who, when faced with a repudiation, resists the lure of immediate damages and decides to 'keep the contract alive' remains 'on risk' in the sense of being obliged to perform its own obligations.[55] There is no justification for adding an open-ended obligation to avoid economic waste in the sense of minimising loss to the defendant, one which would not apply if the defendant's unilateral and wrongful repudiation had never happened.

After all, the courts have no general jurisdiction at common law to strike down substantively unreasonable terms.[56] Nor can the courts rewrite terms under the guise of commercial construction, however substantively 'unreasonable' they are, where the natural meaning of the words is clear and unambiguous. This was clarified by the Supreme Court in *Arnold v Britton*,[57] where Lord Neuberger explained:

---

[54] Subject to the separate policy concern to avoid stalemate and perpetual obligations.

[55] The claimant also remains on risk of the defendant exercising an express right to cancel, as in *Fercometal SARL v Mediterranean Shipping Co SA (The Simona)* [1989] AC 788 (HL), and of supervening frustration, as in *Avery v Bowden* (1855) 5 E & B 714, 119 ER 647 (Court of Queen's Bench).

[56] Cf the specific statutory regimes in the Unfair Contract Terms Act 1977 and the Consumer Rights Act 2015, and the equitable doctrine of penalties.

[57] [2015] UKSC 36, [2015] AC 1619.

Fourthly, while commercial common sense is a very important factor to take into account when interpreting a contract, a court should be very slow to reject the natural meaning of a provision as correct simply because it appears to be a very imprudent term for one of the parties to have agreed, even ignoring the benefit of wisdom of hindsight. The purpose of interpretation is to identify what the parties have agreed, not what the court thinks that they should have agreed. Experience shows that it is by no means unknown for people to enter into arrangements which are ill-advised, even ignoring the benefit of wisdom of hindsight, and it is not the function of a court when interpreting an agreement to relieve a party from the consequences of his imprudence or poor advice. Accordingly, when interpreting a contract a judge should avoid re-writing it in an attempt to assist an unwise party or to penalise an astute party.[58]

What then can be the justification for the courts gaining such a jurisdiction once a serious repudiatory breach has occurred, to be used *in favour* of the repudiating party, *against* the innocent party? The law's astuteness to preserve the bargain in the claimant's favour should, if anything, apply *a fortiori* here. As Lord Hodson[59] said in *White & Carter*:

It is trite that equity will not rewrite an improvident contract where there is no disability on either side. There is no duty laid on a party to a subsisting contract to vary it at the behest of the other party so as to deprive himself of the benefit given to him by the contract. To hold otherwise would be to introduce a novel equitable doctrine that a party was not to be held to his contract unless the court in a given instance thought it reasonable so to do. In this case it would make an action for debt a claim for a discretionary remedy. This would introduce an uncertainty into the field of contract which appears to be unsupported by authority ...[60]

This objection to the 'no legitimate interest' qualification reflects unease at other principles that appear to allow contract-breakers unilaterally to rewrite their bargains by their own wrongdoing. One such is the suggestion, seen for example in *DSND Subsea Ltd v Petroleum Geo Services ASA*,[61] that it is legitimate for a party to threaten to breach a contract, and thereby secure a unilateral variation in its terms, as long as the threat was made in 'good faith'. Bigwood explains the objection perfectly as follows:

To suggest ... that it may not be illegitimate for D to breach or propose to breach his contract with P (in support of D's demands) if D is acting

---

[58] Ibid [20].
[59] Lord Hodson gave a speech for the majority and did not qualify his decision as Lord Reid did.
[60] *White & Carter* (n 1) 445.   [61] [2000] BLR 530 (QB).

'reasonably' and '*bona fide* in a very difficult situation' is effectively to suggest that P's rights are somehow destructible by D unilaterally and without compensation if D is acting from the right commercial motives.[62]

Likewise it mirrors the familiar[63] critique of the troubling proposition that mitigation requires a claimant to accept an offer of varied performance from the repudiating party. In *Payzu Ltd v Saunders*[64] the defendant agreed to sell silk to the claimant. The contract allowed payment on credit terms (a month after delivery) but in breach the defendant refused to make further deliveries other than for cash. The claimant refused, and accepted the defendant's repudiation: this was an odd decision commercially, since the market price of silk had risen since the contract. Under standard damages principles, the claimant ought to be entitled to the difference in value between the contract and market price, but the Court of Appeal held that the claimant failed to mitigate, because it should have accepted the defendant's offer to sell the silk for cash. The upshot was that the defendant could ignore the contract and sell the silk on the market for the higher price, with no obligation to compensate the claimant for its loss of bargain: by repudiating, the defendant was effectively permitted unilaterally to change the payment obligations in the contract from credit to cash terms.[65]

Payzu was subsequently applied in *Sotiros Shipping Inc v Sameiet Soholt*,[66] a decision which is arguably even harder to justify because, unlike *Payzu*, there was no express offer from the party in breach; the Court of Appeal held that mitigation obliged the innocent party to solicit such an offer, even though this made a nonsense of the fact that the defendant had committed a breach of condition. *Sotiros* involved a contract for the sale of a ship, providing for delivery on or before 31 August, where time was of the essence. In breach, the seller delivered the ship on 3 September and so the buyer cancelled. Unusually, and as in *Payzu*, the contract was not a bad bargain for the buyer: the contract price was $5 million and the market price $5.5 million, so it was not clear why the buyer cancelled the contract over such a short

---

[62] Rick Bigwood, 'Economic Duress by (Threatened) Breach of Contract' [2001] 117 LQR 376, 379–80.

[63] See in particular Michael G Bridge, 'Mitigation of Damages in Contract and the Meaning of Avoidable Loss' (1989) 105 LQR 398.

[64] [1919] 2 KB 581 (CA).

[65] An outcome described as 'unintelligible' by Samuel Stoljar, 'Some Problems of Anticipatory Breach' (1974) Melb LR 355, 363.

[66] [1983] 1 Lloyd's Rep 605 (CA).

delay.[67] In any event, both the trial judge and the Court of Appeal held that the buyer could not recover the standard measure of $0.5 million damages because it failed to mitigate its loss: it should have offered to buy the ship at $5 million on 3 September. This would have been reasonable and would have avoided the loss. The upshot again was that the seller could ignore the contract, sell the ship for $5.5 million on the open market with no obligation to compensate the innocent claimant, a unilateral change to the express delivery date, condoned by the court, by virtue of the defendant's repudiation.

It is true that the claimant in both cases had a ready means of avoiding the loss by accepting the defendant's wrongful, unilateral variation in the contract terms, but it is also true that both cases undermine the principle that, where the defendant's breach is a repudiation, the claimant may elect to terminate the contract. The defendant should not, by his repudiation, be entitled to force the claimant to choose between accepting a variation that favours the defendant, or foregoing his right to damages. In the same way, a defendant should not, by his repudiation, be entitled to force the claimant to bring the contract to an end and claim damages, simply because the contract as executed is no longer advantageous to the defendant.

Does the invocation of a principle of good faith alter the position? There is of course no overarching general requirement of good faith in contractual performance in English law,[68] but might there be a specific doctrine – one of Bingham LJ's 'piecemeal devices'[69] – at work here? It will be recalled that Leggatt J in *MSC Mediterranean* sought to justify a version of Lord Reid's qualification requiring the claimant to take account of the defendant's interests, by drawing an analogy with the developing principle[70] that:

[67] There was some evidence that the buyer thought it could use the late delivery to renegotiate the price below $5 million, but it did not succeed in doing so.

[68] Cf *Bhasin v Hrynew* (2014) SCC 71, [2014] 3 SCR 494, where the Supreme Court of Canada held that good faith contractual performance is a general organising principle of the common law of contract which underpins and informs more specific rules and doctrines. But it would seem that *Bhasin v Hrynew* provides no support for the *White & Carter* qualification, since it essentially imposed no more than a minimal standard of honesty on the parties: '[73] ... This means simply that parties must not lie or otherwise knowingly mislead each other about matters directly linked to the performance of the contract. This does not impose a duty of loyalty or of disclosure or require a party to forego advantages flowing from the contract; it is a simple requirement not to lie or mislead the other party about one's contractual performance.'

[69] *Interfoto Picture Library Ltd v Stiletto Visual Programmes Ltd* [1989] QB 433 (CA).

[70] *Abu Dhabi National Tanker Co v Product Star Shipping Ltd (The Product Star) (No 2)* [1993] 1 Lloyd's Rep 397, 404; *Paragon Finance* (n 43) [39]–[41]; *Socimer International*

> [I]n the absence of very clear language to the contrary, a contractual discretion must be exercised in good faith for the purpose for which it was conferred, and must not be exercised arbitrarily, capriciously or unreasonably (in the sense of irrationally).[71]

With respect, it is suggested that this reasoning is unconvincing. First, as Morgan points out:

> It invites the question for what 'legitimate purpose' the *White & Carter* power to affirm is granted by law in the first place. The answer to that is far from obvious. Secondly, to decide on 'abuse', 'caprice' or 'irrationality' etc, the court would be required to assess not just what the promisee has done but *why* they did it. Such an inquiry into parties' motivations and mental states is usually avoided by the law of contract, for very good reason.[72]

For a court to be required to conduct such an inquiry would be productive of considerable uncertainty, as Moore-Bick LJ raised in the Court of Appeal in MSC: There is in my view a real danger that if a general principle of good faith were established it would be invoked as often to undermine as to support the terms in which the parties have reached agreement. The danger is not dissimilar to that posed by too liberal an approach to construction, against which the Supreme Court warned in *Arnold v Britton*.[73]

Moreover the analogy drawn between the contractual discretion cases and a requirement on the claimant to consider the interests of a defendant on repudiation is unconvincing. First, a contractual discretion derives from the agreement between the parties precisely to grant such a discretion. Where a contract is repudiated, however, there is no agreed discretion; rather the innocent party's ability to elect to keep the contract alive is a form of remedy offered by the law. Related to this, the manoeuvring space is potentially much larger for a party with a contractual discretion, than for a party responding to a repudiation. *Paragon Finance* is a good example: if the finance company were permitted to increase interest rates as it pleased, this would leave borrowers at the company's mercy and unable to predict the extent of their obligations. In contrast, when a defendant repudiates a contract, the claimant's choice is both an unwilling one and confined to just two possibilities – keeping the contract alive or terminating it and seeking damages for its losses. The

---

Bank Ltd v Standard Bank London Ltd [2008] EWCA Civ 116, [2008] 1 Lloyd's Rep 558, 575–77; British Telecommunications (n 43) [37].
[71] *MSC Mediterranean* (n 35) [97].   [72] Morgan (n 37) 591.
[73] [2016] EWCA Civ 789 para [45].

defendant is aware of the two possibilities and the extent of its obligation in either case.

Perhaps most significantly, in the *British Telecommunications* case, Lord Sumption's argument centred around the need for the parties to act consistently with the contractual purpose. In instances of repudiation, the repudiation itself is already wholly inconsistent with the contractual purpose, so it would be irrational to place a requirement of consistency with the contractual purpose on the innocent party. Indeed it may be said that the innocent party who opts to keep the contract alive is acting in a manner consistent with the main underlying purpose of the contract, namely performance.

3.6 Conclusion

Taking stock, this chapter has argued that many cases (and examples) reasoned on the basis that the claimant had 'no legitimate interest in performance' are in fact justifiable by reference to a different and more limited principle, namely that the court can intervene on policy grounds to break stalemate between the parties and prevent the creation of perpetual obligations. The claimant can keep the contract alive, but the court will not endorse leaving a life-support machine on in perpetuity.

Outside such a situation, it is suggested that there is no justification for any restriction on the claimant's unfettered right, following a repudiation, to elect to keep the contract alive, perform and claim the price from the defendant.

If we reject the proposition, based either on mitigation or good faith principles, that a claimant is obliged to take account of the defendant's interest in being free of a bad bargain, we are left with Lord Reid's qualification in its own terms, focusing squarely on whether or not the claimant has a legitimate financial interest in performance. And this reveals the most fundamental problem of all with the qualification: who is best placed to judge what is in claimant's interests, the court or the claimant? A claimant who opts to keep the contract alive has already shown, by its choice, what is in its interests. To acknowledge this involves nothing more controversial than upholding freedom of contract and respecting the sanctity of the bargain, in the face of a repudiatory breach by the defendant.

4

Termination and the Agreed Sum

ANDREW SUMMERS

4.1 Introduction

Where a party repudiating a contract refuses to cooperate with further performance by the innocent party, is the contract automatically terminated, or is the innocent party merely prevented from earning the agreed sum? The recent decision in *Société Générale v Geys* has revisited this old controversy.[1] In a forceful dissenting judgment, Lord Sumption argued in favour of automatic termination, relying on Lord Reid's comments in the famous case of *White & Carter v McGregor*.[2] The majority of the Supreme Court instead treated cooperation as a practical limit on recovery of the agreed sum. This chapter sides against Lord Sumption's automatic termination approach, but acknowledges that the majority's view leaves one difficult problem unresolved.

The first section of this chapter describes the cooperation limitation in outline, starting with the dictum of Lord Reid in *White & Carter* and considering its application in *Geys*. The second section assesses and rejects the arguments for regarding cooperation as a limitation on the innocent party's right to affirm the contract. The third section puts forward the argument that cooperation instead provides a practical limitation on the capacity of the innocent party to earn the agreed sum, and shows why this means that the limitation is not universally applicable. The final section acknowledges that the approach of the majority in *Geys* leaves a difficult problem concerning the content of the wage–work bargain in contracts of employment.

---

[1] *Geys v Société Générale* [2012] UKSC 63; [2013] 1 AC 523. See also *MSC Mediterranean Shipping Co SA v Cottonex Anstalt* [2016] EWCA Civ 789, [2016] 2 Lloyd's Rep 494.
[2] Ibid [114], citing *White & Carter (Councils) Ltd v McGregor* [1962] AC 413 (HL).

4.2   The 'Cooperation Limitation'

In *White & Carter v McGregor*, Lord Reid observed that:

> In most cases by refusing co-operation the party in breach can compel the
> innocent party to restrict his claim to damages ... if it had been necessary
> for the defender to do or accept anything before the contract could be
> completed by the pursuers, the pursuers could not and the court would
> not have compelled the defender to act, the contract would not have been
> completed and the pursuers' only remedy would have been damages.[3]

Subsequent cases have referred to this dictum as the cooperation
'qualification',[4] 'exception',[5] 'fetter',[6] or 'limitation'.[7] In *White & Carter*
itself, the claimants had agreed to advertise the defendant's garage business by displaying adverts on litter bins owned by the local council.[8]
The defendant repudiated the contract on the very day that it was
concluded, but the claimants began to display the adverts anyway.[9]
They continued to display the adverts for the full three years of the
contract.[10] Lord Reid noted that 'the peculiarity ... in the present case,
was that the pursuers could completely fulfil the contract without any co-

---

[3] *White & Carter* (n 2) 428–29. See also 445 (Lord Hodson).

[4] *Geys* (n 1) [114], [115], [132], [133], [139] (Lord Sumption); JW Carter, Andrew Phang,
and Sock-Yong Phang, 'Performance Following Repudiation: Legal and Economic
Interests' (1999) 15 *Journal of Contract Law* 97, 106.

[5] *Gator Shipping Corp v Trans-Asiatic Oil SA (The Odenfeld)* [1978] 2 Lloyd's Rep 357 (QB)
372 (Kerr J); *Ocean Marine Navigation Ltd v Koch Carbon Inc (The Dynamic)* [2003]
EWHC 1936 (Comm), [2003] 2 Lloyd's Rep 693, 697 (Simon J); *Ministry of Sound
(Ireland) Ltd v World Online Ltd* [2003] EWHC 2178 (Ch), [2003] 2 All ER (Comm)
823 [25] (Strauss QC); *Isabella Shipowner SA v Shagang Shipping Co Ltd (The Aquafaith)*
[2012] EWHC 1077 (Comm), [2012] 2 All ER (Comm) 461 [10] (Cooke J); *Geys* (n 1)
[114] (Lord Sumption).

[6] *Clea Shipping Corp v Bulk Oil International (The Alaskan Trader) (No 2)* [1984] 1 All ER
129, 137, [1983] 2 Lloyd's Rep 645 (QB) (Lloyd J); *Reichman v Beveridge* [2006] EWCA
Civ 1659, [2007] Bus LR 412 [36] (Lloyd LJ).

[7] *Hounslow LBC v Twickenham Garden Developments Ltd* [1971] Ch 233, 252 (Megarry J);
The Alaskan Trader (n 6) 648 (Lloyd J).

[8] *White & Carter* (n 2).

[9] The contract was concluded on 26 June 1957; the claimants 'prepared the necessary plates
for attachment to the bins and exhibited them on the bins from November 2, 1957,
onwards': Ibid 426 (Lord Reid).

[10] Ibid 432 (Lord Morton): 'The plates ... remained on display during the whole of the
contract period of 156 weeks.' In any case, an acceleration clause in the contract provided
that the whole three-year price became payable if any instalment remained unpaid for
a period of four weeks. There was some debate as to whether this clause amounted to an
unenforceable penalty. Lord Reid thought that it did not (at 427). Lord Keith (dissenting)
found it unnecessary to decide, having concluded that the contract had terminated before
the clause could have been triggered (at 443). See also 446 (Lord Hodson).

operation of the defender.'[11] This 'peculiarity' arose because the defendant garage did not own the bins and their cooperation was not required for the design of the adverts.[12] Consequently, the cooperation limitation did not apply,[13] and the House of Lords upheld the claim for payment of the full contract price by a majority of three to two.

But what, in principle, did Lord Reid's cooperation limitation seek to limit? First, it might be thought to apply to the right of the innocent party to *affirm* the contract following a wrongful repudiation. Secondly (which is the understanding put forward in this chapter), it might apply to the practical capacity of the innocent party to *perform* its obligations under the contract and thereby to earn the agreed sum. Thirdly, it might apply to the right of the innocent party to *recover* the agreed sum (once earned) through the remedy of an action for the agreed sum. The second and third options are formally distinct from the issue of termination.[14] So, one might reframe the central conundrum thus: in a textbook on contract law, should Lord Reid's cooperation limitation be discussed in the chapter on termination or the chapter on the agreed sum?

There is an interconnection between these possible characterisations.[15] If the limitation applies to the right to affirm, such that the contract is 'automatically' terminated by the wrongful repudiation against the wishes of the innocent party, this would also have the effect of limiting recovery of the agreed sum. Upon termination the unperformed primary obligations of both parties are discharged,[16] such that both the innocent party's obligation to perform and the repudiating party's obligation to pay the agreed sum are cancelled. If the agreed sum has not already accrued before termination for repudiatory breach, it cannot be

---

[11] Ibid (n 2) 429.

[12] Lord Morton (dissenting) doubted that performance without cooperation was particularly unusual, noting that 'many examples of such contracts could be given': ibid 432.

[13] Lord Reid also discussed (but declined to apply) the 'legitimate interest' limitation, addressed in this volume by Professor O'Sullivan in ch 3.

[14] Cf Carter, Phang and Phang (n 4) 116–17, who contemplate a binary choice: 'the qualification must relate either to the ability of the promisee to ignore the repudiation or the right to claim a debt'.

[15] Qiao Liu, 'The White & Carter Principle: A Restatement' (2011) 74 MLR 171, 175.

[16] *Photo Production Ltd v Securicor Transport Ltd* [1980] AC 827 (HL) 849 (Lord Diplock). It should be noted that accrued (but unperformed) obligations to pay an agreed sum do survive termination: *Bank of Boston Connecticut (formerly Colonial Bank) v European Grain & Shipping Ltd (The Dominique)* [1989] AC 1056 (HL). However, in this context we are concerned with the innocent party's right to perform a non-monetary obligation and thus to earn the agreed sum from the party in breach.

claimed.[17] This interconnection means that references to the effect of the cooperation limitation can sometimes appear ambiguous.[18]

Despite this interconnectedness, occasionally the stage at which the cooperation limitation applies matters a great deal. This became apparent (if it was not already) in the recent case of *Société Générale v Geys*.[19] The claimant, Raphael Geys, was a banker employed by the defendant bank. Mr Geys' contract of employment provided that he was entitled to a 'substantial'[20] bonus 'if your employment terminates after 31 December 2007 . . .'.[21] The contract expressly provided that the bank could terminate Mr Geys' contract by one of two methods: either 'on the expiry of 3 months' written notice';[22] or alternatively 'with immediate effect by making a payment to you in lieu of notice' (referred to as the 'PILON' clause).[23]

On 29 November 2007, the bank informed Mr Geys that it had decided to dismiss him with immediate effect. They told him to clear his desk and escorted him from the office. This amounted to a wrongful repudiation by the bank. The bank made a payment in lieu of notice on 18 December 2007, but termination under the PILON clause only took effect on 6 January 2008, when notice of the payment was received.[24] Following his dismissal, Mr Geys was unable to continue performance because (amongst other things) he had been denied access to his office. He did not return to work, but nevertheless sought to affirm his contract and claim his bonus on the basis that his employment had not terminated until January 2008.

In the Supreme Court, the majority implicitly interpreted the terms of the bonus clause to mean '*contract of* employment' rather than the de

---

[17] *Sumpter v Hedges* [1898] 1 QB 673 (CA).

[18] See e.g. *MSC Mediterranean Shipping Co SA v Cottonex Anstalt* [2015] EWHC 283 (Comm), [2015] 1 Lloyd's Rep 359 [93] (Leggatt J).

[19] *Geys* (n 1) [15] (Lord Hope): 'there are cases, of which this case is a good example, where it really does matter which of the two theories is adopted'.

[20] Ibid [6] (Lord Hope).

[21] Clause 5.15(b)(iv) of the Contract, discussed by Lord Hope: ibid [6].

[22] Clause 13 of the Contract, discussed by Lady Hale: ibid [47].

[23] Section 8.3 of the Handbook, incorporated by Clause 17 of the Contract, discussed by Lady Hale: ibid [47], [50].

[24] For the majority, Lady Hale determined that the PILON clause impliedly required clear and unambiguous notification that the bank had made the payment in lieu in exercise of the clause, which was only fulfilled on 6 January 2008: ibid [50]–[58]. Lord Sumption (dissenting) took the contrary view that notice was not required and would have held that the PILON clause took effect before the end of 2007: ibid [143].

facto *'relationship of* employment'.[25] Consequently, the main question was whether Mr Geys' contract was automatically terminated as soon as the wrongful repudiation took place, or whether it subsisted until the PILON clause took effect.[26] Lord Wilson highlighted the general importance of the issue:

> [T]he first question must be whether it matters that the contract is terminated forthwith upon repudiation or, instead, survives until some further, terminating, event? The answer is that sometimes it does matter. It depends on the terms of the contract. The date of termination fixes the end of some contractual obligations and, sometimes, the beginning of others. An increase in salary may depend on the survival of the contract until a particular date. The amount of a pension may be calculated by reference to the final salary paid throughout a completed year of service or to an aggregate of salaries including the final completed year. An entitlement to holiday pay may similarly depend on the contract's survival to a particular date. In some cases an award of damages will compensate the employee for any such loss. But often it will fail to do so.[27]

A majority of four to one in the Supreme Court held that the contract was *not* automatically terminated by the wrongful repudiation; Mr Geys' employment only terminated on 6 January 2008 when the requirements of the PILON clause were finally fulfilled.[28] Consequently, the bank was liable to pay Mr Geys' substantial bonus. However, in a dissenting judgment, Lord Sumption held that the contract *was* automatically terminated on 29 November 2007. Lord Sumption's argument expressly relied on Lord Reid's cooperation limitation in *White & Carter*.[29] In essence, it rested on the view that the cooperation limitation applied to the innocent party's right to affirm the contract, such that where cooperation was withheld (and could not be compelled) the contract was brought automatically to an end. The old controversy regarding the characterisation of the cooperation limitation was thus revived.

4.3   A Limit on the Right to Affirm?

This section assesses the argument that the withdrawal of cooperation places a limit on the innocent party's right to affirm its contract. In *Geys*, Lord Sumption (dissenting) held that a contract will be automatically

---

[25] See e.g. ibid [14] issue 2 (Lord Hope). By contrast Lord Sumption expressly took the latter view, although this was not crucial to his decision: ibid [137].

[26] Ibid [111] (Lord Sumption). See similarly [14] (Lord Hope).

[27] Ibid (n 1) [64] (Lord Wilson).   [28] See n 23.   [29] *Geys* (n 1) [114] (Lord Sumption).

terminated where the repudiating party's cooperation is required to continue performance of the contract but where such cooperation has been withdrawn and cannot be compelled.[30] Lord Sumption derived this conclusion from Lord Reid's cooperation limitation, in conjunction with a line of employment cases concerning automatic termination. The argument deserves close scrutiny, because if correct it implicates not only contracts of employment but potentially all contracts in which continued performance depends on cooperation by the repudiating party.

4.3.1   Orthodoxy: An Unfettered Right to Elect

The proposition that an innocent party has an unfettered right to affirm its contract in the face of wrongful repudiation was first articulated in *Hochster v De la Tour*.[31] In many early cases 'the need for the innocent party to elect whether to accept the repudiation ... was taken as read'.[32] Several cases in the mid-twentieth century put this point explicitly. In *Heyman v Darwins*, Viscount Simon LC emphasised that termination for repudiatory breach required acceptance: 'repudiation by one party standing alone does not terminate the contract. It takes two to end it, by repudiation, on the one side, and acceptance of the repudiation, on the other.'[33] Most memorably, in *Howard v Pickford Tool*, Asquith LJ held that 'an unaccepted repudiation is a thing writ in water and of no value to anybody'.[34]

The majority in *White & Carter* seemed quite clear in upholding this orthodoxy. Lord Reid held that 'the general rule cannot be in doubt ... If one party to a contract repudiates it ... the innocent party, has an

---

[30] Ibid (n 1) [116]. See also *MSC* (n 1) [60], where Tomlinson LJ expressed support for Lord Sumption's understanding.

[31] *Hochster v De La Tour* (1853) 2 E & B 678, 118 ER 922 (QB). See also, in Scotland, *Howie v Anderson* (1848) 10 D 355 (Court of Session). In *Geys* (n 1) [113], Lord Sumption noted that the principle had already been applied in earlier cases.

[32] *Geys* (n 1) [80] (Lord Wilson), citing *Boston Deep Sea Fishing & Ice Co v Ansell* (1888) 39 Ch D 339 (CA) 365 (Bowen LJ); *General Billposting Co Ltd v Atkinson* [1909] AC 118 (HL) 122 (Lord Collins). See also *Frost v Knight* (1871–72) LR 7 Ex 111 (EC); *Michael v Hart & Co* [1902] 1 KB 482 (CA).

[33] *Heyman v Darwins Ltd* [1942] AC 356 (HL) 361, citing with approval *Golding v London & Edinburgh Insurance Co Ltd* (1932) 43 Ll L Rep 487 (CA) 488 (Scrutton LJ): 'I have never been able to understand what effect the repudiation of one party has unless the other party accepts the repudiation.' It should be noted that Viscount Simon's statement was not necessary for the decision in *Heyman*, because the case concerned an arbitration clause, which would have survived termination even if the repudiation had been accepted.

[34] *Howard v Pickford Tool Co* [1951] 1 KB 417 (CA) 421.

option. He may accept that repudiation and sue for damages for breach of contract ... or he may if he chooses disregard or refuse to accept it and then the contract remains in full effect.'[35] Later, Lord Reid added: 'It is well established that repudiation by one party does not put an end to a contract. The other party can say "I hold you to your contract, which still remains in force."'[36] Lord Hodson was similarly unequivocal: 'It is settled as a fundamental rule of the law of contract that repudiation by one of the parties to a contract does not itself discharge it.'[37]

In the context of employment contracts, the existence of an unfettered right to affirm was less well-settled prior to the decision in *Geys*. A series of authorities appeared to suggest that in some circumstances an employment contract might *automatically* be terminated by a repudiatory breach. These authorities are further discussed below.[38] Nevertheless, in several other employment cases, the unfettered right to elect was strongly defended: for example, in *London Transport Executive v Clarke*, Templeman LJ rejected the possibility of automatic termination as 'contrary to principle, unsupported by authority binding on this court and undesirable in practice'.[39] Prior to *Geys*, it is fair to say that in relation to employment, the picture was conflicting and complicated. But outside the employment context, the orthodoxy was firmly settled.[40]

In *Geys*, the Supreme Court tasked itself 'to make a difficult and important choice between a conclusion that a party's repudiation (albeit perhaps only an immediate and express repudiation) of a contract of employment automatically terminates the contract ("the automatic

---

[35] *White & Carter* (n 2) 427.   [36] Ibid 432.

[37] Ibid 444. See also 445: 'The true position is that the contract survives and does so not only where specific implement is available.'

[38] See text to n 50 below.

[39] *London Transport Executive v Clarke* [1981] ICR 355 (CA) 368. This statement was expressly approved by Lord Wilson in *Geys* (n 1) [94]. See also *Thomas Marshall (Exports) Ltd v Guinle* [1979] Ch 227 (Ch) (Megarry VC); *Gunton v Richmond upon Thames LBC* [1981] Ch 448 (CA) 468 (Buckley LJ); *Dietmann v Brent LBC* [1987] ICR 737 (QB); *Rigby v Ferodo Ltd* [1988] ICR 29 (HL); *Boyo v Lambeth LBC* [1994] ICR 727 (CA) (Gibson LJ, Purchas LJ). And see KD Ewing, 'Remedies for Breach of the Contract of Employment' (1993) 52 CLJ 405, 415, describing the automatic theory as 'a bastard doctrine, which is difficult to reconcile with the general principles of contract law'.

[40] *Decro-Wall International SA v Practitioners in Marketing* [1971] 1 WLR 361 (CA) 370 (Salmon LJ); *Photo Production* (n 16) (Diplock LJ); *Fercometal Sarl v MSC Mediterranean Shipping Co SA (The Simona)* [1989] AC 788 (HL) 799–801 (Lord Ackner); *The Aquafaith* (n 5) [5] (Cooke J); Francis D Rose, 'The Effects of Repudiatory Breaches of Contract' (1981) 34 Current Legal Problems 235.

theory") and a conclusion that his repudiation terminates the contract of employment only if and when the other party elects to accept the repudiation ("the elective theory")'.[41] A four-to-one majority (Lord Sumption dissenting) settled decisively in favour of the elective theory, thereby concluding the position for employment contracts as well as for the rest of the general law of contract.[42] This position was recently acknowledged by the Court of Appeal in *MSC Mediterranean Shipping*, albeit with some reluctance by Tomlinson LJ.[43]

4.3.2   Lord Sumption's Dissent

At the root of Lord Sumption's dissenting judgment in *Geys* was the proposition that 'the innocent party to a repudiated contract cannot treat it as subsisting unless he can either perform it without the co-operation of the other party or compel that co-operation'.[44] Lord Sumption thought that the elective theory (preferred by the majority) was wrong because 'the right to treat the contract as subsisting has never been absolute. It is subject to important exceptions and qualifications.'[45] He derived this proposition directly and explicitly from the judgment of Lord Reid in *White & Carter*.[46] Whilst affirming 'the general rule . . . that the repudiation of a contract does not necessarily bring the contract to an end',[47] Lord Sumption stated clearly his understanding that Lord Reid's cooperation limitation was an exception to that rule. After citing several authorities from the general law of contract that had applied Lord Reid's cooperation limitation,[48] Lord Sumption concluded:

> These decisions are authority for a general rule that the innocent party to a repudiated contract cannot treat it as subsisting if (i) performance on his part requires the co-operation of the repudiating party, and (ii) the contract is incapable of specific performance, with the result that that co-operation cannot be compelled.[49]

---

[41] *Geys* (n 1) [63] (Lord Wilson).

[42] Ibid [15] (Lord Hope); [42] (Lady Hale); [94] (Lord Wilson); [99] (Lord Carnwarth).

[43] *MSC* (n 1) [36] (Moore-Bick LJ), [60] (Tomlinson LJ). See also *Barclays Bank plc v Unicredit Bank AG* [2012] EWHC 3655 (Comm), [2013] 2 Lloyd's Rep 1 [105] (Popplewell J).

[44] *Geys* (n 1) [130], adding that: 'In the case of a contract of employment, neither condition is satisfied.'

[45] Ibid [114].   [46] Ibid.   [47] Ibid [113].

[48] *Hounslow* (n 7); *Attica Sea Carriers Corp v Ferrostaal Poseidon Bulk Reederei GmbH (The Puerto Buitrago)* [1976] 1 Lloyd's Rep 250 (CA); *The Aquafaith* (n 5) [37]–[41] (Cooke J).

[49] *Geys* (n 1) [116]. In *MSC* (n 1) [60], Tomlinson LJ also expressed support for this understanding of the authorities as they stood prior to *Geys*.

Lord Sumption's analysis of the previous authorities relied on a series of employment cases that (he argued) had applied a doctrine of automatic termination.[50] Lord Sumption also cited some judicial support for automatic termination in employment cases that had ultimately upheld the elective theory.[51] Most significantly, Lord Sumption sought to turn the employment authorities on their head, arguing that the cases adopting automatic termination, 'far from being an exception to the ordinary principles of the law of contract, exemplified the ordinary operation of those principles'.[52] The series of employment cases upholding the elective theory was criticised on the basis that they were 'treating contracts of employment as a special case to which Lord Reid's qualifications do not apply'.[53]

The scope of Lord Sumption's automatic theory rested on a distinction between core and collateral obligations. According to Lord Sumption, core obligations 'are those which are fundamental to the continued existence of the employment relationship, essentially the obligation of the employee to work and the concomitant obligation of the employer to continue to employ and pay him'.[54] Automatic termination applied in *Geys* because 'the contract is a co-operative agreement whose performance requires the engagement and mutual confidence of both sides. It is therefore not possible for the employee to treat it as subsisting once the employer has repudiated it and brought their de facto relationship to an end.'[55] Lord Sumption argued that this would help to improve certainty because, in contrast to the technical difficulties associated with notice and acceptance, 'if the contract ends when the employment relationship ends, the position is clear'.[56]

The crux of Lord Sumption's reasoning was that 'the purpose of the right to treat a repudiated contract as subsisting is to enable it to be performed at the option of the innocent party. It is difficult to see why the law should recognise such a right in a case where the contract cannot be either performed or specifically enforced.'[57] Of course, on the facts of *Geys* itself, Mr Geys had a very clear purpose for affirming other than to

---

[50] *Vine v National Dock Labour Board* [1957] AC 488 (HL) 500 (Viscount Kilmuir); *Francis v Municipal Councillors of Kuala Lumpur* [1962] 1 WLR 1411 (PC) 1417 (Lord Morris); *Ridge v Baldwin* [1964] AC 40 (HL) 65 (Lord Reid); *Denmark Productions v Boscobel Productions* [1969] 1 QB 699 (CA) 726 (Salmon LJ), 737 (Harman LJ); *Sanders v Ernest A Neale* [1974] ICR 565 (National Industrial Relations Court) 571 (Sir John Donaldson). See further authorities cited in *Geys* (n 1) [129]–[131].

[51] *Gunton* (n 39) 459 (Shaw LJ, dissenting); *Boyo* (n 39) 747 (Staughton LJ).

[52] *Geys* (n 1) [130].   [53] Ibid [139].   [54] Ibid [120].   [55] Ibid [131].   [56] Ibid [140].

[57] Ibid [116]; see also [120].

perform: to claim the substantial bonus (which was not conditional upon performance). Nevertheless, Lord Sumption thought that without the possibility of further performance there would be a mere 'husk or shell of a contract devoid of practical content'.[58] Consequently, 'Lord Reid's qualifications to the innocent party's right of election are consistent with principle' because 'in cases where the contract cannot be performed without co-operation, and co-operation is neither forthcoming nor compellable, the contract is in balk unless it comes to an end'.[59]

An ancillary element of Lord Sumption's reasoning concerned the wastefulness of holding open a contract that could not be performed. He argued that the rationale for the cooperation limitation was 'influenced by a strong pragmatic aversion to the specific enforcement of contractual obligations in circumstances where they sterilise productive resources or lead to their wasteful allocation'.[60] In Lord Sumption's view, the decision in White & Carter involved 'waste of resources which could have been avoided'.[61] Unless the automatic theory was adopted in circumstances where cooperation was lacking, this waste would be 'gratuitously extended, at least in the context of contracts of employment, to cases where there can be no contractual performance, because the relationship is dead'.[62]

4.3.3   Criticisms

There is remarkably little authority for Lord Sumption's understanding of the cooperation limitation. None of the other judges in Geys mentioned White & Carter,[63] presumably because they thought that Lord Reid's dictum had no impact on the right to affirm. Lord Hope, who agreed with Lord Wilson's extended analysis of the authorities, expressed the view that the employment cases that seemingly favoured automatic termination were 'not as authoritative or as consistent as Lord Sumption JSC indicates'.[64] In most if not all of those cases, it was unnecessary to decide the termination point directly, because the same conclusion could have been reached on the simpler basis that the salary or wage had not

---

[58] Ibid [139]; see also [110]; Gunton (n 39) 459 (Shaw LJ, dissenting) cited with approval by Lord Sumption at [138].

[59] Geys (n 1) [139].   [60] Ibid [117].   [61] Ibid [139].   [62] Ibid [139].

[63] Apart from Lord Wilson, who expressly rejected Lord Sumption's reliance on the case: Ibid [87].

[64] Ibid [15].

been earned.[65] Furthermore, these employment cases did not draw any connection between automatic termination and Lord Reid's dictum on cooperation; this apparent link was Lord Sumption's innovation.

One argument against recognising automatic termination is the principle that a wrongdoer should not be allowed to benefit from its own wrong.[66] As Lord Hope argued, 'the timing of the repudiation may be crucial, and if the automatic theory were to prevail an employer may well be tempted to play this to his advantage – by getting in first before a rise in pay or pension entitlement takes place or, as in this case, a rise in the entitlement to bonuses'.[67] Lord Wilson and Lord Hope agreed that the elective theory was necessary in order to avoid this injustice.[68] By contrast, Lord Sumption argued that the merits of the dispute lay with the bank. The bank's attempt at summary dismissal was 'a repudiation of the most technical kind' that had caused Mr Geys no loss because the contract could have been validly terminated before January, albeit that in fact it was not.[69]

Lord Sumption's approach may also be criticised on the basis that its scope is uncertain. Lord Wilson argued that 'any proponent of the automatic theory needs to be able to draw the contours of its application and to justify them logically'.[70] The problem is that if the right to affirm is only limited for *some* repudiatory breaches, then the innocent party may not know whether the contract has been terminated or not.[71] A similar problem is already well known where the innocent party is seeking to *terminate* for breach of an innominate term,[72] but Lord

---

[65] For a close analysis of the authorities on this basis, see Rose, 'The Effects of Repudiatory Breaches of Contract' (n 40) 237 and following.

[66] *Geys* (n 1) [15], [18], [19] (Lord Hope); [66] (Lord Wilson). See also Edwin Peel, *Treitel on the Law of Contract* (14th edn, Sweet & Maxwell 2015) [18–006]: 'the argument that the repudiating party should not be allowed to rely on his own wrong to deprive the injured party of valuable rights under the contract has as much force where the contract is one of employment as it has in relation to other contracts'.

[67] *Geys* (n 1) [18].   [68] Ibid [15] (Lord Hope), [66] (Lord Wilson).

[69] Ibid [109] (Lord Sumption).

[70] Ibid [96]. The most extreme version of the automatic theory is that repudiatory breach always presumptively terminates the contract, leaving the innocent party (under some circumstances) with an option to waive the breach and positively affirm the contract: JM Thompson, 'The Effect of a Repudiatory Breach' (1978) 41 MLR 137. For argument against this approach see Rose, 'The Effects of Repudiatory Breaches of Contract' (n 40) 250.

[71] Stephen A Smith, *Atiyah's Introduction to the Law of Contract* (6th edn, Oxford University Press 2006) 203.

[72] See e.g. *Maredelanto Compania Naviera SA v Bergbau-Handel GmbH (The Mihalis Angelos)* [1971] 1 QB 164 (CA) 205 (Megaw LJ).

Sumption's approach would introduce it to circumstances of *affirmation*. Lord Carnwarth thought that the distinction between core and collateral obligations was unworkable.[73] Lady Hale took the view that 'the automatic theory simply cannot work in cases of repudiatory breach which do not amount to express dismissal or resignation'.[74] Any attempt to carve out express dismissal from other forms of repudiatory breach (such as constructive dismissal) would be 'both impracticable and unprincipled'.[75]

Most fundamentally, the reasoning employed by Lord Sumption is circular. As Lord Wilson put it: 'there is no remedy so there is no right so there is no remedy'.[76] The first absent remedy is specific performance to compel cooperation,[77] which will rarely if ever be granted in the employment context. The effect of this reasoning 'was to jump from the absence of some remedies to the absence of all rights, heedless in particular of contractual rights other than to payment of wages or salary'.[78] There are hints that Lord Sumption's approach conflated the subsistence of the contract with the right to recover the agreed sum.[79] On this view, automatic termination would be quite common and certainly not confined to contracts of employment. However, there are many other types of contract, such as sale of goods and charterparties, in which the innocent party may be unable to require full payment under the contract following wrongful repudiation, and yet in which there is no doubt about the continuation of the contract pending election.[80]

A final objection to Lord Sumption's understanding of the cooperation limitation, not raised in the Supreme Court, concerns its implications for withdrawal of repudiation.[81] The orthodox position, in keeping with the election theory, is that a repudiation can be withdrawn until it is accepted. However, if the automatic theory is correct then the contract is terminated immediately upon repudiation whenever the repudiating

---

[73] *Geys* (n 1) [101].   [74] Ibid [42].   [75] Ibid.

[76] Ibid [89], citing Ewing, 'Remedies for Breach of the Contract of Employment' (n 38) 410–11. See also Simon Deakin and Gillian J Morris, *Labour Law* (6th edn, Hart Publishing 2012) [5.38]: the automatic theory is 'a case of the tail wagging the dog'.

[77] *Geys* (n 1) [77] (Lord Wilson). See also Liu, 'The White & Carter Principle: A Restatement' (n 15) 176.

[78] *Geys* (n 1) [89] (Lord Wilson).

[79] See e.g. ibid [121] (Lord Sumption): 'The rule that the innocent party to a repudiated contract of employment was not entitled to treat it as subsisting or recover wages accruing after dismissal was established . . .'

[80] Peel, *Treitel on the Law of Contract* (n 66) [18–006].

[81] Thanks are owed to Professor Robert Stevens, who raised this point in discussions at the BCL Commercial Remedies seminars in Oxford.

party refuses to cooperate and cooperation cannot be compelled,[82] and it must also follow that the repudiation cannot subsequently be withdrawn. It seems implausible to conclude that if the bank had retracted its summary dismissal the same afternoon, and Mr Geys had returned to his desk as normal, the law would nevertheless regard the original contract as at an end.

4.4   A Practical Limitation

This section argues for an alternative characterisation of the cooperation limitation. In short, the withdrawal of cooperation does not give rise to any *legal* limitation; instead it often (but not always) provides a *practical* impediment to fulfilling the requirements necessary to earn the agreed sum. Where the repudiating party's cooperation is required in order to fulfil the contractual conditions for the agreed sum, the innocent party will in practice be unable to earn the sum if that cooperation is refused and cannot be compelled. In these circumstances, it is usually futile to hold open the contract through affirmation; however, there is no legal rule that the contract must be terminated. Consequently, where (as in *Geys*) the conditions for the agreed sum are such that it can be earned without cooperation, the so-called cooperation limitation has no effect.

4.4.1   The Agreed Sum in Outline

The agreed sum goes under various names, for example: price, salary, wage, fee, charge, commission, rent, hire, toll, levy, stipend or subscription. As a matter of law, all these labels simply represent sums payable by agreement. The sum may sometimes be referred to as a debt, although debts can also be imposed by law rather than by agreement: for example a tax or a fine. The remedy of the 'action for an agreed sum' involves enforcement of the primary obligation to pay the sum. It is the monetary equivalent of specific performance.[83] The action is distinct

---

[82] As Lord Sumption identifies, these circumstances account for most cases of employment: *Geys* (n 1) [130].

[83] Peter Birks, 'Rights, Wrongs and Remedies' (2000) 20 OJLS 1, 27; Peel, *Treitel on the Law of Contract* (n 66) [21–001]. Unlike specific performance, the origins of the action for an agreed sum are in common law rather than equity; consequently it is often said that the remedy is available 'as a matter of right' rather than subject to discretion: see *Ministry of Sound* (n 5) [67]–[72]; *White & Carter* (n 2) 445 (Lord Hodson).

from damages, which involve a secondary obligation arising on breach.[84]

In order to bring a successful action for enforcement, the obligation to pay the agreed sum must have accrued; in other words the sum must have 'become due'. The conditions for accrual of the agreed sum are simply a matter of contractual construction. Any set of conditions could be specified. Typically, there are three main types of condition: first, the happening of a specified event; secondly, that the counterparty is ready and willing to perform; or thirdly, through the counterparty's actual performance of its obligations.[85] Where the conditions for accrual of the obligation to pay the agreed sum involve conduct by the party entitled to receive the agreed sum, upon fulfilment of the conditions, the sum is said to have been 'earned'.

4.4.2   No Cooperation Required

Where accrual of the agreed sum is merely conditional upon the innocent party being ready and willing to perform, a lack of cooperation by the repudiating party can never prevent the sum from being earned.[86] This is for the straightforward practical reason that a party's own readiness and willingness to do something is outside the repudiating party's control. There are some common examples of this type of conditionality: for example, section 28 of the Sale of Goods Act 1979 determines accrual of the price (agreed sum) on the basis that 'the seller must be ready and willing to give possession of the goods to the buyer in exchange for the price and the buyer must be ready and willing to pay the price in exchange for possession'.[87] There is a difficult question whether readiness and willingness to work can be sufficient to earn the salary or wage under some employment contracts.[88]

---

[84] See *Photo Production* (n 16) 848–49 (Lord Diplock).
[85] Occasionally, the obligation to pay the agreed sum said to accrue 'independently' i.e. not conditional on any other obligation. However, such circumstances are extremely rare.
[86] See e.g. *Ministry of Sound* (n 5) [49]–[61]; *Mount v Oldham Corp* [1973] QB 309 (CA).
[87] However, under section 49(1), by default the *liability* to pay the price only arises once property in the goods has passed to the buyer. Consequently, the buyer's refusal to cooperate with delivery may prevent recovery of the price: see *The Alaskan Trader* (n 6) 648 (Lloyd J); *White & Carter* (n 2) 438 (Lord Keith); *Colley v Overseas Exporters* [1921] 3 KB 302 (KB). Section 49 has been criticised as 'faulty drafting' by Roy Goode, *Commercial Law* (3rd edn, Penguin 2004) 394.
[88] See further text to n 127 below.

Sometimes the agreed sum may accrue upon the happening of a specified event that does not require any cooperation from the repudiating party. Indeed, the event need not be within the control of either party: for example, we could agree that the sum will accrue if it rains on Sunday, or if England wins the World Cup.[89] Sometimes the only event is the passing of time until a certain date, in which case the liability to pay the agreed sum may be said to arise 'independently'. For example, section 49(2) of the Sale of Goods Act 1979 provides that 'where, under a contract of sale, the price is payable on a day certain irrespective of delivery and the buyer wrongfully neglects or refuses to pay such price, the seller may maintain an action for the price, although the property in the goods has not passed and the goods have not been appropriated to the contract'.[90] In this case, the seller can sue for the price even where the buyer makes it clear that it does not want the goods and will not accept them.[91]

Geys was a case in which accrual of the agreed sum (the bonus) was conditional upon the happening of a specified event, namely where, according to clause 5.15(b)(iv) of the contract, Mr Geys' 'employment terminates after 31 December 2007 . . . '.[92] The majority implicitly interpreted this condition to mean '*contract of* employment' rather than the de facto '*relationship of* employment'.[93] This was the context in which the choice between the automatic and election theories of termination arose for consideration. In this respect the facts of *Geys* were somewhat atypical, because in most employment cases the dispute concerns payment of the wage or salary. The conditions for earning the wage or salary are not always entirely clear,[94] but they usually require some cooperation on the part of the employer. For example, it is very unlikely that Mr Geys could have succeeded in a claim for his salary for December 2007, once he had been barred from the office and had ceased to work.

Accrual of the agreed sum will often be conditional upon actual performance. However, this does not necessarily mean that the repudiating party's cooperation will be required. Depending on the contractual terms of performance,[95] the innocent party may still be able to perform

---

[89] See GH Treitel, '"Conditions" and "Conditions Precedent"' (1990) 106 LQR 185.

[90] See discussion in *Ministry of Sound* (n 5) [52] (Strauss QC).

[91] *Dunlop v Grote* (1845) 2 Car & K 153, 175 ER 64 (Court of Assizes).

[92] Discussed by Lord Hope at *Geys* (n 1) [6].

[93] See e.g. ibid [14] issue 2 (Lord Hope). By contrast Lord Sumption expressly took the latter view, although this was not crucial to his decision: [137].

[94] See further text to n 128 below.

[95] Precisely what is required to fulfil 'performance' again ultimately depends on the construction of the contract. However, the default position appears to be that defects in

without cooperation, in which case the agreed sum can still be earned. This was the case on the facts of *White & Carter* itself. As Lord Reid put it, 'the peculiarity ... in the present case, was that the pursuers could completely fulfil the contract without any co-operation of the defender'.[96] By contrast, as Strauss QC later noted in *Ministry of Sound v World Online*, 'if the advertiser had been in a position to prevent the display of advertisements, for example, by withholding material which was to form part of the advertisements, in the absence of a decree of specific performance, which the court would not have granted, the contractor could not fulfil the contractual pre-condition to payment'.[97]

4.4.3   Cooperation Required

Where the repudiating party's cooperation is needed to fulfil the conditions necessary to earn the agreed sum, the withdrawal of cooperation will prevent recovery. As Lloyd J succinctly put it in *The Alaskan Trader*, 'you cannot claim remuneration under a contract if you have not earned it; if you are prevented from earning it, your only remedy is in damages'.[98] This straightforward explanation of the cooperation limitation provides the key to defining its scope. In several cases following *White & Carter*, counsel attempted to persuade the court that the cooperation limitation should apply whenever *any* cooperation was required.[99] However, once the connection with the capacity to earn the agreed sum is understood, it is clear that this proposition is too broad. In *Ministry of Sound*, Strauss QC correctly concluded that 'Lord Reid's reference to circumstances in which there is "anything" left to do under the contract which requires co-operation indicate that he had in mind only contracts in which the right to payment depended on full prior performance.'[100] Instead, as Cooke J identified in *The Aquafaith*, 'the court must focus upon dependent obligations and whether the contract breaker has to do something before the innocent party can do what is required of him to earn the contract sum'.[101]

---

quality do not prevent accrual of the agreed sum, whereas defects in quantity do: see *Sumpter v Hedges* (n 17) (defect in quantity); *Hoenig v Isaacs* [1952] 2 All ER 176 (CA) (defect in quality).

[96] *White & Carter* (n 2) 429 (Lord Reid); see also 428.   [97] *Ministry of Sound* (n 5) [40].

[98] *The Alaskan Trader* (n 6) 649. See also *Decro-Wall* (n 39) 370 (Salmon LJ).

[99] *Ministry of Sound* (n 5) [41]; *The Aquafaith* (n 5) [7]; *Decro-Wall* (n 40) 375, 380–81.

[100] *Ministry of Sound* (n 5) [61], approved in *The Aquafaith* (n 5) [39] (Cooke J).

[101] *The Aquafaith* (n 5) [39]. See also *Ministry of Sound* (n 5) [41] (Strauss QC).

Several examples may be given in which the agreed sum was irrecoverable because it depended on performance that in turn required cooperation from the (unwilling) repudiating party. In *Hounslow v Twickenham*, the defendant council repudiated its construction contract with the claimant builders, who wished to earn the price by continuing construction.[102] Megarry J justified his conclusion that the cooperation limitation applied on two grounds: 'first, because a considerable degree of active co-operation under the contract by the borough is requisite, and second, because the work is being done to property of the borough'.[103] Active cooperation arose because 'the whole machinery of the contract is geared to acts by the architect and quantity surveyor', which in turn required direction from the defendant.[104] The second ground was said to involve 'passive' cooperation because 'there is no question of the borough being required to do the act of admitting the contractor into possession'.[105] This latter argument is somewhat dubious because the builders had a contractual right (as against the Council) to enter the land,[106] but it was unnecessary for the decision.

The Puerto Buitrago involved an application of the cooperation limitation, properly understood.[107] A useful contrast can be drawn between this case, which concerned a demise charter, and the more recent decision in *The Aquafaith*, which concerned a time charter. In *The Aquafaith*, Cooke J clarified that 'there is a material difference between a demise charter and a time charter'.[108] Explaining *The Puerto Buitrago*, Cooke J noted that 'the very essence of the demise charter is that possession of the vessel is given to the demise charterer so that, as soon as possession is retaken by the owner, the latter can no longer be entitled to hire under the demise charter'.[109] By contrast, in *The Aquafaith* the nature of a time charter meant that 'if the charterers failed to give any orders, the vessel would simply stay where it was, awaiting orders but earning hire. ... In order to complete their side of the bargain, the owners do not need the charterers to do anything in order for them to earn the hire.'[110] Consequently, in *The Puerto Buitrago* cooperation was required to earn the agreed sum, whereas in *The Aquafaith* it was not.

Where cooperation is required but the repudiating party is unwilling to assist, it may very occasionally be possible for the innocent party to

---

[102] *Hounslow* (n 7).   [103] Ibid 254.   [104] Ibid 253.   [105] Ibid 253.
[106] Cf Liu, 'The White & Carter Principle: A Restatement' (n 15) 184.
[107] The case was expressly decided on the basis of both the cooperation and legitimate interest limitations: *Hounslow* (n 7) 256 (Orr LJ).
[108] *The Aquafaith* (n 5) [40].   [109] Ibid [40].   [110] Ibid [37].

compel cooperation by successfully claiming an order for specific performance. Such an order would need to attach to an obligation implied in fact that each party will reasonably cooperate so as to enable the other party to perform.[111] However, a successful claim for specific performance will be very rare in light of the practical restrictions enumerated in *Cooperative v Argyll Stores*,[112] most notably the bars of constant supervision and personal servitude. For example, in the recent case of *Ashworth v The Royal National Theatre*, a group of musicians sought an interim injunction to compel a theatre to allow them to continue to perform in a production of *War Horse*, following their dismissal without notice.[113] Cranston J held that the musicians had no prospect of obtaining an order for specific performance, with the consequence that they were unable to earn their salary.

In some other jurisdictions, where the repudiating party withholds its cooperation the innocent party is simply 'deemed' to have completed performance under a doctrine of 'fictional fulfilment'.[114] This approach appears to have been rejected in English law,[115] albeit without complete consistency.[116] In *Geys*, Lord Sumption concluded that 'the courts have never applied to contracts of employment the doctrine of deemed performance'.[117] However, Lord Hope expressed some sympathy with the rhetorical question 'why should the employee not sue for wages if it is the act of the employer which has prevented his performing the condition

---

[111] *Kleinert v Abosso Gold Mining Co* (1913) 58 SJ (PC) 45, [1913] UKPC 52 (PC); *Alpha Trading Ltd v Dunnshaw-Patten Ltd* [1981] QB 290 (CA). In these cases the claimant recovered damages for breach of the implied term.

[112] *Cooperative Insurance Society Ltd v Argyll Stores (Holdings) Ltd* [1998] AC 1 (HL).

[113] *Ashworth v Royal National Theatre* [2014] EWHC 1176, [2014] 4 All ER 238 (QB).

[114] See e.g. in the United States: *Foreman State Trust & Savings Bank v Tauber* (1932) 180 NE 827; E Allan Farnsworth, *Farnsworth on Contracts* (3rd edn, Aspen 2003) Vol 2, 454. See also French Code Civil, Art 1178; German Bürgerliches Gesetzbuch, s 162(1).

[115] *Colley v Overseas Exporters* (n 87). See also *CIA Barca de Panama SA v George Wimpey & Co Ltd* [1980] 1 Lloyd's Rep 598 (CA) 609 (Bridge LJ); *Thompson v ASDA-MFI Group plc* [1988] Ch 241 (HC) 266 (Scott J); *Little v Courage Ltd* (1995) 70 P & CR 469 (CA) 474 (Millett LJ).

[116] *Mackay v Dick* (1881) 6 App Cas 251 (HL) 270 (Lord Watson): '[The sellers] have been thwarted in the attempt to fulfil that condition by the neglect or refusal of the [buyer] to furnish the means of applying the stipulated test; and their failure being due to his fault, I am of opinion that . . . they must be taken to have fulfilled the condition.' Cf ibid 264 (Lord Blackburn). *Mackay* was a Scottish appeal, but it was subsequently followed by Devlin J in *Tiberghien Draperie Societe A Responsabilite v Greenberg & Sons (Mantles) Ltd* [1953] 2 Lloyd's Rep 739 (HC).

[117] *Geys* (n 1) [131].

precedent of rendering his services?'[118] There may accordingly be some
scope for this issue to be reopened.

4.4.4   The Effect on Termination

Although the so-called cooperation limitation does not impose any
legal limit on the right to affirm a repudiated contract, withdrawal of
cooperation may nevertheless have an important *practical* effect on
the innocent party's election.[119] The inability to earn the agreed sum
will often mean that the innocent party will see no practical utility in
keeping the contract alive rather than terminating and claiming
damages. For example, in *Decro-Wall International v Practitioners in
Marketing*, Salmon LJ doubted whether an unaccepted repudiation
could bring an end to a contract of employment as a matter of law,
'although no doubt in practice it does'.[120] As Sachs LJ clarified in the
same case, 'the truth of the matter is that there are a great many cases
in which it is of no benefit to the innocent party to keep the contract
alive . . . So there are vast numbers of cases where the innocent party can
in one sense be said to be forced to adopt the only practicable course
because any other would be valueless.'[121] Nevertheless, Sachs LJ was
perfectly clear that 'in such cases it is the range of remedies that is
limited, not the right to elect'.[122]

There is a significant risk, if the basis of the cooperation limitation
is not properly understood, that the legal and practical effects of a lack
of cooperation will be conflated. For example, *Chitty on Contracts*
notes that 'the party not in default may be compelled to treat the
prevention of performance as a repudiation of the contract and to sue
for damages for the breach',[123] without clarifying whether this reflects
the position in law or merely in fact. In *Geys*, Lord Sumption's reasoning attempts to draw a direct line between these two effects, arguing
essentially that the reason *why* the contract is terminated in law is
because of its practical futility. However, the facts of *Geys* itself ought
to demonstrate that an inability to continue with performance does
not always render the whole of the contract futile for all purposes.
Consequently Lord Hope was correct to warn that 'one must be careful

---

[118] Quoting *Sanders* (n 50) 571 (Sir John Donaldson).
[119] See Rose, 'The Effects of Repudiatory Breaches of Contract' (n 40) 241.
[120] *Decro-Wall* (n 40) 370.   [121] Ibid 375; see also 376.
[122] Ibid 375. Contra *MSC* (n 1) [60] (Tomlinson LJ).
[123] Hugh Beale (ed), *Chitty on Contracts* (32nd edn, Sweet & Maxwell 2015) Vol 1 [24–033].

not to assume that, just because in practice the employee may have little choice but to accept the repudiation, he has in law no alternative but to do so'.[124]

4.5   Defining the Wage–Work Bargain

One unresolved controversy exposed by the majority's decision in *Geys* concerns the conditions for earning the salary or wage in contracts of employment.[125] This is commonly known as the 'wage–work bargain'. The main possibilities are: actual performance by the employee; mere readiness and willingness to perform; or a third composition of conditions based on subsistence of the employment relationship. The issue did not arise directly on the facts of *Geys*, because the claim was for Mr Geys' bonus rather than his salary. Consequently, after expressing his provisional view, Lord Wilson held that 'even if the question can be said to be unresolved, this court is not invited to resolve it'.[126] Recently, in *Sunrise Brokers LLP v Rodgers*, Longmore LJ again posed a series of open questions that 'Lord Wilson's judgment appears to leave open for further resolution', concerning circumstances in which the salary or wage may be earned.[127]

The prevailing view appears to be that, at least by default, a salary or wage is only earned by actual performance by the employee. This was the provisional conclusion drawn by Lord Wilson in *Geys*, who held that 'the law has been clear that, save when, unusually, a contract of employment specifies otherwise, the mere readiness of an employee to resume work, following a wrongful dismissal which he has declined to accept, does not entitle him to sue for his salary or wages'.[128] In support of this

---

[124]   *Geys* (n 1) [17].

[125]   The problem is not new: in *Cerberus Software Ltd v Rowley* [2001] EWCA Civ 78, [2001] ICR 376, 386, Sedley LJ (dissenting) described it as 'one of the great unresolved questions of employment law'. See also B Napier, 'Aspects of the Wage–Work Bargain' (1984) 43 CLJ 337.

[126]   *Geys* (n 1) [79]. See further David Cabrelli and Rebecca Zahn, 'The Elective and Automatic Theories of Termination in the Common Law of the Contract of Employment: Conundrum Resolved?' (2013) 76 MLR 1106, 1119.

[127]   *Sunrise Brokers LLP v Rodgers* [2014] EWCA Civ 1373, [2015] ICR 272 [58]: '(i) if the employee decides to keep the contract alive, why should he not be allowed to sue for his salary or wages . . .; (ii) if the employer decides to keep the contract alive and seeks an injunction to restrain the employee from working for a rival during the . . . notice period which the employee is bound to give, should the employer not be bound to continue to pay the employee . . . ?'

[128]   *Geys* (n 1) [79].

proposition he cited 'the Victorian work ethic' established in the early authority of *Goodman v Pocock*.[129] More recently, in *Denmark Productions Ltd v Boscobel Productions*, Salmon LJ noted that the employee 'cannot sit in the sun'.[130] This position appears to be supported in other recent Court of Appeal authorities.[131]

However, there are at least some employment contracts in which the salary or wage can be earned where the employee is merely ready and willing to perform. In *Geys*, Lord Hope acknowledged that 'it is not always true that work is the counterpart of the entitlement to wages. In some contracts wages are given to employees for holding themselves available for work.'[132] This is plainly correct with regard to, for instance, the payment of a 'retainer', which might be thought of as a species of salary. In *Boyo v Lambeth LBC*, Staughton LJ criticised the requirement of actual performance and observed that, unconstrained by authority, he would not have accepted it.[133] Support for the sufficiency of an employee being ready and willing to perform can also be found at the level of the House of Lords.[134]

In *Geys*, Lord Sumption robustly held that the requirement of actual performance 'is certainly not a general principle of employment law'.[135] In particular, 'where the contract is subsisting, the employee is entitled to wages provided they are ready and willing to do the work even if the employer does not provide any work'.[136] In support of this conclusion he cited a series of cases concerning sick pay (before the introduction of a statutory entitlement), 'go-slows' and other forms of partial industrial action.[137] From these authorities, he further concluded that 'the only rational explanation of the rule that a wrongfully dismissed employee

---

[129] *Goodman v Pocock* (1850) 15 QB 576, 117 ER 577 (KB) 583–84, 580 (Erle J), cited by Lord Wilson in *Geys* (n 1) [78].

[130] *Denmark Productions* (n 50) 726.

[131] *Henderson-Williams v Davis* Unreported 17 June 1999 (CA); *Masood v Zahoor* [2008] EWHC 1034 (Ch) [279] (Peter Smith J).

[132] *Geys* (n 1) [18], citing Douglas Brodie, *The Contract of Employment* (W Green 2008) [18–09].

[133] *Boyo* (n 39) 747. See also *Henthorn and Taylor v Central Electricity Generating Board* [1980] IRLR 361 (CA); cf *Cummings v Charles Connell & Co (Shipbuilders) Ltd* 1968 SC 305 (Court of Session) (a claim for damages equal to wages).

[134] *Miles v Wakefield Metropolitan DC* [1987] AC 539 (HL) 561 (Lord Templeman), 552 (Lord Brightman), 574 (Lord Oliver).

[135] *Geys* (n 1) [131].   [136] Ibid [131].

[137] *Cuckson v Stones* (1858) 1 El & El 248 (KB) 256; 120 ER 902, 905 (Lord Campbell CJ); *Miles v Wakefield* (n 136) 561 (Lord Templeman); Mark R Freedland, *The Personal Employment Contract* (Oxford University Press 2003) 212–23.

cannot sue for his wages is that once the employee has been dismissed, albeit wrongfully, there is no longer a contractual obligation to pay the wages, and therefore no debt on which to sue'.[138] It therefore appears that Lord Sumption's conclusion on the characterisation of the cooperation limitation was in large part derived from his understanding of the wage–work bargain.

Unfortunately, many of the cases cited by Lord Sumption are very weak authority for the proposition that an employee can earn the salary or wage merely by being ready and willing to perform. The cases on 'go-slows' and partial industrial action could equally concern the interpretation of 'performance' and not whether performance of some kind is required. There is a difficult question as to whether performance that is defective in quality (such as a go-slow) but not quantity is sufficient to fulfil a requirement of actual performance.[139] However, these cases in which the salary or wage have been earned despite the absence of *full* performance do not necessarily demonstrate the sufficiency of being ready and willing to perform; they may instead show that actual performance does not require performance that is complete in both quantity *and* quality.

A third possibility is that the conditions for earning the salary or wage are composite, and include at least in part the requirement that the employment relationship remains subsisting. In *Gunton v Richmond Upon Thames*, Brightman LJ proposed a distinction between the contract of employment and the relationship of employment,[140] the former being a legal construct and the latter being essentially a matter of fact. Another way of putting this requirement may be to say that (i) the employee must be ready and willing to perform and (ii) the employer must be ready and willing to accept performance, since both of these are prerequisites for the employment relationship to subsist as a matter of fact. In circumstances where the employer has sought to terminate the contract (including by wrongful repudiation), it is almost certain that the second condition will be unfulfilled, in which case according to this view the wage or salary could not be earned.

The general answer to the problem of the wage–work bargain must surely be that, in the end, it remains a matter of contractual construction. In this sense the approach is no different from the process by which the

---

[138] *Geys* (n 1) [131].   [139] See further n 96 above.
[140] *Gunton* (n 39) 474–75. See also *Micklefield v SAC Technology Ltd* [1990] 1 WLR 1002 (HC) 1006 (John Mowbray QC).

conditions of any other type of agreed sum are ascertained. However, in the absence of any express agreement, the question arises whether any 'default' solution should be implied. It is not clear that any of the three options canvassed above offer clearly the right approach for *all* types of employment contract. In other words, any solution implied in fact is also likely to be context-dependant. Whilst this flexibility is probably required to reflect the diversity of employment relationships, the uncertainty of the wage–work bargain presents practical difficulties for the employee in deciding whether to exercise their right to affirm, in circumstances where it is not clear whether the agreed sum can continue to be earned without cooperation from the employer.

4.6 Conclusion

In *Geys*, Lord Sumption attempted to re-characterise the cooperation limitation as a restriction on the innocent party's right to affirm its contract in the face of wrongful repudiation. The majority correctly resisted this analysis by reasserting the unfettered right to affirm. The cooperation limitation raised by Lord Reid in *White & Carter* is instead best understood as a practical rather than legal limitation. The withdrawal of cooperation by a repudiating party may prevent the innocent party from taking the steps necessary to earn the agreed sum. However, the effect on the issue of termination is only indirect; a lack of cooperation may make it futile, but never legally impermissible, to hold the contract open. This understanding of the role of cooperation places important emphasis on construing the conditions for earning the agreed sum. In relation to employment contracts, *Geys* leaves this particular controversy unresolved.

5

Specific Performance and Change of Mind

MINDY CHEN-WISHART

When I order a pizza, I want the pizza and not damages for not getting the pizza.[1] So, why will contract law give me damages and not the pizza? One who is tasked with exploring the remedy of specific performance for breach of contract is immediately confronted with its secondary status. Specific performance only kicks in after the primary remedy of damages is assessed to be 'inadequate'. Even then, a host of other considerations may oust specific performance as the appropriate remedy. The common assumptions that the contractual right is to performance and that contract remedies enforce that right make the rarity of specific performance perplexing to some, and outright wrong to others. For someone who seeks to understand the black-letter law, the natural question is: why do courts so rarely require defendants to perform the contract, as opposed to paying damages?

This chapter argues that while there is a contractual right to performance (and a corresponding duty to perform), the remedies awarded by the law do not *simply* aim to enforce that right or duty. Instead, when courts, as emanations of the state, are called on to vindicate contractual rights, they are entitled to take account of a range of factors that we see operating across the entire law of contract remedies. One of these factors explains the adequacy of damages bar, a bar that more than any other consigns specific performance to its secondary status. It is rooted in a more nuanced understanding of individual autonomy that is facilitated by the institution of contract. We take for granted that autonomy requires contract law to enable parties to voluntarily undertake obligations. What is less obvious is that *valuable* autonomy also requires the law

With thanks to Hugh Collins, Simon Gardner, Roderick Bagshaw and John Cartwright for helpful discussions. And, huge thanks to Owen Lloyd, Vinerian Scholar 2015, University of Oxford, for research assistance above and beyond the call of duty.
[1] Daniel Friedmann, 'The Performance Interest in Contract Damages' (1995) 111 LQR 628, 632.

to permit a party's change of mind by not compelling her to actually perform if damages would be 'adequate' to compensate the other party. The law's recognition of the individual's ability to bind herself and also to change her mind is the paradox that lies at the heart of the specific performance remedy. Understanding these propositions not only makes sense of the specific performance remedy, but also provides the intellectual apparatus for understanding many other rules shaping the law's response to breach of contract.

Section 5.1 will discuss the dominant remedies-as-enforcement view and identify the very significant extent to which contract law deviates from it. Section 5.2 explores some explanations for this lack of fit between the right and the remedy and settles on one that creates space for the operation of considerations beyond the simple enforcement of the contractual right. Section 5.3 then makes a start on identifying and justifying these 'other' considerations such as procedural and substantive fairness, the administration of justice and human rights. The focus, however, is on explaining the most important bar of adequacy of damages by reference to the importance of change of mind as constitutive of the valuable autonomy that contract law seeks to enhance.

5.1 Enforcement of the Contractual Right?

5.1.1 The Contract Right and Enforcement of that Right View

The dominant academic opinion is that the contractual right is the right to performance. This is generally rooted in rights-based theories of private law[2] according to which legal rights are grounded in a conception of individual agency and autonomy, and generate corresponding duties that are owed by individuals (as individuals) to the right holder. '[C]ontracts are made to be performed.'[3] Accordingly, Friedmann sees specific performance, injunctions and debt claims as remedies that enforce the performance interest, while compensatory and restitutionary damages are 'substitutional remedies'.

---

[2] See generally, e.g. Jules L Coleman, *Risks and Wrongs* (Oxford University Press 2002) 197–439; Charles Fried, *Contract as Promise* (Oxford University Press 2015); Ernest J Weinrib, *The Idea of Private Law* (Oxford University Press 2013); Randy E Barnett, 'A Consent Theory of Contract' (1986) 86 Colum LR 269; Peter Benson, 'The Unity of Contract Law' in Peter Benson (ed), *The Theory of Contract Law* (Cambridge University Press 2001); Friedmann (n 1); Dori Kimel, *From Promise to Contract. Towards a Liberal Theory of Contract* (Hart Publishing 2003).

[3] Friedmann (n 1) 629.

This reasoning is reflected in European civilian jurisdictions. Their starting point is also that performance is constitutive of, inherent in, or intrinsic to the contractual right, but this is implemented by making specific performance the *primary* response to non-performance. The essence of specific performance is rooted in the idea of enforcement of the right. Indeed, it is alien to regard performance as a 'remedy' that connotes something external to the right, let alone one that is secondary and discretionary.

Although the common law treats specific performance as a secondary right, support can also be found for the position that the contractual right at common law is to performance. The very language of 'breach' used to describe the defendant's non-performance or defective performance presumes that there is a duty to perform, and a correlative right to performance on the claimant's part.[4] Further, the existence of the tort of inducing breach of contract seems to assume that a contract gives rise to a right and correlative duty to performance. That is why it is objectionable for a third party to induce a defendant not to perform, entitling the claimant to sue the third party.

There is also support in the common law for the idea that the remedies for breach enforce the right to performance. First, the very existence of the specific performance remedy is held up as enforcement of the right, with particular emphasis on undertakings to pay money and to transfer interests in land that are routinely specifically enforced. Secondly, damages is presented as *replicating* the right to performance; the classic authority of *Robinson v Harman* states that the claimant 'is, so far as money can do it to be placed in the same situation, with respect to damages, as if the contract had been performed'.[5] On this view, the primary rights live on albeit in mutated form;[6] defendants should pay damages for the same reason that they should perform their primary duties. Thirdly, the possibility of claiming an account of profits for breach of contract has been justified on the basis of protecting the right to performance. In *Attorney General v Blake*[7] Lord Nicholls endorsed the argument of Lionel Smith that the right to contractual performance

---

[4] Charlie Webb, 'Performance and Compensation: An Analysis of Contract Damages and Contractual Obligation' (2006) 26 OJLS 41.

[5] (1849) 1 Exch 850, 855.

[6] See Lord Diplock in *Photo Production Ltd v Securicor Transport Ltd* [1980] AC 827, 848C, 848H, 849C.

[7] [2001] 1 AC 268, 283.

should be protected as strongly as a proprietary right – by entitling the claimant to the defendant's gains from breach.[8]

5.1.2 Departures from Enforcement of the Right to Performance

Despite such support for the idea that contract remedies simply enforce the contract right, the reality deviates significantly from this straightforward picture. Indeed, it is remarkable just how fragile the right to performance is when it is translated into remedial form. Money, land and some negative obligations aside, the claimant's right to performance is rarely awarded. Furthermore, damages, which *are* routinely awarded, will often fall short of putting the claimant in the position she would have been in 'if the contract had been performed'.

The most obvious way of enforcing the contract is by awarding specific performance. Yet, it is acknowledged to be 'an exceptional remedy';[9] despite some moves towards widening its availability, the House of Lords in *Co-operative Insurance Ltd v Argyll Holdings Ltd*[10] has entrenched the bars to its award. Most of these bars are difficult to square with the idea that contract law's task, in the face of breach, is simply to enforce the duty to perform.

5.1.2.1   Impossibility and Inutility

The bar of impossibility is uncontroversial. It is pointless to order performance that is impossible; the defendant cannot fulfil the duty and the claimant cannot realise the right. Likewise, if a contract allows the defendant to revoke, the order will be refused as the defendant can neutralise it by exercising his power to terminate.[11]

5.1.2.2   Vagueness, Constant Supervision and Heavy-handed Enforcement Mechanism

Administrative concerns may also appear to impose legitimate limits on the availability of specific performance; for example, the vagueness of the primary duties may make it too difficult to spell out what must be specifically performed, and ensuring the performance of continuing contracts may overburden judicial resources. However, the extent to which these concerns should bar specific performance depends on the strength of

---

[8] Lionel D Smith, 'Disgorgement of the Profits of Breach of Contract: Property, Contract and Efficient Breach' (1995) 24 Can BLJ 121, 132.

[9] *Co-operative Insurance Ltd v Argyll Holdings Ltd* [1998] AC 1 (HL) 11.   [10] Ibid.

[11] *Wheeler v Trotter* (1737) 3 Swan 174.

the law's commitment to the enforcement of contractual rights and the concomitant strength of will to overcome such difficulties as arise.

In the context of contract formation, courts will strain to cure the vagueness of contract terms by reference to a wide range of techniques, such as the parties' previous dealings, customs of the trade, the standard of reasonableness, and severance. Likewise, in the remedial context, '[i]t is open to the court, in order to give its order specificity and effectiveness, to spell out what performance is required in the particular circumstances of the case', and courts may 'include a liberty to apply, so that the parties can, if it becomes necessary, come back for further directions'.[12] In short, courts can go a very long way to overcome any vagueness *if they want to*. So, the question is why they may not want to.

Likewise, the answer to the question 'how much judicial supervision is too much?' depends on how committed the law is to ensuring performance. Parties will generally obey court orders so that no supervision is required.[13] Moreover, courts have means of overcoming any problems of constant supervision, for example, by appointing a receiver to perform the specified acts,[14] appointing an expert to act as officer of the court, or authorising the claimant to appoint a person to act as agent of the defendant for the purpose of performing those acts.[15] Where the defendant need not personally perform, the court can simply order her to make a contract for a third party to perform.

Lord Hoffmann puts forward 'the heavy-handed nature of the enforcement mechanism'[16] as an important reason against the award of specific performance. But, if the aim of contractual remedies is simply to enforce the primary right, this factor should make courts *more* (rather than less) willing to award specific performance, for defendants are more likely to obey it. The fact that vagueness, constant supervision and the 'heavy-handed' nature of enforcement mechanisms bar specific performance calls into serious question the law's commitment to the enforcement of the right to performance.

---

[12] *Alfa Finance Holdings AD v Quarzwerke GmbH* [2015] EWHC 243 [8]–[9].

[13] Andrew Burrows, *Remedies for Torts and Breach of Contract* (3rd edn, Oxford University Press 2004) 481. And see *Storer v Great Western Rly Co* (1842) 2 Y & C Ch 48; *Kennard v Cory Bros & Co Ltd* [1922] 2 Ch 1 (CA); *Rainbow Estates Ltd v Tokenhold Ltd* [1999] Ch 64 (Ch).

[14] Cf *Gibbs v David* (1875) LR 20 Eq 373.

[15] Cf Law of Property Act 1925, s 101; Insolvency Act 1986, s 44.

[16] *Co-operative Insurance Society Ltd v Argyll Stores (Holdings) Ltd* (n 9) 12.

5.1.2.3 Adequacy of Damages

The adequacy of damages bar signals most clearly the law's lack of commitment to enforcing the right to performance. Fried justifies the availability of expectation damages:

> If I make a promise to you, I should do as I promise; and if I fail to keep my promise, it is fair that I should be made to handover the equivalent of the promised performance . . . [T]his proposition appears as the expectation measure of damages for breach . . . [which] gives the victim of a breach no more or less then he would have had had there been no breach – in other words, he gets the benefit of his bargain.[17]

But, why settle for expectation damages if the 'victim of a breach' prefers actual performance? Late performance (if still sought by the victim) along with any damages for delay is the most obvious way to enforce the contract. Why, then, positively *bar* specific performance and confine victims to 'adequate' damages, especially when damages are often regarded as 'adequate' even when they do not, as touted, put the victim 'so far as money can do . . . in the same situation . . . as if the contract had been performed'[18]? The general default measure of expectation is diminution of value rather than the cost of cure. These measures may (although they need not) produce wildly differing figures.[19] To add insult to injury, the victim's proven losses may not be fully recoverable due to the operation of well-known limits such as the general bar to recovery for non-pecuniary loss, the mitigation and remoteness requirements. Atiyah famously observed that the mitigation requirement 'makes a large dent' in the theory that the claimant is entitled to damages representing his lost expectations.[20] The same principles govern the award of damages 'in lieu' of specific performance or injunctions.[21] Both the common law and equity purport to put the claimant in the position that she would be in if the contract had been performed, but 'neither is followed through to its logical conclusion'.[22]

The mystery deepens. In *Co-operative Insurance v Argyll*, one reason for Lord Hoffmann's refusal to grant specific performance was that the claimant might otherwise be 'unjustly enriched', in the sense that it would strengthen the claimant's bargaining position in settlement negotiations

---

[17] Fried (n 2) 17. [18] *Robinson v Harman* (n 5) 855.
[19] *Tito v Waddell (No 2)* [1977] Ch 106 (Ch) is an example of the latter.
[20] PS Atiyah, *Introduction to Contract Law* (5th edn, Clarendon 1995) 458.
[21] Senior Courts Act 1981, s 50; *Johnson v Agnew* [1980] AC 367 (HL) 400.
[22] Hugh Beale, *Chitty on Contracts* (31st edn, Sweet and Maxwell 2012) [27–080].

and allow her to charge more for release than the value of performance to
the claimant (measured by court-awarded damages).[23] But, if the claimant's right to performance provides the point of reference, it makes no
sense to describe its economic exploitation as either 'unjust', or indeed,
'enrichment'. The value exchanged for waiving performance only constitutes 'unjust enrichment' against the different baseline of (often inadequate) damages.

This baseline of court-assessed damages rather than performance also
makes sense of the bars on affirming the contract on the defendant's
repudiatory breach. *White & Carter v McGregor*[24] holds that a claimant
cannot affirm a contract (so as to complete its own performance and earn
the agreed sum) if she would need the defendant's cooperation or would
have no 'legitimate interest' in completing performance. If the claimant
has a duty to respect the defendant's contractual right to performance,
then she also has a right to do so; ought implies can. So, why should
a claimant who has a contractual duty to perform ever be regarded as
having 'no legitimate' interest in performing? Moreover, why should
a defendant not be required to cooperate even in the most attenuated
form of allowing a claimant onto her land?[25]

5.1.2.4   Contracts of Personal Services

Damages are inadequate, *par excellence*, where contracts are for personal
services and yet specific performance is unavailable for this class of
contracts. The traditional explanation is that enforcement would amount
to slavery,[26] or, less dramatically, would 'interfere unduly with [the
defendant's] personal liberty'.[27] Section 236 of the Trade Union and
Labour Relations (Consolidation) Act 1992 prohibits courts from compelling an employee to do any work.

Likewise, an injunction will not be awarded where the practical effect is
to secure indirect specific performance of contracts of personal services.[28]
But, how can it be 'slavery' to require the defendant to do what she has

---

[23] *Co-operative Insurance v Argyll* (n 9) 15.   [24] [1962] AC 413 (HL) 431.

[25] As in *Hounslow LBC v Twickenham Garden Developments Ltd* [1971] Ch 233 (Ch).

[26] *De Francesco v Barnum* (1890) 45 Ch D 430, 438 (Ch).

[27] *Young v Robson Rhodes* [1999] 3 All ER 524 (Ch) 534. And see Anthony T Kroman,
'Paternalism and the Law of Contracts' (1983) 92 Yale LJ 763, 778–79; JE Penner,
'Voluntary Obligations and the Scope of the Law of Contract' (1996) 2 *Legal Theory*
325, 353.

[28] *Warner Bros Pictures Inc v Nelson* [1937] 1 KB 209 (KB); *Warren v Mendy* [1989] 1 WLR
853 (CA); *LauritzenCool AB v Lady Navigation Inc* [2005] EWCA Civ 579, [2005] 1 WLR
3686.

voluntarily undertaken to do? More tellingly, the fact that even *employers* are generally not required to rehire unfairly dismissed employees[29] shows that slavery cannot be the sole focus of concern here. Rather, the focus shifts to the normative concern to avoid *undue* interference with the defendant's liberty, on which much more will be said below.[30]

5.1.2.5 Want of Mutuality

The mutuality bar is also puzzling if the aim of remedies is to enforce performance. The bar says that if the claimant who has yet to complete performance would not be compelled to perform (and so confining the defendant to damages), then the claimant must also be denied specific performance and be confined to damages. The effect of the bar is to go to the lowest common denominator of damages. The obvious question is why, if the law aims to enforce contractual obligations, specific performance is not made the primary remedy, for this would eliminate the risk of lack of mutuality all around.

5.1.2.6 Procedural and Substantive Unfairness

Procedural and substantive unfairness also operate as bars to specific performance. Specific performance is barred if the claimant has given no consideration;[31] nominal consideration;[32] or inadequate consideration if a court finds a trace of procedural unfairness (which is easily inferred from the inadequacy of consideration itself).[33] The claimant's lack of 'clean hands' can bar specific performance[34] even when this was insufficient to vitiate the contract.[35] Furthermore, even where the claimant is not responsible for them, the defendant's mistake,[36] or facts occurring post-formation and even post-breach, may make it harsh or oppressive to

---

[29] The Employment Rights Act 1996, Pt X, ss 113–117. A tribunal may order the reinstatement or re-engagement of the employee, but the employer can, in the last resort, only be ordered to pay compensation. Likewise, under the Equality Act 2010, s 124 an employer can, in the last resort, be required only to pay compensation. The statutory right to return to work after maternity, parental or paternity leave appears not to be specifically enforceable. Employment Rights Act 1996, Pt VIII; Maternity and Parental Leave Regulations 1999 (SI 1999/3312) reg 18.

[30] See section 5.3.2.3 below.   [31] *Cannon v Hartley* [1949] Ch 213 (Ch).

[32] *Jeffreys v Jeffreys* (1841) Cr & Ph 138; 41 ER 443.

[33] *Griffith v Spratley* (1787) 1 Cox Eq Cas 383, 29 ER 1213; *Falcke v Gray* (1859) 4 Drew 651, 62 ER 250.

[34] See *Chitty* (n 22) [27–032], [27–035]–[27–036], [27–045].

[35] E.g. for misrepresentation, duress or undue influence.

[36] *Denne v Light* (1857) 8 DM & G 774.

order specific performance[37] or injunctions[38] against the defendant. The puzzle: why should requiring the performance of a valid duty be regarded as 'harsh' or 'oppressive'? Even if it is, why should it matter? Why should the right to performance be trumped by these factors when they do not prevent the creation of the rights and duties?

5.1.2.7   Limits on Agreed Remedies

Neither the primary right to performance, nor the right to specific performance on breach agreed by the parties is automatically enforceable *in specie*. Courts will refuse to enforce contract terms that expressly require specific performance on breach; their discretion to refuse specific performance cannot be ousted by the parties' agreement.[39] Furthermore, a sum agreed to be payable on breach is unenforceable as a penalty if it is 'unconscionable and extravagant', is 'out of all proportion to any legitimate interest of the innocent party in the enforcement of the primary obligation' (this may go beyond compensation for breach), and simply punishes the defaulter.[40] The assumption that it is improper for parties to agree a contractual provision for the purpose of ensuring contractual performance is difficult to square with the idea of a right to performance and the enforcement of such performance by the courts. On the other hand, it is entirely consistent with the bars of adequacy of damages and contracts of personal services.

5.1.2.8   Limits on Restitutionary Damages

The award of an account of profit for breach of contract by the House of Lords in *Attorney General v Blake*[41] could have presaged a particularly strong vindication of the right to performance. The idea is to equate the claimant's right to the defendant's performance with a proprietary interest, hence entitling the claimant to trace through to the profits generated by that performance. In reality, far from account of profits becoming routinely available for breach of contract, the remedy is confined to the most exceptional (rarely to be repeated) circumstances.[42] The more

---

[37] *Patel v Ali* [1985] Ch 283.   [38] *Jaggard v Sawyer* [1995] 1 WLR 269.
[39] *Quadrant Visual Communications Ltd v Hutchison Telephone (UK) Ltd* [1993] BCLC 442 (CA).
[40] *Cavendish Square Holding BV v El Makdessi, ParkingEye Ltd v Beavis* [2015] UKSC 67 [19]–[32].
[41] [2001] 1 AC 268 (HL) 285.
[42] *Esso Petroleum v Niad* [2001] EWHC Ch 458 is the one, now quietly abandoned, aberration.

frequently awarded 'Wrotham Park damages'[43] has also been tamed by interpretation. There, the developers who made additional profits by building in excess of a restrictive covenant were required to pay damages at just 5 per cent of their estimated profits. Although Lord Nicholls in Blake appeared to consider this restitutionary,[44] the weight of subsequent judicial opinion is that it is standardly compensatory.[45] It is characterised as 'negotiating damages'[46] which represents such a sum of money as might reasonably have been demanded by the claimant from the defendant as a *quid pro quo* for permitting the continuation of the breach.[47]

However, its quantification proceeds on the assumption that:

> It is a negotiation between a willing buyer (the contract-breaker) and a willing seller (the party claiming damages) ... Both parties are to be assumed to act reasonably. The fact that one or both parties would in practice have refused to make a deal is therefore to be ignored.[48]

All this points to a compulsory purchase of the claimant's contractual right, rather than its enforcement. Moreover, the factors said to be relevant in determining the availability of account of profits[49] also contradict the idea that it is aimed at simply enforcing the primary duty. One such factor is that the claimant should have a 'legitimate interest in preventing the defendant's profit-making activity, and hence, in depriving him of his profit'.[50] But, if the claimant has a right to performance, why should she ever be regarded as *not* having such legitimate interest?[51]

---

[43] *Wrotham Park Estate v Parkside Homes Ltd* [1974] 1 WLR 798 (Ch).

[44] *Blake* (n 41) 286, although his Lordship would 'prefer to avoid the unhappy expression "restitutionary damages".'

[45] *World Wide Fund for Nature v World Wrestling Federation Entertainment Inc* [2007] EWCA Civ 286, [2008] 1 WLR 445 (Chadwick LJ); *Pell Frischmann Engineering Ltd v Bow Valley Iran Ltd* [2009] UKPC 45, [2011] 1 WLR 2370. Even the account of profits awarded in *Blake* has been described by Chadwick LJ in *WWF* at [58]–[59] as compensatory, although this seems rather far-fetched.

[46] *Lunn Poly Ltd v Liverpool & Lancashire Properties Ltd* [2006] EWCA Civ 430, [2007] L & TR 6 [22] (Neuberger LJ).

[47] *Pell Frischmann* (n 45) [48]–[49] *(Lord Walker)*.

[48] Ibid, citing *Wrotham Park* (n 43) 815; *Jaggard* (n 38) 282–83.

[49] See e.g. *World Wide Fund for Nature v World Wrestling Federation Entertainment Inc* [2006] EWHC 184 (Ch), [2006] FSR 38 [174], e.g. the moral character of the breach (whether cynical, deliberate), the ordinary contract remedies must be 'inadequate', each party's reasonable use of their respective bargaining positions, at the time of negotiations, the claimant's loss and the defendant's gain, any delay in making its claim, and what 'practical justice' demands in 'exceptional circumstances'.

[50] *Blake* (n 41) 285 (Lord Nicholls).

[51] See Mindy Chen-Wishart, 'Restitutionary Damages for Breach of Contract' (1998) 114 LQR 363.

5.1.2.9   Consideration and Failure of Consideration

Two other doctrines outside the law on contract remedies reinforce the idea that damages is not the equivalent of performance. First, acceptance of actual performance of a pre-existing contractual duty (or a re-promise to perform which increases the chances of performance) as 'practical benefit',[52] and so 'additional' consideration for a reciprocal promise to pay more, only makes sense if actual performance (or an increased chance of it) is regarded as 'extra' to the default remedy of damages.[53] Secondly, the right to restitution for total failure of consideration shows that the availability of damages does not prevent consideration (i.e. actual performance) from failing; damages is, therefore, not a substitute for that performance.[54]

In sum, far from specific performance being the 'core' remedy from which deviations are exceptionally permitted, damages is the primary remedy, with specific performance being exceptionally available, and only as a 'back-up' when damages would be inadequate. Even then, specific performance may be ousted for a host of other reasons. This position is embedded in other rules of contract law. Cumulatively, the extent to which the law diverges from the notion of contract remedies enforcing the right to performance is striking.

5.2   Structural Explanations for the Gap between the Right and the Remedy

How are we to understand the yawning gap between, on the one hand, the claim that the right is to performance and that the remedies aim to enforce this right, and, on the other hand, the actual remedial rules? There are at least four options.

5.2.1   There is no Right to Performance

The first response is to deny that there is any right to performance, but only one to damages. The argument would run that the remedy defines the right, and there is no right to performance unless the court is willing to award specific performance or award the cost of cure to enable the

---

[52] *Williams v Roffey Bros & Nicholls (Contractors) Ltd* [1991] 1 QB 1 (CA).

[53] Mindy Chen-Wishart, 'A Bird in the Hand: Consideration and Promissory Estoppel' in Andrew Burrows and Edwin Peel (eds), *Contract Formation and Parties* (Oxford University Press 2010) 93.

[54] I am indebted to Owen Lloyd for this point.

claimant to secure substitute performance.[55] This is the gist of Oliver Wendell Holmes' position:

> The only universal consequence of a legally binding promise is, that the law makes the promisor pay damages if the promised event does not come to pass. In every case it leaves him free from interference until the time for fulfillment has gone by, and therefore free to break the contract if he chooses.[56]
>
> ... the so-called primary rights and duties are vested with a mystic significance beyond what can be assigned and explained. The duty to keep a contract at common law means a prediction that you must pay damages if you do not keep it – and nothing else ... [T]here are some cases in which a logical justification can be found for speaking of civil liabilities as imposing duties in an intelligible sense. These are relatively few in which equity will grant an injunction ... But I hardly think it advisable to shape a general theory from the exception.[57]

This view is not without attraction, but set against it is the evidence of a right to performance mentioned above;[58] namely, the very notion of 'breach' of contract, and the tort of inducing breach of contract. More critically, acceptance of this option is tantamount to a rejection of contract as an institution that permits the assumption of self-imposed obligations.

5.2.2 *There is a Right to Performance and the Current Law Enforces that Right*

There are two variants of this argument. Both regard damages as a kind of specific relief akin to awards to repay a debt. The first variant is that damages are a complete substitute for performance,[59] so that the claimant should be indifferent to whether she receives damages or specific performance. The implausibility of this idea, however, is evident no sooner than it is stated. A reasonable person will often *not* be indifferent as between receiving actual performance (or the cost of cure) and receiving damages with all its limitations that result in oft-acknowledged under-compensation.

---

[55] PS Atiyah, *Essays on Contract* (Clarendon Press 1990) 61–62; Catherine Mitchell, 'Remedial Inadequacy in Contract and the Role of Restitutionary Damages' (1999) 15 JCL 133.

[56] Oliver Wendell Holmes Jr, *The Common Law* (Little Brown & Co 1881) 301.

[57] Oliver Wendell Holmes, 'The Path of the Law' (1896) 10 Harv L Rev 457, 462.

[58] See 5.1.1 above.

[59] E.g. Kimel (n 2) 101: 'expectation damages, though a substitutionary remedy in their rationale, are simply just as good'.

The second variant is that courts award damages because the defendant's contractual duty was actually a *disjunctive* duty to either perform the primary duty or, alternatively, to pay damages. On this view, parties either understand themselves to be receiving disjunctive rights,[60] or terms are implied in law to that effect. This is a different iteration of Holmes' view set out above. It is consistent with Lord Hoffmann's view expressed in *Co-operative Store v Argyll*[61] that both parties were large sophisticated commercial organisations who entered the contract for purely financial reasons, knowing that the remedy for breach was likely to be limited to damages.

Three immediate objections can be raised to this construction. First, parties do not generally understand themselves as bargaining for disjunctive rights; to repeat, when I order a pizza, I expect to get a pizza, and not damages for not getting a pizza. Secondly, if the disjunctiveness of the rights arises from terms implied in law, this requires further justification. Thirdly, the idea of disjunctive duties implies that the defendant should either perform or pay the sum signified by damages *at the time that performance is due*. However, the quantum of damages cannot be known at the time of breach, not least because the defendant will not know many of the facts on which the quantum will depend (e.g. the extent of the claimant's lost profits). Moreover, the operation of other limits such as remoteness or mitigation will only be crystallised at adjudication. Indeed, the defendant may not even know that breach has occurred at the time of breach. Again, ought implies can: 'The suggestion that the law recognises a legal duty to do something that individuals cannot reasonably be expected to do should be accepted on only the clearest evidence.'[62]

5.2.3   There is a Right to Performance and the Law should be Reformed to Reflect That

The recognition that the current law does not adequately protect the claimant's right to performance or the defendant's duty to perform has led to calls for the wider availability of specific performance,[63] and more

---

[60] See e.g. Daniel Markovits and Alan Schwartz, 'The Myth of Efficient Breach: New Defenses of the Expectation Interest' (2011) 97 Virginia L Rev 1939, 2006.

[61] See *Co-operative Insurance Ltd v Argyll Holdings Ltd* (n 9), 18.

[62] Stephen S Smith, 'Duties, Liabilities and Damages' (2012) 125 Harvard LR 1727, 1744.

[63] E.g. Seana Shiffrin, 'The Divergence of Contract and Promise' (2007) 120 *Harvard Law Review* 708; Alan Schwartz, 'The Case for Specific Performance' (1979) 89 Yale LJ 271;

fulsome measures of damages (e.g. for breach of contract for the benefit of third party and for non-pecuniary loss).[64] Webb writes:

> If we do not believe breach of contract is a fiction, and so accept that contracting parties acquire a right to performance, then we must allow them to assert that right in cases of breach of contract. The law of contractual remedies will then look very different and leading cases would need to be reconsidered.[65]

This approach does not offer an explanation of the law so much as a rejection of it. If implemented, it would result in a radically different contract world from the one we know, and one of very dubious desirability: specific performance would be automatically available as long as it is possible and wanted by the claimant; alternatively, the full cost of cure would be awarded without being obstructed by such considerations as its reasonableness, or the claimant's intention to cure;[66] recovery of damages for loss sustained would not be restricted for being non-pecuniary, too remote, or for the claimant's failure to mitigate; the parties' agreed remedies would be enforced; and, claimants would be allowed to claim the defendant's profits made from breach.

5.2.4   There is a Right to Performance and the Remedy of Specific Performance is to Enforce the Right but it is Cut Back by Other Legitimate Concerns of the Law at the Remedial End

The claim here is that there is a right to performance, and a duty to perform, but that when courts are asked for remedies in response to breach, courts are rightly concerned with factors beyond the strict enforcement of the duty. As Zipursky explains, the private nature of private law means that '[t]he law does not *impose civil liability*. The law *empowers* private parties to have other private parties held liable to them, *if they*

Randy E Barnett, 'Contract Remedies and Inalienable Rights' (1986) *Social Philosophy & Policy* Vol 4, 179, 182–84.

[64] Ewan McKendrick, 'Breach of Contract and the Meaning of Loss' (1999) 52 CLP 37. See also Ewan McKendrick, 'The Common Law at Work: The Saga of *Panatown Ltd v Alfred McAlpine Construction Ltd*' (2003) 3 OUCLJ 145 and Ewan McKendrick and Katherine Worthington, 'Damages for Non-Pecuniary Loss' in Nili Cohen and Ewan McKendrick (eds), *Comparative Remedies for Breach of Contract* (Hart 2004); Janet O'Sullivan, 'Lost on Penalties' (2014) 73 CLJ 480.

[65] Webb (n 4) 70.

[66] As set out in *Ruxley Electronics & Construction v Forsyth* [1996] AC 344 (HL).

choose.[67] Power is conferred[68] on individuals who satisfy certain conditions to obtain state assistance to coerce another individual to do something (perform a contract, pay damages). Since the state is essentially involved in private actions, the paradigm is one of state subsidisation of an activity that is regarded as worthwhile. But, there is no reason for the state, via the law, to subsidise this activity in an unqualified way. Indeed, there are numerous considerations that legitimately impinge on determinations made by courts. Focus on the courts as emanations of the state explains why enforcing contractual rights is just one element in the normative account of contractual remedies. These 'other' relevant concerns need to be identified and justified, and their relationship to the core value of facilitating personal autonomy articulated.

5.3   The Judicial Imposition of Liability

The view that remedies for breach of contract are not simply aimed at the enforcement of the primary rights creates space for courts to weigh various considerations in determining the shape of the precise remedy awarded. The main task here is to understand the bars to specific performance, especially that of the adequacy of damages.

5.3.1   Limits on Expectation Damages and Bars to Specific Performance

In determining how to vindicate the right breached, it is entirely proper for courts to take into account the seriousness of the breach in the sense of the harm or loss caused to the claimant. This way of valuing the right infringed yields the expectation interest as the starting point. But 'other' factors cut back the expectation measure. Significantly, they find counterparts in the bars to specific performance. Some examples will suffice for present purposes.

5.3.1.1   Avoidance of Harshness

The first cluster of considerations is aimed at the avoidance of undue harshness on the defendant. This is a legitimate concern of courts when

---

[67] Benjamin C Zipursky, 'Philosophy of Private Law' in Jules L Coleman, Kenneth Einar Himma and Scott Shapiro (eds), *The Oxford Handbook of Jurisprudence and Philosophy of Law* (Oxford University Press 2002) 655 (emphasis added).

[68] HLA Hart, *The Concept of Law* (3rd edn, Oxford University Press 2012) 27–38, designates legal rules that recognise private plaintiffs as having rights of action as 'power-conferring rules'.

asked to assist the claimant against the defendant. It engages the broad ideas of substantive fairness (in the sense of the impact of the remedy sought on the defendant in comparison with other available remedies), and procedural fairness (in the sense of whether the claimant has acted in good faith by taking account of the defendant's interests). The same sort of concerns are evident throughout contract law.[69] This would help[70] to explain, for example, the limits on damages based on mitigation and remoteness, the limits to the cost of cure award based on unreasonableness, the refusal to give effect to penalty clauses that exceed a pre-estimate of damages in an exorbitant and unconscionable way, and the limits to the power to terminate or affirm. These mirror such bars to specific performance as impossibility, inutility, no or inadequate consideration, the claimant's lack of clean hands, severe hardship to the defendant, and want of mutuality.

5.3.1.2 Administrative Concerns

Secondly, courts are legitimately concerned about the cost of administering justice in subsidising the activity of contracting. This explains the restriction on compensation for non-pecuniary loss[71] and for speculative losses. The same concern explains the bars to specific performance of constant supervision and vagueness.

5.3.1.3 Public Policy

Thirdly, public policy may also affect the award of contractual remedies. Cranston J recently held that protection of human rights should be relevant to the discretion to award specific relief. In *Ashworth v The Royal National Theatre*,[72] his Honour refused an application by musicians for an order for specific performance or a mandatory injunction requiring the Royal National Theatre to re-engage them, because to do so would have interfered with the theatre's right to artistic freedom. As Cranston J explains, section 12(1) and (4) of the Human Rights Act 1998 'provides that, in considering whether to grant any relief which may affect the right of freedom of expression in Article 10 of the European

---

[69] They provide one explanation for e.g. collateral contracts, implied terms, vitiating factors, and statutory unfair terms.

[70] Of course, other explanations are possible in support of other theses.

[71] Despite the pockets of exceptions, the general rule still bars recovery for non-pecuniary loss. *Watts v Morrow* [1991] 1 WLR 1421 (CA); *Farley v Skinner* [2001] UKHL 49, [2002] 2 AC 732.

[72] [2014] EWHC 1176 (QB), [2014] 4 All ER 238.

Convention on Human Rights, the court must have particular regard to the importance of that right'.[73] Even before the Human Rights Act, English law had given effect to the same sort of consideration by granting specific performance of a contract to allow the National Front to use a hall for a political meeting because, *inter alia*, the remedy would promote freedom of speech and assembly.[74] Similarly, in granting an injunction against a strike called without complying with statutory requirements, account has been taken of the effect of the strike, not only on the employers, but also on the 'wider public'.[75] All of these factors may detract from the enforcement of the contractual right.

5.3.2   The Adequacy of Damages

We now turn to the legal elephant in the room – the bar of 'adequacy of damages' that consigns specific performance to its secondary status. Why should someone who has bargained for performance be forced to settle for damages? Why should someone who has assumed a duty to perform only be required to pay damages? The answer is counter-intuitive. It lies in the importance of the ability to change one's mind to valuable autonomy.

5.3.2.1   Contract and Autonomy

The starting point is the moral, political and economic importance of personal autonomy in modern liberal societies. Its core idea is that of self-authorship; that there is something intrinsically valuable in pursuing freely chosen goals and relationships. Its preservation is a ready justification for state action. This primacy of private ordering receives widespread support from classical liberals and libertarians.[76] The correlative demand in the arena of contract is for the state to provide the necessary framework for making and upholding transactions, but otherwise to

---

[73] Ibid [27].

[74] *Verrall v Great Yarmouth BC* [1981] QB 202 (CA); and see *Imutran Ltd v Uncaged Campaigns Ltd* [2001] 2 All ER 385 (Ch).

[75] *British Airways plc v Unite the Union* [2009] EWHC 3541 (QB), [2010] IRLR 423 [83]. And see *Lawrence v Fen Tigers Ltd* [2014] UKSC 13, [2014] AC 822 [118], [124].

[76] See John Stuart Mill, *On Liberty* (JW Parker and Son 1859); Friedrich A von Hayek, *The Road to Serfdom* (Routledge 1944); Friedrich A von Hayek, *Individualism and Economic Order* (Routledge 1949); Friedrich A von Hayek, *The Constitution of Liberty* (Routledge 1960); Milton Friedman, *Capitalism and Freedom* (University of Chicago Press 1962); Robert Nozick, *Anarchy, State and Utopia* (Basic Books 1974); Fried, *Contract as Promise* (n 2).

refrain from 'interfering' with the choices made *at the time of contract formation*. On this view, specific enforcement (or the cost of cure) is the natural default position where the claimant seeks it.

If enforcing voluntary undertakings were the sole and unqualified value, contract law would have a fraction of its actual content. The answer to all contractual questions (e.g. formation, vitiation, contents and remedies) would depend on the parties' intentions; the only issue being one of fact-finding. This is clearly not the law. It is true that there has been an increasing tendency to derive answers to contract questions from the objectively determined 'intentions of the parties'.[77] But, the traditional techniques for determining the parties' intentions have always given courts enormous latitude to give effect to other policies such as those discussed in the previous section.[78] Even Fried concedes the force of 'other' values such as that of restitution of benefits received, loss sharing in respect of common enterprises,[79] civility, altruism or humanity,[80] and, that these sometimes operate behind the façade of giving effect to the parties' intention.

In a very significant sense, the law of contract can be understood as the law on the *limits* to the freedom to contract. Contract law imposes limits on, for example: what it means to agree, when such agreements will be recognised as contracts, what techniques may be used to induce the other party's agreement, how express terms will be interpreted, what evidence will be taken into account, which express terms will be enforced, and what remedies are available for breach. Not all of this can be rationalised in terms of enforcing the presumed intention of the parties *at the time of the contract*, or can only be done by far-fetched reasoning. More importantly, for present purposes, the defendant's intention at formation may even have to give way to the defendant's change of mind, come the time for performance.

5.3.2.2 Autonomy and Change of Mind

The backstory of most contract disputes that come before courts is either that the defendant can no longer perform (in which case the bar of

---

[77] See e.g. in relation to remoteness in contract, *Transfield Shipping Inc v Mercator Shipping Inc (The Achilleas)* [2008] UKHL 48, [2009] 1 AC 61 [12] per Lord Hoffmann ('It seems to me logical to found liability for damages upon the intention of the parties (objectively ascertained) because all contractual liability is voluntarily undertaken.'); *John Grimes v Gubbins* [2013] EWCA Civ 37, [2013] PNLR 17 [24].

[78] E.g. as to the curing of uncertainty or incompleteness, as to the existence of implied or collateral terms, and as to the assumption of responsibility as to compensation for loss.

[79] Fried (n 2) 69–70.   [80] Ibid 109–10.

'impossibility' is triggered) or the defendant no longer wants to perform. If contract law values freedom of choice in support of individual autonomy, the question is why it should prioritise an individual's *past* choice over her *present* change of mind, when both are equally valid expressions of her freedom.[81] It is not obvious that we enhance an individual's freedom by forcing her to do what she no longer wants to do. Indeed, the individualistic premise suggests the opposite.

Fried's answer is that restricting one's ability to change one's mind 'increase[s] one's options in the long run'[82] and thus, despite appearances to the contrary, is autonomy-respecting. This is premised on 'the continuity of the self and the possibility of maintaining complex projects over time', without which, 'not only the morality of promising but also any coherent picture of the person becomes impossible'.[83] In short, we limit individuals' freedom to change their minds because this increases their freedom *in the long run*. The problem with this reasoning is that it is always vulnerable to the challenge that in particular circumstances the claimed increase in autonomy does not, or will not, occur. The claim is not something that can be ascertained by abstract analysis, but only by examining particular circumstances in their historical context.[84] It is an empirical claim based on an appeal to pragmatic results, and not a deduction from the basic liberal principle of autonomy.

The reality is that while the self may be continuous, it also evolves over time. An integral part of any autonomous life is our ability to learn, mature and recreate ourselves. Over time, parts of ourselves will change: our assumptions, knowledge base, attitudes, values, priorities, or passions. This may entail the alteration or rejection of previous beliefs, commitments or goals that are now, no longer authentically ours. As Kimel observes: 'a person who remains unwaveringly true to past commitments which no longer meaningfully relate to her present vision of how she ought to live [i]s anything but a model of personal autonomy in action'.[85] Long ago, Cohen recognised something amiss in a concept of

---

[81] Alan Brudner, 'Reconstructing Contracts' (1993) 43 University of Toronto LJ 1, 21: 'the decision of the autonomous will to commit itself to a course of action can enjoy no moral privilege over its subsequent decision to change its mind, for both decisions are particular and equally valid expressions of the will'.

[82] Fried (n 2) 14.   [83] Ibid.

[84] Ian R Macneil, 'Values in Contract: Internal and External' (1983) 78 Northwestern University L Rev 340, 356–58, 395.

[85] Dori Kimel, 'Promise, Contract, Personal Autonomy, and the Freedom to Change One's Mind' in Gregory Klass, George Letsas and Price Saprai (eds), *Philosophical Foundations of Contract Law* (Oxford University Press 2014) 100.

autonomy that renders individuals 'bound by every promise, no matter how foolish, without any chance of letting increased wisdom undo past foolishness. Certainly, some freedom to change one's mind is necessary for free intercourse between those who lack omniscience.'[86]

This gives a fresh perspective to the law that voids contracts for fundamental mistaken assumptions, and that discharges contracts when circumstances radically change without the fault of either party (under the rubric of 'frustration'). In both these situations, at least one of the parties will no longer be able, or want, to perform come time for performance. Given the extremity of the circumstances, that party will be entirely relieved from her contractual obligation.[87] In other, perhaps less catastrophic, circumstances recognised by the doctrines of misrepresentation, duress, undue influence and unconscionable contract, a party can change her mind and not perform the contract or be liable for its non-performance (so long as rescission is not barred).

Even in the absence of these recognised vitiating factors, coerced performance of some regretted promises may unduly compromise an individual's integrity, authenticity and self-respect[88] (e.g. working for a cause that one has lost faith in). This may even apply to corporate entities, for example, in relation to their corporate social responsibility. To accommodate this vital aspect of autonomy, individuals must not only have the ability to make commitments, but also some freedom to reassess and to break from past commitments, especially long-term or personal commitments (hence, for example, divorce is possible). Clearly, some changes of mind will not seem particularly momentous, and holding someone to her promise may help her to learn from her mistakes. Nevertheless, there should be what Feinberg calls 'a general presumption in favour of liberty'.[89] This is consistent with the adequacy of damages bar being applicable to *all* cases of breach. This approach has the further advantage of saving judicial time by not having to draw the difficult line between 'worthy' and 'unworthy' changes of mind.

The importance of change of mind is recognised by some utilitarian theorists, albeit in support of different aims. Thus, the basic idea that contract law should aim at maximising overall welfare is said to require

---

[86] Morris R Cohen, 'The Basis of Contract' (1933) 46 Harvard L Rev 553, 572.

[87] Although there may be restitutionary obligations at common law or by statute.

[88] Anthony T Kronman, 'Paternalism and the Law of Contract' (1983) 92 Yale LJ 763, 774–85.

[89] Joel Feinberg, *The Moral Limits of the Criminal Law 1: Harm to Others* (Oxford University Press 1987) 9.

the law to tolerate changes of mind by awarding damages rather than specific performance as the primary remedy for breach.[90] This allows 'efficient breaches'[91] of contract by enabling commodities to move to those who value them the most (rather than keeping them with claimants just because they are entitled to them). However, the significance of change of mind to the identification of welfare raises a paradox that threatens to destroy the welfare basis for the bindingness of contracts. Trebilcock dubs this the 'Paretian dilemma'.[92] Benson explains that:

> Suppose that one party regrets her decision to enter a transaction because, as it turns out when performance is due, she has acted on incomplete or faulty information, or because new opportunities have since arisen, lead-ing to a change in her valuation of the contract's subject matter. At the moment of entering the contract, both parties, we suppose, thought they would be made better off. At that point, *ex ante*, the Pareto criterion is satisfied and the fact that one of them subsequently regrets her decision is not at issue. Enforcement of the agreement seems to be justified. But if we adopt an *ex post* perspective, the fact that one party regrets the agreement does become relevant. We can no longer draw the inference that the agreement is Pareto superior ... the transaction will make one party worse off and that therefore it should not be enforced. If the appropriate standpoint from which to judge transactions is *ex post*, we end up excus-ing most breaches of contract. The Pareto perspective does not lead to a single coherent conclusion as to enforceability, but on the contrary, to two wholly inconsistent answers.[93]

These utilitarian insights are significant given the extent to which individual welfare and individual autonomy are linked; autonomy is usually exercised to access the individual's assessment of her own welfare, and welfare is often a function of individual choices. The law's solution to the Paretian dilemma lies, *not* in excusing breaches of contract, but only in the secondary status of the specific performance remedy achieved by the adequacy of damages bar.

[90] Anthony A Kronman, 'Specific Performance' (1978) 45 *University of Chicago Law Review* 35. But many utilitarian scholars now reject the efficient breach thesis on utilitarian grounds. E.g. Eric A Posner, 'Economic Analysis of Contract Law after Three Decades: Success or Failure?' (2003) 112 Yale LJ 829, 834–39; Schwartz, 'The Case for Specific Performance' (n 63) 278–96.

[91] See Robert L Birmingham, 'Breach of Contract, Damage Measures, and Economic Efficiency' (1970) 24 Rutgers LR 273, 292.

[92] Michael J Trebilcock, *The Limits of Freedom of Contract* (Harvard University Press 1993) 103 and 244.

[93] Peter Benson, 'The Idea of a Public Basis of Justification of Contract' (1995) 33 *Osgoode Hall Law Journal* 273, 281.

5.3.3   Change of Mind, Damages and Specific Performance

The adequacy of damages bar permits the defendant to change her mind, while *still* vindicating the right to performance through the award of damages. The defendant need not actually perform the contract, but absent the recognised vitiating factors, her change of mind is *not cost free* since she is still liable to pay damages to the claimant who has given consideration and is entitled to her expectation. Nevertheless, the cost of the defendant's change of mind is reduced by the operation of rules that limit the amount of damages payable. The most puzzling of these rules is that the claimant cannot recover any actual losses that she is judged to have failed to mitigate. A common justification for the mitigation rule is the avoidance of waste or the increase of efficiency; but, it is difficult to justify the subjugation of the claimant's right to this social policy, especially when it operates to shield the party breaching that right. The requirement to mitigate is said to be a 'cost free' duty,[94] since compliance would leave the claimant no worse off. However, the claimant's effort in mitigating will often be non-trivial. Moreover, the mitigation rule bites precisely when the claimant is judged to have *failed* to mitigate and is denied some or all of her provable losses flowing from the breach: this clearly 'costs' the claimant. Fried explains mitigation as 'a kind of altruistic duty, towards one's contractual partner'.[95] But if enforcement of the right to performance lies at the heart of contract remedies, such an altruistic duty in favour of the party in breach makes little sense.

Acceptance of the importance of the defendant's change of mind provides the explanation for the claimant's 'duty' to mitigate. This is consistent with Burrows' view that the claimant 'should not leave it simply to the courts to ensure fulfillment of his expectations, but should rather take it upon himself to adopt other reasonable means to ensure the fulfillment of his expectations'.[96] There would be no reason to require the claimant to fulfil his own expectations if contract remedies are already supposed to do that. But, if the law recognises the importance of tolerating the defendant's change of mind, then it stands to reason that the

---

[94] Charles J Goetz and Robert E Scott, 'The Mitigation Principle: Toward a General Theory of Contractual Obligation' (1983) 69 *Virginia Law Review* 967.

[95] Fried (n 2) 131.

[96] AS Burrows, 'Contract, Tort and Restitution – A Satisfactory Division or Not?' (1983) 99 *LQR* 217, 266.

claimant should take account of the defendant's legitimate interest to do so by being *required* to act reasonably to minimise the cost of that change of mind.[97]

This baseline of expectation damages, which facilitates the defendant's change of mind, explains many of the other puzzles noted in section 5.1.2. For example, it explains:

- why it may be 'oppressive' to the defendant[98] to award specific performance where damages are 'adequate' – there would be no oppression if the baseline were, instead, performance of the contract;
- why Lord Hoffmann[99] believes that awarding specific performance risks unjust enrichment (by strengthening the claimant's position in negotiating the defendant's release) – again, any enrichment cannot be regarded as 'unjust' if the baseline were, instead, performance of the contract;
- why an injunction to restrain breach will be denied where the injury to the claimant is small, can be adequately compensated in money and the grant of an injunction would be oppressive to the defendant;[100]
- why courts will not require a defendant who has changed her mind to cooperate when the claimant insists on rendering unwanted performance,[101] and why affirmation will also be barred if the claimant's affirmation would be extremely wasteful and costly to the defendant;
- why punitive damages are not awarded and account of profits are only very exceptionally awarded[102] – they would prevent the defendant from moving on to another project;
- why where damages would be 'inadequate', the claimant is only generally entitled to *Wrotham Park* 'negotiating damages'[103] – and the claimant is compelled to permit the defendant's change of mind in exchange for a waiver fee at market price; and

The remoteness limit can be seen in similar terms of allowing the defendant to calculate the cost of her change of mind.
[98] Chitty (n 22) [27–005]; *Re Schwabacher* (1908) 98 LT 127.
[99] In *Co-operative Insurance Ltd v Argyll Holdings Ltd* (n 9) 15.
[100] See *Chitty* (n 22) [27–064]; *Jaggard v Sawyer* (n 38).
[101] *White & Carter (Councils) Ltd v McGregor* (n 24).
[102] If deterrence is especially called for in circumstances of deliberate and cynical breach where damages would be inadequate and the claimant has a particular interest in preventing the defendant from profiting from breach as in *AG v Blake* (n 41).
[103] Neuberger LJ in *Lunn Poly Ltd v Liverpool & Lancashire Properties Ltd* (n 46) [22].

- why there is good consideration when one party promises to pay more if the other foregoes a change of mind by actually rendering the promised performance.[104]

The value of change of mind provides the best explanation for the bar to specific performance of contracts of personal services (where damages are most likely to be inadequate). Here, the language of 'slavery' should be understood to signify the undesirability of forcing someone to do what she no longer wants to do, a concern that is heightened where this involves personal services. Concern about 'slavery' can hardly explain why even *employers* are not generally required to specifically perform and rehire their employees; but, again, tolerated change of mind does. Indeed, Barnett,[105] who adopts a property right view of contractual obligations, is driven to explain the personal services bar by the idea that the future control of one's person is inalienable. The preferable explanation is that you *can* obligate yourself to future performance, but your change of mind will also be tolerated in support of your future freedom, so long as you compensate the other party. This explains:

- why an injunction is barred where it would amount to indirect specific performance of contracts of personal services;[106]
- why unreasonable restraints of trade[107] and agreed specific performance clauses are ineffective;
- why the heavy-handedness of the enforcement mechanism[108] (i.e. contempt and imprisonment) is of such concern;
- why vagueness of the contract bars specific performance – it raises concern about the 'oppression caused by the defendant having to do things under threat of proceedings for contempt' when it is unclear exactly what she must do;[109] and
- why 'constant supervision' bars specific performance, concerned as it is with the complexities and undesirability of compelling people to do what they no longer want to do.

---

[104] Mindy Chen-Wishart, 'A Bird in the Hand: Consideration and Promissory Estoppel' in Andrew Burrows and Edwin Peel (eds), *Contract Formation and Parties* (Oxford University Press 2010). Although *Williams v Roffey Bros (Contractors) Ltd* (n 52) accepts that an increased chance of performance is sufficient.

[105] Randy E Barnett, 'Contract Remedies and Inalienable Rights' (n 63) 185–95, 197–98, 202.

[106] *Warner Bros Pictures Inc v Nelson* (n 28); *Warren v Mendy* (n 28); *LauritzenCool AB v Lady Navigation Inc* (n 28).

[107] Stephen A Smith, 'Future Freedom and Freedom of Contract' (1995) 59 MLR 167.

[108] *Co-operative Insurance v Argyll* (n 9) 12.   [109] Ibid. 13–14.

5.3.4   Land and Money Obligations

Given the thesis of this chapter, how should the routine availability of specific performance for land contracts and the action for the agreed sum be understood?

5.3.4.1   Land

The default remedy for breach of contracts for the sale of land is specific performance, whether the claimant is the purchaser or the vendor.[110] The assumption that each and every piece of land is unique such that damages are inadequate may explain the routine availability of specific performance to *purchasers*. But it does not explain why *vendors* are also entitled to specific performance, and so able to 'thrust the property down the purchaser's throat'[111] when it appears to be a paradigm case where damages would be an adequate remedy.

One response to this is simply to say that the current law is wrong – neither purchaser nor vendor should be automatically entitled to specific performance. The assumption that land is inherently, and indisputably, unique has been rejected or questioned in Canada,[112] New Zealand[113] and Singapore.[114] First, English law's reservation of a special position for land derives from socio-political circumstances that have little relevance today. Land in pre-industrial England accorded its owner the right to vote and also granted its owner considerable political influence; therefore, damages were never adequate because of the intangible rights and social status that each parcel of land in England conferred upon its owner.[115] Secondly, land is often purchased as investment or as a profit-

---

[110] Charles Harpum, Stuart Bridge and Martin Dixon, *Megarry and Wade: The Law of Real Property* (Sweet & Maxwell 2012) 703; *Sudbrook Trading Estate Ltd v Eggleton* [1983] 1 AC 444, 478; *AMEC Properties Ltd v Planning Research & Systems plc* [1992] 1 EGLR 70 (CA).

[111] *Hope v Walker* [1900] 1 Ch 257 (CA) 258 (Lindley LJ).

[112] *Semelhago v Paramadevan* [1996] 2 SCR 415.

[113] *Landco Albany Ltd v Fu Hao Construction Ltd* [2006] 2 NZLR 174 (CA) [43]: specific performance was denied because the claimant only had a 'plainly commercial rather than private or sentimental [interest]' in the property in question. And see earlier *Loan Investment Corporation of Australasia v Bonner* [1970] NZLR 724.

[114] *E C Investment Holding Pte Ltd v Ridout Estate Pte Ltd* [2011] 2 SLR 232 (HC), [2012] 1 SLR 32 (CA). The claimants had been prepared to forgo their right to acquire the property so long as compensation was paid, and only sought specific performance when property prices rose. Further, third parties would suffer hardship if specific performance were granted.

[115] See David Cohen, 'The Relationship of Contractual Remedies to Political and Social Status: A Preliminary Inquiry' (1982) 32 University of Toronto LJ 31.

generating asset, for example by large corporate entities or through buy-to-let schemes. In such circumstances, damages should be regarded as presumptively adequate – both for the vendor and purchaser. Sopinka J, speaking for the majority of the Canadian Supreme Court in *Semelhago v Paramadevan*,[116] goes even further; he observed that: 'Residential, business and industrial properties are all mass produced much in the same way as other consumer products. If a deal falls through for one property, another is frequently, though not always, readily available.'[117] On the facts, the Canadian Supreme Court held that specific performance was inappropriate because the property was not unique, however, since both parties had proceeded on the basis that the claimant was entitled to specific performance, the case was considered on that basis. However, Sopinka J stressed that '[I]n future cases, under similar circumstances, a trial judge will not be constrained to find that specific performance is an appropriate remedy.'[118]

To change the long-established rule that specific performance is routinely available for land contracts would bring land into line with the rest of the law on specific performance; but, the difficulties attendant on such a change may provide a convincing practical, if not principled, reason for the status quo. First, courts would be confronted with very difficult factual questions. For example, how should the court decide whether there are sufficiently similar substitutes readily available in the market, such that damages are adequate, or alternatively, that the land is 'unique' such that damages are inadequate? Should the test be objective or should it take into account the parties' subjective motives or valuation?[119] The calculation of damages may also raise new difficulties. For example, if specific performance is routinely available, damages in lieu are calculated at the date of trial rather than breach and the claimant need not mitigate loss. But, if the availability of specific performance is now unclear, questions arise over the date of assessment and the claimant's duty to mitigate.[120] This may make an enormous difference in a rising market. In particular, it puts the claimant in the impossible position of both pressing for specific performance, and, if this is ultimately denied, being at risk that damages will be assessed as at the date of breach.

Secondly, changing the automatic availability of specific performance in land contracts may also have serious unintended, and unexpected,

[116] *Semelhago v Paramadevan* (n 112) [22].   [117] Ibid [20].
[118] Ibid [23].   [119] Ibid [21].
[120] See *Southcott Estates Inc v Toronto Catholic District School Board* (2012) SCC 51, [2012] 2 SCR 675.

consequences. A specifically enforceable contract for the sale of land gives rise to a constructive trust[121] in advance of the vendor's performance. This constructive trust is a foundation of modern conveyancing around which other rules have evolved. Chambers cautions:[122]

> The rules in question ... apply generally to any specifically enforceable promise to transfer an asset. It is the reason why a contract to grant a lease, mortgage, profit, or easement, produces an equitable version of the promised right. An option to purchase is an equitable interest in land only because the exercise of that option will produce a specifically enforceable contract of sale. Changing the rules for the paradigm case, a contract for the sale of land, may shake the foundations of property law ...

Moreover, the proprietary interest raised by the automatic availability of specific performance is critical when the seller becomes insolvent to give the buyer priority over the generality of creditors.

After *Semelhago* a case-by-case assessment was required in Canada as to the availability of specific performance and so whether an interest arose to be protected. The previous approach to registering or filing interests in Canada was disrupted; without an interest in the land, purchasers could not protect their rights by caveat or registration, enforce their rights against others, or insure against loss. In response, the Alberta Law Reform Institute has recommended statutorily reversing *Semelhago* as a response to these difficulties.[123]

In sum, the automatic availability of specific performance need not be seen as a shining example of the simple enforcement of contract. Rather, the rule has been criticised, and has been kept in place for other reasons. While the historical reasons in support of the rule are largely redundant, important property rules have evolved around it such that change has the potential to wreak havoc with substantial portions of property law.

5.3.4.2 Money

The truly shining example of enforcing the contractual right is the action for the agreed sum, perhaps the most common action brought for breach of contract. Yet, like the rule in respect of land contracts, this rule has also

---

[121] *Lysaght v Edwards* (1876) 2 Ch D 499.

[122] Robert Chambers, 'The Importance of Specific Performance' in Simone Degeling and James Edelman (eds), *Equity in Commercial Law* (Thomson 2005) 431, 433, see also 434–48.

[123] Alberta Law Reform Institute, *Contracts for the Sale and Purchase of Land: Purchasers' Remedies* (Final Report No 97, October 2009).

been the subject of criticism and its continued existence is explicable on grounds other than the mere enforcement of contracts. In *The Puerto Buitrago*[124] Lord Denning MR noted the similarities between the action for the agreed sum and specific performance; on the facts, his Lordship rejected the award of the agreed sum since damages would have been perfectly adequate. Burrows also takes the view that the law here should to be brought in line with that relating to specific performance, chiefly in support of the mitigation requirement.[125]

Retention of the action for the agreed sum must be understood in the following contexts. First, where the contractual obligation is the depersonalised one to pay money, the concern to preserve scope for change of mind (expressed in the bars on personal services, vagueness, constant supervision, impossibility, inutility, or mutuality) are not engaged. Secondly, the defendant will not be compelled to cooperate with the claimant to enable her to complete performance and earn the price, and further, such performance will be barred if it would be grossly wasteful. Thirdly, the action for the agreed sum is an immensely common and simple remedy. If this were to change, there would be an unmanageable clog in the courts. In sum, the award of an agreed sum poses relatively little danger to the claimant's change of mind while having the great advantage of expediting the resolution of a huge class of contract cases.

5.4 Conclusion

Two claims have been advanced here. First, that the remedies for breach of contract are not simply aimed at enforcing the contractual right; rather, in determining how the law will bring its coercion to bear on the defendant in aid of the claimant, courts legitimately weigh it alongside other factors ranging from prevention of undue harshness, the administration of justice and even the protection of human rights. Secondly, the key to understanding the subsidiary status of specific performance lies in the importance of the ability to change one's mind as constitutive of a more nuanced conception of the valuable autonomy promoted by contract law. In principle, there is no reason why this

---

[124] *Attica Sea Carriers v Ferrostaal Poseidon Bulk Reederei GmbH (The Puerto Buitrago)* [1976] 1 Lloyd's Rep 250 (CA) 255, 'by suing for the money, the plaintiff is seeking to enforce specific performance of the contract – and he should not be allowed to do so when damages would be an adequate remedy'.

[125] Burrows (n 13) 440.

reasoning should not also apply to land and money obligations. But, in practice, compelling reasons exist for the departure from this position.

Civil law systems focus on the duty to perform and to repair the harm caused by the breach of duty.[126] Accordingly, specific performance is the primary remedy and represents the enforcement of the right. Given this 'in principle' contrast with the common law, the high degree of functional 'in practice' convergence with the common law position in civil law jurisdictions of both Europe[127] and in Asia[128] (largely via the requirement of good faith and fair dealing) is an important matter of note. Article III.–3:302 of the *European Draft Common Frame of Reference* recognises a general entitlement to specific performance except in a range of circumstances that mirror most of the common law bars to specific performance, including that the contract is 'of such a personal character that it would be unreasonable to enforce it'.[129] Moreover, while specific performance is not strictly barred where damages would be adequate, it is strongly discouraged since,

> the creditor cannot recover damages for loss or a stipulated payment for non-performance to the extent that the creditor has increased the loss or the amount of the payment by insisting unreasonably on specific performance in circumstances where the creditor could have made a reasonable substitute transaction without significant effort or expense.[130]

Thus, while civilian jurisdictions prioritise the enforcement of the contractual right to performance, they too recognise considerable scope for change of mind.

---

[126] See e.g. Barry Nicholas, *The French Law of Contract* (2nd edn, Clarendon 1992) 4.

[127] Konrad Zweigert and Hein Kötz, *An Introduction to Comparative Law* (Tony Weir tr, 3rd edn, Oxford University Press 1998) 484. And see *Co-operative Insurance Ltd v Argyll Holdings Ltd* (n 9) 11.

[128] Mindy Chen-Wishart, 'Comparative Asian Contract Law on the Remedies for Breach of Contract: Transplant, Convergence and Divergence' in Mindy Chen-Wishart, Alexander Loke and Burton Ong (eds), *Studies in the Contract Laws of Asia Vol. I: Remedies for Breach of Contract* (Oxford University Press 2016).

[129] Christian von Bar, Eric Clive and Hans Schulte-Nölke (eds), *Principles, Definitions and Model Rules of European Private Law, Draft Common Frame of Reference (DCFR)*, < http://ec.europa.eu/justice/contract/files/european-private-law_en.pdf > (accessed 25 October 2015), Art III-3:302(3): 'performance would be unlawful or impossible' 'unreasonably burdensome or expensive'; Art III-3:302(4): delay.

[130] Ibid, Art III-3:302(5) DCFR.

6

Injunctions in Tort and Contract

PAUL S DAVIES

An injunction is an order of the court directing a party either to do something (i.e. a mandatory injunction) or to refrain from doing something (i.e. a prohibitory injunction). The availability of injunctive relief is an important issue within the broader subject of 'commercial remedies'. A claimant who obtains an injunction is in a very strong bargaining position with defendants who wish to pay for the relaxation of that injunction; this has led to concerns that right-holders could make 'ransom demands' such that others are 'bound hand and foot' if they seek a release of the injunction.[1] There have been suggestions that injunctions should only be awarded in exceptional cases as a result.[2] This chapter will focus on particular areas of controversy in the context of torts – especially nuisance – and breach of contract. In the former, there is now significant confusion about when damages should be awarded in lieu of an injunction.[3] In the latter, there is some lack of clarity about the availability of specific relief where the contract is one for services. It is suggested that in both areas injunctive relief should be awarded more readily.

6.1   Tort Law

Injunctions are regularly granted to protect property rights.[4] Indeed, prohibitory injunctions have even been said to have been awarded 'as

---

[1] *Isenberg v East India House Estate Co Ltd* (1863) De GJ & S 263, 273; 46 ER 637, 641 (Lord Westbury LC).

[2] See, e.g. the speech of Lord Sumption in *Coventry v Lawrence* [2014] UKSC 13, [2014] AC 822.

[3] And even whether injunctions should be the prima facie remedy at all: see text to nn 10–21.

[4] For discussion of whether a tendency to focus upon property rights is too restrictive in tort law generally, see John Murphy, 'Rethinking Injunctions in Tort Law' (2007) 27(3) OJLS 509.

of course' in the context of trespass.[5] But uncertainty now surrounds the available remedies in nuisance after the decision of the Supreme Court in *Coventry v Lawrence*.[6]

Nuisance is a tort against land; it protects property rights.[7] Property rights are concerned with land use rather than land value,[8] and should generally be protected by 'property rules' rather than 'liability rules'.[9] Injunctions should therefore be the prima facie remedy available in response to an ongoing nuisance. However, in *Coventry v Lawrence*, Lord Sumption said:

> There is much to be said for the view that damages are ordinarily an adequate remedy for nuisance and that an injunction should not usually be granted in a case where it is likely that conflicting interests are engaged other than the parties' interests. In particular, it may well be that an injunction should as a matter of principle not be granted in a case where a use of land to which objection is taken requires and has received planning permission.[10]

To take such a step would involve a significant re-appraisal of the law of nuisance.[11] Lord Mance in particular was uncomfortable with this idea,[12] and it is inconsistent with the approach of the majority in the Supreme Court. Injunctive relief to restrain a nuisance remains the starting point for a court when determining what remedies to award.

Lord Sumption's approach places great weight on the relevance of planning permission.[13] Yet the planning authorities have no power to authorise a nuisance, and are concerned solely with the negative question of whether there is a good reason, from the 'community perspective', not to allow a proposed development to go ahead. If there is no such reason, planning permission is granted, but that does not necessarily indicate

---

[5] *Anchor Brewhouse Developments Ltd v Berkley House (Docklands Developments) Ltd* [1987] 2 EGLR 173 (Ch) 176C, 178K (Scott J). See too *Redland Bricks Ltd v Morris* [1970] AC 652 (HL) 665 (Lord Upjohn).
[6] [2014] UKSC 13, [2014] AC 822.   [7] *Hunter v Canary Wharf* [1997] AC 655 (HL).
[8] Martin Dixon, 'The Sound of Silence' [2014] Conv 79, 84.
[9] This language appears in Guido Calabresi and A Douglas Melamed, 'Property Rules, Liability Rules and Inalienability: One View of the Cathedral' (1972) 85(6) Harvard LR 1089.
[10] *Coventry* (n 6) [161].
[11] Emma Lees, '*Lawrence v Fen Tigers*: Where Now for Nuisance?' [2014] Conv 449.
[12] *Coventry* (n 6) [168].
[13] The other judges saw planning permission as a relevant factor when deciding whether to award damages in lieu of an injunction, but with differing emphasis: see *Coventry* (n 6) [125] (Lord Neuberger); [167]–[168] (Lord Mance); [169] (Lord Clarke); [240]–[246] (Lord Carnwath).

that the authorities positively desire that the development proceed. Nor does planning permission purport to determine the validity or strength of any person's private law rights; such rights require protection from the courts through the law of nuisance.[14] It is therefore unsatisfactory for planning permission to be dispositive against an injunction.[15]

Shifting the generally available remedy for the tort of nuisance away from injunctions towards damages effectively replaces a 'property rule' with a 'liability rule'. This might undermine, in some respects, the proprietary nature of the tort of nuisance. A person who enjoys a property right protected by a property rule has the ability to choose whether or not to relax his or her property rights.[16] If the right-holder chooses to sell that right, that party is able to set his or her own value on that right. If X owns a plot of land, and Z wants to build on neighbouring land such that the development will encroach upon X's land, then X can prevent Z from proceeding. X's property right allows it to exclude others and to refuse to sanction the deprivation of its property rights by Z. It is also X's prerogative to ask for an extortionate amount before allowing the development to proceed. X cannot be forced to give up its property rights simply because it might be considered to be acting unreasonably.[17] As AL Smith LJ observed in *Shelfer v City of London Electric Lighting Company*, 'a person by committing a wrongful act . . . is not thereby entitled to ask the Court to sanction his doing so by purchasing his neighbour's rights'.[18] One private actor should not be able to appropriate another's property without public backing.[19]

Admittedly, nuisance is different from trespass; it is unclear whether a party can 'possess' an easement.[20] Nevertheless, nuisance is indubitably

---

[14] Lord Neuberger noted (*Coventry* (n 6) [90]): 'it seems wrong in principle that, through the grant of a planning permission, a planning authority should be able to deprive a property-owner of a right to object to what would otherwise be a nuisance, without providing her with compensation, when there is no provision in the planning legislation which suggests such a possibility'.

[15] See too Dolan Nolan, 'Nuisance, Planning and Regulation: The Limits of Statutory Authority' in Andrew Dyson, James Goudkamp and Frederick Wilmot-Smith (eds), *Defences in Tort* (Hart 2015).

[16] Unless the compulsory purchase regime applies: see text to nn 39–44.

[17] *Bradford Corporation v Pickles* [1895] AC 587 (HL) 597.

[18] [1895] 1 Ch 287 (CA) 322. See similarly 315–16 (Lindley LJ).

[19] In the Court of Appeal in *Bradford Corporation v Pickles* (n 17), Lord Herschell LC, after hearing argument, informed counsel for the Corporation that if it were to apply to Parliament for compulsory power to take the water, the Court of Appeal would adjourn the decision on the appeal until Parliament had decided upon the appropriate course to take. The Corporation refused to avail itself of this opportunity.

[20] Cf Louis Kaplow and Steven Shavell, 'Property Rules versus Liability Rules: An Economic Analysis' (1996) 109(4) Harvard LR 713, 771–73.

concerned with the use of property, and the ability to enjoy proprietary rights needs to be protected.[21] It is also important to remember that not every interference with another's use of property will be sanctioned by the law of nuisance: the interference must be unreasonable for there to be a tortious wrong at all. Injunctions should be awarded as the general response to nuisance.

6.2 Damages in Lieu of an Injunction

An injunction is a discretionary remedy, and, as a result of Lord Cairns' Act, courts are able to award damages in lieu of an injunction.[22] It is important to establish what principles and factors inform the exercise of a court's discretion not to award an injunction but rather damages in lieu.[23] The traditional 'working rule' was laid out in *Shelfer v City of London Electric Lighting Company*.[24] That case concerned a nuisance caused by the defendants' carrying out noisy and disruptive work. The claimants sought an injunction to prevent further work continuing the nuisance. Kekewich J, at first instance, thought that an injunction was inappropriate on the facts and that damages should be preferred. The Court of Appeal disagreed, and awarded an injunction.

The judgment of the Court of Appeal was very conservative. Lindley LJ thought that the jurisdiction to award damages 'ought not to be exercised … except under very exceptional circumstances'.[25] Lord Halsbury and AL Smith LJ also adopted a narrow approach, thereby limiting the very wide discretion that seems to be afforded to judges on the face of Lord Cairns' Act. AL Smith LJ set out what he termed a 'good working rule' when determining whether damages ought to be awarded in lieu of an injunction:

(1) if the injury to the plaintiff's legal rights is small;
(2) and is one which is capable of being estimated in money;
(3) and is one which can be adequately compensated by a small money payment;

[21] Howarth has criticised Lord Sumption's approach in *Coventry* (n 6): 'A long-running academic debate rages about whether Lord Sumption's world might be more economically efficient … but in the post-Great Crash era that debate seems increasingly outdated. A further bout of financialisation now looks not economically literate but irresponsible': David Howarth, 'Noise and Nuisance' [2014] CLJ 247, 250.
[22] Chancery Amendment Act 1958, s 2. See now: Senior Courts Act 1981, s 50.
[23] JA Jolowicz, 'Damages in Equity – A Study of Lord Cairns' Act' (1975) 34(2) CLJ 224.
[24] See n 18.   [25] Ibid 316.

(4) and the case is one in which it would be oppressive to the defendant to grant an injunction;

then damages in substitution for an injunction may be given.

This 'working rule' has tended to be adopted as a useful framework when deciding whether or not damages should be awarded in lieu of an injunction.[26] It is helpful for judges to have some guidance, rather than to be cast adrift with an unfettered discretion.

Shelfer has nevertheless proven to be controversial and, at times, has not been followed. It has sometimes been perceived as weighting the scales too heavily in favour of injunctive relief. There appears to be some concern that the willingness of courts to grant injunctive relief can hamper the viability of certain desirable development schemes. This may be particularly acute in the commercial environment, where large-scale developments might run into severe difficulties if they interfere with easements which benefit neighbouring land.[27] Many disputes concern an infringement of a right to light:[28] the belief of developers that some parties were simply exploiting property rights for unreasonable reasons to extort vast sums from developers led to the Law Commission examining this particular area.[29] Given the importance of new homes, schools, hospitals and so on, there may be some sympathy for the developers' plight; indeed, the increasingly crowded nature of the country was one factor raised by Lord Sumption in favour of damages over specific relief.[30]

Two particular criticisms of *Shelfer* must be noted. The first is that the tendency to award injunctive relief discourages economically efficient results.[31] The efficiency equation might be influenced by how many

---

[26] *Coventry* (n 6) [102]. Lord Neuberger recognised that 'the case which is probably most frequently cited on the question' of whether to award damages in lieu of an injunction is *Shelfer* (n 18).

[27] See, e.g. *Regan v Paul Properties Ltd* [2006] EWCA Civ 1391; [2007] Ch 135; *HKRUK II (CHC) Ltd v Heaney* [2010] EWHC 2245 (Ch), [2010] 3 EGLR 15.

[28] See generally Paul Davies, 'Lighting the Way Ahead: The Use and Abuse of Property Rights' in Susan Bright (ed), *Modern Studies in Property Law*, Vol 6 (Hart 2011).

[29] Law Commission, *Rights to Light* (Law Com No 356, 2014) paras 1.7–1.8.

[30] *Coventry* (n 6) [161].

[31] For some discussion of this issue, see, e.g. Calabresi and Melamed (n 9); A Mitchell Polinsky, 'Resolving Nuisance Disputes: The Simple Economics of Injunctive and Damage Remedies' (1980) 32(6) *Stanford Law Review* 1075; Kaplow and Shavell (n 20); James E Krier and Stewart J Schwab, 'Property Rules and Liability Rules: The Cathedral in Another Light' (1995) 70 NYULR 440; Richard A Epstein, 'A Clear View of *The Cathedral*: The Dominance of Property Rules' (1997) 106 Yale LJ 2091.

neighbours the developer would need to negotiate with in order to build in infringement of the neighbours' property rights: the greater the number of neighbours, the higher the negotiation costs, and the stronger the inclination to protect the neighbours' rights through liability rules. However, even in such situations, liability rules may not ensure the most economically efficient results. After all, the 'assessment costs' required when calculating damages may be high, particularly since it is very difficult to know how and on what basis damages in lieu of an injunction are calculated.[32] If damages are assessed on a 'hypothetical bargain' measure of damages, then this necessarily involves the fictional exercise of pretending that the parties acted as reasonable parties (thereby implying, perhaps unfortunately, that in reality the parties have not actually acted reasonably) and is bound to be imprecise.[33] Moreover, damages may not include the 'idiosyncratic value' a particular claimant places upon its rights.[34] It may well be contended that awarding injunctions can incentivise efficient outcomes since the parties would be encouraged to bargain amongst themselves and thereby reduce assessment and litigation costs.[35] Even if economic efficiency is a relevant goal in this context, arguments based upon economic efficiency are ultimately inconclusive on the question of whether it would be desirable to protect a claimant's rights through property rules or liability rules.

The second criticism of *Shelfer* is that it fails to take into account the 'public interest' since this factor is absent from AL Smith LJ's 'working rule'. Prior to *Coventry v Lawrence*, the public interest only seemed to be relevant in tipping the scales in favour of damages rather than an injunction in the 'marginal' case.[36] A difficult example is *Dennis v Ministry of Defence*,[37] where an injunction was not granted to restrain a nuisance caused by aircraft based at RAF Wittering, since the public

---

[32] See text to nn 89–107 below.

[33] It has been said that the final award must simply 'feel right': see, e.g. *Tamares (Vincent Square) Ltd v Fairpoint Properties (Vincent Square) Ltd* [2007] EWHC 212 (Ch), [2007] 1 WLR 2167 [22] (Gabriel Moss QC), citing *Amec Developments Ltd v Jury's Hotel Management (UK) Ltd* [2001] 1 EGLR 81 [35] (Anthony Mann QC).

[34] Kaplow and Shavell (n 20).

[35] Krier and Schwab (n 31); Richard Craswell, 'Property Rules and Liability Rules in Unconscionability and Related Doctrines' (1993) 60(1) U Chicago LR 1. And parties' bargains do tend to be efficient: see, e.g. Elizabeth Hoffmann and Matthew L Spitzer, 'The Coase Theorem: Some Experimental Tests' (1982) 25(1) JL & Economics 73.

[36] *Watson v Croft Promo-Sport* [2009] EWCA Civ 15, [2009] 3 All ER 249 [51] (Sir Andrew Morritt C). Cf *Miller v Jackson* [1977] QB 966 (CA) and *Kennaway v Thompson* [1981] QB 88 (CA).

[37] [2003] EWHC 793 (QB), [2003] 2 EGLR 121.

interest in the defence of the realm and therefore the training runs of the fighter jets was so important that the nuisance should be tolerated. Although the result of the case may be explained on the basis of an obvious and important public interest, even this is not entirely convincing: as Beever has argued, the Ministry of Defence could easily have carried out its training exercises elsewhere, and was already planning to relocate to America.[38]

It is problematic to make a judge the arbiter of what is in the public interest. This seems to involve considerations concerning parties who are not before the court, and may be beyond the competence of any particular judge.[39] It is difficult for a judge to assess wider considerations of public interest in what is essentially a dispute between neighbouring landowners. Indeed, in *Shelfer* itself the injunction hindered works on the local electricity supply, and it is perhaps telling that Lindley LJ noted that '[e]xpropriation, even for a money consideration, is only justifiable when parliament has sanctioned it. Courts of Justice are not like Parliament, which considers whether proposed works will be so beneficial to the public as to justify exceptional legislation, and the deprivation of people of their rights with or without compensation.'[40] If a defendant wishes to introduce the public interest as a reason for not awarding an injunction, it should be incumbent upon the defendant to make use of compulsory purchase regimes.

Admittedly, this does put a burden on private developers to seek the support of public bodies in agreeing that there is a public interest such that compulsory purchase should be favoured, but this does not seem to be unreasonable. Nor should it be unduly onerous: recommendations to improve the compulsory purchase procedure have been made by the Law Commission,[41] and these should be exploited. If a public body is not convinced that the proposed development really is in the public interest, then a judge should not be put in the position, in the context of a private dispute, of overriding that exercise of discretion and judgment by a local authority.[42]

Developers should not struggle to gain the support of local authorities if their developments truly are in the public interest. In *Standard*

---

[38] Allan Beever, *The Law of Private Nuisance* (Hart 2013) 149.

[39] See too RA Buckley, 'Injunctions and the Public Interest' (1981) 44 MLR 212, 213.

[40] *Shelfer* (n 18) 316.

[41] Law Commission, *Towards a Compulsory Purchase Code: (2) Procedure: Final Report* (Law Com No 291, 2004).

[42] Indeed, to do so may infringe the claimant's human rights: *United Kingdom v James* (1986) 8 EHRR 123 [40].

Commercial Property Securities Ltd v *Glasgow CC*,[43] the House of Lords offered support for 'back-to-back' agreements with local authorities: public bodies can agree to exercise their powers of compulsory purchase in order to ensure that the land can be developed, and later lease the land back to the developer, in return for the developer undertaking to indemnify the public authority for the costs incurred in the process.[44]

However, in *Coventry v Lawrence* there was significant criticism of the marginalisation of the 'public interest' as a factor that the court should consider when deciding whether to exercise its discretion to award damages in lieu of an injunction. For example, Lord Carnwath said: 'I agree with Lord Neuberger PSC and the rest of the court that the opportunity should be taken to signal a move away from the strict criteria derived from *Shelfer*', largely because it was necessary to allow in considerations of 'public interest', with the result that 'the Court of Appeal in *Watson*[45] was wrong to hold that the judge had no power to make the order he did, and to limit public interest considerations to cases where the damage to the claimant is "minimal"'.[46]

Nevertheless, Lord Sumption did recognise that a judge 'will usually lack the information to [take into account the public interest] effectively, and is in danger of stepping outside his main function of deciding the issue between the parties'.[47] This is an important point. It is unclear what a judge is to do when considering the 'public interest' as part of the exercise of his or her discretion in awarding an injunction. Nor is it clear what the 'public interest' means, or the weight to be attached to it. Some of the contrasting opinions about the 'public interest' of cricket matches which disrupt the peaceful enjoyment of a neighbour's property were infamously made clear in *Miller v Jackson*.[48]

---

[43] [2006] UKHL 50, 2007 SC (HL) 33.

[44] Furthermore, greater use may be made of Part IX the Town and Country Planning Act 1990; especially, in this context, s 237. See too *R (Sainsbury's Supermarkets Ltd) v Wolverhampton CC* [2010] UKSC 20, [2011] 1 AC 437; Emma JL Waring, 'Private-to-Private Takings and the Stability of Property' (2013) 24(2) KLJ 237; Jonathan Gaunt and the Hon Mr Justice Morgan, *Gale on Easements* (19th edn, Sweet & Maxwell 2012) 12–16–12–19.

[45] *Watson v Croft Promo-Sport* [2009] EWCA Civ 15, [2009] 3 All ER 249.

[46] *Coventry* (n 6) [239]. See too [118] (Lord Neuberger): 'The notion that it [i.e. the public interest] can be relevant where the damages are minimal, but not otherwise, as stated in *Watson*, seems very strange. Either the public interest is capable of being relevant to the issue or it is not.' See also [124] (Lord Neuberger), [157] (Lord Sumption), [169] (Lord Clarke); cf Lord Mance [167]–[168].

[47] *Coventry* [158].   [48] See n 36.

The 'public interest' appears to encompass consideration of whether or not planning permission was granted, although the judges in *Coventry v Lawrence* differed as to the weight to be placed upon this.[49] As was suggested above, the powers and nature of planning authorities are such that it would be unsatisfactory for planning permission to override a claimant's property rights which are protected by the private law.[50] Indeed, the Supreme Court Justice with the most experience of planning matters, Lord Carnwath, said that he 'would not regard the grant of planning permission for a particular use as in itself giving rise to a presumption against the grant of an injunction'.[51]

The difficulty now lies in determining what principles the court should apply when deciding whether to award damages in lieu of an injunction. The guidance from the Supreme Court is somewhat nebulous. *Shelfer* is viewed as too restrictive; the court's equitable discretion should not be fettered by a rigid or mechanical application of AL Smith LJ's 'working rule'. Considerations of 'public interest' can be taken into account, and in some situations planning permission might be a factor to be considered. Lord Neuberger observed that 'each case is likely to be so fact-sensitive that any firm guidance is likely to do more harm than good',[52] but clearly some direction for judges would be helpful, otherwise how is it possible to know whether a decision has been 'correctly' reached? Indeed, Lord Neuberger himself commented that 'it is appropriate to give as much guidance as possible so as to ensure that, while the discretion is not fettered, its manner of exercise is as predictable as possible'.[53] Given the disparate judgments in the Supreme Court in *Coventry v Lawrence*, and the disparagement of *Shelfer* without a clear replacement, it is unclear how predictable the resolution of the issue of damages in lieu of an injunction currently is.

There is even some lack of clarity concerning which party bears the burden in this area. Lord Neuberger accepted that 'the prima facie

---

[49] *Coventry* (n 6) [125] (Lord Neuberger), [157]–[161] (Lord Sumption), [167]–[168] (Lord Mance), [169] (Lord Clarke), [240]–[246] (Lord Carnwath).

[50] See too Nolan (n 15) 204–05. Cf Maria Lee, 'Private Nuisance in the Supreme Court: *Coventry v Lawrence*' [2014] *Journal of Planning & Environment Law* 705, 708–10.

[51] *Coventry* (n 6) [246]. His Lordship continued: 'As I have said, the circumstances in which permissions may be granted differ so much as to make it unwise to lay down any general propositions. I would accept however that the nature of, and background to, a relevant planning permission may be an important factor in the court's assessment.'

[52] Ibid [120].

[53] Ibid [121]. This is particularly important since an appellate court will be very reluctant to interfere with a trial judge's exercise of discretion: *Ottercroft Ltd v Scandia Care Ltd* [2016] EWCA Civ 867.

position is that an injunction should be granted, so the legal burden is on the defendant to show why it should not',[54] but then went on to say that 'when a judge is called on to decide whether to award damages in lieu of an injunction, I do not think that there should be any inclination either way'.[55] This is, potentially, a stark departure from *Shelfer*, under which damages in lieu of an injunction would be awarded only rarely. However, a similar approach to that of Lord Neuberger might be found in the speech of Lord Sumption,[56] whilst Lord Clarke 'would wish to reserve the question upon whom the burden of proof should be placed on the question how that discretion should be exercised'.[57]

It is suggested that the balance should still firmly lie in favour of injunctive relief, and the defendant should have to prove why the court should exercise its discretion to award damages in lieu. Property rights should not lightly be taken away by the courts, which is the practical effect of allowing the defendant to pay damages and thereby continue to commit the nuisance.[58]

It will be interesting to see what the lower courts make of the decision of the Supreme Court in *Coventry v Lawrence*. In *Higson v Guenault*, which concerned an interference with a right of way, Aikens LJ, giving the only reasoned judgment in the Court of Appeal, noted that '[t]here was some debate as to the correct test to apply when considering whether there should be an injunction or an award of damages in lieu'.[59] His Lordship applied the *Shelfer* test and held that an injunction should be granted, but also said that '[i]f the test is whether to exercise a more general discretion' then an injunction would still be awarded.[60] It therefore did not matter on the facts of the case whether the 'working rule' of *Shelfer* should still be applied or not,[61] but the relevance and

---

[54] Ibid [121]. This was cited with approval in *Gott v Lawrence* [2016] EWHC 68 (Ch) [70].

[55] Ibid [122].

[56] Who noted that 'it is unfortunate that it has been followed so recently and so slavishly': ibid 161.

[57] Ibid [170].

[58] As Buckley J once observed: 'The Court has affirmed over and over again that the jurisdiction to give damages where it exists is not so to be used as in fact to enable the defendant [in an action for disturbance of an easement] to purchase from the plaintiff against his will his legal right to the easement ... To refuse to aid the legal right by injunction and to give damages instead is in fact to compel the plaintiff to part with his easement for money.': *Cowper v Laidler* [1903] 2 Ch 337 (Ch) 341. See too *Manchester Corporation v Farnworth* [1930] AC 171 (HL) 194–95 (Viscount Sumner); cf *Jaggard v Sawyer* [1995] 1 WLR 269 (CA) 287.

[59] [2014] EWCA Civ 703, [2014] 2 P & CR DG13 [51].   [60] Ibid [51].

[61] Nor was it important in *Sunrise Brokers LLP v Michael William Rodgers* [2014] EWCA Civ 1373, [2015] ICR 272 [51]–[55] (Underhill LJ).

status of *Shelfer* does not seem to have been obvious to the Court of Appeal. This could prove problematic in later cases where the outcome under the *Shelfer* test clashes with that which would be reached under a broader discretion.

Further discussion about the test to be employed when deciding whether to award damages in lieu of an injunction has occurred in other contexts. For instance, in *Prophet plc v Huggett*, David Donaldson QC, sitting as a Deputy High Court Judge, thought that the comments in *Coventry v Lawrence* were not limited to nuisance, and could be applied to a post-termination restrictive covenant.[62] The judge said that 'the *Shelfer* formula is to be applied as no more than the working rule which AL Smith LJ conceived it to be',[63] but nevertheless commented that 'satisfaction of the four tests [in *Shelfer*] will normally lead to a refusal of an injunction in the absence of other relevant circumstances'.[64] The judge was clearly reluctant to be left without any guidance or principles to apply; although he recognised that the *Shelfer* factors 'are neither exhaustive nor to be applied mechanistically', he insisted that they remained relevant.[65] On the other hand, in *Comic Enterprise Ltd v Twentieth Century Fox Film Corp*,[66] an intellectual property dispute, Roger Wyand QC, sitting as a Deputy High Court Judge, cited passages from Lord Neuberger's speech in *Coventry v Lawrence* and concluded:

> From all of this I extract the conclusion that I have to apply a multi-factorial exercise balancing the two competing fundamental rights[67] with no presumption that either one automatically trumps the other. There is, however, a legal burden on the Defendant to show why an injunction should not be granted. It will depend upon the facts of the case.[68]

---

[62] [2014] EWHC 615 (Ch), [2014] IRLR. 618 [28]. This decision was reversed by the Court of Appeal, which did not consider the issues concerning damages in lieu of an injunction: [2014] EWCA Civ 1013, [2014] IRLR 797.

[63] [2014] EWHC 615 (Ch), [2014] IRLR 618 [27].   [64] Ibid [27].   [65] Ibid [28].

[66] [2014] EWHC 2286 (Ch)), [2014] ETMR 51. Compare *Kerry Ingredients (UK) Ltd v Bakkavor Group Ltd* [2016] EWHC 2448 (Ch), in which Newey J only cited *Shelfer* and did not refer to *Coventry v Lawrence* at all in a case concerning injunctive relief for breach of confidence.

[67] As the judge said at [5]: 'The grant of an injunction in IP cases requires a balancing of the various fundamental rights under EU law. The right of intellectual property, which is to be protected in accordance with Article 17(2) of the EU Charter, is to be balanced against the right to freedom of expression, which is to be respected in accordance with Article 11 of the EU Charter, and the right of the arts to be free from constraint as provided under Article 13 of the EU Charter.'

[68] See n 66 [15].

Such a 'multifactorial' approach allows the court great freedom.[69] But it also makes it difficult to predict what factors the court will consider relevant, and what weight will be placed upon them.

Although the comments regarding *Shelfer* in the Supreme Court were strictly obiter, it is clearly likely that they will be followed by the lower courts. But it is important that stable and clear guidance be developed. One of the great virtues of *Shelfer* was its relative predictability:[70] an injunction would be granted unless there was a very good reason not to do so. It is suggested that this was particularly appropriate in the context of nuisance disputes: the claimant's rights were infringed, but there was no corresponding right of the defendant which was sacrificed, since the defendant simply never had the right to use its property such as to cause a nuisance. For instance, the defendant developer never had the right to build in a way that would infringe neighbours' property rights, so injunctive relief would not deprive the defendant of a right he once had. On the other hand, limiting the claimant to damages rather than an injunction would effectively deprive the claimant of its property right. It is also important to remember that a property right, once lost, is lost to successors in title as well. A strict interpretation of the *Shelfer* test meant that this result only arose in very limited circumstances.

Although the 'working rule' of *Shelfer* was considered to be too weighted in favour of injunctive relief, this conclusion was not, in fact, entirely obvious. The first limb could have ensured a de minimis exception to the presumptive award of an injunction,[71] but some sizeable awards were made,[72] allowing the courts greater leeway. The second limb was a necessary requirement for an award of damages to be made, but the third limb could be viewed as somewhat defendant-friendly: after all, a claimant may well not agree that its injury can truly be adequately compensated by a small money payment. The fact that the claimant considers that its rights are worth more than the defendant is prepared to pay (and perhaps the objective value of the right) should not lightly be

---

[69] This has been championed by some commentators, too: see, e.g. Ian Spry, *Equitable Remedies* (9th edn, Sweet & Maxwell 2013) 665; Mark L Wilde, 'Nuisance Law and Damages in Lieu of an Injunction: Challenging the Orthodoxy of the Shelfer Criteria' in Stephen GA Pitel, Jason W Neyers, Erika Chamberlain (eds) *Tort Law: Challenging Orthodoxy* (Hart 2013); Stephen Tromans, 'Nuisance-Prevention or Payment?' [1982] 41(1) CLJ 87.

[70] Cf *Rights to Light* (n 29) para 4.64, citing the comments of Morgan J

[71] For instance, in *Regan* (n 27), the Court of Appeal held that £5,000 was not 'small', overturning the decision of the judge below.

[72] See, e.g. *Lane v O'Brien Homes* [2004] EWHC 303 (QB). See too *Jaggard* (n 58).

cast aside: it is unclear why the court should order the claimant to forego its property rights.[73] The fourth limb[74] was also not entirely pro-claimant: even if an injunction might be oppressive to a defendant, it might also be considered oppressive to a claimant to be deprived of a choice whether or not to sell its rights.[75] Moreover, it should be remembered that the availability of injunctive relief rarely means that desirable developments are entirely jettisoned: defendants are simply in a worse bargaining position when negotiating with claimants for a fee for the relaxation of the claimant's rights.[76]

In any event, to seek to return to a stricter approach in favour of injunctive relief seems to go very much against the current tide of opinion. In the wake of *Coventry v Lawrence*, the Law Commission published its 'Report on Rights to Light', in which it recommended the following approach to whether damages should be awarded in lieu of an injunction in Clause 2 of its Draft Rights to Light (Injunctions) Bill:[77]

(2) The court must not grant an injunction if, in all the circumstances of the case, an injunction would be a disproportionate means of enforcing the claimant's right to light.

(3) The circumstances to be considered in assessing whether that is the case include –

    (a) the claimant's interest in the dominant land;

    (b) the loss of amenity attributable to the infringement;

    (c) whether or not damages would be adequate compensation for the injury to the claimant;

    (d) the claimant's conduct;

    (e) any unreasonable delay in claiming an injunction;

    (f) the defendant's conduct;

---

[73] See text to nn 16–19.

[74] Which tended to be the 'key question': see, e.g. *Site Developments (Ferndown) Ltd v Barratt Homes Ltd* [2007] EWHC 415 (Ch) [64] (Richard Arnold QC).

[75] Of course, it might be said that if the first three limbs are satisfied there is no oppression of the claimant, but this deprivation of the ability to choose what to do with one's property rights may nonetheless be considered a significant intrusion.

[76] See generally Ben Pontin, *Nuisance Law and Environmental Protection: A Study of Nuisance Injunctions in Practice* (Lawtext 2013) 187. See too Ben Pontin, 'Nuisance injunctions after *Coventry v Lawrence*: Revisiting the Question of "Prevention or Payment"?' (2013) 25(6) ELM 209. Even after an injunction was awarded in *HKRUK II* (n 27), which would have led to part of an office block being pulled down, the parties simply negotiated a settlement which was reached just before the case was due to be heard by the Court of Appeal.

[77] *Rights to Light* (n 29) Appendix B.

(g) the impact of an injunction on the defendant;

(h) the public interest, so far as relevant.

This list of factors is not exhaustive. But it is intended to be much wider than the approach in *Shelfer*.[78] The claimant's conduct even includes consideration of whether or not the claimant was willing to accept damages at an earlier stage of negotiations with the defendant.[79]

At the time of writing, it remains to be seen whether this Bill receives support from the Government. Despite some suggestion in *Coventry v Lawrence* from Lord Carnwath[80] and Lord Mance[81] that rights to light raised particular issues, Lord Neuberger did not think cases concerning rights to light involved 'special rules'.[82] It is suggested that it would be unfortunate if different approaches to damages in lieu of an injunction were applied to different easements, for instance. *Coventry v Lawrence* may be the catalyst for a new approach to damages in lieu of an injunction, and judges should be able to develop this at common law. If the Draft Rights to Light (Injunctions) Bill were to be passed, it is likely that judges would be tempted to apply it by analogy in the context of other easements, since it provides clearer guidance than the decision of the Supreme Court. But this is not obviously appropriate – the Law Commission's work was narrowly confined to rights to light without considering other easements – and it is suggested that it would now be preferable to leave this issue for judicial development.

The dispute in *Coventry v Lawrence* itself may give the courts scope to elaborate on the principles applicable when deciding whether to grant damages in lieu of an injunction. The defendants obtained planning permission for a stadium which was to be used for speedway racing. The stadium was later used for stock car racing. This was very noisy, and the claimants sought an injunction to restrain the nuisance. Richard Seymour QC granted an injunction;[83] the Court of Appeal disagreed;[84] the Supreme Court allowed the appeal. At first instance, the judge was not asked to grant damages in lieu of an injunction, probably because there was little realistic possibility of success if *Shelfer* was applied.[85] However, Lord Neuberger said that the defendants should be free to argue that the injunction granted should be discharged, and damages awarded in lieu. His Lordship emphasised that he was 'not in any way seeking to fetter the

---

[78] See generally ibid ch 4.   [79] Ibid paras 4.107–4.109.   [80] *Coventry* (n 6) [247].
[81] Ibid [167].   [82] Ibid [122].   [83] [2011] EWHC 360 (QB), [2012] LLR 53.
[84] [2012] EWCA Civ 26, [2012] 1 WLR 2127.
[85] *Coventry* (n 6) [149]–[150] (Lord Neuberger).

judge's discretion when deciding whether to award damages instead, or seeking to suggest how that discretion might be exercised'.[86] It is therefore an open question what and how the judge may decide.[87] It is perhaps possible to derive hints from the Supreme Court that the fact that planning permission had been granted, coupled with the public interest in the events being held at the stadium, might well tip the balance in favour of damages in lieu of an injunction. But it is not clear that such a result would be satisfactory. It seems more appropriate to force the defendants actually to negotiate with the claimants for permission to continue to infringe the latter's property rights. If such negotiations fail, it would appear that the defendants could still hold events in the stadium in a way which complied with the injunction granted and did not cause a nuisance.[88]

In any event, greater use of the discretion to award damages in lieu of an injunction will make it necessary to establish precisely how such damages should be calculated. Lord Neuberger[89] and Lord Clarke[90] were sympathetic to including some reference to the benefit gained by the defendant, whereas Lord Carnwath was much more circumspect.[91] The issue was not argued before the Supreme Court and so no decision on this point was required.[92]

It is suggested that damages in lieu of an injunction should be calculated by reference to the hypothetical bargain which would have been reached between the claimant and defendant if they had acted reasonably and been willing to make a deal. Much has been written about whether the basis of the loss of bargain measure is restitutionary or compensatory.[93] Regardless of the theoretical basis of such damages, the monetary award should take into account both the claimant's loss and the defendant's gain, as any

---

[86] Ibid [152].

[87] The case may well settle out of court: the claimant's house was destroyed by a fire and has not been rebuilt, and the costs in the case have already become 'disturbingly' large: *Coventry v Lawrence (No 2)* [2014] UKSC 46, [2015] AC 106 [34] (Lord Neuberger).

[88] Or alternatively the defendants could exploit the compulsory purchase procedures already in place: see text to nn 39–44.

[89] *Coventry* [128].   [90] Ibid [173].   [91] Ibid [248].

[92] Ibid [132]. Although the Law Commission did not recommend specific reform in the context of rights to light, it did express dissatisfaction with how damages in lieu of an injunction are quantified: *Rights to Light* (n 29) ch 5.

[93] E.g. Craig Rotherham, 'Wrotham Park Damages and Accounts of Profits: Compensation or Restitution?' [2008] LMCLQ 25; Andrew Burrows, 'Are 'Damages on the Wrotham Park Basis' Compensatory, Restitutionary or Neither?' in Ralph Cunnington and Djakhongir Saidov (eds), *Contract Damages: Domestic and International Perspectives* (Hart 2008).

sensible course of negotiations should.[94] This approach has been employed
where damages have been awarded in lieu of an injunction after the tort of
nuisance has been established.[95] In *Forsyth-Grant v Allen*, however,
Toulson LJ thought that:

> [T]here was every reason not to give the appellant compensation on the
> basis of what she could have bargained for, because the respondent had
> been willing to bargain but she refused his invitation to do so. Since she
> refused that opportunity I cannot see, as a matter of justice, why she
> should be entitled to any greater remedy for the infringement of her rights
> to light than damages for loss which she actually suffered as a result of the
> infringement.[96]

But if the claimant was unwilling to enter into a bargain or negotiate
a settlement, that may simply be because the claimant did not wish to
accept money in substitution for the right itself. It seems very hard then
to force the claimant to release his or her property rights and, on top of
that, not to allow the claimant to recover the 'loss of bargain' measure.[97]
After all, this measure of damages is by its very nature hypothetical, and
assumes that both the claimant and defendant acted as reasonable negotiating parties. The doubts cast on this approach by the Court of Appeal
in *Forsyth-Grant* should not be heeded.[98]

The approach of Millett J in *Carr-Saunders v Dick McNeil Associates
Ltd*[99] and Gabriel Moss QC, sitting as a Deputy High Court Judge, in
*Tamares (Vincent Square) Ltd v Fairpoint Properties (Vincent Square)
Ltd*[100] is to be preferred. In *Carr-Saunders*, Millett J found that the loss of
light caused by a nuisance would lead to a minimum award of £3,000. But
he thought that the claimant should recover more than this, since he
'would have a bargaining position because, unless he were bought out,
the defendants would be inhibited in their development'.[101] Thus the
judge increased the size of the award to £8,000, without giving precise
reasons as to why this figure was chosen.[102] It is suggested that the uplift

---

[94] *Inverugie Investments v Hackett* [1995] 1 WLR 713 (PC), 717–18 (Lord Lloyd); *Horsford
v Bird* [2006] UKPC 3; [2006] 1 EGLR 75.
[95] See, e.g. *Carr-Saunders v Dick McNeil Associates Ltd* [1986] 1 WLR 922 (Ch) (Millett J);
Tamares (n 33).
[96] [2008] EWCA Civ 505, [2008] 2 EGLR 16 [39]; see too [32] (Patten J).
[97] Cf *Wrotham Park Estate Co Ltd v Parkside Homes Ltd* [1974] 1 WLR 798 (Ch).
[98] Cf *Rights to Light* (n 29) paras 4.107–4.109.   [99] *Carr-Saunders* (n 95).
[100] [2007] EWHC 212 (Ch), [2007] 1 WLR 2167.   [101] *Carr-Saunders* (n 95) 931.
[102] In *Tamares* (n 33), the judge suggested, at [20], that: 'The method used by Millett J was to
start with the loss of amenity and then build upwards, in effect guessing at the boost
given to the claimant by his bargaining position in the absence of evidence relating to the

can be justified by the strong bargaining position of the claimant, which should be reflected by allowing the claimant to recover a proportion of the gains the defendant would expect to make.[103] In *Tamares* this was around 30 per cent, and in Forsyth-Grant around 15 per cent. How can the courts decide on the figure to be awarded? There is no straightforward answer to this question. Gabriel Moss QC usefully set out a series of considerations to be taken into account:

(1) The overall principle is that the court must attempt to find what would be a 'fair' result of a hypothetical negotiation between the parties.
(2) The context, including the nature and seriousness of the breach, must be kept in mind.
(3) The right to prevent a development (or part) gives the owner of the right a significant bargaining position.
(4) The owner of the right with such a bargaining position will normally be expected to receive some part of the likely profit from the development (or relevant part).
(5) If there is no evidence of the likely size of the profit, the court can do its best by awarding a suitable multiple of the damages for loss of amenity.
(6) If there is evidence of the likely size of the profit, the court should normally award a sum which takes into account a fair percentage of the profit.
(7) The size of the award should not in any event be so large that the development (or relevant part) would not have taken place had such a sum been payable.
(8) After arriving at a figure which takes into consideration all the above and any other relevant factors, the court needs to consider whether the 'deal feels right'.[104]

---

profit being made from the development.' Lee has contended that 'some form of elevated damages may be necessary if private nuisance is to remain a realistic response to neighbourhood amenity problems': Lee (n 50) 711.

[103] It is clear that the date of assessment should normally be at the time of the infringement: *Lunn Poly Ltd v Liverpool and Lancashire Properties Ltd* [2006] EWCA Civ 430; [2006] 2 EGLR 29 [29]; *Pell Frischmann Engineering Ltd v Bow Valley Iran Ltd* [2011] 1 WLR 2370 (PC). Where the developers present the claimants with a fait accompli, in some circumstances a full account of profits may even be desirable: see generally Craig Rotherham, 'Gain-based Relief in Tort after *AG v Blake*' (2010) 126 LQR 102.

[104] *Tamares* (n 33) [22]. The case concerned the infringement of a right to light; cf *Amec Developments Ltd v Jury's Hotel Management (UK) Ltd* [2001] 1 EGLR 81 (Ch) 87.

Such guidance is undoubtedly helpful, but it remains uncertain how much the court will award when quantifying damages in lieu.[105] It is obviously impossible to know what 'reasonable' people would consider to be a 'fair' result, and whether or not a particular sum 'feels right' to the judge is little more than educated guesswork. Some degree of uncertainty is inevitable, but given that this is an area where negotiated settlements of disputes should be encouraged, a large degree of uncertainty is problematic: parties could have very different understanding of the strengths of their respective positions. The difficulties of assessment strengthen the suggestion that the courts should strongly favour the award of an injunction;[106] this puts the onus on the parties themselves to strike a reasonable bargain, and absolves the courts from the need to do so.

The Supreme Court in *Coventry v Lawrence* recognised that the law surrounding damages in lieu of an injunction more generally is very difficult. Indicating that the principles need to be developed more clearly by subsequent cases, Lord Neuberger observed that:

> There are differences between the various members of the court on this final issue. Most, probably all, of these differences are ones of emphasis and detail rather than of principle, but I none the less accept that we are at risk of introducing a degree of uncertainty into the law. The nature of the issue, whether to award damages in lieu of an injunction, is such that a degree of uncertainty is inevitable, but that does not alter the fact that it should be kept to a reasonable minimum. Given that we are changing the practice of the courts, it is inevitable that, in so far as there can be clearer or more precise principles, they will have to be worked out in the way familiar to the common law, namely on a case by case basis.[107]

6.3   Breach of Contract

In *Doherty v Allman*, Lord Cairns LC said:

> If parties, for valuable consideration, with their eyes open, contract that a particular thing shall not be done, all that a Court of Equity has to do is to say, by way of injunction, that which the parties have already said by way of covenant, that the thing shall not be done; and in such case the

---

[105] As regards rights to light, the Law Commission thought that 'there is to some extent a problem with equitable damages' given the uncertainties in the law, but did not propose reform given a lack of clear economic evidence: *Rights to Light* (n 29) ch 5, esp 5.76–5.79.

[106] This is perhaps even stronger where there are potentially multiple claimants: cf *Forsyth-Grant v Allen* [2008] EWCA Civ 505, [2008] Env LR 41 [46] (Toulson LJ).

[107] *Coventry* (n 6) [132].

injunction does nothing more than give the sanction of the process of the Court to that which already is the contract between the parties.[108]

Prohibitory injunctions are often awarded to enforce restrictive covenants against departing employees such that they cannot work for a competitor for a specified period.[109] However, the award of even a prohibitory injunction is always discretionary and never automatic.[110] It is therefore important to consider further the principles that guide the exercise of the court's discretion.

One particularly controversial issue concerns the granting of equitable relief in the context of contracts for services. This is because restraining a party from committing a breach of contract might have the practical effect of forcing that party to perform the contract.[111] Yet in *Lumley v Wagner*, Lord St Leonards LC said: 'I disclaim doing indirectly what I cannot do directly.'[112] In that case, Johanna Wagner, an opera singer, had agreed with Mr Lumley not to sing at any theatre other than his without written permission, and this term was enforced by the court via an injunction. It is notable that the contract was of very short duration (only three months) and Miss Wagner was therefore not prevented from plying her trade for very long. More onerous was the decision in *Warner Bros Pictures Inc v Nelson*,[113] in which Branson J restrained the film star Bette Davis from making movies for anyone other than Warner Brothers for three years. It was perhaps unrealistic to expect Bette Davis to do anything other than work as an actress for Warner Brothers following that ruling.

There appeared to be some retreat from injunctive relief in *Page One Records Ltd v Britton*,[114] where Stamp J was not prepared to prevent the pop group 'The Troggs' from hiring another manager as he did not wish to force unwilling persons to have to work with each another. Similar reasoning was employed in *Warren v Mendy*.[115] However, injunctive relief clearly remains available to prevent a breach of contract, and was given something of a boost by the important decision of the Court of Appeal in *LauritzenCool AB v Lady Navigation Inc*.[116]

---

[108] (1878) 3 App Cas 709 (HL) 720.

[109] See, e.g. HG Beale (ed), *Chitty on Contracts* (31st edn, Sweet & Maxwell 2012) para 27–069.

[110] Cf *Redland Bricks* (n 5) (Lord Upjohn).

[111] Mandatory injunctions will not be considered here; they raise issues similar to those encountered within specific performance: see ch 5.

[112] (1852) 1 De GM & G 604, 620; 42 ER 687, 693.   [113] [1937] 1 KB 209 (KB).

[114] [1968] 1 WLR 157 (Ch).   [115] [1989] 1 WLR 853 (CA).

[116] [2005] EWCA Civ 579, [2005] 1 WLR 3686.

LauritzenCool concerned a time charter. The claimants managed two of the defendants' vessels as part of a shipping pool. The defendants sought to use their vessels outside the pool, but were restrained from doing so by a prohibitory injunction. The Court of Appeal accepted that the practical effect of this would be that the defendants would continue to provide the vessels to the pool and perform the charter.[117] A time charter is a contract for services, but Mance LJ emphasised that there is no firm rule that an injunction cannot be granted where the contract is for services; injunctive relief remains a matter for the court's discretion.[118]

The result in *LauritzenCool* should be welcomed: the vessels, as commercially valuable assets, were clearly going to be employed in some form, and whether they were hired out by the claimants or by another party did not affect any particular individual. There was therefore no 'human necessity' in the case,[119] so there was no fear of forcing an individual to perform work in anything resembling a modern form of slavery.[120] Indeed, on the facts of *LauritzenCool*, the claimants and defendants had managed to maintain a workable professional relationship, and it was highly unlikely that the parties would be unable to make their contractual agreement function pursuant to the injunction. This will often be the case in the commercial environment: commercial parties tend to be able to manage difficult relationships,[121] and it is unrealistic to suppose that they will deliberately fail to comply with equitable orders.

Mance LJ in *LauritzenCool* cited the pertinent comments of Ackner LJ in *Regent International Hotels (UK) Ltd v Pageguide Ltd*:

> [T]his action raises the further serious question, as yet unresolved by English authority, as to the extent to which a commercial arrangement of this kind between two independent companies, which does not provide for the employment of any named individuals and is part of a larger package . . . can be properly treated as analogous to a contract of personal service.[122]

The distinction between contracts where a particular individual is named as being bound to perform, and contracts between corporate entities who promise to ensure a service is provided, is significant.

---

[117] Mance LJ (ibid [7]) accepted that there was 'no realistic alternative'.   [118] Ibid [33].

[119] Ibid [22]; cf *Warren v Mendy* [1989] 1 WLR 853 (CA), cited by Mance LJ (ibid [21]).

[120] See, e.g. Robert S Stevens, 'Involuntary Servitude by Injunction' (1921) 6 Cornell LQ 235.

[121] In *LauritzenCool*, the trial judge was confident that this was true even though 'the parties, in the course of their dispute, have been abusive about one another': [2004] EWHC 2607 (Comm), [2005] 1 All ER (Comm) 77 [26] (Cooke J).

[122] *The Times*, 13 May 1985 (CA).

In the latter situation, no individual is forced to work against his or her will. For example, if Company A contracts with Company B to provide a venue and staff for an event, it is not unreasonable to assume that the staff of Company A would be happy (and possibly contractually bound) to work regardless of whether the event is for Company B or Company Z.

This issue remains important. In *Société Générale v Geys*, Lord Wilson noted that '[t]he big question whether nowadays the more impersonal, less hierarchical, relationship of many employers with their employees requires review of the usual unavailability of specific performance has been raised ... but is beyond the scope of this appeal'.[123] It is suggested that the thrust of the reasoning in *LauritzenCool* should be exploited such that, where damages would be an inadequate remedy, injunctions should be granted even in the context of contracts to provide services.[124] After all, injunctive relief has been granted to enforce contracts of personal service in some instances.[125]

Nevertheless, in some situations the overall exercise of the court's discretion might lead to a refusal to grant equitable relief, even though damages may seem to be inadequate. This is most likely to be the case where '"the services are so linked to some special skill or talent whose continued display is essential to the psychological material or physical well being of the servant" so as to make negative injunctions restraining breach of the contracts of service impossible'.[126] Yet even here it is important to remember that injunctions may still be awarded where the 'servant' is only restrained from acting over a short period. Thus in *Araci v Fallon*[127] the Court of Appeal overturned the decision of the trial judge and granted an injunction to prevent the champion jockey Kieren Fallon from riding another's horse in breach of his contract with the claimant, even though this had the effect of preventing Fallon from riding in the Derby. Although a very prestigious event, Fallon was only prevented from competing on that one day. The result may have been

---

[123] [2012] UKSC 63, [2013] 1 AC 523 [77].

[124] Compare the opening sentence of *Warren* (n 119) 857 (Nourse LJ): 'It is well settled that an injunction to restrain a breach of contract for personal services ought not to be granted where its effect will be to decree performance of the contract.'

[125] E.g. *Hill v CA Parsons & Co* [1972] Ch 305 (CA); *Irani v Southampton and South West Hampshire HA* [1985] ICR 590 (Ch).

[126] *Isabella Shipowner SA v Shagang Shipping Co Ltd (The Aquafaith)* [2012] EWHC 1077 (Comm), [2012] 2 All ER (Comm) 461 [38] (Cooke J), citing the first instance decision in *LauritzenCool* (n 121) [27] (Cooke J).

[127] [2011] EWCA Civ 668, [2011] LLR 440.

different if the period of time during which Fallon could not exercise his trade had been one year and Fallon's skills could have gone stale.

It appears that the courts now consider whether or not there has been a loss of confidence between the parties such that, if an injunction were granted and the practical effect would be that the parties had to work together, that relationship would be impossible. This approach is preferable to a blanket rule[128] that injunctions will not be granted where contracts for services are concerned.[129] Courts should be sceptical about arguments that commercial actors will be unable to make a relationship work, and therefore more willing to grant injunctions.[130] It is generally only where close co-operation and trust between the parties is required that the balance will be tipped in favour of refusing injunctive relief.[131]

LauritzenCool is an important decision that indicates greater scope for injunctive relief where contracts for services are concerned. But the result was not obvious. The defendants relied upon the decision of the House of Lords in *The Scaptrade*.[132] Lord Diplock held that:

> To grant an injunction restraining the shipowner from exercising his right of withdrawal of the vessel from the service of the charterer, though negative in form, is pregnant with an affirmative order to the shipowner to perform the contract; juristically it is indistinguishable from a decree for specific performance of a contract to render services; and in respect of that category of contracts, even in the event of breach, this is a remedy that English courts have always disclaimed jurisdiction to grant.[133]

---

[128] The idea that there was a 'jurisdictional bar' where contracts for services are concerned was again rejected in *Akai Holdings Ltd v RSM Robson Rhodes LLP* [2007] EWHC 1641 (Ch) [39] (Briggs J).

[129] *Ferrara Quay Ltd v Carillion Construction Ltd* [2009] BLR 367 [74]–[77]; *Vertex Data Science Limited v Powergen Retail Ltd* [2006] EWHC 1340 (Comm), [2006] 2 Lloyd's Rep 591.

[130] Especially since the parties may bargain for the relaxation of an injunction if necessary.

[131] A recent example is *Ashworth v Royal National Theatre* [2014] EWHC 1176 (QB), [2014] 4 All ER 238 [23]–[25] (Cranston J), which concerned the production of the play *War Horse* and an injunction sought by musicians: 'The plain fact is that the production of a play necessarily entails close cooperation between all those involved, the actors and those directing and producing the play ... That to my mind is precisely the type of situation where on the authorities it would be inappropriate for the court to enforce a contract by specific performance or analogous injunction. There is clearly an absence of personal confidence on the part of the National Theatre. In addition the claimants themselves would be affected by knowing that the National Theatre does not want them and believes that the play is better without them.'

[132] *Scandinavian Trading Tanker Co AB v Flota Petrolera Ecuatoriana (The Scaptrade)* [1983] 2 AC 694 (HL).

[133] Ibid 701.

In *The Scaptrade*, equitable relief to restrain a party from exercising its contractual right of withdrawal was refused. It was distinguished in *LauritzenCool* on the facts: *The Scaptrade* did not consider the question of whether a party could be restrained from employing its vessel outside the charter. Nevertheless, there seems to be a tension between the two judgments. It is suggested that the House of Lords' insistence that contracts of services cannot be specifically performed is outdated and should be jettisoned; the fact that a contract is for personal services is simply another factor that informs the exercise of the court's discretion.[134] The approach in *LauritzenCool* should be preferred to that of *The Scaptrade*.

The more recent decision in *AB v CD*[135] might also confirm a greater willingness to award injunctions than may previously have been supposed. The parties entered into a licensing agreement, under which AB obtained the right to market CD's internet-based platform. A clause in the contract purported to exclude liability for loss of profits in the event of a breach, or of any cause of action, and also to cap the recoverable damages under any head of claim according to a prescribed formula. AB sought an interim injunction[136] to require CD not to terminate the agreement. At first instance, the judge refused to grant an injunction as he considered that AB would be adequately compensated by damages.[137] A unanimous Court of Appeal allowed AB's appeal, insisting that the clause in the contract should be taken into account when deciding whether or not the remedies which would be available at common law were adequate to reflect the substantial justice of the situation.[138] This was consistent with previous guidance from the Court of Appeal[139] and was thought to be right in principle. As Underhill LJ put it:

> The primary obligation of a party is to perform the contract. The requirement to pay damages in the event of a breach is a secondary obligation, and an agreement to restrict the recoverability of damages in the event of a breach cannot be treated as an agreement to excuse performance of that primary obligation ... The primary commercial expectation must be that the parties will perform their obligations. The expectations created (indeed given contractual force) by an exclusion or limitation clause are

---

[134] Spry (n 69) 70.   [135] [2014] EWCA Civ 229, [2015] 1 WLR 771.

[136] The thrust of the reasoning seems equally applicable to final injunctions: see, e.g. [2014] EWCA Civ 229, [2015] 1 WLR 771 [32] (Ryder LJ).

[137] [2014] EWHC 1 (QB) (Stuart-Smith J).

[138] *AB* (n 135) [27]. See too PG Turner, 'Inadequacy in Equity of Common Law Relief: the Relevance of Contractual Terms' [2014] 73(3) CLJ 493, 495–96.

[139] *Bath and North East Somerset DC v Mowlem plc* [2004] EWCA Civ 115, [2015] 1 WLR 785.

expectations about what damages will be recoverable in the event of
breach; but that is not the same thing.[140]

The logic of this reasoning is clear. Contracts should be performed, and
clauses which limit the amount of damages payable do not undermine
this point: such clauses restrict the secondary obligation to pay damages
in the event of breach, but not the primary obligation to perform.
Injunctive relief therefore remains available, and the court is entitled to
consider wider losses which would be irrecoverable if an injunction were
not granted. The court clearly did not think such a result was 'uncommercial'. The decision does perhaps make it more difficult for a draftsman to know whether including a limitation clause in a contract would
make injunctive relief more likely,[141] but this does not undermine the
reasoning in *AB v CD*. Indeed, Underhill LJ was clear that even if it is
established that damages are inadequate – perhaps in part because of
a limitation clause – that 'only opens the door to the exercise of the
court's discretion'.[142] It will still need to be established what the parties'
liabilities would have been in the absence of a limitation clause, for
example. Although parties cannot bind the courts to grant an injunction
through their contractual arrangement,[143] *AB v CD* usefully highlights
that equitable relief cannot easily be sidelined by a term in the contract.
Injunction remains an important remedy in commercial disputes.

[140] *AB* (n 135) [27]–[28].   [141] See, e.g. ibid [33] (Laws LJ).   [142] *AB* (n 135) [30].
[143] *Warner Brothers Pictures, Incorporated v Nelson* [1937] 1 KB 209 (KB) 221 (Branson J).

7

Rescission

NICHOLAS J MCBRIDE

The Bible tells us of two occasions when a king of Persia was tricked by his advisers into passing a decree that had the effect of condemning to death someone close to him.[1] Neither king could undo his decree because the laws of the Medes and the Persians were unchangeable. We are more privileged than the Persian kings. Where the law gives C a legal power to do *x* (such as a power to make a gift, or enter into a contract), if C does *x*, there are circumstances in which the law will allow C to cancel, or *rescind*, her doing *x* so that if C does this: (1) the law will treat C as though she never did *x*; and (2) the law will, as best it can do it, put C and those affected by C's doing *x* back in the position that they were in before C did *x*. So the distinctive feature of rescission as a remedy is that it is *retrospective* in its effect: it rewrites history. However, as numerous stories and films about time travel show, rewriting history is never easy and frequently gives rise to complications; so it proves in the case of rescission. Sarah Worthington has observed that 'Almost every aspect of the law of rescission is now contentious.'[2] The task of this chapter is to see if we can provide a rational basis for resolving some of the controversies surrounding the remedy of rescission.

7.1 Overview

Rescission is an area of law that is particularly affected by the division between law and equity.

My thanks to Robert Stevens, Frederick Wilmot-Smith, Paul Davies, Jason Neyers, and Irit Samet for their comments on earlier drafts of this chapter.
[1] Daniel 6:6–23; Esther 3:6–9:5.
[2] Sarah Worthington, 'The Proprietary Consequences of Rescission' [2002] RLR 28, 28.

7.1.1   Grounds of Rescission

Where C makes a contract with D, or makes a gift to D, the contract/gift can be rescinded at law where D procured it through fraud or duress, while it can also be rescinded in equity where the gift/contract was induced by D's innocent misrepresentation, undue influence, unconscionable behaviour, or breach of equitable duty. A contract that C has entered into because of a mistake that was not induced by anyone else cannot be rescinded in equity;[3] however, a gift can be – but only where C's mistake in making that gift was of 'sufficient gravity' that 'it would be unconscionable, or unjust, to leave the mistake uncorrected'.[4] Where it was not D but a third party, T, who induced C to make a gift to/contract with D by using (say) fraud or undue influence, C will be able to rescind any gift she made to D, but she will only be allowed to rescind a contract she made with D if D *knew*[5] of T's fraud or undue influence at the time C contracted with D; the burden of establishing that D had such knowledge will fall on C if she wishes to rescind.[6]

7.1.2   Effects of Rescission

The general rule is that where a contract or gift between C and D is rescinded, C and D must be restored to the position they were in before

---

[3] *Great Peace Shipping Ltd v Tsavliris Salvage (International) Ltd* [2002] EWCA Civ 1407, [2003] QB 679.

[4] *Pitt v Holt* [2013] UKSC 26, [2013] 2 AC 108 [122], [128] (Lord Walker), endorsing *Ogilvie v Littleboy* (1897) 13 TLR 399 (CA), 400 (Lindley LJ).

[5] Dominic O'Sullivan, Steven Elliott and Rafal Zakrzewski, *The Law of Rescission* (2nd edn, Oxford University Press 2014) ('OEZ'), [9.05]. There is an exception where the contract made with D involved C's giving security for a loan made by D; in such a case the contract can be rescinded by C merely on showing that D knew *or ought to have known* that C was entering into the contract because of T's misbehaviour: *Barclays Bank v O'Brien* [1994] 1 AC 180 (HL). Where D purchases a debt that was incurred by C because of T's misbehaviour, C will still be entitled to rescind the debt whatever D's state of knowledge in purchasing the debt: *Stoddart v Union Trust Ltd* [1912] 1 KB 181 (CA).

[6] *Whitehorn Brothers v Davison* [1911] 1 KB 463 (CA); *Barclays Bank plc v Boulter* [1999] 1 WLR 1919 (HL). C's inability to rescind her contract/gift unless she can prove such knowledge on D's part cannot be explained as being an application of the defence of *bona fide* purchase: (1) that defence exists to allow D to get a better title than he could obtain from C under the *nemo dat* rule and there is no question here of C's being unable to give D a good title; and (2) that defence has to be pleaded by D, whereas C has to establish D's knowledge to rescind her contract with D. See William Swadling, 'Restitution and *Bona Fide* Purchase' in William Swadling (ed), *The Limits of Restitutionary Claims: A Comparative Analysis* (UKNCCL 1997); Peter Birks, 'Notice and Onus in *O'Brien*' (1998) 12 TLI 2, 5–7; Dominic O'Sullivan, 'Developing *O'Brien*' (2002) 118 LQR 337, 342.

the contract/gift in question was made: in Latin, *restitutio in integrum* must follow rescission. Where *restitutio in integrum* is not possible, rescission will be barred and the contract/gift will stand.

Where C made a gift to/contract with D because of D's fraud or duress, and as a result transferred to D legal title to an item of property X, C will normally be entitled to rescind the gift/contract at law; if she does, title to X will automatically and retrospectively revest in C so that C will be held to have been the legal owner of X even after she transferred X to D. However, C will be barred from rescinding the gift/contract at law: (1) where title to X is not capable of automatically revesting in C; or (2) where title to X was acquired by a *bona fide* purchaser before C managed to rescind her gift/contract.

Where (1) is true (because, for example, only the registered owner of X counts as being the owner, and D is the registered owner), C will be barred from rescinding *at law* because C will not, by rescinding, be able to recover title to X and achieve *restitutio in integrum*. However, C will be able to go to court and have the gift/contract rescinded *in equity*, as equity can effect *restitutio in integrum* by holding that D held X on trust for C from the moment that D received X from C.[7] A retrospective trust will also arise over property that has been transferred by C to D (and is still in D's hands) under a gift/contract that has been rescinded in equity on a purely equitable ground.[8]

Where (2) is true, the traditional explanation as to why C will not be allowed to rescind her contract/gift at law is that it is no longer possible to effect *restitutio in integrum* as between C and D: the *bona fide* purchaser's title to X is unimpeachable (even at law) and so title to X can no longer be revested in C. However, it has been argued that in such a case: (a) C should still be able to rescind, and (b) the process of effecting *restitutio in integrum* should take the form of 'pecuniary rescission', under which D would be held liable to C for the value of X.[9] In support of (a), it can be pointed out that: (i) contracts can be rescinded in equity

---

[7] OEZ (n 5) [14.21]–[14.28]. C cannot sue D for committing a breach of trust under this retrospective trust: [16.41]. (The same rule will apply if C is allowed to rescind her contract with/gift to D at law, with the result that she is held to have legally owned X even after she transferred X to D – she will not be able to sue D in conversion for anything D did to X before C rescinded: [14.15].)

[8] OEZ (n 5) [16.39].

[9] See Nyuk Yin Nahan, 'Rescission: A Case for Rejecting the Classical Model?' (1997) 27 WALR 66; Peter Birks, 'Unjust Factors and Wrongs: Pecuniary Rescission for Undue Influence' [1997] RLR 72; Worthington (n 2), 41–42, 65–67; Birke Häcker, 'Rescission and Third Party Rights' [2006] RLR 21.

even after property conveyed under the contract has disappeared into the hands of a *bona fide* purchaser;[10] (ii) where C has been fraudulently induced by D to enter into a contract under which she pays D £1,000, C can rescind the contract at law even if D no longer has the very £1,000 C paid him; (iii) it is hard to see why the impossibility of putting C back in the position she was in before she made her gift to/contracted with D should prevent C rescinding that gift/contract, if that is what she wants to do. So far as (b) is concerned, it has been observed that while 'pecuniary rescission' can be supported where D is still enriched as a result of receiving X, it can operate unfairly where D is no longer enriched as a result of receiving X and did not act reprehensibly when C entered into her contract with/made her gift to D.[11]

7.1.3   Timing of Rescission

A final difference between law and equity relates to *when* a contract/gift will be rescinded. The power to rescind *at law* will be effectively exercised when C gives D notice that she is rescinding; where D is untraceable, this requirement of notice will be dispensed with in favour of requiring C to make a public act indicating an unequivocal intention to rescind.[12]

Though the authorities on the issue are all over the place, the balance of academic opinion favours the view that a contract/gift can only be rescinded *in equity* by going to court.[13] This seems right: given the looser categories of situation where rescission in equity is allowed – and consequent uncertainties in a given case as to whether rescission is justified on equitable grounds – it makes sense to defer the moment rescission is effective in equity until a court can determine the facts of the case. In the case where C seeks to rescind a gift/contract in equity for *fraud or duress*

---

[10] OEZ (n 5) [15.14]–[15.24].   [11] OEZ (n 5) [15.31]–[15.32].

[12] *Car and Universal Finance Co Ltd v Caldwell* [1965] 1 QB 525 (CA). Janet O'Sullivan (in 'Rescission as a Self-help Remedy: A Critical Analysis' (2000) 59 CLJ 509, 531–33) criticises this aspect of the law, arguing that where C has been fraudulently induced to sell a car to D, if C is allowed to rescind and revest title to the car in herself merely by announcing her intention to do so, a third party T who subsequently buys the car from D in ignorance of C's election to rescind will be prejudiced under the *nemo dat* rule. However, as Worthington (n 2) points out (31–32, n 24) T is no more caught out than someone who buys stolen goods in good faith, and this 'does not seem wholly unreasonable'.

[13] JD Heydon, MJ Leeming and PG Turner, *Meagher, Gummow and Lehane's Equity: Doctrines and Remedies* (5th edn, LexisNexis 2014) ('MGL'), [25–105]–[25–110]; O'Sullivan, 'Rescission as a Self-help Remedy' (n 12) 517–18; OEZ (n 5) [11.108] (at least where fraud is not involved).

because title to the property X that she passed to D under that gift/contract is incapable of automatically revesting in C, C's interests are not prejudiced by a rule that she has to go to court in order to rescind her gift/contract – even were she allowed to rescind in equity by simply telling D she is rescinding,[14] doing this would merely result in D's holding X on trust for C, and C would therefore still be vulnerable to someone's subsequently purchasing X in good faith.

7.2 Rationale

It seems unlikely that we can come to any intelligent conclusions as to how the law on rescission should operate without knowing why we have a law on rescission in the first place. To discuss this issue, let us consider a case where *Granny* owns a painting that has been in her family for years. Unknown to *Granny*, the painting is by Rembrandt, and worth £20 million. *Granny* is hard up for money, and takes the painting to *Dealer* to be valued; *Dealer* recognises the painting for what it is, but lies to *Granny* and tells her it is by an undistinguished nineteenth century Flemish painter, and offers to buy it from her for £25,000. *Granny* happily sells the painting to *Dealer* but soon after discovers the truth when she reads about an upcoming auction where *Dealer* is putting her painting up for sale as a recently rediscovered Rembrandt. *Granny* rings *Dealer* and tells him she wants her painting back. By doing this *Granny* will have effectively rescinded her contract with *Dealer*, with all the effects specified above. The question is: why is *Granny* allowed to rescind her contract with *Dealer*?

7.2.1 Consent

Consent-based theories of rescission argue that *Granny* is allowed to rescind her contract with *Dealer* because she did not properly consent to enter into that contract. Lionel Smith argues that *Granny*'s lack of consent means that she has not validly made a contract with *Dealer*;[15] however, plainly she has, otherwise there would be nothing to rescind. Worthington argues that rescission is allowed in cases where we cannot tell, until C stands up and tells us so, whether C validly consented to make

---

[14] Which OEZ think is the position where fraud or duress is involved: OEZ (n 5) [11.108], [16.37]–[16.38].

[15] Lionel Smith, 'Unjust Enrichment – Big or Small?' in Simone Degeling and James Edelman (eds), *Unjust Enrichment in Commercial Law* (Thomson Reuters 2008), 40–41.

a gift or enter into a contract; before C does this, our default position will be to assume that C has validly consented to the gift or contract.[16] But here we know everything about what happened to *Granny*, and we would still not find that *Granny's* contract with *Dealer* was null and void *until Granny* said she wanted to avoid it. More generally, consent-based theories of rescission founder on the fact that rescission is available in circumstances where we cannot say that C's consent to exercising a legal power to do *x* was absent: for example, in cases where C exercised that power in favour of D in ignorance of facts that D was duty-bound to tell C about;[17] or cases where C acted in breach of an equitable duty in exercising that power.[18]

7.2.2   Unjust Enrichment

Unjust enrichment-based theories of rescission argue that *Granny* is allowed to rescind her contract with *Dealer* in order to prevent *Dealer* being unjustly enriched at her expense. The argument goes as follows. It seems undeniable that *Dealer* has been unjustly enriched at *Granny's* expense in that he has obtained a benefit from her by lying to her about the provenance of her painting. This gives us a reason to want to give back to *Granny* what *Dealer* has obtained from her. However, so long as the *Granny–Dealer* contract remains in place, we cannot. To say that *Granny* and *Dealer* have a valid contract between them, but we are going to reverse the effects of that contract, seems to involve us in a contradiction.[19] Before we can prevent *Dealer* being unjustly enriched, we have to wipe out the contract – and that is what rescission is there to do.

The same would apply in an alternative scenario where *Granny* gives her painting – not knowing it is worth £20 million – to her favourite

---

[16] Worthington (n 2), 29–30.

[17] *Sybron Corp v Rochem Ltd* [1984] Ch 112 (CA) (wrongful failure to disclose breaches of contract of employment); *Demerara Bauxite Co Ltd v Hubbard* [1923] AC 673 (PC) (wrongful failure to disclose full information regarding value of land which solicitor obtained option to purchase from his client). By way of comparison, neither the criminal law (*R v Dica* [2004] EWCA Crim 1103, [2004] QB 1257), nor tort law (*Chatterton v Gerson* [1981] QB 432 (QB)) requires consent to be informed before it will be regarded as being valid.

[18] *Holder v Holder* [1968] Ch 353 (CA) 398 (sale by trustee to himself of trust property voidable within reasonable period of time by beneficiary); *Pitt* (n 4) [93] (distribution of trust property in breach of equitable duty).

[19] See Daniel Friedmann, 'Valid, Voidable, Qualified, and Non-existing Obligations: An Alternative Perspective on the Law of Restitution' in Andrew Burrows (ed), *Essays on the Law of Restitution* (Oxford University Press 1991), 247–48.

Nephew as a twenty-first birthday present and shortly after discovers the
true value of the painting. We might think that *Granny*'s mistake means
that *Nephew* has been unjustly enriched at *Granny*'s expense, and this
gives us a reason to want to give *Granny* back what *Nephew* has obtained
from her. However, we cannot do this so long as the law says that *Granny*
has made a valid gift to *Nephew*.[20] Before we can reverse *Nephew*'s unjust
enrichment, the gift must be wiped out – and, again, that is what rescission is there to do.

There are three problems with this theory. First, it seems to have the
law backwards. On this theory, we allow rescission in order to reverse
what has happened between *Granny* and *Dealer/Nephew*. However, the
conventional understanding is that we reverse what has happened
between *Granny* and *Dealer/Nephew* because *Granny* has rescinded her
contract with *Dealer*, or her gift to *Nephew*.[21]

The second is that we can easily envisage scenarios where we know
rescission will be allowed, but where it is difficult to say that the effects of
rescission being allowed is to reverse an unjust enrichment. For example,
suppose that *Dealer* got it wrong and the painting he bought from
Granny turns out not to be by Rembrandt at all, but by an obscure
contemporary of Rembrandt's and is worth about £15,000 – £10,000
less than *Dealer* paid *Granny* for it. If, for whatever reason, *Granny*
seeks to rescind her contract with *Dealer*, it is hard to say that we allow
Granny to rescind her contract with *Dealer* in order to prevent *Dealer*
being unjustly enriched.[22]

---

[20] *Allcard v Skinner* (1887) 36 Ch D 145 (CA). OEZ (n 5) argue (at [29.34]–[29.35]) that had
Granny given *Nephew* money (perhaps intending to pay £200 electronically into his bank
account, but sending him £20,000 through a 'fat finger' accident), rescission of the gift is
not necessary to allow *Granny* to sue *Nephew* in unjust enrichment for the value of the
money.

[21] Of course, it could be that when we are reversing what has happened between *Granny* and
Dealer or *Granny* and *Nephew*, we are seeking to prevent unjust enrichment *because*
Granny's act of rescission has made it so that if we do not reverse then *Dealer* or *Nephew*
will be unjustly enriched. Those who think that the receipt of rights or value will be
unjustly enriching when there was no legal basis for that receipt will be particularly
attracted to this view. However, that still does not explain why *Granny* is allowed to
rescind in the first place.

[22] Chambers acknowledges that at the level of *value* we cannot say *Dealer* has been enriched
in this case, but argues that we can still say that *Dealer* has been enriched by virtue of the
rights (over the painting) that he has received from *Granny*: Robert Chambers, 'Two
Kinds of Enrichment', in Robert Chambers, Charles Mitchell and James Penner (eds),
Philosophical Foundations of the Law of Unjust Enrichment (Oxford University Press
2009), 258–61. However, both McFarlane and Bant have pointed out that even in the
realm of rights it is difficult to say that *Dealer* has been enriched under his contract with

The third problem is an extension of the second. There are circumstances where *Bride* – who has got married to *Groom* – can rescind her marriage. The circumstances are very similar to those that allow rescission of a contract/gift: in particular, *Bride* can rescind the marriage if at the time of the marriage 'she did not validly consent to it, whether in consequence of duress, mistake, unsoundness of mind or otherwise'.[23] And *Bride* will lose her ability to rescind her marriage with *Groom* in circumstances very similar to those that will result in someone losing the ability to rescind a contract/gift: in particular, she will not be allowed to set the marriage aside if she does not seek to have it set aside within three years of entering into it.[24] It is hard to imagine anyone would seek to argue that when *Bride* is allowed to rescind her marriage with *Groom* she is allowed to do so in order to prevent *Groom* being unjustly enriched. So why should we adopt such an analysis in cases where people are allowed to rescind contracts or gifts?

7.2.3   Unconscionability

Tony Weir sought to draw an analogy between the law on rescission and the Roman *exceptio doli*, which instructed a Roman judge to allow a claim in debt:

> 'Unless the plaintiff has acted or is acting in bad faith.' It is the conjunction of the perfect and present tense which is so genial ... [W]e have here the explanation for the fact, otherwise a little surprising, that equity would rescind a transaction not only where the misrepresentation was fraudulent, but also where it was entirely innocent. Telling deliberate lies, of course, is manifestly bad, and making an honest mistake is not, but if you do make an honest mistake in what you say and the other party believes you and contracts on that basis, it would be very bad of you to try to take advantage of the mistake you innocently caused, and equity will not allow you to do it. Although there is no fraud in the transaction, there is fraud in the action ... [25]

Granny given that *Dealer*'s rights against *Granny* were matched by rights that *Granny* had against *Dealer*: see Ben McFarlane, 'Unjust Enrichment, Rights and Value' in Donal Nolan and Andrew Robertson (eds), *Rights and Private Law* (Hart Publishing 2011), 584–85 and Elise Bant, 'Rights and Value in Rescission' in Donal Nolan and Andrew Robertson (eds), *Rights and Private Law* (Hart Publishing 2011), 614–15.

[23] Matrimonial Causes Act 1973, s 12(c).   [24] Matrimonial Causes Act 1973, s 13(2).

[25] Tony Weir, 'Contracts in Rome and England' (1992) 66 Tulane LR 1615, 1624 (footnotes omitted). Cf *Redgrave v Hurd* (1881) 20 Ch D 1 (CA) 12–13 (Jessel MR): 'Even assuming that moral fraud must be shewn in order to set aside a contract, you have it where a man, having obtained a beneficial contract by a statement which he now knows to be false, insists upon keeping that contract. To do so is a moral delinquency: no man ought to seek to take advantage of his own false statements.'

RESCISSION   159

What is being advanced here is an unconscionability-based theory of the law on rescission: C is allowed to rescind a contract/gift in order to prevent D from taking unfair advantage of some weakness of C's. This theory works best where: (1) C's contract/gift was procured by some unfair advantage-taking by D (as in our example of *Granny* and *Dealer*), or by a third party where D was aware of what the third party was doing; or (2) D seeks to enforce a contract knowing that C entered into it because of an innocent misrepresentation that D made.[26]

However, the theory works a lot less well where: (3) D receives a gift that was made by C under the influence of an innocent misrepresentation or a spontaneous mistake (i.e. a mistake that was not induced by anyone), or as a result of unfair advantage-taking by a third party of which D was unaware at the time the gift was made; (4) C seeks to rescind a contract that she entered into with D because of an innocent misrepresentation where the contract has been completely performed; (5) rescission is sought of a contract or distribution of property made by C, a trustee, in breach of an equitable duty. In all of these cases, it is hard to say that D is taking unfair advantage of any weakness of C's because D is not actually doing anything – in (3) and (5) he was, and continues to be, the passive recipient of C's largesse; in (4) he is not seeking to hold C to her contract with him because the contract has already been performed.[27] Moreover, it is hard to see what 'weakness' of C's is being taken advantage of in (5), where C was entirely responsible for her breach of duty and may have actively sought to commit that breach of duty.

7.2.4   The Balance Theory

None of the existing theories of why we have a law of rescission works that well. I think a better theory of rescission would start from the idea that the law endows us with powers to make contracts or gifts in order

---

[26] A lot of the relevant authorities and *dicta* supporting the idea that rescission in situations (1) and (2) is allowed to prevent unconscionable conduct are usefully gathered together in Pauline Ridge, 'Third Party Volunteers and Undue Influence' (2014) 130 LQR 112, 120–21. See also MGL (n 13) [13–010]–[13–015]; and *Earl of Chesterfield v Janssen* (1750) 2 Ves Sen 125, 155; 28 ER 82, 100 (rescission of contract 'such as no man in his senses and not under delusion would make on the one hand, and as no honest and fair man would accept on the other').

[27] Cf *Seddon v The North Eastern Salt Co Ltd* [1905] 1 Ch 326 (Ch), holding that rescission would not be allowed in (4), a position reversed by s 1(b) of the Misrepresentation Act 1967. See also *Selway v Fogg* (1839) 5 M & W 83, 151 ER 36 (no remedy for claimant wishing to rescind executed contract for services).

that certain goods might be achieved that cannot be achieved, or can only be achieved with much more difficulty, in the absence of those powers. This idea suggests that:

Where C has formally exercised a legal power P, but:

(a) the circumstances in which C exercised that power mean that (i) the goods which the exercise of power P was meant to realise for C are likely to be absent or (ii) are accompanied by harms for C that we are not normally happy to tolerate as a side effect of allowing people to exercise power P, and

(b) allowing C to undo her exercise of P would not do more harm than the good we are trying to do by allowing C to escape what she has done,

then we have good reason to allow C to undo her exercise of power P, if that is what she wants to do. Let us call this the 'balance theory' of rescission (or 'BT' for short) as giving effect to it involves balancing a number of different considerations.

According to BT, then, in order to determine whether or not C should be allowed to rescind the exercise of a particular power P, we first have to ask why that power exists. Once again, the comparison with rescinding a marriage is illuminating – the factors that allow a marriage to be rescinded (lack of consummation, lack of genuine consent, mental disorder on the part of one of the parties, the fact that the other party had a venereal disease or was pregnant by someone else at the time of the marriage)[28] reflect a particular vision of what goods are sought to be achieved by allowing people to marry each other (namely, providing a platform for two people to achieve the closest kind of union – physical, emotional, and biological – that any two people can achieve with each other) and where the power to marry is formally exercised in circumstances that mean those goods are unlikely to be realised, there is a case for allowing the exercise of that power to be rescinded.

BT argues that we allow *Granny* to rescind her contract with *Dealer* because, while the goods that are supposed to be realised through the exercise of the power to make a contract with another – enabling people to coordinate in a reliable way the production and exchange of goods and services[29] – are present in *Granny*'s case, they are accompanied by a very

---

[28] Matrimonial Causes Act 1973, s 12.

[29] Cf Jonathan Morgan, *Contract Law Minimalism* (Cambridge University Press 2013), chs 1–2.

substantial harm (*Granny*'s being cheated of her property) that we are not prepared to tolerate as a side effect of our endowing people with the power to make contracts with others. All cases where C is allowed to rescind a contract/gift that has been procured through unfair advantage-taking by D can be explained on a similar basis.

BT also explains why, when C makes a gift to D as a result of unfair advantage-taking by T, the gift can be rescinded without proving that D was aware of the unfair advantage-taking at the time of the gift,[30] whereas if C enters into a contract with D under similar circumstances, the contract cannot be rescinded if D was not aware of T's unfair advantage-taking at the time the contract was entered into.[31] Where C makes a gift to D, and everything else is equal, the gift can be undone without doing more harm than good whatever D's state of knowledge was of how that gift came to be made. The same is not true where D entered into a contract with C not knowing that the contract was a result of T's unfair advantage-taking – in such a case, allowing the contract to be rescinded would undermine the goods that we are trying to achieve by allowing people to make contracts: D's ability to rely on his expectation that he has a good contract with C would be frustrated.

BT can also explain why we allow rescission of contracts or distributions of property that have been made by a trustee in breach of duty: almost by definition, the exercise of a power in breach of duty must be accompanied by harms we are not prepared to tolerate as a side effect of giving people that power, and give us reason to want to undo the exercise of that power.

So BT can account for all that the unconscionability-based theory of rescission can, and much that it cannot. But what does BT imply as to when C should be allowed to rescind a contract/gift that she has made because of a mistake – either a spontaneous mistake, or a mistake innocently induced by someone else?

7.3 Rescission for Mistake

7.3.1 Spontaneous Mistake

The authorities on when a gift can be rescinded because C made that gift as a result of a spontaneous mistake (or 'SM' for short) as to the circumstances existing at the time of the gift, and the pre-*Great Peace*

---

[30] *Bridgeman v Green* (1757) Wilm 58, 97 ER 22. [31] See text at n 6.

authorities on when a contract could be rescinded on similar grounds, are spectacularly opaque.

Gifts made because of an SM can only be rescinded where C's mistake was so grave that it would be unconscionable not to allow C to rescind her gift.[32] Lord Walker indicated in *Pitt v Holt* that this test would 'normally be satisfied only when there is a mistake either as to the legal character or nature of a transaction, or as to some matter of fact or law which is basic to the transaction'.[33] Beyond this, Lord Walker was unwilling to go, emphasising instead that everything would depend on the facts of the case.[34] Given this, it is impossible to say whether *Granny*'s gift to her *Nephew* of a painting that turns out to be by Rembrandt and worth £20 million could be rescinded. So far as contracts are concerned, the decision of the Court of Appeal in *Solle v Butcher*[35] opened the door to the possibility of a contract entered into by C with D being rescinded on the basis that C entered into that contract because of an SM where (1) D shared in C's mistake, (2) C was not at fault for the mistake, and (3) the mistake was 'fundamental'.[36] Neither *Solle* nor the subsequent cases applying *Solle*[37] give us any idea as to what amounts to a 'fundamental' mistake.

Faced with this uncertainty, it is unsurprising that academics should be in favour of adopting a simple rule under which gifts made because of an SM can always be rescinded (other things being equal);[38] and that the Court of Appeal in *Great Peace* should have, in the interests of commercial certainty, declared that the courts have no jurisdiction to rescind a contract on the basis that it was entered into because of an SM.[39] However, neither position is based on a principled understanding as to why rescission is allowed.

What does BT have to tell us about: (1) when a gift should be rescinded because it was made because of an SM, and (2) whether *Great Peace* was correct to rule out the rescission of contracts made because of an SM? In order to answer these questions, we need to make use of something

---

[32] *Ogilvie* (n 4) 400 (Lindley LJ); *Pitt* (n 4) [122], [128] (Lord Walker).   [33] Ibid [122].
[34] Ibid [126].   [35] [1950] 1 KB 671 (CA).
[36] Ibid 693 (Denning LJ); also 686 (Bucknill LJ).
[37] *Grist v Bailey* [1967] Ch 532 (CA) (rescission of sale of land where price fixed in belief that land subject to protected tenancy); *Magee v Pennine Insurance Co Ltd* [1969] 2 QB 507 (CA) (rescission of settlement of claim on voidable insurance policy); *Laurence v Lexcourt Holdings Ltd* [1978] 1 WLR 1128 (CA) (rescission of lease of floors of building entered into in belief that floors could be used as offices).
[38] Birke Häcker, 'Mistaken Gifts after *Pitt v Holt*' (2014) 67 CLP 333.
[39] *Great Peace* (n 3) [153]–[157].

like the table set out below, which details the goods that are sought to be achieved by empowering people to make gifts/contracts (column (1)), the harms attendant on people making gifts/contracts because of an SM (column (2)), and the harms that might be caused by allowing people to rescind gifts/contracts because of an SM (column (3)). Where a gift/contract is made by C because of an SM in circumstances that mean:

(a) the goods specified in column (1) are likely to be missing, or the harms specified in column (2) are present and sufficiently weighty as to be intolerable; *and*
(b) the harms specified in column (3) are missing or are not significant enough to deter us from allowing C to rescind;

then the case for allowing C to rescind her gift/contract is very strong.

	(1) Goods sought to be achieved by empowering people to make ...	(2) Harms that might be attendant on making ... because of SM	(3) Harms that might be caused by allowing rescission of ... because of SM
Gifts	Allowing D to benefit from C's surplus wealth	(i) Regret by C (ii) Regret by D	(i) Turning gifts into a mixed blessing (ii) Depriving C of chance to learn from her mistakes
Contracts	Enabling D and C to co-ordinate in a reliable way production and exchange of goods and services	Regret by C	(i) Making contracts unreliable (ii) Depriving C of chance to learn from her mistakes

Applying this table to the case of *Granny* unwittingly gifting a Rembrandt painting to *Nephew*, there is a strong case for allowing rescission as *Granny's* SM means that the good to be achieved through allowing people to make gifts has not been achieved here (she has not donated any of her *surplus* wealth to *Nephew* but the overwhelmingly vast majority of the wealth that she in fact possessed), and the facts of *Granny's* case are so unusual that (i) allowing her to rescind the gift will not generally make people fear that every time they receive a gift they are also making themselves a potential target for a lawsuit, thus turning the gift into a mixed blessing, and (ii) refusing to rescind the gift will not teach *Granny* to take more care in the future about checking the value of the gifts she makes. Rescission of the gift in *Lady Hood of Avalon v Mackinnon*[40] can be supported on a similar basis – the fact that the claimant in that case made her gift forgetting that the same gift had already been made a few years before meant that she was not sharing her surplus wealth with the defendant daughter, but was instead (and unwittingly) making a sacrifice.

Rescission of the gifts in *In re Griffiths*[41] and *Pitt v Holt*[42] – which attracted inheritance tax that could have been avoided had they been made differently – cannot be justified on the basis that the goods sought to be achieved by allowing people to make gifts were not achieved in those cases, but can be justified by reference to the harms attendant on making a gift because of an SM. Of the harms listed in column (2), C's regret at making the gift is a harm we are usually prepared to tolerate as a side effect of giving people the power to make gifts; we do this in order to ensure that gifts do not turn into mixed blessings and in order to give people like C the chance to learn from their mistakes.[43] So there is no case – according to BT – for allowing rescission of the gift in Andrew Tettenborn's example where *Uncle* gives a wedding present to *Niece* not knowing that she is marrying a man he hates.[44] However, where D regrets C's making the gift to D – because C could have made it in a way that would have been much more beneficial for D – and C is no longer alive to learn from her mistake in making her gift to D in the way she did, the case for allowing rescission becomes very one-sided in favour of rescission.

Turning to contracts made because of an SM by C, the above table indicates that the Court of Appeal was right to rule in *Great Peace* that where C and D entered into a contract based on an SM that was shared between C and D, rescission should not be available – C's regret at entering the contract is not sufficient ground to justify disrupting D's reasonable expectation that he had a valid contract with C. However, a much

---

[40] [1909] 1 Ch 476 (Ch).   [41] [2008] EWHC 118 (Ch), [2009] Ch 162.   [42] *Pitt* (n 4).

[43] The need to ensure that people are given the chance to learn from their mistakes is why 'Children quickly learn that if they give their toys away they cannot expect to get them back.': Peter Birks, *An Introduction to the Law of Restitution* (rev edn, Oxford University Press 1989), 9.

[44] Andrew Tettenborn, *Law of Restitution in England and Ireland* (3rd edn, Cavendish Publishing 2002), 76.

stronger case for allowing rescission can be made where D was *aware* of C's SM.[45] This is because D would not have any reasonable expectation that he had a valid contract with C if (a) he was aware of C's SM, and (b) there existed a rule that a contract entered into as a result of an SM could be rescinded by C where (i) D was aware of C's SM, and (ii) D's superior knowledge was not the result of any exercise of skill and judgment on D's part for which D should be rewarded. The only objection to allowing C to rescind in such a case would be that doing so would not give C any incentive to learn from her mistakes. In order to accommodate this objection, a third requirement – that (iii) C was not at fault for her SM – could be added to the first two.

7.3.2 Innocently Induced Mistake

Something like the rule I have suggested should apply to determine whether C can rescind a contract that she entered into with D because of an SM *does* apply where C entered into a contract with D because of a mistake induced by a third party T who made a misrepresentation to C. If C can prove that D was aware of her mistake at the time he contracted with C, then she will be entitled to rescind her contract with D.[46]

In contrast, if C's contract with D was induced by D's making a misrepresentation to C, then C will be entitled to rescind the contract even if D made the misrepresentation innocently, without knowing that he was inducing C to make a mistake. Michael Bridge questions why this is so, arguing that 'Serious consideration should be given to the abolition of rescission for innocent misrepresentation.'[47] However, if BT is correct, we can support the idea of C's being allowed to rescind a contract entered into with D as a result of an innocent misrepresentation by D. One of the harms attendant on C's entering into such a contract (which is not present when C enters into a contract with D as a result of an SM) will

---

[45] Cf Christian von Bar, Eric Clive and Hans Schulte-Nölke (eds), *Principles, Definitions and Model Rules of European Private Law, Draft Common Frame of Reference (DCFR)*, <http://ec.europa.eu/justice/contract/files/european-private-law_en.pdf> (accessed 14 October 2015), II-7:201(1)(b)(ii), and the (currently withdrawn) draft Common European Sales Law: Commission, 'Proposal for a Regulation of the European Parliament and of the Council on a Common European Sales Law', COM (2011) 635 final, Art 48(1)(b)(iii), both of which contemplate that D's knowledge of C's SM could provide a basis for C's rescinding her contract with D.

[46] See n 6.

[47] Michael Bridge, 'Innocent Misrepresentation in Contract' (2004) 57 CLP 277, 303.

be a residual suspicion on C's part that D *may* have *deliberately* lied to her, and consequent distrust of D. Allowing C to rescind her contract with D will not remove this harm, but locking C into her contract with D and telling C that she can only be released *if* D deliberately lied to her will certainly encourage C to entertain and make the most of her suspicions far more than is the case than under the current law, which allows C amicably to escape her deal with D without recriminations and accusations.

On similar grounds, BT would support C being allowed to rescind a gift made to D as a result of an innocent misrepresentation made by D. BT has the most difficulty, however, with the question of whether C should be allowed to rescind a gift made to D as a result of an innocent misrepresentation made by T of which D was ignorant at the time of the gift. However, it may be that rescission can be supported on the basis that: (1) T's misrepresentation will often have the effect of inducing C to make a mistake that, had it been spontaneous, would have entitled C to rescind anyway under the analysis developed in the previous section; (2) the cases where this is not true[48] will be so few and far between that allowing rescission across the board in cases where C makes a gift as a result of an innocent misrepresentation made by T will not make people who receive gifts fear that receiving a gift will make them a target for a lawsuit, thus turning the gift into a mixed blessing.

7.4 Proprietary Claims and Rescission

Let us now consider what position the law should take on whether C can make a proprietary claim where C transferred to D title to an item of property X under a contract/gift that has been rescinded. For simplicity's sake, we will initially assume the contract/gift has been rescinded for D's *fraud*, before going on to consider more complex cases. Two proprietary claims will be considered: (1) a claim to X; and (2) a claim to any substitutes (S) obtained by D in return for X.

---

[48] This will be the case in an adaptation of Tettenborn's example (text at n 44), where *Uncle* is on his guard against making a gift to *Niece* that he will later regret, so he asks his wife what *Niece*'s fiancé does and she says 'He's a writer' (which is what *Niece* told her, not wanting to confess the full truth that her fiancé writes pornographic scripts and then turns them into films) and *Uncle*, satisfied that *Niece* has nothing to do with his hated enemy the pornographer, gives her a valuable painting as a wedding present.

7.4.1   Claim to X

So long as X has not, before C rescinded, ended up in the hands of a *bona fide* purchaser, the law is clear that once C has rescinded her contract/gift, C can make a proprietary claim to X: if title to X is capable of automatically revesting in C, then she will be held to be the legal owner of X (and to have owned X both before and after she transferred X to D); if it is not so capable (call this situation '*Sticky Title*') then title to X will be held on trust for C (and will be regarded as having been held on trust for C as soon as she transferred it to D).

In the case where C transferred (say) a car to D under a contract with D which she then rescinded for D's fraud, William Swadling has questioned whether C should be allowed to claim that she is now (and always was) the legal owner of that car.[49] He argues that the fact that C's contract with D has been wiped out does not mean that D cannot establish a good title to the car. To establish a good title, he can simply rely on the fact that C physically delivered the car to D, intending to transfer title to the car to D.[50] If Swadling's argument is right, then the rewriting of history that we engage in when we allow C to rescind her contract with D will not work to establish that she never gave up title to her car, and if C wants to make a proprietary claim in relation to the car, she will have to argue that the car is, and was, held on trust for her – as she would in a *Sticky Title* situation.

Swadling's argument does not seem to work in the case where it is established as a matter of fact that D obtained title to C's car when he *entered* into the contract to buy it from her (call this case, '*Transfer of Car by Contract*', or 'TCC' for short).[51] In TCC, wiping out the contract also wipes out the basis of D's title to C's car, with the result that C can claim the car always belonged to her, even after she transferred physical possession of it to D. But what about the case where *making* the contract did not give D title to C's car, but it was C's subsequent act of delivery that gave D title to the car (call this case '*Transfer of Car by Delivery*', or 'TCD' for short)?

In TCD, some academics argue that just as C can rescind her contract with D for fraud, she can *also* rely on D's fraud to rescind whatever she did to transfer to D title to her car.[52] However, while you can rescind

[49] William Swadling, 'Rescission, Property, and the Common Law' (2005) 121 LQR 123.
[50] Ibid 139–42; see also Tony Weir, 'Taking for Granted – The Ramifications of *Nemo Dat*' (1996) 49 CLP 325, 339–43.
[51] This will be the case where Sale of Goods Act 1979, s 18 rule 1, applies.
[52] Birke Häcker, 'Rescission of Contract and Revesting of Title: A Reply to Mr Swadling' [2006] RLR 106, 110; Michael Bridge, Louise Gullifer, Gerard McMeel and Sarah Worthington, *The Law of Personal Property* (Sweet & Maxwell 2013), [13–035]; OEZ [1.27].

a *legal* act such as making a contract, or making a gift, it is not clear that you can rescind a *bare* act such as physically handing over a car to D, or an *intention* such as an intention to transfer title to the car to D. The same point applies where D fraudulently induces C to *give* him a car, and C subsequently rescinds the gift. We are not *logically compelled* to find that C's rescinding the gift means that she is now (and always was) legal owner of the car. We *could* find that: (i) C's physical act of delivering the car to D with the requisite intention to transfer was effective to transfer title to the car to D, and (ii) C's subsequent rescission of her gift does not have any effect on that – C's act of rescission simply means that D did not receive title to the car *as a gift*, with the result that D is personally liable to C for the value of the car, or (perhaps) holds the car on trust for C.

So it seems that the *only* situation where we are *logically compelled* to find that C can make a proprietary claim to an item of property X that she has transferred to D under a transaction that has been rescinded for fraud is where title to X is capable of automatically revesting in C, and C transferred title to X to D by performing a legal act, such as making a contract with D or making a deed, the effect of which act has been wiped out by rescinding it. In all other cases, whether C can make a proprietary claim to X must be decided as a matter of *principle* rather than logic.

As a matter of principle, Swadling cannot see why the victim of fraud should not be confined to making a personal money claim against the fraudster, whether the claim is based on the wrongness of the fraud, or the fact that the fraudster has been unjustly enriched at his victim's expense.[53] However:

(1) Given that we *must* find that C can claim legal ownership of the car in TCC, the law would operate in an arbitrary fashion if it did not *also* allow C to claim legal ownership of the car in TCD given that 'the parties [to a contract to sell a car], as lay people, will probably give no thought to the exact mechanism of conveyance [of the car]'.[54]

(2) Where C has transferred title to an item of property X to D under a contract that has been rescinded for fraud in a *Sticky Title* situation, the only way C can make a claim to X is to argue that title to X is held on trust for her. Given that C *will* be able to assert a proprietary interest in the car in TCC and (I argue) in TCD, it would again seem

---

[53] Swadling, 'Rescission, Property, and the Common Law' (n 49) 135–36.
[54] Häcker, 'Rescission of Contract and Revesting of Title' (n 52) 109.

arbitrary for the law not to allow C to assert a proprietary/trust interest in X in *Sticky Title*: it would seem irrational for C to be confined to a personal remedy simply because, as a matter of property law, title to X cannot automatically revest in her on rescinding her contract with D.

(3) And if we say (as we have ended up saying) it is the case that when C transfers an item of property X to D under a *contract* that she subsequently rescinds for D's fraud, C will – other things being equal – be entitled to claim a proprietary interest in X, it would again seem arbitrary to deny that C can claim a proprietary interest in X if she has *given* X to D and has subsequently rescinded the gift because of D's fraud. Gift-givers are not worthy of less protection than contracting parties.

Only one question remains, which is whether C should be able to claim a proprietary interest (which will necessarily be a trust interest) in an item of property X that was transferred to D as a result of a contract/ gift that has been rescinded not for fraud (or duress, for that matter) but on some purely equitable ground such as innocent misrepresentation or undue influence. Here there seems much more justification for Swadling's anti-proprietary stance, as there seems no reason why rescission in equity *needs* to give rise to a proprietary response.[55] Worthington points out that it used to be the case that 'Equity could not order money remedies [against D]: it was confined to proprietary remedies unless the defendant was a fiduciary or a confidant.'[56] However, once we admit the possibility of 'pecuniary rescission'[57] there seems no reason why C should not be confined to making money claims against D to be restored to the position she was in before she contracted with/made a gift to D that she subsequently rescinded in equity. Writing extra-judicially, Lord Millett has suggested a qualification to this – that C should be able (and only be able) to claim a trust/ proprietary interest in X where X is 'land or other property of special value [to C]';[58] in such a case 'pecuniary rescission' would not be

---

[55] Cf *Westdeutsche Landesbank v Islington LBC* [1996] AC 669 (HL), where the House of Lords rejected the suggestion that if there were no legal basis for C's transferring title to X to D (i.e. C did *not* transfer title to X to D as a gift, or under a valid contract, or pursuant to some other valid legal obligation) then D would necessarily hold title to X on trust for C. To similar effect, see *Re Goldcorp Exchange Ltd* [1995] 1 AC 74 (PC) 102.

[56] Worthington (n 2) 41.   [57] Discussed above, text at nn 9–11.

[58] PJ Millett, 'Restitution and Constructive Trusts' (1998) 114 LQR 399, 416.

adequate to restore C to her position she was in before contracting with/
making a gift to D.[59]

7.4.2 *Claim to S*

Let us now turn to the case where C transferred to D title to X under
a gift/contract but before C rescinded the gift/contract, D transferred title
to X to a *bona fide* purchaser and in return obtained title to S. Once again,
for the sake of simplicity, we assume that C's gift/contract was fraudulently induced by D. Whatever difficulties C might experience in attempt-
ing to rescind her gift/contract at law,[60] C will be allowed to rescind her
gift/contract in equity, and there is clear authority – most of it emanating
from Lord Millett, who, given what has just been said, must now take
a different view – that when C rescinds, she will acquire a retrospective
trust interest in X, which will then allow her to claim an equitable
proprietary/trust interest in S.[61]

Despite the weight of authority in favour of C's being allowed to
claim a proprietary interest in S, it is difficult to justify applying the logic
of 'hard-nosed property rights'[62] to allow C to make a claim to S where
the basis of that claim – C's being recognised as having had a proprietary interest in X at the time D disposed of X in return for S – only exists
because of our desire to allow C to *undo* what she has done. Allowing
C to make a claim to S is not necessary to allow C to escape the
consequences of her having contracted with/made a gift to D unless,
as Worthington suggests, C is claiming a *charge* over S, securing
a money claim for 'pecuniary rescission' against D.[63] So allowing C to

---

[59] It should be noted that Lord Millett has subsequently endorsed Swadling's anti-
proprietary stance without any qualification: Peter Millett, 'Proprietary Restitution' in
Simone Degeling and James Edelman (eds), *Equity in Commercial Law* (Law Book Co
2005), 320, n 31.

[60] See above, text at nn 9–11.

[61] *El Ajou v Dollar Land Holdings* [1993] 3 All ER 717 (Ch) 734; *Bristol & West Building
Society v Mothew* [1998] Ch 1 (CA) 23; *Halifax Building Society v Thomas* [1996] Ch 217
(CA) 226; *Shalson v Russo* [2003] EWHC 1637 (Ch), [2005] Ch 281 [122]. OEZ (n 5) argue
(at [14.33]) that where: (i) D has bartered X for S, or sold X and used the very same cash
from the sale to buy S, and (ii) title to S is capable of automatically vesting in C, C's
rescinding her gift to/contract with D at law should result in C's acquiring legal title to
S. They also argue (at [15.17]–[15.19]) that rescission of C's gift/contract with D in *equity*
will allow her to bring a personal claim for the value of S, as well as a proprietary/trust
claim to S.

[62] *Foskett v McKeown* [2001] 1 AC 102 (HL), 109 (Lord Browne-Wilkinson).

[63] Worthington (n 2) 60.

make a proprietary claim *to* S cannot be justified on the basis that it is a logical outcome of C's having a proprietary claim to X – it has to be justified on some other ground, such as a desire to ensure that fraudsters like D are not allowed to profit from their fraud. However, even if the recognition of proprietary interests *could* be justified on policy-based grounds,[64] it is unlikely that a proprietary claim to S *can* be justified here as a means of ensuring that D cannot profit from his fraud. The reason is that the courts will not even allow a *personal* money claim to be made against a fraudster to strip him of the profits of his fraud.[65] Given this, there seems no justification for allowing a *proprietary* claim to S to be made on exactly the same basis.

If, on rescinding for fraud, the most C should be able to claim by way of a proprietary interest is a charge over S designed to secure a claim for 'pecuniary rescission' against D, then that should be the most C can claim after rescinding on some purely equitable ground. However, in such a case, even a charge over S should be denied C if, had C rescinded earlier, C would not have obtained a proprietary interest in X: C cannot, by rescinding, secure a greater proprietary interest in S than she could ever have had in X.

7.5 Unfinished Business

This chapter has sought to address three controversies over the law of rescission, relating to its rationale, grounds, and effects. We have also touched on two other controversies, over whether 'pecuniary rescission' should be possible,[66] and over when rescission of a contract/gift should be held to have taken place.[67] Two further controversies remain to be resolved: (1) whether *partial rescission* should be allowed (e.g. in a case where C is deceived into thinking that she was entering into a contract on terms *x*, but was in fact entering into a contract on terms *y*, should she should be allowed to rescind the terms *x* contract but be required to fulfil a terms *y* contract instead?);[68] and (2) whether D's *change of position*

---

[64] For criticism, see William Swadling, 'Policy Arguments for Proprietary Restitution' (2008) 28 LS 506.

[65] *Halifax BS v Thomas* (n 61); *Devenish Nutrition Ltd v Sanofi-Aventis SA* [2008] EWCA Civ 1086, [2009] Ch 390.

[66] Text at nn 9–11.   [67] Text at nn 12–14.

[68] Against: OEZ (n 5) [19.34]–[19.35]. For: Jill Poole and Andrew Keyser, 'Justifying Partial Rescission in English Law' (2005) 121 LQR 273. Very doubtful: Peter Watts, 'Partial Rescission: Disentangling the Seedlings, But Not Transplanting Them' in Elise Bant and Matthew Harding (eds), *Exploring Private Law* (Cambridge University Press 2010).

subsequent to his innocently receiving a gift from C that was induced by
T's misbehaviour, or where D induces C to contract with him by making
an innocent misrepresentation, should operate to bar C from rescinding
her gift/contract or limit what the effects will be of rescinding that
gift/contract.[69] However, the foundations laid in this chapter for understanding the law of rescission will, I hope, make the resolution of these
remaining points of dispute relatively straightforward.

---

[69] Theorists who take the view that rescission exists to prevent unjust enrichment are
unsurprisingly in favour: Peter Birks, *Unjust Enrichment* (2nd edn, Oxford University
Press 2005), 210; Andrew Burrows, *The Law of Restitution* (3rd edn, Oxford University
Press 2011), 252; Elise Bant, *The Change of Position Defence* (Hart Publishing 2009),
108–14. But adopting BT will not necessarily result in a different conclusion: someone
who adopts BT will resist allowing rescission where doing so will prejudice an innocent D.

8

Remedies for Vindicating Ownership Rights in Real Property

AMY GOYMOUR

8.1 Introduction

'Firmly embedded in English folklore' is the idea that an 'Englishman's home [or, more broadly, his land] is his castle.'[1] This encapsulates two key propositions: (i) an owner may do as he pleases in his castle; and (ii) the law 'provides a remedy to enable the owner ... to secure the eviction of trespassers from [his castle]'.[2] There are numerous, well-documented exceptions to the first proposition. Most obviously, an owner cannot murder, build in breach of planning regulations, or annoy neighbours by committing the tort of nuisance on his land. By contrast, the second proposition – that owners can recover their land *in specie* from unauthorised interferers – is relatively under-explored. It forms the focus of this chapter.

At first glance, the proposition seems correct.[3] Real property, unlike personal property, can indeed be specifically vindicated, via the common law's 'action for the recovery of land'. This action has been described as 'essentially a [classical Roman law] *vindicatio*', which responds to an owner's 'direct assertion of his ownership'.[4]

However, a deeper examination of the landowner's position vis-à-vis interferers reveals a more complex and puzzling remedial landscape.

I am extremely grateful to Simon Gardner, Rachel Leow, Graham Virgo and Stephen Watterson for their helpful comments on earlier drafts, and to the participants at the 2015 Commercial Remedies Workshop. All errors are my own.
[1] *Malik v Fassenfelt* [2013] EWCA Civ 798 [1] (Ward LJ).
[2] Ibid; also *Entick v Carrington* (1765) 19 Stat Tr 1029, 1060; 95 ER 807, 817.
[3] See Graham Virgo, *Principles of the Law of Restitution* (3rd edn, Oxford University Press 2015) 632; Andrew Burrows (ed), *Principles of the English Law of Obligations* (Oxford University Press 2015) 388.
[4] Burrows (n 3) 211–12.

The 'recovery' action is more limited than its name might suggest, and, furthermore, sits alongside an untidy assortment of other remedial options, such as injunctions, self-help, and monetary awards. This is strikingly uncharted territory for land law scholarship which typically focuses on land law as a subject about property 'rights' and 'priorities between rights', leaving relatively neglected the remedies afforded to right-holders if things go wrong. And yet these remedies are clearly crucial: rights are meaningless for their owners unless they can be practically enforced. In our capitalist economy, land is a highly prized asset, whether as store of wealth, a generator of wealth, or for more strategic or personal reasons. A stable and commercially sensitive legal system should ensure that landowners' rights receive adequate and coherent remedial protection against adverse interferences.

Sections 8.2 and 8.3 of this chapter expose the remedial responses available for the various 'ills' that may befall a landowner. Cumulatively, they resemble the contents of a disorderly 'medicine cabinet'. Over the years, various potions – old and new, legal and equitable, common law and statutory – have been shoved into the cabinet, without any real consideration of the problems that may result from this haphazard strategy: problems of remedial duplication, inconsistency or gaps. Section 8.4 exposes four of the most pressing of these problems, as a starting-point for future resolution.

8.2   Setting the Scene: 'Ills' Requiring a Remedy

This chapter focuses on the remedial protection(s) afforded to a *private* (rather than public) owner of an *unencumbered registered freehold*[5] estate in land, in the event of unauthorised interference by another private party. It also proceeds on the well-established basis that most landowners would prefer *in specie* protection to a monetary award.[6]

Typically, ownership of an unencumbered freehold confers two major entitlements: (i) an abstract freehold right; and (ii) a concomitant right to enjoy physical possession of the land. Both entitlements are vulnerable to interference. A '*legal* interference' occurs where the owner's abstract right is affected; conversely, '*physical* interferences' involve unauthorised

---

[5] The freehold is 'for almost all practical purposes, equivalent to full ownership of the land itself': *Mabo v Queensland (No 2)* [1992] HCA 23; (1992) 175 CLR 1, 80.

[6] E.g. Robert Chambers, 'The Importance of Specific Performance', in Simone Degeling and James Edelman (eds), *Equity in Commercial Law* (Thomson Reuters 2005) 431–62.

factual intrusions onto the owner's land, as contemplated by the 'castle' mantra. A complete picture of the law's remedies requires both dimensions to be surveyed.

8.2.1 Physical Interferences

Unauthorised physical intrusions broadly fall into two categories: *possessory* and *non-possessory* physical interferences. This distinction is reflected in the law's remedies.

8.2.1.1 Possessory Interferences

A *possessory interference* occurs when a third party ('X') *possesses* land without the true owner's ('O') authority, to the exclusion of O. For example, X may enter and possess the land as a squatter, or he may possess as a purported tenant or licensee after the lease/licence has expired, or was void *ab initio*. For reasons of space, this chapter will focus on possessory interferences by squatters. Notably, a squatter (X) acquires his own possessory freehold estate on entering into adverse possession, which is exigible against everyone except O: O's freehold is relatively superior, unless and until defeated by the rules of adverse possession.[7] How far can O can vindicate his superior right *in specie*, and recover his 'castle' from X?

8.2.1.2 Non-possessory Interferences

Non-possessory interferences are more common. They arise when X intrudes on O's land without permission, but without taking possession from O. Examples include walking across O's land or swinging a crane into O's airspace.[8] Such conduct is clearly unlawful, but can O obtain an *in specie* remedy to prevent future intrusions?

8.2.2 Legal Interferences

Whilst physical interferences existed in the days of castles and sieges, *legal interferences* are a more modern problem: an unfortunate by-product of our land registration system. The Land Registration Act

---

[7] *Turner v Chief Land Registrar* [2013] EWHC 1382 (Ch), [2013] 2 P&CR 12 [13]–[15] (Roth J).

[8] NB this chapter is not concerned with nuisances, which do not necessarily involve *physical* intrusions.

2002 ('LRA') provides for the 'conclusiveness' of registration, meaning that the Land Register is not only a *reflection* of title, but also a constitutive *source* of legal title. Section 58 provides:

> If, on the entry of a person in the [R]egister as the proprietor of a legal estate, the legal estate would not otherwise be vested in him, it shall be deemed to be vested in him as a result of the registration.

Accordingly, if X manages to procure registration of O's land into his own name, without O's consent or other lawful authority, X becomes the new legal owner by 'statutory magic',[9] thereby usurping O's former ownership rights. A common example is where O's signature on a document apparently transferring the land from O to X is forged, resulting in X's mistaken registration as proprietor.[10] X may afterwards dispose of his registered title to an innocent purchaser, Y. Full *in specie* reversal of X's legal interference requires O to be re-registered as proprietor. How readily should that option be available?

8.2.3   Comparing the Nature of In Specie *Remedies for Physical and Legal Interferences*

In legal interference cases, O seeks to *recover* registered rights *lost* as a result of the interference (termed here a '*reinstatement remedy*', whereby O obtains a *new* version of the right he lost). In contrast, in purely physical interference cases, O seeks to vindicate his *pre-existing, continuing* property rights (a '*vindicatory remedy*').[11] Despite these differences, both remedial forms ultimately aim to put O back into the position he enjoyed pre-interference. Any rationalisation of real property's remedies must confront whether, and to what extent, there should be consistency between the two remedial forms.

8.3   The Content of the Law's Medicine Cabinet

Building on section 8.2, this section examines the individual remedies lying inside the law's 'medicine cabinet', so far as relevant to

---

[9] *Odogwu v Vastguide Ltd* [2008] EWHC 3565 [3] (Rattee J).

[10] See further Amy Goymour, 'Mistaken Registrations of Land: Exploding the Myth of "Title by Registration"' (2013) 72 CLJ 614, 619–20.

[11] NB this distinction loosely corresponds to the distinction between reversing factual and legal enrichments in Andrew Lodder, *Enrichment in the Law of Unjust Enrichment and Restitution* (Hart Publishing 2012) 58–59.

landowners.[12] The remedies can be usefully grouped into four categories: declaratory, *in specie*, monetary and miscellaneous remedies.

8.3.1 Declaratory Remedies

Declaratory remedies involve courts articulating the nature of O's rights in the property as against a defendant, e.g. that O owns a freehold estate and/or is entitled to possession.[13] They equate to a mere 'diagnosis' of the claimant's current legal position; they do not themselves furnish any kind of enforceable 'cure' for physical/legal interferences suffered.[14] In fact, declarations seem futile in *legal interference* cases: they will merely confirm that X, having unlawfully taken O's registered title, is deemed by 'statutory magic' to be the lawful owner of O's land. However, declarations have practical significance in *physical interference* cases: a judicial statement of O's ownership rights might steer defendants away from O's land in the future.

8.3.2 In Specie *Remedies*

In specie remedies form the second remedial category. They remove, either fully or partially, ills that have befallen O's estate. There are four sub-types. Three are vindicatory remedies; the fourth reinstates rights.

8.3.2.1 Self-help

O is sometimes at liberty to physically reclaim his land, by using reasonable force to evict trespassing intruders. Just as certain medicines are self-administered, self-help remedies are effected solely by the owner's *own acts*, without a court order.[15] However, the availability of self-help is limited, in three respects.

First, criminal offences circumscribe the availability of self-help. For example, it is unlawful for O to exercise violence to recover property from X, if someone present at the property opposes O's entry.[16]

Secondly, self-help cannot reverse a *legal interference*. Reversal of a fraudster's mistaken registration in the Land Register requires the

---

[12] See generally Emma Godfrey and Adrian Davis, *Tolley's Claims to the Possession of Land* (5th edn, LexisNexis 2000) (updated regularly).

[13] *Wensley v Persons Unknown* [2014] EWHC 3086 (Ch).

[14] Rafal Zakrzewski, *Remedies Reclassified* (Oxford University Press 2005) 158–64.

[15] Cf Zakrzewski (ibid) 22, 33, 46, for whom 'remedy' means 'right arising from certain *court* orders', concludes that self-help is not a remedy.

[16] Criminal Law Act 1977, s 6.

involvement of the Chief Land Registrar (acting via one of his appointed registrars)[17] and, in some cases, a court.[18]

Thirdly, although the position is unclear,[19] the self-help remedy is probably confined to *non-possessory physical interference* cases. Slade J explained in *Powell v McFarlane* that an owner can exercise self-help against trespassers 'until the possession of land has actually passed to the trespasser'.[20] Accordingly, the intruder's position 'becomes that much more secure' once he takes possession: 'if he will not leave voluntarily, the owner will find himself obliged to bring proceedings for possession'.[21] Two explanations might be offered for this limitation. First, it aligns with other areas of land law, which also specifically protect those who develop significant ties with the relevant land, by occupation or possession: e.g. the European Convention on Human Rights (ECHR), Article 8 protects those occupying land as their 'home'; the LRA prohibits rectification of the Land Register against certain proprietors in 'possession';[22] and the LRA provides that interest-holders in 'actual occupation' enjoy priority against future owners.[23] Secondly, limiting self-help to non-possessory interferences might be explained historically. Out-of-court remedies are only justifiable, if at all, where it is manifestly clear, without a court decision, that the party exercising self-help (O) has a superior entitlement to the land than the intruder (X). This is plainly so where O maintains possession of the land and X is a non-possessory intruder, without entitlement to the land. However, the picture changes once X dispossesses O. On taking possession, X acquires his own freehold estate, which, being second in time, is relatively inferior to O's.[24] Although O has better rights than X, self-help is arguably only warranted where the superiority of O's rights is patently clear. Today, the Land Register provides that proof: O's registered title is patently superior to the squatter's later title. However, in the days prior to land registration, O's superior title was inevitably less obvious. Indeed, unless the title deeds were readily accessible, the outside world might assume that X, the possessor, was owner, rather than O. To avoid protracted uncertainty as to title to the land, it seemed appropriate to channel the dispute through the courts, so that title and

---

[17] LRA, ss 99–100, 132(1) and Sch 7.   [18] Ibid Sch 4.

[19] *Secretary of State for the Environment, Food and Rural Affairs v Meier* [2009] UKSC 11, [2009] 1 WLR 2780 [30] (Lady Hale).

[20] (1977) 38 P&CR 452, 476; also *Lambeth LBC v Rumbelow* (Ch, 25 January 2001). For opposing views, see Ken Oliphant (ed), *The Law of Tort* (2nd edn, LexisNexis 2007) 512.

[21] *Powell* (n 20).   [22] LRA, Sch 4, para 3.   [23] LRA, Sch 3, para 2.   [24] *Turner* (n 7).

remedial solutions could be determined simultaneously. Today, it is questionable (i) whether self-help should continue to have a place in the law's medicine cabinet at all; and, if so, (ii) whether the historic distinction between possessory and non-possessory interferences should be maintained.

8.3.2.2   Action for the Recovery of Land, Leading to a Possession Order

The 'action for the recovery of land' (formerly the 'action for ejectment'),[25] leading to a 'possession order', is one of the most commonly sought remedies in local courts. However, it has received little academic attention to date.[26] This is surprising: the remedy bristles with thorny issues that make it ripe for analysis.

8.3.2.2.1   Conditions for Bringing Action   Procedurally, the action for the recovery of land is exercised by bringing a 'possession claim' within Part 55 of the Civil Procedure Rules ('CPR').[27] 'Recovery' actions and 'possession claims' are seemingly one and the same thing: the CPR is merely a procedural framework for the underlying common law action.[28]

Crucially, the claim is limited to *possessory physical interferences*, more particularly, situations where: (a) O has a right to possess; and (b) X currently possesses the relevant land. Accordingly, the claim cannot be brought against non-possessory intruders,[29] nor against defendants who do not currently possess the land, but who threaten to do so in the future. In *Secretary of State for the Environment v Meier*,[30] for example, the Supreme Court refused the Forestry Commission's possession claim in respect of New Forest land, which protesters were imminently intending to occupy.

---

[25] Until Supreme Court of Judicature Act 1875: *Meier* (n 19) [33].

[26] Exceptions include Mark Wonnacott, *Possession of Land* (Cambridge University Press 2012), David Elvin and Jonathan Karas, *Unlawful Interference with Land* (2nd edn, Sweet & Maxwell 2002), Gary Webber and Daniel Dovar, *Residential Possession Proceedings* (9th edn, Sweet & Maxwell 2013).

[27] Possession proceedings take three forms: ordinary (requiring full trial); summary (this chapter's focus); and interim possession order proceedings: Godfrey and Davis (n 12) ch A4.

[28] This is rarely articulated, but see *Meier* (n 19) [60] (Lord Neuberger); *University of Essex v Djemal* [1980] 1 WLR 1301 (CA) 1304 (Buckley LJ). Cf *Manchester Airport plc v Dutton* [2000] QB 133 (CA) 149 (Laws LJ), suggesting that possession claims be detached from the 'rattling chains of history'/the action for ejectment.

[29] *Meier* (n 19) [4]–[12] (Lord Rodger); cf [35]–[37] (Lady Hale).   [30] Ibid.

Whether these limitations are appropriate is questionable. Indeed, both are showing signs of strain. In *Manchester Airport v Dutton*, the Court of Appeal controversially undermined limitation (a), by extending the remedy to mere contractual licensees, whose licence entitled them to take up *occupation*, rather than possession, of the relevant land.[31] In *Meier*, Lord Neuberger also expressed discomfort with limitation (b): it might lead to 'defect[ive]' remedial protection of owners' rights and, and was 'ripe for consideration' by the relevant reform committee.[32]

8.3.2.2.2 Consequences of a Successful Action Being Brought

A successful possession claim leads to a court making a 'possession order' against X. If X refuses to leave, the court can issue a further 'writ' or 'warrant' of possession, requiring 'the bailiffs or the sheriff physically to remove [X]' from O's land.[33]

Opinions differ as to whether the remedy operates *in personam* or *in rem*. The better view is that it is peculiarly hybrid in nature: the order itself operates *in personam* (it binds only X, the intruder(s)) but is enforced *in rem* (the bailiff/sheriff will 'in principle . . . remove all those who are on the relevant land, irrespective of whether they were parties to the action').[34]

8.3.2.2.3 Availability/Withholding of the Remedy

The most striking feature of the remedy is that a possession order is, at least at common law, available *as of right* whenever the conditions for bring a possession claim are met, even if eviction would cause the trespasser grave hardship and/or homelessness. Thus, a court has 'no discretion' to suspend/withhold a possession order against a squatter;[35] the Englishman can recover his castle. Even Lord Denning MR, normally sympathetic to the plights of the needy, confirmed the remedy's non-discretionary nature, explaining that:

> [i]f homelessness were . . . admitted as a defence to trespass, no one's house could be safe. . . . So the courts must, for the sake of law and order, take a firm stance.[36]

---

[31] *Dutton* (n 28) 150 (Laws LJ).   [32] See n 19 [59], [94].   [33] Ibid [22] (Lady Hale).
[34] Ibid [6] (Lord Rodger).
[35] *McPhail v Persons Unknown* [1973] Ch 447 (CA) 460 (Lord Denning MR); *Boyland & Son Ltd v Rand* [2006] EWCA Civ 1860, [2007] HLR 24.
[36] *Southwark LBC v Williams* [1971] Ch 734 (CA) 744.

This rigid common law rule is, however, being threatened by recent human rights jurisprudence. The Supreme Court has recognised that defendants to possession actions brought by *public* bodies can raise Article 8 of the ECHR in their defence, if they occupy the land as their 'home'.[37] This means that in 'exceptional' cases, where it is 'seriously arguable' that eviction might constitute a disproportionate interference with X's home, the court might deviate from the normal remedy, e.g. by refusing a possession order, temporarily or indefinitely. Such deviation is nevertheless rare: courts attach 'real weight' to claimant owners' property rights (which are themselves protected rights within Article 1 of the ECHR's First Protocol) when assessing the proportionality of possession claims.[38] This rarity notwithstanding, some cases have suggested, without deciding the issue, that possession claims by *private* claimants might be similarly vulnerable to occupiers' human rights arguments.[39] Were such a development to occur, as is assumed in the remainder of this chapter, the remedy would, in theory, cease to be automatically available, 'as of right'.[40]

Further, it should be noted that the rules of adverse possession[41] may also defeat an 'owner's' possession claim; a registered owner who has lost his title to squatters has no standing to bring such a claim.

8.3.2.2.4 Juridical Basis Perhaps surprisingly for such an important remedy, there is little consensus as to the juridical basis of possession claims.[42] Ben McFarlane argues that they are *wrongs*-based: they respond to torts committed by X, such as trespass.[43] The very conduct that establishes a possession claim (X's possessing land, which O is entitled to possess) typically also constitutes a trespass (committed when X interferes with someone else's possession). This view also gleans support from history, for the former ejectment action (the precursor to

---

[37] *Manchester CC v Pinnock* [2010] UKSC 45, [2011] 2 AC 104; *Hounslow LBC v Powell* [2011] UKSC 8, [2011] 2 AC 186. Other ECHR human rights/freedoms may also constitute defences to possession actions, e.g. speech/assembly: *Sun Street Property Ltd v Persons Unknown* [2011] EWHC 3432 (Ch).

[38] *Pinnock* (n 37) [54] (Lord Neuberger). Exceptionally, X's human rights argument succeeded in *Southend-on-Sea BC v Armour* [2014] EWCA Civ 231, [2014] HLR 23.

[39] *Malik* (n 1); *Manchester Ship Canal Developments Ltd v Persons Unknown* [2014] EWHC 645 (Ch); cf *McDonald v McDonald* [2016] UKSC 28, [2016] 3 WLR 45 [40] (Lord Neuberger and Baroness Hale), limiting X's human rights ability to raise a human rights argument where O's superior rights arose from a contract between O and X, which itself was governed by a legislative framework.

[40] *Malik* (n 1) [26] (Ward LJ).   [41] LRA, ss 96–97, Sch 6.

[42] By contrast, chattel recovery undoubtedly requires proof of wrongdoing/conversion.

[43] Ben McFarlane, *The Structure of Property Law* (Hart Publishing 2008) 358.

the possession claim) was itself grounded in trespass.[44] However, many more commentators characterise possession claims as *title*-based: they respond to the mere fact that X possesses land to which O has a superior entitlement, without proof of wrongdoing.[45] Lord Neuberger MR also tends towards this view in *Meier*.[46] Looking ahead, the proper foundation of possession claims needs clarification, so that claimants know what facts must be alleged and proven.

8.3.2.3   Equitable Injunctions

Equitable injunctions offer a third form of *in specie* relief against harm to O's rights as landowner. This section focuses on some key points, relevant to real property interferences. Compared with possession claims/orders, injunctions are both more expansive, and more limited, in their reach.

Injunctions are potentially available in a much wider range of cases than possession claims/orders: they can be sought for both *physical interferences* (*possessory* and *non-possessory*) and *legal interferences*.

In *physical interference* cases, O can seek an injunction against X either as an end in itself, by way of a 'final injunction' (e.g. to order X to remove his trespassing crane from O's airspace), or as a temporary measure, by way of an 'interim injunction', to protect O's position whilst he brings a claim for a final remedy which awaits court resolution. Thus, in *possessory interference cases*, O can apply for an interim injunction against X, whilst seeking a possession order.

Injunctions have a more limited, but still useful, role in *legal interference* cases. Here, O's primary concern is to recover the registered title from X (or Y, X's successor in title) via 'alteration' of the Land Register. Pending resolution of the alteration claim, O can seek an interim injunction against X (or Y, where appropriate), preventing further dealings with the property until the alteration issue is resolved.[47]

Crucially, injunctions, unlike possession orders, do not just cure existing ills. They can also be sought (by way of a '*quia timet* injunction') to prevent imminent future ills. Thus, in *Meier*,[48] the Forestry Commission was denied a possession order against future trespassers on their land, yet obtained injunctive relief.

---

[44] *Meier* (n 19) [33] (Lady Hale).
[45] E.g. Virgo (n 3) 632; Zakrewski (n 14) 117–18; Godfrey and Davis (n 12) 3; Elvin (n 26) 347.
[46] See n 19 [60]–[78].   [47] E.g. *Fretwell v Graves* (HC, 2005).   [48] See n 19.

However, whilst O can apply for an injunction against interferers in a wide range of situations, this equitable remedy is weakened by the fact that courts have a discretion as to whether to grant an injunction: O is not guaranteed his castle back. Where courts refuse injunctive relief, they can award damages *in lieu* in respect of future interferences with O's rights.[49] Thus, in *Horsford v Bird*,[50] X, O's neighbour, encroached on O's land by building a wall. O was refused an injunction to remove the wall, but was awarded damages instead, representing the capital value of the encroached-upon land. The factors guiding judicial decisions to grant/withhold injunctions are widely discussed in the case-law and surrounding literature.[51] Rather than revisiting that familiar ground, this chapter, in section 8.4 focuses on the *effect* of the granting/withholding of injunctions.

The remedial strength of injunctions is further weakened by the manner of their enforcement. Whereas possession orders are enforceable *in specie* by bailiffs/sheriffs physically evicting X *from the land*, injunctions are enforced *in personam* against X, by sequestering his assets, or committing him to prison for contempt.[52] Thus, a mandatory injunction compelling X to leave O's land does not actually guarantee that outcome.

8.3.2.4 Rectification of the Land Register

The final *in specie* remedy applies to *legal interference* cases, where X has unlawfully acquired O's registered title. Here O, having typically lost legal and beneficial title to X,[53] cannot rely on any 'vindicatory remedy':[54] he has no current title to vindicate. Happily for O, Schedule 4 of the LRA provides for a 'reinstatement remedy', permitting O to seek 'alteration', or more specifically 'rectification', of the Land Register to 'correct a mistake'. Where X was registered as proprietor pursuant to a forged or non-existent deed of transfer, there is a 'mistake' in the Register, which may be corrected via rectification, seemingly with prospective effect.[55]

---

[49] Supreme Court Act 1981, s 50.   [50] [2006] UKPC 3, (2006) 22 Const LJ 187.
[51] *Lawrence v Fen Tigers Ltd* [2014] UKSC 13, [2014] AC 822; Paul S Davies, 'Injunctions in Tort and Contract', ch 6 in this volume.
[52] *Meier* (n 19) [59], [94] (Lord Neuberger).
[53] *Swift 1st Ltd v Chief Land Registrar* [2015] EWCA Civ 330, [2015] Ch 602.
[54] Except interim injunctions, which can be sought alongside alteration.
[55] *Gold Harp Properties Ltd v MacLeod* [2014] EWCA Civ 1084, [2015] 1 WLR 1249; Amy Goymour, 'Resolving the Tension between the Land Registration Act 2002's "Priority" and "Alteration" Provisions' [2015] Conv 253.

It also seems – after a period of judicial prevarication – that O can also bring a rectification claim against a remoter party, Y, to whom X may have since transferred the registered title.[56]

The success of O's alteration claim against X/Y is not, however, guaranteed. The LRA strikes a balance between defrauded parties (like O), and the interest in security of those currently on the Register (X or Y), who may believe they have an indefeasible title. The LRA provides that O's claim can be defeated (i) by 'exceptional circumstances',[57] or (ii) where X/Y currently possesses the land, unless X/Y carelessly caused/ contributed to the Registry's error, or it would be 'unjust' not to alter the Register.[58] Recent cases have tended to construe narrowly the provisions allowing X/Y to defeat O's claim, thereby preferring O.[59] Nevertheless, the fact remains that O is never guaranteed to recover his castle from such legal interferers.

8.3.3   Monetary Remedies

Monetary remedies form the next major remedial category. They are a second-order medicine. Unlike *in specie* relief, they do not *remove* specific ills that befall O's land; rather, they help relieve O's general suffering. The relationship between the two remedial forms in land-interference cases is complex and under-explored. Two key forms of monetary remedy are identifiable.

8.3.3.1   Civil Monetary Award against Interferer

First are civil monetary claims, brought against the alleged interferer. Two forms are particularly relevant in the land-interference context: claims brought in respect of a wrong (e.g. where X commits trespass to O's land, by interfering with O's possession); and claims to reverse an unjust enrichment (e.g. where X, via his interference, has been unjustly enriched at O's expense). The interaction between these monetary claims and *in specie* relief raises fundamental, unsolved questions. For example, how far can O choose a monetary remedy over *in specie* recovery (i.e. in *legal interference* cases, can O elect to sue X in unjust enrichment for

---

[56] See *Gold Harp* (ibid); *Ajibade v Bank of Scotland plc* [2008] EWLandRA 2006/0163; and Goymour 'Mistaken Registrations' (n 10), and Law Commission, *Updating the Land Registration Act 2002* (Law Com. No 222, 2016) [13.29].

[57] LRA, Sch 4, para 3(3).   [58] LRA, Sch 4, para 3(2).

[59] *Gold Harp* (n 55) (discussing 'exceptional circumstances'); and *Baxter v Mannion* [2011] EWCA Civ 120, [2011] 1 WLR 1594 (discussing the possession defence).

acquiring title to his land, rather than bringing a statutory claim to rectify the Land Register?); and what happens to O's underlying property rights if/when a monetary award is made?

8.3.3.2 Indemnity Award against HM Land Registry

In *legal interference* cases, an alternative monetary remedy is available, grounded in statute, and awarded against the Land Registry, rather than the interferer. The LRA gives O a right to a Registry indemnity whenever he has a *prima facie* rectification claim to recover his title from X/Y, but that claim is defeated, e.g. by exceptional circumstances, or X/Y being in possession. Unless O fraudulently or carelessly authored his own misfortune, the Registry must indemnify O for 'loss' suffered, leaving the Registry to pursue whoever is ultimately responsible for the unfortunate state of affairs.[60] The relationship between the two types of monetary remedy in *legal interference* cases is difficult. For example, could O, who desires a monetary award, bypass the statutory indemnity scheme and bring a direct civil monetary claim against X/Y instead?

8.3.4 *Other Miscellaneous Remedies*

Alongside the main remedies, already discussed, are some further, miscellaneous remedies, mentioned here for the sake of completeness.

In some[61] *legal interference* cases, X's conduct might generate a constructive trust over X's registered legal title, in O's favour, which will lead to further *in specie* remedies. For example, a trust may arise where X has acted 'unconscionably' in taking X's legal title.[62] The imposition of a trust enables O to recover the land, bring a monetary claim for breach of trust, and apply to be re-registered as proprietor.[63]

Finally, in some *physical interference* cases, X might commit an arrestable criminal offence. If arrested, X's arrest will indirectly open the door for O to re-enter the land.[64]

---

[60] LRA Sch 8, para 5. The Registry may recoup its loss from those ultimately responsible for the problem: Sch 8, para 10.

[61] A trust is not *automatically* generated by a mistaken registration: *Swift* (n 53).

[62] *Westdeutsche Landesbank Girozentrale v Islington LBC* [1996] AC 669 (HL) 705 (Lord Browne-Wilkinson).

[63] Via a claim for alteration for 'bringing the register up to date': LRA, Sch 4.

[64] E.g. Criminal Law Act 1977, s 7; Public Order Act 1994, ss 61, 62A, 68; Legal Aid, Sentencing and Punishment of Offenders Act 2012, s 144.

8.4   Making Sense of the Medicine Cabinet: Four Key
Controversies

Opening the medicine cabinet door has revealed a hotchpotch of potions, developed ad hoc by courts and Parliament, to deal with particular situations, with no apparent oversight as to the overall scheme. This strategy is not necessarily problematic: much of the common law's success is down to its organic growth, and ability to respond to new situations. However, the array of remedies relating to land interferences has been left unscrutinised for too long: there are inconsistencies, duplications, potential gaps, and uncertainty as to certain remedies' fields of application and/or theoretical bases. Furthermore, as section 8.3 revealed, the current law does not reflect the common perception that owners can always recover their 'castle' from strangers: in various situations, courts can and do deny owners *in specie* relief. This section exposes four key controversies which require resolution, namely: (1) the effect that denying specific relief might have on O's pre-court ownership rights; (2) the effect of O obtaining or being denied specific relief on the parties' future property rights; (3) the circumstances in which specific relief ought to be withheld; and (4) the relationship between *in specie* and monetary remedies. Understanding the current law and its problems is an essential first step towards much-needed future rationalisation of the law's remedies.

8.4.1   *What Effect Does the Denial of Specific Relief have*
on the Nature of O's Pre-Court Ownership Rights?

Section 8.3 showed that the most powerful right in land – freehold ownership – is not guaranteed absolute *in specie* remedial protection. Each court-ordered *in specie* remedy can be withheld, for different reasons: possession claims are vulnerable (exceptionally) to human rights defences; injunctions are inherently discretionary; and the LRA specifies circumstances in which Register-rectification can be refused. This prompts a fundamental question: is it consistent with the concept of freehold ownership that owners are not guaranteed *in specie* relief? 'Ownership' is typically thought to comprise (a) a 'positive' right to use the land; and (b) a 'negative' right (imposing a corresponding duty) that others not interfere with the land.[65] Does the fact that specific remedies

---

[65] Tony Honoré, 'Ownership' in Anthony G Guest (ed), *Oxford Essays in Jurisprudence* (Oxford University Press 1961) 113.

might be denied force us to re-conceptualise this orthodox understanding of the nature of freehold ownership?

These questions engage a wider theoretical debate in remedies scholarship, concerning the proper relationship between private rights and their remedies. Stephen Smith has argued that opinions broadly divide between (i) 'realists' – for whom private rights are defined by reference to their remedial protection; and (ii) 'formalists' – who define private rights by reference to some abstract, formal standard, notwithstanding that a judicial remedy is not always forthcoming.[66] Realists and formalists will have divergent responses to cases like *Horsford v Bird*[67] where O received damages *in lieu* of an injunction against a neighbour who had built a wall on O's land, or *Woollerton and Wilson Ltd v Richard Costain Ltd*,[68] where O obtained neither an injunction nor damages against a developer whose crane was swinging in his airspace. For realists, withholding *in specie* relief fundamentally undermines the quality of O's pre-court entitlement: as rights and remedies are inextricably linked, the fact that O is refused a *specific remedy*, ordering a third party to leave the land, demonstrates that such third parties never owed any pre-court *specific duty* to leave the land (as opposed to merely paying damages), and that O never enjoyed the corresponding *specific right*, typical of ownership, that others not interfere with his land.[69] For formalists, however, rights are not co-extensive with their remedies. O can have a specific private law right that others not interfere with his land even though he may not, and does not, obtain a specific court-ordered remedy against them. Although the competing views are finely balanced, the formalist approach might be preferred, for two reasons.

First, it might be understood as a better reflection of the current law. In physical interference cases, for example, there is always a *possibility* that O might obtain specific relief against X (by injunction or possession order), which remains until a court decides whether to award a specific remedy. It might be understood as unhelpful, and misleading, to treat a court's subsequent decision to withhold specific relief as retrospectively re-characterising/diminishing O's pre-court rights. Imagine that X1 and X2 independently but simultaneously interfered with O's land. As the law stands, a court could conceivably grant O injunctive relief against X2, whilst refusing it against X1 (perhaps because X1's interference was less

---

[66] Stephen A Smith, 'Rights and Remedies: A Complex Relationship' in Robert J Sharpe and Kent Roach (eds), *Taking Rights Seriously* (Canadian Institute for the Administration of Justice 2010) 31, 38–39.
[67] See n 50.   [68] [1970] 1 WLR 411 (Ch).   [69] Smith (n 66) 38–39.

serious). If so, the court's refusal to injunct X1 seems to have no impact on O's pre-court specific entitlement against other third parties (e.g. X2) – contrary to the realist view.

Secondly, there may be compelling policy justifications for decoupling private rights from their judicial remedies. As Smith has argued, our reasons for respecting *private* ownership *rights* are not necessarily the same as courts' reasons, as *public bodies*, to award/deny *remedies* to/ against particular individuals, in particular circumstances. Private rights might exist to guide private citizens' behaviour among themselves, whereas courts may have other legitimate concerns (e.g. concerns that particular remedial orders can be adequately and efficiently policed, concerns about wasting valuable resources, concerns to dis/incentivise certain behaviour etc).[70] Arguably, it is the mark of an advanced property law system, regulating a densely populated land-mass, that absolute property rights do not always command absolute *in specie* remedial protection, and that remedies might be tailored to the particular circumstances.[71] Of course, such a strategy is justified only if the 'tailoring' happens coherently.

8.4.2   What are the Legal Effects of O (a) Obtaining; or (b) being Denied In Specie *Relief on the Parties' Future Property Rights?*

The previous section examined the effect of denying specific relief on O's *pre*-court entitlement. But what about the legal effects of granting/withholding a remedy on O's and X's rights, *going forward*? The effects can be significant, in some cases amounting to a judicial transfer, or expropriation, of title. Remarkably, however, this topic has yet to receive proper judicial or academic attention.

8.4.2.1   Legal Effect of Specific Relief Being Granted/Obtained

In any *physical interference* case, the obtaining/grant of specific relief – via injunctions, possession orders or self-help – has no effect on O's underlying rights. These remedies are purely 'vindicatory': O was, and remains, the owner, and the remedy merely ensures that O can enjoy that right in practice, going forwards. Additionally, to remedy the effects of X's past unauthorised interference, O's continuing ownership may, of course, give

---

[70] Ibid 43–45.
[71] For similar analysis in nuisance context, see *Lawrence v Fen Tigers Ltd* (n 51) [238]–[240] (Lord Carnwath).

him standing to sue X for a monetary award in trespass and/or unjust enrichment. This possibility is addressed below.

The picture is different, and more complicated, in *legal interference* cases, where X has been registered as the owner of O's title without O's authority. Here, the LRA's 'statutory' magic deems X to be the legal proprietor upon registration, with the concomitant loss of O's ownership rights.[72] The legal effect of a successful *in specie* claim for 'rectification' of the Register is therefore to 'reinstate' O's lost rights, rather than to merely 'vindicate' continuing rights. However, the timing of this legal transformation is uncertain. Is O's re-registration (and therefore his title) backdated to the date when X first deprived O of his title, or does it only operate prospectively, from the date the Register is changed, such that X is treated as the true owner during his unlawful registration?

The answer hinges on the meaning and breadth of LRA Schedule 4, paragraph 8, which provides that, in cases concerning '[r]ectification and derivative interests', the power to 'alter the register ... extend[s] to changing *for the future* the priority of any interest affecting the registered estate' (emphasis added). This difficult provision was considered recently by the Court of Appeal in *Gold Harp Properties Ltd v MacLeod*,[73] albeit in a slightly different context to the legal interferences discussed in this chapter. T1 held a registered long lease over O's freehold title. That lease was mistakenly deregistered, after which O granted T2 a registered lease which, according to the LRA's priority rules, was unburdened by T1's unregistered lease.[74] T1 thus brought a rectification claim, seeking re-registration of his lease, with priority over T2's leasehold interest. The Court of Appeal accepted T1's claim: paragraph 8 meant that rectification could 'chang[e] ... the priority' of derivative interests, so that T1's lease bound T2's, but only *prospectively* – 'for the future' – from the date of T1's re-registration. This meant that until rectification occurred, T2 was entitled to use the land, and any use by T1 would have infringed T2's (temporarily) superior rights; after rectification, their relative entitlements were reversed.

The *Gold Harp* case fitted squarely within paragraph 8, being a contest between two 'derivative' interests, both leases deriving from O's freehold. Unfortunately, it is unclear, whether the decision that rectifications operate merely *'for the future'* applies in other contexts too. In particular, what happens in the legal interference cases discussed in this chapter, where O seeks reinstatement as outright freehold proprietor as against X – not

---

[72] O retains a mere (proprietary) 'right to alter' the Register: *Swift* (n 53).   [73] See n 55.
[74] LRA, ss 28–29.

a case of competing derivative interests? Many commentators have assumed, following *Gold Harp*, that O's re-registration operates prospectively in all contexts,[75] but the better view is that the point remains unsettled.[76] It therefore remains intolerably uncertain whether X's use of the land prior to rectification constitutes an infringement of O's rights, potentially actionable in trespass and/or unjust enrichment.

8.4.2.2   Legal Effect of Denying Specific Relief

The legal effect of O being denied *in specie* remedies against X or others is also underexplored. The moderate language of 'withholding' or 'denying' specific remedies tends to mask the profound impact that refusing such relief may have on O's underlying property rights.

8.4.2.2.1 Legal Interference Cases Legal interference cases are straightforward: denying O's rectification claim means that X's current position as the registered legal owner is secure and absolutely indefeasible against O. The principle of *res judicata* should shield X from further claims by O.

Cases concerning physical interferences raise more difficult problems. Possessory and non-possessory interferences need to be distinguished.

8.4.2.2.2 Possessory Physical Interference Cases Where X has physically dispossessed O, X acquires a relatively inferior title upon going into possession. O, relying on his superior title, can seek a possession order, an injunction, or both, against X. Denying O specific relief broadly affords X full enjoyment of his own freehold estate, unencumbered by O's technically superior rights.

(a)   Withholding Possession Orders

Possession orders are available 'as of right', unless it is possible for X to raise a defence asserting that evicting him would violate his human rights, e.g. his right to respect for his 'home', under Article 8 of the ECHR. The existence of a human rights defence against private possession claims is controversial. But if accepted, its consequences are potentially significant. According to Lord Neuberger in *Pinnock*:

---

[75] Martin Dixon, 'Rectification and Priority: Further Skirmishes in the Land Registration War' (2015) 131 LQR 207; Emma Lees, 'Rectification of the Register: Prospective or Retrospective?' (2015) 78 MLR 361.

[76] Goymour, 'Resolving the Tension' (n 55).

> [The] effect of [A]rticle 8 may, albeit in exceptional cases, justify (in
> ascending order of effect) granting an extended period for possession,
> suspending the order for possession on the happening of an event, or even
> refusing an order altogether.[77]

Subsequent cases indicate that a temporary postponement of O's
possession claim is much more likely than an outright, indefinite
refusal.[78] In either case, the consequences are underexplored. Two difficult problems arise.

First, it is unclear whether an outright refusal of O's possession claim
(i) merely affects O's ability to evict X, or (ii) would prevent O from
recovering the land indefinitely *from anyone*.

According to analysis (i), X can possess the land, as against O, for an
indefinite period, until X ceases occupying the land as his 'home' and the
human rights defence expires. O's successors (O2) would probably also
be prevented from repossessing against X – either because the court's
refusal to grant possession orders binds O2 *de iure*,[79] or because *de facto*
X's continued occupation affords X a secure human rights defence
against O2's future possession claims. The indefinite suppression of O's
ability to enjoy the land whilst X occupies amounts *in substance* to an
expropriation, in X's favour, of O's present right to enjoy the land.
Determining what *technically* happens to the parties' property rights
whilst the defence is 'live' is trickier. A possible explanation is that X's
defence effects a reversal of the priority of O's and X's relative freehold
titles,[80] so that X's title becomes superior to O's; once X leaves and the
defence expires, O's title will regain its former priority.

Analysis (ii) goes rather further. It would amount *in substance* to a full,
permanent expropriation of O's rights. Again, this might be explained on
the basis that X's defence effects a reversal of the priority of O's and X's
relative freeholds, this time *permanently*. A further corollary is that
X could seek to become the registered proprietor.[81]

Secondly, what happens where X's human rights defence merely
results in a *temporary* postponement of O's possession order? Here

---

[77] *Pinnock* (n 37) [62]; *Powell* (n 37) [103] (Lord Hope).
[78] *Thurrock BC v West* [2012] EWCA Civ 1435, [2013] HLR 5 [31] (Etherton LJ); *Malik* (n 1) [27]–[28] (Ward LJ).
[79] By analogy with injunction-withholding, which binds O2: text to n 82.
[80] NB X's freehold would be unregistered. See Amy Goymour and Robin Hickey, 'The Continuing Relevance of Relativity of Title under the Land Registration Act 2002' in Martin Dixon, Amy Goymour and Stephen Watterson (eds), *Land Registration: Contemporary Problems and Solutions* (Hart forthcoming).
[81] X could obtain alteration, 'bringing the Register up to date': LRA, Sch 4.

again, the relative priority of O's owner's freehold and X's inferior free-hold seems to be temporarily reversed: in substance, a temporary expropriation of O's rights.

Where O's possession claim against X is refused on human rights grounds, further difficult questions arise as to whether O can obtain monetary compensation from X. This is discussed below.

(b) Withholding Injunctive Relief

What happens to the parties' rights when O elects for a final injunction (rather than a possession order) against an unauthorised possessor, X, and that relief is refused? Some answers are beginning to emerge from recent cases.

First, a court's refusal to grant an injunction apparently binds not only O and X, but also, their respective successors in title.[82] This is most obviously justified where X is ordered to pay O damages *in lieu* of injunction – e.g. it would be unjust for X to pay O damages representing the land's value, but later face being injuncted by O's successor in title.[83] However, the principle applies whether or not money is paid.[84]

Secondly, there is growing judicial acceptance that refusal of a final injunction has the significant effect of expropriating property rights from O to X. Thus, in *Horsford v Bird*, where X encroached on (and seemingly possessed) O's land by building a wall, the Privy Council said that:

> The [trial judge's] refusal ... of the mandatory injunction and her decision to award damages in lieu had the consequence of, in effect, expropriating that piece of land from [O] and enabling it to become thenceforth, *de jure* as well as *de facto*, part of [X's] garden.[85]

Finally, *Horsford* also confirms that this 'expropriation' occurs prospectively from the date the injunction is refused,[86] meaning X may be liable to a monetary claim for his unlawful occupation up to that point.

Piecing these points together, refusal of an injunction effectively amounts to a forced judicial sale if damages awarded in lieu, and otherwise a forced gift, of the land from O to X. But some awkward questions

---

[82] *Jaggard v Sawyer* [1995] 1 WLR 269 (CA) 286 (Millett LJ).

[83] Vice versa, it is unjust for O to receive the land's value *and* be able to injunct X's successor.

[84] *Jaggard* (n 82) [285] (Millett LJ).

[85] See n 50, [11] (Lord Scott). See also *Ramzan v Brookwide Ltd* [2010] EWHC 2453 (Ch) [14]: the trespasser in *Horsford* had 'in effect become the lawful owner of the expropriated property' (Geraldine Andrews QC).

[86] *Horsford* (n 50) [11] (Lord Scott).

remain unresolved. For example, how does the expropriation technically work? In analogous cases concerning chattels, legislation expressly provides for a judicial extinction of O's title, leaving the current possessor as the default owner.[87] What of land cases? One plausible explanation is that refusal of the injunction turns O's registered freehold into an empty shell of a title, leaving X, who has a squatter's possessory freehold, holding the best title to the land. X would then have a right to be registered as proprietor.[88]

8.4.2.2.3 Non-possessory Physical Interference Cases

The impact of denying *in specie* relief is more complicated where X physically interferes with O's land, *without* taking possession – e.g. by repeatedly walking over O's land. Here, O's options for specific relief are restricted to self-help and injunctions. In practice, self-help is frequently precluded by the criminal law.[89] What happens when the sole remaining option (the injunction) is refused by a court?[90]

This occurred in *Jaggard v Sawyer*, where, *inter alia*, O was refused an injunction preventing X (a neighbour) driving across his land; O received damages *in lieu*. Millett LJ opined that the '*practical* effect' was to expropriate rights from X: X (and his successors) could no longer sue O (nor implicitly O's successors) in trespass. However, his Lordship rejected the idea that this amounted to vesting a *legal* right in X to use O's land, e.g. an easement.[91]

This analysis of X's position seems unsatisfactory. First, couching X's position negatively (in terms of immunity from trespass liability) rather than positively (in terms of rights) fails adequately to explain why X can continue to drive on the land when O conveys the land to another. Whilst *proprietary* rights are capable of binding successors in title, it is far from clear that *immunities* from liability (often equated to licences) also have this effect. Secondly, Millett LJ's analysis seemingly masks the truth: if X's ability to enjoy the land behaves like an easement, fair labelling supports calling it an easement. This chimes with Lord Neuberger's recent reappraisal of *Jaggard* as a case where the court's refusal of an injunction 'effectively gave [X] a right of way ... over [O's] land'.[92] Thirdly,

---

[87] Torts (Interference with Goods) Act 1977, s 5.
[88] To 'bring the [R]egister up to date': LRA, Sch 4.
[89] Because self-help is exercised without resort to the courts, its non-availability has no impact on O's property rights.
[90] NB self-help is precluded once a mandatory injunction is refused.
[91] *Jaggard* (n 82) 280.   [92] *Lawrence* (n 51) [111].

recognising that X has an easement brings further, welcome consequences. For example, it would no longer be correct to assert, as Millett LJ did, that X is *guaranteed* protection against O's successors in title – a blunt strategy. The priority between X's easement and O's successor's freehold title would be determined by the LRA's priority rules, which strike a more delicate balance between the interests of competing parties.[93]

In short, looking ahead, it is vital to recognise that denying injunctions has a real, non-trivial effect on parties' property rights. However, difficult technical questions remain. For example, (i) in a case like *Jaggard*, would the easement that arises be legal or equitable, and could it be registered?; (ii) what right would X obtain if, in a different case, the nature of his interference with O's land did not fit any recognised form of property right, such as an easement?

8.4.3   When Should Specific Relief be Available/Withheld?

The last section showed that the withholding of specific relief has an important substantive effect on O's and X's property rights, (i) *confirming* that O has lost his registered title to X, in legal interference cases; or (ii) *effecting* what amounts to a transfer of property rights (permanent or temporary), in physical interference cases. As such, 'withholding of specific relief' arguably stands alongside consent-based acquisition, prescriptive acquisition, and original acquisition, as a mode of acquiring/creating property rights. It also becomes obvious that withholding of specific relief must be closely monitored, to ensure that property rights are re-distributed in a coherent and justifiable manner.

8.4.3.1   Current Inconsistencies

There are four sorts of problems of consistency concerning remedy-availability/withholding in the current law.

First, there are inconsistencies *within individual remedy types*. Most obviously, one finds conflicting judicial statements as to the circumstances in which injunctive relief against a trespasser might be withheld. Some suggest that whenever O is entitled to possession, injunctions are 'plainly' available and must be awarded.[94] Nevertheless, this approach is not universal: *Horsford* demonstrates that courts can, and sometimes do,

---

[93] LRA, ss 28–29, Sch 3.
[94] E.g. *Patel v WH Smith (Eziot) Ltd* [1987] 1 WLR 853 (CA); *Higson v Guenault* [2014] EWCA Civ 703.

refuse injunctions against trespassers.[95] Similarly divergent responses emerge in rectification claims. The LRA provides that O's rectification claim against a possessor must be refused, unless it would be 'unjust' not to rectify the Register. Some cases suggest that it is inherently 'unjust' not to alter a mistaken registration, thus suggesting O will always obtain rectification.[96] Other cases regard the assessment of 'unjust[ness]' as a more factual matter, determined on a case-by-case basis.[97]

Secondly, there are inconsistencies *between different remedies*, applied to the same facts. Most problematic are physical possessory interference cases, for which claimants can seek specific relief via a possession order and/or an injunction against X. Possession orders are available 'as of right', unless X exceptionally has a human rights defence, whereas injunctions, on one view, are inherently discretionary. The same facts may therefore yield different responses, with different proprietary consequences for the parties, according to whether O elects for an injunction or a possession order. In *Horsford*, O's injunction against X possessor was refused – resulting in *de facto* and *de iure* loss of title – whereas a possession claim would apparently have succeeded. Why should O's retention/loss of title depend on which remedy he chooses to seek?

Thirdly, the likelihood of a court ordering/withholding a specific remedy varies with the nature of the interference. Relief is most likely in possessory physical interference cases (via a possession claim), less likely in non-possessory physical interference cases (when an injunction is sought), and less likely still in legal interference cases (where Register-rectification is sought). Is this variation justified?

Finally, there are potential inconsistencies between remedy-withholding and other areas of the law, such as prescriptive acquisition of title. The LRA protects registered owners against squatters, requiring an adverse possessor to wait ten years before he can apply (usually unsuccessfully) to take over O's registered title. Despite this, the earlier discussion of remedy-withholding suggests that the same squatter may become owner prior to the ten-year point, if O seeks, but is permanently refused, injunctive relief. In the latter case, X might be ordered to pay O damages in lieu of the injunction. Yet we must wonder whether such remedy-withholding undermines the owner's typical ten-year protection against squatters.

---

[95] Also *Ketley v Gooden* (1997) 73 P&CR 305 (CA).　　[96] E.g. *Baxter* (n 59).
[97] E.g. *Walker v Burton* [2013] EWCA Civ 1228, [2014] 1 P&CR 9.

8.4.3.2   A More Principled Way Forward?

These concerns/inconsistencies require resolution. Once the expropria-
tory/acquisitive effect of remedy-withholding is appreciated, it becomes
important to place this mode of acquisition on a surer footing. Party-
consent usually justifies derivative acquisition, whilst a need to 'clothe'
longstanding 'fact with law'[98] justifies prescriptive acquisition, but what
justifications underpin acquisition via remedy-withholding? Although
somewhat nebulous, the answer seems to rest directly on public policy/
policies. Sometimes, society's interests dictate that X be favoured over O,
for example: to prevent waste, if X has since built on the land; to promote
certainty of land registration, if X is currently owner; or to protect those
who will make the best use of the land, e.g. as a home, or as essential
business property. Looking ahead, it will be essential to identify which
policy factors indeed justify depriving O of his land (is it defensible, for
example, to expropriate O's land in X's favour for purely environmental
or public planning reasons?)[99] and ensure that these factors are woven
together into a coherent, non-arbitrary strategy.

8.4.4   When are Monetary Remedies Available?

The final controversy concerns the availability of monetary remedies, an
under-examined topic, brimming with difficulties. O may seek a money
award for two major reasons: (i) *in lieu* of specific recovery of the land
(either O would prefer a monetary remedy, or O's claim for specific
recovery has failed); and/or (ii) as compensation/restitution in respect of
X's past interference, whether or not O recovers the land.[100] This section
focuses on monetary awards *in lieu* of recovering the land. Their availability
is not, of course, an isolated issue: it may influence the circumstances in
which courts are justified in withholding specific recovery from O.

Different problems emerge in relation to physical and legal interferences.

8.4.4.1   Physical Interferences

8.4.4.1.1   O Claims, but is Refused, In Specie Relief   First, when
might courts award a monetary remedy against a physical interferer, X,
in lieu of O's preferred claim for specific recovery of the land? In

---

[98] *Moody v Steggles* (1879) 12 Ch D 261, 265 (Fry J).
[99] For parallel discussions in the tort of private nuisance context, see *Lawrence* (n 51) [124],
[161], [240], [247].
[100] *Ramzan v Brookwide Ltd* [2011] EWCA Civ 985, [2012] 1 All ER 903 [44] (Arden LJ).

principle, the case for awarding a monetary award seems strong: X should pay O for the rights he, in effect, obtained when the court refused to grant a specific remedy. However, in practice, the law permitting monetary relief is under-examined and patchy.

The availability of monetary relief might depend on which specific remedy O originally sought: whilst courts can award damages *in lieu* of granting O a claimed-for injunction,[101] it is unclear whether that jurisdiction extends to awarding damages directly *in lieu* of possession orders. This is a critical issue. Possession orders may be refused on human rights grounds, bringing a temporary or permanent loss of O's rights, and yet neither of the traditional bases for monetary relief against X – trespass and unjust enrichment – may be available to O. X's human rights defence legitimises his presence on O's land, meaning he is neither an unlawful trespasser[102] nor, it seems, 'unjustly' occupying at O's expense. O's recovery therefore turns on whether courts have the power to award damages directly *in lieu* of possession orders, in the absence of a tort/unjust enrichment.

Human rights law may require domestic law to develop in this direction. O's property rights themselves command human rights protection (within ECHR, Article 1, First Protocol); and Strasbourg jurisprudence suggests that 'deprivations'[103] of property generally require compensation, to be Convention-compliant. Arguably, O's being refused a possession order amounts to a relevant 'deprivation', and O's loss merits compensation under English law.

8.4.4.1.2 O Directly Elects for Monetary Relief

Secondly, in physical interference cases, what happens where O directly elects for monetary relief against X instead of bringing a claim for a specific remedy? The question rarely arises: owners normally want their land back. However, it may be relevant where O planned to sell (or grant some lesser right, e.g. an easement) and prefers monetary relief. Policy and logic might dictate that O should have a choice between claiming specific and monetary relief, as with chattels. However, O's two possible grounds for claiming direct monetary relief – trespass or unjust enrichment – raise difficulties.

Trespass has stringent standing requirements: O must be in actual possession of the land, or be 'deemed' to have possession by the doctrine

---

[101] Seemingly without O having to prove an underlying wrong.

[102] *Parshall v Hackney LBC* [2013] EWCA Civ 240 suggests that statutory permission to occupy prevents trespass.

[103] *Sporrong and Lonnroth v Sweden* (1982) 5 EHRR 35. NB mere 'controls of use' do not necessitate compensation.

of 'relation back', which applies to give O retrospective possession when O brings an *in specie* possession claim.[104] Plainly, O can sue X in trespass for *non-possessory interferences*. Whether trespass claims lie in *possessory interference* cases is more doubtful: O has neither actual possession nor, having chosen monetary over *in specie* relief, is he deemed to have possession by 'relation back'. Despite the technical differences, it seems incoherent from O's perspective for the trespass tort to discriminate between possessory and non-possessory interferences; indeed some judicial statements suggest trespass might already extend to both interference types.[105] However, even if trespass is thus extended, a problem remains: O should not receive the monetary value of the land from X, whilst retaining unencumbered ownership. Regrettably, there is no obvious existing legal mechanism for divesting O of title/rights in favour of X, following a trespass claim. To justify a monetary award for liability in trespass, some new solution to the title problem must be found. Options include: (a) deeming that O voluntarily renounces his title by bringing a trespass claim for the land's value (although renunciation normally results in escheat to the Crown rather than a transfer to a private party); (b) introducing legislation stating that title transfers whenever a successful monetary claim is brought, akin to legislation applicable to chattels; or (c) recognising that, by operation of law, a successful trespass claim for the land's value automatically results in a transfer of property rights between the parties. Whatever the 'transfer' mechanism, X would subsequently need to apply for registration as the new owner.

Might O bring a claim in unjust enrichment for the value of the land instead? There is little authority on the question. A wide-ranging unjust enrichment liability could certainly plug the gaps in any trespass liability. However, there are difficulties. To bring an unjust enrichment claim, O must show that X was unjustly enriched at O's expense. Any enrichment seems 'unjust', since X has acted 'without authority',[106] but whether X is 'enriched' 'at O's expense' by property, title to which remains with O, is hotly contested.[107] The enrichment problem could be overcome by, for example, recognising that X has been *factually* enriched by using O's

---

[104] Elvin (n 26) 8–9.

[105] E.g. *Lord Fitzhardinghe v Purcell* [1908] 2 Ch 139 (Ch D) 145 (Parker J).

[106] See Charles Mitchell, Paul Mitchell and Stephen Watterson, *Goff and Jones: The Law of Unjust Enrichment* (8th edn, Sweet & Maxwell, 2011) ch 8.

[107] E.g. William Swadling, 'A Claim in Restitution' [1996] LMCLQ 63; Ross Grantham and Charles Rickett, 'Restitution, Property and Ignorance: A Reply to Mr Swadling' [1996] LMCLQ 463.

land.[108] However, we still re-encounter the familiar dilemma that O should not recover the land's value from X, whilst remaining owner. As with trespass liability, the law should not countenance O's monetary claim unless there is a mechanism for simultaneously transferring O's title to X. It is not obvious that such a mechanism exists under the current law.

8.4.4.2 Legal Interferences

The availability of monetary relief is even more problematic in legal interference cases, where X is mistakenly registered as owner of O's land. Here, the LRA's indemnity regime adds an extra layer of complexity. The key question is whether O can bypass the Act's indemnity provisions and sue X under the common law, in trespass/unjust enrichment.

Trespass can be immediately rejected. *Parshall v Hackney* holds that mistakenly registered owners have lawful authority to use the land, via their registration, and cannot be trespassers.[109] However, whether X is liable in unjust enrichment remains a live issue.

O might prefer to sue X in unjust enrichment rather than seek a Registry indemnity for two reasons. First, if O's loss is partly due to his carelessness, he is disqualified from receiving an indemnity, but he may successfully sue in unjust enrichment, for which O's carelessness is irrelevant.[110] Secondly, unlike monetary relief via unjust enrichment, a Registry indemnity is not a directly available remedial option under the LRA: before qualifying for an indemnity, O must seek *in specie* relief against X, via a rectification claim.[111] Only if rectification is denied on the facts (e.g. owing to 'exceptional circumstances') might an indemnity be payable, as a fallback remedy.

Whether O can bring a direct unjust enrichment claim in such circumstances is controversial. O probably has a *prima facie* claim against X: X is enriched at O's expense (X's registered title having derived from O's title), and X's enrichment may be unjust: O's complete non-participation in the transaction means he may plead 'ignorance' or 'want of authority' as the unjust factor.[112] But would any bar or defence defeat O's claim? X could certainly plead change of position, insofar as he paid for the land, ignorant of O's rights. Beyond that, would X's *registration* as owner itself constitute a blanket bar/defence to O's claim? There are two options.

---

[108] See Lodder (n 11) 97–98.   [109] See n 102 [91]–[94] (Mummery LJ).
[110] *Kelly v Solari* (1841) 9 M&W 54; 152 ER 24.   [111] LRA, Sch 8, para 1(3).
[112] Mitchell, Mitchell and Watterson (n 106) ch 8.

First, X's registration might be regarded as a *basis/justifying ground* for X's enrichment, which automatically *bars* O's unjust enrichment claim. This argument, however, may be too formalistic. Although registration confers a statutory title on X, it offers no *substantive basis/justification* for the *transfer* of wealth/enrichment from O to X.

A second option is more plausible: X's registration might supply a policy-based *defence* to O's claim. Whether such a defence should be recognised is much-discussed in Torrens-based literature,[113] but under-explored in English law.[114] The Law Commission's pre-LRA reports certainly envisaged the continuing existence of *personal* claims against registered proprietors.[115] Liability for knowing receipt and for tortious wrongdoing were expressly mentioned; unjust enrichment was not, but the Law Commission may have contemplated restitutionary claims lying against registered proprietors, at least where they had behaved improperly. Against this, allowing unjust enrichment claims against registered owners would arguably stultify the LRA's own policy ambitions. The LRA protects registered owners, like X, against *in specie* rectification claims in carefully defined situations. Allowing an unjust enrichment claim to succeed against X where he is statutorily immune from rectification might undermine the protection Parliament intended for him: unless X has unusually deep pockets, he will need to sell the land to meet the unjust enrichment liability. A registration defence therefore might be justifiable, to prevent the Act's policy goals being thwarted, at least where X's registration would be immune from rectification.

8.5 Conclusions

The analysis in this chapter has sought to shine a light into dusty, often-neglected corners of the law's 'medicine cabinet' of real property remedies. The search-light has revealed that the remedial potions are not necessarily as strong as traditionally perceived to be: landowners are not always guaranteed their 'castle' back if things go wrong. The same exploration has also thrown up a host of important, as yet unresolved controversies concerning the remedies' proper ambits and functions,

---

[113] E.g. Jonathon Moore, 'Equity, Restitution and In Personam Claims under the Torrens System: Part II' (1999) 73 ALJ 712.
[114] Cf Elise Bant, 'Registration as a Defence to Claims in Unjust Enrichment: Australia and England Compared' [2011] Conv 309.
[115] Law Commission, *Land Registration for the Twentieth Century* (Law Com No 254, 1998) [3.48]–[3.49].

which are of theoretical and practical importance: the impact which the granting – or withholding – of specific relief might have on an owner's past or future property rights; the circumstances in which specific relief might appropriately be granted/withheld; and the troubled relationship between specific and monetary relief.

It is striking that in our modern legal system so much remains uncertain – although perhaps not surprising, given the ad hoc historical evolution of the remedies. Looking ahead, it would be regrettable if this obscurity were allowed to continue. If this chapter has achieved anything, it has hopefully brought some sense of order to the medicine cabinet, and illuminated paths for future research and thought.

PART III

Monetary Remedies

Performance Damages

CHARLIE WEBB

9.1 Duties and Coercion

Contracting parties have an interest in receiving the performance they are due under their contracts and, when a contract is breached, this interest can support an award of damages. This performance interest is not the only interest which contracting parties have and upholding contractors' interests is not the only objective of contract law. Nonetheless the recognition and protection of this interest in receiving performance has a good claim to be the defining role of the law of contract. I will not seek to defend that claim here and the arguments which follow do not depend on it. They do, however, suppose that protecting the performance interest is at least one of contract law's aims. Some doubt even this. 'The duty to keep a contract at common law means a prediction that you must pay damages if you do not keep it, – and nothing else.'[1] Perhaps Holmes did not mean what his words here appear to mean: that the law gives contracting parties the option not to perform but instead to pay damages.[2] But others have endorsed this view and with it the idea that the law has no particular concern to see that parties obtain the performance they were promised so long as they are not prejudiced by not receiving that performance.

Why think this? The law's standard response to breaches of contract, outside of contractual undertakings to pay money, is not to compel performance but to order damages, even where performance remains possible and is preferred by the claimant. Moreover, these damages will

[1] OW Holmes, 'The Path of the Law' (1897) 10 *Harvard Law Review* 457, 462.
[2] For the suggestion that this misinterprets Holmes, see Joseph M Perillo, 'Misreading Oliver Wendell Holmes on Efficient Breach and Tortious Interference' (2000) 68 *Fordham Law Review* 1085. If it is a misinterpretation, it is nonetheless an understandable one given Holmes' broader view of laws and legal duties: 'If you want to know the law and nothing else, you must look at it as a bad man, who cares only for the material consequences which such knowledge enables him to predict.': Holmes (n 1) 459.

often be insufficient for the claimant to obtain the object of the promised performance from another source. Here then, when it comes to the crunch, the law chooses to give contracting parties not performance but merely compensation for non-performance. Does this not mean that there is, in truth, no legal duty on the defendant to perform, no legal right in the claimant to that performance? No. It would no doubt be possible for a legal system to provide that contracting parties have the option not to perform their 'contractual' undertakings, expressly leaving them at liberty to pay damages instead. But this is not what English contract law says. Instead it says that contracting parties are, in all cases, obligated to perform their contracts, that a failure to perform is, in all cases, a breach of that obligation, a breach of contract.

Thinking that there is no such duty reflects the more basic thought that the content of law and so of our legal duties is fixed by the content of the coercive measures which legal institutions do (or would) in fact impose on us: we owe legal duties only where the law in fact compels us to act and those duties extend only to what the law in fact compels us to do. The deficiencies of this way of thinking were laid out long ago by Hart.[3] When the law identifies some action as obligatory, it is not simply foreshadowing the imposition of some penalty or other coercive measure on those who fail so to act; it is saying that this is something we must do, marking out the relevant conduct as non-optional. Of course, the law's designation of certain conduct as obligatory is not simply rhetorical but is aimed at prompting those upon whom that obligation is imposed to act in this way. The law's threat to visit unwanted consequences upon those who do not plays a big part in securing that end result. But the fact that the law will often use such threats as part of its strategy to promote conformity with its obligations should not lead us to reduce those obligations to the demands made of those who default. So there is a difference between a tax and a fine even though each means that the relevant conduct will trigger a demand to pay over a sum of money, which a judge will, if called on, enforce.[4] No doubt there may be border-line cases, so too cases where conduct labelled as obligatory is or comes to be, in practice, treated (not only by those to whom these norms are addressed, but by officials) as instead licensed upon payment of a fee. Nonetheless it is a mistake to reframe all legal obligations in this way, precisely because this is not how they are, in the vast majority of

---

[3] HLA Hart, *The Concept of Law* (3rd edn, Oxford University Press 2012), 38–42, 82–91.
[4] Ibid 39.

cases, held out by the law or indeed how they are understood by their addressees.

When the law designates some action as obligatory, it speaks to those whose conduct it is seeking to direct. The addressees of the law's directives include legal officials. Judges charged with resolving legal disputes are subject to legal norms determining how they are to do so. But the law is not only for judges and many of its duties are directed not (or not only) to officials but to the rest of us in our everyday deliberations as to what we should do. So while one job for the law of contract is to tell judges charged with deciding contract cases how they should be deciding them, it also speaks to contracting parties and, more broadly, all of us thinking about entering into such arrangements. And if we ask what it says to us, the message we find is, at root, simple: perform your contracts. The view that contracting parties owe only duties to pay damages in the event of non-performance imagines that the law speaks to us only through its sanctions and penalties, and so disregards everything else the law says and does, not least the reasons officials give when applying those sanctions. For when courts award damages in contract claims they are unequivocal: these are damages for breach of contract, providing compensation for losses caused by the defendant's failure to perform his contractual obligations.

Of course, given that the law says that we are all obligated to perform our contracts, we can ask why it is nonetheless so reluctant to compel performance. But it is a mistake to think that, unless the law makes us perform, it cannot really mean what it says when it identifies performance as obligatory. The question contracting parties face, and which the law answers by stipulating that there is a duty to perform one's contractual undertakings, is 'must I do as I promised?' For judges resolving claims for breach of contract, however, the question they must answer is not (or not simply) 'should the defendant have kept his promise?' but 'should *I*, as a state official and backed by its coercive machinery, now compel that defendant to perform?' These questions need not receive the same answer. There will sometimes be good reason for the state to tell us to do things which it would be unreasonable for it to compel us to do, and so it may be reasonable for the law to direct us to perform our contracts even where it would not be reasonable to enforce that obligation by compelling performance.[5] To put the point the other way around: that

---

[5] See too Stephen A Smith, 'The Law of Damages: Rules for Citizens or Rules for Courts?' in Ralph Cunnington and Djakhongir Saidov (eds), *Contract Damages: Domestic and International Perspectives* (Hart Publishing 2008).

it would (for example) be oppressive and costly to compel me to perform my employment contract are not reasons for the law to tell me that turning up for work is optional.

So legal obligations are not to be reduced to the coercive measures that attend their breach or to the threat of those measures. Nor does the obligatoriness of legal obligations extend only so far as the measures legal officials will in fact impose on those in breach. The fact that a court will, in the end, require me only to pay damages should I fail to turn up to work does not mean that my duty is, in reality, *either* to go to work *or* to pay damages, still less a bare duty to pay those damages in the event that I do not go to work. Indeed, the truth is that the content of the sanction which follows breach says nothing at all about the content of the obligation, and I can be under a legal obligation even where no sanction at all attaches to its breach. If *ubi ius, ibi remedium* is true of English positive law, it is not because it captures any necessary aspect of the relationship between legal rights and duties and their remedies.

It is possible, though unreasonable, to pay attention to the law only where it puts its money where its mouth is and forcibly compels compliance with its norms, and so it is possible for contracting parties to take their cue only from the judicial orders which follow claims for breach of contract. Perhaps many contracting parties think in just this way. But even though the law may be, in part, responsible for encouraging this sort of attitude, through its failure to do more to promote performance, it should be clear that this is not how it directs us to think or to act. Would it be better if the law authorised us to 'break' our contracts, so long as we made adequate compensation? Should it go further still and direct us *not* to perform where this would (say) maximise utility or increase social welfare? Showing that English law gives clear recognition and expression to the interest of contracting parties in receiving contractual performance does not show that it is right to do so, let alone that it should do more to see that interest secured in claims following breaches of contract. Nonetheless, the position English law has taken is clear: contracting parties are obligated to perform their contracts; the law of contract remedies support this, even in those cases where performance is not compelled, not least through the clear statement that these are remedies for *breach* of contract; and there should, therefore, be no doubt that the law recognises contracting parties' interest in contractual performance.

9.2 Performance and Compensation

Just as it is a mistake to think that the law's reluctance to order performance reveals the performance interest to be an illusion, it is likewise a mistake to conclude that, since contracting parties *do* have an interest in performance, it must be a deficiency of English contract law that it so often fails to secure it. Providing the claimant with the performance he is due is one good to which contract law and its remedial rules are properly directed. But it is not a good to be pursued at any cost. Courts faced with claims for breach of contract must make an all-things-considered judgment as to how, if at all, that breach should be remedied. That all-things-considered judgment requires consideration of the full range of reasons which bear on the law's resolution of such claims. The claimant's performance interest provides, in all cases, a court with a reason to see that the claimant is provided with that performance. But this is just one consideration and it must, in all cases, be weighed against other considerations which are likewise implicated in the law's response to these claims. Sometimes there will be competing goods and goals which outweigh the good of upholding the claimant's performance interest and so justify denying the claimant any redress. (Hence it is sometimes reasonable for the law to hold a contract to be valid but unenforceable.) At other times, the claimant's interest in obtaining performance is not overridden but its protection is rightly limited to accommodate other goods and goals whose pursuit would be compromised if performance were compelled. A claimant's performance interest is not denied simply by virtue of the fact that a court denies him performance.[6] Where full protection of the claimant's interest in performance would be unreasonable or is in any event impossible, it may yet be both possible and reasonable to protect it in part, and so his performance interest may play a role in grounding and shaping the court's response to a breach of contract even where it refuses to compel that performance.

We can, therefore, accept that contracting parties have an interest in receiving performance without committing ourselves to the view that the

---

[6] So it is wrong to say that, if contracting parties have a right to performance, 'we must allow them to assert that right in cases of breach of contract' (where 'assert' is to be read as 'enforce'); so too that, where a claimant 'is barred from enforcing his right to performance', '[i]t would be more honest to admit that ... the claimant acquired no such right upon contract formation' (Charlie Webb, 'Performance and Compensation: An Analysis of Contract Damages and Contractual Obligation' (2006) 26 OJLS 41, 70–71). A claimant can have a right that the defendant perform without also having a right that the court compel the defendant to perform.

primary or default response to breaches of contract should be to compel that performance. Indeed recognition of the performance interest is compatible with a legal framework which routinely denies claimants that performance. The reasons typically given for the common law's preference for damages over specific performance – the cost of policing such orders, the excessive state interference with defendants' liberty they sometimes entail, the severity of the penal consequences of failing to comply with the order – are sound reasons and should embarrass no defender of the performance interest.

Those who have argued that the performance interest should be better protected in remedying breaches of contract have tended to grant, if only by implication, the reasonableness of the law's subordination of specific performance and focused their attention instead on how the performance interest may be secured through an award of damages, where these concerns have little or no bite. But while it is clear how specific performance realises the claimant's interest in receiving performance, how this may be achieved through damages is not. One way to see this is to look again at the view of contractual obligation associated with Holmes. On this view, the primacy of damages signals a rejection of the performance interest: faced with a claim for breach of contract, the law opts to deny the claimant performance and instead to give him compensation for the losses he is caused by the contract not being performed. As we have seen, this view goes wrong by not attending to other features of contract law, including the reasons judges give when awarding damages to contract claimants, which show that this option is one not granted to contracting parties. If I contract to do work for you, the law tells me I am obligated to do that work, even where no court would, if called upon, compel me to perform. The fact that a court would only ever order me to pay you damages does not mean that the law licences me to abandon the job and write you a cheque instead.

But what Holmes got right was that, if the law did give me that option, it would mean that I was under no legal obligation to perform. Of course, I might still opt to perform and, if I did, your interest in receiving that performance would be realised. But the law would be expressing no preference between my performing and my providing you instead with its monetary equivalent: so long as I leave you with something of equal value and hence no worse off than you would have been had I performed, I have done all that is required of me. And, if this were the position the law took, we could not say that it granted any particular protection to your interest in performance.

There is, in short, a basic difference between having one's contract performed and receiving compensation for its non-performance. In this respect if no other, the Holmes view offers, or points toward, a clearer understanding of the diverse objectives of contract law and contract remedies than the orthodoxy which takes both specific performance and standard damages awards as alternative means of securing a single 'expectation' interest. For if compensatory damages really were no more and no less than an alternative means of realising the claimant's (one) interest, an alternative form of the 'performance' the claimant is due, then Holmes was right: one can fulfil one's contractual duty and the law can protect a contracting party's interests just as fully through the payment of compensatory damages. Again, it does not follow that, if the law is to recognise contracting parties as having an interest in performance, it must do what it can to provide them with that performance. That the claimant has an interest in performance and not simply in performance or its monetary equivalent does not mean that the law is unreasonable in its preference for damages over specific performance or in its assessment of the damages claimants are then due. But it does mean that we must reject the view that compensatory damages are simply an alternative means of providing performance and instead acknowledge that a claimant who is awarded such damages receives something other than the performance he is due.

9.3 Loss

All remedies for breach of contract, as remedies *for breach of contract*, provide some recognition of a claimant's performance interest. Even an award of nominal damages serves to give expression to the fact that the promisee did not receive the performance he was due. So far as these remedies play their part in encouraging performance, they serve to advance the performance interests of contracting parties generally. But not all of these remedies secure or advance the claimant's own performance interest. There is, to repeat, a difference between having one's contract performed and being compensated for the loss one suffers on account of its non-performance and an award of damages aimed at providing such compensation will often do little to advance the claimant's interest in obtaining that performance.

This point stands however those losses are measured. One criticism sometimes levelled at English contract law is that it adopts too narrow a view of loss. One way this argument is made is to say that, when assessing damages, the court should attend to the claimant's interest in performance and not just to the financial returns performance would bring. This is true enough. But putting it in this way risks running together two distinct arguments, providing two distinct bases for a damages claim. While the first concerns how we identify and measure loss for the purposes of compensatory awards to ensure that they properly compensate those who do not receive the performance they are due, the second looks beyond compensation to see how damages can provide a claimant with that performance.

Not all losses are balance-sheet losses. Sometimes this is because the balance-sheet or market valuation of some commodity does not match the claimant's own valuation of that commodity. *Ruxley Electronics and Construction Ltd v Forsyth* is an example.[7] Forsyth contracted for Ruxley to build him a swimming pool. The pool Ruxley provided was not of the specified depth. The evidence was that the difference in depth made no difference to the market value of the property to which the pool was appended and that the pool was safe to be used in all the ways Forsyth intended to use it. Forsyth was nonetheless dissatisfied with the pool and refused to pay Ruxley the balance outstanding under the contract. When Ruxley sued for this money, Forsyth counterclaimed for damages for breach. The court had to determine what damages were payable. Forsyth argued that he should be awarded the £21,560 it would cost to get another builder in to dig out the pool to the specified depth. Ruxley, by contrast, contended that no substantial damages were payable as the breach had caused no loss. The trial judge awarded Forsyth £2,500 as damages for his 'loss of amenity', an award upheld on appeal to the House of Lords.

One reason given for the award was that, while the market considered there to be no difference between the value of the pool he wanted and the value of the pool he got, for Forsyth there was a difference.[8] So far as he was concerned, the pool he ended up with was worse – worth less – than the pool he was promised and the damages he was awarded represented this difference in value. This idea is commonly expressed, as it was in *Ruxley*, in terms of the claimant's 'consumer surplus': the additional value he placed on performance beyond its market value. But the same issue arises where the claimant places a value lower than the market on

<hr>

[7] [1996] AC 344 (HL).
[8] Ibid 360–61 (Lord Mustill). Cf ibid 374 (Lord Lloyd) where the award is explained as compensation for Forsyth's consequential losses: the disappointment and lost enjoyment he suffered as a result of not getting the pool he wanted.

the (defective) performance he receives. Indeed this seems to be the better reading of *Ruxley*: the loss Forsyth suffered came not from him placing a higher value on the pool he was promised than the market but from his valuing the pool he got less.

It is not only those whose valuations differ from the market who risk being undercompensated by an approach to loss which looks only to the claimant's balance-sheet position. The same is also true in cases where the claimant contracts for a 'pure' service: one that leaves no 'marketable residuum' in the claimant's hands, no increase in his patrimonial wealth. Say you hire me to give you a contract law tutorial. You are not planning to act on the information I give you and so you are looking to derive no financial profit from what you will learn. This is just something you are interested in knowing about. So my tuition will leave you, in balance-sheet terms, no richer. By the same token, my failure to give you the tutorial leaves you no poorer. Nonetheless, it is clear my services have a value: a market value and so a value to those who, like you, have agreed to pay the market rate for them. If I do not provide the tutorial, you then lose something of value.

The courts have, on occasion, recognised that someone who receives substandard services may suffer a loss even where this makes no difference to his balance-sheet position and that, in such cases, the claimant should be compensated by an award of damages measured by the difference in value between the services promised and those provided.[9] Elsewhere, however, such claims are routinely denied. Say you want to know more about contract law because you are in a contractual dispute and you want to know whether you have a claim. You hire me to advise you. But I advise you badly. What damages can you recover? It depends. If you act on my advice, you can recover for the losses you suffer as a result: for instance, the wasted expense of doomed litigation. But if you ignore my advice or if it otherwise makes no difference to the decision you make, you recover only nominal damages.

It is right to ask what difference my advice made. If my advice caused you to take a course of action you would not otherwise have taken, any losses resulting from that course of action are losses resulting from my

---

[9] See e.g. *White Arrow Express Ltd v Lamey's Distribution Ltd* [1995] CLC 1251 (CA) 1255–56 (Lord Bingham MR); *Attorney General v Blake* [2001] 1 AC 268 (HL) 286 (Lord Nicholls); *Giedo van der Garde BV v Force India Formula One Team Ltd* [2010] EWHC 2373 (QB). As the last of these cases shows, when measuring this difference in value, we again face the question of whether value is to be measured by reference to the market or by the claimant's own valuation of the services.

breach, losses for which I am responsible. If it made no difference to your decision-making, then whatever loss followed from your decisions cannot be attributed to me. Yet even where you do not rely on my advice, the fact remains that the advice you were given was worse than the advice you should have received. If bad legal advice has any value at all, it clearly has less value than good advice. And so, here too, you contracted and paid for a particular service of undoubted value and received something worse, something of little or no value at all.

Isn't this a loss to you? Perhaps not. In the tuition example, you suffer a loss when I do not perform, notwithstanding that the tutorial would add nothing to your balance sheet. One way that this loss is evidenced is by the money you were willing to pay to have the tutorial. But the value of the tutorial to you does not lie in the money you spent on it. Quite the opposite: you made the choice to spend money on it because it was – or you judged it would be – of value to you. Valuable how? In the contribution it makes to your goals, its advancement of your interests. You have an interest in knowing about contract law, an interest which you wish to advance by having me give you tuition. This interest, for you, is not instrumental; the knowledge you wish to acquire is not a means to some other end. You value it for its own sake. When I do not give the tutorial, I thereby fail to advance your interests in the way I would have advanced them had I done as I had agreed, leaving you worse off than you would and should have been. This is your loss.

The advice example is different. Here too you want to be informed about the law. But this time you want this information to assist you in making a particular decision. The value to you of this information is not intrinsic but instrumental and the interests you are looking to advance through obtaining my advice are the interests affected by that decision: (say) your financial interests and the broader range of interests to which your financial resources may be directed. So this time your interests (as you take them to be) are not set back simply by my failure to advise you properly. Instead my bad advice harms your interests only if you act on that advice and the decision you then make turns out worse than the decision you would have made had I, in proper performance of our contract, advised you well.

So contractual performance can have a value even where, as in cases of pure services, it does nothing to improve your balance-sheet position. Being denied such performance can therefore cause you loss – deny you something of value, leave you worse off – even if it leaves you, in balance-sheet terms, no poorer. But whether and by how much you are left worse off as a result of breach depends, *inter alia*, on your reasons for entering into that contract, on the interests of yours that its performance will serve. Accordingly, if a court is to see that you are properly compensated for the losses breach caused you, it needs to attend to these reasons, to these interests.

Yet when attending in this way to the interests which performance serves, the court is doing nothing to advance your performance interest. To compensate a claimant in full is to see that his interests, considered in the round, end up suffering no setback as result of the defendant's breach. But this does not mean that the claimant obtains the performance he contracted for, nor even any greater part of that performance. The pool Ruxley built for Forsyth was safe to dive into. However Forsyth said he did not feel safe. The damages the court awarded him didn't get him the pool he contracted for, nor did they do anything to advance his interest in having a pool he would feel safe diving into. Instead Forsyth was left with the same imperfect pool and a sum of money he could then spend as he wished to secure other benefits, advancing other interests of his, equal in measure though different in kind to those he was denied by Ruxley's breach.

9.4   Securing Performance

Receiving something of equal value to one's contracted-for performance is not to have one's contract performed, and so compensation is not performance, however sensitive that compensation is to the circumstances and interests of the claimant. Nonetheless, *Ruxley* does help to show how the claimant's interest in performance could have been realised, at least in its greater part, through a damages award.[10] Forsyth argued that he should be given the money it would take to have another builder come in to complete the work, an argument the House of Lords rejected. One reason given for refusing Forsyth this sum was that it was in excess of the loss he suffered.[11] So it was. The breach did not leave Forsyth £21,560 out of pocket or with a pool worth £21,560 less to him than the pool he requested. And if Forsyth had gone ahead and spent that money getting the pool fixed, so that he did end up down by this amount, the court (and the defendant) could reasonably have objected that this increased loss was one which Forsyth brought on himself and for which Ruxley should not be held accountable.

[10] For the full argument see Webb (n 6).   [11] *Ruxley* (n 7) 359 (Lord Jauncey).

But there is a different case to be made for awarding Forsyth that sum. Ruxley undertook to provide Forsyth with a pool of the specified depth. By failing to do this, it breached its contract with Forsyth. This breach left Forsyth with something worse, something of less value to him, than the pool he had contracted for, and this loss could be made good by an award of damages measured by reference to this difference in value. But Ruxley's duty was not simply to provide Forsyth with something of equal value to the promised pool; it was to provide him with that pool. Moreover, that pool could still be supplied and Forsyth could still, to this extent, receive the performance he was due. One way to do this would have been to order specific performance, compelling Ruxley to go back and complete the work it had started. But much the same result could be achieved by ordering Ruxley to provide Forsyth with the money it would take to pay someone else to do the job. Far from conferring on Forsyth an 'uncovenanted profit', this would, to this extent, secure for him the very performance he was promised. Or it would do provided the money was indeed used in this way. So damages can achieve a partial realisation of the claimant's performance interest – partial because that performance will likely be delayed and come via a different route to that stipulated in the contract – through a cost of cure award which is then in fact used to cure the defect in the performance initially provided.

Perhaps the closest we get to an expression of this idea in the English cases comes from Oliver J's judgment in *Radford v De Froberville*.[12] Radford sold part of his land to De Froberville, with De Froberville promising to build a wall on the boundary with the land Radford retained. The wall was not built and Radford sued. De Froberville argued that Radford had suffered no loss as the wall was not for his benefit but for the benefit of tenants who were in possession of the land. Oliver J found that Radford intended to have an equivalent wall built on his own side of the boundary and held that he was entitled to damages measured by the cost of getting this done. To the argument that Radford's only loss was the diminution in the value of his reversionary interest, such as there was, which resulted from the breach, Oliver J responded:

> Whilst I see the force of this, I do not think that it really meets the point that, whatever his status, the plaintiff had a contractual right to have the work done and does in fact want to do it.[13]

---

[12] [1977] 1 WLR 1262 (Ch). See too *Tabcorp Holdings Ltd v Bowen Investments Pty Ltd* [2009] HCA 8, (2009) 236 CLR 272.
[13] Ibid 1285.

In other words, independent of whatever loss the breach may have caused him, Radford had an interest in having the contract performed. And so, regardless of whether the sum could be regarded as the proper measure of that loss, there was reason to award him cost of cure damages because he had an interest in obtaining the performance he contracted for and this was one way to give it to him.

In *Radford*, Oliver J considered that cost of cure damages should be awarded only where it would be reasonable to have the work done. In *Ruxley* it was held that it would not be reasonable to award Forsyth damages on a cost of cure basis. Though the court considered that it was applying the test identified in *Radford*, asking whether it would be reasonable for the claimant to have the work done is not the same as asking whether it would be reasonable for the court to order the defendant to fund that work. (For example, the suggestion, taken up in *Ruxley*, that the claimant's intention to have the work done is relevant to the application of the reasonableness test makes little sense if the question is whether it would be reasonable for the claimant to have that work done.) But since the question for the court is whether to make such an order, it is right for the court to ask itself whether this would be a reasonable thing for it to do.

When is it reasonable? In *Ruxley* the court was concerned that awarding Forsyth cost of cure damages would give him an unjustified windfall. But, as mentioned already, it would constitute such a windfall only if the money were not then used to have the pool rebuilt to his specifications. If it were, Forsyth would be in no better a position than he would have been in had the contract been performed. The courts typically impose no conditions on how a claimant uses his damages. This approach makes sense in the standard case, where the damages award is not aimed at securing for the claimant some specific item or performance.[14] But where the object of awarding the claimant this sum of damages is to provide him with the means to obtain some such performance, there is a case for making the award conditional on the money being so used.[15] If it is thought that the award would cause problems similar to those which count against specific performance – problems of supervision, the prospect of further litigation – the next best approach is for the court to order cost of cure damages only if it is satisfied that the claimant intends to use the money to effect repairs. This is the approach *Ruxley* adopts.

[14] See further Charlie Webb, 'Justifying Damages' in Jason W Neyers, Richard Bronaugh and Stephen GA Pitel, *Exploring Contract Law* (Hart Publishing 2009), 164–65.
[15] See Webb (n 6) 62–63.

But an intention to have the defective performance put right may not be enough. On one view the court should go on to ask whether it is worthwhile to see this sum of money spent in this way. The trial judge found that Forsyth did not intend to have the pool rebuilt. But even after Forsyth gave an undertaking to use his damages in this way, the court held that awarding him the £21,560 to fix the pool would be unreasonable. The pool was substantially fit for purpose; was it really worth spending all that money to have it rebuilt to the agreed specifications? Often this line of thinking is seen as directed towards the prevention of economic waste, but it may also reflect a concern not to be unfair to the defendant by requiring him to bear a significant financial burden for no corresponding benefit to the claimant. Either way, there is nothing incoherent or unreasonable about courts taking such considerations into account. As we have seen, the claimant's performance interest provides a reason for the law to take measures directed to securing that performance for the claimant. But this may yet be outweighed by competing considerations, identifying other goods and values which would be threatened by such an award. Damages provide a means of protecting the claimant's performance interest which avoids some of the concerns which attend orders of specific performance, but there may be other reasons which count against its protection in this form too.

Much, though not all, of the work done by the reasonableness requirement might, however, be rationalised on a different basis. Consider the example discussed in *Ruxley* of a contract to build a house with a provision that one of the lower courses of bricks is to be blue.[16] The builder uses yellow bricks instead – a clear breach – but the house is completed and is in all other respects in conformity with the terms of the contract. Replacing the yellow bricks with blue would require substantial demolition work at very high cost. For this reason, there is no doubt having the bricks replaced would be considered unreasonable and cost of cure damages would be denied. We might, as we have seen, explain this by saying that spending time and money on this would be wasteful or that it would be unfair to the builder. But considerations like this come into the balance only if there is something for them to be balanced against, only if there is indeed an argument in favour of ordering cost of cure in the first place. Now the case for cost of cure damages here is that they enable the claimant to obtain the performance he is due under the contract: the claimant is entitled to blue bricks and cost of cure damages would allow him to get them.

---

[16] For the leading real-world example see *Jacob & Youngs, Inc v Kent* 230 NY 239 (1921).

If, however, the contract does not provide for blue bricks, the cost of cure claim does not get off the ground as it would no longer give him performance.

Isn't it clear that the claimant *is* entitled to the blue bricks? Not necessarily. What matters is not what the claimant was due at the date of contract formation or at the point work commenced but what he is due now. The builder undertook to provide blue bricks and so there is no doubt that he was in breach of contract when he used yellow bricks instead. But now the house is built and the blue bricks can be incorporated only at immense cost and inconvenience. Should we take the builder to have undertaken to provide the blue bricks even in these circumstances? Contract lawyers have long been reluctant to read in qualifications to apparently absolute undertakings. But this approach is questionable: it is rarely reasonable to understand 'I undertake to φ' to mean 'I undertake to φ unconditionally'.[17] Treating such statements as grounding unconditional obligations is to supplement the parties' intentions just as much as we would were we to read in certain unstated conditions. The fact that it would be unreasonable (whether on the basis of waste or unfairness) to require the builder to pay for the building to be demolished and rebuilt with blue bricks does not mean that this cannot be what the parties have agreed. But it does mean that we should be slow to conclude that this is the proper implication of their express undertakings.[18]

9.5   *Panatown*: Loss

The leading judicial discussion of the use of damages to protect a claimant's performance interest shows only an imperfect grasp of these points. In *Alfred McAlpine Construction Ltd v Panatown Ltd*, Panatown had contracted for McAlpine to construct an office block and car park on land owned by UIPL, like Panatown, a subsidiary of Unex Corporation.[19] At the same time as entering into the contract with Panatown, McAlpine executed a duty of care deed with UIPL, by which it undertook to exercise reasonable care in doing the work. There were serious defects with the buildings McAlpine constructed and Panatown

---

[17] Cf Charlie Webb, *Reason and Restitution: A Theory of Unjust Enrichment* (Oxford University Press 2016), 128–29.

[18] Making the broad point: *L Schuler AG v Wickman Machine Tool Sales Ltd* [1974] AC 235 (HL) 251 (Lord Reid).

[19] [2001] 1 AC 518 (HL).

sued for breach of contract. By majority, the House of Lords held that Panatown had suffered no loss and so could recover no more than nominal damages.

The common law has long struggled with contracts such as this, where the beneficiary of the promisor's performance is not the promisee but a third party. For here it seems that the party who suffers if the contract is not performed is the intended beneficiary of that performance. With privity denying any claim to the third party, the defendant could breach without meaningful sanction. The party with the claim has no loss to be compensated, the party who has suffered the loss has no claim: the possibility of an effective remedy disappears into a 'legal black hole'. Putting it this way suggests that the problem lay with the doctrine of privity not the law on damages.[20] That breach causes the promisee no loss is just the fact of the matter; it is the rule of law denying the beneficiary a claim which creates the injustice. On this basis, the solution was to reform or abolish privity. No adjustments to the remedies available to the promisee were needed, save where they might offer a temporary workaround, providing an indirect means to what privity's abolition would achieve directly.[21]

But if allowing the third party to enforce the contract provides an adequate solution, it does so only where and only because this serves the promisee's interests too.[22] The promisee does not cease to have an interest in performance where that performance is directed to advancing some other beneficiary's interests and that performance does not cease to have a value to the promisee simply because it has a value to that beneficiary too. And while the promisee's interests – in performance and in his not being disadvantaged by the contract's non-performance – may on occasion be secured by allowing the third-party beneficiary to sue, more often their protection requires that we provide a direct remedy to the promisee. Indeed, we can, in the arguments set out already, identify two distinct grounds upon which the promisee in such a contract may be able to make out a claim for substantial damages.

First: we have seen that not all losses are balance-sheet losses. Accordingly, the fact that performance brings the promisee no balance-sheet gain does not

---

[20] See e.g. ibid 534–35 (Lord Clyde).
[21] Such as the rule developed in *The Albazero* [1977] AC 774 (HL).
[22] Indeed, the strongest case for privity reform was that by denying a third-party beneficiary the cause of action the contracting parties intend him to have compromised the promisee's own interest in the contract's performance. There's no reason for the law to give you a claim simply because I don't make the gift I intended to make to you. This does not change where my reason for making the gift was that someone else paid me to.

PERFORMANCE DAMAGES 221

mean it has no value to him and the fact that breach leaves the promisee no worse off in balance-sheet terms does not mean that it causes him no loss. If I contract for you to deliver some flowers to Erika and you do not make the delivery, it is not only Erika who's the worse for your breach. What I have contracted for is, from my perspective, tantamount to a pure service. The mere fact that pure services leave no balance-sheet gain does not mean they have no value and the value they have does not lie only in the prospect that they may bring balance-sheet gains down the line. So there is a value to me in Erika getting the flowers: indeed this is why I was willing to use my own (valuable) resources to that end. If you do not then perform, I am denied something I value and so, unless some equivalent is provided in its stead, I am left worse off. Accordingly, I suffer a loss if you fail to deliver the flowers to Erika no less than had I contracted for you to deliver them to me and I have as strong a claim that you should compensate me for that loss in the former case as I do in the latter. The proper measure of that loss is in turn the same as we find elsewhere: the difference between the value of the performance contracted for and the value of the performance in fact rendered, combined with any consequential losses the breach went on to cause.

Second: the promisee in these cases no less than in others has an interest in the contract being performed. This interest is secured not by seeing that he is left no worse off in the event of the promisor's breach but by ensuring that the contract is, so far as possible, performed. Therefore, whatever losses the breach might have caused to the promisee and so independently of whatever compensation he may be due, the promisee can call for damages to be awarded so as to provide him with the performance he is due. As we have seen, this can be achieved by an award which provides me with the means to purchase that, or some such, performance from another source, at least if the money is then so used. In *Ruxley* this was the cost of hiring another builder to come in and dig out the pool to the agreed depth; in our example this would be the money it would take for me to pay someone else to deliver such flowers to Erika.

The judgments in *Panatown* were hampered on both sides by a failure to tell these two arguments apart. The question that divided the court was whether Panatown could make out a claim to substantial damages simply by virtue of not having received the performance it contracted for. The answer to this question was taken to turn on whether McAlpine's breach could be said to have caused Panatown loss. The focus of the case then became whether such a loss could be identified, with the result that the best case for awarding Panatown substantial damages was never properly considered.

Panatown had suffered no balance-sheet loss. It had no interest in the land, it had not paid for repairs and there was no evidence that it would, so it was, by this measure, in no worse a position than it would have been had the contract been performed. Nonetheless, as we have seen, not all losses are balance-sheet losses and often breach will cause the promisee a loss despite it making no difference to his balance-sheet position. This is true with our contract to give flowers to Erika. I value Erika getting the flowers and suffer a loss if she does not. It is also true in the example, discussed in *Panatown*, of the husband who contracts for a new roof for the matrimonial home owned by his wife.[23] If the work is not completed, the husband is left worse off.[24] Indeed this case is even clearer: as if the only benefit of having a roof on your home is the difference this makes to its resale value.

Could the same be said of Panatown? Absent truly exceptional circumstances, whenever individuals contract on their own account, they do so with a view to advancing their own interests, even where the performance they contract for is also intended to benefit some third party. I have an interest in seeing Erika happy, which I intend that our contract for you to deliver her flowers will serve. As we have seen, it is because my interests and not only Erika's are served by your performance that your breach causes not only her but also me loss. Unless I took this performance to be in my interests, my decision to enter into this contract with you and to deploy my own resources to this end would be irrational.[25]

This is not true when companies contract. Companies exist to advance human interests. But the mechanism by which company law advances these interests involves treating corporations as legal entities with proprietary and financial interests of their own, distinct from those whose interests they exist to serve.[26] Companies often contract to advance these

---

[23] The example comes originally from Lord Griffiths' judgment in *St Martin's Property Corporation Ltd v Sir Robert McAlpine Ltd*, reported as *Linden Gardens Trust Ltd v Lenesta Sludge Disposal Ltd* [1994] 1 AC 85 (HL) 96–97.

[24] Though the measure of this loss is not, as Lord Griffiths thought, the cost of completing the work, unless the husband does indeed incur this expense, but the difference in value between the work done and the work promised: cf *Panatown* (n 19) 533–34 (Lord Clyde).

[25] Hence the suggestion that we might take the fact that the promisee contracted for a particular performance as presumptive evidence that that performance is of value to the promisee: see *Woodar Investment Development Ltd v Wimpey Construction UK Ltd* [1980] 1 WLR 277 (HL) 300–01 (Lord Scarman), *Panatown* (n 19) 592 (Lord Millett).

[26] Notwithstanding that, in other respects, a company's interests are identified with the interests of its shareholders or of other groups: see e.g. *Gaiman v National Association for Mental Health* [1971] Ch 317 (Ch); *Greenhalgh v Arderne Cinemas Ltd* [1951] Ch 286 (CA); Companies Act 2006, s 172.

distinct corporate interests and, where they do, breach may set those interests back, causing the company loss. But companies may alternatively contract to benefit those whose interests the company exists to serve and without any mediating or collateral benefit to the company itself. *Panatown* provides what appears to be an example of this. There was no indication that Panatown had any interest in – indeed anything at all to gain from – the development of UIPL's land. Why then contract to have this work done? Presumably because it was in the interests of Panatown's and UIPL's parent company, Unex, to have this work done and to have it funded in this way. That the contract was in the financial interests of Unex does not mean that it was also in Panatown's interests. Unex's profits are not Panatown's profits. By the same token, where the contract is not performed and these profits are not realised, Unex's loss is not Panatown's loss.

None of this calls into question Panatown's right to performance of the contract. One can have an interest in performance even where that performance is not in one's broader interests and a contracting party is not denied a right to performance simply on the basis that that performance would not in fact make him better off. But, if this argument is correct – if, that is, it is true to say that the contract was in the interests of Unex but not in Panatown's own interests – then, though Panatown was denied the performance it was indeed due, the majority were right on the facts to hold that Panatown suffered no loss as a result of McAlpine's breach.

9.6   *Panatown*: Performance

There was no basis for awarding Panatown substantial damages as compensation since there was no loss to compensate. Nonetheless, it had an interest in the contract being performed and this interest provided an alternative basis for an award of damages. The nearest we get to an expression of this idea is in the minority judgments. The minority, like the majority, considered that Panatown could recover damages on its own account only if it had suffered a loss. Unlike the majority, they thought that it had. What explains this difference? Not any disagreement on the facts. Rather it seems that the majority and minority diverged because they had different understandings of what counts as a loss: what the minority considered a loss was not thought to be a loss by the majority.

The idea that the minority endorsed and Lords Clyde and Jauncey in the majority rejected was that a contracting party may suffer a loss just by

virtue of not receiving the performance he contracted for.[27] This proposition can, however, be read in two different ways. One is that, since the
promisee will typically value performance, breach can cause him loss on
the basis that it leaves him instead with something less valuable. This is
the idea we have encountered already: you suffer a loss when I do not give
you the tutorial you contract for; I suffer a loss when you do not deliver
Erika the flowers. But another way to read this suggestion is to say that
the fact the promisee did not receive the performance he was due is itself
the loss. Understood in this way, it does not matter what value is to be
attached to that performance; if the contract is breached, the promisee
suffers a loss just by virtue of not getting – and so losing out on – what he
contracted for. So, while on the first reading the promisee's loss lies in his
getting something worse than what he contracted for, on the second it lies
simply in his getting something different.

The minority judgments show no clear commitment to either one of
these readings and indeed seem by and large oblivious to the difference
between them. Understanding their references to loss in the second of
these two senses would, however, help explain why they took the proper
measure of the promisee's loss in such cases as the cost of obtaining
performance elsewhere. If the promisee's loss comes from getting something worse than the performance he contracted for, he can be compensated by giving him something as good, as valuable. But this does not
require supplying him with the funds to purchase that performance from
another provider. This is one lesson of *Ruxley*. If, however, we understand the promisee's loss to lie simply in the fact that he did not get the
performance he was due, that loss can be made good only if the claimant
ends up with that performance. If the defendant is not to be compelled to
perform himself, much the same result may still be achievable through
a cost of cure award by which the defendant effectively purchases that
performance for the claimant from another source.

So if the loss lies in the very fact that the contract has not been
performed, the only compensation for that loss is performance of the
contract. But we can capture the same idea just as well – indeed better –
without reference to loss and compensation by saying that the claimant is
entitled to performance of the contract and so should be awarded

---

[27] The third majority judge, Lord Browne-Wilkinson, appeared also to endorse the idea that
there could be a loss simply in not receiving the performance one is due. Yet he held that
Panatown suffered no such loss because UIPL had a claim of its own under the duty of
care deed. How this loss, however understood, was precluded by UIPL's right to sue is
unclear.

substantial damages so as to provide him with that performance. These two senses in which a promisee may be said to suffer a loss on account of not receiving the performance he contracted for then map on to the two arguments for damages set out in the previous section: one aimed at ensuring the promisee is not left worse off as a result of breach, the other directed to providing him with the performance he contracted for. So to the extent that the minority judgments took Panatown's loss to lie in the simple fact that it did not obtain the performance it contracted for, they can be taken to endorse the view that a contracting party's performance interest provides an independent basis for an award of substantial damages.

Framing what was in substance a claim for damages which would give Panatown the performance it was due as a claim for compensation for the loss of that performance came at a cost, for it made it possible for the majority to reject this argument without full consideration of its merits. As Lord Clyde noted, this idea of a loss of performance comes 'very close to a way of describing a breach of contract':

> A breach of contract may cause a loss, but it is not in itself a loss in any meaningful sense. When one refers to a loss in the context of a breach of contract, one is in my view referring to the incidence of some personal or patrimonial damage.[28]

All this is right. Panatown had not received the performance it was due but it was no worse off for it. Awards of nominal damages presuppose the possibility of breach without loss. So, even if it is possible to extend the term 'loss' to cover the mere fact that one did not get what one was due, it is clear that this is not the idea of loss that the courts use. As such, it looked like the minority were engaged in a sort of subterfuge – reaching their preferred answer by redefining the terms of the question – or were simply mistaken. Once this was exposed, their argument was undermined. If, however, the references to loss had been avoided and the argument made instead in terms of Panatown seeking damages to enable it to obtain the performance it contracted for, the majority could still have pointed out that Panatown had been caused no loss. But then the rejoinder would more clearly have been: so what? As Oliver J had said in *Radford*, the claimant has a right to the work being done and it still wanted it done. At the very least, the majority would have had to do more to show why Panatown's claim should be rejected.

---

[28] *Panatown* (n 19) 534.

Should Panatown have succeeded? If cost of cure damages were to be awarded to provide Panatown with the performance it was due, it mattered that the money would indeed be used to secure that performance. But while the court believed that the reparative work would be done, it was not clear who would be paying for it. No doubt the money would come from somewhere within the Unex group, but there was nothing to suggest that it would be Panatown. It matters ordinarily that it is the claimant who will pay: neither the majority nor the minority welcomed the possibility that 'the employer in such a case could recover the cost of effecting the necessary repairs and then put the money in his own pocket'.[29] However, given the relationship between Panatown, UIPL and its parent, it was likely that the internal accounting of the Unex group would see that, in substance if not in form, those damages were used to pay for that work and Panatown would be left with no windfall. For the minority, this was enough. But, contrary to the suggestion of the minority, the award would not extend to damages for delay. True, Panatown's performance interest extended to having the work done on time. Necessarily, however, this part of the performance it contracted for could no longer be provided. The only basis for awarding damages for delay was for the losses this delay caused. If these losses were not Panatown's, these damages were not Panatown's to recover.

9.7   Conclusion

How far the cases acknowledge that contracting parties have an interest in their contracts being performed and how far they recognise that the protection and realisation of this interest is one possible, and proper, aim of an award of damages is unclear. It is unclear not simply on account of the mixed messages coming from the cases but, more broadly, because those cases show significant confusion about these ideas; confusion also found in, and encouraged by, the academic writing. One such confusion is the thought that recognition of the performance interest provides what is just another head of damage for which the claimant may recover compensation or that it gives us an alternative, and broader, understanding of the loss which breach may cause and which such damages can aim to make good. No doubt, the courts' understanding of loss *is* at times too narrow and there is good reason to attend to the non-financial, non-balance-sheet interests performance may serve. But the fact that

[29] Ibid 571 (Lord Jauncey), see too 560 (Lord Goff).

claimants may contract for more than financial reasons and that the losses they suffer from breach may go beyond their financial, balance-sheet losses does not mean that the proper measure of their losses is always, or even often, the cost of having the defective performance cured.

The case for making a cost of cure award is instead that the claimant has an interest in performance irrespective of the value he attaches to that performance and so whatever the losses he may suffer in the event of breach. The second confusion comes in here, with the thought that contracting parties' legal rights and duties are determined by and co-extensive with the remedial measures the courts adopt. This is Holmes' confusion but it is also the confusion of those who think that, if the claimant is to have a right to performance – and the defendant a duty to perform – the court has no option but to see that he gets that performance. The truth is that a claimant's right that the defendant perform need not be accompanied by any right against the court that it intervene to secure that performance for him. Accordingly, whether the court should then intervene to this end is a question which remains live even once we accept that, as between claimant and defendant, performance is not optional but obligatory. So recognising a claimant's performance interest does not alone determine how breaches of contract should be remedied. Nonetheless, its recognition is significant, for it provides a basis for an award of damages which is distinct from compensatory awards, one which is neither addressed to nor limited by the losses which result from the breach. There will, as we have seen, be times when it reasonable to deny such awards. But if they are to be denied, it will not do simply to point out that such an award would exceed the claimant's losses.

10

Proving Contract Damages

ADAM KRAMER

In commercial claims the balance of probabilities test has very little to say about the proof of what would have happened but for the breach, and so what loss was suffered. The fair-wind principle and presumptions such as that of breaking even mean that the claimant is given the benefit of the doubt. And the loss of chance principle holds much of the field, although its application to commercial disputes – especially where the market or trading is involved – requires careful unpacking.

10.1 Introduction

The legal principles governing damages – remoteness, legal causation, mitigation – are frequently explored and understood. But there has been very little consideration of the law's approach to proof of loss in contract and tort cases, despite its huge importance to practitioners and to the outcome of disputes, save for those thickets of the proof field apparently governed by a distinct legal principle (such as the *Lavarack* principle). A short section in Harvey McGregor's encyclopaedic work on damages is a rare exception.[1] If they thought about it, most people would probably assume that the burden falls on the claimant to prove all loss to the civil standard of the balance of probabilities in the usual way, subject only to a minor wrinkle of loss of chance. They would be wrong.

I would like to thank Andrew Summers, Sarah Green, Sir George Leggatt and an anonymous reviewer for comments on a draft of this chapter.

[1] Harvey McGregor, *McGregor on Damages* (19th edn, Sweet & Maxwell 2014) [10–001]–[10–007]. It would be impossible and wrong to write any chapter on damages at this time without referring to Harvey's recent death, which is a sad loss to the damages field and all of us in it.

10.2   The Difficulties of Proving the Non-breach Position

Once a claimant has proven that a contract has been breached or tort committed, attention turns to loss.[2] The claimant must then prove a difference between the position he is in ('the breach position') and the position he would have been in but for the breach ('the non-breach position'[3]).

The breach position is a question of historical and actual fact – what happened, what was spent, and what was received.[4] It can be established with precision and the claimant has the burden of doing so.[5] And proving it means proving that on the evidence it was more likely than not that the event did happen.[6] Probability here is used in the sense of 'you are probably right'. The uncertainty is only epistemic.

But the non-breach position is of its nature a hypothetical. Proof of it is a different type of exercise – proof of how the world would have operated in a counterfactual situation. It is necessarily more uncertain – or uncertain in a more profound way – than the breach position.

10.3   Resolving Uncertainty in the Claimant's Favour

The law is highly sympathetic to the difficulties the claimant faces in proving the non-breach position. It relaxes the burden on the claimant. And this approach appears to have started with the eighteenth-century case of *Armory v Delamirie*,[7] in which the defendant to a claim for trover of a jewel refused to produce it, thwarting the claimant chimney-sweep's attempt to prove its value. In the circumstances, the court gave the claimant the benefit of any uncertainty. The core of this principle is

---

[2] Of course, some torts cannot be established until the necessary element of damage has been proven.

[3] See further Adam Kramer, *The Law of Contract Damages* (Hart 2014) 14–15.

[4] There is also the question of what will happen (see further ibid 246–47). This is uncertain in a similar way to the non-breach position, and although there is less authority on the point, it appears that the same approach as described below (giving the claimant a fair wind in relation to uncertainties) applies: *Wardle v Credit Agricole Corporate and Investment Bank* [2011] EWCA Civ 545, [2011] IRLR 604, [50], [52].

[5] See *Parabola Investments Ltd v Browallia Cal Ltd* [2010] EWCA Civ 486, [2011] QB 477 (CA) [23] (Toulson LJ), contrasting this with the non-breach position as discussed below.

[6] E.g. *Re H* [1996] AC 563, 586 (Lord Nicholls); *Re B* [2008] UKHL 35, [2009] 1 AC 11 [13] (Lord Hoffmann).

[7] (1722) 1 Strange 505, 93 ER 664. See more recently and with not dissimilar facts *Zabihi v Janzemini* [2009] EWCA Civ 851.

that where a party deliberately spoils[8] or withholds[9] relevant evidence, that party will not be allowed to benefit from the wrongdoing and the other party will get the benefit of the uncertainty.

The *Armory* principle has been extended to the situation where the defendant's breach meant that it had failed to keep records it should have kept and which would have helped the claimant to prove its case, even if this was not a deliberate attempt to thwart the process of proof in court.[10] It is said that it does not 'lie in the mouth' of the defendant to object to the lack of evidence in such a case,[11] even though the defendant did not deliberately hold back evidence. Likewise where the defendant's breach led to a mixing of the claimant's oil with the defendant's so that the claimant could not prove the quantity or quality of what had originally belonged to it.[12]

Whether or not this extension is justified – deliberately obstructing an opponent's ability to prove the case is very different to the wrong itself putting the claimant in difficulty in discharging the burden of proof – the extension is well-established. It has a huge impact on the burden of proof of the non-breach position. This is because in every case the defendant's breach means that the claimant faces the difficulty of having to prove what would have happened. And so the law holds that the fact of breach, without more, is (subject to the limitations discussed below) enough for the courts to lean towards the claimant and in effect err on the side of the claimant.

This policy of favouring the claimant has a very long history in US law at the highest level,[13] where it is explicitly founded on *Armory* and has been applied to contract cases among others: 'The defendant who has

---

[8] The destruction principle is known by the maxim '*omnia preasumuntur contra spolia-torem*' – everything is presumed against the spoiler.

[9] Adverse inferences will be drawn where a party has relevant evidence but chooses not to call it: *British Railways Board v Herrington* [1972] AC 877 (HL); *Wisniewski v Central Manchester Health Authority* [1998] Lloyd's Rep Med 223 (CA).

[10] *Keefe v Isle of Man Steam Packet Co Ltd* [2010] EWCA Civ 683.

[11] Ibid [19] (Longmore LJ).

[12] *Indian Oil Corporation Ltd v Greenstone Shipping SA* [1988] QB 345 (Com Ct). More generally, this approach of visiting the burden of proof or similar consequences on the defendant as a result of their causing the claimant's evidential difficulties is close to the concept of evidential damage described in Ariel Porat and Alex Stein, *Tort Liability under Uncertainty* (Oxford University Press 2001) ch 6.

[13] *Story Parchment Co v Paterson Parchment Paper Co* 51 S Ct 248 (1931); *Bigelow v RKO Radio Pictures Inc* 66 S Ct 574 (1946); *Locke v US* 283 F 2d 521 (US Court of Claims 1960); *Schonfeld v Hilliard* 218 F 3d 164 (2d Cir 2000) at 174–75; Restatement (Second) of Contracts (1981) comment a in §352.

wrongfully broken a contract should not be permitted to reap advantage from his own wrong by insisting on proof which by reason of his breach is unobtainable.'[14] And as Chief Justice Learned Hand put it: 'It is often very hard to learn what the value of the performance would have been; and it is a common expedient, and a just one, in such situations to put the peril of the answer upon that party who by his wrong has made the issue relevant to the rights of another.'[15]

It is also clearly established in English law. Many of the cases are professional negligence cases, where the defendant's negligence cost the claimant the chance of pursuing litigation against a third party[16] or pursuing an insurance claim against a third-party insurer.[17] But the principle has been applied more generally to the questions of what profits would have been made but for a trademark infringement or breach of confidence,[18] or had a licence been continued as it should have been,[19] or had goods continued to be supplied under an exclusive distribution agreement,[20] and of whether a third-party bidder would have proceeded with a deal if approached.[21]

Despite a few doubts as to its general applicability,[22] the principle, as Parker LJ put it:

> raises an evidential (i.e. rebuttable) presumption in favour of the claimant which gives him the benefit of any relevant doubt. The practical effect of

[14] *Locke* (n 13) 524 (Jones CJ).
[15] *L Albert & Son v Armstrong Rubber* 178 F 2d 182 (2d Cir 1949).
[16] *Allen v Sir Alfred MacAlpine & Sons Ltd* [1968] 2 QB 229 (CA); *Mount v Barker Austin* [1998] PNLR 493 (CA) obiter; *Sharif v Garrett & Co* [2001] EWCA Civ 1269, [2002] 1 WLR 3118; *Dixon v Clement Jones* [2004] EWCA Civ 1005, [2005] PNLR 6; *Feakins v Burstow* [2005] EWHC 1931 (QB); *Browing v Brachers* [2005] EWCA Civ 753, [2005] PNLR 44; *Pritchard Joyce & Hinds v Batcup* [2008] EWHC 20 (QB), [2008] PNLR 18 (appeal allowed [2009] EWCA Civ 369, [2009] PNLR 28); *McFaddens v Platford* [2009] EWHC 126 (TCC), [2009] PNLR 26; *Hirtenstein v Hill Dickinson LLP* [2014] EWHC 2711 (Comm).
[17] *Phillips v Whatley* [2007] UKPC 28, [2007] PNLR 27 [45]; *Ramco Ltd v Weller Russell & Laws Insurance Brokers Ltd* [2008] EWHC 2202 (QB), [2009] PNLR 14.
[18] *Fearns v Anglo-Dutch Paint & Chemical Co Ltd* [2010] EWHC 1708 (Ch); *Intercity Telecom Ltd v Solanki* [2015] EWHC B3 (Mercantile), [2015] 2 Costs LR 315.
[19] *Double G Communications Ltd v News Group International Ltd* [2011] EWHC 961 (QB); *Gul Bottlers (PVT) Ltd v Nichols plc* [2014] EWHC 2173 (Comm) [86].
[20] *Yam Seng Pte Ltd v International Trade Corp Ltd* [2013] EWHC 111 (QB), [2013] 1 Lloyd's Rep 526 [188] (Leggatt J).
[21] *Rosserlane Consultants Ltd v Credit Suisse International* [2015] EWHC 384 (Ch).
[22] *Mathieson v Clintons* [2013] EWHC 3056 (Ch) [189] (Asplin J); *Porton Capital Technology Funds v 3M UK Holdings Ltd* [2011] EWHC 2895 (Comm) [244] (Hamblen J); *McGregor on Damages* (n 1) para 10–006.

that is to give the claimant a fair wind in establishing the value of what he has lost.[23]

Or in Leggatt J's words: 'The court is aided in this task by what may be called the principle of reasonable assumptions – namely, that it is fair to resolve uncertainties about what would have happened but for the defendant's wrongdoing by making reasonable assumptions which err if anything on the side of generosity to the claimant where it is the defendant's wrongdoing which has created those uncertainties.'[24]

10.4   The Scope of the Principle

The principle only applies where there is uncertainty – meaning here a difficulty of evidence – that is created by the defendant, i.e. where the uncertainty is a necessary characteristic of the claimant's having to prove the non-breach position. It does not apply where there is evidence available to the claimant which the claimant has not deployed. This means in practice that the principle is limited in a couple of ways.

First, plainly the *Armory* principle will have little or no application to the question of what choices the claimant would have made but for the breach, as to which the claimant will be able and so expected to lead substantial evidence largely unhampered by the breach. And when proving what the defendant would have done,[25] the claimant can rely on adverse inferences if the defendant does not lead evidence. In practice this means that the *Armory* principle is mainly applicable to the question of what third parties (including the market) would have done, which is the same field as is (thought to be) occupied by the loss of chance doctrine, discussed below.

Secondly, the principle does give the claimant a fair wind, but it does not give a free ride. The law still expects and requires the claimant to deploy the best evidence reasonably available to it.[26] It will not engage in

---

[23] *Browing* (n 16) [210] (Parker LJ).

[24] *Yam Seng* (n 20) [188] (Leggatt J), quoting at [189] from *Wilson v Northampton and Banbury Junction Railway Co* (1873–74) LR 9 Ch App 279 (Court of Appeal in Chancery) 285–86 where Lord Selborne LC again tied this to the *Armory* principle. See also *Fearns* (n 18) [70] (Leggatt QC).

[25] Subject to the *Lavarack* principle, to the extent there still is one: see Kramer (n 3) 256ff.

[26] *Ratcliffe v Evans* [1892] 2 QB 524 (CA) 532–33 (Bowen LJ); *Biggin v Permanite* [1951] 1 KB 422, 438 (Devlin J). Moore-Bick LJ counselled against a strict requirement that the claimant produce the absolutely best evidence in *Capita Alternative Fund Services (Guernsey) Ltd v Driver Jonas* [2012] EWCA Civ 1417, [2013] 1 EGLR 119 [80].

'pure guesswork'[27] and will only give as fair a wind as is justified by the evidence.[28] This latter qualification can mean that in a particular case the court is often slightly freer than usual in making reasonable assumptions about what would have happened, while not going so far as to actually operate a presumption in favour of the claimant.[29]

10.5   Where Does the Loss of Chance Principle Fit in?

Where commercial losses depend upon the decision of a particular third-party person, as they did in *Allied Maples Group Ltd v Simmons & Simmons*[30] (Would the negotiating counterparty have agreed to amend the draft clause if asked?), the law is clear (including from that case) that the loss of chance principle applies and the claimant can recover the size of the lost chance of gain (even if less than 50 per cent) multiplied by the size of the gain.[31] In *Allied Maples* itself, the appeal was on a preliminary issue and the size of the percentage had to be decided at a later date,[32] but the principle was applied by the House of Lords in *Jackson v RBS*,[33] where the relevant lost chance was that the dog-chew customer would have ended its supply arrangement with the claimant early even if the defendant bank had not prematurely revealed to the customer the mark-up that the claimant middle-man was taking.[34]

---

[27] *Double G Communications* (n 19) [15] (Eady J).

[28] *Porton Capital* (n 22) [349] (Hamblen J). See also *Double G Communications* (n 19) [97] (Eady J).

[29] Putting the emphasis not on the words quoted at the text to n 24, but rather the words that immediately preceded that quotation (*Yam Seng* (n 20) [189]): 'courts will do the best they can not to allow difficulty of estimation to deprive the claimant of a remedy, particularly where that difficulty is itself the result of the defendant's wrongdoing. . . . Accordingly the court will attempt so far as it reasonably can to assess the claimant's loss even where precise calculation is impossible.'

[30] [1995] 1 WLR 1602 (CA).

[31] Sarah Green contends in ch 12 of this book that loss of chance applies wherever the matter is outside the parties' control, not only whenever it depends upon third parties.

[32] See *Allied Maples* (n 30) 1614. (Millet LJ dissented. He thought the claimant had not proven a real chance that the counterparty would have agreed to adjust the draft wording.)

[33] [2005] UKHL 3, [2005] 1 WLR 377.

[34] The judge found a different percentage chance that the customer would have terminated the relationship after one year, two years, three years and four years, and applied that (increasing) percentage to the profits that would have been made each year if the relationship had continued: see ibid [28], [37]; also the Court of Appeal decision: [2000] CLC 1457 [16]. The judge's approach was approved in the House of Lords (allowing the appeal from the Court of Appeal's approach), although the figures were found to have been too generous (but that did not avail as it would have been too costly to

Even in these cases in which what would have happened depends upon the decision of one third person, the evaluation of the chance is not straightforward. In *Jackson* the contract counterparty would have either continued or ended the contract with the claimant, but in many or most cases the third party's decision is not a binary one, but involves many possible outcomes. Thus in *Allied Maples* Hobhouse LJ pointed out that:

> The judge will have to assess the plaintiffs' loss on the basis of the value of the chance they have lost to negotiate better terms. This involves two elements: what better terms might have been obtained – there may be more than one possibility – and what were the chances of obtaining them. Their chance of obtaining some greater improvement, although signifi-cant, may be less good than the chances of obtaining some other lesser improvement. It will be a question for the judge, on the basis of the evidence already adduced together with any further evidence which the parties place before him at the further trial to make his assessment of the value of what the plaintiffs lost.[35]

The court may wish to 'show its working' by adding up the different products of the chance and the possible loss, e.g. (10% chance × £50) + (40% chance × £60) + (10% chance × £70) + (40% chance × £0). Thus in one case where the question was whether the claimant investment bank-ing headhunter would have secured a contract with a particular custo-mer, the court found that there was 15 per cent chance it would have secured the contract as sole service provider (on an exclusive mandate) and earned £3.26 million profit, 45 per cent chance it would have secured the contract as partial provider (on a shared mandate with others) earn-ing £1.26 million profit, and 40 per cent that it would not have secured the mandate at all.[36]

But in most cases, the court will instead prefer to take the most likely outcome (of the negotiations etc) and multiply the chance of loss by that one outcome.[37] Where the possible outcomes sit on a bell curve (as they appear to in the example I gave in the previous paragraph), this approach (e.g. 60% × £60) will yield the same result as the more nuanced

---

remit the matter for reconsideration of the figures after all the time that had passed, so the judge's figures were upheld).

[35] *Allied Maples* (n 30) 1621.

[36] *Wellesley Partners Ltd v Withers LLP* [2014] EWHC 556 (Ch), [2014] PNLR 22 [208], [233]; upheld by the Court of Appeal in *Wellesley Partners LLP v Withers LLP* [2015] EWCA Civ 1146. Or see, e.g. *Langford v Hebron* [2001] EWCA Civ 361, [2001] PIQR Q13, a personal injury case.

[37] See especially *Browning* (n 16) [212]; *Earl of Malmesbury v Strutt & Parker* [2007] EWHC 999 (QB), [2007] PNLR 29 [149].

calculation, because the chances of a lower figure are balanced by the chances of a higher figure.[38]

10.6 Loss of Chance and the Market

But the situation is rather different where the question is not what an individual would have decided but what the market would have paid for something. The market is a collection of individuals with free choice, but aggregated together their behaviour can be assessed to give a clear individual outcome – the market price – usually with the assistance of expert evidence.

In *Owners of the 'Front ACE' v Owners of the 'Vicky 1'*,[39] a collision with a very large crude oil carrier put it out of action for a time. It was found that the vessel would certainly have been employed – the vessel already had a fixture for the first period, which was cancelled as a result of the collision, and would have had little problem obtaining fixtures thereafter, having a 96 per cent utilisation rate historically and there being a ready market for chartering such a vessel.[40] In the circumstances, the Court of Appeal overturned the first instance Registrar's reduction of the lost profit figure by 20 per cent for the chance that the vessel would not have been profitably employed or would have been employed at a lower price.[41]

This decision makes an important point. A market means that there would have been a customer and so a deal. The employment of the vessel is certain and it is only the price which is uncertain. And once the market rate has been established (in this case by looking at the various voyage charter rates available at the time), that is the sum that would have been earned and, unless the costs that must be deducted to calculate the net profit lost were uncertain, there is no need for a further reduction for contingencies.

Hence the typical valuation case of the market price (e.g. in a property non-delivery or destruction case) does not involve the language of loss of a chance. The valuer identifies a single 'most probable' figure. And that is

---

[38] This is because the most likely figure (the mode average) is the same as the weighted average figure (the mean) and the middle figure reached by measuring half of the area under the graph (the median). For a little further discussion, see Kramer (n 3) 276–78.
[39] [2008] EWCA Civ 101, [2008] 1 CLC 229.   [40] Ibid [70].
[41] The Registrar's approach was summarised at ibid [5], [68] and the Court of Appeal's at ibid [71], [73].

2

ADAM KRAMER

the end of it, at least assuming a bell curve, as Lord Hoffmann has
explained:

> A forecaster who predicts that profits in a given period will be, say,
> $2,223,000, is not doing anything so silly as to say that in his opinion
> the profits will be precisely that figure. He is saying that $2,223,000 is in his
> opinion the most probable outcome, but that figures slightly higher or
> lower are almost equally probable and that on either side of them there is
> a range of possible figures which become increasingly less probable as they
> deviate from the mean ... The same is true of a valuation of property,
> which is no more than an estimate of what a property would fetch on
> a given date, based upon induction from information about what similar
> property has fetched.[42]

However, the market will not always give such a clear answer. Where
there is a volatile market or limited access to it (due to a forced or urgent
sale), it may not be realistic merely to fix on a single market price that
would have been obtained and that provides a balance of all other
possible prices. In *First Interstate Bank of California v Cohen Arnold &
Co*,[43] it was proven on the balance of probabilities that if the defendant
had properly advised as to a borrower's worth, the bank claimant would
have taken the decision to put the security property on the market at
a particular date (June 1990). At that date the market was undergoing
a property crash. Accordingly, the Court of Appeal preferred the
approach of identifying a two-thirds chance that a sale at £3 million
would have been achieved in September 1990,[44] leaving a one-third
chance that the sale achieved would have been no better than the
actual sale achieved at a price of £1.4 million, after marketing that
began in September 1990 (this actual sale taking place in lots
between October 1990 and June 1992).

10.7 Loss of Chance and Trading Losses

It is not easy to apply these lessons of how to determine what profit would
have been made from selling or leasing/chartering valuable property to
the more complicated situation of a trading business. With such
a business there is no simple market price to help the court. Trading
a business is an aggregate of many different transactions, and profitability
is as much about the number of trades and their costs as it is about the

---

[42] *Lion Nathan Ltd v C-C Bottlers Ltd* [1996] 1 WLR 1438 (PC) 1445–47.
[43] [1996] PNLR 17 (CA). [44] Ibid 25, 31.

market price (and so revenue) of each trade. The strongest evidence of what would have happened is usually the ability and pedigree of the trader (including historical trading figures), and a general discussion of the competitiveness and profitability of the market, without the court ever getting into the minutiae of how (from whom in what transactions) the profit would have been earned.

In *Parabola Investments Ltd v Browallia Cal Ltd*[45] the claimant was an equities trader with a very successful history. When establishing the loss that would have been suffered but for the defendant stockbroker's fraud, the court had the difficulty of knowing that the claimant had a gift for making very good choices that beat the stock market but not really knowing how he did it. Of course, each of these investment choices required a market upon which a trade could be performed, but the profit was not made by selling something for the market price at a profit against the costs of that thing or service (as in *Vicky 1* or *First Interstate Bank of California*), but rather by speculating on market movements by buying and selling. The market movements are the aggregate of the behaviour of various third parties – and so the sort of thing to which the loss of chance approach should apply – but here the court could not open the black box and investigate what would have happened following a particular choice by the claimant. From the court's point of view, this was akin to asking whether a gambler with a history of winning would continue winning.

Not being able to point to exactly how he made money or what decisions would have been made, one might have thought that the court would make some sort of deduction for the possibility that the claimant would have done worse than he did in the past. But, consistent with the fair-wind principle mentioned earlier (although it was not mentioned in this case), the first instance judge and Court of Appeal were willing to accept without too much difficulty that the claimant would have done broadly as well as he had done in the past.

In quantifying the amount of loss, the Court of Appeal seemed to confirm that the loss of chance approach applied,[46] the establishment of a figure being a matter of 'reasonable assessment',[47] and upheld Flaux J's

---

[45] See n 5.

[46] Ibid [23]. That the loss of chance approach was intended is fairly clear from the text of this paragraph but is also confirmed by the passages of *Davies v Taylor* [1974] AC 207 (HL) and *Gregg v Scott* [2005] UKHL 2, [2005] 2 AC 176 cited therein.

[47] *Parabola* (n 5) [24].

figure for loss which had been reached after taking (said that judge) 'sufficient account of the inherent risks in any trading'.[48]

In the course of reaching this result, the court confirmed that the balance of probability approach does not apply to the measurement of loss,[49] and rejected the submission[50] that the claimant must prove on the balance of probabilities that at least the sum awarded would have been earned but for the breach. This decision of the court is in principle right, because the loss of chance and not balance of probabilities approach applies and because the claimant has a fair wind, meaning that uncertainties are within reason resolved in the claimant's favour.

But it is important to realise that the loss of chance approach, subject to the fair-wind principle, awards the mean of all possible outcomes. And where, as must be fairly common, the possible outcomes are distributed on a bell curve or any other symmetrical probability curve, the sum which it is more likely than not the claimant would have earned (the median, the figure with half the area under the curve to the left of it and half to the right) is the same as the mean.[51] In those situations the balance of probabilities approach is not wrong,[52] and indeed the balance of probabilities and loss of chance approaches are the same.[53]

With *Vasiliou v Hajigeorgiou*,[54] we turn to the rather different situation of a Greek-Cypriot restaurant, although it suffers from some of the same difficulties as the trader in *Parabola*. Although restaurant trading operates in a market, knowing the market value of a plate of moussaka and cost of a Greek waiter will not help the court to establish whether a Greek restaurant would have traded profitably. The claimant tenant had been deprived by the landlord's breaches of the ability to operate a new restaurant for eighteen months. The Court of Appeal confirmed that a discount should be made for uncertainty where the prospects of trading at profit are uncertain.[55] In this case, however, the judge had found that the claimant definitely (i.e. with a 100 per cent probability) would have

---

[48] See the quotation from Flaux J's judgment: ibid [11].   [49] Ibid [22], [24].

[50] Made by a counsel team including this author. As to these submissions, see the note of argument: ibid 480D.

[51] And indeed where the curve is a bell curve, the mean and median are the top of the curve, the modal average.

[52] This is true of all symmetrical probability distributions – the weighted average is the midpoint of the graph.

[53] Provided we are not talking about proving on the balance of probabilities that the claimant would have earned a particular figure, but proving on the balance of probabilities that the claimant would have earned *at least* that figure.

[54] [2010] EWCA Civ 1475.   [55] Ibid [47].

made a profit,[56] so no discount was required.[57] It is still necessary to fix a figure for the lost profits, and this was done by the trial judge (and upheld on appeal) following evidence of Mr Vasiliou's competence and track record as a restaurateur, and allowing for the likely (on a balance of likelihoods) number of covers per week, the growth rate, and other factors.[58]

Accordingly, in most cases the calculating and reasoning is opaque and the court does the best it can to fix a figure.[59] This will frequently not involve a particular multiplier (probability) and multiplicand (gain). It will take into account the chances of things going well or badly, and the different possible outcomes. The judge may occasionally show some of the working by indicating a percentage deduction to apply where profits were not certain,[60] but usually the judge will just come up with a figure. This sort of approach is an evaluative task the result of which is quite properly very difficult to appeal.[61] So it is a loss of chance approach without the outward signs of one. And there is nothing wrong with any of that.

Trading cases have a key difference from the pure chance of gain case such as *Chaplin v Hicks*[62] or *Allied Maples*, namely that the worst that can happen is not merely that the claimant is left without a gain, but rather the claimant might make a loss. And the chance of making a loss must be set against the chance of making a gain.

That being the case, it is frequently worth working out first whether it is more likely than not that the claimant would have made a profit. If the probability graph is symmetrical, the median (the more likely than not figure) is also the mean (the loss of chance award figure), and so if it is more likely than not that the claimant would not have made a profit it follows that there will be no award, as on the weighted loss of chance approach the claimant would have been worse off but for the breach. And so, as the case law indicates,[63] and perfectly properly, in cases of bell or other symmetrical probability curves, the court as a first stage frequently

---

[56] Ibid [44].   [57] Ibid [39].

[58] See the discussion: ibid [16]–[18]. For more detail, see the first instance judgment, which is unreported but available on Lawtel.

[59] For an example from the 'figure in the air' end of the scale see *Giedo van der Garde BV v Force India Formula One Team Ltd* [2010] EWHC 2373 (QB) [410]–[412].

[60] *Salford City Council v Torkington* [2004] EWCA Civ 1646, [2004] 51 EG 89 (CS) [55] (Potter LJ in obiter) as discussed in the *Vasiliou* case (n 54).

[61] *Wellesley CA* (n 36) [125]–[126].   [62] [1911] 2 KB 786 (CA).

[63] *Parabola* (n 5) [23]; *Vasiliou* (n 54) [14] (the reference to balance of probability) [19], [24], [26], [28]. *Fiona Trust & Holding Corp v Privalov* [2016] EWHC 2163 (Comm) [53]–[57].

asks whether on the balance of probabilities the claimant would have made a profit.[64]

But no one should confuse this with there being some sort of separate hurdle of proving the fact of loss on the balance of probabilities before engaging with a second hurdle of proving the extent of the loss (on a loss of chance basis). Some of the language in the case law suggests this,[65] but it is misguided.[66] The short point is that, when it comes to third parties and lost profits, '[a]ll that remain[s] on the issue of causation was for [the claimant] to establish whether there was a real and substantial chance' that it would have made a profit, and '[t]hat was the beginning and end of its case on causation' and 'the evaluation of the chance' of obtaining the profit is then 'part of the process of the quantification of damages'.[67]

First, it is necessary for some purposes to distinguish the fact from the extent of loss, such as fixing the accrual of the cause of action in tort cases from which date the limitation period runs. But in loss of chance cases the actionable loss is (at least on one view, and if one looks at the effect of the law) the loss of an opportunity to make a gain (providing it is a more than de minimis opportunity[68]), and it is that loss (the opportunity) which must be proven on the balance of probabilities.[69] It matters not for those purposes that there was a less than 50 per cent chance that the opportunity would have in fact yielded a gain. The loss of chance principle makes an award nevertheless, and the balance of probabilities test has nothing in practice to say.

Secondly, plainly it would be illogical and undesirable for the beauty contest candidate to have to show that on the balance of probabilities she would have won a prize as a prior hurdle to then having to show a substantial chance (which can be under 50 per cent) that she would

---

[64] Text to n 52.

[65] See the comments at first instance in *Wellesley*, discussed below at n 67. And see the US cases, which suggest that the *Armory* principle applies to the extent of the loss but not the fact of the loss: *Story Parchment* (n 13) 250; *Bigelow* (n 13) 581, 524; *Bagwell Coatings Inc v Middle South Energy Inc* 797 F 2d 1298 (US C of A 5th Circuit 1986) 1308–09.

[66] See further Andrew Burrows, 'Uncertainty about Uncertainty: Damages for Loss of a Chance' (2008) JPI Law 31, 42–43.

[67] *Wellesley CA* (n 36) (Floyd LJ) [109]–[110]. The Court of Appeal did not repeat the muddled language of the first instance judge (*Wellesley HC* (n 36) [188(2), (5)-(7)] (Nugee J)), which seemed to support a balance of probabilities test.

[68] *Davies* (n 46) 212 (Lord Reid). This 'de minimis' language evolved in *Allied Maples* and other cases into the language of 'real or substantial' and not 'merely speculative'. See more recently *Wellesley CA* (n 36) (Floyd LJ) [94].

[69] *Gregg v Scott* (n 46) [17] (Lord Nicholls). See further Sarah Green's discussion of the 'Access Question' in ch 12.

have won a prize, with damages then assessed as that latter chance multiplied by the amount of the prize. The loss of chance approach replaces the balance of probabilities test. In the beauty contest example the curve is not symmetrical (it has a heavy right-skew) and so the median figure is not the same as the mean. It may be more likely than not that the claimant would have earned zero (the median), but the weighted average allowing for the possible large gains (the mean) is a positive figure, and therefore so is the damages award.

10.8 The Presumption that Everything is Worth what the Claimant was Willing to Pay for It

But even removing the usual requirements of the standard of proof and resolving uncertainties in favour of the claimant sometimes is not enough to reach a realistic conclusion as to the non-breach conclusion. This is especially true in cases where the claimant has expended money on a business venture, project or transaction. In such cases the court is mindful of the need to balance the unfairness to the defendant of awarding a speculative sum for lost profits, against the unfairness to the claimant of awarding nothing and therefore leaving the claimant not just having missed out on an opportunity to gain but nursing a monetary loss. Of course, this is only unfair if the claimant would but for the breach have recouped that expenditure in revenue, but the court tends to presume that it would.

Accordingly, what Leggatt J called in *Yam Seng* the court's 'attempt so far as it reasonably can to assess the claimant's loss even where precise calculation is impossible'[70] finds its most powerful expression in the presumptions the court makes as to the benefit that would have been obtained from the defendant's performance.[71]

And the most powerful of those presumptions, as Leggatt J explained, is the:

> (rebuttable) presumption that the claimant would have recouped expenditure incurred in reliance on the defendant's performance ... in the expectation of making a profit. Where money has been spent in that expectation but the defendant's breach of contract has prevented that expectation from being put to the test, it is fair to assume that the claimant would at least have recouped its expenditure had the contract

---

[70] *Yam Seng* (n 20) [189].
[71] See Leggatt J's quotation of Lord Selborne LC in *Yam Seng* referred to in n 24.

been performed unless and to the extent that the defendant can prove otherwise'.[72]

This is based on the presumption that the claimant was rational in its business and correct in its expectation, which is a fair starting point, although evidence can be led by the defendant to defeat these premises and the presumption.

This presumption was not identified in England in this modern form until as recently as the 2010 decision of Teare J in *Omak Maritime Ltd v Mamola Challenger Shipping Co*,[73] explaining the well-known 'reliance damages'/'wasted expenditure' cases such as *Anglia Television v Reed*.[74] The leading decision of an ultimate court on the point is the High Court of Australia's *Commonwealth v Amann Aviation Pty Ltd* from 1991.[75]

This presumption that the claimant would have broken even provides a baseline recovery of lost revenue in a large variety of commercial cases, and proves determinative where (even with a fair wind) the claimant cannot demonstrate that it would have made a profit and the defendant cannot prove that the claimant would have made a loss.[76] I have explored this elsewhere,[77] and for the purposes of this chapter it suffices to summarise below some of the situations in which the presumption operates.

10.8.1 Recouping the Cost of Diverted Time

Where the defendant's breach diverted the claimant's employees from work in the claimant's business, it will usually be next to impossible to show what contribution their ordinary work would have made to an amount of profits of the business. In the circumstances, the court sensibly presumes that the claimant's employees are worth – whether their contribution to revenue is direct or indirect – what they are paid. As Wilson

---

[72] *Yam Seng* (n 20) [190].

[73] [2010] EWHC 2026 (Comm), [2011] 2 All ER (Comm) 155. See further David McLauchlan, 'The Redundant Reliance Interest in Contract Damages' (2011) 127 LQR 23.

[74] [1972] 1 QB 60 (CA). [75] (1992) 174 CLR 64.

[76] This book on commercial damages is not the place to investigate non-commercial contracts, but in passing it is worth noting that it is at least as difficult in non-commercial cases to prove what would have been received but for the breach – the enjoyment or other non-financial equivalent of revenue. There, too, the costs expended on the price or otherwise provide an appropriate and useful starting point, via the presumption that the non-financial value to the claimant was at least what the claimant spent to get the performance and enjoyment of it, for measuring the claimant's non-breach position and so its loss. See further Kramer (n 3) 503–04, 511–13.

[77] Ibid 29–34, 480–87.

LJ summarised in the leading case on such claims, *Aerospace Publishing v Thames Water Utilities Ltd*:

> [I]t is reasonable for the court to infer from the disruption that, had their time not been thus diverted, staff would have applied it to activities which would, directly or indirectly, have generated revenue for the claimant in an amount at least equal to the costs of employing them during that time.[78]

Cases in which the costs of in-house lawyers and claims managers[79] are recoverable are probably explicable on the same basis.

10.8.2 Recouping the Cost of Property Put out of Use

Where property is kept out of use, a standard measure of damages is the 'standing charge' method, by which the court calculates the costs of running and maintaining the property, including overheads, on the 'assumption that this figure must represent approximately the value [to] the operators'.[80] Such an award should also include an allowance for depreciation, i.e. the relevant proportion of the capital cost of the property when divided by the life of the property, since that too is a cost attributable to having the property for the relevant period that would have to be recouped for the business or other venture to have broken even.[81]

10.8.3 Recouping the Price Paid to the Defendant

Sometimes the presumption operates simply to return to the claimant in damages the price (or relevant part of the price) paid to the defendant, on the assumption that the claimant would have recouped it in revenue but for the breach.

This is how the Court of Appeal fixed the damages for breach of a commercial landlord's covenant of repair that kept a tenant's business closed for two months in *Savva v Hussein*: it was presumed that the tenant would have earned enough to recoup the rent he had paid the defendant landlord.[82] And this was how the damages were calculated in

---

[78] [2007] EWCA Civ 3, [2007] Bus LR 726 [86]. See further Kramer (n 3) 30–33.

[79] See e.g. *Portman Building Society v Bevan Ashford* [2000] 1 EGLR 81 (CA).

[80] *Birmingham Corp v Sowsbery* [1970] RTR 84 (QB), approved in *Beechwood Birmingham Ltd v Hoyer Group UK Ltd* [2010] EWCA Civ 647, [2011] QB 357; *Hunt v Optima (Cambridge) Ltd* [2013] EWHC 681 (TCC), 148 Con LR 27.

[81] *West Midlands Travel Ltd v Aviva Insurance Ltd* [2013] EWCA Civ 887, [2014] RTR 10.

[82] [1996] 2 EGLR 65 (CA) 67 (Staughton LJ).

Playup Interactive Entertainment (UK) Pty Ltd v Givemefootball Ltd,[83] where a football awards sponsor was not given a certain proportion of the fan contact details and other benefits promised in the sponsorship contract. The damages were measured by that proportion of the price paid on the assumption that what would have been received would have been worth what was paid for it. It is how the award in *Giedo van der Garde BV v Force India Formula One Team Ltd*[84] should have been explained, when the claimant was only given a certain proportion of the Formula One track test laps he was promised, and the court awarded that proportion of the price he paid.[85]

In contrast with service cases, usually there is ample evidence as to the value of property that has not been supplied. But in *McRae v Commonwealth Disposals Commission*,[86] where the purchase was of an oil tanker wreck that did not exist (so could not be valued), the presumption of breaking even proved determinative: the claimant recovered the costs spent on the salvage expedition.

10.8.4   Recoupment of the Full Cost of the Venture

Where a venture has been abandoned it is often difficult to prove what the outcome would have been. Thus in *Anglia TV Ltd v Reed*[87] the claimant recovered all its expenditure on the unrebutted presumption that the planned film would have broken even. The same applied in *Yam Seng* to the costs that had been sunk into the distribution of Manchester United fragrances that had to be abandoned upon non-supply by the defendant.[88] Where the defendant failed properly to provide a car bodyshop trade show at which the claimant was to advertise in *Dataliner Ltd v Vehicle Builders & Repairers Association*,[89] the claimant was awarded its expenditure as it was presumed that it would have earned enough new business to recoup that expenditure.

---

[83] [2011] EWHC 1980 (Comm), [2011] Info TLR 289 [272].   [84] See n 59.
[85] Instead the presumption of breaking even was not mentioned. The court apparently concluded that the chance of profit the claimant received in return for the laps was well below the price paid (hence the small loss of chance award – although note that Mr van der Garde did in fact go on to a professional Formula One career). Nevertheless, the court correctly awarded a proportion of the price paid albeit on a legally unsound 'market value of the service' basis, or in the alternative a sounder *Wrotham Park* basis (discussed below). See further Kramer (n 3) 35–39.
[86] (1951) 84 CLR 377 (High Court of Australia).   [87] See n 74.   [88] See n 20.
[89] *The Independent*, 27 August 1995 (CA).

In these cases the expenditure was wholly or partly spent on third parties. But, if the claimant has paid the defendant for a service and that service has not been provided, and the claimant cannot recoup its money (e.g. because the claim in unjust enrichment fails on the grounds that there was only a partial failure of consideration), the claimant should also be able to rely on the presumption of breaking even to assist in proving that it lost revenue equal to the price it paid for the service that was not provided.

10.9   Other Presumptions

As the structure of this chapter makes clear, the presumption of breaking even is merely one (although probably the most important) permissible presumption that the court can apply to resolve uncertainty or, where justifiable, give the wronged claimant a fair wind. One of the more interesting other presumptions is the presumption that the claimant would have received as much revenue (or non-financial benefit) from the performance as the amount it would have been willing to sell the performance for – i.e. the amount it would have been willing to accept to waive the right to performance – by a sanitised hypothetical bargain.[90] This is, in this author's opinion, the best explanation of the *Wrotham Park* measure, applied mainly in cases of negative promises (like *Wrotham Park* itself) where there is no easy apportionment of the price paid by the claimant that would allow the presumption of breaking even to assist.[91]

Another presumption that can apply in some cases is that the claimant would not only have broken even but made a certain return. This is most obviously applied to cases of loss of use of money, where the ease of quantifying what can be earned from employing money (especially by lending it to a bank by depositing it) means the courts are quick to presume that a certain return would have been made from money during a particular period.[92] But it can also apply in cases of loss of use of other property.[93]

---

[90] There must be an assumption that the claimant would have agreed to waive, even if contrary to fact, in order to get the economic measure off the ground.

[91] Kramer (n 3) 554–56.

[92] *Sempra Metals Ltd (formerly Metallgesellschaft Ltd) v Inland Revenue Commissioners* [2007] UKHL 34, [2008] 1 AC 561 and the statutory awards such as under section 35A of the Senior Courts Act 1981. In fact, the courts are usually willing to award the higher amount reflecting the cost to the claimant of borrowing a replacement sum.

[93] *British Columbia and Vancouver Island Spar, Lumber and Saw Mill Company Ltd v Nettleship* (1867–68) LR 3 CP 499 (Common Pleas).

10.10   Conclusion

Frequently when litigating or arbitrating disputes the most practically important questions for the parties – i.e. those that have the greatest impact on success or failure of the claim or on the amount of the recovery – are not the legal principles of remoteness, mitigation and legal causation, or even the application of those principles to the facts, but rather the messy and largely unappealable business of proving with evidence as a matter of fact what would have happened. But as this chapter has sought to show, the law is not insensible to the difficulties claimants face in such cases. On the contrary, the court is willing to make certain presumptions or otherwise to stack the deck in the claimant's favour, making it much easier than a strict balance of probabilities test would entail to recover the expenditure incurred or revenues that merely might have been earned but for the breach. Before parties fire the arrows of their lengthy factual and expert evidence, and before judges look to see whether they have struck home, they should all make sure they are focusing on the right target. That target is often an easier one for claimants than all might have supposed.

11

Interest

ANDREW BURROWS

11.1 Introduction

By the time I had got my act together, all the topics on commercial remedies that I would have liked to write on had been chosen by other contributors. So here I am with a chapter on interest which, at least at first sight, may be thought to be of little, if any, interest. In fact, the topic throws up a surprising number of intriguing issues that are important both in practice and theoretically. These include: are there and, if so, what are the principles that govern the award of statutory interest; what did *Sempra Metals Ltd v IRC*[1] decide; and what is the relationship between statute and common law in this area? In practice, interest can make a huge difference to the quantum of claims. So in the recent decision in *Littlewoods Ltd v HMRC*[2] the Court of Appeal pointed out that the difference between the compound interest claimed, and the simple interest that the defendant accepted was payable, amounted to over £1.1 billion.[3] It is also noteworthy at the outset that, apart from leading cases on interest, some of the leading cases on general principle within the law of obligations have turned on questions of interest, such as *Woolwich Equitable Building Society v IRC (No 2)*.[4]

The initial task of this chapter is to provide an overview of an area of the law that for many academics and students is relatively unfamiliar. We then move to the heart of the chapter (those who already know the basics on interest may choose to skip the overview and go straight to section 11.3) which considers a number of specific questions, some of which are both topical and difficult.

---

[1] [2007] UKHL 34, [2008] 1 AC 561. [2] [2015] EWCA Civ 515, [2015] 3 WLR 1748.
[3] Ibid [2] (Arden LJ). [4] [1993] AC 70 (HL).

11.2   Overview

11.2.1   Post-judgment Interest

11.2.1.1   Judgment Debt Interest

A court's award of damages or an agreed sum constitutes a 'judgment debt'. Under section 17(1) of the Judgments Act 1838 simple[5] interest automatically runs on a 'judgment debt' at a rate of what, since 1993,[6] has been 8 per cent.[7] By the Civil Procedure Rules (CPR) 40.8, the interest on a judgment debt runs from the date of the judgment unless the court orders otherwise. Under section 17(2) of the 1838 Act, rules of court may provide for the court to disallow all or part of any interest otherwise payable.[8] There is no discretion for a court to award judgment debt interest at a different rate than 8 per cent (other than where the award is being made in a currency other than sterling).[9]

11.2.1.2   Contractually Agreed Post-judgment Interest

Where the claim is for a contractual debt (or even damages for breach of contract) contracting parties may agree that, in addition to judgment debt interest, post-judgment interest (whether simple or compound) may be payable at an agreed rate on a sum due under the contract.[10] In other words, the claimant may be entitled to both judgment debt interest and contractual post-judgment interest (although, depending on the construction of the contract, the contractual interest may take into account the judgment debt interest).[11] The relevant rate of interest is also commonly set out in the contract. Contractually agreed interest is, and always

---

[5] Although not explicitly stated, it has always been assumed that this Act merely permits simple interest. This is not least because, as the statute fixes a rate per annum, it must have in mind simple interest because if compound interest were in mind one would need to specify the periods of rest.

[6] Judgment Debts (Rate of Interest) Order 1993, SI 1993/564.

[7] From 1838 until 1971 the rate was fixed at 4 per cent. It was then raised to 7.5 per cent and went to a high of 15 per cent in 1985 before being reduced to the present rate of 8 per cent in 1993.

[8] E.g. CPR 47.8 (sanction for failure to commence detailed assessment proceedings in time).

[9] This is provided for in s 44A of the Administration of Justice Act 1970.

[10] In *Director General of Fair Trading v First National Bank plc* [2001] UKHL 52, [2002] 1 AC 481, it was decided that such an agreement to pay post-judgment interest was not unfair under the Unfair Terms in Consumer Contracts Regulations 1994, SI 1994/3159.

[11] For the relationship between the two, see e.g. *Economic Life Assurance Society v Usborne* [1902] AC 147 (HL).

has been, enforceable in the same way as any other contractually agreed sum. Nothing special applies to it or needs to be said about it.

11.2.2   Pre-judgment Interest

11.2.2.1   Contractually Agreed Pre-judgment Interest

What we have just said about contractually agreed post-judgment interest applies equally to contractually agreed pre-judgment interest, which is even more commonplace. This interest is enforceable in the same way as any other contractually agreed sum and no special rules apply.

11.2.2.2   Pre-judgment Statutory Interest on Damages or Debts

Putting to one side contractually agreed interest, there was no power at common law to award interest on damages or debts. In other words, as first laid down in *Page v Newman*[12] and confirmed in the leading decision of *London Chatham and Dover Rly Co v South Eastern Rly Co*,[13] the courts did not recognise a claim for damages for the failure to pay a sum of money (whether a debt or damages) even though it might be clear that this failure caused the claimant to suffer loss.

Statute first intervened in the Civil Procedure Act 1833 (Lord Tenterden's Act) and then more comprehensively in the Law Reform (Miscellaneous Provisions) Act 1934 and subsequently in the Administration of Justice Act 1982. The 1934 and 1982 provisions on interest were then consolidated in what is now section 35A of the Senior Courts Act 1981. By this:

(i) Under section 35A(1) and (3),[14] the courts have a discretion (rarely if ever not exercised) to award simple interest at such rate as the court thinks fit where a judgment is being given for a debt or damages for all or any part of the period between when the cause of action arose and the date of judgment; and the same applies (with the relevant period being up to the date of payment) where there has been full or part payment after proceedings have been commenced

---

[12] (1829) 9 B & C 378, 109 ER 140.   [13] [1893] AC 429 (HL).

[14] Where a payment, other than under a judgment, has been made (where there is a judgment, s 35A(1) alone applies), the relationship between s 35A(1) and (3) is not clear. Section 35A(1) refers to 'or payment is made' which presumably includes a (part) payment of damages or a debt; whereas s 35A(3) refers to the paying of 'the whole debt'. For an attempt to explain the relationship, see *Edmunds v Lloyds Italico & l'Ancora Co* [1986] 1 WLR 492 (CA).

but before judgment. Although this is a matter for the discretion of the court, a commercial borrowing rate of simple interest is normally applied so that the usual rate awarded is 1 per cent over the base rate for claimants which are larger companies[15] and up to 3 per cent over base rate for smaller companies.[16] The explanation for these rates is considered below.[17]

(ii) Under section 35A(2), the courts must award simple interest in relation to a judgment given for damages for personal injuries or death which exceed £200 unless the court is satisfied that there are special reasons to the contrary. For personal injury damages for non-pecuniary loss, the courts apply a fixed rate of 2 per cent.[18] For personal injury or death damages for pre-trial pecuniary loss, interest is normally payable from the date of the accident or death until trial at half the average rate on the special account (formerly called the short-term investment account)[19] which tends to follow behind changes in commercial market rates and presently stands at 0.5 per cent.

(iii) Under section 35A(4) interest in respect of a debt is not to be awarded under the 1981 Act for a period during which interest on the debt already runs. It is not entirely clear what this is referring to. It may be that it is principally concerned to make clear that contractually agreed interest will continue to be awarded unaffected by the statute. However, as we shall see later,[20] this subsection may have a more wide-ranging significance in working out the precise relationship between section 35A and the common law.

(iv) Under the 1934 Act, there was no power to award interest where the sum in question had already been paid before judgment. Assuming no contractually agreed interest, debtors could therefore in effect obtain interest-free credit if they withheld payment until sued but then paid up before the claimant could obtain judgment. In *President*

---

[15] See e.g. *BP Exploration v Hunt (No 2)* [1979] 1 WLR 783 (QB), affd [1983] 2 AC 352 (HL); *Tate & Lyle Food and Distribution Ltd v Greater London Council* [1982] 1 WLR 149 (QB), 154–55; *Metal Box Ltd v Currys Ltd* [1988] 1 WLR 175 (QB); *Shearson Lehman Hutton Inc v Maclaine Watson & Co Ltd (No 2)* [1990] 3 All ER 723 (QB); *Kuwait Airways Corp v Kuwait Insurance Co SAK (No 2)* [2000] 1 All ER (Comm) 972 (QB); *JSC BTA Bank v Ablyazov* [2013] EWHC 867 (Comm) (QB).

[16] See e.g. *Catnic Components Ltd v Hill & Smith Ltd* [1983] FSR 512 (Ch); *Bridge UK Com Ltd v Abbey Pynford plc* [2007] EWHC 728 (TCC), (2009) 25 Const LJ 150; *Jaura v Ahmed* [2002] EWCA Civ 210 (CA).

[17] See section 11.3.1.1 point (v).

[18] *Wright v British Railways Board* [1983] 2 AC 773 (HL).

[19] *Cookson v Knowles* [1979] AC 556 (HL).   [20] See the final paragraph of section 11.3.3.

of India v La Pintada[21] it was held that, applying the *London Chatham and Dover Railways* rule of 'no damages for failure to pay', the common law could not fill the gap left by statute. Taking a needlessly restrictive view of Parliamentary intention, it was in any event thought to be inappropriate for the common law to be developed where this would be inconsistent with the statute (the relevant statute being the Law Reform (Miscellaneous) Provisions Act 1934).[22] As we have seen under point (i), reform was effected by section 35A(1) and (3) of the 1981 Act (which had actually been passed prior to the decision of their Lordships but did not apply to the facts of the case).

(v) However, section 35A does not apply, so that no interest can be awarded, in respect of payments made by the defendant before the creditor has commenced proceedings to recover the debt (or damages). This means that, as regards interest under section 35A, debtors can still obtain some interest-free credit if they withhold payment of their debts until the moment before the creditor commences proceedings.

Two developments, one statutory and the other common law, have narrowed, or arguably removed, that remaining lacuna.

As regards statute, the Late Payment of Commercial Debts (Interest) Act 1998 gives the creditor an automatic right to simple interest on an unpaid commercial debt, which starts to run from the day after 'the relevant day'.[23] The Act applies to contracts for the supply of goods or services (other than excluded contracts, such as a consumer credit agreement) where the purchaser and supplier each act in the course of a business. The rate of interest has been fixed at the base rate plus 8 per cent. The method by which this statutory interest becomes payable is intriguing. The legislation

---

[21] [1985] AC 104 (HL). [22] Ibid 129–30 (Lord Brandon).
[23] The period from when the statutory interest runs – which turns on the definition of the 'relevant day' – is extremely complex. It is principally laid down in s 4 (and for advance payments in s 11) of the 1998 Act but complexity has been added by the amendments to s 4 by the Late Payment of Commercial Debts Regulations 2013, SI 2013/395 and the Late Payment of Commercial Debts (Amendment) Regulations 2015, SI 2015/1336. By s 4 it appears that where no date for payment has been agreed, the interest normally runs from 30 days after the date (which, for shorthand, may be referred to as the 'performance/notice date') on which the creditor performed or on which the debtor had notice of the amount of the debt, whichever is the later, but if the parties have agreed a date for payment, interest runs from the day after that date or, if earlier than the agreed payment date, 60 days from the performance/notice date (or if the debtor is a public authority 30 days from the performance/notice date). By reason of s 3(2), interest under this Act does not run after there is a judgment debt because then s 17 of the Judgments Act 1838 applies.

rests the right to statutory interest on the law of contract by implying a term into a contract to which the Act applies that simple interest shall be payable; and the relationship to other statutes (in particular the 1981 Act) is dealt with by saying that the interest shall be treated as if it were provided for under an 'express contract term'. That apparent contradiction between saying, on the one hand, that the term is implied and yet, on the other, that it should be treated as 'express' seems unnecessary. The essential point is that the interest is treated as if contractually agreed so that e.g. it is not inconsistent with section 35A of the Senior Courts Act 1981.

Potentially more wide ranging still has been the decision of the House of Lords in *Sempra Metals*. This will be touched on further in the next subsection and then discussed in detail later. Suffice it to say at this point that that decision has removed the *London Chatham and Dover Railways* rule and has overruled *La Pintada*. What arguably remains unclear is the relationship between the interest, including compound interest, that can now be awarded at common law and interest under section 35A.

11.2.2.3 Damages to Cover Pre-judgment Interest Paid or Lost ('Interest as Damages')

The statutory regimes that we have so far considered concern an award of interest in addition to damages or in addition to the recovery of a debt. In shorthand, they are concerned with interest *on* damages (or debts). But what about an argument that interest should be recoverable *as* damages? It was that precise argument which was rejected in *London Chatham and Dover Railway*. That case laid down that interest paid or lost could not be recovered as damages: in other words, it established the rule of 'no damages for a failure to pay'. It is precisely because interest could not be recovered *as* damages at common law that statute has intervened by allowing the recovery of interest *on* damages (and debts).

The rationale for the *London Chatham and Dover Railway* rule was unclear. It may have been linked to the common law's traditional refusal to compensate losses consequent on one's own impecuniosity as most famously illustrated by the (now overruled) decision in *The Liesbosch*.[24] Given its uncertain basis, it is not surprising that, even before *Sempra Metals*, exceptions had been recognised to the *London Chatham and Dover Railway* rule. Perhaps the best known example was *Wadsworth v Lydall*.[25]

---

[24] [1933] AC 449 (HL), departed from in *Lagden v O'Connor* [2003] UKHL 64, [2004] 1 AC 1067.

[25] [1981] 1 WLR 598 (CA).

Here the defendant failed to pay all of a sum of money owing to the claimant. As a result, the claimant had to take out a loan in order to finance a contract to purchase some land. The claimant was awarded damages for interest charges paid on the loan (and legal costs) even though these followed from the defendant's failure to pay the sum of money. The Court of Appeal distinguished *London Chatham and Dover Railway* on the ground that, while it prevented general damages for failure to pay a sum of money, it did not prevent 'special damages'.[26] What was meant by special damages was unclear. One interpretation was that, apart from the general loss of the use of money (as dealt with by awards of interest on damages in section 35A), all other losses (most obviously specific interest charges paid) were recoverable as damages. But while approving *Wadsworth v Lydall*, the House of Lords in *La Pintada* (which may lay claim to be the worst decision of the highest court in the last fifty years) interpreted 'general' and 'special' damages as correlating to the first and second rules of remoteness in *Hadley v Baxendale*.[27] Bizarrely, this meant that interest paid or lost could only be recovered as damages if it did not arise naturally or in the normal course of things and yet, because of the defendant's special knowledge, was not too remote.

In the light of *Sempra Metals* we no longer need to concern ourselves with what is here meant by general or special damages. *La Pintada* was overruled in *Sempra Metals* and the rule (although not the actual decision) in *London Chatham and Dover Railway* was disapproved. Although the decision in *Sempra Metals* concerned an award of restitution for money paid, and not damages, part of the central reasoning was that interest, including compound interest, can be awarded as damages. We will return in detail to what *Sempra Metals* decided in due course.[28]

11.3 Specific Questions

11.3.1 What is the Purpose of Interest on Damages or Debts under Section 35A Senior Courts Act 1981?

11.3.1.1 Compensation for Not being Paid Money Owed

The principles applicable to the award of simple interest under section 35A have been considered in a number of leading cases.[29]

---

[26] Ibid 604–05.   [27] (1854) 9 Exch 341, 156 ER 145.   [28] See section 11.3.2.

[29] Most importantly, *BP Exploration v Hunt* (n 15); *Tate & Lyle Food and Distribution Ltd v Greater London Council* (n 15), 154–55; *Jaura v Ahmed* (n 16); *Fiona Trust and Holding*

It is worth citing straightway from Forbes J in *Tate & Lyle Food and Distribution Ltd v Greater London Council*[30] which sets out very clearly the modern position. He said:

> One looks, therefore, not at the profit which the defendant wrongfully made out of the money he withheld – this would indeed involve a scrutiny of the defendant's financial position – but at the cost to the plaintiff of being deprived of the money which he should have had. I feel satisfied that in commercial cases the interest is intended to reflect the rate at which the plaintiff would have had to borrow money to supply the place of that which was withheld. I am also satisfied that one should not look at any special position in which the plaintiff may have been; one should disregard, for instance, the fact that a particular plaintiff, because of his personal situation, could only borrow money at a very high rate or, on the other hand, was able to borrow at specially favourable rates. The correct thing to do is to take the rate at which plaintiffs in general could borrow money. This does not, however, to my mind, mean that you exclude entirely all attributes of the plaintiff other than that he is a plaintiff. There is evidence here that large public companies of the size and prestige of these plaintiffs could expect to borrow at 1 per cent over the minimum lending rate, while for smaller and less prestigious concerns the rate might be as high as 3 per cent over the minimum lending rate. I think it would always be right to look at the rate at which plaintiffs with the general attributes of the actual plaintiff in the case (though not, of course, with any special or peculiar attribute) could borrow money as a guide to the appropriate interest rate. If commercial rates are appropriate I would take 1 per cent over the minimum lending rate as the proper figure for interest in this case.[31]

Very significantly Robert Goff J in *BP Exploration v Hunt*[32] had applied the same compensatory approach a few years earlier to statutory interest (under what is now section 35A of the Senior Courts Act 1981) in respect of a restitutionary claim for the value of services (equivalent to a *quantum meruit*) under section 1(3) of the Law Reform (Frustrated Contracts) Act 1943. Stressing that, in the light of the very large sums involved, it was important to consider the principles underlying the discretion to award statutory interest, he said: 'The fundamental principle is that interest is not awarded as a punishment, but simply because the plaintiff has been deprived of the use of the money which was due to him.'[33]

Although the claim was for restitution for unjust enrichment Robert Goff J focused, throughout his discussion of interest, on the loss of the

---

Corp v Privalov [2011] EWHC 664 (Comm), [13]–[16], [31] (Andrew Smith J); *West v Ian Finlay* [2014] EWCA Civ 316, [2014] BLR 324, [75]; *JSC BTA Bank v Ablyazov* (n 15).
[30] See n 15.   [31] Ibid 154.   [32] See n 15.   [33] Ibid 845.

claimant, not the enrichment of the defendant. His decision was to award 1 per cent over the bank rate on the restitutionary award from when the claimant made clear its intention to bring a claim (which was some years after the accrual of the cause of action which was the date of the frustration).[34]

That a particular type of compensation explains statutory interest is also made clear by Edelman and Cassidy in their excellent book *Interest Awards in Australia*: 'Statutory interest is . . . to provide compensation to the plaintiff for the loss of the use of the verdict moneys.'[35]

Looking across all the leading cases, they may be said to establish the following five principles.

(i) Statutory interest is to compensate the claimant for being deprived of the money which it should have had. It is not concerned to remove the benefit to the defendant of withholding the money owed, i.e. it is compensatory not restitutionary. In the light of *BP Exploration v Hunt*, this is so even where the principal remedy is restitutionary, not compensatory.

(ii) The money which the claimant should have had is money that was due to the claimant whether as a debt or damages. So this may cover money owed under a contract (a contractual debt); damages (for a civil wrong whether breach of contract or a tort or a statutory wrong); or a restitutionary monetary remedy for unjust enrichment including not only for money paid by the claimant to the defendant but also a *quantum meruit*.

(iii) The money (whether a debt or damages) must be treated as being due for these purposes as soon as the cause of action accrues and even though no award has yet been made by the courts. Hence, interest under the 1981 Act may be awarded from the date of the accrual of the cause of action. This is not to deny that the courts, in the exercise of their discretion, may postpone the running of interest until e.g. the claimant has commenced proceedings or has made clear its intention to make a claim.

(iv) The best measure of compensation in this context is the cost to the claimant of borrowing that sum of money rather than the rate of return that the claimant would have had from investing that sum. So it is a cost of cure rather than a difference in value compensatory measure.

(v) In considering the cost to the claimant of borrowing, courts have taken a pragmatic broad-brush largely objective approach whereby one

---

[34] Ibid 847–49.
[35] James Edelman and Derek I Cassidy, *Interest Awards in Australia* (LexisNexis Butterworths 2003), 128 (footnotes omitted).

ignores the particular characteristics or position of the claimant and the conventional simple interest rate taken is a commercial rate of borrowing. One should ignore, for example, as Andrew Smith J made clear in *Fiona Trust and Holding Corp v Privalov*,[36] that the claimant might have been able to borrow at lower rates because it is 'asset-rich' and would therefore have given security for the borrowing. However, one can take into account the general character of the claimant as being either a major commercial borrower (which would have been able to borrow at cheaper rates) or a small company (which would only have been able to borrow at higher rates). In the former case the rate of interest will therefore generally be 1 per cent over the base rate, whereas in the latter case the rate will generally be 3 per cent over base.[37] An even higher rate over the base rate may be applied in respect of an individual, as in *West v Ian Finlay* where 4.5 per cent over base was awarded to the claimant.[38] This mix of objectivity and subjectivity is designed pragmatically to avoid fine-tuning while not departing altogether from the factual position of the claimant. Rix LJ explained the position as follows in *Jaura v Ahmed*:

> The history in the business context of the movement in recent decades [has been] away from a purely conventional rate to one which more closely reflects the claimant's costs of borrowing ... Thus a rate of 1 per cent above base rate prevailing from time to time has become the practice of the Commercial Court, albeit this is only a presumption and can be varied up or even down to meet the fairness of the parties' particular situation. It is right that defendants who have kept small businessmen out of money to which a court ultimately judges them to have been entitled should pay a rate which properly reflects the real cost of borrowing incurred by such a class of businessmen.[39]

Of course, the statute only permits simple not compound interest[40] so that, to that extent, even the more careful consideration of the class of borrower to which the claimant belongs does not end up with an award of interest that reflects the 'real cost of borrowing'.

In conclusion, therefore, it is clear that a compensatory approach is being taken by the courts to statutory interest under section 35A. The award is standardised to a greater or lesser extent. But even where

---

[36] See n 31 [31].

[37] This was the rate awarded for the claimant who was a small businessman in *Jaura v Ahmed* (n 16), [25] (Rix LJ).

[38] [2014] EWCA Civ 316, [2014] BLR 324, [75].   [39] See n 16 [20], [26].

[40] Contrast s 49 of the Arbitration Act 1996, which permits an arbitrator to award compound interest.

the claim is for restitution, it is the position of the claimant, albeit largely objectivised, that is being focused on.

11.3.1.2   How Can One Justify the Compensatory Approach to Statutory Interest?

Compensation is easy to justify where there is a civil wrong. The commission of the wrong to the claimant by the defendant explains why it is the defendant who is legally liable to put the claimant into as good a position as if the wrong had not occurred. Examples of compensation in the law where there is no wrong in play are hard to find and may not exist at all. So in justifying the compensatory approach to interest under the 1981 Act, one naturally searches for a civil wrong. But is there always a civil wrong in play?

Where the sum is contractually owed, the failure to pay that sum will constitute a breach of contract and one might therefore regard the interest as compensation for that breach of contract. Again, where the interest is payable on damages, at least for a pecuniary loss, one may regard the interest as another layer of pecuniary loss consequential on the wrong (e.g. the tort or breach of contract) that triggered the damages.

But it is hard to see how interest on damages for a non-pecuniary loss (e.g. pain, suffering and loss of amenity in a personal injury action) can be regarded as compensating for an extra loss caused by the wrong that triggered those damages.

Again, at least at first sight, there is no wrong involved where the interest is being paid on a restitutionary remedy for unjust enrichment. Where the interest is in respect of money paid by the claimant to the defendant, one might more naturally regard the interest as a restitutionary remedy, to reflect an additional unjust enrichment conferred on the defendant by the claimant, rather than as compensation for the claimant's loss. So, for example, where C has paid money to D by mistake, one can also say that C has mistakenly transferred the use of the money to D, and interest may be regarded as reflecting that unjust enrichment of D at C's expense.

However, where there is a *quantum meruit* or an analogous remedy as in *BP Exploration v Hunt*, it is not at all clear how one treats the interest on that restitutionary sum as reflecting an extra enrichment of D at the expense of C. The enrichment in not paying the restitutionary sum is an enrichment that has not come from C (nor is there a correspondence of loss and gain in the required sense). There is also no conventional unjust factor.

One might conclude from this analysis that, where there is no underlying civil wrong or, even if there is, where the loss is non-pecuniary,
there is no principled explanation for the award of statutory interest
under the 1981 Act; that the compensation that the courts say underpins
the award of interest is *sui generis* because it does not involve a civil
wrong; and that one does not need to agonise further because this is all
a matter for the discretion of the courts as conferred by statute. However,
coherence in the law demands that, if it all possible, the exercise of
a statutory discretion ought to adopt a principled approach.

   With that in mind, it is submitted that the best explanation (on the
assumption that the interest is indeed compensating a loss of the claimant) is that the failure to pay a sum that is legally due (whether a debt or
damages) *is in itself being treated as a wrong for the purposes of the 1981
Act*. It is a wrong that, under the statute, triggers compensation for loss of
the use of money caused by the failure to pay the sum legally owed with
the wrong being committed at the date of the accrual of the cause of
action for the debt or damages (i.e. at the date when the debt or damages
were payable). The recognition of that wrong readily explains why
statutory interest compensating the claimant is being awarded not only
on damages for a pecuniary loss, but also on damages for a non-
pecuniary loss. It further explains how it is that one can regard interest
on restitutionary remedies as compensatory.[41]

   One might go on to say that a similar explanation applies to explain the
award of interest under the Judgment Debts Act 1838. As this statute
imposes a fixed rate of award, there has been no real discussion of the
justification for the interest. However, if it is seen as compensating a loss
of the claimant – even though the award is highly objective and not finely
tuned to the position of the claimant – there is again the apparent
objection that compensation is normally triggered only by a wrong.
As with the 1981 Act, one might therefore suggest that the failure to
pay a judgment debt (including an award of damages) is itself a type of

---

[41] Cf Stephen Smith, 'Why Courts Make Orders (and What This Tells us about Damages)'
     (2011) 64 CLP 51, 72 and Stephen A Smith, 'A Duty to Make Restitution' (2013) 26
     Canadian Journal of Law and Jurisprudence 157, 166 arguing that one reason why one
     cannot regard the legal requirement to pay damages or to make restitution as a 'duty' is
     precisely because there is no compensation for the loss of use from not being paid the
     damages or restitutionary sum. That is, as the mirror image of the argument that I am
     here making, Smith is arguing that there is no wrong because interest is not being
     awarded as compensation for that loss of use. But this, of course, is contradicted by the
     judicial interpretation of s 35A (albeit correct at common law).

wrong, for the purposes of the 1838 Act, which triggers compensation for the loss of use of the judgment debt owed.

The conclusion to be reached therefore is that, although not straight-forward, interest payable on a debt or damages under section 35A of the Senior Courts Act 1981 (and on a judgment debt under the Judgments Debt Act 1838) is best rationalised as compensating the claimant for the loss of use of the money owed where the failure to pay the money owed is itself being treated as a type of wrong.

11.3.2   What Did Sempra Metals Decide?

We here move away from statute to the common law and to the great and important case of *Sempra Metals*. The question is, what precisely did the House of Lords decide in that case, recently described by the Court of Appeal in *Littlewoods* as 'historic'?[42]

It is apparent from the judgments, and has been confirmed by con-versations with the counsel involved, that there was considerable confu-sion in *Sempra Metals* as to what the claimant's cause of action was. In general terms, the claimants were seeking a remedy for the premature payment of corporation tax paid to HMRC that had been obtained (as advanced corporation tax) contrary to EU law. The question was how, applying the notion of procedural autonomy, the undisputed right to 'repayment' (the EU right required by *San Giorgio*)[43] was to be translated into a cause of action recognised by English domestic law.

Ultimately, it was recognised by the House of Lords that there were three possible causes of action: (i) compensatory damages for (a serious) breach of statutory duty; (ii) restitution for unjust enrichment under the *Woolwich* principle; (iii) and restitution for unjust enrichment for pay-ments made by mistake of law. I understand that it was not until part-way through the hearing in the House of Lords that the claimants made clear that they were seeking restitution for mistake of law, so as to take the benefit of the postponement of the limitation period under section 32(1)(c) of the Limitation Act 1980, rather than either of the other two causes of action.

This partly explains why so much time was spent in the leading speech of Lord Nicholls in considering the law on damages for loss of interest

---

[42]   See n 2 [151] (Arden LJ).
[43]   Case 199/82 *Amministrazione delle Finanze dello Stato v SpA San Giorgio* [1983] ECR 3595.

even though the main claim was recognised as being one for restitution of unjust enrichment. As it was, Lord Nicholls saw that discussion as useful background to understanding the restitutionary claim for interest that was directly in issue but it is nevertheless correct that there is some issue as to whether, strictly speaking, everything said about damages and the rule in *London Chatham and Dover Railway* was obiter dicta. Lord Hope's speech made clear that that was not the issue: 'In my opinion a decision on this point [on damages for interest losses] is not essential to the resolution of the question which is at issue in this case, as the cause of action with which we are concerned here is different.'[44] However, it would seem that Lord Nicholls did regard the damages discussion as part of the ratio because he stressed that the judge's order on damages awarding compound interest should be upheld.[45]

In truth, this debate about the ratio is no longer of practical importance because, not surprisingly, in the light of the careful consideration given to that rule and to the law on damages for interest, *Sempra Metals* has inevitably been treated as binding in respect of the law of damages as well as in relation to the law on unjust enrichment. In practice, it has been interpreted as having overruled *La Pintada* and as having rid the law of the rule in *London Chatham and Dover Railway*.

It is submitted that, in a nutshell, what *Sempra Metals* decided was that, subject to any clash with section 35A, no special rules apply to deny or restrict the recovery of interest, including compound interest, as damages (for a tort or breach of contract) or as restitution for unjust enrichment. The special rule of denial in *London Chatham and Dover Railway* no longer applies. So, subject to any clash with section 35A, if applying normal common law principles, interest as damages would be awarded for a tort of breach of contract, or interest would be awarded as restitution for unjust enrichment, that interest should be awarded.

Talking of non-statutory interest, and of Australian law (which through *Hungerfords v Walker*[46] was ahead of *Sempra Metals*), Edelman and Cassidy helpfully express the essential point (recognised subsequently in *Sempra Metals*) as follows: 'Interest awards in private law operate as a means of perfecting responses or remedies to legal obligations.'[47]

I leave aside until the next main subsection the question of any clash with section 35A which did not have to be resolved on the facts of *Sempra Metals*. What we are then left with is a simple proposition: normal rules

---

[44] *Sempra* (n 1) [16].   [45] Ibid [127].   [46] [1989] HCA 8, (1989) 171 CLR 125.
[47] Edelman and Cassidy, *Interest Awards in Australia* (n 38), 12.

apply when considering the question of interest at common law. What is perhaps not so simple is what that then means in practice. It is to that issue that we now turn.

11.3.2.1 Applying *Sempra Metals* to Compensatory Damages for a Tort or Breach of Contract

As regards (compensatory) damages, it would appear that the correct approach is to ask whether, applying the normal rules of compensatory damages for a tort or breach of contract, the claimant has suffered a loss that is best measured by interest (whether simple or compound) and which is not ruled out by standard limiting principles: so, for example, that loss must not be too remote and must not be a loss that could reasonably have been avoided applying the 'duty to mitigate'. Such a loss will cover, most obviously, interest charges on borrowings incurred or interest that would have been earned but has not been. These losses may include compound interest paid or foregone that would not be recoverable under section 35A. As with all awards of compensatory damages, the loss has to be proved.

If that analysis is correct, it is perhaps surprising – although on one view this may reflect a concern about the clash with section 35A – that there appear to have been only three reported cases since *Sempra Metals* in which damages for a loss of compound interest have been awarded.

The first was a county court patent case, *Xena Systems Ltd v Cantideck*, where HHJ Birss QC awarded compound interest at 8 per cent as damages.[48]

The second and more important decision was that of Males J in *Equitas Ltd v Walsham Bros & Co Ltd*.[49] This dealt with an arrangement that had been entered into to deal with some of the fallout from the huge losses suffered by Names at Lloyd's in the 1990s. The claimant was entitled, either in its own right or as an assignee, to certain premiums and claims that should have been paid across by the defendant brokers before and after 1996. In addition to the principal sums (most of which had now been paid) the claimant sought damages (in contract and tort) for their loss of investment income from not having had those payments. Even though the claimant did not seek to provide precise details of that loss, it was held that, applying *Sempra Metals*, the claimant was entitled to damages for that loss calculated at the LIBOR rate plus 1 per cent and

---

[48] [2013] EWPCC 1, [2013] FSR 41, [116].
[49] [2013] EWHC 3264 (Comm), [2014] PNLR 8.

compounded. Faced with the argument that the claimant had not provided proof of that compound interest loss, Males J said the following:

> [I]t is not necessary for the claimant to produce specific evidence of what
> it would have done with the money or what steps if any it took to borrow
> or otherwise to replace the money of which it was deprived ... [I]t may
> often be impossible or at any rate extremely difficult to produce such
> evidence, especially if that would mean attempting to disentangle
> a claimant's overall business operations in an artificial attempt to attribute
> specific activity such as borrowing to the non-remittance of specific funds.
> Instead, at any rate in commercial cases and unless there is some positive
> reason to do otherwise, the law will proceed on the basis that the measure
> of the claimant's loss is the cost of borrowing to replace the money of
> which the claimant has been deprived regardless of whether that is what
> the claimant actually did. A conventional rate will be used which represents
> the cost to commercial entities such as the claimant and is not
> necessarily the rate at which the claimant itself could have borrowed or
> did in fact borrow. This avoids the need for protracted investigation of the
> particular claimant's financial affairs. As with other conventional measures
> (e.g. the assessment of damages by reference to a market price in sale
> of goods cases) this approach has the advantage of certainty and predictability
> which is always important in the commercial context, as well as
> being broadly fair in the great majority of cases and avoiding expensive
> and often ultimately unproductive litigation ... If a conventional borrowing
> cost is to be adopted in this way, the question whether interest should
> be simple or compound answers itself. While simple interest has the virtue
> of simplicity ... it also has the certainty of error and injustice ... it is
> impossible to borrow commercially on simple interest terms.
> I respectfully agree with Lord Nicholls that the law must recognise and
> give effect to this reality if it is to achieve a fair and just outcome when
> assessing financial loss. To conclude that, at least in a typical commercial
> case, the normal and conventional measure of damages for breach of an
> obligation to remit funds consists of compound interest at a conventional
> rate is therefore both principled and predictable, as well as being in
> accordance with what was actually awarded in *Sempra Metals*.[50]

Yet six months earlier in *JSC BTA Bank v Ablyazov*,[51] which was not
cited to or mentioned by Males J, it would appear that a different
approach to this question of proof was taken by Teare J in applying
Sempra Metals. His decision was that the loss, represented by compound
interest, must be explicitly proved and that one could not presume a loss
based on compound interest rates so that the claim for compound
interest failed. The claim was for damages for fraud and the claimant

[50] Ibid [123].   [51] See n 15.

bank sought interest on the sums paid away at compound interest rates applying *Sempra Metals* or, alternatively, at simple interest rates under section 35A. It was held that only the latter could be awarded because the claim for compound interest had not been sufficiently pleaded and proved: the claimant had not alleged what it would otherwise have used the money for or any borrowing that it had now had to make because of the loss of the money paid out. In a very clear judgment, Teare J said:

> It is to be observed that in none of the actions is there any allegation of the use to which the monies paid away as a result of the Defendants' fraud would have been put had there been no fraud. There is no allegation of losses the Bank had suffered in addition to having paid away the principal sums. Thus the Bank, in my judgment, has not alleged 'its actual interest losses'. It may be that the monies paid away would have been lent to bona fide borrowers but that has not been alleged. It may be that the sums would have been used to augment the Bank's capital base and so reduced the extent of the Bank's own borrowings but whether that was done and if so what savings would have been made (and therefore lost) has not been alleged. It may be that but for the fraud the monies would not have been borrowed by the Bank in the first place and so the interest it paid has been thrown away but that has not been alleged. [Counsel for the Bank] submitted that the pleadings, whilst not perhaps perfect, nevertheless were sufficient to entitle the Bank to claim interest as damages. I am unable to accept that submission. There has been, no doubt for very good reason, no attempt to plead as damages the Bank's actual interest losses over and above the paying away of the principal sums. There has merely been a claim for damages. But that, as was clearly stated by Lord Nicholls in *Sempra Metals*, is insufficient for the purpose of claiming actual interest losses.[52]

And later he concluded:

> To require actual interest losses to be specifically pleaded might be regarded by the Bank as unrealistic and unduly formalistic. But Lord Nicholls expressly accepted this 'reproach' to the common law and said that in the absence of a specific plea of actual interest losses the remedy lay in the statutory provisions for interest. This is clear guidance for trial judges which I must follow. I have therefore concluded that there has been no plea of actual interest losses. It follows that the Bank can only claim simple interest pursuant to section 35A of the Senior Courts Act 1981.[53]

It is possible that one can reconcile these apparently conflicting decisions by saying that in the former the loss had been pleaded and proved and it was merely the quantum that was in dispute whereas in the latter it

[52] Ibid [12]–[13], [18]–[19].   [53] Ibid [18]–[19].

was the loss that had not been pleaded or proved. But that is a strained distinction. Perhaps more convincing is that Teare J was clearly troubled, and rightly so, by the relationship between *Sempra Metals* and section 35A of the Senior Courts Act 1981, whereas Males J made no reference at all to this. We shall return to this clash below.[54]

11.3.2.2   Applying *Sempra Metals* to Restitution for Unjust Enrichment

In contrast to the application of *Sempra Metals* to compensatory damages for a tort or breach of contract, which (leaving aside the possible clash with section 35A and the issue of proof) is relatively easy – because the rules on compensatory damages for a tort of breach of contract are well known and long-established – the application of *Sempra Metals* to restitution for unjust enrichment is exceedingly difficult. This is because it raises unexplored issues of general principle in the law of unjust enrichment relating to enrichment, the measurement of enrichment and, in the view of some commentators, the 'at the expense of' requirement. These issues have given rise to very careful analyses by Henderson J in no fewer than three separate cases involving claims for overpaid tax against the Revenue.[55] One of these three cases, *Littlewoods Ltd v HMRC*[56] has since been appealed on, amongst other points, the question of interest, with the Court of Appeal upholding Henderson J's decision on interest (and indeed on all other points appealed) albeit not all his reasoning.

The analysis of Henderson J in the three cases has been as follows:

  (i) Interest as restitution is concerned to measure the enrichment to the defendant from having the (unjust) use of money.
 (ii) The use of money is a separate enrichment from the payment of money and raises more complex issues in establishing that the defendant has been enriched.
(iii) More specifically, the objective enrichment that is being measured is the defendant's opportunity to use the money.
 (iv) The Revenue (which was the defendant in all three cases) cannot 'subjectively devalue' that enrichment by showing that the money

---

[54] See section 11.3.3.
[55] *Prudential Assurance Co v HMRC* [2013] EWHC 3249 (Ch), [2014] STC 1236; *Littlewoods Retail Ltd v HMRC* [2014] EWHC 868 (Ch), [2014] STC 1761; *Test Claimants in the FII Group Litigation v HMRC (No 2)* [2014] EWHC 4302 (Ch), [2015] STC 1471.
[56] See n 2. Since this chapter was written, the *Prudential* and *FII (No 2)* cases have also gone to the Court of Appeal: see, respectively, [2016] EWCA Civ 376, [2016] STC 1798; and [2016] EWCA Civ 1180. In the latter, the Court of Appeal considered itself to be bound by *Littlewoods* which, in any event, it agreed with.

was spent rather than being invested or otherwise lent for a return. To that extent at least, it is irrelevant to show what the defendant did with the money or what actual benefit it derived from having received the payment (or having received it early).

(v) The appropriate measure is the compound rate of interest which the government would have had to pay to borrow an equivalent sum of money. This is lower than the commercial rate of borrowing because the government can borrow at a lower rate than commercial borrowers. That was the measure of restitution awarded in *Sempra* and was considered to be the correct amount to award in the other tax cases against the Revenue with which Henderson J was concerned.

(vi) A complication is that EU law in this area requires that interest is an adequate indemnity for the claimant's loss so that the focus in EU law is on compensating the claimant for its loss of interest not reversing the defendant's unjust enrichment by having had the opportunity to use the money. Nevertheless, provided compound interest is awarded as the restitutionary measure, Henderson J considered that that was an adequate indemnity so that there was no need to adjust the English law of unjust enrichment to comply with the need to comply with the EU principle that there must be an equivalent and effective remedy and hence an 'adequate indemnity'.

Henderson J's judgments are always a delight to read because of the rigour and clarity of his analysis. With great respect, however, it seems to me that his analysis of the English law of unjust enrichment is flawed to the extent that it applies, from start to finish, a notional or objective approach to the defendant's enrichment.[57] That may be correct as the starting point but it is not correct as the end point. It should always be open to a defendant to show that it has not been benefited by the objective benefit. Put another way, the law of unjust enrichment is concerned with the actual benefit to this defendant and not the notional benefit to a hypothetical defendant. So, for example, Lord Nicholls in *Sempra* accepted that a defendant who made no use of the money (e.g. if she hid the sum of money received under the bed) could not be said to have been enriched by the use value of the money.[58] Although objectively she

---

[57] I should make clear that I was one of the counsel representing the Revenue in the *Prudential* and *FII* cases.

[58] See n 1 [118]. On this example, one must also assume that the defendant would not otherwise have borrowed that sum of money so that it has not been saved that borrowing cost.

had the opportunity to use the money, in that example she could show that that opportunity was of no benefit to her.

In the light of that example, it appears to follow that the Revenue, if it can show that it has spent the money (non-profitably and provided it can show that it has not saved having to borrow other equivalent sums of money), thereby establishes that it has not been benefited by the use value of the money and certainly has not been benefited from the use of the money for the whole of the claimed period. Indeed if one were to step back from the complex detail, the result of Henderson J applying compound interest on all the mistaken payments from the date of receipt appears to be tantamount to saying that, had the Revenue not been paid those sums, it would have borrowed the same sums at a compound interest rate for five decades. Surely that cannot be right.

Nevertheless the Court of Appeal (Lady Justice Arden and Lord Justices Patten and Floyd) in *Littlewoods*[59] upheld the decision of Henderson J, albeit without endorsing some of his central reasoning. Contrary to Henderson J, the Court of Appeal stressed that it was important to focus on the actual benefit to the defendant in question so as to respect the defendant's freedom of choice. The court recognised that this is what, probably inaptly, has been labelled 'subjective devaluation', its own preferred terminology being a 'defendant-focused rate'.[60] So, in disagreeing with the reasoning of Henderson J, the Court of Appeal said:

> [S]ince HMRC proved to the satisfaction of the judge that the actual benefit it obtained from Littlewoods' overpayments was less than [the] market value of the time value of that money, actual use value could be relevant to valuing the benefit which the government received as a result of the overpayments.[61]

Yet the Court of Appeal came to the same decision as Henderson J. Unfortunately their precise reasoning on this is, with respect, far from transparent and is contained in two mysterious paragraphs.[62] These paragraphs contain the following three points, none of which is easy to follow.

(i) The government was not an involuntary recipient of the benefit. It is hard to see what the relevance of this was thought to be, let alone what was here meant by a voluntary as opposed to an involuntary recipient.

(ii) Even if the overpayment was used for government spending or reducing taxation – and not in repaying borrowing or placing the money

---

[59] See n 2.   [60] Ibid [158].   [61] Ibid [187].   [62] Ibid [196]–[197].

on deposit – the government had none the less been free to use the money for those latter purposes. However, this appears to be the same as saying that what matters is that the government had the opportunity to use the money for those purposes which was the approach of Henderson J that the Court of Appeal had said it was rejecting.

(iii) Even if the money were spent on public projects, it could be assumed that that money was well spent and it would be difficult to value the benefit which the government obtains by spending the money for the benefit of others. But this did not appear to meet HMRC's argument that precisely because the money was spent (non-profitably) on the assumption that it would not need to be repaid (and whether well or badly spent was immaterial), it would be inappropriate to treat the government as if it had taken out a long-term loan.

With great respect, the conclusion to be reached is that the reasoning of the Court of Appeal is deeply puzzling.

Some commentators argue that, in any event, there can be no claim for the interest as restitution of unjust enrichment because the use of the money by the defendant is not 'at the expense of the claimant' in the relevant sense. Professor Robert Stevens takes this approach.[63] I disagree. As their Lordships clearly recognised in *Sempra Metals*, there has been a transfer of the use of the money, or the opportunity to use the money, from the claimant to the defendant. The use value to the defendant has come from the claimant. Put another way, there is a direct causal correlation between the claimant's loss of use and the defendant's use of, or opportunity to use, the money. In any event, it is plain that the House of Lords in *Sempra Metals* authoritatively took the view that there is a claim for restitution of unjust enrichment in this situation, so that the Stevens' view is contradicted by the reasoning of their Lordships. Indeed that 'at the claimant's expense' was satisfied was thought to be so obvious that there was no overt discussion of it.

---

[63] Although his view has not been published, this is the approach he has adopted in numerous seminars and conferences at which I have been present. He regards the facts of *Sempra* as equivalent to the following hypothetical example. There are two stamps of a certain type in the world, each owned by C and D; C mistakenly destroys his stamp the effect of which is to increase hugely the value of D's stamp. Does C have a claim in unjust enrichment against D? The answer is plainly 'no'. Stevens argues that this is because D's gain is not at the expense of C in the relevant sense. But surely that is because there has been no transfer of value from C to D in that stamp example, whereas there was such a transfer of use value in *Sempra*. Alternatively in the stamp example the enrichment of D is an incidental benefit, whereas that is not so as regards the use value in *Sempra*.

11.3.3 *Is There an Unacceptable Clash between* Sempra Metals *and Section 35A?*

One of the difficulties of the law of interest in this jurisdiction is that statute has reacted to the deficiencies of the common law. If the common law is then reformed judicially, or consideration is being given to such a judicial reform, it may be regarded as clashing with the statute. Indeed it can be argued – and indeed this was the argument accepted in *La Pintada* – that the only way to avoid a clash with the statute is not to reform the common law at all but rather to amend the statute. So it is that an argument that has still not been finally resolved is whether there is an unacceptable clash between the extended application of *Sempra Metals* and section 35A of the Senior Courts Act 1981 in relation to compound interest.

So if one asks, how can it be that simple interest only is permitted under section 35A whereas compound interest can be awarded as compensatory damages for a tort or breach of contract or as restitution for unjust enrichment under *Sempra Metals*, there appear to be two main possible answers.

(i) One approach is to say that there is no clash because, on the facts of *Sempra Metals*, the claim for compound interest – that is, the claim for the premature payment of tax (or as it may otherwise be termed, the interest for the 'pre-utilisation' period) – was the principal sum of restitution sought. There was no other sum for repayment of tax in issue because the mainstream tax, against which the advanced corporation tax was set off, was lawfully due. Section 35A did not therefore apply. Interest was not being added to a debt or damages. The interest was the debt in issue. Section 35A would only have come into play once it had been determined that restitution corresponding to the premature payment of tax was owed and interest was then sought to be added to that sum. In *Sempra Metals* it had been accepted at first instance by Park J that that additional interest (which may be termed interest for the 'post-utilisation' period) fell within section 35A so that, in contrast to the principal sum claimed for the 'pre-utilisation period' (which was best measured by compound interest) simple interest only could be awarded.[64] Lords Nicholls and Walker in the House of Lords said that they did not necessarily agree with that confinement of the additional interest to simple interest but left the question open because it was not in

---

[64] [2004] EWHC 2387 (Ch), [2004] STC 1178, [46].

issue, as did Lord Mance.[65] However, one might argue that one way of resolving the 'clash' is to say that, in line with Park J's judgment, where interest *can* be awarded under section 35A, such interest can only be simple. *Sempra Metals* does not clash with section 35A because no interest for the pre-utilisation period could have been awarded under section 35A. The only award for that period could have been at common law. This approach to avoiding a clash has the added advantage that it does not require the overruling of several past cases in the law of unjust enrichment, including most importantly, *Westdeutsche v Landesbank Girozentrale v Islington London BC*[66] in the House of Lords, in which the majority held that simple interest only under section 35A could be added to the principal sum of restitution being awarded. This would also mean that, in general, interest on damages will continue to be governed by section 35A and will be simple only. In effect, this approach argues that, where it applies, section 35A has replaced the common law: within its sphere of application it is an exclusive regime. Indeed one might ask, if the common law is to outflank section 35A, does it also outflank the Judgment Debtors Act 1838 so that compound interest is now to be awarded on judgments debts? If not, why not?

(ii) The main alternative approach is to say that, even though simple interest can be awarded under section 35A, that does not preclude compound interest being awarded at common law. The claimant who wishes to recover compound interest will have the burden of establishing and proving on the evidence that at common law compound interest is the correct measure of damages for a tort or breach of contract, or that compound interest is the correct measure of restitution for unjust enrichment; but that, if it can do so, a claimant is entitled to compound interest. The clash with section 35A is resolved by in effect treating section 35A as the straightforward default position which does not require evidence or significant legal argument by the claimant. But a claimant who wishes to

---

[65] See n 1. Lord Nicholls said at [129]: 'The order provided for payment of simple interest pursuant to section 35A for the period from the date of set off until judgment. Sempra did not challenge this provision. So this provision in the order will stand. But I am not to be taken as accepting that compound interest was unavailable for this period. Sempra's financial losses caused by payment of ACT did not wholly cease at the date of set off. Sempra remained out of pocket for the unpaid interest, and its financial losses in this regard continued to accrue up to judgment. Similarly, as to the restitutionary claims: after the date of set off the Inland Revenue continued to derive interest benefits from the benefits it had already obtained from having use of the ACT payments.' See also Lord Walker at [156] and Lord Mance at [228].

[66] [1996] AC 669 (HL).

go beyond the simple interest available by statute, may do so. On this view, *Sempra Metals* is applicable across the board and was in no sense confined to where the principal sum claimed is for interest.

The latter approach is more attractive in terms of principle in allowing full recognition to the obvious fact that, in the commercial world, a claimant's loss and a defendant's enrichment, represented respectively by borrowing costs incurred or saved, are likely to be more accurately measured by compound rather than simple interest. Certainly one might think that the claimant should have the option to prove that loss or enrichment. This was the approach taken by Henderson J in the three restitution cases mentioned above; it may also be said to underpin the approach of both Males J and Teare J in the damages cases referred to above in the sense that in both cases it was possible to award simple interest under section 35A and yet it was accepted that, if proved as a loss, compound interest as damages should be awarded (albeit that, as we have seen, the two judges took a different approach to the standard of proof required with Males J's view appearing to obliterate completely section 35A in commercial cases).

The important point to stress, however, is that that principled approach does tend to undermine the application of the statute and requires the overruling of past cases. Some might argue that, given that Parliament has laid down that the interest should be simple and not compound in all relevant statutes dealing with interest (the Judgment Debts Act 1838 and the Late Payment of Commercial Debts (Interest) Act 1998 as well as section 35A of the Senior Courts Act 1981), it would be inappropriate for the courts to contradict that in situations where the statute applies. The constitutionally appropriate route is for Parliament to amend section 35A to allow compound interest. At the very least the apparent clash is surely an issue that merits argument by the Supreme Court rather than being resolved in the lower courts.

Is there anything in the wording of section 35A that assists? One may think that section 35A(4) has some relevance. That reads: 'Interest in respect of a debt shall not be awarded under this section for a period during which, for whatever reason, interest on the debt already runs.' This might be thought to suggest that the statute is not seen as comprehensive and that, if interest (including compound interest) can be awarded at common law, there is no objection to that. In other words, it might be argued that this subsection reinforces the idea that section 35A sets up a default position only. But the subsection is confined to debts and does not extend to damages so that, if it were setting up a default position, it would be defective as covering part of the field only. In the light of this, the better interpretation is that the subsection offers no help on the central question which we are discussing. Certainly what appears to be principally in mind in section 35A(4) is that contractually agreed interest, or interest available under a different statute (e.g. a statute dealing with the repayment of overpaid tax), overrides interest under section 35A.[67]

11.4   Conclusion

The patchwork of common law and statute that comprises our law on interest throws up some difficult questions. It has principally been argued or observed in this chapter that:

(i) The well-accepted compensatory function of an award of statutory interest under section 35A of the Senior Courts Act 1981 may be best rationalised by regarding the non-payment of a debt or damages as itself being for these purposes a wrong (constituted by a failure to pay what is owed) from the moment of the accrual of the cause of action for the debt or damages.

(ii) Applying *Sempra Metals*, there is an unresolved clash of first instance decisions on the standard of proof of loss required for an award of compound interest as damages.

(iii) The award of compound interest as a restitutionary measure in *Sempra Metals* requires that the defendant in question has itself been enriched and one cannot simply apply an objective approach from start to finish based on the idea that the defendant was enriched, objectively, by the opportunity to use the money received.

(iv) Different approaches may be taken to the possible clash between the development of the common law on interest in *Sempra Metals* and section 35A of the Senior Courts Act 1981. On the facts of *Sempra Metals*, the clash did not arise and it is important to appreciate that interest could not have been awarded under section 35A. Certainly, that possible clash needs to be examined and resolved by the Supreme Court. It provides a classic example of our need to understand fully the intriguing relationship between statute and the common law.

---

[67] For consideration of the former provision under the Law Reform (Miscellaneous Provisions) Act 1935 to the effect that 'interest could not be awarded upon interest', see *Bushwall Properties Ltd v Vortex Ltd* [1975] 1 WLR 1649 (Ch) 1660, rvd on a different point [1976] 1 WLR 591 (CA).

12

Actionable Loss of a Chance

SARAH GREEN

There are three types of factual situation which have been characterised as 'lost chance' scenarios. In forensic terms, only one of these is an appropriate characterisation. The first type of situation involves a defendant who has denied a claimant access to an opportunity which exists independently of the claimant–defendant relationship. The second situation is based on the measure of the claimant's inability to reach the balance of probabilities standard in trying to prove that the defendant caused her any injury at all. The third is one in which a defendant has caused a claimant to suffer a present detriment, where the magnitude of that detriment needs quantifying. The importance of the distinction should not be underestimated; the first situation is one in which the claimant has lost *only* the possibility of realising a future chance of benefit; the second is, by definition, one in which no *legally recognised* loss has occurred; and in the third, the claimant has suffered a legally relevant loss which requires quantification.

The difference between those 'lost chance' claims which should succeed and those which should not has variously been identified as being dependent upon whether the chance lost is that of avoiding an adverse physical outcome or of making a commercial gain,[1] or whether the outcome of the chance concerned is dependent upon the actions of the claimant herself or of a third party.[2] The true means of distinction is simpler than this:

I am grateful to all the participants in the Commercial Remedies workshop at Trinity College, Cambridge, in July 2015 for their questions, comments and criticisms in response to an earlier version of this chapter. I would like to thank Nicholas McBride and Adam Kramer in particular for their detailed and constructive suggestions.

[1] See, e.g. *Hotson v East Berkshire AHA* [1987] AC 750 (HL); *Gregg v Scott* [2005] UKHL 2, [2005] 2 AC 176; and *Kitchen v RAF Association* [1958] 2 All ER 241 (CA).
[2] *Allied Maples Group Ltd v Simmons & Simmons* [1995] 1 WLR 1602 (CA).

Type 1 – the only cases to which the 'loss of a chance' label can accurately be applied Those situations in which the relevant chance is one that exists independently of the litigants,[3] so that whilst the breach affects a claimant's ability to avail herself of that chance, the substance of the chance itself is beyond the control of either party, e.g. *Chaplin v Hicks*,[4] *Allied Maples*.[5] There are two criteria which must both be met for a situation to fit this category:

- primary loss has to be a chance, defined as the *possibility* of detriment or benefit;
- that chance has to be independent of the relationship between the litigants.

Type 2 Those situations in which the 'chance' and the breach are causally interdependent because the breach affects the existence and content of the chance itself, e.g. *Gregg v Scott*.[6] These are not in fact loss of chance cases at all, because to claim that a chance has been lost here is to beg the question.

Type 3 Those situations in which the claimant has proved on the balance of probabilities that the defendant's breach has caused her loss, but the extent of that loss remains to be quantified, e.g. *Golden Strait Corp v Nippon Yusen Kubishika Kaisha (The Golden Victory*[7]*)*. Cases of this type are simply orthodox cases of quantification, and are included here to distinguish them clearly from loss of chance cases proper (Type 1 cases).

12.1 Two Separate Questions

The only *causal* question of legal relevance in this context is: 'But for the breach, would the claimant have had access to an opportunity independent of the parties?' This is the Access Question, and determines whether a claimant has suffered a legally recognised loss. By contrast, the question 'But for the breach, what were the claimant's chances of an ultimately favourable outcome?' is the Magnitude Question and is purely quantitative. As such, it should *not* be asked independently of the Access Question. In negligence, and other torts of which damage is the gist,

---

[3] See *Chester v Afshar* [2004] UKHL 41, [2005] 1 AC 134 [81] (Lord Hope): 'the risk of which she should have been warned was not created by the failure to warn. It was already there, as an inevitable risk of the operative procedure itself however skilfully and carefully it was carried out.'

[4] [1911] 2 KB 786 (CA).   [5] See n 2.   [6] See n 1.

[7] [2007] UKHL 12, [2007] 2 AC 353.

the Access Question governs the actionability of a claim. In contract and torts actionable per se, the Access Question determines whether any substantial damages will be payable (but not what those damages should be). As such, the Access Question is one which must be established on the balance of probabilities if a claimant is to prove that he is any worse off as a result of the breach.[8] Any consequent damages will be calculated by asking the Magnitude Question, and so calculating the value of the chance which has been lost, regardless of whether it exceeds 50 per cent.[9] This is because, in true lost chance cases, the uncertainty inherent in the chance itself is not affected by anything the defendant has done, and it is not, therefore, necessary for the law to resolve it one way or another: in legal terms, such a chance is relevant only in terms of quantification.

12.2   Type 1 Cases Explained

Allied Maples Group Ltd v Simmons & Simmons is one of the clearest examples of a Type 1 case.[10] The defendants therein were solicitors, whose negligence in drafting an acquisition contract had deprived the claimants of the opportunity to negotiate for more advantageous terms. The claimants, relying on the negligently drafted agreement, believed they were protected from liabilities arising from the acquisition when in fact they were not. Had they known of their vulnerability, they would have attempted to acquire such protection from the vendor before the contract was concluded. The Court of Appeal decided in favour of the claimants, and determined that damages should be assessed by reference to the chance of any negotiations (had they been possible) being success-ful. It concluded that, as long as there was a real, as opposed to speculative chance of success, there was no need for a positive outcome to be more likely than not. These facts fall squarely within the Type 1 classification

---

[8]   A question which necessarily involves the claimant establishing that she would have, on the balance of probabilities, taken the chance had she been able to: *McWilliams v Sir William Arrol & Co Ltd* [1962] 1 WLR 295 (HL). This is what the claimant failed to establish in *Sykes v Midland Bank Executor and Trustee Co Ltd* [1971] 1 QB 113 (CA) and justifies the finding therein in favour of the defendant. Cf Sandy Steel, 'Rationalising Loss of a Chance in Tort' in Stephen GA Pitel, Jason W Neyers and Erika Chamberlain (eds), *Challenging Orthodoxy in Tort Law* (Hart 2013), particularly 247–53, in which he seems to suggest that the uncertainty inherent *in the chance itself* is a problem for proving causation; something that analysing in this way would avoid.

[9]   As long as it is more than speculative: see *Allied Maples* (n 2) 1614 (Stuart-Smith LJ).

[10]   Ibid. Other examples include *Kitchen v RAF Association* (n 1) and *Yardley v Coombes* (1963) 107 SJ 575.

because the solicitors' breach of duty had no effect whatsoever on the substance or content of the chance itself; its existence was extraneous to, and independent of, the solicitors' actions. The magnitude of the chance *eo ipso*, therefore, is of no relevance to the question of causation, but only to the subsequent question of quantification. The breach of duty did, however, affect the claimant's ability to avail itself of that chance:

> On the evidence before him the judge was justified in concluding that the defendants' breach of duty did have a causative impact upon the bargain which the plaintiffs and the vendors struck. He was entitled to find that, if the plaintiffs had negotiated further, they had a measurable chance of negotiating better terms which would have given them at least some protection against the liability on assigned leases which they were to assume on the draft agreement as it then stood, and as ultimately signed.[11]

Another classic Type 1 case is *Chaplin v Hicks*,[12] in which the claimant was granted damages corresponding to the one in four chance that, had she been granted the appointment with the defendant to which her contract entitled her, she would have been chosen as one of the 12 most attractive finalists in his beauty/talent competition. The answer to the Access Question on these facts is straightforward: but for the defendant's failure to inform the claimant of the date of the appointment, she would have been able to avail herself of the opportunity to win the contest. Her chances of winning that contest have nothing whatsoever to contribute to that inquiry, but of course do answer the Magnitude Question, which was used quite properly in *Chaplin*, to assess the quantum of damages to which the claimant was entitled as a result. At this point, it is necessary to deal with a slight complication of the facts of *Chaplin*, as accepted by the court. As Burrows points out,[13] given that the contingency in fact turned on the decision of the defendant himself, as opposed to an independent panel, no damages at all should have been awarded, on the basis of the principle that a court is entitled to assume that a defendant will make the decision most favourable to himself. This fits with the analysis herein, that in order for any lost chance to be actionable, it must exist independently of the claimant–defendant

---

[11] *Allied Maples* (n 2) 1620 (Hobhouse LJ).

[12] See n 4. This is the clearest statement of the point, but see also *Hotson v East Berkshire AHA* (n 1) 785 (Lord Mackay); and Helen Reece, 'Losses of Chances in the Law' (1996) 59 MLR 188, 197.

[13] Andrew Burrows, *Remedies for Torts and Breach of Contract* (Oxford University Press 2004) 54 fn 4. See also Andrew Burrows, 'Uncertainty about Uncertainty: Damages for Loss of a Chance' [2008] JIPL 41 fn 44.

relationship. On its true facts, therefore, *Chaplin* would not be a classic Type 1 case, or in fact a Type 1 case at all. On the facts as pleaded and accepted, however, in which the claimant's chances of winning were in the hands of a panel independent of Hicks, the case fits the Type 1 category.

An essential feature of Type 1 cases is that the opportunity in question must not be a possibility which has been realised, but only one whose outcome can never, as a result of the breach, be known.[14] This accords with the well-known distinction made by Lord Diplock in *Mallett v McMonagle* between those uncertainties on which the law needs to take a certain view, and those which it can accept as uncertain:

> The role of the court in making an assessment of damages which depends upon its view as to what will be and what would have been is to be contrasted with its ordinary function in civil actions of determining what was. In determining what did happen in the past a court decides on the balance of probabilities. Anything that is more probable than not it treats as certain. But in assessing damages which depend upon its view as to what will happen in the future or would have happened in the future if something had not happened in the past, the court must make an estimate as to what are the chances that a particular thing will or would have happened and reflect those chances, whether they are more or less than even, in the amount of damages which it awards.[15]

Similarly, Lord Reid said in *Davies v Taylor*:

> You can prove that a past event happened, but you cannot prove that a future event will happen and I do not think that the law is so foolish as to suppose that you can. All that you can do is to evaluate the chance. Sometimes it is virtually 100 per cent: sometimes virtually nil. But often it is somewhere in between.[16]

In order to qualify as a loss for which a claimant can recover in its own right, therefore, the relevant opportunity must be unrealised and independent of the relationship between the litigating parties. This goes further than the explanation of *Allied Maples* which has come to be accepted. Whilst it is often said that possibilities dependent upon the hypothetical action of a third party may form the basis of a damages award whether or not they exceed 50 per cent, this is only part of the full

---

[14] See Steel (n 8) 236.

[15] [1970] AC 166 (HL) 176. See also *Malec v JC Hutton Pty Ltd* [1990] HCA 20, (1990) 169 CLR 638; and Geoff Masel, 'Damages in Tort for Loss of a Chance' (1995) 3 *Torts Law Journal* 43.

[16] [1974] AC 207 (HL) 213.

story. Clearly, such third-party chances will often fulfil the independence criteria identified here, but independent contingencies need not involve third parties at all, since they could equally be dependent on pure fortune, physiological make-up or other natural, non-human intervention. It is far more accurate, therefore, to describe chances which can be lost in a legal sense as those that are independent, and therefore beyond the control of, the litigants in any given case.

12.3 Type 2 Cases Explained

In substance, Type 2 cases present the orthodox causal question. It is only as a consequence of claimants' attempted reformulation of this question, in response to an otherwise certain no-liability result, that such factual situations have been represented as involving lost chances.[17] On the basis of such a reformulation, however, almost every negligence scenario could be recast as one in which a so-called chance has been lost because the forensic process does not deal in certainties,[18] meaning that any conclusion established on the balance of probabilities will necessarily admit of there being a 'chance' that it is not an accurate representation of actual events. In such situations, it makes sense to talk of 'probabilities' rather than 'chances', since this is really what the interaction between the defendant and the claimant has affected.

Where that probability is not independent of the parties, it means nothing as a standalone estimation of likelihood. As a result of the civil law's standard of proof, and its inherent fiction of certainty, there is no such thing as an actionable chance of ≤50 per cent between litigating parties. Either the claimant had a greater than evens chance, of which she was deprived by the defendant's breach, or she never had a greater than evens chance, and so had nothing of which the defendant could deprive her. Since, in the former situation, the claimant is taken to have proved that the defendant's breach definitely caused her injury and, in the latter that the breach definitely did not cause her injury, probabilities have no further part to play in the forensic process. That this has nothing to do with whether the purported chance is that of financial gain or of avoiding an adverse physical outcome can be illustrated by reference to a few real and hypothetical examples.

---

[17] As in *Hotson v East Berkshire AHA* (n 1) and *Gregg v Scott* (n 1).

[18] As recognised by Baroness Hale in *Gregg v Scott* (n 1) [224]. See also Lord Hoffmann, 'Causation' in Richard Goldberg (ed), *Perspectives on Causation* (Hart 2011) 8.

Hotson v East Berkshire AHA,[19] and *Gregg v Scott*,[20] are the most well-known examples of cases in which claimants argued that they had lost chances. In the first case, the thirteen-year-old claimant fell from a tree and injured his left hip.[21] The defendant's hospital, from which he sought treatment, negligently failed to diagnose or treat him correctly for five days. Ultimately, the claimant suffered avascular necrosis of the epiphysis, involving disability of the hip joint with the virtual certainty that osteoarthritis would later develop. At trial, Simon Brown J found that, even had the injury been properly diagnosed and treated in a timely manner, there remained a 75 per cent risk that avascular necrosis would have developed, but he awarded the claimant damages corresponding to the 25 per cent chance of which the defendant's negligence had supposedly deprived him. Whilst the Court of Appeal concurred, the House of Lords decided in favour of the defendant and held that the trial judge's finding, that at the time of the fall there had already been a 75 per cent chance of avascular necrosis developing, amounted to a finding on the balance of probabilities that the fall was the sole cause of the injury. The court did not, however, expressly exclude the possibility that 'loss of a chance', as it was presented therein, could form the basis of a successful claim in negligence.[22]

In *Gregg v Scott*, the claimant visited the defendant GP, complaining of a lump under his left arm, which the defendant diagnosed as a benign lipoma. In failing to refer the claimant to a specialist at that point, the defendant was held to have been in breach of his duty of care. It was not until a biopsy was carried out by a specialist, following a referral by another GP nine months later, that the claimant discovered that he had cancer in the form of non-Hodgkin's lymphoma. The trial judge found that the claimant's chance of being 'cured' (defined in this context as a period of ten years' remission) was 42 per cent when he made his visit to the defendant, but that the nine-month delay, consequent upon the defendant's negligent failure to diagnose his illness correctly, reduced his chance of being cured to 25 per cent. As the claimant had only a 42 per cent chance of a cure in the first place, however, he was unable to prove on the balance of probabilities that the defendant's negligence caused him to be in a worse state than he would have been in, had his treatment not been delayed by nine months. In the light of this fact, the claimant argued that he had suffered the loss of a 17 per cent chance of

---

[19] See n 1.   [20] Ibid.   [21] More specifically, his left femoral epiphysis.
[22] *Hotson* (n 1) 786.

being cured as a result of the defendant's negligence. In so doing, he invited the court to address a similar question to the one first considered by the House in *Hotson* as to whether or not such a loss should be recoverable.

By a majority of three to two (Lord Hope and Lord Nicholls dissenting), the House of Lords dismissed the claimant's appeal and held that it was (still) not prepared to find defendants liable in such cases. Whilst, on the facts as found by the trial judge, it had been established that the defendant's breach of duty had reduced the epidemiological likelihood of survival by 17 per cent, the House of Lords correctly declined to recognise this as actionable damage. As Lord Hoffmann put it, 'a wholesale adoption of possible rather than probable causation as the criterion of liability would be so radical a change in our law as to amount to a legislative act'.[23]

In refusing to depart from the orthodox approach to causation, the court recognised that it is our epistemic limitations which pose the most consistent problem for the causal inquiry and, to use Lord Hoffmann's words once more: 'What we lack is knowledge and the law deals with that lack of knowledge by the concept of the burden of proof.'[24] In other words, although the law cannot expect to deal in certainties, the least it can do is expect outcomes to be more or less likely than not. Common to both *Hotson* and *Gregg* is the fact that the claimants could not have established their claims on the basis of the orthodox approach to causation, since in neither case was it more likely than not that the claimant was any worse off as a result of the defendant's breach of duty. The formulation of both claims, misleadingly couched in terms of 'lost chances', was an attempt to sidestep the standard of proof on the basis that the claimants had lost something of value to them in having their 'already likely to suffer an adverse outcome' position made, by the defendant's breach, into 'even more likely to suffer an adverse outcome'. That this argument was made is, at least from a human interest point of view, easily understandable, since most individuals would class even the tiniest percentage chance of avoiding an adverse physical outcome as being something of significant value to them.[25] In legal terms, however, such a 'chance' is less a prediction of what would have happened to

---

[23] *Scott* (n 1) [90]. See also *Tabet v Gett* [2010] HCA 12, 240 CLR 537; *Naxakis v Western General Hospital* [1999] HCA 22, 197 CLR 269; *Laferrière v Lawson* [1991] 1 SCR 541 (Supreme Court of Canada).
[24] *Scott* (n 1) [79].   [25] See Steel (n 8) 263–68.

a particular claimant than it is an approximation of the forensic margin of error:

> If it is proved statistically that 25 per cent of the population have a chance of recovery from a certain injury and 75 per cent do not, it does not mean that someone who suffers that injury and who does not recover from it has lost a 25 per cent chance. He may have lost nothing at all. What he has to do is prove that he was one of the 25 per cent and that his loss was caused by the defendant's negligence. To be a figure in a statistic does not by itself give him a cause of action. *If the plaintiff succeeds in proving that he was one of the 25 per cent and the defendant took away that chance*, the logical result would be to award him 100 per cent of his damages.[26]

As the emphasis shows, what is uncertain in these cases is whether the claimant ever had a greater than evens chance of recovery, and whether the defendant's breach affected the substance of that possibility, making it into a less than evens chance.[27]

In Type 2 situations, it is crucial for the law to distinguish between the cardinal result of a defendant's breach and its ordinal effect on the claimant's evidential position. A claimant has a legally recognised chance to lose only where she *starts off* in a position in which it is more likely than not that she will avoid the adverse outcome. If a breach of duty reduces this chance to a level at which it is still greater than evens, the defendant in question is not liable in negligence, despite having affected the likelihood of that outcome occurring, because the claimant is still in the same position as far as the balance of probabilities is concerned. If a breach of duty brings the claimant's chances below the evens threshold, however, that defendant will be liable in negligence for having taken from the claimant a *legally recognised* chance. In *McGhee v National Coal Board*, Lord Salmon gave the following well-known illustration:

> Suppose . . . it could be proved that men engaged in a particular industrial process would be exposed to a 52% risk of contracting dermatitis even when proper washing facilities were provided. Suppose it could also be proved that that risk would be increased to, say, 90% when such facilities were not provided. It would follow that . . . an employer who negligently failed to provide the proper facilities would escape from any liability to an employee who contracted dermatitis notwithstanding that the employers had increased the risk from 52% to 90%. The negligence would not be

---

[26] *Hotson v East Berkshire HA* [1987] 2 WLR 287 (CA) 303 (Croom-Johnson LJ) (emphasis added).

[27] Another reason why the common law's balance of probabilities standard renders the award of damages proportional to the 'chance' lost inappropriate.

a cause of the dermatitis because even with proper washing facilities, i.e. without the negligence, it would still have been more likely than not that the employee would have contracted the disease – the risk of injury then being 52%. If, however, you substitute 48% for 52% the employer could not escape liability, not even if he had increased the risk to, say, only 60%. Clearly such results would not make sense; nor would they, in my view, accord with the common law.[28]

Fortunately, in *Sienkiewicz v Grief (UK) Ltd*, Lord Phillips made direct reference to this argument, and said of it:

> I can understand why Lord Salmon considered that to base a finding of causation on such evidence would be capricious, but not why he considered that to do so would be contrary to common law. The balance of probabilities test is one that is inherently capable of producing capricious results.[29]

Although this comment has the obvious merit of aligning the result in Lord Salmon's example with the orthodox common law position, it also has the unfortunate effect of fortifying the view that such a position is capricious. It is not. Whilst the balance of probabilities approach might sometimes produce results which seem harsh either to a particular claimant or defendant considered discretely, those results will at least be consistent across the spectrum of *causal relationships between parties*. That is, a defendant found liable in negligence on the basis of having caused a 4 per cent reduction in the probability of a favourable outcome for the claimant (say, from 52 per cent to 48 per cent)[30] might look hard done by, as compared to another who was found not liable, despite having caused a 42 per cent reduction (say, from 48 per cent to 6 per cent) in another claimant's chances. Comparing the positions of defendants alone, however,[31] is not an authentic means of evaluating a mechanism intended to allocate the risk of error as between defendants and claimants as distinct, but related, classes. If the positions of claimants are considered alongside those of the defendants with whom they are correlative,[32] results will be consistent, and this is the comparison which really matters. For every losing defendant whose breach reduces the probability of a favourable outcome from 51 per cent to 49 per cent, for instance (an instance of orthodox causation, to which no loss of

---

[28] [1973] 1 WLR 1 (HL) 12.   [29] [2011] UKSC 10, [2011] 2 AC 229 [26].

[30] A case which would not, of course, require any resort to a lost chance analysis.

[31] Or indeed claimants, to whom the argument applies with equal force.

[32] See Ernest J Weinrib, *Corrective Justice* (Oxford University Press 2012) 20.

chance analysis would need to be applied),[33] there will be a losing claimant whose probability of a favourable outcome has been reduced by, say, 45 per cent, but who only ever had a chance amounting to 46 per cent. In other words, the potential for harsh results cut both ways. But it *always* cuts both ways, so it cannot accurately be described as 'capricious'. Indeed, since we are all potential claimants in negligence as much as we are potential defendants, splitting the risk of error in this way is the *least* capricious way of dealing with the inherent imperfections of the forensic process.[34] Consequently, it is not open to claimants to re-characterise a claim which does not reach this evidentiary standard as being a claim for a lesser *degree* of loss,[35] because the legal result of falling short of this standard is that no loss has been suffered. Claimants in Type 2 cases, therefore, are not those who have lost a less-than-evens chance, but those for whom there is a less-than-evens chance that they have lost anything at all.

In Type 2 situations, there is no such thing as an independently quantifiable opportunity which can be divorced from the question of whether the defendant's breach made the claimant worse off. In the Type 2 cases of *Gregg* and *Hotson*, for instance, the claimants' chances of avoiding an adverse physical outcome were inextricably bound up with the effects of the defendant's negligent diagnosis. The relevant 'chance' therefore is not assessable independently of the breach, since it is defined and determined by it. Given that there is nothing extraneous from which the claimant can be excluded, the causal question is not whether, on the balance of probabilities the claimant has been denied access to an opportunity, but whether the claimant ever had such an opportunity in the first place, and whether the defendant's breach deprived her of it. The only

---

[33] That this is causation proved on orthodox grounds can sometimes be obscured by the 2 per cent change in the claimant's position, leading to the question of how this amounts to a cause in forensic terms. The shift of 2 per cent is, however, redundant, since the starting point of a greater than 50 per cent chance of a positive outcome means that the pre-breach position, or background event, was not 'the' cause on the balance of probabilities. Erroneous 'loss of chance' formulations, created for the very purpose of dealing with situations where the claimant starts off with a less than 50 per cent chance of a positive outcome (meaning that proof of the breach of duty's causal valence cannot be achieved on causal grounds) distract from this basic point by focusing, as they are forced to do, on the percentage shift. On an all-or-nothing basis, however, it is the starting position which determines causation, as the House of Lords in *Hotson* emphasised.

[34] See *Sienkiewicz* (n 29) [187] (Lord Brown).

[35] As the claimants in both *Hotson* and *Gregg* did; they claimed not for the full extent of their final injury, but for a proportion of it, calculated according to the 'chance of avoiding it' they claimed to have lost.

way, therefore, in which the claimants in *Hotson* and *Gregg* could have recovered would have been to have established causation on orthodox causal grounds; that is, to have proved that they had a greater than 50 per cent chance before they interacted with the defendant, which the defendant's breach then reduced to a less than 50 per cent chance.

This last point explains why the 'type' of chance itself is not determinative of whether it can be lost in a legal sense. It has nothing to do with whether the outcome is that of making a financial gain, or of avoiding an adverse physical result (a distinction which has sometimes been mooted). The only true distinguishing criterion is that the magnitude of the chance is not something which is itself directly affected by the interaction between the parties. The following hypothetical gives a clear illustration of this. TA, a travel agent, specialises in activity holidays. There are three bungee jump operators on a particular remote island, X, Y and Z. TA contracts with X because X is cheaper than Y and Z, even though Y and Z both have a policy of investing far more money than X in maintaining equipment. TA nevertheless promises in its contract with C 'only to engage the safest contractors available'. C does a bungee jump with X and is horribly injured when her worn-out bungee stretches too far. Neither Y nor Z has ever had any accidents, despite each doing twice as many jumps per day as X. In this example, C has lost a chance of avoiding an adverse physical outcome, and TA's breach has, on the balance of probabilities, caused her to lose it. This is actionable, and damages should be quantified according to the magnitude of the chance she has been denied. That chance (the probability of her not being injured by either Y or Z) is not affected in its magnitude by TA's breach, and remains a chance of which the claimant has been denied.

It is easy to see why the red herring of the adverse physical outcome explanation has taken root: most situations in which the issue of avoiding adverse physical outcomes arises are those in which the parties are medical professionals and patients. This means not only that the interaction between them is almost bound to affect the probability of a positive outcome for the claimant, but also that the claimant's chances are to a greater or lesser extent already playing out when their interaction with the defendant begins. By contrast, in Type 1 cases in which the law recognises the loss of a chance, the whole basis of the claim is that the claimant has been unable to take her chances. In Type 2 cases, therefore, the probability wheels are in motion, but in Type 1 cases the point is that they never will be. The explanation that the distinction is based here on the independence of the chance, as opposed to its being a question of personal injury, is far more palatable. Given the general hierarchy of interests protected by the common law, a distinction which allowed claimants to recover for pure economic loss whilst applying a bright-line exclusion to comparable personal injury claims would be hard to defend.

12.4   Type 3 Cases Explained

These are simply orthodox cases in which the real question is that of quantification. Here, a claimant has proved on the balance of probabilities that the defendant's breach has caused her to suffer a loss and the precise value of that loss has yet to be quantified. Such quantification might need to take the form of evaluating the extent to which the setback is likely to affect the claimant's interest. Consider, for example, a defendant who negligently injures a promising young cricketer to the extent that he will never again be able to play competitively. This is in itself a current loss. The question of its magnitude, the answer to which requires evaluation of, *inter alia*, the chances that he would have played first class or international cricket, and for how long, is a consequential and quantitative question. This chance does not need to satisfy the balance of probabilities, since it is not a causal issue, and the claimant can recover for any future chances that are more than negligible.[36] This, therefore, is a question which accommodates lost chances, but does not in itself represent the primary loss suffered by the claimant. It is therefore distinct from both Type 1 and Type 2 cases. This point of distinction is the sole reason for its inclusion in this analysis, given that it is not in itself a contentious issue, unless and until it is misleadingly referred to as a 'loss of a chance' analysis. Such a label makes it liable to be confused with a causal analysis.

The Court of Appeal has very recently considered the analysis discussed here, and the judgment illustrates well the difference between the Access (causal) Question of 'Has the defendant caused the claimant to suffer the possibility of a future detriment?' and the Magnitude (quantification) Question of 'Has the defendant caused the claimant to suffer a present detriment which now needs quantifying?' In *Wellesley Partners LLP v Withers LLP*,[37] the claimant executive search firm sued the

---

[36] See, for example, *Brown v Ministry of Defence* [2006] EWCA Civ 546, [2006] PIQR Q9; *Dixon v John Were* [2004] EWHC 2273 (QB); *Thomas v Albutt* [2015] EWHC 2187 (Ch), [2015] PNLR 29.

[37] [2015] EWCA Civ 1146, [2016] CILL 3757.

defendant solicitors for negligently failing to follow their instructions in drafting an LLP agreement, with the result that one of the investors withdrew its funds earlier than anticipated, thereby reducing the claimant's ability to expand its business in the United States (an expansion found to be largely dependent upon securing mandates from a particular entity – Nomura). In concluding that a loss of chance analysis was applicable to such facts, Floyd LJ emphasised the following distinction:

> WP had, first, to prove that its own actions would have been such as to place itself in a position to obtain that work, and it had to do so on the balance of probabilities. It did so. All that remained on the issue of causation was for WP to establish whether there was a real and substantial chance that Nomura would have awarded some part of the mandates to WP. It did so. That was the beginning and end of its case on causation ... It does not follow at all, however, that it is no longer relevant to consider the chances that WP would have obtained the mandates. The evaluation of that chance is part of the process of the quantification of damages. It would be wrong in principle to treat the conclusion on causation as if it meant that the chances of obtaining some part of the mandate were 100%. The judge was correct to reflect his view of the chances of WP obtaining the mandate in his quantification of damages.[38]

12.5 Contract and Tort Distinguished

In Type 1 cases, as we have seen, the claimant aims to prove that the defendant's breach has prevented her from taking advantage of an opportunity which exists independently of the relationship between claimant and defendant. There is an important distinction to be made here between, on the one hand, contract and torts actionable per se, and, on the other, those torts, such as negligence, of which damage is the gist. In the case of the former, the Access Question addresses whether substantial damages will be available. Where the latter is concerned, that same question tells us whether there is an action at all. Whilst this might look like a considerable theoretical difference, its practical significance is minimal, as long as the loss of a chance concept is properly applied.

For instance, the distinction between a contract claim and a negligence claim could be thought to be especially problematical in a healthcare context, since privately treated patients might be seen to have an easier route to recovery than those treated on the NHS, given that the former do not have to prove actionable damage in order to have a claim. It remains

---

[38] Ibid [109]–[110].

the case, however, that claimants in contract nevertheless have to prove a causal link between a defendant's breach and any loss for which they seek substantial damages. What is more, breaches of contract must be proved to have been an *effective* cause of a claimant's loss,[39] leaving a claimant in contract with more to do than those claiming in negligence, who have only the balance of probabilities to satisfy. The same distinction between the Access Question and the Magnitude Question applies, therefore, *a fortiori*, to contract claims:[40] loss of a chance cannot act as a surrogate for effective cause. For it to do so would be to undermine the causal integrity of the inquiry, just as it would in negligence if the claimants in *Gregg* and *Hotson* had been successful. In contract, as much as in negligence, a true lost chance is the denial of access to an independent opportunity, and not a means of sidestepping the anterior inquiry of whether a defendant has made a claimant worse off. A claimant's inability to prove that a defendant's breach of contract has been an effective cause of her failure to recover, therefore, means that she should not be awarded substantial damages. So, a patient who claims that her private consultant's breach of contract has reduced her chances of recovery from 42 per cent to 25 per cent has not proved that the breach was an effective cause of her failure to recover any more than the NHS patient, claiming in negligence, could prove actionable damage on the balance of probabilities. In fact, the private patient on the same facts is further away from such satisfaction. The reformulation of such a claim as a 'lost chance' of 17 per cent is forensically meaningless, since it does no more than illustrate in percentage terms that the breach of contract is not an effective cause of the claimant's ultimate loss.

Where, as in this example, the damage in question is the alleged loss of a chance of avoiding an adverse physical outcome, that is not a chance which exists independently of the parties because it is (or has been) affected in its magnitude by the interaction between the defendant healthcare provider and the claimant patient. Proving a breach of contract without more is of little practical value to a claimant, and yet this is the only causal advantage accruing to those in a contractual relationship, as compared to those for whom negligence is the only option. The same would apply to commercial situations in which one claimant has, for

---

[39] *Galoo Ltd v Bright Grahame Murray* [1994] 1 WLR 1360 (CA) 1374–75.

[40] Although in contract and torts actionable per se, the Access Question determines access to substantial damages, rather than to a claim itself. Its clear distinction from the Magnitude Question, relevant to quantification, remains as crucial regardless of the nature of the claim.

instance, a contractual relationship with an agent or adviser and another does not. As long as a loss of chance analysis is applied only to those situations in which the chance concerned is independent of the parties, it will not serve to create arbitrary distinctions between recovery in contract and in tort. To some extent, this accords with the established approach to loss of a chance in contract: 'In contrast with past facts and the hypothetical behaviour of the claimant and defendant, the hypothetical behaviour of third parties is to be determined on a loss of chance basis ... '[41]

As suggested above, however, the reference to the actions of third parties is simply too narrow to describe in its entirety the potential reach (and conceptual extent) of the loss of a chance doctrine. In justifying the distinction made between third parties and contracting parties, Kramer says, 'there is an intuitive appeal to the distinction between claimants and third parties that is captured in Lord Nicholls' observation that the loss of a chance doctrine applies to the loss of an opportunity to achieve a result "whose achievement was outside [the claimant's] control"'.[42] This is an argument which applies with equal force to *any* chance whose result lies outside of the parties' control.[43] There is no reason to restrict it to the actions of third parties when it could equally apply to naturally occurring events, such as market movements,[44] weather conditions (or the interaction of the two), or the insolvency of a potential judgment debtor.[45] Consequently, it is far better to circumscribe recovery for loss of a chance by reference to the concept of independence from the claimant and defendant; a broader, and more authentic, criterion.

In torts requiring proof of damage, however, there is a difficulty in accommodating claims for the loss of a chance in a Type 1 sense. Does the loss of such an opportunity itself amount to actionable damage? If the magnitude of the independent chance constitutes the quantification, the question of what constitutes the harm itself remains open.[46] An answer

---

[41] Adam Kramer, *The Law of Contract Damages* (Hart 2014) 271.   [42] Ibid 273.

[43] Subject, of course, to the *SAAMCO* requirement that recoverable loss should lie within the scope of a defendant's duty: *South Australia Asset Management Corp v York Montague Ltd* [1997] AC 191 (HL). There is no reason, however, to exclude lost chances from that scope as a matter of principle.

[44] *John D Wood & Co (Residential & Agricultural) Ltd v Knatchbull* [2002] EWHC 2822 (QB), [2003] PNLR 17.

[45] *Pearson v Sanders Witherspoon* [2000] PNLR 110 (CA).

[46] This is a function of the tort of negligence, of which damage is the gist. It does not affect, for instance, the law of contract, which is actionable per se: Burrows, *Remedies* (n 13) 59; and Harold Luntz, 'Loss of Chance' in Ian Freckleton and Danuta Mendelson (eds), *Causation in Law and Medicine* (Ashgate 2002) 153.

can be found, however, in both *Chester v Afshar*,[47] and *Allied Maples v Simmons & Simmons*.[48] In substantive terms, these are Type 1 cases, and decisions which amount in effect to common law recognition of an individual's right to autonomy. Neither case is framed in this way, but a proper analysis of those situations in which there is an independent chance to be lost (Type 1), leads to the inescapable conclusion that the damage in such cases is really the claimant's ability to make a free choice. Any quantification subsequent to this recognition should then compare the chance (if any) available to the claimant as a result of the breach to the chance which would have been available but for the breach,[49] thereby establishing whether the claimant is any worse off for having been denied a chance. Lord Hoffmann, in alluding to this in his dissenting judgment in *Chester*,[50] was the only panel member involved in that decision who recognised (at least explicitly) the implications of a decision in favour of liability.

In *Chester v Afshar*, the defendant performed elective surgery upon the claimant in order to alleviate her severe back pain. Although he did so without negligence, she suffered significant nerve damage and was consequently left partially paralysed. The defendant breached his duty of care by failing to warn his patient of the 1–2 per cent risk of such paralysis occurring as a result of the operation. The causal problem arose in this case because the claimant did not argue that, had she been warned of the risk, she would *never* have had the operation, or even that, duly warned, she would have sought out another surgeon to perform the operation.[51] Her argument was simply that, had she been properly warned of the risks inherent in the procedure, she would not have consented to having the surgery within three days of her appointment, and would have sought further advice on alternatives. The House of Lords (Lord Bingham and Lord Hoffmann dissenting) held Mr Afshar liable on the basis that, since the ultimate injury suffered by the claimant was a product of the very risk of which she should have been warned, it could therefore be *regarded* as having been caused by that failure to warn. In the course of his dissent,

---

[47] See n 3.

[48] See n 2, discussed below. See also *Sellars v Adelaide Petroleum NL* (1994) 179 CLR 332.

[49] This, as we shall see, is where the judgment in *Chester v Afshar* went wrong.

[50] Which ultimately, of course, he did not support.

[51] Cf *Chappel v Hart* [1998] HCA 55, (1998) 195 CLR 232 in which Kirby and Gaudron JJ found that the claimant's hypothetical actions in that case, in seeking out a more experienced surgeon, would have decreased her risk of injury as a result of the procedure. There was no agreement on this point.

Lord Hoffmann made the following point: 'Even though the failure to warn did not cause the patient any damage, it was an affront to her personality and leaves her feeling aggrieved. I can see that there might be a case for a modest solatium in such cases.'[52]

The very fact that the majority decision on the facts in *Chester* was one in favour of liability suggests that what the claimant was being compensated for was the denial of her right to make a free choice, since that denial led in her case to no consequential loss.[53] It is not, however, a straightforward exercise to justify *Chester* in this way. First, although in *Rees v Darlington Memorial NHS Trust* there is an explicit recognition at the highest level that an infringement of autonomy can amount to actionable damage in negligence,[54] none of the judgments in *Chester* made reference to that decision.[55] Second, the House of Lords in *Chester* departed substantively from the *Rees* approach in any event by awarding substantial damages for the infringement, far in excess of the £15,000 conventional award granted in the earlier case. Finally, these contextual issues aside, the outcome in *Chester v Afshar* is simply not presented as one based on the idea of autonomy as a freestanding right; rather, it is presented as a conclusion reached on causal grounds.

Similarly, *Allied Maples*, although decided before *Rees*, is deficient in explicit references to the concept of autonomy. Nevertheless, Type 1 situations such as these in negligence can *only* be satisfactorily explained by reference to a claimant's right of autonomy, since there is no other 'damage' to form the gist of the tort. Such situations should be described therefore as 'lost autonomy' cases, after the nature of the damage itself. To use the 'lost chance' label in such a context is somewhat misleading, since it refers only to the (potential) loss consequent upon the wrong. Whilst there is scant judicial support for the idea of reduced autonomy being actionable in its own right, it is an idea of which Joseph Raz is an advocate:

> Respect for the autonomy of others largely consists in securing for them adequate options, i.e. opportunities and the ability to use them. Depriving

---

[52] *Chester* (n 3) [33]–[34].

[53] Because the chance available to her as a result of the breach was identical to the one that would have been available to her but for the breach. See Robert Stevens, *Torts and Rights* (Oxford University Press 2007) 76–78; and *Chappel v Hart* (n 51) [40]–[43] (McHugh J).

[54] [2003] UHKL 52, [2004] 1 AC 309. See also *Montgomery v Lanarkshire Health Board* [2015] UKSC 11, [2015] 2 WLR 768 particularly Lady Hale at [108].

[55] Despite the fact that both counsel in *Chester* referred directly to *Rees* in their respective submissions. For an assessment of the implications of *Rees*, see Donal Nolan, 'New Forms of Damage in Negligence' (2007) 70 MLR 59, 71–80.

a person of opportunities or of the ability to use them is a way of causing him harm ... Needless to say a harm to a person may consist not in depriving him of options but in frustrating his pursuit of the projects and relationships he has set upon.[56]

12.6   Why Loss of Chance and Increase in Risk are Not the Same Thing

This analytical distinction detailed here explains why the loss of a chance is not the same thing as a material increase in risk.[57] The latter concept, as a term of art, is associated with the exceptional causal principle originating in the negligence case of *McGhee v National Coal Board*,[58] and made infamous by *Fairchild v Glenhaven Funeral Services Ltd.*[59] In brief, the principle applies only in exceptional factual circumstances; where a claimant is suffering from an indivisible injury, where that injury is caused by a single agent, and where medical knowledge about that disease is unable to generate a causal conclusion about the source of the agent responsible for the disease. On such facts, the exception allows a claimant to satisfy the causal element of the negligence inquiry by proving on the balance of probabilities that the defendant materially increased the risk of her damage occurring, rather than having to prove the impossible by establishing on the balance of probabilities that the defendant caused the injury itself. Currently, this approach tends only to apply to cases involving mesothelioma, given that the aetiology of this disease is something about which medical knowledge is still very limited.[60] The exception was developed in *Fairchild* largely because mesothelioma sufferers who had been exposed to asbestos from more than one source would otherwise *never* be able to prove their case on causal grounds: this particular factual circumstance is one on which it is currently impossible *in principle* for claimants to establish causation. It is not, therefore, merely an instance in which a given claimant cannot produce the requisite evidence to satisfy the balance of probabilities standard. Since multiple employment

---

[56] Joseph Raz, *The Morality of Freedom* (Oxford University Press 1986) 413.
[57] As argued by Burrows, 'Uncertainty about Uncertainty' (n 13); and Edwin Peel, 'Lost Chances and Proportionate Recovery' [2006] LMCLQ 289.
[58] See n 28.
[59] [2002] UKHL 22, [2003] 1 AC 32. Although it has now been considerably extended by *Sienkiewicz* (n 29); see Sarah Green, *Causation in Negligence* (Hart 2014) ch 6.
[60] Although not quite as limited as it was when *Fairchild* was decided. See *Jones v Secretary of State for Energy and Climate Change* [2012] EWHC 2936 (QB); and *Amaca Pty Ltd v Booth* [2011] HCA 53, (2011) 283 ALR 461.

patterns, asbestos exposure and instances of mesothelioma were relatively high in most of the industries concerned, a strict adherence to orthodox casual principles on *Fairchild* facts would have had dire implications for corrective justice.

The defining characteristic of the material increase in risk or *Fairchild* principle is, therefore, that the claimant has suffered a loss, and that the interaction between the claimant and the defendant probably increased the risk of that loss occurring. Any 'chance' the claimant might have had of avoiding that loss is no longer in existence; it was not in any event ever independent of the litigating parties' relationship, nor is it the primary harm for which the claimant is suing. The material increase in risk is merely an *ex post facto* description of what underlies the defendant's liability for the claimant's harm (for which it or they are held liable in full and not according to the percentage risk increase). This extraordinary *Fairchild* principle, therefore, fulfils none of the criteria for lost chances in law. This is no surprise, given that the two situations are analytically separate. Whilst, semantically, a 'lost chance' might be argued to be synonymous with a 'material increase in risk', the legal meanings of the two phenomena are fundamentally different. As Sandy Steel succinctly puts it, damages awarded in the material contribution to risk context 'are for the chance of causation, not causation of a lost chance'.[61]

12.7 Conclusion

The legal concept of 'loss of a chance' needs to be given a clear and discrete definition as a legal term of art. Given that the label is currently applied indiscriminately to three situations which are analytically distinct from one another, it is unsurprising that it is a term so often subject to misunderstanding. Were a consistent and independent definition to be established, the concept could play a far more decisive and useful role in the law, particularly in relation to commercial remedies, where it will most often be required. As this discussion suggests, this would both entail and enable the clarification of other legal issues, such as whether interference with autonomy is a right explicitly and directly protected by the tort of negligence, and where the notion of a material increase in risk begins and ends. Resolving three issues for the price of one is surely a chance not to be lost.

---

[61] Steel (n 8) 242.

13

Gain-based Remedies

GRAHAM VIRGO

In *Jetivia SA v Bilta (UK) Ltd*,[1] Lord Neuberger said, albeit as regards the defence of illegality, that there is a spectrum of strongly held differing views which epitomises 'the familiar tension between the need for principle, clarity and certainty in the law with the equally important desire to achieve a fair and appropriate result in each case'. This statement could equally apply to the award of gain-based remedies. When and why such remedies should be awarded raise a number of long-standing controversies which need to be resolved, since the award of gain-based remedies is of real commercial significance.

Although the focus of this chapter is on the award of gain-based remedies, it is important to be clear at the outset what the underlying claim might be for their award. There are three possible claims. First, those grounded on the reversal of the defendant's unjust enrichment, for which the only remedies are gain-based and operate to restore to the claimant the value of any benefit received by the defendant. Secondly, a proprietary claim in respect of property received by the defendant in which the claimant has a proprietary interest. Thirdly, where the remedy is sought following the commission of a wrong by the defendant, whether breach of contract, the commission of a tort or an equitable wrong. Whilst each claim raises controversies in its own right, it is in the context of gain-based remedies for wrongdoing that the most significant remedial controversies relevant to commercial practice arise. Consequently, the focus of this chapter is on gain-based remedies for wrongs. But it must not be forgotten that the division between these three claims is not absolute; they may overlap and the claimant might then have a choice as to which one to pursue. So, for example, where the defendant has wrongly taken the claimant's property, the claimant may have alternative claims for gain-based remedies

---

[1] [2015] UKSC 23, [2016] AC 1 [13].

founded both on wrongdoing and on their continuing proprietary rights in assets held by the defendant.

Three particular controversies will be examined in this chapter. The first concerns the meaning and relevance of the requirement that gain-based remedies following the commission of a wrong are only available where compensatory remedies are inadequate. The second controversy concerns the determination of the range of gain-based remedies and their relationship with compensatory remedies. The third controversy relates to when and why proprietary gain-based remedies should be available where the defendant has committed a wrong.

13.1 Restitution and Disgorgement

The assessment of gain-based remedies turns on the identification of a gain made by the defendant rather than of a loss suffered by the claimant. In analysing such remedies it is essential to distinguish between restitution and disgorgement functions.

13.1.1 Restitution

Restitutionary remedies operate to restore to the claimant the value of that which the defendant had obtained from the claimant. Although such remedies are assessed by reference to the defendant's gain rather than the claimant's loss, their effect will be to correct an injustice by restoring to the claimant that which he or she had lost. As Bastarache J recognised in *Kingstreet Investments Ltd v New Brunswick (Finance)*:

> Restitution is a tool of corrective justice. When a transfer of value between two parties is normatively defective, restitution functions to correct that transfer by restoring parties to their pre-transfer positions.[2]

The award of restitutionary remedies consequently operates as a mechanism to rectify an imbalance between the claimant and defendant, by requiring the defendant to give back what had been subtracted from the claimant.

13.1.2 Disgorgement

In some cases, however, the remedy awarded, although still assessed by reference to the defendant's gain, results in the claimant obtaining

---

[2] [2007] 1 SCR 3 [32].

something of value which he or she did not have before. For example, the
defendant may have obtained some money from a third party in breach
of duty to the claimant. In such circumstances, the claimant may claim
the money, but, since it had not been taken from the claimant, it is
inappropriate to describe the remedy as restitutionary, because it is not
possible to restore to the claimant that which he or she never had in the
first place. These remedies should instead be described as disgorgement
remedies, since they require the defendant to disgorge benefits to the
claimant, involving a giving-up rather than a giving-back of a gain.[3]

The award of such disgorgement remedies can be justified on
a different basis to that of restitutionary remedies. Justice demands that
the defendant should disgorge gains obtained as a result of a breach of
a duty because no defendant should profit from their wrongdoing.
So disgorgement remedies have a deterrent or distributive function.[4]
But disgorgement remedies can also be justified on the basis that they
operate as a mechanism to secure corrective justice between the parties.
That is because the claimant is the victim of a wrong and requiring the
defendant to disgorge gains obtained as a result of committing the wrong
is an appropriate mechanism for protecting the claimant's rights.[5]
Edelman[6] has asserted that the award of restitutionary remedies are
easier to justify than disgorgement remedies and disgorgement remedies
should only be awarded where the defendant has acted cynically, which,
as will be seen, has sometimes been reflected in English law.

13.2   Inadequacy of Compensatory Damages Principle

The first controversy relating to the award of gain-based remedies for
wrongdoing concerns the relationship of such remedies with compensatory damages. The orthodox position is that gain-based remedies are only
considered to be appropriate where compensatory remedies are inadequate. This 'inadequacy of compensation principle' is potentially a very
significant restriction on the award of gain-based remedies, although the

---

[3] See E Allen Farnsworth, 'Your Loss or My Gain? The Dilemma of the Disgorgement
    Principle in Breach of Contract' (1985) 94 Yale LJ 1339, 1342; Lionel D Smith,
    'The Province of the Law of Restitution' (1992) 71 CBR 672, 696.
[4] Kit Barker, 'Understanding the Unjust Enrichment Principle in Private Law: A Study of
    the Concept and its Reasons' in Jason Neyers, Mitchell McInnes, and Stephen Pitel (eds),
    Understanding Unjust Enrichment (Hart 2004) 101.
[5] Kit Barker, 'Unjust Enrichment: Containing the Beast' (1995) 15 OJLS 457, 473.
[6] James Edelman, *Gain-based Damages: Contract, Tort, Equity and Intellectual Property*
    (Hart 2002) ch 3.

reason for its recognition is unclear: why should compensation be regarded as the prime remedy, to the exclusion of all others, when it is considered to operate adequately?

The inadequacy of compensatory damages principle was recognised by the House of Lords in *Attorney-General v Blake*,[7] where it was held that a gain-based remedy for breach of contract could only be awarded exceptionally where the normal remedies for breach, namely compensatory damages, specific performance and injunctions, were inadequate. Since specific performance and injunctions are themselves only available where compensatory damages are inadequate, this affirms the vital significance of the inadequacy of compensation principle.

The operation of this principle was subsequently clarified in *Devenish Nutrition Ltd v Sanofi-Aventis SA (France)*,[8] where it operated to deny an account of profits as a remedy for the tort of breach of statutory duty because compensatory damages remained an adequate remedy. The dispute in *Devenish* arose from cartel agreements amongst competing suppliers of vitamins to increase their prices, which contravened EU competition law. The claimant had purchased vitamins from one of the suppliers to the prohibited agreements and resold them at a profit. The claimant sued the defendant for breach of statutory duty and sought an account of the defendant's profits rather than compensatory damages, because it had mitigated its loss by passing the overcharge on to its customers. The Court of Appeal held that a gain-based remedy was precluded where compensatory damages were an adequate remedy. In determining whether compensatory damages are adequate, the court identified two principles:

(i) Difficulties in proving loss do not automatically render damages inadequate,[9] save where the evidential difficulties are not the responsibility of the claimant.[10]

(ii) Where no loss is suffered, as distinct from not being proven, it may be possible to treat compensatory damages as an inadequate remedy.[11] But, as in that case, where loss was not suffered because it had been passed on to customers, compensatory damages are not necessarily rendered inadequate,[12] since allowing the claimant to obtain an account of profits in such circumstances would result in a windfall,[13] which was considered to be unacceptable because the

---

[7] [2001] 1 AC 268 (HL) 285 (Lord Nicholls).   [8] [2008] EWCA Civ 1086, [2009] Ch 390.
[9] Ibid [146] (Longmore LJ); [157] (Tuckey LJ).   [10] Ibid [106] (Arden LJ).
[11] Ibid [111] (Arden LJ).   [12] Ibid.   [13] Ibid [147] (Longmore LJ); [158] (Tuckey LJ).

law should not transfer monetary gains from one undeserving recipient to another.[14]

As a result of this second principle it was held that an account of profits was unavailable. But surely if the claimant has not suffered loss, regardless of whether or not it has been passed on to another, compensatory damages cannot be considered to be an adequate remedy to right the wrong and a gain-based remedy should have been available.

The requirement that compensatory damages are not adequate is not recognised as a limitation on the award of gain-based remedies in equity, for example for breach of fiduciary duty, even though the requirement exists for the award of other equitable remedies, such as injunctions and specific performance.[15] That is presumably because injunctions and specific performance can be used to enforce common law rights, whereas the right arising from breach of fiduciary duty is recognised within the primary equitable jurisdiction and does not involve any extra-jurisdictional enforcement. This explains the real function of the inadequacy of compensation principle: where the award of compensatory damages is available in principle, it should have priority over the award of any other remedy, which will consequently only be available exceptionally where compensatory damages are considered to be inadequate, thus severely restricting the ambit of gain-based awards. It follows that *Devenish* is suspect because compensatory damages were plainly inadequate, since the claimant had suffered no loss, so rendering the award of a gain-based remedy appropriate. That compensatory damages should be considered to be inadequate when the claimant has suffered no significant loss is consistent with the approach adopted when determining whether specific performance should be ordered.[16] It is also consistent with the approach of the House of Lords in *Blake*, where a gain-based remedy for breach of contract was justified precisely because the claimant had suffered no loss as a result of the breach. But, regardless of whether *Devenish* was correctly decided, it is clear that, at least as a matter of remedial orthodoxy, there is a hierarchy of pecuniary remedies available for wrongdoing, with compensatory damages trumping all others. Whether the inadequacy of compensatory damages principle is still

---

[14] Ibid [158] (Tuckey LJ).

[15] *American Cyanamid Co v Ethicon Ltd (No 1)* [1975] AC 396 (HL) 408 (Lord Diplock); *Co-operative Insurance Society v Argyll Stores (Holdings) Ltd* [1998] AC 1 (HL) 11 (Lord Hoffmann).

[16] *Beswick v Beswick* [1968] AC 58 (HL) 102 (Lord Upjohn).

needed to restrict the award of gain-based remedies is a controversy which requires careful consideration. Before doing so, it is first necessary to consider what the gain-based remedies are and how they operate in practice.

13.3 Personal Gain-based Remedies

13.3.1 Range and Function

In *Devenish*,[17] Arden LJ recognised that recent decisions of the courts had produced 'a cultural change in the law in favour of the classification of remedies on a coherent basis rather than on the basis of some formulaic division between different wrongs'. Consequently, when analysing personal gain-based remedies for wrongs, emphasis should be placed on the nature of the remedies and their function regardless of the underlying wrong. There are potentially three categories of personal gain-based remedies: an account of profits; restitutionary damages; and what can usefully be called 'negotiation damages'. Here a second controversy emerges, namely whether these remedies really are gain-based or whether they are actually compensatory or possibly, even more controversially, a hybrid of the two.

13.3.1.1 Account of Profits

An account of profits is a remedy which involves the taking of a literal account, to determine the net profit made by the defendant from the wrong, which the defendant is then required to disgorge to the claimant. An account of profits is an equitable remedy[18] which consequently may be defeated by equitable defences, such as laches, or the claimant's unconscionable conduct, such as where the claimant stood by whilst the defendant made the profit and then claimed to be entitled to it.[19] An account of profits is not confined in its operation to equitable wrongs, since it is clearly available[20] in respect of some torts and for breach of contract.

---

[17] See n 8.

[18] *Seager v Copydex Ltd* [1967] 1 WLR 923 (CA) 932 (Lord Denning MR); *Blake* (n 7) 285 (Lord Nicholls).

[19] *Re Jarvis (deceased)* [1958] 1 WLR 815 (Ch) 820–21 (Upjohn J).

[20] Through the operation of equity's auxiliary jurisdiction, in the same way that the equitable remedy of an injunction is available to restrain tortious conduct and specific performance to enforce contractual obligations.

Whilst an account of profits is clearly gain-based, since it requires the defendant's gain to be ascertained and transferred to the victim of the wrong, it can operate either as a restitutionary or a disgorgement remedy. The restititutionary function will be engaged, for example, where the claimant paid money to the defendant as the result of the commission of a wrong and an account of profits is taken to identify and to restore the value of the defendant's gain to the claimant. The disgorgement function will be engaged, for example, where the defendant has obtained money from a third party as the result of a wrong and the defendant is required to give up the value of that gain to the claimant. In *Murad v Al-Saraj*,[21] which involved depriving a defendant of profits made as a result of a breach of fiduciary duty, Arden LJ described the operation of an account of profits as a 'procedure to ensure the restitution of profits which ought to have been made' for the principal. But that is not correct where the claimant has not suffered any loss, since then there is nothing which can be restored to the claimant, in which case it should be treated as having a disgorgement function. This was recognised by Jonathan Parker LJ in the same case,[22] who described an account of profits as being neither restitutionary nor compensatory but designed to strip the fiduciary of profits. This reflects the disgorgement function of the remedy, which is still plainly gain-based. The remedy cannot be characterised as compensatory, because it is irrelevant that the claimant could not have obtained the profit for themselves.[23] Despite this, there has been an unfortunate recent tendency to characterise an account of profits as a compensatory remedy. For example, in *FHR European Ventures Ltd v Cedar Capital Partners LLC*,[24] in the context of a claim relating to a secret commission received by a fiduciary from a third party in breach of fiduciary duty, the Supreme Court described the personal remedy available as 'equitable compensation',[25] which is to be assessed as a sum equal to the value of the secret commission. But, since the secret commission will typically have been received from a third party, it is inappropriate to describe the remedy as compensatory, even with the prefix 'equitable'. It is a disgorgement remedy which operates to deprive the defendant of the gain rather than to compensate the claimant for loss suffered.

---

[21] [2005] EWCA Civ 959, [2005] WTLR 1573 [85].   [22] Ibid [108].
[23] Ibid [59] (Arden LJ).
[24] [2014] UKSC 45, [2015] AC 250. See also *WWF – World Wide Fund for Nature v World Wrestling Federation Entertainment Inc* [2007] EWCA Civ 286, [2008] 1 WLR 445 [59] (Chadwick LJ).
[25] [2014] UKSC 45, [2015] AC 250 [1] (Lord Neuberger).

13.3.1.2 Restitutionary Damages

Whereas an account of profits focuses on depriving the defendant of an actual gain made, there will be circumstances where the defendant has saved money through the commission of a wrong. Such a defendant may be ordered to pay the value of the amount saved to the claimant and this remedy might usefully be characterised as 'restitutionary damages'. Although the use of this phrase has been criticised, most notably by Lord Nicholls in *Attorney-General v Blake*,[26] the Court of Appeal in *Blake*[27] had used that term, as did Lord Steyn in the House of Lords.[28] This accords with the recommendation of the Law Commission that the term should be used to describe the gain-based remedy awarded for wrongdoing.[29] But Lord Nicholls may have subsequently changed his mind about the use of the term 'restitutionary damages'. In *Commercial Remedies: Current Issues and Policies*[30] it is reported that he pronounced, extra-judicially at a conference, that 'the measure of recovery could extend from expense saved through to stripping a proportion of the profits made through to stripping all of the profits made from the breach'. Once it is accepted that a remedy should be available where expense has been saved, that remedy needs to be described. It cannot be called an account of profits, because there was no profit obtained, and so 'restitutionary damages' is appropriate.

Whether the award of damages in circumstances where the defendant has saved money is necessarily a restitutionary remedy has proved to be controversial, since often it will be possible to characterise the remedy as both compensatory, by reference to the amount lost by the claimant, and restitutionary, by reference to the amount saved by the defendant. So, for example, if the defendant had taken the claimant's property without the claimant's permission, the appropriate remedy may be what the defendant would have had to pay to the claimant for the use of that property. Such a remedy will both reflect the claimant's loss, for not receiving payment for the use of the property, and the defendant's gain in what he or she had saved in not paying for the use; loss and gain will correspond precisely, which suggests that it will not matter in practice whether the remedy is characterised as compensatory or restitutionary.

[26] *Blake* (n 7) 284. [27] *Attorney-General v Blake* [1998] Ch 439, 459.
[28] *Blake* (n 7) 291.
[29] Law Commission, *Aggravated, Exemplary and Restitutionary Damages* (Law Com No 247, 1997) 51–52. Katy Barnett, *Accounting for Profit for Breach of Contract* (Hart 2012) 1 prefers the expression 'disgorgement damages'.
[30] Andrew Burrows and Edwin Peel (eds) (Oxford University Press 2003) 129.

It has been argued by Sharpe and Waddams[31] that the damages which the claimant receives in such circumstances are properly analysed as compensatory rather than gain-based. This is because such damages seek to compensate the claimant for the loss of the opportunity to bargain with the defendant for an appropriate fee for the use of the claimant's property. Such a compensatory analysis might sometimes be appropriate, at least where the claimant would have been willing to hire the property to the defendant or somebody else, but a principle of lost opportunity to bargain cannot be used to explain the nature of the remedy which has been awarded in every case where the defendant has saved money by interfering with the claimant's proprietary rights. This is because damages have been awarded in a number of cases where the defendant has interfered with the claimant's proprietary rights even though there was no evidence that the claimant would have bargained with the defendant,[32] so the opportunity to bargain cannot be considered to have been lost. If the damages which were awarded in such cases are to be treated as compensatory rather than restitutionary, it is necessary to introduce a fiction that the claimant would have been prepared to bargain with the defendant, even though this might be contradicted by the evidence. Such artificiality can be avoided simply by concluding that the claimant may be awarded a remedy which is assessed by reference to the amount saved by the defendant as a result of the wrongdoing; in other words that the remedy is restitutionary rather than compensatory.

A further danger in analysing these remedies as operating only to compensate the claimant for loss suffered is that such an analysis increasingly depends on an artificial notion of loss to ensure that the claimant obtains a remedy. Where the defendant has benefited from the commission of a wrong, but the claimant suffered no real financial loss, it is appropriate to consider the award of a restitutionary remedy which explicitly focuses on the defendant's benefit, rather than create a constructive loss.[33]

13.3.1.3   Negotiation Damages

'Restitutionary damages' is, however, gradually morphing into a new type of pecuniary remedy, which has been described as the hypothetical

---

[31] Robert J Sharpe and SM Waddams, 'Damages for Lost Opportunity to Bargain' (1982) 2 OJLS 290.

[32] See in particular *Strand Electric and Engineering Co Ltd v Brisford Entertainments Ltd* [1952] 2 QB 246 (CA); and *Penarth Dock Engineering Co Ltd v Pounds* [1963] 1 Lloyd's Rep 359 (QB).

[33] *Blake* (n 7) 279 (Lord Nicholls).

bargain measure, but is more elegantly called 'negotiating damages',[34] or simply 'negotiation damages', which describes precisely what the damages are providing for, namely what the claimant has lost and the defendant has gained by not negotiating with each other to release the claimant's right. This is a court-imposed hypothetical bargain which seeks to determine the price which the parties would reasonably have agreed for the claimant to allow the defendant to interfere with the claimant's rights.

The foundations of this remedy can be identified in *Wrotham Park Estate Co Ltd v Parkside Homes Ltd*,[35] where the remedy awarded for building houses in breach of a restrictive covenant was damages in lieu of an injunction to demolish, which was assessed with reference to the price which the claimant would reasonably have demanded of the defendant to agree to a waiver of the covenant. This bargain was most definitely hypothetical because it was acknowledged that the claimant would not have agreed to relax the covenant on any terms.[36] The price was assessed as 5 per cent of the defendant's profit from building the house, although it is unclear how this figure was determined. Subsequent decisions have sought to identify the principles underpinning the assessment of this measure of damages. In *Pell Frischmann Engineering Ltd v Bow Valley Iran Ltd*[37] in particular the Privy Council recognised that it should be assumed that the parties would have acted reasonably in the negotiations and the focus should be on how those negotiations would have progressed in the light of the information known to the parties at the time and the particular commercial context of the dispute.

The determination of the essence of negotiation damages is fraught with controversy, particularly as to their characterisation. Although they are regularly characterised as compensatory,[38] by reference to what the

---

[34] *Primary Group (UK) Ltd v Royal Bank of Scotland plc* [2014] EWHC 1082 (Ch), [2014] 2 All ER (Comm) 1121 [385] (Arnold J). See also *Lunn Poly Ltd v Liverpool and Lancashire Properties Ltd* [2006] EWCA Civ 430, [2006] 2 EGLR 29 [14] (Neuberger LJ); *Force India Formula One Team Ltd v 1 Malaysia Racing Team Sdn Bhd* [2012] EWHC 616 (Ch); [2012] RPC 29 [383] (Arnold J).

[35] [1974] 1 WLR 798 (Ch).   [36] This was recognised by Brightman J, ibid 815.

[37] [2009] UKPC 45, [2011] 1 WLR 2370 [49] (Lord Walker). See also *Vercoe v Rutland Fund Management Ltd* [2010] EWHC 424 (Ch), [2010] Bus LR D141 [292] (Sales J); *Force India* (n 34) [386] (Arnold J).

[38] This was how Megarry V-C in *Tito v Waddell (No 2)* [1977] Ch 106 (Ch) 335 characterised the remedy awarded in *Wrotham Park*, as did Millett LJ in *Jaggard v Sawyer* [1995] 1 WLR 269 (CA) 291 and Lord Hobhouse in *Blake* (n 7) 298. See also *Severn Trent Water Ltd v Barnes* [2004] EWCA Civ 570, [2004] 2 EGLR 95 [36]–[39]; *Harris v Williams-Wynne* [2006] EWCA Civ 104, [2006] 2 P and CR 27 [27]–[29]; *Lunn Poly*

claimant had lost in not being able to bargain with the defendant, and even as equitable compensation,[39] the remedy has also been treated as restitutionary,[40] by reference to what the defendant had saved in not bargaining with the claimant. The appropriate characterisation matters, both because it will influence the determination of the hypothetical bargain but also because, if characterised as restitutionary, the award of the remedy will apparently be curtailed by the inadequacy of compensatory damages principle.

The arguments relating to the appropriate characterisation of this remedy as either compensatory or gain-based are unconvincing. For example, although it was suggested earlier that the damages awarded in *Wrotham Park* could not be compensatory because the claimant would never have bargained with the defendant to vary its contractual right, and so could not have suffered any loss, it equally does not follow that the defendant had necessarily obtained a benefit by not negotiating with the claimant. For, if the claimant would not have made a bargain with the defendant, how can be it be concluded that the defendant had gained by not negotiating with the claimant? The hypothetical bargain is determined against a backdrop of there not having been any negotiation, but it is necessary to determine what the parties would have agreed had they been forced to do so. Nothing can be gained by artificially treating negotiation damages as being necessarily either compensatory or restitutionary. A more subtle analysis should be adopted which constructs the claimant's loss and the defendant's gain on the assumption that a bargain should have been made between the parties.

In many situations the appropriate characterisation is of no significance, since the loss suffered by the claimant is the same as the benefit obtained by the defendant in not making the bargain. But treating the remedy as only compensatory, and so focused on what the claimant has lost does not reflect the reality of how the hypothetical bargain is actually determined with regard to the defendant's gain as well. This is illustrated

---

(n 34) [34] (Neuberger LJ); *World Wide Fund* (n 24) [59] (Chadwick LJ); *Pell Frischmann* (n 37) [50]; *Force India* (n 34) [383] (Arnold J); *One Step (Support) Ltd v Morris-Garner* [2016] EWCA Civ 180, [2017] QB 1, [81] (Christopher Clarke LJ).

[39] *Gott v Lawrence* [2016] EWHC 68 (Ch) [76] (Recorder Halliwell), although in that case the damages were awarded in lieu of the equitable remedy of an injunction.

[40] *Blake* (n 7) 283–84 (Lord Nicholls of Birkenhead); *Experience Hendrix LLC v PPX Enterprises Inc* [2003] EWCA Civ 323, [2003] 1 All ER (Comm) 830, 839 (Mance LJ); *Giedo van der Garde BV v Force India Formula One Team Ltd* [2010] EWHC 2373 (QB) [507] (Stadlen J). See also *Strand Electric* (n 32) 254 (Denning LJ).

by *Horsford v Bird*,[41] where the defendant was held liable for the tort of trespass to land through the building of a boundary wall which significantly encroached on the claimant's land. Damages in lieu of an injunction to remove the wall were awarded, representing the price which the claimant would reasonably have demanded for the defendant to purchase part of the claimant's property. This price was initially assessed by reference to the value of the land which the defendant had appropriated, but this was doubled because the appropriation of the land had enhanced the amenity value of the defendant's own property by providing vehicular access and a garden, plus the defendant had saved money in not having to demolish the wall and rebuild it along the proper boundary.[42] This analysis is significant because there was explicit reliance on the benefit obtained by the defendant in committing the tort; this is consistent with the remedy having a gain-based component.

That a hybrid characterisation of remedies, as being both compensatory and gain-based, is possible had previously been explicitly recognised by the Privy Council in *Inverugie Investments Ltd v Hackett*.[43] The defendant in that case had excluded the claimant for fifteen years from apartments which the claimant had leased from the defendant. During this period the defendant rented the apartments to others, but only achieved an occupancy rate of 40 per cent. It was held that damages should be assessed by reference to a reasonable rental value of all the apartments which the claimant had leased whilst the defendant was committing the trespass, after deduction of what the claimant had saved in not having to pay rent as a result of the defendant's trespass. Crucially, it was recognised that the damages 'need not be characterised as exclusively compensatory, or exclusively restitutionary; it combines elements of both'.[44] Although this case did not explicitly consider the negotiation measure, it supports a more sophisticated approach to characterisation of remedies beyond binary compensation or gain-based. In *Inverugie* the award could not be considered solely compensatory, because the claimant's loss was confined to the income which it did not receive from the apartments. Since the defendant's occupancy rate was only 40 per cent, awarding the claimant the full rental value of the apartments would have over-compensated him. Similarly, the remedy could not be characterised as purely gain-based because, as the Privy Council recognised, the defendant had not derived a benefit from all of the apartments all the time, but it was still expected to pay a reasonable

---

[41] [2006] UKPC 3.   [42] Ibid [12]–[13].   [43] [1995] 1 WLR 713 (PC).   [44] Ibid 718.

rent for the use of the apartments throughout the period during which the tort had been committed.

Consequently a holistic approach to the characterisation of negotiation damages should be adopted:[45] it has gain-based characteristics, but is not limited by them. Recognition of the compensatory component means that the inadequacy of compensation principle should not exclude the operation of this remedy, because there will always be a loss to be compensated, albeit a constructed one. The recognition of the hybrid nature of negotiation damages also means that there remains scope for the recognition of restitutionary damages as a distinct remedy, which is explicitly gain-based.

13.3.2   The Operation of the Remedies

It follows that there are three categories of personal remedy which can be considered to have gain-based characteristics in whole or in part. It is then necessary to resolve a consequent controversy, namely how these remedies interrelate. This can be examined by considering the award of such remedies for breach of contract and the tort of trespass to land.

13.3.2.1   Breach of Contract

In *Attorney-General v Blake*[46] the House of Lords awarded an account of profits for breach of contract. It was acknowledged that this was an exceptional remedy which was available where compensatory damages were an inadequate remedy and where the claimant's legitimate interest in the performance of the contract made it just and equitable that the defendant should not benefit from the breach.[47] The Crown was held to have such an interest in preventing a former spy from profiting from breaches of an undertaking not to divulge official information gained from his employment. An account of profits was further justified because the defendant had deliberately breached his contract in publishing his autobiography; the contractual obligations owed by him were considered to be closely akin to those of a fiduciary; and also because Blake had compromised national security and committed a serious crime.

Despite the revolutionary significance of *Blake* in recognising the award of gain-based remedies for breach of contract, the principles

---

[45] Stephen Waddams, 'Gains Derived from Breach of Contract: Historical and Conceptual Perspectives' in Djakhongir Saidov and Ralph Cunnington (eds), *Contract Damages: Domestic and International Perspectives* (Hart 2008) 192. This was close to being acknowledged in One Step (Support) (n 38) [128] (Christopher Clarke LJ).

[46] See n 7.   [47] Ibid 285 (Lord Nicholls).

underpinning their award were unclear. Subsequent judicial developments have significantly restricted the award of a full account of the
defendant's profits made from breach of contract, such that it will only be
in cases with such exceptional facts as *Blake* itself that this remedy will be
awarded. In the commercial context a full account of profits is unlikely
ever to be available, and, with one exception which is properly considered
to be an aberration,[48] has not been awarded.[49] In *One Step (Support) Ltd
v Morris-Garner*,[50] for example, an account of profits was not awarded for
breach of a non-competition covenant, even though the breach was
deliberate, since the defendants had planned to compete even before
the covenant was made, because the breaches were characterised as
being relatively straightforward and did not satisfy the *Blake* test of being
exceptional.[51]

Some cases decided since *Blake* have adopted a gain-based analysis of
the remedy available for breach of contract, but without requiring the
defendant to make full disgorgement of profits. In *Experience Hendrix LLC
v PPX Enterprises Inc*,[52] for example, the defendant had repeatedly breached a settlement agreement. A gain-based remedy was justified in principle because there was no evidence of financial loss suffered by the
claimant as a result of the breach,[53] so compensatory damages were
inadequate. Further, as in *Blake*, the defendant had deliberately[54] done
what it had promised not to do and the claimant was considered to have
a legitimate interest in preventing the defendant from profiting from the
breach. The defendant was not, however, ordered to account for all the
profits which derived from the breach, since the case was not considered to
be exceptional. This was because the dispute did not concern a sensitive
subject such as national security, the defendant was not in a fiduciary or
quasi-fiduciary relationship with the claimant[55] and the breaches occurred
in a commercial context. The defendant was instead required to pay
a reasonable sum assessed with reference to what the claimant would
reasonably have demanded for modification of the settlement; what
today would be considered to be negotiation damages.

---

[48] *Esso Petroleum Co Ltd v Niad Ltd* [2001] All ER (D) 324 (Ch).
[49] See, for example, *The Sine Nomine* [2002] 1 Lloyd's Rep 805 (CA) 807; *University of
Nottingham v Fishel* [2000] ICR 1462 (QB) 1488; *WWF-World Wide Fund for Nature
v World Wrestling Federation Entertainment Inc* [2002] FSR 32 (Ch) [63].
[50] [2014] EWHC 2213 (QB), [2015] IRLR 215.
[51] Ibid [103] (Phillips J). This was confirmed as the 'just response' by the Court of Appeal
(n 38), [121] (Christopher Clarke LJ).
[52] [2003] EWCA Civ 323, [2003] 1 All ER (Comm) 830.   [53] Ibid 845 (Mance LJ).
[54] Ibid 848 (Peter Gibson LJ).   [55] Ibid 843 (Mance LJ).

In *Vercoe v Rutland Fund Management Ltd*,[56] Sales J identified a number of principles to determine when an account of profits or negotiation damages should be available. The key aim is to ensure that the remedy awarded is not disproportionate to the wrong done to the claimant. This is to be determined by assessing whether the claimant's objective interest in performance of the relevant obligation makes it just and equitable that the defendant should retain no benefit from the breach. Where the claimant has a particularly strong interest in full performance, he or she should be entitled to choose between compensatory or negotiation damages and account of profits. But this is at odds with the inadequacy of compensation principle which states that a gain-based remedy is only available where compensatory damages is an inadequate remedy. The claimant might have a strong interest in full performance of the contract where, for example, the breach involves infringement of property rights, or where it would not be reasonable to expect the contractual right to be released for a reasonable fee, such as where the contractual right arises under a fiduciary relationship.[57] If the claimant does not have a strong interest in performance, as is more likely in a commercial context,[58] an account of profits should not be available and the claimant should be confined to the negotiation measure. In assessing the hypothetical bargain it may be appropriate to have regard to the defendant's anticipated profits arising from the breach of contract,[59] if this would have reasonably been taken into account by the parties in conducting their negotiations, confirming that even negotiation damages have a gain-based component. But, crucially, account of profits for breach of contract remains a very exceptional remedy.[60]

13.3.2.2   Trespass to Land

The tort of trespass to land can be committed in a variety of ways, including the temporary use of the claimant's land without permission or its unlawful expropriation. The nature of the trespass will have an effect on the remedy which is awarded. Whilst the typical remedy is undoubtedly compensatory, with reference to the loss suffered by the claimant, the award of restitutionary and even disgorgement remedies

---

[56] [2010] EWHC 424 (Ch) [339]–[343].
[57] See *Jones v Ricoh Ltd* [2010] EWHC 1743 (Ch) [89] (Roth J); *Luxe Holding Ltd v Midland Resources Holding Ltd* [2010] EWHC 1908 (Ch) [55] (Roth J).
[58] *Jones* (n 57) [89] (Roth J).   [59] *Giedo van der Garde* (n 40) [507] (Stadlen J).
[60] *One Step (Support)* (n 38) [126] (Christopher Clarke LJ).

has been recognised. In *Stadium Capital Holdings v St Marylebone Properties Co plc*[61] Peter Smith J said:

> there has been a development ... of awarding damages not on the basis of the land to be used by the plaintiff but the basis upon which the defendant has used the land, and this starts basically with the decision in *Penarth Dock Engineering Co Ltd v Pounds* [62] ... where Lord Denning MR says precisely that. The test of the measure of damages is not what the plaintiff had lost but what benefit the defendant obtained by having the use of the berth. This introduces a flexible basis for assessment because it requires the court to look at the use that was made. It is fair to say, in the cases that we have been taken through, that the vast majority of those resolve it by charging a reasonable fee for the occupation of the land by the trespasser; but, in the light of these authorities, which end up in *Attorney General v Blake* ... my view is that this area is flexible, and in an appropriate case it is possibly arguable that the measure of damages can represent 100%. It is equally possible that the measure of damages could be debated [sic] by the amount of expenditure the wrongdoer incurs in obtaining the benefit, and in between it is possible that damages could be assessed by a license fee that would be artificially negotiated by the parties in the lines of *Wrotham Park* above and succeeding authorities.

It follows that there is a range of remedial options open to the court which can be restitutionary and may even involve full disgorgement of all gains made from the trespass.

Where the trespass involves the temporary deprivation of land, the remedy will relate to the defendant's use of the land in the form of 'mesne profits'. Where the trespass involves permanent expropriation, the defendant may be required to restore the land to the claimant and pay for the use of the land until restoration, or the court may decline to restore the land to the claimant but require the defendant to pay the capital value and pay for the use of the land until the order for payment of the capital value has been made. In either case the remedy will typically take the form of negotiation damages.[63]

The capital value of the land will typically be determined by reference to its market value, which will reflect both the claimant's loss and the defendant's gain. In some circumstances, however, the capital value may

---

[61] [2010] EWCA Civ 952 [14].   [62] See n 32.

[63] See *Horsford v Bird* (n 41) [13]; *Field Common Ltd v Elmbridge BC* [2008] EWHC 2079 (Ch); *Stadium Capital Holdings v St Marylebone Properties Co plc*, (n 61) [16] (Peter Smith LJ), [17] (Sullivan LJ); *Ramzan v Brookwide Ltd* [2010] EWHC 2453 (Ch), [2011] 2 All ER 38 [29]–[30] (Geraldine Andrews QC); *Jones v Ruth* [2011] EWCA Civ 804, [2012] 1 WLR 1495 [39] (Patten LJ).

exceed the market value if the defendant would have been willing to pay more for it. So, in *Ramzan v Brookwide Ltd*,[64] it was recognised that the defendant would have been willing to pay more than the market value for the claimant's storeroom which had been unlawfully incorporated into the defendant's property to form a residential flat which was then leased. This reflects a restitutionary analysis. Increasing the capital value of the property to reflect the particular advantage to the defendant in having the storeroom is consistent with the general approach to the identification and valuation of an enrichment for purposes of a claim in unjust enrichment. This involves two tests to determine the value of a benefit, namely market value and objective value where the market would have taken into account particular circumstances of the defendant in valuing the enrichment.[65] Similarly, if a person in the position of the defendant would gain particular advantages from trespassing on the land, this should be taken into account when valuing the defendant's benefit.

When assessing the use value of land on which the defendant has trespassed, the negotiation measure is typically used and, although this may operate to compensate the claimant for his or her loss of use of the land, the benefit to the defendant is taken into account as well. So, for example, in *Ramzan v Brookwide Ltd*,[66] although the annual market rent for the storeroom was £190 per annum, it was held that the reasonable value should reflect the particular value of the room to the defendant. This was assessed as 4.5 per cent of the capital value of the land.[67] Although this was explicitly analysed as damages to compensate the claimant for loss suffered, which was found to be higher than the gross profits which the defendant had made from renting the flat, it is difficult to see why the measure is exclusively compensatory, especially because the judge emphasised that the claimant would not have been willing to enter into an agreement for the defendant to use the storeroom,[68] so there was no loss of an opportunity to bargain, and because the judge had explicit regard to the benefit to the defendant from the use of the room. Surely this reflects negotiation damages as having both compensatory and restitutionary components, with regard to constructed losses and gains.

The significance of the restitutionary component of negotiation damages is also reflected in *Jones v Ruth*,[69] where the defendant had trespassed on the claimant's land in a variety of ways over a four-year

---

[64] [2010] EWHC 2453 (Ch), [2011] 2 All ER 38. See also *Horsford v Bird* (n 41).
[65] *Benedetti v Sawiris* [2013] UKSC 50, [2014] AC 938 [15]–[17] (Lord Clarke).
[66] [2010] EWHC 2453 (Ch), [2011] 2 All ER 38.   [67] Ibid [35] (Geraldine Andrews QC).
[68] Ibid [34] (Geraldine Andrews QC).   [69] See n 63.

period whilst the defendant was rebuilding his neighbouring property. Negotiation damages were awarded in lieu of an injunction for the defendant's use of the claimant's land, which was assessed as one-third of the increase in the net value of the defendant's land as a result of the trespass.[70] This assessment has a clear restitutionary focus on the value of the defendant's gain as a result of the trespass. In assessing this amount, Patten LJ emphasised that the parties would be assumed to have negotiated reasonably, so the defendant would not have agreed to give up all of the profit which was attributable to the building works and the claimant would be assumed to have been willing to allow interference with her proprietary rights.[71] This again reflects the hybrid nature of the negotiation measure.[72]

Sometimes the remedy which has been awarded following trespass to land has been entirely gain-based, such that the remedy is properly characterised as restitutionary rather than negotiation damages. This is illustrated by *Ministry of Defence v Ashman*,[73] where Hoffmann LJ recognised that the claimant may elect to recover restitutionary damages measured by reference to the value of the benefit obtained by the defendant as a result of committing the tort, namely, in that case, what the defendant had saved by continuing to occupy the claimant's premises, which was valued at what she would have had to pay for local authority housing. This conclusion does cause some difficulties, however, because compensatory damages remained an adequate remedy. Also, since the decision in *Ashman*, negotiation damages has become recognised as the appropriate measure of the use of land. It does not follow that restitutionary considerations are excluded; they are simply incorporated within the negotiation measure.

There will be certain exceptional circumstances where the defendant will be liable to account for profits made as a result of the trespass to land, but only where the commission of the tort is considered to be particularly serious. This is also illustrated by *Ramzan v Brookwide Ltd*,[74] where an account of profits would have been awarded had not the negotiation measure been more lucrative for the claimant.[75] The trespass to land in

---

[70] Ibid [41] (Patten LJ).   [71] Ibid [39].
[72] See also *Inverugie Investments Ltd v Hackett* (n 43).
[73] [1993] 2 EGLR 102. Affirmed in *Ministry of Defence v Ashman* [1993] 2 EGLR 107 (CA).
[74] [2010] EWHC 2453 (Ch), [2011] 2 All ER 38.
[75] See n 74 [48]–[49] (Geraldine Andrews QC). There was no appreciation of the significance of the inadequacy of compensation principle such that, if compensatory damages did provide an adequate remedy, there was no scope for any gain-based remedy.

that case was characterised as particularly serious because it involved cynical expropriation of the claimant's property, which was amalgamated with the defendant's property to make a profit which could not have been made but for the expropriation.[76] This was considered to be more serious than the trespass to land in *Horsford v Bird*,[77] because in that case the expropriation of land was for the personal benefit of the defendant and not for commercial reasons to make a profit. It is significant that an account of profits is limited to the most serious cases of trespass to land, involving significant culpability and motivated by a desire to deter such wrongdoing. This is similar to the exceptional award of account of profits for breach of contract.

13.3.3   Conclusions

This analysis of the gain-based pecuniary remedies available for wrong-doing reveals a significant shift in the nature and function of the remedies and, crucially, a shift which is largely unaffected by the nature of the wrong which has been committed. It also reveals that the debate about whether a remedy is compensatory or gain-based is ultimately sterile. There is a hierarchy of pecuniary remedies for wrongdoing, but this is flatter than is often appreciated. At the apex is compensation; if compensatory damages are adequate then there is no scope for a purely restitutionary or a disgorgement remedy. This principle does not, however, exclude restitutionary considerations, since this forms a key component of the negotiation measure. The prevalence of that measure in the recent authorities suggests that there is no longer a need for a separately identified restitutionary remedy for wrongdoing; restitutionary damages should be considered to have been subsumed within the negotiation measure. The hybrid nature of that remedy does not contradict the inadequacy of compensation principle, because the compensatory function forms a key component of the negotiation measure.

The rise of the negotiation measure of damages and the restrictive approach to the award of gain-based remedies for wrongdoing suggests that there is no longer any need to recognise the inadequacy of compensation principle as a mechanism for limiting gain-based awards. The only pure gain-based remedy which is available for wrongdoing is the account of profits. Since that remedy will only be awarded very exceptionally, at least at common law as the cases on breach of contract and trespass to

---

[76] Ibid [50] (Geraldine Andrews QC).   [77] See n 41.

land reveal, there is no need to limit its operation by the inadequacy of compensation principle. The recognition of that principle initially might have been motivated by a concern about the dramatic expansion of the so-called 'restitutionary project'. That expansion has not occurred. Other mechanisms have been identified for restricting the award of gain-based remedies, particularly the cynical nature of the wrong, making it unnecessary to rely on the inadequacy of compensation principle, and so it should consequently be rejected.

It follows that the controversies relating to the award of gain-based remedies for wrongdoing can be readily dissipated. There is no longer any useful function for the inadequacy of compensation principle. Pure gain-based awards themselves are only relevant in the most exceptional of circumstances. Finally, the dispute about whether particular remedies should be characterised as compensatory or gain-based is easily resolved. At one end of the spectrum of pecuniary remedies are compensatory damages, which are focused solely on quantifying the claimant's loss. At the other end is an account of profits, which is focused solely on identifying the defendant's gain. Between these two extremes is the negotiation measure, which is properly treated as a hybrid remedy encompassing both compensatory and gain-based elements, since loss and gain would be taken into account by the parties when negotiating for the defendant's interference with the claimant's right.

13.4   Proprietary Remedies

Much of the last section focused on the award of gain-based remedies for common law wrongdoing. The desire to restrict such remedies has not been replicated in equity, where the natural tendency has been to deprive the defendant wrongdoer of gains made by breach of an equitable duty rather than to compensate the claimant for loss suffered.[78] That is why the account of profits has proved to be so significant in equity. But equitable remedies for wrongdoing are even more significant, because they may have proprietary consequences,

Sometimes, where the defendant has obtained profits through the commission of an equitable wrong, he or she will be required to hold the profits on constructive trust for the claimant. Although the recognition that the defendant holds property on constructive trust is not

---

[78] This is changing, with a growing focus on compensatory awards in equity. See *AIB Group (UK) plc v Mark Redler & Co* [2014] UKSC 58, [2015] AC 1503.

a remedy as such, it does have remedial consequences because the claimant will have an equitable proprietary interest which can be vindicated by means of a proprietary claim, enabling the claimant to assert proprietary rights in respect of assets held by the defendant. Whilst the constructive trust appears to be obviously gain-based, with either literal restitutionary or disgorgement implications, it has sometimes been described as compensatory.[79] This is an abuse of the language of compensation, which should consequently be rejected; the constructive trust should be recognised for what it is, namely a mechanism which operates to deprive the defendant of a gain.

Where the defendant holds property on constructive trust, there are potentially three proprietary advantages for the claimant. First, on insolvency of the trustee, the beneficiary of the trust gains priority over the trustee's unsecured creditors. Secondly, the beneficiary can benefit from any increase in the value of the asset which is held on trust. Thirdly, the beneficiary can assert proprietary rights against innocent third parties who have received and retained the asset or its traceable substitute but who have not provided value, as well as recipients who received but have not retained the asset or its traceable substitute in circumstances where his or her initial receipt can be considered to have been unconscionable.

In England the constructive trust is characterised as institutional, since it arises by operation of law by virtue of clearly defined principles, rather than judicial discretion. In other jurisdictions, notably Australia, the constructive trust is characterised as a remedial trust which arises by operation of judicial discretion. England is notoriously suspicious of the judge exercising such a discretion. So, for example, Lord Camden in *Doe v Kersey*[80] said:

> The discretion of a Judge is the law of tyrants; it is always unknown; it is different in different men; it is casual, and depends upon constitution, in temper and passion. In the best it is often times caprice; in the worst it is every vice, folly and passion to which human nature is liable.

As a consequence of this scepticism about judicial discretion, in England the remedial constructive trust is not recognised, as recently confirmed by the Supreme Court.[81] Interestingly, the Supreme Court cited the judgment of Lord Browne-Wilkinson in *Westdeutsche Landesbank*

---

[79] See *FHR* (n 25) [1] (Lord Neuberger).

[80] (1795)(CP), quoted in *Bower's Law Dictionary* (1839).

[81] *FHR* (n 25) [47]. See also *Angove's Pty Ltd v Bailey* [2016] UKSC 47, [2016] 1 WLR 3179, [27] (Lord Sumption).

Girozentrale v Islington LBC[82] in support of this conclusion, but, whilst he did not formally recognise the remedial constructive trust in that case, he was not adverse to its recognition, just not at that point in time.

Extra-judicially, Lord Neuberger has expressed his concerns about the remedial constructive trust,[83] noting that it 'displays equity at its flexible flabby worst'. He considered it to be 'unprincipled, incoherent and impractical' and was opposed to its recognition in England because it would render the law unpredictable; it would be an affront to the common law view of property rights and interests; and it would involve the courts usurping the role of the legislature, since the creation of new property rights should be left to Parliament.[84]

But the real concern about the recognition of the remedial constructive trust is simply that it would involve unrestrained judicial discretion. This concern does not appear to be shared in Australia.[85] In fact, when the constructive trust in both jurisdictions is carefully examined, the extreme stereotypical characterisations of it being either a rigid institution or an embodiment of unrestrained judicial discretion is a false dichotomy. As Deane J recognised in *Muschinski v Dodds*: 'for the student of equity, there can be no true dichotomy between the two notions'.[86] He went on to recognise that, although the constructive trust is primarily remedial, it is not a 'medium for the indulgence of idiosyncratic notions of fairness and justice' and 'it is available only when warranted by established equitable principles'.[87] In England, the characterisation of the constructive trust as an institution which cannot be modified through the exercise of judicial discretion is equally false. For example, where a proprietary estoppel is established, the claimant's rights might be vindicated by recognising a constructive trust;[88] or the constructive trust might be modified by the award of an equitable allowance to reflect the value of the defendant fiduciary's work in making a profit, albeit in breach of

---

[82] [1996] AC 669 (HL) 714–16.

[83] Lord Neuberger, 'The Remedial Constructive Trust – Fact or Fiction' (Banking Services and Finance Law Association Conference, New Zealand, 10 August 2014) <www .supremecourt.uk/docs/speech-140810.pdf> accessed 15 April 2016, [6]. See also Peter Birks, 'The Remedies for Abuse of Confidential Information' [1990] LMCLQ 460, 465.

[84] Lord Neuberger (n 83) [27]–[28]. But the Supreme Court in *FHR* (n 25) did create a new property right in bribe money which had not existed previously.

[85] See, especially, *Grimaldi v Chameleon Mining NL (No 2)* [2012] FCAFC 6, (2012) 200 FCR 296 [569] (Finn J).

[86] (1985) 160 CLR 583, 614.

[87] Ibid [8]. See also *State Trustees Ltd v Edwards* [2014] VSC 392 [143] (McMillan J).

[88] *Thorner v Major* [2009] UKHL 18, [2009] 1 WLR 776.

duty;[89] and, if a fiduciary had made a profit in breach of fiduciary duty which would continue to accrue over a period of time as the result of the fiduciary's continued work, surely the court would modify the constructive trust in some way, such as to limit it to the profits obtained over a specific period of time.[90]

The reality of the constructive trust is that it arises by operation of law at the point when the defendant's conduct can be characterised as unconscionable, as defined with reference to recognised principles, but this constructive trust (institutional if we have to call it that) should be open to modification through the exercise of judicial discretion, but in a principled way. This does not subvert the statutory insolvency regime; what equity has created, equity can take away, as long as it is done on a principled basis.

The legitimacy of this analysis depends on the identification of the appropriate underlying principles. Whether a constructive trust should be recognised in the first place should turn on the court's characterisation of the defendant's conduct. Subjective unconscionability, judged by reference to the defendant's knowledge of the circumstances in which property was received, should be the standard for the recognition of the constructive trust. This will not be an absolute standard, however, since there will be circumstances where an objective test of unconscionability can be justified, especially where a fiduciary is liable for breach of duty, because of the high standard of conduct expected of fiduciaries. The defendant's fault should be the trigger for recognising the constructive trust because an unconscionable defendant should be deprived of all benefits arising from their conduct; the claimant's claim to the assets is stronger than that of the defendant; the defendant's conscience should be purged by disgorging all benefits obtained from the unconscionable conduct; and all those claiming through the defendant should likewise have their conscience purged from all possible unconscionability. These justifications become increasingly unconvincing, but that is why the constructive trust should not be absolute but should be modified. There may be other considerations to take into account, such as whether other remedies can do the same work more effectively or whether third parties, such as creditors of the defendant, have pure consciences which do not need to be purged.

The appropriate model of the constructive trust consequently is one where the trust arises by operation of law where the defendant's receipt or

---

[89] *Boardman v Phipps* [1967] 2 AC 46 (HL).

[90] See the Australian case of *Warman International Ltd v Dwyer* [1995] HCA 18, (1995) 182 CLR 544.

retention of property can be characterised as unconscionable, actual or deemed, but this trust can be modified with reference to recognised principles. This model of modification can be assessed with reference to the three identified advantages of recognising the constructive trust, to determine whether each of them can be justified in all the circumstances. The operation of this model of the constructive trust can be tested with reference to two particular scenarios where the trust has an important role to play in the commercial context.

13.4.1   Theft

It is recognised in both Australia[91] and England[92] that a thief holds stolen assets on a constructive trust for the victim. This can be justified on the ground that, although the victim will typically have retained title to the stolen asset, the thief's unconscionable conduct in committing theft justifies treating the thief as holding the stolen asset on trust for the victim. The court sees the fault and, from a desire to purge the defendant's conscience, deprives him or her of all benefits. Should such a constructive trust be modified in any way?

(i)   If the thief has become insolvent, should the thief's creditors be able to assert a claim against the stolen assets? Since the stolen property did not legitimately form part of the thief's pool of assets, there is no reason why the creditors of the thief should gain priority over the victim.

(ii)   If the stolen asset has increased in value, then, since the thief should not benefit from their crime in any way, there is no reason why the claimant should be deprived of the benefit of this increase.

(iii)   The claimant should be able to assert a proprietary claim against third parties, who are not *bona fide* purchasers for value but who have received and retained the stolen asset. Innocent third parties who have obtained possession of the asset should not have any better claim than the thief. But this is simply assertion. Against the trend of the authorities, if the third party's conscience was not affected in any way at the time of receipt then, since the thief was unaware that the property had been stolen or constituted the

---

[91] *Black v S Freedman & Co* [1910] HCA 58, (1910) 12 CLR 105.

[92] *Westdeutsche* (n 82) 716 (Lord Browne-Wilkinson); *Armstrong DLW GmbH v Winnington Networks Ltd* [2012] EWHC 10 (Ch), [2013] Ch 156 [276] (Stephen Morris QC).

proceeds of crime, surely the third party's claim should be at least as good and possibly even better than that of the victim of the theft.

It follows that the constructive trust should not be modified to benefit either the thief or his or her creditors, but there might be a case to treat the constructive trust as revoked once the asset has been received by an innocent third party who has not provided value for the receipt. Of course, if they are a *bona fide* purchaser for value, the claimant's equitable title will be defeated anyway.

13.4.2   Bribed Fiduciary

Whether a fiduciary who has received a bribe or secret commission should hold it on constructive trust has proved to be controversial for many years, but it has now been recognised that the bribe will be held on an institutional constructive trust for the principal.[93] This is justified because the fiduciary should be treated as though he or she had acquired the bribe on behalf of the principal, although this does involve the creation of rights in property which did not exist before, but only because of the defendant's unconscionable conduct, which is deemed because of the high standards of fidelity expected of fiduciaries.[94] But should this constructive trust be modified?

(i) Lord Millett has asserted that, where the fiduciary has become insolvent, his or her creditors should not claim that to which they are not entitled and so the claimant should have priority over them.[95] In a very significant dictum in *FHR European Ventures Ltd v Cedar Capital Partners LLC*,[96] however, the Supreme Court recognised that concern about the position of unsecured creditors of the defendant fiduciary has considerable force in some contexts, but only limited force in the context of bribes and secret commissions. The court did not elaborate as to what these circumstances might be, or explain why constructive trusts of bribes are different. But, acknowledging that the position of the unsecured creditors of the constructive trustee might need to be considered in some cases, is highly significant. Does it not suggest that sometimes the constructive trust will be recognised in principle, but its effect might be

---

[93] *FHR* (n 25).
[94] Lord Peter Millett, 'Bribes and Secret Commissions Again' (2012) 71 CLJ 583, 592.
[95] Ibid 611.   [96] *FHR* (n 25) [43].

modified so that the claims of the claimant and the creditors of the trustees are treated equally?

(ii) Where the fiduciary has profited from investment of the bribe, the bribed fiduciary should not benefit in any way. Receipt of a bribe is a serious crime[97] which undermines the essence of fiduciary law and so the fiduciary should be required to disgorge all the profit obtained directly or indirectly from the breach of fiduciary duty.

(iii) Where the asset which has been held on constructive trust has been transferred to an innocent volunteer, the constructive trust should be treated as defeated. Where, however, the recipient is aware that what they had received were the proceeds of bribery, their conscience should be considered to be tainted such that they should be bound by the constructive trust.

13.5   Resolution of Controversies

This chapter has identified three particular controversies relating to the award of gain-based remedies. The first concerns the role of the inadequacy of compensation principle in restricting gain-based awards. This principle is suspect in its interpretation and is not applied consistently. Since gain-based remedies are much less extensive than once thought, there is no need to restrict their application further by reference to such a principle, which should be rejected. The second controversy concerns the appropriate characterisation of gain-based remedies. An account of profits is clearly gain-based. Although there is evidence that restitutionary damages are recognised, there is growing evidence they have been subsumed within negotiation damages, which are properly treated as a hybrid remedy, embodying compensatory and gain-based components. The third controversy relates to the appropriate function of the constructive trust which, whilst characterised as an institution which arises by operation of law, should sometimes be subject to judicial modification where the proprietary connotations of the constructive trust are contradicted by countervailing policy considerations.

---

[97] Contrary to the Bribery Act 2010.

14

Exemplary Damages

JAMES GOUDKAMP

The criminal law and private law differ from each other in numerous ways, one of which concerns the things that these areas of the law aim to achieve in responding to liability. According to well-established principles, the main goals of sentencing offenders are (or include) meting out punishment and deterring the commission of offences.[1] It is obvious that private law's priorities in responding to liability are rather different. Despite the many remedies known to private law, most remedies are, at least on their face, unconcerned with punishment and deterrence. This is perhaps especially true of the award of compensatory damages, which is often regarded as private law's central response to liability.[2] According to conventional wisdom, compensatory damages are awarded, not in order to punish or deter, but to undo losses. Consistently with this understanding, Sir Thomas Bingham MR wrote that 'In the ordinary way, damages bear no resemblance to a criminal penalty.'[3] Probably the clearest departure in private law from the foregoing pattern concerns exemplary damages. Such damages, the courts tell us, exist in order 'to punish and deter'.[4] Although it is certainly arguable (and it has, indeed,

Robert Stevens generously provided me with detailed and illuminating comments on a draft of this chapter. I am most grateful to have had the benefit of them. I am also indebted to Eleni Katsampouka for reading an early version of this chapter and offering suggestions for improvement.

[1] Section 142(1) of the Criminal Justice Act 2003 identifies 'the punishment of offenders' and 'the reduction of crime (including its reduction by deterrence)' as 'purposes of sentencing' to which 'any court dealing with an offender in respect of his offence must have regard'.

[2] John Gardner, for instance, speaks of the 'primacy of reparative damages as a remedy in the law of torts': John Gardner, 'Torts and Other Wrongs' (2011) 39 *Florida State University Law Review* 43, 57.

[3] *AB v South West Water Services Ltd* [1993] QB 507 (CA) 528.

[4] *Rookes v Barnard* [1964] AC 1129 (HL) 1221.

strenuously been argued) that other private law remedies also pursue these objectives,[5] exemplary damages do so most visibly.

Received wisdom has it that English courts rarely award exemplary damages. They are supposedly 'a remedy of last resort'.[6] If this is true,[7] the attention that scholars have lavished on exemplary damages is plainly disproportionate to their practical importance. Commentators have discussed exemplary damages very extensively.[8] The literature is

---

[5] It has long been contended, of course, that all private law remedies exist in order to deter particular types of behaviour. The most sustained analyses in this regard have been made by law-and-economics scholars. Speaking very generally, these scholars' position is that all of private law (including the law of remedies) can be explained as an attempt to reduce the incidence of inefficient conduct, which is defined as conduct that causes a net loss of societal wealth. The *locus classicus* is Richard Posner, 'A Theory of Negligence' (1972) 1 *Journal of Legal Studies* 29. The suggestion that private law remedies beyond exemplary damages are concerned, at least to some extent, with punishment is less frequently embraced. For insightful analysis in this regard, see Tony Honoré, 'The Morality of Tort Law: Questions and Answers' in David Owen (ed), *Philosophical Foundations of Tort Law* (Oxford University Press 1995) 73; Peter Cane, 'Retribution, Proportionality and Moral Luck in Tort Law' in Peter Cane and Jane Stapleton (eds), *The Law of Obligations: Essays in Celebration of John Fleming* (Clarendon Press 1998) 141; RA Duff, 'Torts, Crimes, and Vindication: Whose Wrong is it?' in Matthew Dyson (ed), *Unravelling Tort and Crime* (Cambridge University Press 2014) 146.

[6] *Kuddus v Chief Constable of Leicestershire Constabulary* [2001] UKHL 29, [2002] 2 AC 122, 145 [63].

[7] Recent cases in which exemplary damages were awarded include *Merson v Cartwright* [2005] UKPC 38 (police battery); *Muuse v Secretary of State for the Home Department* [2010] EWCA Civ 453, *The Times*, 10 May 2010 (unlawful detention); *Ramzan v Brookwide Ltd* [2011] EWCA Civ 985, [2011] 2 P & CR 22 (appropriation of property); *2 Travel Group plc v Cardiff City Transport Services Ltd* [2012] CAT 19, [2012] Comp AR 211 (infringement of competition laws); *Tasneem v Morley* (unreported, County Court (Central London) 30 September 2013) (fraudulent insurance claim); *R (Lamari) v Secretary of State for the Home Department* [2013] EWHC 3130 (QB) (unlawful detention); *Choudhury v Garcia* [2013] EWHC 3283 (QB) (unlawful eviction); *Hassan v Cooper* [2015] EWHC 540 (QB), [2015] RTR 26 (fraudulent insurance claim). The fact that exemplary damages have been granted so frequently as of late casts doubt upon whether they are truly exceptional.

[8] For a small sample of the literature, see Nicholas McBride, 'A Case for Awarding Punitive Damages in Response to Deliberate Breaches of Contract' (1995) 24 *Anglo-American Law Review* 369; Nicholas McBride, 'Punitive Damages' in Peter Birks (ed), *Wrongs and Remedies in the Twenty-First Century* (Oxford University Press 1996) 175; Law Commission, *Aggravated, Exemplary and Restitutionary Damages* (Law Com No 247, 1997); Allan Beever, 'The Structure of Aggravated and Exemplary Damages' (2003) 23 *Oxford Journal of Legal Studies* 87; Andrew Tettenborn, 'Punitive Damages – A View from England' (2004) 41 *San Diego Law Review* 1551; Jonathan Morgan, 'Reflections on Reforming Punitive Damages in English Law' in Lotte Meurkens and Emily Nordin (eds), *The Power of Punitive Damages: Is Europe Missing Out?* (Intersentia 2012) 183.

on a staggeringly large scale. A newcomer to the field would likely feel overwhelmed and at a loss to know where to start reading. Given the outpouring of analysis regarding exemplary damages, it is unsurprising that debates have broken out about essentially every conceivable facet of the law in this connection. The purpose of this chapter is to address five disagreements and to suggest how they should be resolved. These disagreements are as follows. First, should exemplary damages be available as a remedy for breach of contract? Secondly, should the 'categories test' developed in *Rookes v Barnard*[9] be retained? Thirdly, does the apportionment provision for contributory negligence apply to awards of exemplary damages, and should it apply to such awards? Fourthly, should a defendant ever incur vicarious liability in respect of exemplary damages? Fifthly, are exemplary damages masquerading as another form of damages? The analysis that follows seeks to shine new light on these areas of persistent difficulty. Despite the scale of the literature that exists in relation to exemplary damages, theorising in relation to all five of these debates has (it will be argued) gone awry. There is hence room for this chapter to contribute something worthwhile.

There is an important terminological issue that needs to be mentioned at the outset. As will be apparent from what has been said so far, the remedy with which this chapter is concerned will be referred to as 'exemplary damages'. An alternative label, which is preferred in the United States, is 'punitive damages'.[10] Although these terms are often used interchangeably,[11] the clear trend in the English case law is in favour of 'exemplary damages'. Judges have suggested that the phrase 'punitive damages' is outdated.[12] Because (and only because) English judges have indicated a preference for 'exemplary damages', that label has been adopted in this chapter.

---

[9] See n 4.

[10] Additional but less common terms have been used. McCardie J in *Butterworth v Butterworth* [1920] P 126 (Divorce) 136 noted that the type of damages in question 'have been variously called exemplary, vindictive, penal, punitive, aggravated or retributory'.

[11] The very existence of two labels may reflect the dual functions of the remedy. Arguably, 'punitive damages' reflects the goal of punishment, while the label 'exemplary damages' points to that of deterrence.

[12] See, e.g. *AB* (n 3) 528 (Sir Thomas Bingham MR). Cf *R v Secretary of State for Transport, ex p Factortame Ltd (No 5)* [1998] 1 CMLR 1353, 1414 [157] ('The phrase "exemplary damages" is misleading: the appropriate phrase is "penal damages".').

14.1 Exemplary Damages in Contract

14.1.1 Addis v Gramophone Co Ltd

Addis v Gramophone Co Ltd[13] is widely regarded as the leading authority in support of the proposition that exemplary damages are unavailable in an action for breach of contract.[14] For example, the Law Commission wrote, citing *Addis*, that exemplary damages 'are clearly unavailable in a claim for breach of contract'.[15] The authors of *Chitty on Contracts* contend that the principle in *Addis* 'prevents the recovery of exemplary damages for any breach of contract'.[16] Whether or not this prevailing understanding of *Addis* is correct is debatable. The defendants in that case had dismissed the claimant employee from their service. The claimant sued for breach of contract. A jury awarded the claimant, relevantly, £600. The defendants challenged that sum. In the House of Lords, Lord Loreburn LC did not say anything explicit about exemplary damages. His Lordship focused on the extent to which the award included a sum to compensate the claimant for injured feelings owing to the circumstances of his dismissal and a sum to reflect the difficulty that the claimant may encounter in finding future employment owing to his having been dismissed. The Lord Chancellor held that to the extent that the award 'include[d] compensation' in respect of those losses, it should not stand. Lord Shaw agreed with the Lord Chancellor. Lord James also concurred with the Lord Chancellor and added that he did not think that the claimant could recover damages in contract on account of the manner in which he had been dismissed.[17] Lord Atkinson wrote: 'I have always understood that damages for breach of contract were in the nature of compensation, not punishment.'[18] His Lordship concluded that exemplary damages 'ought not to be, and are not according to any true principle of law, recoverable in such an action as the present'.[19] Conversely, Lord Collins opined that exemplary damages were available in contract. Lord Gorell in brief reasons remarked that he could find neither 'authority nor principle for the contention that [the claimant] is entitled to have damages for the manner in which his discharge took

---

[13] [1909] AC 488 (HL).

[14] Exemplary damages are available where the claimant has concurrent claims in both tort and contract: *Drane v Evangelou* [1978] 1 WLR 455 (CA).

[15] Law Commission (n 8) 63, para 1.112.

[16] Hugh Beale (ed), *Chitty on Contracts*, vol 1 (31st edn, Sweet & Maxwell 2012) 1787 [26–044].

[17] *Addis* (n 13) 492.   [18] Ibid 494.   [19] Ibid 496.

place'.[20] The result of the decision was that the claimant could not recover damages for the manner of his dismissal.

It is clear from the foregoing that *Addis* provides only weak support for the proposition that exemplary damages are unavailable in contract. Only two of the Law Lords (Lord Atkinson and Lord Gorell) discussed exemplary damages directly, and they split on the availability of exemplary damages in proceedings in contract. The other Law Lords left it unclear whether they were discussing the availability of compensatory damages for injured feelings or exemplary damages, although the former seems more likely. It is, accordingly, something of a mystery how *Addis* came widely to be regarded as laying down the rule that exemplary damages are unavailable in an action for breach of contract.[21] One suspects that judges and scholars have unthinkingly repeated the mantra that *Addis* establishes that exemplary damages cannot be awarded for a breach of contract.

14.1.2 Subsequent Developments

The understanding that exemplary damages are unavailable as a remedy for breach of contract has never, it seems, been challenged before English courts. This situation is probably largely attributable to the decisions in *Rookes v Barnard*[22] and *Broome v Cassell & Co Ltd*.[23] *Rookes* radically restricted the circumstances in which exemplary damages can be awarded in private law generally. Lord Devlin, with whom the other Law Lords agreed, limited the award of exemplary damages to just three categories of case: (1) cases involving oppressive, arbitrary or unconstitutional actions by the government; (2) cases involving conduct calculated by the defendant to make a profit; and (3) cases in which a statute authorises the court to grant exemplary damages.[24] This control

---

[20] Ibid 501.
[21] One writer who has successfully resisted the herd mentality that dominates thinking regarding *Addis* is Ralph Cunnington, 'Should Punitive Damages be Part of the Judicial Arsenal in Contract Cases?' (2006) 26 *Legal Studies* 369, 373.
[22] See n 4.   [23] [1972] AC 1027 (HL).
[24] Parliament has rarely provided for exemplary damages to be awarded. When it legislates in relation to exemplary damages, it usually provides that they are unavailable in a given situation or in order to impose additional restrictions on their award: see, e.g. Law Reform (Miscellaneous Provisions) Act 1934, s 1(2)(a)(i); Competition Act 1998, s 47C(1); Civil Liability Act 2002 (NSW), s 21; Defamation Act 2005 (NSW), s 35. Examples of statutes that authorise the award of exemplary damages include the Reserve and Auxiliary Forces (Protection of Civil Interests) Act 1951, s 13(2) and the Crime and Courts Act 2013, s 34(4).

device is known as the 'categories test'. It is clear that Lord Devlin thought that exemplary damages should, ideally, be killed off entirely but that he felt constrained by precedent to allow them to be awarded in the categories that he identified. Given the decision in *Rookes*, it must have been thought by practising lawyers that the courts would be hostile to the suggestion that the bar on awarding exemplary damages for breach of contract should be lifted.[25] This perception would have been reinforced by *Broome*, in which the House of Lords held that *Rookes* should be understood as laying down a 'cause of action test' too. Pursuant to that test, exemplary damages can be awarded only if the cause of action in which a given claimant sues is one in which it had been held, before *Rookes* was decided, that exemplary damages were available. The cause of action test meant that exemplary damages could not be awarded in proceedings in, for example, public nuisance and negligence.[26]

At least two subsequent developments have made the possibility of challenging *Addis* much more promising. The first is the decision of the House of Lords in *Kuddus v Chief Constable of Leicestershire*.[27] That case jettisoned the cause of action test. The removal of that constraint on the award of exemplary damage was entirely justified. It was nonsensical for a remedy to be denied simply on the ground that it had not previously been granted in relation to the cause of action in question. The change in the law effected by *Kuddus* is important for present purposes because it signals a fundamental change of attitude in the courts towards exemplary damages. It is also significant because the abolition of the cause of action test makes the bar on awarding exemplary damages in actions in contract particularly fragile. Given that the award of exemplary damages is no longer confined to particular causes of action, why should exemplary damages be unavailable in contract? Tantalisingly, in *Kuddus* Lord Mackay,[28] Lord Nicholls[29] and Lord Scott[30] appeared to be willing to engage in a more widespread review of the law governing exemplary damages. However, they declined to do so on account of the limited scope of the parties' submissions.

The second development that suggests that *Addis'* days may be numbered is the decision of the Supreme Court of Canada in *Royal Bank of*

[25] This perception continues to the present day in some quarters: see, e.g. *Crawfordsburn Inn Ltd v Graham* [2013] NIQB 79 [18] ('the longstanding restrictions applied by the House of Lords render it inappropriate to extend the award of exemplary damages' to an action in breach of contract).
[26] *AB* (n 3) 530 (Sir Thomas Bingham MR).   [27] See n 6.   [28] Ibid 137–38 [35]–[36].
[29] Ibid 145 [68].   [30] Ibid 156 [106].

Canada v W Got & Associates Electric Ltd.[31] In that landmark case[32] the Supreme Court unanimously held that exemplary damages could be awarded in proceedings in contract, although it stressed that it would be only in unusual cases that a breach of contract would justify such an award.[33] These developments in Canada are important for present purposes primarily because they show that awarding exemplary damages for breach of contract would be unlikely to have any adverse consequences for the justice system or society more generally. There is no evidence, for example, that *Got* has resulted in Canada in intolerable uncertainty, a deluge of claims for exemplary damages or exponential growth in liability insurance premiums.[34]

14.1.3   Is the Bar on Awarding Exemplary Damages in Contract Justified?

Numerous arguments have been marshalled in support of withholding exemplary damages as a contract law remedy. The arguments on offer hold a powerful spell over many theorists. However, they are unconvincing, some spectacularly so.[35] They are nothing more than distractions that impede clear thinking about this corner of the law. This section canvasses a selection of the most important arguments in this regard. It will be explained why they fail. The purpose of this section is not to make out a positive case for accepting exemplary damages as one of the remedies that courts can award for breach of contract. Its goal is more

---

[31] [1999] 3 SCR 408.

[32] It is discussed perceptively in James Edelman, 'Exemplary Damages for Breach of Contract' (2001) 117 *Law Quarterly Review* 539.

[33] *Got* (n 31) 422 [29]. The Supreme Court has repeatedly affirmed *Got*: *Whiten v Pilot Insurance Co* [2002] SCC 18, [2002] 1 SCR 595; *Performance Industries Ltd v Sylvan Lake Golf & Tennis Club Ltd* [2002] SCC 19, [2002] 1 SCR 678.

[34] Canada is the only major common law jurisdiction in which exemplary damages are available for a breach of contract. §355 of the Restatement (Second) of the Law of Contracts provides: 'Punitive damages are not recoverable for a breach of contract unless the conduct constituting the breach is also a tort for which punitive damages are recoverable.' (The Reporters note, however, the existence of some statutory deviations from this rule: see cmt a.) The same principle obtains in Australia: *Hospitality Group Pty Ltd v Australian Rugby Union Ltd* [2001] FCA 1040, (2001) 110 FCR 157, 191 [142]–[143].

[35] Nicholas McBride engages in a thorough demolition in McBride (1995) (n 8) and McBride (1996) (n 8). What follows here has been influenced by his analyses. I agree with McBride that the arguments for withholding exemplary damages as a contract law remedy are unconvincing. However, I find most of the arguments in question unsatisfactory for rather different reasons from McBride.

modest, principally due to the limited amount of space available. It aims
merely to move out of the way some influential arguments in favour of
maintaining the status quo.

The first argument for withholding exemplary damages as a remedy
for breach of contract is that awarding exemplary damages 'would lead to
confusion and uncertainty in commercial affairs'.[36] This contention goes
nowhere. It does not explain why exemplary damages are available in
those parts of tort law which are of commercial significance. Neither does
this argument explain why 'confusion and uncertainty' is more objectionable in the case of commercial contracts than other types of contracts.
Nor does it supply a reason to think that awarding exemplary damages
would be liable to breed uncertainty. It is a pure assertion to say that
confusion and uncertainty would be the inevitable result of awarding
exemplary damages. The experience in Canada[37] suggests that this assertion is groundless. Finally, this argument does not demonstrate that any
'confusion and uncertainty' that might result is not worth tolerating in
return for whatever benefits may flow from recognising exemplary
damages as a contract law remedy.

A second argument has to do with the fact that exemplary damages are
available in tort.[38] The idea is as follows. Where the defendant's conduct
in breaching a contract is sufficiently reprehensible to warrant an award
of exemplary damages, the defendant will often incur liability in tort.
Because exemplary damages are available in tort, it is said to follow that it
is unnecessary to recognise exemplary damages in the law of contract.
This argument is bad. For one thing, a person can breach a contract
maliciously without committing a tort.[39] Hence, it will not always be the
case that exemplary damages will be available in tort where there is
a particularly egregious breach of contract. More importantly, this argument proceeds inconsistently with the common law's traditional
approach to concurrent liability. When a defendant incurs concurrent

[36] *Addis* (n 13) 495 (Lord Atkinson).   [37] Text to n 34.

[38] Lord Atkinson seemed to be attracted to this argument in *Addis* although he did not
endorse it explicitly: (n 13) 496. His Lordship pointed out that where the defendant
breaches a contract maliciously or fraudulently, he may 'sustain an action of tort as an
alternative remedy'. The Law Commission also appeared to find this argument attractive:
Law Commission (n 8) 119, para 1.73.

[39] If illustrations of this point are needed, consider an insurer who refuses to pay what is, to
the insurer's knowledge, a genuine claim, in order to apply pressure to a financially
vulnerable claimant. As another example, take a manufacturer who sells a product that he
knows is, because of a defect, highly dangerous, in circumstances where the product
happens not to cause any damage.

liability, the law's concern is usually only to prevent double recovery rather than to deny a particular type of remedy in one cause of action simply because that remedy happens to be available in the other.

A third argument is that exemplary damages should not be available in an action for breach of contract because such damages have not previously been awarded in that action. This argument was accepted by the Law Commission.[40] However, it clearly is unpersuasive. The mere fact that something has not been done before is not a compelling reason against doing the thing concerned. Precisely the same defective logic underpinned the cause of action test,[41] which the Law Commission rightly condemned.[42]

A fourth argument concerns the nature of loss that tends to be suffered in contract and tort. The Law Commission put this argument in the following way: 'contract primarily involves pecuniary, rather than non-pecuniary, losses; in contrast, the torts for which exemplary damages are most commonly awarded, and are likely to continue to be most commonly awarded, usually give rise to claims for non-pecuniary losses'.[43] This argument suffers from formidable difficulty. The implicit suggestion seems to be that non-pecuniary loss is more serious than pecuniary loss[44] and, hence, that the award of exemplary damages should be available in tort law but is not required in contract law. However, the proposition that non-pecuniary loss is more serious than pecuniary loss is obviously highly contestable. The criteria by which seriousness is measured are not indicated. Additionally, while it is of course true that contractual claims are generally in respect of pecuniary loss, the suggestion that claims in tort 'for which exemplary damages are most commonly awarded' tend to be in respect of non-pecuniary loss is contentious. Certainly, this proposition is unsupported by any empirical evidence. There is no shortage of tort cases that were substantially about pecuniary loss in which exemplary damages were awarded.[45]

A fifth argument concerns supposed differences between contractual and tortious obligations. The Law Commission argued: 'a contract is

---

[40] Law Commission (n 8) 118, para 1.72.   [41] See section 14.1.2 above.

[42] Law Commission (n 8) 93, para 1.2. The Commission wrote that the cause of action test meant that 'the availability of exemplary damages [was] ... dictated by what are arguably the accidents of precedent, rather than sound principle'.

[43] Ibid 118, para 1.72.

[44] Although consider *Southport Corporation v Esso Petroleum Co Ltd* [1953] 3 WLR 773 (QB) 779 where Devlin J suggested that non-pecuniary interests (specifically the interest in human life) were qualitatively more important than pecuniary interests.

[45] See, e.g. *Tasneem* (n 7); *Ramzan* (n 7).

a private arrangement in which parties negotiate rights and duties, whereas the duties which obtain under the law of tort are imposed by law; it can accordingly be argued that the notion of state punishment is more readily applicable to the latter than to the former'.[46] The Law Commission evidently had only individually negotiated contracts in mind. It did not appear to consider this argument to extend to standard-form contracts. So, even if this reason is a good one, it supports excluding exemplary damages as a remedy for breach of only one type of contract. A further point to observe is that it is not at all clear that the Law Commission was correct to say that contractual obligations are imposed by the parties while tortious obligations are imposed by the law.[47] This way of understanding the difference between obligations in tort and contract has been trenchantly criticised as overly simplistic.[48] It is arguable, for instance, that obligations in contract are ultimately imposed by the law because the law determines when there is an agreement and the effect of that agreement. Finally, the Law Commission left unexplained the relevance of the fact that a contract has been individually negotiated. It is unclear why the mere fact that negotiations have taken place renders it inappropriate for the law to punish one of the parties on account of the way in which he later conducted himself.

Sixthly, it is sometimes suggested that the fact that breaking promises is not a criminal offence supports the current rule.[49] The idea is that breaking promises is not sufficiently reprehensible to warrant criminal punishment and that it would, therefore, be odd if breaches of promises were punished by way of exemplary damages awards. This argument is unpersuasive. There is no requirement that tortious behaviour also be criminal before exemplary damages will be awarded in tort. This argument cannot explain the absence of such a rule. More fundamentally,

---

[46] Law Commission (n 8) 118, para 1.72.

[47] This suggestion can be traced at least to Winfield, who argued that: 'Tortious liability arises from the breach of a duty primarily fixed by the law.': Percy Winfield, *The Province of the Law of Tort* (Cambridge University Press 1931) 32. This way of separating obligations in tort from contractual duties holds a powerful grip on the minds of many judges and writers. Lord Goff, for example, contended that 'the tortious duty is imposed by the general law, and the contractual duty is attributable to the will of the parties': *Henderson v Merrett Syndicates Ltd* [1995] 2 AC 145 (HL) 194.

[48] For thoughtful discussion, see Andrew Robertson, 'On the Distinction between Contract and Tort' in Andrew Robertson (ed), *The Law of Obligations: Connections and Boundaries* (UCL Press 2004) ch 6.

[49] Ewan McKendrick, for example, gestures towards this argument in Ewan McKendrick, *Contract Law* (10th edn, Palgrave Macmillan 2013) 332.

simply because the criminal law does not punish people for failing to keep their promises does not mean that any given failure is undeserving of punishment. The truth of the matter is that the fact that a given act is legal or illegal is only a very rough indicator as to the blameworthiness of the actor. There are likely many good reasons why the breaking of promises does not attract criminal liability that have nothing to do with the issue of blame. These include, for example, difficulties in specifying with precision sufficient to satisfy the criminal law's fair warning principle the circumstances in which criminal liability will arise in respect of a breach of contract.

A final argument invokes the doctrine of efficient breach. On this analysis, public wealth is maximised by allowing the defendant to breach his contract and pay damages where he calculates that he will make a net gain by doing so. The defendant's liability should not exceed the claimant's loss since, if it does so, the law would not optimally encourage efficient breaches. This argument was endorsed by the Law Commission[50] and it is widely accepted in the United States.[51] Nicholas McBride criticises it on the basis that English courts have not embraced the efficient breach doctrine.[52] However, this criticism is misconceived. If the efficient breach doctrine is a good reason for refusing to award exemplary damages, that fact is wholly unaffected by whether the doctrine has been approved by the courts. A key difficulty with the efficient breach argument is simply that it is at best a partial justification of the unavailability of exemplary damages in contract law. This is because it does not explain the unavailability of exemplary damages as a response to a breach of contract where the defendant's breach is inefficient and the award of compensatory damages alone would be inadequate to optimally deter (e.g. due to the fact that the breach is of a kind that is often undetected).

14.1.4   Conclusion

Three main points have been made in this section. First, contrary to received wisdom, it is most doubtful whether *Addis* establishes that exemplary damages are available in an action for breach of contract. Scholars and judges have been too quick to reach the conclusion that

---

[50] Law Commission (n 8) 118–19, para 1.72.
[51] See, e.g. Restatement (Second) of Contracts (1981) ch 16, Introductory Note.
[52] McBride (1995) (n 8) 384–85. See also Cunnington (n 21) 387–89.

Addis lays down any such principle. Secondly, the scene is set for the view that exemplary damages are unavailable in an action in contract to be challenged. Developments in both England and Canada suggest that the bar on awarding exemplary damages in contractual claims is ripe for reconsideration. Thirdly, it was suggested that the most prominent reasons for refusing to award exemplary damages in contract are either nonsensical or at best partial justifications. The analysis stopped short of arguing, definitively, that exemplary damages should be available as a remedy for breach of contract. Showing that arguments against awarding exemplary damages in contract are bad does not establish that exemplary damages should be available as a response to a breach of contract. There is insufficient space available fully to develop an argument in support of the recognition of exemplary damages as a contract law remedy. The analysis has, however, sought to show that the door that leads to the outcome that exemplary damages should be recognised is wide open.

14.2   The Categories Test

The central principles established by *Rookes* were outlined above.[53] To recap, in that case, as understood by *Broome*, Lord Devlin imposed a cause of action test and a categories test. Both tests had to be satisfied before exemplary damages could be awarded. While the cause of action test was jettisoned in *Kuddus*, the categories test survives to the present day. This section addresses the categories test.

The categories test has been rejected forcefully in several other jurisdictions. The High Court of Australia refused to accept it in *Uren v John Fairfax & Sons Pty Ltd*.[54] On appeal to the Privy Council, the Judicial Committee held that the High Court was entitled to do so.[55] The courts in Canada[56] and New Zealand[57] similarly held that the test was wrong. Academic commentators have often been unkind to the categories test. The Law Commission wrote that the test is inconsistent with 'sound principle'.[58] Andrew Tettenborn called it 'curious' and 'arbitrary' and said that it was 'difficult to see much logic' in it.[59] Peter Jaffey argued that, in embracing the categories test, *Rookes* left the law 'in an awkward

---

[53] See section 14.1.2 above.   [54] (1966) 117 CLR 118.
[55] *Australian Consolidated Press Ltd v Uren* [1969] 1 AC 590 (PC).
[56] *Vorvis v Insurance Corp of British Columbia* [1989] 1 SCR 1085.
[57] *Taylor v Beere* [1982] 1 NZLR 81 (CA).   [58] Law Commission (n 8) 93, para 1.2.
[59] Tettenborn (n 8) 1554–55.

state'.[60] In view of the foregoing, Lord Nicholls's remark in *Kuddus* that *Rookes*, in laying down the categories test, had 'received a generally negative reception' is a significant understatement.[61] *Rookes* was regarded outside of England as so disastrous that it was, arguably, a major catalyst for the significant weakening in the precedential status of Privy Council and House of Lords' decisions in Commonwealth jurisdictions that occurred during the twentieth century.[62]

The categories test is vulnerable to formidable objections. As these have been well rehearsed elsewhere, it is unnecessary to set them out in detail here. It will suffice to say that the central difficulty with the test is that no compelling reason exists for it, given the stated purposes of awarding exemplary damages. The courts have indicated that the purpose of awarding exemplary damages is to punish and deter. A need for punishment or deterrence can obviously exist in circumstances that fall outside the three situations in which the categories test permits exemplary damages to be awarded.[63] Therefore, the categories test is an irrational constraint on the availability of exemplary damages. The courts have proceeded inconsistently in saying both that exemplary damages are about punishment and deterrence and in limiting the availability of exemplary damages by way of the categories test. As Lord Nicholls put it, 'the availability of exemplary damages should be co-extensive with its rationale'.[64] Unless the courts change their position on the purposes to be served by awarding exemplary damages, the categories test should be abolished.

In order to avoid the analysis in this section from being misunderstood, it is stressed that the point that has been made is not that the categories that constitute the categories test are themselves unjustified. It may be that they are justified. (The third category – situations identified by statute where exemplary damages can be awarded – is plainly defensible. It is arguable that first category – oppressive, arbitrary or unconstitutional actions by the government – is warranted on the ground

---

[60] Peter Jaffey, 'The Law Commission Report on Aggravated, Exemplary and Restitutionary Damages' (1998) 61 *Modern Law Review* 860, 863.

[61] See n 6 [64].

[62] Regarding this weakening, see James Goudkamp and John Murphy, 'Divergent Evolution in the Law of Torts: Jurisdictional Isolation, Jurisprudential Divergence and Explanatory Theories' in Andrew Robertson and Michael Tilbury (eds), *The Common Law of Obligations: Divergence and Unity* (Hart Publishing 2015) 283–89.

[63] For a recent illustration see *Breslin v McKevitt* [2011] NICA 33 (terrorist bomb attack held not to satisfy the categories test).

[64] *Kuddus* (n 6) [65].

that it would be inappropriate, where the state is a wrongdoer, for the sanctioning of the state to be solely under the control of the executive branch of government. The second category – conduct calculated by the defendant to make a profit – is perhaps more difficult to defend. It is hard to see why it should matter that the defendant was motivated by the prospect of making a profit as opposed to some other reason.) But the goal of this section has not been to demonstrate that these categories make no sense. Its purpose has been to show that it is nonsensical that the availability of exemplary damages is restricted to just these categories.

14.3 Exemplary Damages and Contributory Negligence

Two questions will be addressed in this short section. They are: (1) whether the apportionment provision for contributory negligence[65] applies to awards of exemplary damages; and (2) whether awards of exemplary damages should be susceptible to reduction for contributory negligence. Neither of these questions has received much consideration. The Law Commission thought that it was arguable that the apportionment provision extends to exemplary damages but did not engage with the issue.[66] Michael Tilbury and Harold Luntz consider that the provision is 'capable of encompassing' exemplary damages but, likewise, did not develop this claim.[67] The second question has been little discussed. It has recently been explored by Victor Schwartz and Christopher Appel.[68] Those authors contend that exemplary damages should be brought within the net of apportionment.

Admittedly, the practical significance of these questions is fairly limited. This is for at least two reasons. The first reason is that if there is contributory fault on the part of the claimant, the likelihood may be low that a court will think that exemplary damages should be awarded.[69] Significant fault on the part of the claimant may suggest that the defendant is less culpable than would otherwise be the case, particularly if the claimant's contributory fault is in the nature of highly provocative

[65] Law Reform (Contributory Negligence) Act 1945, s 1.
[66] Law Commission (n 8) 81, para 1.168 fn 475.
[67] Michael Tilbury and Harold Luntz, 'Punitive Damages in Australian Law' (1995) 17 *Loyola of Los Angeles International & Comparative Law Journal* 769, 790.
[68] Victor Schwartz and Christopher Appel, 'Two Wrongs Do Not Make a Right: Reconsidering the Application of Comparative Fault to Punitive Damages Awards' (2013) 78 *Missouri Law Review* 133.
[69] 'The plaintiff's conduct may serve to exclude exemplary damages altogether.': Law Commission (n 8) 69, para 1.132.

conduct. The second reason is that wrongs that tend to attract awards of exemplary damages are often wrongs in respect of which contributory negligence is not an answer to liability. For example, the doctrine of contributory negligence does not apply to liability in battery,[70] deceit[71] or defamation.[72] These wrongs are all wrongs that appear to attract exemplary damages more regularly than some others. Nevertheless, the questions raised in this section are not without interest. They are worth addressing even if their importance in practice is limited.

The issue of whether the apportionment provision applies to awards of exemplary damages needs to be resolved by reference to the statutory language. Unfortunately, the language does not offer much guidance. The provision states:

> Where any person suffers damage as the result partly of his own fault and partly of the fault of any other person or persons, a claim in respect of that damage shall not be defeated by reason of the fault of the person suffering the damage, but the damages recoverable in respect thereof shall be reduced to such extent as the court thinks just and equitable having regard to the claimant's share in the responsibility for the damage . . .[73]

It might be thought that the fact that the provision indicates that the '*damages* recoverable' shall be reduced where there is fault on both sides suggests that it extends to exemplary damages. The word 'damages' is unqualified. However, other aspects of the apportionment provision stand in the way of this construction. The provision refers to 'damages' being awarded in respect of 'damage' and to 'damages' being reduced in line with 'the claimant's share in the responsibility for the damage'. The legislation does not define 'damage' beyond saying that it includes personal injury and death.[74] Nevertheless, it is hard to see how 'damage' could, in the context of the apportionment provision, mean anything other than 'loss'. If 'damage' means loss, then 'damages' awarded in respect of damage must mean, and mean only, compensatory damages, these being the only type of damages that are awarded in respect of loss. The stronger view is, therefore, that the apportionment provision does not extend to exemplary damages.

---

[70] *Co-operative Group (CWS) Ltd v Pritchard* [2011] EWCA Civ 329, [2012] QB 320.

[71] *Standard Chartered Bank v Pakistan National Shipping Corp (Nos 2 and 4)* [2002] UKHL 43, [2003] 1 AC 959.

[72] Contributory negligence is not even addressed in the most comprehensive book on defamation: Richard Parkes et al (eds), *Gatley on Libel and Slander* (12th edn, Sweet & Maxwell 2013).

[73] Law Reform (Contributory Negligence) Act 1945, s 1(1).   [74] Ibid s 4.

This conclusion says nothing about whether the apportionment provision should extend to exemplary damages. How should the second of the two questions posed be answered? It is strongly arguable that provision should not apply to exemplary damages. Exemplary damages are awarded, according to conventional wisdom, in order to punish and deter. The realisation of those goals will be jeopardised if exemplary damages are apportioned on the ground of claimant fault. The defendant will be punished less than he deserves and he will be sub-optimally deterred if an award of exemplary damages is cut back. It is undoubtedly for these reasons that the criminal law does not recognise a defence of contributory fault.[75]

One counterargument to the foregoing is that apportioning exemplary damages would not result in the goals of punishment and deterrence being undermined because apportionment will result in the *claimant* being punished and deterred. There are various possible replies to this counterpoint. One reply is that apportioning exemplary damages for contributory negligence is unjustified because apportionment would aggravate the harshness of the doctrine of contributory negligence from the perspective of claimants. The doctrine already treats claimants to whom it applies severely given that it usually leaves them with uninsured losses.[76] While findings of liability usually do not impact upon defendants personally because defendants are usually insured, claimants are typically without relevant insurance and so suffer directly reductions in their damages. Apportioning exemplary damages is therefore prone to punish claimants disproportionately. Another reply is that apportioning exemplary damages on account of claimant fault is unlikely to have any deterrent impact given that exemplary damages are supposedly awarded only rarely.

14.4 Exemplary Damages and Vicarious Liability

The interaction between exemplary damages and vicarious liability has attracted considerable controversy.[77] Generally speaking, the courts have

---

[75] On this point, see Ken Simons, 'The Relevance of Victim Conduct in Tort and Criminal Law' (2005) 8 *Buffalo Criminal Law Review* 541.

[76] For illuminating discussion, see Peter Cane, *Atiyah's Accidents, Compensation and the Law* (8th edn, Cambridge University Press 2013) 50–51.

[77] For a recent treatment, see Stephen Todd, 'Vicarious Liability, Personal Liability and Exemplary Damages' in Simone Degeling, James Edelman and James Goudkamp (eds), *Torts in Commercial Law* (Thomson Reuters 2011).

accepted that a defendant can be vicariously liable to pay exemplary damages.[78] The Law Commission supported this position.[79] By contrast, Allan Beever contends that: 'If exemplary damages serve to punish the wrongdoer, then it seems both senseless and unjust to hold his innocent employer liable.'[80] Beever clearly is correct to say that the punishment goal of awarding exemplary damages is not served if someone other than the wrongdoer is required to pay exemplary damages. Does that mean, however, that liability to pay exemplary damages should never be imposed on a defendant who is vicariously liable? Two short points are worth briefly noting in this connection. The first point concerns deterrence, which is the other judicially accepted function of exemplary damages. It is true that it is nonsensical as a matter of retributive justice to punish someone who is not a wrongdoer. However, punishment is not the only reason why exemplary damages are awarded. Arguably, the deterrent function of exemplary damages can be promoted by requiring a defendant who is vicariously liable to pay them. Such a defendant may be in a position to influence the actual wrongdoer and might be incentivised to do so by way of awards (and the threat of awards) of exemplary damages. In short, Beever's critique of holding defendants vicariously liability to pay exemplary damages is incomplete because it engages with only one of the purported goals of awarding exemplary damages.

The second point is that the strength of Beever's objection to imposing vicarious liability to pay exemplary damages depends on how vicarious liability is understood. There are two ways of understanding vicarious liability. According to the servant's tort theory, the only tort is that of the servant, and the liability of the servant is simply duplicated on the master. On the master's tort theory, the acts of the servants are attributed to the master with the result that the master is a tortfeasor. The way in which one should feel about imposing vicarious liability to pay exemplary damages depends in part on which of these theories one accepts. If the master's tort theory is correct,[81] 'vicarious liability' is not truly vicarious. The master is a wrongdoer, and it follows that the puzzle presented by the interaction between vicarious liability and exemplary damages dissolves. Conversely, if the servant's tort theory is embraced, vicarious liability involves imposing liability on someone who is not a wrongdoer. If the

---

[78] Consider *Racz v Home Office* [1994] 2 AC 45 (HL).

[79] Law Commission (n 8) 159, para 1.212.   [80] Beever (n 8) 96.

[81] For argument in favour of the master's tort theory, see Robert Stevens, *Torts and Rights* (Oxford University Press 2007) ch 11; Ernest Weinrib, *The Idea of Private Law* (Harvard University Press 1995) 185–86.

servant's theory is correct, therefore, it becomes much more controversial to pin liability for exemplary damages on a person who is held vicariously liable.

14.5 What are Exemplary Damages?

According to the case law, exemplary damages are awarded in order to punish and deter. However, various important challenges have been made to this way of viewing exemplary damages. This section engages with two alternative ways in which theorists have suggested exemplary damages should be understood.

14.5.1 Restitutionary Damages

Ernest Weinrib argues that exemplary damages, or at least certain awards of exemplary damages are, properly understood, restitutionary damages. Weinrib develops this analysis in the course of promoting his corrective justice theory of private law. Corrective justice, Weinrib tells us, involves placing 'the defendant under the obligation to restore the plaintiff, so far as possible, to the position the plaintiff would have been in had the wrong not been committed'.[82] It follows that damages that are awarded to punish or deter do not effect corrective justice. This is rightly conceded by Weinrib.[83] Weinrib attempts to mitigate the problem from which his theory suffers in this regard by suggesting that, in at least some situations, exemplary damages are in reality restitutionary damages. He points out that, under the second category identified in *Rookes v Barnard*,[84] exemplary damages can be awarded where the defendant has sought to make a gain. In Weinrib's words: 'In Cassell & Co. v. Broome, [1972] App. Cas. 1027 (HL), Lord Diplock explained this second category in terms of unjust enrichment. This explanation would make this category, at least, consistent with corrective justice's treatment of illegitimate gains.'[85]

Fatal difficulties afflict the suggestion that exemplary damages awarded under the second category of the categories test are actually restitutionary damages. For one thing, exemplary damages may be awarded under the second category in *Rookes* even if the defendant has not in fact made any gain (a mere intention to make a gain can be sufficient to

---

[82] Weinrib (n 81) 135 (footnote omitted).   [83] Ibid 135 fn 25.   [84] Text to n 24.
[85] Weinrib (n 81) 135 fn 25. Lord Diplock wrote that the second category in *Rookes v Barnard* is 'analogous to the civil law concept of enrichessement indue': *Broome* (n 23) 1129.

bring a case within that category[86]). The test, as laid down by Lord Devlin in *Rookes*, is whether the defendant 'with a cynical disregard for a plaintiff's rights has calculated that the money to be made out of his wrongdoing will probably exceed the damages at risk'.[87] The crucial issue according to Lord Devlin's formula is the defendant's motivation, not the result.[88] Furthermore, even where a defendant has made a gain as a result of his wrong, the award of exemplary damages is calculated according to the need to punish and deter the defendant rather than the size of the gain made, which is what would be necessary in order for Weinrib's attempt to accommodate the second category in *Rookes v Barnard* within his theory to be viable. Andrew Burrows observes that this 'crucial additional point [shows] that damages under [the] second category are not concerned merely to reverse the defendant's unjust enrichment'.[89]

14.5.2 Substitutive Damages

Robert Stevens in a thought-provoking and engaging analysis argues that damages awarded in tort are substitutive of the right of the claimant that the defendant violated.[90] They are, in other words, awarded to vindicate the infringement of the claimant's right. Exemplary damages, as they are conventionally understood, are inconsistent with this thesis. Stevens is alive to the challenge that exemplary damages present. He acknowledges: 'it may be objected that exemplary damages are ... inconsistent with a rights-based model of the law. If the courts are concerned to punish the defendant for his wrongdoing, it can be argued that this goes beyond mere vindication of the claimant's rights.'[91] Stevens responds to this challenge by contending that exemplary damages are, along with compensatory damages, substitutive for the right that is infringed.[92] The idea is that '[t]he more outrageous the defendant's conduct, the greater the infringement of the right and the greater the substitutive award'.[93] Stevens then draws attention to aspects of the law on exemplary damages that are consistent with this way of understanding them. Good

---

[86] 'I do not think that the argument that the defendant could not make a profit here defeats the plaintiff's claim.': *Archer v Brown* [1985] QB 401 (QBD) 423 (Peter Pain J).
[87] See n 4 1227.
[88] For an illustration of a case in which the defendant had a profit motive but made no profit yet was nonetheless required to pay exemplary damages, see *Drane v Evangelou* [1978] 1 WLR 455 (CA).
[89] Andrew Burrows, *Remedies for Torts and Breach of Contract* (3rd edn, Oxford University Press 2004) 414.
[90] Stevens (n 81).   [91] Ibid 85.   [92] Ibid.   [93] Ibid.

illustrations (Stevens's not mine[94]) include the fact that exemplary damages are paid to the victim rather than to, for example, the state and the fact that the procedural and evidential protections conferred upon defendants that are found in criminal law proceedings are not given to tort defendants who are sued for exemplary damages. These rules are understandable if the focus in awarding exemplary damages is on the violation of the claimant's right.

However, as Stevens concedes[95] other rules governing the award of exemplary damages stand in the way of his interpretation of them. Several such rules are as follows, not all of which are acknowledged by Stevens:

(1) It is a well-established principle that the defendant's wealth is a material factor to consider in determining the quantum of exemplary damages.[96] This rule contradicts Stevens's explanation of exemplary damages. It shows that exemplary damages are not driven by a concern to vindicate the claimant's rights. The economic wealth of the defendant has nothing to do with the claimant's rights.

(2) The courts in awarding exemplary damages take account of the need to deter the defendant and others from engaging in the conduct in question.[97] This approach cannot be explained by a rights-based account of tort law. This is because it is aimed at incentivising the defendant and third-parties to act in particular ways rather than with ensuring that exemplary damages vindicate any right enjoyed by the claimant.

(3) The categories test is problematic for Stevens's account of exemplary damages. If, as he claims, exemplary damages are awarded to vindicate the claimant's rights, why are they available only in the three situations isolated by the categories test? Those are plainly not the only situations in which a claimant's rights might be egregiously infringed.

(4) It is well established that the courts must exercise significant restraint both in deciding to award exemplary damages and, if the decision is made to award them, in determining their quantum.[98] This constraint is inexplicable from a rights-based approach. If egregious violations of rights require a larger award of damages than would

---

[94] Ibid 86–87. [95] Ibid 87.

[96] See, e.g. *Rookes* (n 4) 1228; *John v MGN Ltd* [1997] QB 586 (CA) 625.

[97] See, e.g. *Broome* (n 23) 1073.

[98] *Rookes* (n 4) 1227; *Gray v Motor Accident Commission* (1998) 196 CLR 1, 9 [20].

be provided by compensatory damages in order to vindicate the right
concerned, the award of exemplary damages should not be confined
in this way.

(5) Stevens's explanation cannot account for the fact that where the
defendant has been punished by the criminal law (or by other
means) in respect of the conduct about which the claimant com-
plains, an award of exemplary damages might be reduced or precluded for that reason.[99] If the concern is with the vindication of the
claimant's rights, the fact that the defendant has already been punished ought to be irrelevant.

(6) Stevens's account cannot explain the rules that apply where there are
multiple claimants who are deserving of an award of exemplary
damages. The law here is that the court should allocate the exemplary
damages awarded equally between the claimants.[100] This is inconsistent with Stevens's rights-based explanation of exemplary damages.
It means that only by chance will the quantum of the exemplary
damages award reflect the gravity of the violation of any given right.

As has been observed, Stevens concedes that the evidence in favour of his
explanation of exemplary damages is not 'all one way'.[101] There are some
aspects of the law on exemplary damages that he can explain. However,
there is a great deal more that he cannot. The clash between the principles
that govern exemplary damages and the suggestion that exemplary
damages are, in reality, substitutive damages, is significant. The fact of
the matter is that unless the foregoing features of the law of exemplary
damages are disregarded, exemplary damages cannot be brought within
the scope of his rights theory. Allan Beever accurately summed up the
insurmountable obstacles that rights theorists face as a result of exemplary
damages well when he said that in awarding exemplary damages, 'a court
cannot be taken to be concerned with the rights of the claimant. The court
is expressing condemnation of the defendant, but condemnation of the
defendant does not imply vindication of the claimant.'[102]

14.5.3 Summary

This section has described two attempts to present exemplary damages as
being other than about punishment and deterrence. The first attempt

---

[99] *Walker v CFTO* (1987) 39 CCLT 121 (Ont CA); *AB* (n 3); *Gray* (n 98).
[100] *Riches v News Group Newspapers Ltd* [1986] 1 QB 256 (CA).   [101] Stevens (n 81) 87.
[102] Beever (n 8) 99.

addressed was Weinrib's analysis. It endeavours to show that exemplary damages, at least in some situations, are restitutionary damages. The other attempt is that made by Stevens. He contends that exemplary damages are really about vindicating the claimant's rights. Both accounts draw support from various features of the law. But, equally, they both suffer from significant obstacles. It has been argued that they do not do enough to displace the conventional understanding of exemplary damages.

14.6   The Future

In 1986 in *Riches v News Group Newspapers* Stephenson LJ lamented the state of the law governing exemplary damages. His Lordship wrote that this corner of the law 'cries aloud . . . for Parliamentary intervention'.[103] This is just one of a multitude of similar remarks that were made in the wake of *Rookes* and *Broome*.[104] A raft of important proposals for change were advanced by the Law Commission in 1997. The Law Commission properly recommended that the cause of action and categories tests be abolished. It also recommended that exemplary damages be assessed only by judges rather than by juries. However, these proposals were not acted upon. The government stated in the House of Commons that due to a lack of a clear consensus as to how the law should be changed, it had opted not to implement the Law Commission's proposals.[105] The Law Commission's report gathered dust. Judicial reform was effected by the House of Lords in *Kuddus* in 2001, which saw the abolition of the cause of action test. In order to save money, the legislature progressively restricted the use of civil juries generally to the point where civil juries are now effectively a thing of the past.[106] This restriction yielded indirectly the change in the law concerning juries that the Law Commission sought.

As is apparent from the foregoing, some of the central difficulties that the Law Commission perceived in the law on exemplary damages have

---

[103] See n 100 269.   [104] See, e.g. *Kuddus* (n 6) [61].

[105] HC Deb 9 November 1999, vol 337 col 502 (Written Answers to Questions). Mr Lock, Parliamentary Secretary, Lord Chancellor's Department, wrote: 'In the absence of a clear consensus on the issue the Government have decided not to take forward the Law Commission's proposals for legislation on exemplary damages. It may be that some further judicial development of the law in this area might help clarify the issues.'

[106] See, e.g. Senior Courts Act 1981, s 69 (as amended by, *inter alia*, the Defamation Act 2013, s 11).

been removed. But much more needs to be done by way of reform. This chapter has identified several areas of the law where change is required. Most obviously, the categories test remains. That test is a glaring defect in the law. It should be jettisoned. The apportionment legislation should be amended to clarify that the apportionment regime does not extend to exemplary damages. Perhaps the most far-reaching reform canvassed in this article concerns the bar on awarding exemplary damages in response to a breach of contract. That bar owes its existence to a decision – *Addis* – that arguably says next to nothing about exemplary damages. Arguments that have been offered in support of the bar are, on the whole, so weak that it is surprising that they are taken seriously. The bar's existence should be re-examined by the Law Commission.

This chapter discussed important theoretical attempts that have been made to come to grips with the essential nature of exemplary damages. It was noted that the scholars in question – Ernest Weinrib and Robert Stevens – have suggested that exemplary damages are not, despite what the courts tell us, about punishment or deterrence. It is worth emphasising that these theorists have made these claims in the course of developing theories of private law generally (or at least of significant parts of it). It seems, therefore, that the law of exemplary damages is emerging as a major battleground in terms of how private law should be understood. Exemplary damages, despite raising intractable problems and supposedly being of minimal practical relevance, may paradoxically hold the answer to how private law generally should be comprehended.

PART IV

Agreed and Party-Specific Remedies

15

Express Termination Clauses

RICHARD HOOLEY

15.1 Introduction

An express termination clause (an 'ETC') is an express term of a contract which gives either or both of the parties the right to terminate the contract.[1] ETCs are found in many long-term commercial contracts.[2] It is the aim of this chapter to increase the level of confidence that commercial parties may have when relying on an ETC by resolving a number of legal uncertainties associated with their use.

Commercial parties will be reluctant to rely on an ETC if uncertainty surrounds its application. This may be because the events which 'trigger' the clause are not precisely defined, or because the procedure to be followed when relying on the clause leaves room for doubt, as where the clause requires one party to give the other the opportunity to remedy a breach before termination and there is uncertainty as to whether the breach can be, or has been, remedied. There is also potential uncertainty as to whether one party's reliance on an ETC prevents that party from relying on any right to terminate that it may have under the common law. Concern that mistaken reliance on an ETC may lead to potential liability in damages to the other party is often matched by concern that mistaken reliance on an ETC will cause reputational damage within the market in which the parties operate.[3]

---

[1] There may also be provision for automatic termination on the happening of a specified event beyond the control of the parties.

[2] Following the book's theme of 'commercial remedies', this chapter will concentrate on commercial, as opposed to consumer, contracts.

[3] In *Woodar Investment Development Ltd v Wimpey Construction UK Ltd* [1980] 1 WLR 277, the House of Lords held that a bona fide but mistaken reliance on a contractual term to terminate a contract did not manifest an intention to abandon the contract, and so was not repudiatory. But this (relatively rare) situation, which might apply where there is an

The application of an ETC by one party can lead to what may appear to be a 'harsh' outcome for the other. For example, depending on the wording of the clause, a relatively minor breach by one party might give the other a right of termination that it would not otherwise have under the common law.[4] Some ETCs even allow one party to terminate the contract at its own convenience without having to establish breach by the other party or any other cause. Should the courts be able to interfere, and risk increased uncertainty of outcome, through the implication of a good faith requirement in such cases?

15.2   Functions of an ETC

There are a number of reasons why the parties may wish to include an ETC in their contract. First, the principal function is to increase certainty of outcome. It may not be clear whether a right to terminate has arisen under the common law. Has one party renounced its obligations under the contract? Has breach by one party deprived the other of substantially the whole benefit of performance or, as is commonly said, 'gone to the root of the contract'? Getting the answers to these questions wrong can be catastrophic.[5] An error can lead the supposedly innocent party to commit a repudiatory breach, thereby giving the other party the right to terminate and a claim in damages. These questions can be avoided by an ETC. Secondly, the parties are given greater scope for termination than would arise under the common law. An ETC can apply where there has not been a breach of contract, or even a failure to perform, and also where there has been a breach that does give a right to terminate at common law, e.g. where the breach is not repudiatory. Thirdly, the fact that one party has the right to terminate for breach under an ETC may encourage the other party to perform.[6]

---

anticipatory breach, must be distinguished from those cases where there is an actual breach of contract that constitutes a repudiation: see *Mercuria Energy Trading Pte Ltd v Citibank NA* [2015] EWHC 1481 (Comm) [146], applying *Dalkia Utilities Services plc v Celtech International Ltd* [2006] EWHC 63 (Comm), [2006] 1 Lloyd's Rep 599 [149]–[150].

[4] See, e.g. *Mardorf Peach & Co Ltd v Attica Sea Carriers Corp of Liberia (The Laconia)* [1977] AC 850 (HL).

[5] John E Stannard and David Capper, *Termination for Breach of Contract* (Oxford University Press 2014) para 8.01.

[6] Hugh Beale, 'Penalties in Termination Provisions' (1988) 104 LQR 355, 359; JW Carter, 'Termination clauses' (1990) 3 Jcl 90, 93–94.

15.3 Types of ETCs

The basic distinction is between those ETCs triggered by an event which constitutes a breach of contract, and those triggered by an event that does not constitute a breach.[7] The second category includes ETCs for convenience which give one (or even both) of the parties the right to terminate the contract at their own convenience (at their will) and without having to show cause. Such clauses are found mainly in building and engineering contracts.[8] They go well beyond what would be allowed under the common law, which does not usually permit termination in the absence of breach.[9] Does a party with a right to terminate for convenience, effectively with complete discretion whether or not to perform, provide consideration for the other party's promise to perform?[10] But, as Carter observes, 'termination for convenience clauses do not work in that way': an ETC for convenience usually requires the party relying upon it to pay a fee for termination or to make a payment for partially completed performance by the other party.[11] On the other hand, a clause giving one party the unilateral right to choose to perform or not to perform at will, with no express or implied limitation on its exercise, would constitute 'illusory' consideration.

15.4 Construction of an ETC

Proper construction of the ETC will be vital for a number of reasons. First, it will be necessary to construe the clause in order to ascertain whether the right to terminate has accrued or been 'triggered' in the first place. Secondly, the clause may (and very often does) contain an express time period for, and/or procedures that must be followed on, termination. These must be construed and complied with. Thirdly, the clause may contain express provisions dealing with the consequences of termination under the clause, e.g. payment of financial compensation by one party to the other, which require construction.

---

[7] Remembering that some 'hybrid' clauses contain both breach and non-breach triggers.

[8] In the US they are also found in government procurement contracts.

[9] Without breach, discharge by termination must be based on the doctrine of frustration, occurrence of a condition subsequent or agreement of the parties.

[10] Edwin Peel, *Treitel's Law of Contract* (14th edn, Sweet & Maxwell 2015) (hereafter '*Treitel*') para 3–030: 'illusory consideration'. There may also be a question over contractual intention: *Treitel* para 4–020.

[11] JW Carter, 'Partial Termination of Contracts' (2008) 24 Jcl 1, 23–24.

An ETC should be construed in the same way as any other term of the contract. The principles set out by Lord Hoffmann in *Investors Compensation Scheme Ltd v West Bromwich Building Society* apply.[12] They require an objective construction of the clause in the light of the background facts reasonably available to the parties at the time they contract. In the context of a commercial contract, this does not mean that the express words used by the parties should be ignored because of reliance on some broad (and amorphous) principle of commercial common sense.[13] When clear words are used by the parties they are the best evidence of their intention, and a court should not search for ambiguities in order to depart from the natural meaning of those words.[14]

15.5 Triggering Event

Yet it seems that the courts continue to take a strict approach when construing the words of an ETC. *Rice (t/a Garden Guardian) v Great Yarmouth BC* is a prime example.[15] A local authority purported to terminate a four-year service contract under an ETC, which stated that:

> If the contractor ... commits a breach of any of its obligations under the Contract; ... the Council may, without prejudice to any accrued rights or remedies under the Contract, terminate the Contractor's employment under the Contract by notice in writing having immediate effect.[16]

The Court of Appeal concluded that the notion that the clause entitled the council to terminate this contract for any breach, however minor, of any term flew in the face of commercial common sense.[17] It was held that the clause only gave the Council the right to terminate if the breach was

---

[12] [1998] 1 WLR 896 (HL) 912–13.
[13] *Arnold v Britton* [2015] UKSC 36, [2015] 2 WLR 1593 [17] (Lord Neuberger: 'save perhaps in a very unusual case').
[14] Ibid [18]. Even Lord clarke's statement in *Rainy Sky SA v Kookmin Bank* [2011] UKSC 50, [2011] 1 WLR 2900 [21] that '[i]f there are two possible constructions, the court is entitled to prefer the construction which is consistent with business common sense and reject the other', assumes that the commercially more sensible meaning can be ascertained by the court (*BMA Special Opportunity Hub Fund Ltd v African Minerals Finance Ltd* [2013] EWCA Civ 416 [24]; *Cottonex Anstalt v Patriot Spinning Mills Ltd* [2014] EWHC 236 (Comm), [2014] 1 Lloyd's Rep 615 [52]–[58]).
[15] [2003] TclR 1 (CA); applied in *Dominion Corporate Trustees Ltd v Debenhams Properties Ltd* [2010] EWHC 1193 (Ch).
[16] *Rice* (n 15) [15].
[17] Ibid [24], applying *Antaios Compania SA v Salen Rederierna AB (The Antaios)* [1985] AC 191 (HL) 201 (Lord Diplock).

a repudiatory breach and that the trial judge had been entitled to conclude that the breach in question had not been repudiatory.[18]

The decision has been subjected to severe criticism.[19] Two objections stand out.[20] First, if the Council had the right to terminate under the general law on the occurrence of a repudiatory breach, what was the point of inserting a clause into the contract if its only effect was to replicate a right that already existed under the common law? Secondly, the Court of Appeal did not give sufficient weight to the word 'any' in the clause. The Court of Appeal said that such a construction, which allowed a long-term contract to be terminated for any breach of any term, flew in the face of commercial common sense. But this seems to be an unnecessary and, with respect, an illegitimate invocation of 'commercial common sense' to override the ordinary meaning of the words in the contract.[21] There seems little doubt that the Court of Appeal 'read down' the scope of the termination clause in order to control its operation.[22]

The draftsman is left to work around *Rice*. This may be possible if the contract is clear as to the particular term(s) that must be breached for the right of termination to arise. In *BNP Paribas v Wockhardt EU Operations (Swiss) AG*,[23] Christopher Clarke J held that the draftsman of an ISDA Master Agreement had achieved this by providing that any non-payment or non-delivery had that consequence. Alternatively, the draftsman may be tempted to refer to a 'material' breach?[24] But this hardly increases the level of certainty when the courts have said that what is material 'must depend on all the facts of the particular case'[25] and that 'it is relevant to consider not only of what the breach consists but also the circumstances

---

[18] *Rice* (n 15) [39].

[19] Simon Whittaker, 'Termination clauses' in Andrew Burrows and Edwin Peel (eds), *Contract Terms* (Oxford University Press 2007) 277–83; Michael Bridge, 'Freedom to Exercise Contractual Rights of Termination' in Louise Gullifer and Stefan Vogenauer (eds), *English and European Perspectives on Contract and Commercial Law: Essays in Honour of Hugh Beale* (Hart Publishing 2014) 87, 98–100.

[20] See Ewan McKendrick, *Contract Law: Text Cases and Materials* (7th edn, Oxford University Press 2016), 786–7.

[21] See *Arnold* (n 13).

[22] Whittaker (n 19) 258, 283. See also *Fu Yuan Foodstuff Manufacturer Pte Ltd v Methodist Welfare Services* [2009] 3 SLR(R) 925 (Sing CA) [36].

[23] [2009] EWHC 3116 (Comm) [42].

[24] See generally Neil Andrews, Malcolm clarke, Andrew Tettenborn and Graham Virgo, *Contractual Duties: Performance, Breach, Termination and Remedies* (Sweet & Maxwell 2012) paras 9-018–9-028.

[25] *Glolite Ltd v Jasper Conran Ltd, The Times*, 28 January 1998 (Ch) (Neuberger J), cited in Andrews (n 24) para 9-024.

in which the breach arises, including any explanation given or apparent as to why it has occurred'.[26] The Court of Appeal's more recent guidance, that a material breach is 'more than trivial but need not be repudiatory', does not do much to narrow the search for this elusive concept.[27] Unfortunately, the uncertainty created by *Rice* continues.[28]

15.6   Procedures for Termination

The party seeking to terminate must act strictly in accordance with the term of the contract.[29] What is required of that party will be a matter of construction of the ETC, and in some cases a construction that takes account of context might enable the court to avoid the consequences of literal non-compliance.[30]

It is common for an ETC to require termination to be exercised by notice. In fact, the ETC may go further and require the promisee to give the promisor an opportunity to remedy the breach before termination can take place.[31] Should the promisor remedy the breach, there is no ground for termination. This raises several questions: When is a breach remediable? Does the promisee have to give the promisor notice to remedy when the breach is not remediable, or can it simply go straight to termination?

Most breaches are remediable, at least where they can be remedied within any express time period in the contract or, where no period is expressed, within a reasonable time. But not all can be remedied. For example, in *Force India Formula One Team Ltd v Etihad Airways*

---

[26] *Dalkia* (n 3) [102] (Christopher clarke J).

[27] *Mid Essex Hospital Services NHS Trust v Compass Group UK and Ireland Ltd (t/a me direst)* [2013] EWCA Civ 200 [126]. Similarly, a court would have to search for the meaning of a 'substantial' breach.

[28] See also Bridge (n 19) 98–100.

[29] *Treitel* (n 10) para 18–064. See, e.g. *The Mihalis Angelos* [1971] 1 QB 164 (CA). Note also the general requirement, applicable to notices of all kinds, that the other party be 'notified in clear and unambiguous terms that the right to bring the contract to an end is being exercised, and how and when it is intended to operate': *Geys v Société Générale* [2012] UKSC 63, [2013] 1 AC 523 [52] (Baroness Hale).

[30] *Ellis Tylin Ltd v Co-operative Retail Services Ltd* [1999] BLR 205. See also Carter, 'Termination clauses' (n 6) 101.

[31] Unless provided for in the terms of the contract, there is no general common law rule that gives a breaching party the opportunity to remedy or cure a breach: see, e.g. *Bournemouth University Higher Education Corp v Buckland* [2010] EWCA Civ 121, [2011] QB 323 [52]–[53]. There are 'exceptions' to this principle: see Solène Rowan, *Remedies for Breach of Contract: A Comparative Analysis of the Protection of Performance* (Oxford University Press 2012) 79, n 59.

PJSC,[32] a question arose whether breaches were remediable for the purposes of an ETC which allowed for termination on 'any material breach of this Agreement which, if capable of remedy, has not been remedied within ten business days of receipt of written notice'. Rix LJ, delivering the judgment of the Court of Appeal, agreed that the authorities favoured a practical rather than an unduly technical test when deciding whether or not a breach was remediable.[33] He held that the breaches – the new owner of a Formula 1 racing team changing the team's name and livery – could not be remedied. These changes could have been reversed to some extent, i.e. going back to old name and reverting back to original livery, but, looking at the matter pragmatically and not technically, as the team had been 'persistently marketed' under the new name and livery 'the marketing genie cannot be put back in the bottle', and so the beach was held to be irremediable.[34] Rix LJ regarded the situation as analogous to that identified by Lord Reid in L Schuler AG v Wickman Machine Tool Sales Ltd,[35] who said that breach of a confidentiality clause through disclosure of confidential information could not be remedied by a promise not to do it again.

Following the Supreme Court's decision in Wickland (Holdings) Ltd v Telchadder,[36] where a statute provided the contract breaker with a right to remedy his breach, we might now say that the 'mischief' resulting from the breach in the Force India case could not be redressed.[37] In Telchadder, the licensee of a mobile home site breached the terms of a covenant against anti-social behaviour. The site owner's contractual right to terminate the licence was subject to the Mobile Homes Act 1983, which allowed termination only where the licensee had not complied with 'a notice to remedy the breach'.[38] The Supreme Court unanimously held that the breach could be remedied, despite the fact that the anti-social behaviour had already taken place and could not be undone. Lord Wilson took a practical, rather than technical, approach to the issue[39] and said:

---

[32] [2010] EWCA Civ 1051.   [33] Ibid [108].   [34] Ibid.   [35] [1974] AC 235 (HL).

[36] [2014] UKSC 57, [2014] 1 WLR 4004.

[37] Telchadder involved the interpretation of a statute, and the language of 'mischief' might seem more appropriate in that context. However, it is submitted that the same principle captures the nature of the test that should be applied when deciding whether a breach of contract is remediable.

[38] Mobile Homes Act 1983, Sch 1, Pt 1, para 4(a). Unlike s 3(g) of the Mobile Homes Act 1975, the 1983 Act did not expressly state that the breach had to be 'capable of being remedied'.

[39] See also Akici v LR Butlin Ltd [2005] EWCA Civ 1296 [64] (Neuberger LJ).

> In my view the answer is to be found by a practical inquiry whether and if
> so how (to adapt the words of Staughton LJ in the *Savva* case[40]) the
> mischief resulting from Mr Telchadder's breach could be redressed.[41]

He held that it could be redressed 'by [Mr Telchadder] committing no
further breach of his covenant against anti-social behaviour for a reasonable
time'.[42]

The answer to the second question – does the promisee have to give the
promisor notice to remedy when the breach is not remediable? – turns on
construction of the ETC. In *Telchadder*, Lord Wilson, who was part of the
majority on this issue, said (obiter) that '[i]t would be nonsensical to require
service of a notice to remedy a breach which is incapable of remedy'.[43] He
drew on *L Schuler AG v Wickman Machine Tool Sales Ltd*,[44] where a clause,
which entitled either party to determine the contract on the other's material
breach if the other 'shall have failed to remedy the same within 60 days of
being required in writing so to do', was construed by Lord Reid as 'intended
to apply to all material breaches of the agreement which are capable of being
remedied'.[45] The point turns on construction of the contract term,[46] but
avoiding a nonsensical meaning is an established principle of construction
and so it would seem likely that a court would restrict a requirement to serve
a notice to remedy a breach to breaches that are capable of remedy.
The situation will be clearer where, as in *Force India*,[47] the ETC makes
express reference to the breach being 'capable of remedy'.[48]

15.7 Consequences of Termination

The ETC may make express provision for what is to happen on termination.
But first we shall consider the position where no such provision is made.

15.7.1 Unliquidated Damages

It is trite law that termination for a repudiatory breach releases the parties
from primary obligations which have not yet fallen due at the time of

---

[40] *Savva v Hussein* (1997) 73 P & CR 150 (CA) 154.   [41] *Telchadder* (n 37) [31].

[42] Ibid [32].   [43] Ibid [20]. Baroness Hale ([44]) and Lord Toulson ([62]) agreed.

[44] *Schuler* (n 35).   [45] Ibid 249.

[46] See JW Carter, *Carter's Breach of Contract* (Hart Publishing 2012) para 10–13.

[47] *Force India* (n 32). See also *Vinergy International (PVT) Ltd v Richmond Mercantile Ltd FZC* [2016] EWHC 525 (Comm) [35].

[48] In *Telchadder* (n 36), the relevant statute, perhaps due to the Parliamentary draftsman's oversight, did not (see [22], and n 38). By contrast, the position will be otherwise where the contract expressly sets out a procedure for dealing with breaches that are incapable of being remedied: see *Dalkia* (n 3) [15].

termination, and the breaching party is placed under a secondary obligation to pay damages.[49] The same principle applies when termination takes place under an ETC. However, there is a distinction to be made between the position under the general law and that under an ETC with regard to the recovery of damages. The position is summarised in *Treitel* as follows:

> Where the injured party terminates under the general law, he can recover damages in respect of any loss suffered by reason of the premature determination of the contract, i.e. for 'loss of bargain', but he has (unless the contract otherwise provides) no such right where he terminates for a non-repudiatory breach under an express contractual provision entitling him to do so.[50]

This has been referred to as the 'bifurcated' principle.[51]

The locus classicus is *Financings Ltd v Baldock*,[52] where a contract for the hire-purchase of a lorry gave the owners an express contractual right to terminate if any instalment was over ten days late. The hirer defaulted on the first two instalments. The owners exercised their contractual right to terminate and recovered the lorry. The Court of Appeal restricted the owners to recovery of the unpaid instalments outstanding at the date of termination. There was no award of loss of bargain damages because the non-payment did not amount to repudiation of the contract.

Three reasons were given for this decision. First, the hirer's future obligations were said to have been discharged by termination, which meant there was no breach thereafter for which damages could be claimed.[53] Secondly, the loss was said to have been caused not by the breach, but by the owner's decision to terminate.[54] Thirdly, it was said that an ETC should not necessarily be construed as giving the innocent party anything more than a right to terminate.[55]

This reasoning is flawed. First, as we have just seen, the outstanding obligations of the party in default may be discharged by termination, but they are replaced by a secondary obligation to pay damages for resultant loss. Secondly, Carter has rightly said that, in the commercial context, the

---

[49] The concepts of primary and secondary obligations come from Lord Diplock: see, e.g. *Moschi v Lep Air Services Ltd* [1973] AC 331 (HL) 354–55; *Photo Production Ltd v Securicor Transport Ltd* [1980] AC 827 (HL) 848–49. Some rights and obligations may survive termination, either by implication or express provision, e.g. an arbitration clause.

[50] *Treitel* (n 10) para 18–070.

[51] Brian R Opeskin, 'Damages for Breach of Contract Terminated under Express Terms' (1990) 106 LQR 293.

[52] [1963] 2 QB 104 (CA). There is an excellent summary and analysis of the decision in Stannard and Capper (n 5) paras 10.11–10.15.

[53] *Baldock* (n 52) 110 (Lord Denning MR).   [54] Ibid 111–12 (Lord Denning MR).

[55] Ibid 120–21 (Diplock LJ).

causation argument 'seems naïve'.[56] Carter notes that '[a] common law right to terminate in the commercial contract often arises for reasons of commercial convenience', and adds that '[i]t is somewhat artificial to draw a contrast between what the common law permits by reference to commercial convenience and what the parties agree for reasons of commercial convenience'.[57] Thirdly, as Tettenborn and Wilby point out, the party terminating for breach is entitled to be compensated for that breach, and if the result of that breach has been to cause a loss of bargain then it should not matter whether the innocent party terminates for repudiatory breach or under an express power.[58]

Treitel tries to justify the decision on policy grounds arguing that 'it alleviates the sometimes harsh operation of express provisions which allow a party to terminate even for a minor breach'.[59] Nevertheless, *Baldock* is a product of its time. In the early 1960s, the courts were still coming to terms with hire-purchase and other forms of consumer finance, and there was undoubtedly a desire to protect consumers from what might be seen to be 'oppressive' behaviour by a finance company.[60] The Consumer Credit Act 1974 was some way off.

---

[56] Carter (n 49) para 13–07. See also *Stocznia Gdynia SA v Gearbulk Holdings Ltd* [2009] EWCA Civ 75, [2009] 3 WLR 677 [36]. See further, Opeskin (n 55) 315–20.

[57] Carter (n 46) para 13–07.

[58] Andrew Tettenborn and David Wilby (eds), *The Law of Damages* (2nd edn, LexisNexis 2010) para 19.31; and see generally, Opeskin (n 51). Cf Edwin Peel, 'The Termination Paradox' [2013] LMCLQ 519, 523–24, who stresses the forward-looking aspect of a repudiatory breach (which is lacking with a non-repudiatory breach) and argues that only a repudiatory breach *prior* to termination allows the claimant to terminate and say there has been a loss of bargain (the opportunity for a repudiatory breach being lost after termination). But there are three responses: (i) termination under an ETC, whether or not constituting a repudiatory breach, has the effect of denying the innocent party access to the future bargain (and so why should that party be denied damages which reflect that loss?); (ii) denying loss of bargain damages could put the innocent party in an uncertain position when it has to decide whether to terminate under an ETC in an adverse market or continue to deal with a difficult counterparty and wait until a repudiatory breach takes place (see Flaux J in *The MV Astra* [2013] EWHC 865 (Comm), [2013] 2 Lloyd's Rep 69 [115]; but contrast Popplewell J in *Spar Shipping SA v Grand China Logistics Holding (Group) Co Ltd* [2015] EWHC 718 (Comm), [2015] 2 Lloyd's Rep 407 [205], noted with approval by E Peel (2016) 132 LQR 177, and upheld on appeal [2016] EWCA Civ 982, [2016] 2 Lloyd's Rep 447 [64]–[65], [93]–[94], [97]–[100]); and (iii) the fact that loss of bargain damages are recoverable where there is breach of a term that the parties have expressly classified as a condition makes the distinction artificial.

[59] *Treitel* (n 10) para 18–070.

[60] In *Baldock* (n 52) 117–18, Diplock LJ noted that hire-purchase was designed by finance companies to avoid the statutory requirements relating to money-lending and to bills of sale.

The utility of *Baldock* must also be questioned. It is easily circumvented by the parties expressly agreeing in the contract to make the term that is later breached a 'condition' of the contract, or by expressly making time of performance 'of the essence', so that it becomes a condition of the contract. In such cases, breach of the condition will be considered to be a 'repudiatory breach', thereby giving the innocent party the right to claim damages for loss of bargain.[61] The fact that the courts allow a breach of condition to be treated as the equivalent of a substantial failure to perform, means that the innocent party can terminate and claim loss of bargain damages for even a minor breach, thereby removing the justification for *Baldock*.

There are two issues in play here. First, the question whether the parties should be able expressly to designate a term a condition and, in doing so, circumvent the bifurcated principle. It is submitted that the principle of party autonomy allows the parties to contract on the basis that a term should be a condition if this reflects their intention as objectively assessed.[62] The second, arguably more important, question is whether the parties should have to engage in express classification of a term as a condition in order to avoid the effect of *Baldock*. It is submitted that they should not. The ETC itself allows for termination for breach and if, as a result of that breach, the innocent party has been caused loss, including loss of bargain, it should be able to recover damages for that loss. Nevertheless, the bifurcated principle continues to be part of the English law of contract.[63]

---

[61] *Lombard North Central plc v Butterworth* [1987] QB 527 (CA) (albeit reaching that decision reluctantly: see 540 and 546).

[62] Other terms of the contract may show that the parties did not intend breach of the term to have the same consequences as breach of a condition, however, they described the term: see *Schuler* (n 35). See generally, A Burrows, *A Restatement of the English Law of Contract* (Oxford University Press 2016) 114, cited with approval by Gross LJ on appeal in *Spar Shipping* (n 58) [20].

[63] See, e.g. *Spar Shipping SA v Grand China Logistics Holding (Group) Co Ltd* (n 58) [97–104], [190], upheld on appeal (n 58); *C&S Associates UK Ltd v Enterprise Insurance Co plc* [2015] EWHC 3757 (Comm) [103]. It has been rejected in Canada: *Keneric Tractor Sales Ltd v Langille* [1987] 2 SCR 440, 454. But not in Australia and New Zealand: *Shevill v Builders Licensing Board* [1982] HCA 47, (1982) 149 CLR 620, 627; *Progressive Mailing House Pty Ltd v Tabali Pty Ltd* [1985] HCA 14, (1985) 157 CLR 17, 31; *Wallace-Smith v Thiess Infraco (Swanston) Pty Ltd* [2005] FCAFC 49, (2005) 218 ALR 1; *Morris v Robert Jones Investments Ltd* [1994] 2 NZLR 275 (CA). See generally, John Randall, 'Express Termination Clauses in Contracts' [2014] CLJ 113, 129–38, who favours the Canadian approach (which has 'the great merits of realism and clarity': 137).

15.7.2   Liquidated Damages

The ETC may expressly provide for the consequences of termination and allow for recovery of liquidated damages. This will be a matter of construction of the ETC in question. However, there is a risk that a court may consider such a provision to be an unenforceable penalty.[64]

In *Lombard North Central plc v Butterworth*,[65] where a computer was supplied under a contract of hire, the contract contained a clause (clause 6(a)) by which, following repossession of the goods, the hirer was to pay: (i) all arrears of rentals; (ii) all further rentals which would have fallen due less discount for accelerated payment; and (iii) damages for breach, including expenses and costs incurred by the owners in taking possession. The Court of Appeal agreed that the clause would have been penal in so far as it allowed the owners to claim a sum equivalent to full loss of bargain damages, even in cases of termination under an express right, contrary to the principle in *Financing Ltd v Baldock*.[66]

In fact, the Court of Appeal held that clause 6(a) was not penal because clause 2(a) made time of payment of rental instalments of the essence. The hirer was held to have breached a condition of the contract allowing recovery of full loss of bargain damages, which would have been a much larger sum than the amount of the one instalment which had not been paid. As Peel rightly observes, the enforceability of clause 6 was very much dependent on the inclusion of clause 2.[67] This point is of great commercial significance because it enables the parties to insulate a liquidated damages clause from the adverse application of the penalty clause jurisdiction.[68] Nevertheless, it would be unnecessary if English law were to be liberated from *Baldock*.

15.8   Distinguishing Termination under an ETC and under the Common Law

The interplay between contractual rights of termination and rights of termination arising under the common law has recently been described

---

[64] For the law on penalties generally, see Sarah Worthington's ch 16.   [65] *Lombard* (n 61).

[66] Ibid 542–43 (Nicholls LJ). Whether a clause is penal must now be assessed in the light of the decision of the Supreme Court in *Cavendish Square Holding BV v Makdessi* [2015] UKSC 67, [2016] AC 1172.

[67] Edwin Peel, 'The Common Law Tradition: Application of Boilerplate clauses under English Law' in Giuditta Cordero-Moss (ed), *Boilerplate clauses, International Commercial Contracts and the Applicable Law* (Cambridge University Press 2011) 129.

[68] See, e.g. *BNP Paribas v Wockhardt EU Operations (Swiss) AG* (n 23), where the close-out provisions in the ISDA Master Agreement were challenged as a penalty.

as 'an area which is not free from difficulty'.[69] In order to understand that interplay, we shall (a) examine the extent to which an ETC may constitute an exhaustive statement (or 'complete code') of the innocent party's rights against the party in breach, and (b) how far the way the innocent party exercises its rights reduces the range of remedies available.

15.8.1   A 'Complete Code'?

The English courts have been reluctant to hold that express contractual rights of termination were intended to exclude common law rights even where this was suggested by the contract.[70] It is a matter of construction.[71] If the parties intend to exclude the common law regime, they should do so in clear and unambiguous terms.[72]

In *Dalkia Utilities Services plc v Celtech International Ltd*, the contract for the construction of a power plant contained detailed terms allowing termination for material breach, including:

> The consequences of termination set out in this clause represent the full extent of the parties' respective rights and remedies arising out of any termination save for those rights remedies and liabilities which arise prior to termination.[73]

It was held that the clause did not provide a 'complete code' as to the rights and remedies enjoyed by the parties in the event of termination,

---

[69] *Newland Shipping and Forwarding Ltd v Toba Trading FZC* [2014] EWHC 661 (Comm) [48] (Leggatt J).

[70] See Stannard and Capper (n 5) para 8.19. But criticised by JW Carter and Yihan Goh in their article 'Concurrent and Independent Rights to Terminate for Breach of Contract' (2010) 26 Jcl 103, 132, on the ground that the parties do not go to all the trouble of setting out a contractual regime for termination with the intention of still leaving the common law regime in place. On the other hand, it is just as likely that the parties merely intend to increase the options available rather than limit them (and commercial parties often include an express 'savings provision' in their contracts to make this clear).

[71] See e.g. *Lockland Builders Ltd v Rickwood* (1995) 46 Con LR 92 (CA).

[72] *Gearbulk* (n 56) [23]. Even where there are two possible meanings the intention of the parties may still be clear after the court has applied 'all its tools of linguistic, contextual, purposive and common sense analysis to discern what the clause really means': *Scottish Power UK plc v BP Exploration Operating Co Ltd* [2016] EWCA Civ 1043 [29], Christopher clarke LJ citing the words of Briggs LJ in *Nobahar-Cookson v The Hut Group Ltd* [2016] EWCA Civ 128 [19]. An express reference in the ETC that the contractual right to terminate is 'without prejudice to other rights and remedies' is probably enough: HG Beale (gen ed), *Chitty on Contracts* (32nd edn, Sweet & Maxwell 2015) vol 1, para 22–049, fn 217.

[73] *Dalkia* (n 3) [19].

because it only related to the express rights mentioned in the clause.[74] The clause did not exclude the right of the parties to terminate for repudiation.[75] There is a presumption against the abandonment of common law remedies for breach and clear express words are needed to rebut it.[76]

15.8.2   Exercise of the Right

Where the innocent party has concurrent rights to terminate under an ETC or under the common law, does the exercise of one right rule out the other? The issues can be of immense practical importance where the innocent party is later held not to have complied with some procedural requirement under the ETC. Can the innocent party now claim that termination was, after all, under the common law? In many cases the innocent party will serve notice of termination, but not make it clear whether it is doing so under an ETC or under the common law. Does this prevent that party from relying on one or other or even both grounds?

In some (older) cases the courts have held that termination for breach in reliance on an ETC prevents the innocent party from accepting that breach as repudiatory under the common law. The exercise of the contractual right is deemed to be some form of affirmation of the contract. For example, in *United Dominions Trust (Commercial) Ltd v Ennis*,[77] the hirer under a hire-purchase agreement was entitled to terminate on payment of an agreed sum. The finance company sued the hirer for the agreed sum. The finance company then (in the alternative) claimed loss of bargain damages. The Court of Appeal held that the clause giving the claim for the agreed sum was a penalty.[78] However, the Court of Appeal also held that the hirer's repudiation had not been accepted by the finance company, which had elected to affirm the contract by suing for the agreed sum.[79]

This leads to an oddly paradoxical position.[80] The exercise of the right to contractual termination is said to prevent termination for repudiatory

---

[74] Ibid [21].   [75] Ibid.
[76] Ibid, citing *Gilbert-Ash (Northern) Ltd v Modern Engineering (Bristol) Ltd* [1974] AC 689 (HL) 717 (Lord Diplock). See also *Gearbulk* (n 56) [23]: 'The more valuable the right, the clearer the language will need to be.' But 'the strength of the presumption is reduced in proportion to the degree of derogation from the common law position': *Scottish Power* (n 72) [30] (Christopher Clarke LJ), where the presumption was held to have been rebutted.
[77] [1968] 1 QB 54 (CA).   [78] Ibid 65–66 (Lord Denning MR).
[79] Ibid (Lord Denning MR); 68 (Harman LJ).
[80] *Newland* (n 69) [52] (Leggatt J). See also Edwin Peel, 'Affirmation by Termination' (2009) 125 LQR 378, and 'The Termination Paradox' (n 62).

breach at common law because reliance on the terms of the contract is deemed to be affirmation of the contact; and yet the very act that constitutes affirmation – reliance on the contractual right of termination – actually brings about termination of the contract! This cannot be right.[81]

The law has moved on. It is now recognised that there is in general no inconsistency between terminating a contract pursuant to an ETC and doing so under the common law where there has been a repudiatory breach.[82] In *Stocznia Gdynia SA v Gearbulk Holdings Ltd*,[83] shipbuilders entered into three (materially identical) contracts with the same buyers, each for the construction of a ship. Each contract was subject to a clause allowing termination if the ship was not completed within 150 days after the delivery date, and provided for a 'refund guarantee' under which the builders agreed to refund all previous instalments of the purchase price. When the builders failed to complete the ships, the buyers issued notices of termination and duly received payment under the refund guarantee. The question arose whether the buyers could also claim damages at common law. This turned on whether they had terminated under the express right or at common law. The Court of Appeal held that there was nothing in the contract to show that the parties intended to displace the right to terminate for breach at common law,[84] that the refund guarantee was not intended to operate in isolation or in a manner inconsistent with common law rights,[85] and that the buyers' reliance on the ETC did not bar them from relying on their common law rights.[86] We are reminded that acceptance of a repudiatory breach only extinguishes those primary obligations which define performance of the contract; it does not end other ancillary rights and obligations which regulate termination and its consequences or which, as a matter of construction, are intended to survive terminations.[87]

In *Gearbulk*, there was held to be no inconsistency between the exercise of a right to terminate under the ETC and under the common law on account of repudiatory breach. Moore-Bick LJ said they were 'in effect one

---

[81] In *Gearbulk* (n 56) [34], Moore-Bick LJ said of the Court of Appeal's decision in *Ennis*: 'these were ex tempore judgments delivered at a time when the principles of discharge by breach had not received the detailed analysis and exposition provided in the more recent authorities'.

[82] *Newland* (n 69) [52]. A different, but related, question is whether express notice requirements for operation of the ETC also apply to termination for repudiatory breach at common law. The answer turns on the intention of the parties as revealed by construction of the notice provision: *Vinergy* (n 47) [20].

[83] See n 56.   [84] Ibid [18]–[20].   [85] Ibid [21]–[25].   [86] Ibid [26]–[42].

[87] Ibid [37].

and the same'.[88] However, as we have seen,[89] the bifurcated principle means that an innocent party cannot recover loss of bargain damages when terminating for a non-repudiatory breach under an ETC. By contrast, there is a different outcome when termination takes place following a repudiatory breach, when loss of bargain damages may be awarded. One answer to this apparent inconsistency is to say that it would be removed if *Financing Ltd v Baldock* were to be overruled.[90] But does a different remedial outcome necessarily mean that there is real inconsistency between the exercise of the contractual right and the common law right such as to require election between them? It is submitted that it does not.

Sometimes there is real inconsistency between the exercise of a contractual right of termination and the exercise of a common law right of termination because the consequences of their exercise conflict. In such a case, the innocent party must elect between the two inconsistent rights and communicate his choice to the other party in clear and unambiguous terms.[91] For example, in *Dalkia Utilities Services plc v Celtech International Ltd*,[92] contractual termination and acceptance of a repudiation would have had 'markedly different consequences' as the former allowed the defaulting party to retain possession of the power plant (provided it paid a termination sum), whereas the latter would have entitled the innocent party to take it back. In these circumstances, Christopher Clarke J found that the single termination notice could not be taken to have produced two 'diametrically opposing consequences' and held that there had been a contractual termination only.[93]

There seems to be no reason why an innocent party should not be entitled to exercise both his right to terminate under the contract and his right to terminate under the common law, so long as the consequences of exercising those termination rights are not inconsistent.

---

[88] Ibid [20].   [89] See main text to n 51.
[90] For the reasons given in the main text to nn 52 et seq. Alternatively, *Treitel* (n 10) submits (para 18–073, fn 497) that the only way to explain Moore-Bick LJ's statement in *Gearbulk* (n 56) is to restrict it to cases where the ETC is itself based on a repudiatory breach, i.e. the parties have agreed that the breach in question amounts to a breach of condition.
[91] *Newland* (n 69) [53]. In fact, even in cases of inconsistency, it might still be possible for the innocent party to put the breaching party on notice that it is terminating under the common law but also, in the alternative, under the ETC, if it turns out there is no repudiatory breach (*Treitel* (n 10) para 18–073, citing *Shell Egypt West Manzala GmbH v Dana Gas Egypt Ltd* [2010] EWHC 465 (Comm) [34]).
[92] *Dalkia* (n 3).
[93] Ibid [144]. Cf Carter (n 46) para 12–06, 'the question is one of election between remedies, not election between rights'.

The consequences of exercising one right might be different from the consequences of exercising the other right without those consequences necessarily being inconsistent.[94] In *Newland Shipping and Forwarding Ltd v Toba Trading FZC*,[95] Leggatt J held that the claimant had by a single notice to the breaching party exercised both its right to terminate under the contract and its right to terminate under the common law for repudiatory breach. The judge held that the consequences of exercising each termination right were different but not inconsistent: the ETC (clause 7) allowed the innocent party to terminate and claim compensation for all losses and demurrage, but there could be no claim to damages under the common law because of another clause in the contract (clause 12) which excluded liability to pay such damages.[96] Leggatt J made the following general observation:

> Cases where both rights can be exercised simultaneously themselves seem to me to be of two kinds. In cases where the consequences of contractual termination and termination under the general law are identical, it is not necessary to specify which right is being exercised in order to bring about an effective termination. In such cases there is no difference in substance between the two rights which are, as Moore-Bick LJ put it in the *Gearbulk* case at [20], 'in effect one and the same'. However, in cases where the consequences of exercising the two rights are different, but not inconsistent, it is necessary to make it clear which right is being exercised or that both rights are being exercised; otherwise there will not be the certainty required for an effective termination.[97]

Leggatt J found that the single notice used in the case before him constituted termination under both clause 7 and under the common law.[98] He did note, however, that a notice that failed to convey a clear intention to terminate

---

[94] In *Gearbulk* (n 56) [44], Moore-Bick LJ (obiter) said there must be an election if the contract and the general law provide the innocent party 'with alternative rights which have different consequences: as was held to be the case in the *Dalkia* case'. It is argued in this chapter that 'different consequences' do not necessarily mean there has to be an election: the issue turns on whether there are 'inconsistent consequences' and *Dalkia* is an example of such inconsistency.

[95] *Newland* (n 69). Contrast that notice with the one in *Comau UK Ltd v Lotus Lightweight Structures Ltd* [2014] EWHC 2122 (Comm) [6], [16(a)], which only made reference to termination under the ETC and did not mention termination for repudiatory breach (the judge said at [16(f)] that '[i]t was open to Comau to send a further letter making quite clear that it was proposing now to rely on its rights at common law').

[96] As Leggatt J said (*Newland* (n 69) [59]): 'Termination for repudiatory breach would therefore add nothing of value. But that is no reason why it could not be done.'

[97] Ibid [54].   [98] Ibid [66].

under clause 7, and also failed to convey a clear intention to terminate under the common law, would not terminate the contract at all.[99]

15.9 Good Faith

Would the courts imply a term into the contract which controlled the use of an ETC through a requirement of good faith and/or reasonableness? Let us start with an ETC triggered by breach. In such circumstances, the chances of the courts implying a good faith or reasonableness requirement are slim, almost to the point of non-existence, whether on the traditional tests of 'business efficacy' or that it was 'obvious', or on the basis of Lord Hoffmann's more recent approach in *A-G of Belize v Belize Telecom Ltd*[100] that a term will be implied because it 'spells out in express words what the contract, read against the relevant background, would reasonably be understood to mean'.

It is well established that where a party has a contractual right to terminate, there is generally no requirement for it to act reasonably in exercising that contractual right.[101] However, in recent years, following the lead taken by Leggatt J in *Yam Seng Pte Ltd v International Trade Corp Ltd*,[102] the courts have sometimes been prepared to imply a duty of good faith into a 'relational' contract (such as distributorship agreements) on the ground that it reflects the intention of the parties.[103] Nevertheless, the

---

[99] Ibid [60].

[100] [2009] UKPC 10, [2009] 1 WLR 1988 [21]. Lord Hoffmann's approach to implied terms in *Belize Telecom* must now be reconsidered in light of *Marks & Spencer plc v BNP Paribas Securities Services Trust Company (Jersey) Ltd* [2015] UKSC 72, [2015] 3 WLR 1843.

[101] *Financings Ltd v Baldock* (n 52) 115 (Upjohn LJ) and 122–23 (Diplock LJ). See also *The Solholt* [1983] 1 Lloyd's Rep 605, 607–08 (Sir John Donaldson MR: 'unfettered right'), but note the mitigation point made by Tettenborn and Wilby (n 58) 35–36. Contrast the position in Australia following *Renard Constructions (ME) Pty Ltd v Minister for Public Works* (1992) 26 NSWLR 234, 258 (Priestley JA, NSWCA): see e.g. *Burger King Corp v Hungry Jack's Pty Ltd* [2001] NSWCA 187, reported in part (2001) 69 NSWLR 558; cf *Hunter Valley Skydiving Centre Pty Ltd v Central Coast Aero club Ltd* [2008] NSWSC 539 [48].

[102] [2013] EWHC 111 (QB).

[103] *Bristol Groundschool Ltd v Intelligent Data Capture Ltd* [2014] EWHC 2145 (Ch) [196]; *D & G Cars Ltd v Essex Police Authority* [2015] EWHC 226 (QB) [173]–[176]; cf *Hamsard 3147 Ltd v Boots UK Ltd* [2013] EWHC 3251 (Pat) (no implied duty of good faith in nascent joint venture); *Carewatch Care Services Ltd v Focus Caring Services Ltd* [2014] EWHC 2313 (Ch) (franchise agreements not to be construed as containing implied duty of good faith); *Acer Investment Management Ltd v The Mansion Group Ltd* [2014] EWHC 3011 (QB) (simple agency agreement was not 'relational contract').

general rule in commercial contracts is that 'if the parties wish to impose such a duty [of good faith] they must do so expressly'.[104]

The issue arose in the context of an ETC in *TSG Building Services plc v South Anglia Housing Ltd*,[105] where there was a four-year contract between a housing association (South Anglia) and a contractor (TSG) for the provision by TSG of a gas servicing and associated works programme relating to South Anglia's housing stock. Clause 1.1 required the parties to work together in a spirit of 'trust, fairness and mutual cooperation' and to 'act reasonably and without delay'. Under clause 13.3 each party 'may terminate . . . at any time during the term'. South Anglia terminated the contract early under clause 13.3. Two questions arose: (i) whether, as a matter of construction, clause 1.1 provided for any constraint, condition or qualification on either party's right to terminate under clause 13.3, and (ii) whether there was an implied term of good faith.

Akenhead J held that, properly construed, clause 1.1 did not require South Anglia to act reasonably as such in terminating under clause 13.3 (clause 1.1 was directed to other matters such as performance of its roles, expertise and responsibilities under the partnering documents). He said that clause 13.3 gave each party an unqualified right, and it would have been obvious to each of them, if they had applied their mind to it prior to entering into the contract, that the other could terminate at any time.[106] The judge also held that there was no reason to imply a term of good faith. The parties had gone as far as they wanted in expressing terms in clause 1.1. An implied term of good faith could not circumscribe or restrict what they had expressly agreed in clause 13.3, which was effectively that either of them for any reason could terminate at any time before the four-year term was complete.[107]

Akenhead J said with regard to *Yam Seng*:

> Because cases and contracts are sensitive to context, I would not draw any principle from this extremely illuminating and interesting judgment which is of general application to all commercial contracts. I do not see

---

See also *Monde Petroleum SA v Westernzagros Ltd* [2016] EWHC 1472 (Comm), [2016] 2 Lloyd's Rep 229 [250]: 'the mere fact that a contract is a long-term or relational one is not, of itself, sufficient to justify such an implication' (Richard Salter QC, sitting as a deputy High Court judge).

[104] *Mid Essex* (n 27) [105] (Jackson LJ). See also *Greenclose Ltd v National Westminster Bank plc* [2014] EWHC 1156 (Ch) [150], Andrews J: 'there is no general doctrine of good faith in English contract law and such a term is unlikely to arise by way of necessary implication in a contract between two sophisticated commercial parties negotiating at arm's length'.

[105] [2013] EWHC 1151 (TCC), [2013] BLR 484.   [106] Ibid [42].   [107] Ibid [51].

that implied obligations of honesty or fidelity to the contractual bargain impinge in this case at all. There is certainly no suggestion or hint that there has or might have been any dishonesty in the decision to terminate. So far as fidelity to the bargain is concerned, that depends upon what the bargain actually was. In any event, fidelity to the bargain is largely already covered by the expressed terms of clause 1.1 and, at least to that extent, does not have to be implied as well.[108]

The ETC in this case allowed either party to terminate for convenience. ETCs for convenience are widely used in the construction industry. They are potentially useful in that they allow the site owner an escape route should funds run out or where drastic design changes are required. But they are also potentially 'open to abuse', e.g. where termination is effected simply to get a cheaper deal from someone else. In *South Anglia*, Akenhead J was not prepared to imply a term of good faith into the contract to control the use of the clause. He said that each party had voluntarily undertaken the risk of premature termination by the other party when entering into the contract, even though each might have thought, hoped and assumed that the contract would run its full term.[109] However, the judge did add that:

> if (and there is similarly no suggestion of this) there was some material fraud or dishonesty on the part of South Anglia in and about the termination that might well give rise to some cause of action. Thus, if there were extreme and unusual facts (none being adumbrated so far), the law might provide TSG with some other remedy.[110]

It should be noted that in *South Anglia* the contractor was entitled to payment for all the work that it had done pursuant to the agreement at rates which had been agreed. It was suggested by Judge Humphrey Lloyd QC in *Abbey Developments Ltd v PP Brickwork Ltd*,[111] that if an ETC for convenience does not provide for compensation for the other party it risks being treated 'as leonine and unenforceable as unconscionable'. But the legitimacy of that statement has been questioned due to the fact that the doctrine of unconscionability is of limited application.[112] In *Hadley*

---

[108] Ibid [46].   [109] Ibid [51].   [110] Ibid.

[111] [2003] EWHC 1987 (TCC) [54]. In *Timeload Ltd v British Telecommunications plc* [1995] EMLR 459 (CA) 468, Sir Thomas Bingham MR thought it 'at least arguable' that the common law could invalidate or restrict the operation of an 'oppressive clause in a situation of the present, very special kind'. The tentative nature of Bingham MR's opinion, and the fact BT was in a very special position, limit the utility of this statement.

[112] Martin Hirst, 'Termination for Convenience clauses – A Shield or a Sword in Times of Economic Downturn' [2010] IclR 419, 422.

Design Associates Ltd v The Lord Mayor and Citizens of the City of Westminster,[113] Judge Seymour QC, without reference to the *Abbey* case, upheld the ETC for convenience despite the fact that it did not provide for compensation.[114]

A key question is whether an ETC for convenience should be subject to *Socimer* implied terms requiring the party relying on the clause to act in good faith for the purpose for which the power was conferred, and not arbitrarily, capriciously, perversely or irrationally.[115] In so far as we are dealing with an ETC triggered by breach, there is Court of Appeal authority to say that it should not.[116] The party is exercising an absolute contractual right and that right should not be fettered.[117] The position would change to some extent where the ETC provides that the promisee must give the promisor notice to remedy the breach, and that the breach must be remedied to the satisfaction of the promisee. Then *Socimer* terms are likely to be implied to fetter the subjective view of the promisee.[118]

In contrast to an ETC triggered by breach, it might be argued that an ETC for convenience is more akin to a discretionary power and that *Socimer* terms should be implied to control the exercise of that discretion.

---

[113] [2003] EWHC 1617 (TCC). The judge (at [61]–[73]) distinguished *Timeload* (n 118) and refused to imply a duty of good faith.

[114] But see also main text to n 10 on 'illusory' consideration.

[115] *Socimer International Bank Ltd (in liq) v Standard Bank London Ltd* [2008] EWCA Civ 116, [2008] Bus LR 1304 [66], Rix LJ (with whom Lloyd and Laws LJJ agreed). See also *British Telecommunications plc v Telefónica O2 UK Ltd* [2014] UKSC 42 [37]. In *Braganza v BP Shipping Ltd* [2015] UKSC 17, [2015] 1 WLR 1661, Baroness Hale (in the majority) explained at [24] that the 'rationality' test had two distinct limbs: the first focusing on the decision-making process (whether the right matters had been taken into account in reaching the decision) and the second focusing upon its outcome (whether, even though the right things had been taken into account, the result was so outrageous that no reasonable decision maker could have reached it). See also Lord Hodge (in the majority) at [53] and Lord Neuberger (in the minority) at [103], both agreeing with Baroness Hale on this point. The precise nature of the term to be implied to control the exercise of the decision-making power will depend on the terms and the context of the particular contract (Baroness Hale at [18] and [31]). See also Richard Hooley, 'Controlling Contractual Discretion' [2013] CLJ 65.

[116] *Mid Essex* (n 27), although it should be noted that the Court of Appeal did not have to consider whether there was an implied term that the discretion must be exercised in good faith, i.e. 'with subjective honesty, genuineness and integrity', per Cooke J in *SNBC Holding v UBS AG* [2012] EWHC 2044 (Comm) [72]. See also *Lomas v JFB Firth Rixson Inc* [2012] EWCA Civ 419 [46]; *Sucden Financial Ltd v Fluxo-Cane Overseas Ltd* [2010] EWHC 2133 (Comm), [2010] 2 CLC 216 [50].

[117] *Mid Essex* (n 27) [83] (Jackson LJ), [140] (Lewison LJ).

[118] *Bluewater Energy Services BV v Mercon Steel Structures BV* [2014] EWHC 2132 (TCC) [55]–[56]; *Sucden* (n 116) [49].

Indeed the apparently unfettered nature of an ETC for convenience gives the party relying upon it total discretion to terminate at its will, with some versions of the clause even making express reference to that party's 'absolute discretion' to terminate. There is arguably more scope for a court to imply duties of good faith and rationality, albeit falling short of objective standards of reasonableness, in such a case.[119] Tempting though this argument might appear to be, it should be rejected.[120] Unlike in the *Socimer*-type situation, where the discretion 'involved making an assessment or choosing from a range of options, taking into account the interest of both parties', the party exercising its rights under an ETC (whether for breach or for convenience) takes 'a simple decision whether or not to exercise an absolute contractual right'.[121] The party has a 'binary choice'.[122] In such a case, there is no 'necessity' for the implication of *Socimer* terms.[123] Furthermore, if commercial parties sign up to a contract that contains an ETC for convenience, they take the risk that the other party will exercise it in a way that suits that party's interests rather than their own.[124] Above all, the exclusion of any considerations of good faith, proper purpose and rationality in the exercise of rights under an ETC, promotes greater commercial certainty 'which is the most indispensable quality of mercantile contracts'.[125]

Identifying whether or not a clause is intended to give one party an absolute contractual right may not always be straightforward. The clause must be construed in context,[126] and the 'less clear' the clause is the more likely it is to be construed *contra proferentem*.[127] There will always be

---

[119] See Hooley (n 115) 87, rejecting the implication of an objective standard of reasonableness as favoured by Priestley JA in *Renard* (n 101).

[120] The *Mid Essex* (n 27) decision has led me to change my own views on this, as expressed in my 2013 clJ article (n 115) 83–89. But note that in *MSC Mediterranean Shipping Co SA v Cottonex Anstalt* [2015] EWHC 283 (Comm) [97]–[98], Leggatt J adopts a similar approach to that taken in my article (his approach was criticized on appeal: [2016] EWCA Civ 789 [45]).

[121] *Mid Essex* (n 27) [83] (Jackson LJ). See also *Brogden v Investec Bank plc* [2014] EWHC 2785 (Comm) [99].

[122] *Myers v Kestrel Acquisitions Ltd* [2015] EWHC 916 (Ch) [61].

[123] *Mid Essex* (n 27) [140] (Lewison LJ).   [124] *South Anglia* (n 105) [51].

[125] *Monde Petroleum* (n 103) [274], citing Lord Wilberforce in *Bunge Corp v Tradax Export SA* [1981] 1 WLR 711, 751.

[126] Bridge (n 19) 98–103.

[127] *Arnold* (n 13) [18]. I question Professor Bridge's submission (n 19 at 101) that the ETC in *Rice* (n 15) might be interpreted 'as vesting a discretionary power in the council, a power that is not to be exercised except where there exist good grounds to do so as perceived by a fair-minded contracting party' because, on his own assessment (at 99), the clause was 'clear and simple'.

exceptional cases where the parties are held to have intended that an apparently unfettered right of termination be subject to *Socimer* controls, but those cases should be the exception and not the rule. This approach respects party autonomy and the fact that 'the advantage of easy exit is likely to have been priced into the bargain'.[128]

15.10 Conclusion

ETCs are commercially useful. A well-drafted clause reduces uncertainty of outcome that might otherwise arise when termination takes place under the common law. In some cases, an ETC can operate harshly against the interests of one party and in favour of those of the other, but this should not be a reason for unjustified interference by the courts in the proper operation of the clause. This is part of the warp and woof of commercial affairs. It is what the parties signed up to.

---

[128] Sarah Worthington, 'Common Law Values: The Role of Party Autonomy in Private Law' in Andrew Robertson and Michael Tilbury (eds), *The Common Law of Obligations: Divergence and Unity* (Hart Publishing 2016) 311.

16

Penalty Clauses

SARAH WORTHINGTON

16.1   Introduction

This chapter sets out to describe the law on penalties. That itself might seem ambitious, given that the penalties doctrine has been described as 'an ancient, haphazardly constructed edifice which has not weathered well',[1] and which even Lords Eldon and Diplock and Sir George Jessel MR were unable to explain.[2] But the jurisdiction has been subjected to recent and sustained review by the Supreme Court in the conjoined appeals in *Cavendish Square Holding BV v Talal El Makdessi; ParkingEye Ltd v Beavis*[3] ('*Makdessi*') and has now, the court suggests, been set on more realistic and principled grounds than previously.[4]

---

[1] *Cavendish Square Holding BV v Talal El Makdessi; ParkingEye Ltd v Beavis* [2015] UKSC 67, [2015] 3 WLR 1373 [3]. The case has attracted substantial comment; see in particular Carmine Conte, 'The Penalty Rule Revisited' (2016) 132 LQR 382; Francis Dawson, 'Determining Penalties as a Matter of Construction' [2016] LMCLQ 207; William Day, 'A Pyrrhic Victory for the Doctrine against Penalties: Makdessi v Cavendish Square Holding BV' [2016] JBL 115; William Day, 'Penalty Clauses Following Makdessi: Postscript' [2016] JBL 251; James C Fisher, 'Rearticulating the Rule against Penalty Clauses' [2016] LMCLQ 169; Jonathan Morgan, 'The Penalty Clause Doctrine: Unlovable but Untouchable' [2016] CLJ 11. The modern UK and Australian approaches are compared and contrasted in Sarah Worthington, 'The Death of Penalties in Two Legal Cultures?' (2016) 7 *UK Supreme Court Yearbook* 129–151.

[2] *Makdessi* (n 1) [3].

[3] Ibid. This is the leading UK case, and is referred to extensively throughout the chapter. Where quotations are pinpointed merely by an unattributed paragraph reference, it is to this case. To identify the relevant judges: [1]–[115] (Lord Neuberger P and Lord Sumption, with Lord Carnwath agreeing); [116]–[214] (Lord Mance); [215]–[290] (Lord Hodge); [291] (Lord Clarke agreeing with Lords Neuberger, Sumption, Mance and Hodge generally, although on identifying 'secondary obligations' and on issues on forfeiture inclining towards Lords Mance and Hodge); [292]–[316] (Lord Toulson, agreeing with Lord Mance at [116]–[187] and Lord Hodge at [216]–[283], and in particular agreeing with Lord Hodge's definition of a penalty at [255]).

[4] Ibid [39].

The penalties jurisdiction entitles courts to review an agreed contractual term and declare it void if it is a penalty. A clause is a penalty if, in substance, it imposes consequences for breach of contract that are extravagant, exorbitant, unconscionable or out of all proportion to any legitimate interest of the innocent party in performance of the contract.[5] It is irrelevant that the parties have fully agreed to the term, or that its inclusion has been priced into the contract. Such interference is clearly 'a blatant interference with freedom of contract',[6] undermining 'the certainty which parties are entitled to expect of the law'.[7] Such draconian consequences ensure the jurisdiction retains its fascination, yet examples of successful claims are rare, and perhaps those that exist might all be better explained on alternative grounds.[8]

There is an enormous literature in this area,[9] but this chapter focuses on *Makdessi*, except to the extent that the Supreme Court has confirmed that earlier cases remain illustrative. As Lord Hodge put it, 'the rule against penalties is based on public policy and has developed over time, [so] its current form is of more significance than its historical

[5] Ibid [32], [152], [155], [291], [293]. The law in Australia is different: see n 14.

[6] *Makdessi v Cavendish Square Holdings BV* [2013] EWCA Civ 1539, [2013] 2 CLC 968 [44] (Christopher Clarke LJ).

[7] *Makdessi* (n 1) [33].

[8] None of the major penalties cases discussed in this chapter was successful. The claim succeeded in *Bridge v Campbell Discount Co Ltd* [1962] AC 600 (HL), although by contrast see *Cadogan Petroleum Holdings Ltd v Global Process Systems LLC* [2013] EWHC 214 (Comm), [2013] 2 Lloyd's Rep 26; *Else (1982) v Parkland Holdings* [1994] 1 BCLC 130 (CA); *Scandinavian Trading Tanker Co AB v Flota Petrolera Ecuatoriana (The Scaptrade)* [1983] 2 AC 694 (HL); and *Stockloser v Johnson* [1954] 1 QB 476 (CA). And although relief was granted in *Workers Trust & Merchant Bank Ltd v Dojap Investments Ltd* [1993] AC 573 (PC) (return of a 25 per cent deposit); *Jobson v Johnson* [1989] 1 WLR 1026 (CA) (retransfer of shares on payment default); and *Public Works Comr v Hills* [1906] AC 368 (PC) (forfeiture of a retention fund), all of these have some parallels with relief against forfeiture: see section 16.5.

[9] See in particular Tony Downes, 'Rethinking Penalty Clauses' in Peter Birks (ed), *Wrongs and Remedies in the Twenty-First Century* (Oxford University Press 1996); Louise Gullifer, 'Agreed Remedies' in Andrew Burrows and Edwin Peel (eds), *Commercial Remedies: Current Issues and Problems* (Oxford University Press 2003) ch 16; Anthony Gray, 'Contractual Penalties in Australia after Andrews: An Opportunity Missed' (2013) 18 *Deakin Law Review* 1; Elisabeth Peden and JW Carter, 'Agreed Damages Clauses – Back to the Future?' (2006) 22 *Journal of Contract Law* 189; Sarah Worthington, 'Common Law Values: The Role of Party Autonomy in Private Law' in Andrew Robertson and Michael Tilbury (eds), *The Common Law of Obligations: Divergence and Unity* (Hart Publishing 2016) ch 14; and other references cited below. For the history, see Joseph Biancalana, 'The Development of the Penal Bond with Conditional Defeasance' (2005) 26(2) J Leg Hist 103; and Joseph Biancalana, 'Contractual Penalties in the King's Court 1260–1360' [2005] CLJ 212.

development'.[10] This is all the more so given the changes wrought by *Makdessi*.[11]

Summarising what is to come, the Supreme Court in *Makdessi* declined to abolish the penalties rule either generally or in the commercial context,[12] with Lords Neuberger and Mance adding: 'We rather doubt that the courts would have invented the rule today if their predecessors had not done so three centuries ago. But this is not the way in which English law develops, and we do not consider that judicial abolition would be a proper course for this court to take.'[13] Equally, the Supreme Court says it has not expanded the rule. In particular, it emphatically refused to follow the Australians in explicitly expanding the jurisdiction beyond clauses operating on breach.[14] Nevertheless,

---

[10] *Makdessi* (n 1) [250].

[11] For the earlier UK approach, see the text at nn 29, 58–65; and for the current Australian approach see n 14.

[12] *Makdessi* (n 1) [36]–[39], [162]–[170], [256], [291], [292]. This is reminiscent of the Supreme Court's approach in *Prest v Petrodel Resources Ltd* [2013] UKSC 34, [2013] 2 AC 415, there declining to abolish the jurisdiction to pierce the corporate veil, a jurisdiction also existing elsewhere, but unable to suggest instances where it was really needed and where no other intervention already did the job equally well and on a more principled basis. For suggestions that the penalties jurisdiction should be abolished, see Janet O'Sullivan, 'Lost on Penalties' [2014] CLJ 480; Edwin Peel, 'Unjustified Penalties or an Unjustified Rule against Penalties?' (2014) 130 LQR 365; Worthington, 'Common Law Values: The Role of Party Autonomy in Private Law' (n 9). And implicitly to the contrary, discussing the common law more generally, see Lord Neuberger MR, 'The Life of the Law: The Logic of Experience' (Lionel Cohen Lecture, Jerusalem, May 2010).

[13] *Makdessi* (n 1) [36], Lords Carnwath and Clarke ([291]) agreeing.

[14] Ibid [41]–[42], [130], [163], [241], [291], [292]. For the modern Australian approach, see *Andrews v ANZ Banking Group Ltd* [2012] HCA 30, (2012) 247 CLR 205 and *Paciocco v Australia and New Zealand Banking Group Ltd* [2016] HCA 28. In the former case the Australian High Court took the radical step of removing the 'breach' requirement, allowing courts to review as penalties any stipulation which was collateral (or accessory) to a primary stipulation, and which imposed a penalty intended to deter breach of the primary stipulation: [10]. Interestingly, despite this extension, Gordon J in *Paciocco v Australian and New Zealand Banking Group Ltd* [2014] FCA 52, (2014) 309 ALR 249, applying the new tests, reached identical conclusions to those reached in the initial trial applying orthodox tests: i.e. of all the various banking charges in issue, only the late payment fees were illegal penalties. By contrast, honour fees, dishonour fees, overlimit fees and non-payment fees were not. On further appeal, even the late payment fees were upheld as legitimate terms in the contract: *Paciocco v Australia and New Zealand Banking Group Ltd* [2015] FCAFC 50 (FCFCA) ('*Paciocco*'), aff'd on appeal to the HCA (see above). The *Andrews* decision has been trenchantly criticised in JW Carter and others, 'Penalties: Resurrecting the Equitable Jurisdiction' (2013) 30 *Journal of Contract Law* 99; also see Gray (n 9). The HCA justified its expanded view of the penalties jurisdiction by resort to equity's historical interventions against penal bonds, but that jurisdiction had already been conceived more narrowly by the courts during the eighteenth and

there is at least some move in that direction, given the courts's broad 'substance over form' approach to breaches.[15] There is also a more expansive attitude to the varieties of detriment embraced within the notion of a penalty.[16] But, going against that, in unequivocally freeing the penalties rule from its old and exclusive benchmark comparator of liquidated damages, and also in expressly allowing that deterrence may be a legitimate purpose in formulating a contract term, the Supreme Court has probably gone as near to abolishing the rule as it could without expressly saying as much.[17] Nevertheless, in deliberately leaving the vestiges intact, the Supreme Court may have created a number of new and unintended uncertainties. The most obvious of these are addressed in this chapter, alongside the new jurisdictional rules themselves.

The analysis is assisted by some understanding of the typical facts in penalties cases. The *Makdessi* appeals provide pointed illustrations of the vastly different contexts in which the penalties jurisdiction might have a role. The first case, *Cavendish Square Holding BV v Talal El Makdessi*, concerned a claim worth ~$40 million relating to contract terms which, on one view, defined the sale price for shares delivering a controlling interest in an advertising group, and, on another view, imposed a penalty for breach by the seller of otherwise legitimate contractual restraint of trade clauses.[18] The second case, *ParkingEye v Beavis*, concerned an £85 parking ticket issued for overstaying the permitted period of free parking in a shopping centre car park. The conjunction of the $40 million *Makdessi* claim alongside the £85 *ParkingEye* claim, and the selection of a Supreme Court panel of seven,

---

nineteenth centuries (David Ibbetson, *A Historical Introduction to the Law of Obligations* (Oxford University Press 1999) 213–14) before the jurisdiction was later expanded once again, but on a different basis, in *Dunlop Pneumatic Tyre Co v New Garage & Motor Co Ltd* [1915] AC 79 (HL). See too *Makdessi* (n 1) [4]–[10], [41]–[42]. The UK and Australian approaches are compared and contrasted in Worthington (n 1).

[15] See below, section 16.3.   [16] See below, section 16.5.

[17] See too Day, 'A Pyrrhic Victory for the Doctrine against Penalties: Makdessi v Cavendish Square Holding BV' (n 1); Morgan (n 1).

[18] Makdessi agreed to sell to Cavendish a controlling stake in what had become the largest advertising group in the Middle East. The agreement contained restrictive covenants designed to ensure Makdessi did not compete in defined ways. Makdessi breached these. As a result, under clause 5.1, Makdessi would forfeit the final two instalments of deferred consideration payable by Cavendish for his shares. And under clause 5.6, he would be required to transfer all his remaining shares to Cavendish at a price which excluded any value referable to goodwill. Makdessi unsuccessfully claimed that clauses 5.1 and 5.6 were unenforceable penalty clauses. The Supreme Court reversed the Court of Appeal, which had in turn overturned the trial judge's conclusions.

made it clear that the Supreme Court was open to a fundamental review of the area. But earlier cases are equally diverse. They illustrate penalties claims being advanced in the context of fees charged for late completion of contracts,[19] breach of restraint of trade clauses,[20] or breach of film screening licences;[21] interest rate hikes for breach of loan contracts;[22] and liquidated damages for wrongful dismissal.[23] In *none* of these cases was the claim of a penalty upheld. That perhaps suggests that contracting parties have little to fear from the jurisdiction and its potential for interference with freedom of contract. But the waters which must be negotiated are choppy.

In successive sections, this chapter considers (i) the policy and principles underpinning the penalties rule; (ii) the threshold issue of the breach requirement; (iii) the key issue of what makes a clause penal, and the new requirement to balance 'legitimate interests' against imposed detriments; (iv) the varieties of detriment which are embraced by the penalties rule; (v) the consequences of a finding that the clause is indeed penal; and (vi) concluding remarks.

16.2   Policy and Principle: When and Why Does the Court Intervene?

In order to define the limits of any legal rule, its underpinnings must be clear. If they are not, then hard cases cannot be dealt with confidently, and the rule of law suffers. The Supreme Court conceded as much, setting its own homework in the opening paragraphs of the leading judgment in *Makdessi*: 'But unless the [penalties] rule is to be abolished or substantially extended [neither of which was advocated], its application to any but the clearest cases requires some underlying principle to be identified.'[24]

What that principle is remains troublingly unclear. The Supreme Court noted that it is a principle based on public policy[25] (but all legal

---

[19] *Philips Hong Kong Ltd v Attorney General of Hong Kong* (1993) 61 BLR 41 (PC), [1993] UKPC 3; *Clydebank Engineering & Shipbuilding Co Ltd v Don Jose Ramos Yzquierdo y Castaneda* [1905] AC 6 (HL).

[20] *Dunlop* (n 14).   [21] *Metro-Goldwyn Mayer Pty Ltd v Greenham* [1966] 2 NSWR 717.

[22] *Lordsvale Finance plc v Bank of Zambia* [1996] QB 752 (QB).

[23] *Murray v Leisureplay plc* [2005] EWCA Civ 963, [2005] IRLR 946.

[24] *Makdessi* (n 1) [3] (Lords Neuberger and Sumption, Lords Carnwath and Clarke agreeing).

[25] Ibid [7], [9], [243], [250], [253] and generally throughout the judgments.

principles are surely based on public policy[26]), and that 'everyone else does it too' (my words).[27] Neither advances matters in any useful sense.

More should have emerged from the Supreme Court's discussion of the rule's history, but there too there is little to latch on to. Before *Makdessi*, the leading case on penalties was the House of Lords' decision in *Dunlop Pneumatic Tyre Co v New Garage and Motor Co Ltd*.[28] There the House of Lords held that a retail price maintenance clause with a fee of £5 per breach was a liquidated damages clause, not a penalty clause. The case has been substantially reinterpreted in *Makdessi*, and the emphasis moved squarely from Lord Dunedin's formulaic approach (at least as expressed in later cases) to Lord Atkinson's more pragmatic one. That shift was more concerned with the breadth of interests that the parties to a contract may legitimately protect rather than with the policy or principle which motivated the rule itself, and can be left until later. Ignoring all its subtleties, the early *Dunlop* rule might have been formulated as follows: the courts will not enforce a contractual provision which operates on breach and provides for the payment of a sum of money which is manifestly in excess of what would otherwise be recoverable by way of default common law damages for that breach.[29]

Such a rule is clear, even if its principled basis is not. At root it seems to insist that common law damages – as would have been assessed by the court had the parties been silent – are not only contract law's default rule, but also its mandatory rule. In short, it is not possible to recover more in damages for a breach of contract than the common law default rules would deliver. Why this should be so was not explained, nor why the damages default rule is special when all other default rules (statute permitting) can be contracted around at will.[30] And worse, because the underlying principle was not exposed, the limits of the rule could not be settled with any confidence. The rule could be avoided entirely by clever drafting,[31] with courts then refusing to intervene no matter how unfair

---

[26] Rules might be different, such as whether to drive on the left or right side of the road, or whether uniforms should be blue or green.

[27] *Makdessi* (n 1) [37], [164]–[166], [263]–[265].   [28] *Dunlop* (n 14).

[29] See *Robophone Facilities Ltd v Blank* (1996) 1 WLR 1428 (CA) 1446H–47A (Diplock LJ): there is a rule of public policy which does not 'permit a party to a contract to recover in an action a sum greater than the measure of damages to which he would be entitled at common law'. Also see *Exports Credits Guarantee Department v Universal Oil Products Co* [1983] 1 WLR 399 (HL) 403 (Lord Roskill).

[30] *Photo Production Ltd v Securicor Transport Ltd* [1980] AC 827 (HL) 848.

[31] *Makdessi* (n 1) [15], [258]. All that is needed is that the agreed 'penalty' is payable not on breach, but on some other eventuality: e.g. the price is simply X *or* Y, depending on the

the terms.[32] The rule could also be evaded because the courts allowed parties to include (and quantify) losses which would not normally be recoverable under the default rule,[33] and to value other losses at idiosyncratic personal levels rather than at market levels.[34] Left to spin out, this approach could potentially obliterate the penalties rule entirely. So what were the limits?

By way of answer, it was typically suggested that the parties could not insert terms into their contract which were intended to deter breach rather than simply provide for a genuine pre-estimate of actual likely loss, interpreted increasingly liberally and also with all the margin for error that an *ex ante* decision necessarily requires. Why deterrence was so objectionable was never explained, but the assertion looks questionable, especially when it is merely the flip side of an incentive to perform: recall that a 'discount for early payment' is acceptable, but not a 'penalty for late payment'.

Indeed, in other contexts the courts themselves often recognise that performance can be better than damages, and that sometimes damages will not do. This is the basis of specific performance and injunctions. Indeed, it seems very likely that an injunction to prevent breach could and would have been awarded in a good number of penalties cases if only the innocent party had been on notice early enough. But after the event it is too late to shut the stable door – and why should the parties not recognise that fact, and agree between themselves what the consequences should then be? But none of this goes to explain why deterrence is so objectionable, and indeed so objectionable only if the parties try to put a price on it. Contrast the courts' liberal approach to termination clauses or to the setting of contractual 'conditions', which are surely equally compelling incentives or deterrents. Yet, pre-*Makdessi*, this was the undeviating judicial line, even in the face of cases where any reasonable layperson might have thought that the only reason for the clause in dispute was to deter one form of behaviour and incentivise another (whether conditioned on breach or not). Thankfully the Supreme

---

context; or the full price is Y, with a substantial discount to X for early payment (rather than a potential penalty for late payment). But see below, section 16.3.

[32] *Thomas v Thomas* (1842) 2 QB 851, 114 ER 330.

[33] *Robophone* (29) 1447–48. This has parallels with *Hadley v Baxendale* (1854) 9 Exch 341, 156 ER 145, even as affected by the difficult 'assumption of responsibility' ideas in *Transfield Shipping Inc v Mercator Shipping Inc (The Achilleas)* [2008] UKHL 48, [2009] 1 AC 61.

[34] See the discussion in *Astley v Weldon* (1801) 2 B & P 346, 126 ER 1318 (Court of Common Pleas).

Court in *Makdessi* has now recognised these realities, and indeed so much so that it accepts that some contracts may even have deterrence as their primary purpose (as in *ParkingEye*). However, this then raises a still more difficult problem: what degree of deterrence is permissible and what might go too far?

We are then immediately thrown back to the foundational issue: why are courts interfering in these agreements at all? Until we know that, how can we assess what limits should be imposed? In seeking answers, the principle most often called in aid is 'private punishment' or 'oppression': one party to a contract cannot be allowed to punish or oppress the other.[35] Of course that is right. A great deal of public and private law is devoted to ensuring exactly that. But the law of contract is designed to ensure that parties' agreed expectations are met. Punishment in that particular context can surely only mean the imposition of an unexpectedly severe consequence. This is precisely the focus of the default damages rule. But where the parties have specifically agreed the consequences, and priced them into their contract, then *not* delivering them seems to be punishing their intended recipient. Perhaps 'oppression' is supposed to explain why that might be merited. If the intended recipient of the penal sum has oppressed the other party in order to obtain the agreement, then the agreement should not stand. In that context, oppression is linked to real consent; this is also how the word is used in other contexts in private law, both in contractual contexts and outside them. If that were the focus here, then there would be no complaint. And indeed the judges themselves cannot quite cut loose from this linkage.[36] In particular, it is sometimes suggested that the courts need to strike a blow against rampant freedom of contract precisely in order to protect weaker contracting parties.[37] But if this were the real basis, then there

---

[35] *Makdessi* (n 1) [31], [32], [34], [77], [82], [148], [223], [243]–[254], [262], [278], [282], [287]. See also *AMEV UDC Finance Ltd v Austin* (1986) 162 CLR 170 (HCA) 193 (Mason and Wilson JJ), cited with approval by Lord Woolf in *Philips* (n 19) 57–58, 59. Also see *Elsley v JG Collins Insurance Agencies Ltd* (1978) 83 DLR (3d) 1 (Supreme Court of Canada) 15. Favouring this, in the interests of ensuring good faith, see Mindy Chen-Wishart, 'Controlling the Power to Agree Damages' in Peter Birks (ed), *Wrongs and Remedies in the Twenty-First Century* (Oxford University Press 1996); JW Carter and Elisabeth Peden, 'A Good Faith Perspective on Liquidated Damages' (2007) 23 *Journal of Contract Law* 157. Similarly, see Day (n 1).

[36] *Makdessi* (n 1) [35], [100], [152], [167], [198], [262], [273], [282], [287] and no doubt elsewhere; *Makdessi v Cavendish Square Holdings BV* (n 6) [75] (Christopher Clarke LJ); *Philips* (n 19) 59 (Lord Woolf); *Robophone Facilities Ltd v Blank* (n 29) 1447 (Diplock LJ).

[37] See the much cited comments in *AMEV* (n 35) 190.

would be no need for restrictive links to a breach requirement and its remedial consequences: oppression and flawed consent range well beyond one type of contractual term. And there would be no judicial insistence that consent does not provide a safe route out of the penalties jurisdiction.[38] Nor equally any insistence that the common law rule is one of substance, depending on the effect of the clause, not upon whether it was agreed.[39]

The Supreme Court in *Makdessi* indicated that the rule's underlying rationale is that a provision operating on breach is unenforceable if its consequences are out of all proportion to any legitimate interest of the parties.[40] But this states (or restates) the rule; it does not provide a rationale. And even as a rule, it faces problems. If *this* rule makes sense, then surely it would make still more sense to refuse enforcement of *any* provision if its consequences were out of all proportion to any legitimate interest of the parties. But where would that get us? And surely the most basic 'legitimate interest' of contracting parties lies in having the law uphold the terms of their arrangements provided they are within the law and properly agreed?

Effectively, therefore, the courts are saying that such arrangements, even if properly agreed, are not 'within the law'. So we are full circle – there is something special about remedies.[41] But what that is has not been explained, and it is tempting to suggest that it cannot be explained. This failure to nail the underpinnings of the penalties jurisdiction will undoubtedly come back to haunt the courts. I hazard a guess at the eventual outcome in the final section of this chapter.

16.3   Threshold Issues: The 'Breach' Requirement

The penalties jurisdiction only bites on provisions that operate on breach. *Makdessi* describes these as 'secondary obligations' conditional on breach of a 'primary obligation'. If a provision does not have that character, then courts have no jurisdiction to review the fairness of its terms.[42]

---

[38] *Makdessi* (n 1) [266].   [39] Ibid [34].   [40] Ibid [29], but generally too.

[41] Ibid [13]: 'There is a fundamental difference between a jurisdiction to review the fairness of a contractual obligation and a jurisdiction to regulate the remedy for its breach. . . . the courts do not review the fairness of men's bargains either at law or in equity. The penalty rule regulates only the remedies available for breach of a party's primary obligations, not the primary obligations themselves.'

[42] Ibid [13]. Also see [239], [241]. In England the courts have not given a rationale for focusing the review regime on secondary obligations alone: ibid, [40]–[43], [129]–[130]. This is stated to be in contrast to the contrary Australian 'no breach limitation' as

It is thus crucial to know what counts as a 'secondary obligation' and what is 'primary'. A lot turns on the difference. Pre-*Makdessi*, the distinction was purely a matter of form: an obligation worded as conditional on breach was open to scrutiny; the same obligation avoiding that phraseology was not. That was – quite reasonably – seen as yet another flaw in the penalties jurisdiction. The Supreme Court has avoided that complaint by revising the penalties rule so that the question is one of substance, not form.[43] Despite that, it still concedes, a little inconsistently it might be thought, that clever drafting might nevertheless enable an escape.[44]

The obvious warning in 'substance over form' is that some obligations identified as primary by form may be construed as secondary (or remedial) by substance, and then subjected to the penalties jurisdiction. *Makdessi* did not concern such facts, so there is no judicial guidance on the likely approach, but such recharacterisation is unlikely to be easy in the absence of a rationale for the distinction being sought.

Perhaps surprisingly, the *Makdessi* judgment instead pushes the other way, suggesting that obligations which are secondary in form may sometimes be construed as primary, thus escaping review under the penalties rule entirely, no matter how draconian their terms. This is because the parties can, it was suggested, provide for alternative performance options, each being primary obligations. Under the old penalties rule, where form was crucial, this strategy was often engaged: care was taken to ensure no mention of 'breach', only of alternative modes of performance. But this form says nothing of the underlying substance. Substance now governs, and characterisation across the dichotomy is thus vastly more difficult. Consider the context. In most penalties cases, the parties structure the first delivery option to be more attractive to both parties, and the second less so (often far less so); this second option will then in practice be conditional on failure to deliver according to the first option.

The trouble with this is immediately obvious. When one party fails to perform under the first option, is there *any* test which can determine whether the second option is, at law, a 'secondary obligation' (conditional on failure to perform the primary obligation, but then defining the ensuing remedies for this breach of the first option, and so reviewable

---

expounded in *Andrews* (n 14), although the HCA's focus on 'collateral obligations' does not appear far removed from the SC's focus on 'secondary obligations'. To the same effect, see *Makdessi* (n 1) [153] (Lord Mance).

[43] *Makdessi* (n 1) [15], [34], [77], [130], [258], [270], [280].

[44] Ibid [43]. Also see, more generally, [14], [15], [77], [258].

under the penalties rule) or a 'conditional primary obligation' (conditional on failure to perform the primary obligation, but still itself primary, and merely providing an alternative mode of performance, and therefore not so reviewable)?[45] And yet the distinction is crucial. It determines whether the penalties jurisdiction can be invoked or not.

If substance not form governs, then either construction seems equally open, and the choice by the courts must be made in circumstances where the rationale for intervening, and indeed for intervening only in relation to secondary obligations, has never been successfully articulated. The approach implicit in the *Makdessi* judgments is that the distinction turns on whether the initial primary obligations is mandatory (so failure constitutes a breach, and the second option is then remedial and secondary) or permissive (so failure does not constitute a breach, and the second option is therefore an alternative conditional primary obligation). But this distinction is itself flawed. If the contract expressly provides for alternative modes of performance, then the primary obligation *cannot* be mandatory in the sense which seems necessary here, and the distinction falls away.[46]

If proof were needed that the distinction is difficult, note that the seven judges of the Supreme Court who offered up this 'breach'/'not breach' dichotomy could not themselves agree on whether the conditional clauses in the Makdessi contract should be classified as conditional primary obligations (i.e. redefining the sale price and reshaping the primary relationship between the parties) or as secondary obligations (i.e. defining the remedial consequences following a breach of the primary obligations).[47]

How did we get into this jumble? Part of the problem is simply terminology, and using words without thinking carefully about their significance. But the consequences are significant. On any sensible analysis, agreed contractual obligations are all primary obligations. The parties agree who will do what, and when they will do it, and what will count as proper performance. All contractual obligations are inherently conditional; that is

---

[45] This is notwithstanding the attempt in *Makdessi*, ibid [14], but contrast [280] (Lord Hodge).

[46] If a threatened breach of the initial primary obligation is discovered early enough, a court may order injunctive relief (e.g. in relation to restraint of trade or non-disclosure clauses) or specific performance (e.g. in relation to timely transfer of assets)? But this form of enforcement has no impact on the questions in issue here, however.

[47] See *Makdessi* (n 1) [73]–[88], [180]–[183], [270] and [280], [291], [292]. A useful summary of the divisions on the different clauses is provided by Day, 'Penalty Clauses Following Makdessi: Postscript' (n 1).

what consideration requires: if A does X then B will do Y. Equally, however, the promise may be that if A does X then B will do Y, and if B does not do Y (or fails to do Y) then B will do Z. Despite the added complication, these too are all primary obligations agreed by the parties. The difference between them is simply their different conditionalities.

Obligations which are truly secondary are different. They may be imposed by the courts or agreed by the parties. On the first, the relatively modern jargon is to speak of primary obligations under a contract, and secondary obligations arising upon breach of those primary obligations. These secondary obligations are *not* obligations either expressly or impliedly agreed by the parties, but obligations (liabilities) imposed by the law as default remedies. In a contractual context, they typically require payment by the wrongdoer of expectation damages, although the court can make other orders in certain circumstances. This use of the term 'secondary obligations' defines a liability to a range of judicially imposed default remedies. It defines a different source of obligations, and has nothing to do with the penalties jurisdiction.

Secondary obligations agreed by the parties are different again. Agreements to provide security (either legal security or third-party personal security by way of guarantee) fall into this category. So too do insurance contracts. These agreements certainly specify primary obligations between the parties, but their protective objective is secondary in that the required performance is necessarily defined and quantified by some other (primary) obligation. These obligations are therefore secondary in the sense that they are supportive only, and fall away completely if there is no underlying primary obligation. These obligations also have nothing to do with the penalties jurisdiction. Many illustrations could be given. Forfeiture cases very often fall within this category (and in these circumstances any suggested overlap with the penalties rule seems doubtful[48]). The penal bonds which provided the genesis of the equitable penalties jurisdiction also fall into this category.[49] This may seem odd, but these penal bonds enabled the contracting party to provide an instrument (the penal bond) which described a secondary obligation designed to act as security for performance of the primary obligation defined in the main contract. This was admittedly an atypical security (it did not provide insolvency protection), but it did provide a more ready means of securing

---

[48] See section 16.5.

[49] *Makdessi* (n 1) [4]–[7], citing AWB Simpson, 'The Penal Bond with Conditional Defeasance' (1966) 82 LQR 392. Also see Worthington (n 1), fn 35 and associated text.

a remedy for breach of the primary contract than enforcing the primary obligation itself, or claiming common law damages for its breach. Given these secondary security objectives, it is not difficult to see why the courts intervened to ensure that this form of security delivered no more than required to compensate for breach of the primary contract, regardless of the magnitude of the obligation described in the penal bond.

There are no analogies between these approaches and the distinctions the judges are identifying between 'primary', 'conditional primary' and 'secondary' obligations in the types of contracts before the courts in the English penalties jurisdiction. Whatever the judges say about how obvious these distinctions are,[50] and absent a complete descent to arid formalism, there is – I suggest – no legal or practical substantive distinction in play at all.[51] Whatever the nuances in wording, *all* these contracts provide that if you don't do X then you must do Y. This is true whenever the parties themselves provide for alternative modes of performance, whatever form it takes.[52] I would prefer to say that *all* these choices describe primary obligations. On the test adopted in *Makdessi*, this would leave the penalties jurisdiction with no content. That would be no bad thing in my view, but it makes plain that if the penalties jurisdiction is to have teeth, and if the courts are not to tie themselves in knots or proceed in unending circles, then they will need to take the opposite stance, and say that *every* time a contract provides for alternative modes of performance, then the courts will regard one mode as primary and the other as secondary.[53] Logically, the option which is more attractive to its promisor will be primary, and its alternative secondary. The court's job will then be to decide whether the secondary alternative should be declared void under the penalties jurisdiction. That is a matter for the next section, but it makes plain the radical judicial intervention in play under the penalties jurisdiction.

This is effectively what the Supreme Court did in *Makdessi*, since even the judges who had decided that the alternative Makdessi provisions should be classified as 'conditional primary obligations', not 'secondary

---

[50] See especially ibid [13] and [130] ('a real distinction, legal and psychological'), notwithstanding their own failure to achieve consensus.

[51] As Lords Neuberger and Sumption said in a different context, 'the law relating to penalties has become the prisoner of artificial categorisation': ibid [31].

[52] This is reinforced by comments at [42], criticising the unworkability of the Australian no breach approach.

[53] Except perhaps in those very rare circumstances where both sides are indifferent to the choice to be made, but in truth these cases will simply never come to court, so a formal exception is unnecessary.

obligations', nevertheless considered their fate under the rules applicable had they been classified as 'secondary obligations'. The answers, thankfully, were the same: the clauses were not penal. What remains inexplicable is why, when alternatives are offered, obligation X is not substantively reviewable by the courts, but obligation Y is. The inference in the next section is that the courts are wary of the parties' use of onerous terms to incentivise performance; what is less clear is why the courts are not simply wary of onerous terms themselves (although addressing these is best achieved via the rules on consent, not penalties).

The Supreme Court recognised that one of the advantages of maintaining the 'breach' limitation was precisely because it limited the scope for judicial review. Lords Neuberger and Sumption expressed a desire to keep certain common commercial arrangements beyond review,[54] implicitly suggesting that these clauses could be interpreted as conditional primary obligations, not remedial secondary ones. That might be doubted, given the new rules' altered emphasis on substance over form.[55]

16.4 When is a 'Secondary Obligation' Penal?

Having established a jurisdiction to intervene, the court must then decide whether the identified 'secondary obligation' in its sightlines is penal. The test is simple. Does the secondary obligation impose a detriment which is either 'out of all proportion to any legitimate interest of the innocent party in the enforcement of the primary obligation',[56] or 'exorbitant or unconscionable when regard is had to the innocent party's interest in the performance of the contract'?[57]

This new *Makdessi* test marks a sea change in judicial approach. Under the old rules, a penalty was any secondary obligation which required the offending party to pay a sum that was extravagant and unconscionable in comparison with the greatest provable loss that could conceivably flow from breach of the primary obligation.[58] It made no difference that the

---

[54] *Makdessi* (n 1) [43].

[55] Parties should not worry unduly, however: most of these commercial arrangements would not be seen as imposing disproportionate, unconscionable or extravagant detriments under the tests described in section 16.4.

[56] *Makdessi* (n 1) [32].

[57] Ibid [255]; similarly, see [152]. The onus of proof is on the party in breach: [143]. Also see [31]–[33], [162], [293].

[58] *Dunlop* (n 14); *Makdessi v Cavendish Square Holdings BV* (n 6). By contrast, a secondary obligation which merely provided for a reasonable pre-estimate of the likely loss would survive as a liquidated damages clause. For literature on this earlier rule, see n 9.

parties had consented to the extravagance, nor that their contractual objectives went beyond recovery of compensatory damages. This rule attracted its own subtle accretions, especially in relation to the extent of the permitted deviation from normal contract damages,[59] and – more recently – the possibility that there might be acceptable commercial[60] or social[61] justifications for deviation from the compensatory norm.

This latter trend has crystallised with a vengeance in the new test, which explicitly recognises that parties may have legitimate interests in performance, not merely in compensation for non-performance.[62] Since parties cannot provide for performance itself,[63] they must instead provide incentives to perform or deterrents to breach.[64] Under the old rules, deterrence was outlawed; now deterrence is acceptable.[65] Indeed, *ParkingEye* confirms that deterrence can be the sole objective of the engagement. It is hard to overstate the significance of this move for the penalties jurisdiction.

Perhaps trying to keep the genie in the bottle, Lord Sumption suggested in his oral handing down of the *Makdessi* judgment that parties do not normally have a legitimate interest in performance or deterrence beyond the recovery of compensation for breach. But, to the contrary, a surprising number of contracts fall outside this category. Consider contracts designed to ensure attendance and participation, or timely delivery, or business continuity, or strict confidentiality; alternatively, consider contracts designed to protect the value of underlying assets (as in *Makdessi* and *Dunlop*) or to ration the distribution of limited assets (as in *ParkingEye*). Whenever parties agree to prescribe alternative modes of

[59] *AMEV* (n 35) 193 (Mason and Wilson JJ); *Philips* (n 19).
[60] *Lordsvale* (n 22); *Leisureplay* (n 23); *Philips* (n 19); *United International Pictures v Cine Bes Filmcilik ve Yapimcilik AS* [2003] EWCA Civ 1669, [2004] 1 CLC 401.
[61] *ParkingEye Ltd v Beavis* [2015] EWCA Civ 402, [2015] RTR 27 [30].
[62] This is not to deny the advantages of a liquidated damages clause. These are common, and such contracts are unlikely to come before the court for review under the penalties jurisdiction. This was true under the old penalties rule, and remains true. By contrast, litigated penalties cases invariably reflect objectives going beyond recovery of compensation.
[63] *Quadrant Visual Communications v Hutchison Telephone (UK)* [1993] BCLC 442 (CA) (Stocker LJ). The only exception is promises to pay a sum of money: these promises can be specifically enforced (with recoveries compromised if the claim puts the defendant into insolvency).
[64] Noting that in any form/substance arguments, one is simply the flip side of the other.
[65] *Makdessi* (n 1) [23], [28], [75], [81], [82], [98]–[99], [172], [198], [248], [271]–[278], [282], [285].

performance, one alternative is frequently designed to deter breach of the other. This is true of all the leading penalties cases.[66]

This is the easy part of the new penalties rule: it is permissive; the parties may have legitimate interests in securing performance, and to that end their secondary obligations may impose incentives or deterrents.

The Supreme Court suggested that this change reflected a more 'principled' approach to the interests which can be protected by contract, and that it would eliminate many of the problems with the penalties jurisdiction.[67] It is not clear that the change is principled, since the principle cannot be described, but it is certainly a practical and pragmatic recognition that parties enter into contracts with different goals, and if the law is to support contracts then it should support such goals provided they are legal.

But the difficult aspect of the new rule is the next step: evaluating quantum. Under the new penalties rule, the adopted deterrent must not be wholly disproportionate or exorbitant or unconscionable in view of the interest in performance which is being protected. Judicial assessment of this is undoubtedly made easier by the wide margin of appreciation allowed to the parties. Nevertheless, in assessing contractual terms against this new standard of acceptability, there is now no longer the easy quantum benchmark provided by compensatory damages, so courts must make their own assessments.

In *ParkingEye*, the court was fortunate that people often used the parking centre and thus impliedly confirmed that its fees were reasonable; other parking centres adopted similar fees; and the Protection of Freedoms Act 2012 suggested equivalent scales. Similar benchmarking is often possible with deterrents appearing in financial instruments, loan contracts, standard employment contracts, and so on.

In *Makdessi*, the problem was more difficult as there are no obvious benchmarks. Without these, courts are typically thrown back on the wisdom of the parties themselves. See Lords Neuberger and Sumption:

> It is clear that this business was worth considerably less to Cavendish [the buyer] if that risk [of competition from Makdessi in breach of his primary obligations] existed than if it did not. How much less? There are no juridical standards by which to answer that question satisfactorily. We cannot know what Cavendish would have paid without the assurance of the Sellers' loyalty, even assuming that they would have bought the

[66] And in every single one the court concluded that the clause was valid, and not a penalty. See the cases cited earlier.
[67] *Makdessi* (n 1) [39].

business at all ... We cannot know what other provisions of the agreement would have been different, or what additional provisions would have been included on that hypothesis. These are matters for negotiation, not forensic assessment (save in the rare cases where the contract or the law requires it). They were matters for the parties, who were, on both sides, sophisticated, successful and experienced commercial people bargaining on equal terms over a long period with expert legal advice and were the best judges of the degree to which each of them should recognise the proper commercial interests of the other.[68]

Makdessi is not unusual in this regard. Courts often lack appropriate benchmarks. But the real difficulties go well beyond this. Courts cannot sensibly decide whether a deterrent is wholly disproportionate or exorbitant or unconscionable without knowing why the overly deterred victim is being protected. Judicial protection against payment of an exorbitant sum can be ruled out, since an effective rule would then need much broader reach. So too can protection from punishment, despite claims to the contrary:[69] such a rule might have been defensible under the earlier penalties rule, but it makes little sense now that courts have conceded that deterrence is acceptable: the essence of deterrence is presenting an option which the counter-party will seek to avoid, and one which will therefore seem punitive if applied.

Of course, the focus could then turn to whether this chosen scale of punishment is excessive, but then the entire edifice seems to collapse under the straightforward logical inconsistency in one party insisting that a term in a contract is 'extravagant and unconscionable' or a 'punishment', when it is no more than the parties have agreed as the terms of their deal at the time of contracting. The only ground for complaint ought to be that agreement is apparent, not real. Otherwise, by contrast, it seems unconscionable to insist that a term properly priced into the contract should *not* now bind. This is all the more so when the judges cannot articulate reasons for finding this contrary approach unconscionable, nor for distinguishing between the appropriate forms of review for secondary and primary obligations (with the added problem that this line is itself widely contested).

Finally, a substantive penalties-style review of these particular forms of deterrent looks all the more odd when judged against review of other equally effective deterrents and incentives (e.g. discounted prices for

---

[68] Ibid [75].
[69] The Supreme Court continues to suggest that the objective of the secondary obligation must not be punitive: ibid [31], [77], [82], [243], [251], [278] and [282].

early payment, insurance concessions for safe operators, legal security arrangements, termination clauses, forfeiture clauses, etc). These latter clauses are only ever subjected to procedural review and interpretive assistance, not to substantive review.

This is all a rather longwinded way of saying that since parties can make their own arrangements concerning all their primary obligations, it is difficult to see why they cannot equally make their own arrangements in pricing the incentives or deterrents designed to promote their performance (i.e. their secondary obligations).[70]

If *Makdessi* gives any hope in this direction, it is that the judges acknowledged that contracting parties are typically the best judges of their own commercial interests,[71] and that generally matters should be left to their judgement. (Although that itself surely suggests interference only where there are flaws with consent.) Furthermore, no major penalty cases were successfully brought under the old and rather draconian penalties rules, so it is perhaps difficult to see that any will be successful under these far more liberal modern rules.

16.5   Varieties of Detriment

The previous sections addressed jurisdiction issues (the breach/'secondary obligation' requirement) and the legitimate interest/quantum balancing exercise. This section considers the *types* of detriment (i.e. the forms of secondary obligations) which can be reviewed by the court.

Logically it might be thought that *any* form of detriment imposed by way of secondary obligation is open to review. The entire gist of the previous sections is that where the parties have specified alternative modes of performance, then there is a likelihood that one alternative has been designed to deter breach of the other, or to incentivise its performance. Such incentives or deterrents are reviewable under the penalties rule.

If these secondary obligations are reviewable, then logic suggests that every form they might take should be equally reviewable. The form of detriment does not alter the substance of the clause, and so should not affect its review by the courts. Admittedly, some forms of detriment are more common than others. Most often the detriment is payment

---

[70] Assuming that these secondary obligations can be convincingly distinguished from conditional primary obligations: section 16.3.

[71] See the frequent references in *Makdessi* (n 1), including at [35] and the cases cited there, [75], [82], [100], [152], [181], [185], [274] and [282].

of money[72] or transfer of assets.[73] The Supreme Court in *Makdessi* confirmed both these forms of detriment as reviewable under the penalties rule, and noted that it would be illogical to differentiate between the two.[74]

Perhaps surprisingly, the court hesitated a little over deposits.[75] Their hesitation seems unwarranted. Deposit clauses were undoubtedly difficult to accommodate under the old penalties rules (where deterrence was objectionable, and quantum was assessed against default compensation), but they are completely at home under the new rules (where incentives and deterrents are acceptable, subject to quantum). With deposits, accepted benchmarks suggest that a 10 per cent deposit is typically the norm, and that greater sums then need special justification if they are not to risk being judged extravagant.[76] The only other oddity with deposits in the context of the penalties rule is that the sum is paid in advance of anticipated performance of the primary obligation, but since substance trumps form this seems of little moment.

Moving on, the Supreme Court was far more divided over detriments consisting in the withholding of sums of money otherwise due, or the withholding of assets otherwise due to be transferred. The suggestion was that these detriments overlap with forfeiture clauses, so that care is needed to ensure that the law deals with the potentially different applications of distinct legal principles appropriately.

This issue needs to be approached carefully, and space does not permit full treatment here.[77] The equitable doctrine providing relief against forfeiture is very narrow, far narrower than the loose use of the words 'forfeiture clause' might suggest. Used loosely, this term often simply indicates that one party may be forced to give up rights which they expected to acquire or to exercise. By contrast, the equitable doctrine addresses the narrow situation where proprietary interests (including

---

[72] Whether expressed as a simple sum in its own right (as in *Dunlop*), or as a default interest rate, an upside fee, a make-whole clause or a take-or-pay clause, etc.

[73] As in bad-leaver provisions, or as with non-refundable deposits (unusually, transferred in advance of any likely performance of the primary obligation).

[74] *Makdessi* (n 1) [16], [170], [183], [233].   [75] Ibid [16], [156], [234]–[238].

[76] *Barnard v Zarbafi* [2010] EWHC 3256 (Ch). Working through each of the requirements of the penalties rule seems preferable to the proposition that the penalties rule is not brought into play unless the deposit is excessive: ibid [234].

[77] See Charles Harpum, 'Equitable Relief: Penalties and Forfeitures' [1989] 48 CLJ 370; and Sarah Worthington, 'What is Left of Equity's Relief against Forfeiture?' in Elise Bant and Matthew Harding (eds), *Exploring Private Law* (Cambridge University Press 2010) ch 11 and the authorities cited in both of these.

possessory interests) are transferred to X subject to their revocation or determination in the event of specified breaches by X. *If* X can remedy the breaches in full, by performing according to the terms of the contract and providing full compensation for delay, etc, then a court may grant relief from the agreed forfeiture. Such relief is therefore typically granted (and perhaps only granted) where the forfeiture clause has been inserted by way of security to ensure performance of an underlying primary obligation (i.e. it is a true secondary obligation, providing security for the primary obligation, as in *Cukurova*[78]). Relief is far less common if the forfeiture is intended to operate by way of an agreed termination clause should nominated circumstances come to pass (as is often the intention in charterparties, leases of real property, conditional assignments of intellectual property, etc).[79] Of course, either form will also provide an incentive to perform according to the agreed terms, but should the incentive be reviewable under the penalties rule, or only under more general contractual review rules which apply to security agreements and termination clauses?

In short, should withholding money or property due to be transferred be reviewed under either the penalties jurisdiction, or the forfeiture jurisdiction, or both?[80] Clause 5.1 in the Makdessi contract was in this form, providing for the withholding of purchase price instalments in certain circumstances.[81] Given the new test for a penalty, it would seem impossible to deny that these types of clauses are potentially reviewable under the penalties jurisdiction, although the analysis is a little clumsier than might be thought. As in all penalty clauses, it is necessary to consider the primary and secondary obligations imposed on the contract breaker. Here, Makdessi was required under the primary obligation to sell his shares at a certain price and comply with certain side arrangements; should he fail to perform, then he was subject to a secondary obligation to sell his shares at a lower price. Given the Supreme Court's insistence

---

[78] *Cukurova Finance International Ltd v Alfa Telecom Turkey Ltd* [2013] UKPC 20, [2015] 2 WLR 875 and *Cukurova Finance International Ltd v Alfa Telecom Turkey Ltd* [2013] UKPC 2, [2015] 2 WLR 875.

[79] *Union Eagle Ltd v Golden Achievement Ltd* [1997] AC 514 (PC).

[80] In *Makdessi* (n 1), Lords Mance and Hodge, with the majority agreeing, held that the penalty rule applied to such clauses: [170], [228], [291], [294]. Lords Neuberger and Sumption were less certain ([73]), worrying that such clauses were instead caught only by the forfeiture rule ([18]), and similarly with clauses withholding the transfer of property ([17]).

[81] See n 18.

that analysis under the penalties rule requires attention to substance, not form, the question then becomes whether the detriment imposed by the secondary obligation (i.e. the shortfall in purchase money received) is exorbitant, unconscionable or out of all proportion to any legitimate interest of the innocent purchaser in enforcing the primary obligations. In *Makdessi*, the Supreme Court held that if this alternative clause did indeed define a secondary obligation rather than an alternative conditional primary one, then it was not exorbitant, etc.

The next question is whether such clauses withholding money or property are reviewable under the equitable forfeiture rules. Generally they are not. It is usually impossible to analyse such contracts as ones which give the disappointed claimant some proprietary or possessory interest in the money or property, which interest will subsequently be withheld.[82] Forfeiture of a personal contractual entitlement is not sufficient.[83] An exception may exist where sale contracts are specifically enforceable, so that purchasers may be regarded in certain circumstances as having proprietary interests in the sale property in advance of its transfer. In these circumstances, forfeiture of that interest may be reviewable under the equitable forfeiture rules.

Finally, can a contract be reviewable under both the penalty and the forfeiture rules? In principle it is difficult to see why not, assuming the facts indicate that both rules are potentially applicable. This is notwithstanding various assertions in older cases that particular facts are subject to the forfeiture rules and not the penalties rules, or vice versa.[84] As a matter of empirical outcome, especially under the old penalties rules, that may well have been true; but it surely cannot have been true as a matter of legal principle. Additionally, in principle, it is difficult to see why this potential overlap should present any problems beyond those already faced by the law in the very many circumstances where factual scenarios are open to analysis in different ways: claimants can, for example, sue in contract, tort or unjust enrichment, often on the same set of facts. There is one added difficulty here, however, which is that both the penalties rule and the forfeiture rule provide for review by the courts. This is not quite the same as an election by the claimant as to which of several remedies she prefers to pursue. The problem is highlighted given

---

[82] But note *Makdessi* (n 1) [69].

[83] *Sport Internationaal Bussum BV v Inter-Footwear* [1984] 1 WLR 776 (HL). Also see *Makdessi* (n 1) [17], [69]–[71] and the cases cited there.

[84] See the comments and cases cited in *Makdessi* (n 1) [17], [31].

the different outcomes under each rule: a penalty clause is void; a forfeiture clause may be disapplied if the claimant can deliver adequate performance of the primary obligation so as to make the innocent party whole. The Supreme Court judges in *Makdessi* who favoured the potential for review under both heads were unanimously of the view that review should take place first under the penalties rule, and only then – if the clause were still left standing, so to speak – should review take place under the forfeiture rules.[85] This does not seem quite right. As noted earlier, some forfeiture clauses are, in substance, security arrangements; others are, in substance, termination clauses. It would be most odd if the penalties rule was used to render these clauses void. There are simply too many cases on security and termination where never a thought had been given to review under the penalties rule – although that was under the old rule, not this new version.

To my mind, this final issue reinforces a point made earlier: the jurisdictional issue seems flawed to its core. In principle, every time the parties provide alternative modes of performance, review would seem to be possible. Yet swathes of contract cases attest to the contrary. The reason this flaw has been kept under wraps for so long is because the old penalties rule operated on form, not substance, and insisted on a form by which the secondary obligation under review must be a provision operating on breach and providing for a monetary payment in lieu of compensatory damages. Once those moorings are lost (as undoubtedly they should be, since they themselves are not defensible), the irresistible conclusion is that there is logically no stopping point other than judicial review of the substance of all subsidiary contracting arrangements or none. The former, as everyone appreciates, would be completely unacceptable to all sides; the latter found no favour with the Supreme Court.

16.6 Consequences of a Finding that the Clause is 'Penal'

If a clause is found to be a penalty, then it is void.[86] In this respect too, *Makdessi* has altered the previous law. In the past, a penalty clause was simply unenforceable to the extent that it was penal;[87] now it is simply void. By contrast, if the clause is not a penalty then it is enforced to full effect. This was the case with all the clauses in *Makdessi* and *ParkingEye*.

---

[85] Ibid [160]–[161], [227], [291], [292].   [86] Ibid [9], [84]–[87], [283], [291], [292].
[87] *Jobson v Johnson* (n 8).

16.7   Conclusion

A pessimist might say that the law on penalties is now far more uncertain than it was in 2015. To that extent one should heed the old adage to be careful what you wish for. Several points can be made.

First, the penalties jurisdiction is not attracted unless the clause in question operates on breach (i.e. it defines a 'secondary obligation' rather than a 'primary' one). This characterisation is made by the courts, and substance trumps form. It follows that an obligation which is secondary in form may be held primary in substance, although even the Supreme Court seems uncertain when this might be so. On analysis, this important jurisdictional test for the penalties regime seems fatally flawed. Taken to its logical ends, it would seem to suggest that whenever a contract makes alternative provisions for performance, then the subsidiary/secondary term must inevitably be open to review as a penalty. This has the potential to swallow whole areas of contract law which were previously safe under the old formulaic rule. The alternative is to review none of these clauses, but that too was met with little warmth by the Supreme Court.

Secondly, contracting parties can protect their 'legitimate interests', and these interests go well beyond concern for recovery of losses flowing from the breach. In particular, parties can include contractual clauses designed as incentives and deterrents.

Thirdly, the deterrence which is used must not be out of all proportion or exorbitant or unconscionable, but without any yardstick such as compensatory damages, that assessment is rather at large.

Finally, if the parties get this wrong and their arrangement falls foul of the penalties rule, then the impugned secondary obligation will be void.

Short of abolishing the penalties rule, the Supreme Court could not have been more liberal. That is a plus. But vestiges of the jurisdiction remain, and neither the Supreme Court nor any of the courts before it have managed to nail a rationale for the penalties rule. This means that all the difficult distinctions just noted must be made without any sense of principle or purpose. In most circumstances this would be a recipe for disaster, not a recipe for the rule of law. With luck, however, the courts will continue to hold that properly consenting parties are generally the best arbiters of what they want, and will leave matters to them, just as they have done for most of the past century in this area.

But in an ideal world it may be better to return to the analysis adopted in the early equity cases in this area. There the focus was on procedural unfairness, not substantive unfairness. Overly onerous remedies simply raised an inference that the compromised party had not properly agreed to the particular term: there was an inference of impaired consent. This approach has obvious parallels elsewhere; it is routinely adopted by the common law to deal with the problem of onerous exclusion clauses. An approach that relies on procedural unfairness, rather than substantive unfairness, is both easier to implement and easier to justify.

17

Deposit Clauses

CARMINE CONTE

As conventionally understood, a 'deposit clause' is a provision that requires B to pay a sum of money to A as an earnest of performance of the contract, and to give up her right to recover that sum if A terminates the contract for B's default. If the deposit clause is valid, the deposit payment is immune from any repayment requirement; otherwise, it is not so immune. The main contemporary controversy in the English law of deposits surrounds why it operates in this way. The orthodox view is that the penalty rule, contextually applied, decides the fate of the clause.

This chapter will show that, properly understood, the penalty rule does not and cannot apply to deposit clauses. In other words, there is no such thing as a 'penal deposit'. Rather, the English law of deposit clauses operates as it does by reason of the true nature of these clauses, which nature fundamentally differs from that of part payment forfeiture clauses and extinguished compensation fund clauses. Viewed in this light, English law is perfectly explicable, coherent and uncontroversial. Though the chapter will concentrate on English law, it will also consider recent developments in Australian law. This is because such an approach is necessary to resolve the current issues in English commercial law.

The argument put in this chapter will proceed in three stages. First, it will outline the penalty rule jurisdiction, as best understood. Secondly, the chapter will examine deposit clauses. After considering how such clauses are conventionally analysed, it will evaluate the case law supporting the orthodox view that the penalty rule applies to deposit clauses. It will then illustrate why the penalty rule does not and cannot apply to such clauses. Finally, the chapter will explore security deposit clauses. It will demonstrate that this concept does not provide a counterexample to the argument advanced, because in truth security deposit clauses do

I am grateful to Professor Andrew Burrows for his valuable comments. The usual disclaimers apply.

not involve 'deposits' at all. Rather, they are compensation fund clauses, which do not fall within the penalty rule's ambit. However, an associated type of clause is an extinguished compensation fund clause, which clause a court may properly review under the rule.

17.1   The Penalty Rule Jurisdiction

Under the penalty rule, a court can only review an 'agreed damages clause'.[1] As traditionally understood, an agreed damages clause obligates B to pay to A a fixed sum of money upon B's breach of her contractual duty owed to A. As such, the conventional view is that the court's review jurisdiction under the rule arises where B must *pay money* to A upon *breach*.

However, as best understood, the penalty rule jurisdictional test contains two requirements. B must suffer a 'detriment'.[2] Also, B's breach of contract must trigger that detriment. An analysis of each requirement is set out below.

17.1.1   Detriment

Recent case law has established that an obligation to pay money is merely a species of the detriment genus. Two other types of detriment suffice to satisfy this element of the jurisdictional test, as follows.

The first type is an obligation to transfer a right.

In English law, an obligation to transfer a *proprietary* right clearly satisfies the first limb of the test.[3] The classic example is *Jobson v Johnson*.[4] In that case, the relevant clause of the share sale contract provided that, if the purchaser defaulted in paying an instalment of the purchase price, he was obliged to retransfer to the vendor the proprietary rights to shares for a stipulated sum. The Court of Appeal held that there was no distinction between a penalty clause that required B to pay money, and one that obligated B to transfer a proprietary right, either for no consideration or at an undervalue. In Nicholls LJ's words: 'In principle . . . there can be no

---

[1] For a detailed examination of the penalty rule, see ch 16 in this book.
[2] *Cavendish Square Holdings BV v Makdessi; ParkingEye Ltd v Beavis* [2015] UKSC 67, [2015] 3 WLR 1373 [32]; *Andrews v Australia and New Zealand Banking Group Ltd* [2012] HCA 30, (2012) 247 CLR 205 [10].
[3] Australian law is similar: *Ringrow Pty Ltd v BP Australia Pty Ltd* [2005] HCA 71, (2005) 224 CLR 656 [21]; *Andrews* (n 2) [12]–[13].
[4] [1989] 1 WLR 1026 (CA).

difference between an obligation to pay a stipulated sum of money arising on a default and an obligation to transfer specified property arising on a default. The essential vice is the same in each case.'[5] In *Cavendish Square Holdings BV v Makdessi*, the Supreme Court similarly held that the penalty rule applies to a clause that imposes on B 'an obligation to transfer assets (either for nothing or at an undervalue)'.[6]

If an obligation to transfer a proprietary right suffices, then an obligation to transfer a *personal* right must also do. Here, one cannot rationally distinguish between these two forms of rights. Further, as commercial parties usually intend that B will satisfy her obligation to pay money to A by an electronic funds transfer, and not in cash, arguably most agreed damages clauses require the transfer of a personal right.

Accordingly, a relevant detriment exists if the agreed damages clause imposes upon B an obligation to pay a sum of money, or to transfer a personal or proprietary right, to A. This will satisfy the first limb of the jurisdictional test.

The second – presently more important – type of detriment is an obligation to extinguish a right.

Three preliminary points arise.

To start, an extinguishment occurs when a party gives up a pre-existing right that she held before the story began. For example, a party may hold a right to be paid money. That party may then enter a contract containing a clause whereby she 'contracts out' of her pre-existing right to be paid. Consequently, once the event triggering the clause occurs, that party's pre-existing right is destroyed for the future. Her entitlement is extinguished.

Next, a counterfactual test applies to determine whether an extinguishment has happened. One must ask whether, but for the relevant clause, a party would have held a right against another party (for instance, a right to be paid money). If the answer is 'yes', then an extinguishment has occurred.

Lastly, when discussing the issue of extinguishing rights, some Anglo-Australian judges and commentators have used the language of 'forfeiture'.[7] However, to increase precision and avoid confusion, in this context it is best to avoid the forfeiture terminology.

---

[5] Ibid 1042.

[6] *Cavendish* (n 2) [16] (Lord Neuberger and Lord Sumption) and see also [170], [183] (Lord Mance), [233] (Lord Hodge).

[7] E.g. Harvey McGregor, *McGregor on Damages* (19th edn, Sweet & Maxwell 2014) [15–096].

Leading academics have argued that the penalty rule is exclusively concerned with executory promises, and so it does not apply to benefits 'liable to forfeiture on breach'.[8] Not so. Correctly understood, under the penalty rule a court has the power to review a clause that imposes an obligation to extinguish an accrued contractual right to be paid.

The leading case is *Gilbert-Ash (Northern) Ltd v Modern Engineering (Bristol) Ltd*.[9] The facts concerned a building contract between a main contractor and a sub-contractor. Clause 14 of the sub-contract stated that the main contractor was entitled to 'suspend or withhold [the] payment of any monies due' to the sub-contractor if the latter breached the sub-contract's terms.[10] The House of Lords held that the clause fell within the court's review jurisdiction. According to Lord Salmon, a court is entitled to review a clause that, upon B's breach, would enable A to suspend or withhold the payment of money due from A to B.[11]

English appellate judges have consistently supported the decision. For example, in *Firma C-Trade SA v Newcastle Protection and Indemnity Association (The Fanti)*, the court followed the decision in *Gilbert-Ash*, holding that there is 'no distinction between withholding or disentitling a person to a sum of money which is due to him and requiring him to pay a sum of money ...'.[12] Further, in *Cavendish*, Lord Hodge approved the decision, ultimately concluding that the penalty rule applies to a clause that authorises 'the withholding of sums otherwise due to the contract-breaker'.[13]

Stevens and McFarlane have argued that the agreed damages clause in *Gilbert-Ash* 'attempted to remove the subcontractor's accrued right to be paid if [it] committed any breach of contract ... It was, therefore, functionally equivalent to a penalty payable upon breach of contract.'[14] This passage makes two fundamental points.

---

[8] JW Carter and others, 'Contractual Penalties: Resurrecting the Equitable Jurisdiction' (2013) 30 JCL 99, 100.

[9] [1974] AC 689 (HL). In Australia, see *Bysouth v Shire of Blackburn and Mitcham (No 2)* [1928] VLR 562 (VSCFC) 573–74, 585. See also *Interstar Wholesale Finance Pty Ltd v Integral Home Loans Pty Ltd* [2008] NSWCA 310, (2008) 257 ALR 292 [93], [104].

[10] *Gilbert-Ash* (n 9) 703.   [11] Ibid 723.

[12] [1989] 1 Lloyd's Rep 239 (CA) 262, revd [1991] 2 AC 1 (HL).

[13] *Cavendish* (n 2) [228]. In *Cavendish*, Lord Mance also supported the decision, and came to the same conclusion: *Cavendish* (n 2) [154], [170]. Conversely, Lord Neuberger and Lord Sumption expressed some reservations about the judgment, though in the end their Lordships were 'prepared to assume, without deciding' that the rule is engaged by a provision that 'disentitles the contract-breaker from receiving a sum of money which would otherwise have been due to him [or her]': *Cavendish* (n 2) [73].

[14] Robert Stevens and Ben McFarlane, 'In Defence of *Sumpter v Hedges*' (2002) 118 LQR 569, 581.

For one, a clause entitling A to suspend or withhold the payment of money due from A to B, or disentitling B to receive a payment otherwise due to B, is in fact a clause that *extinguishes B's accrued right* to be paid by A.[15] So, in *Gilbert-Ash*, clause 14 satisfied the definition of an extinguishment, as it effectively provided that, upon the sub-contractor's breach, it would give up its pre-existing claim right against the main contractor to be paid for services it had rendered. Further, clause 14 also passed the counterfactual test as, but for the clause, the sub-contractor would have held that claim right against the main contractor.

For another, the passage raises an important point regarding functional equivalency. Clearly, a clause requiring B to transfer a proprietary right to A for no consideration is functionally equivalent to one providing for B to pay money to A. Why? Because the former clause operates to leave B factually worse off, and to leave A factually better off, to the same extent as the latter clause. The same reasoning applies to the clause in *Gilbert-Ash*. Thus, clause 14 attempted to cancel the subcontractor's accrued right to be paid. Accordingly, clause 14 was functionally equivalent to an agreed damages clause requiring payment as the clause operated to leave the sub-contractor factually worse off, and to leave the main contractor factually better off, to the same extent as a clause requiring the sub-contractor to pay money to the main contractor. Put differently, a clause entitling A to extinguish an accrued right that B holds against A is functionally equivalent to a clause providing for B to pay money to A.

If an obligation to extinguish an accrued contractual right to be paid *money* satisfies this element of the test, then an obligation to give up an accrued contractual right to be transferred *property* must also suffice. For instance, assume a clause states that, if B breaches her obligation to do act X by Wednesday, A is entitled to withhold transferring to B the proprietary right to shares worth £500, a transfer to which B has an accrued right. In other words, A is entitled to extinguish B's accrued right to be transferred the shares.[16] Precedent and principle support the view that such a clause creates a sufficient detriment.

As to precedent, in *Interstar* the New South Wales Court of Appeal held that it was 'a small step from accepting that the doctrine applies to

---

[15] See *Lancore Services Ltd v Barclays Bank plc* [2009] EWCA Civ 752, [2010] 1 All ER 763 [29].

[16] In some cases, if B holds an *accrued* contractual right to the transfer of shares, then B in fact may hold a proprietary right to the shares (as the beneficiary under a trust). If so, then pursuant to the clause, A would be entitled to extinguish B's *proprietary* right to the shares. This possibility need not be explored further here.

a transfer of property ... to applying it to [a] forfeiture of property ... ', and as such the court assumed that the rule applies to the 'forfeiture of rights or property'.[17] This passage is difficult. It is best interpreted as follows. An obligation to transfer a proprietary right is analogous to an obligation to extinguish a right to have transferred a proprietary right. Hence, both situations properly fall within the review jurisdiction.

As to principle, in the context of obligations to transfer, English private law does not distinguish between personal and proprietary rights. Rationally, it must follow that the law does not refuse to review an obligation to extinguish merely on the basis that it is connected to a proprietary right. In other words, when applying the jurisdictional test, the distinction between personal and proprietary rights is not a meaningful one.

Consequently, a relevant detriment exists if: B holds a right against A that obligates A to transfer money or property to B; and the agreed damages clause provides A with a right to extinguish B's right to the payment or to have transferred the property, and imposes upon B the concomitant obligation to give up the particular right. This will satisfy the first limb of the jurisdictional test.

17.1.2 Breach

It is universally agreed that the court's power to review an agreed damages clause arises upon B breaching a contractual duty owed to A. It has long been debated whether a rights infringement also delimits the court's review jurisdiction. However, in *Cavendish*, the Supreme Court unanimously held that a breach of contract is both sufficient and necessary to engage the rule.[18] Thus, the review jurisdiction properly includes agreed damages clauses that are triggered by an actual breach, and a 'causal breach'.

On the one hand, a breach of contract provides the 'core case' of judicial review. On the other hand, a 'causal breach' refers to a breach that is the causally operative trigger for B's detriment. For example, assume a clause states that A has the right to terminate a contract pursuant to an express contractual right arising upon B's non-repudiatory breach. A separate clause states that, if A does so, B must pay agreed damages to A. Strictly, when such an agreed damages is

---

[17] *Interstar* (n 9) [104].
[18] *Cavendish* (n 2) [12], [129]–[130], [239]–[241], [291]–[293] cf *Andrews* (n 2) [78].

engaged, it is A's election to exercise her right to terminate, not B's breach, that causally triggers B's obligation to pay. Despite this, the clause is reviewable upon orthodox principles.[19] The reasoning is that, in substance, it is the underlying breach that triggers B's duty to pay, transfer or extinguish, such that termination for breach is essentially tantamount to breach, and rightly treated similarly.

In short, the review power properly extends to clauses activated by an actual breach, or a causal breach. Either will satisfy the second limb of the jurisdictional test.

17.2 Deposit Clauses

17.2.1 Conventional Analysis

Deposit clauses most commonly arise in sale contracts. In that context, a conventional analysis of deposit clauses suggests that the term in fact refers to two separate clauses: a deposit *payment* clause and a deposit *forfeiture* clause. Further, it is thought that where a contract contains these two clauses, the following three rights arise.

First, a deposit payment clause obligates the purchaser to transfer a deposit payment, and provides the vendor with a *payment right*: that is, a right to that payment on the due date. Secondly, absent the contract containing a forfeiture clause, upon the vendor terminating the contract for the purchaser's breach the purchaser would obtain a *recovery right*: that is, a right to recover the deposit payment. Finally, if the contract contains a deposit payment clause it must also contain an express or implied deposit forfeiture clause,[20] which provides that upon termination the vendor obtains a *forfeiture right*: that is, the right to forfeit the purchaser's recovery right. As a result, the vendor may retain the deposit payment.

It is important to note three points regarding the traditional view.

To begin with, in the sale contract context, the purchaser forfeits the right *to recover* the deposit payment, not the right to the payment itself, which is

---

[19] *Cooden Engineering Co v Stanford* [1953] 1 QB 86 (CA) 96–97, 116. See also *AMEV-UDC Finance Ltd v Austin* [1986] HCA 63, (1986) 162 CLR 170, 184–85, 197, 205, 211.

[20] This is because if the contract contains a correctly labelled deposit (payment) clause and no express deposit forfeiture clause, the court *necessarily* will imply a deposit forfeiture clause unless the contract contains an express contrary provision: Keith Mason, JW Carter and Greg J Tolhurst, *Mason and Carter's Restitution Law in Australia* (2nd edn, LexisNexis 2008) [1138] cf McGregor (n 7) [15–097] (sale of land contracts only).

transferred to the vendor before he terminates.[21] The recovery right is a prima facie claim right to restitution for unjust enrichment. The unjust factor grounding the claim is a failure of basis: the purchaser has transferred the payment on the basis that she will receive counter-performance, and the vendor renders nothing in exchange for the payment.

Next, the deposit forfeiture clause excludes the purchaser's unjust enrichment claim right. The reasoning is that, by including that clause, the purchaser 'contracts out' of her prima facie entitlement to restitution.[22]

Lastly, the judicial enquiry regarding deposit clauses contains two stages.[23] The first stage is one of construction (or interpretation). The court will ask: was the clause correctly labelled as a 'deposit clause'? The second stage concerns validity. Thus, if the clause is correctly labelled, the judge must determine whether the putative deposit clause is valid or not.

17.2.2 Does the Penalty Rule Apply to Deposit Clauses?

Presently the orthodox view is that the penalty rule, contextually applied, determines whether a putative deposit clause is valid or not.[24] If it is invalid, the vendor must return the deposit payment to the purchaser, subject to a deduction for general compensatory damages.

The leading case espousing the conventional view is the Privy Council's decision in *Workers Trust and Merchant Bank Ltd v Dojap Investments Ltd*.[25] In that case, under a mortgagee sale the vendor bank contracted to sell to a purchaser the proprietary right to Jamaican land. The contract provided that the purchaser was to transfer a deposit payment of 25 per cent of the contract price, and that the contract was to complete within 14 days of the contract date. The agreement contained a clause making the time of the essence. It further stipulated that if the purchaser defaulted, its 'deposit [would] be forfeited to the vendor'.[26] The purchaser transferred the right to the deposit payment to the vendor. It then failed to complete. The vendor terminated the contract and exercised its forfeiture right. The purchaser sought relief.

---

[21] *Howe v Smith* (1884) 27 Ch D 89 (CA) 101 (Fry LJ); *Amble Assets LLP (In Administration) v Longbenton Foods Ltd* [2011] EWHC 3774 (Ch), [2012] 1 All ER (Comm) 764 [81].

[22] Andrew Burrows, *The Law of Restitution* (3rd edn, Oxford University Press 2011) 355; Elisabeth Peden, 'Forfeiture of Deposits: Where Law and Equity Collide?' (2012) 6 J Eq 161, 161.

[23] *Coates v Sarich* [1964] WAR 2 (WASCFC) 15.

[24] *Cavendish* (n 2) [16], [238] but see [170] cf *Cadogan Petroleum Holdings Ltd v Global Process Systems LLC* [2013] EWHC 214 (Com Ct), [2013] 2 Lloyd's Rep 26 [34].

[25] [1993] AC 573 (PC).   [26] Ibid 577.

The Privy Council held that the putative deposit clause was a 'plain penalty'[27] and invalid. As such, the vendor was not entitled to retain the deposit payment. Accordingly, the Board ordered that the vendor repay the entire sum to the purchaser. However, the vendor was entitled to subtract from the repayment any general compensatory damages for losses it had suffered as a result of the purchaser's breach.

In the Privy Council's advice, Lord Browne-Wilkinson analysed the penalty rule in terms of a general rule, and an exception.

Starting with the general rule, his Lordship stated:

> In general, a contractual provision which requires one party in the event of [her] breach of the contract to pay or forfeit a sum of money to the other party is unlawful as being a penalty, unless such provision can be justified as being a payment of liquidated damages being a genuine pre-estimate of the loss which the innocent party will incur by reason of the breach.[28]

Accordingly, the Board recognised that *putative* deposit clauses are agreed damages clauses, such that the penalty rule generally applies to them. Many courts and commentators have supported this analysis.[29]

Moving to the exception, Lord Browne-Wilkinson held:

> One exception to this general rule is the provision for the payment of a deposit by the purchaser on a contract for the sale of land ... [T]he forfeiture of such a deposit (customarily 10 per cent of the contract price) does not fall within the general rule and can be validly forfeited even though the amount of the deposit bears no reference to the anticipated loss to the vendor flowing from the breach of contract.[30]

In short, although under the general rule *true* deposit clauses are penal and invalid, they are in fact exceptional, and therefore valid. Again, much support for this view exists.[31] In fact, in a later case, the Privy Council forcefully rejected an argument that the law is otherwise.[32]

---

[27] Ibid 582.   [28] Ibid 578.

[29] *The General Trading Co (Holdings) Ltd v Richmond Corp Ltd* [2008] EWHC 1479 (Com Ct), [2008] 2 Lloyd's Rep 475 [113]; *Barnard v Zarbafi* [2010] EWHC 3256 (Ch) [15]–[16]; *Ng v Ashley King (Developments) Ltd* [2010] EWHC 456 (Ch), [2011] Ch 115 [22]; Edwin Peel, *The Law of Contract* (14th edn, Sweet & Maxwell 2015) [20–148]–[20–149]; JW Carter, 'Two Privy Council Cases' (1993) 6 JCL 260, 267. See also *Coates* (n 23) 14; *Manufacturers House Pty Ltd v Ashington No 147 Pty Ltd* [2005] NSWSC 767, (2005) 12 BPR 23, 913 [55], [60]. But cf *Amble Assets* (n 21) [75].

[30] *Workers Trust* (n 25) 578.

[31] *Midill (97PL) Ltd v Park Lane Estates Ltd* [2008] EWCA Civ 1227, [2009] 1 WLR 2460 [32]; *Ng* (n 29) [22]. See also *Manufacturers House* (n 29) [55], [60].

[32] *Union Eagle Ltd v Golden Achievement Ltd* [1997] AC 514 (PC) 518.

In *Workers Trust*, Lord Browne-Wilkinson also articulated the following rules of validity, to be applied at the second stage of the judicial enquiry. To be valid, a putative deposit clause must be objectively 'reasonable'. A customary deposit payment of 10 per cent is prima facie reasonable. However, a reasonable deposit may be greater than this. So, a vendor may recover a deposit payment exceeding 10 per cent if he can show that 'special circumstances' exist[33] (e.g. the contract provides for a long pre-completion period,[34] or the contractual subject matter may substantially deteriorate or devalue during the pre-completion period[35]). It necessarily follows that if the purchaser can show that the deposit payment is unreasonable, it is penal and invalid.

In *Union Eagle*, the Privy Council confirmed this analysis. In the Board's advice, Lord Hoffmann held that if a deposit clause permits a vendor to retain an amount exceeding a reasonable deposit payment – if the amount is unreasonable – it will constitute a penalty. His Lordship added that any relief against the 'forfeiture' of a deposit payment is, in fact, a form of 'restitutionary relief against penalties'.[36]

For several reasons, the Privy Council's analysis in *Workers Trust* is problematic.

The general rule propounded is inaccurate, too narrow and contradicted by authority. It is inaccurate because it suggests that the penalty rule applies where a clause requires one party to 'forfeit a sum of money' upon breach. But a purchaser cannot 'forfeit' her right to the deposit payment; if she 'forfeits' anything at all, she 'forfeits' her recovery right. It is too narrow because the general rule assumes that liquidated damages clauses are exclusively concerned with loss. They are not. For instance, judges have recognised that liquidated *substitutionary* damages clauses exist.[37] Authority contradicts it because, although the general rule implies that agreed damages clauses are prima facie *invalid*, courts have held that such clauses are in fact presumed *valid*: the party alleging that the clause is penal bears the onus of demonstrating this.[38]

More importantly, the exception is arbitrary, discordant with practice, and incoherent. So, why is a conventional deposit payment of 10 per cent

---

[33] See similarly *James v Hill* [2004] NSWCA 301 [48].   [34] *Barnard* (n 29) [23].
[35] *Re Hoobin (deceased)* [1957] VR 341 (VSC) 347–48.   [36] *Union Eagle* (n 32) 520.
[37] E.g. *Alfred McAlpine Construction Ltd v Panatown Ltd* [2001] 1 AC 518 (HL) 554–55 (Lord Goff).
[38] *Murray v Leisureplay plc* [2005] EWCA Civ 963, [2005] IRLR 946 [69] (Arden LJ), [106(vii)] (Clarke LJ); *Spiers Earthworks Pty Ltd v Landtec Projects Corporation Pty Ltd (No 2)* [2012] WASCA 53, (2012) 287 ALR 360 [86].

automatically valid? Any principled justification is impossible. In the
Board's advice, for example, Lord Browne-Wilkinson admitted that the
exception is 'anomalous'.[39] Instead, writers plead in support an unexplained notion of 'pragmatism'.[40] In addition, the Privy Council treated
the enforcement of deposit forfeiture clauses as an exception to the
general rule. However, as Carter notes, the position in practice regarding
such clauses is that 'enforcement is the rule and relief the exception'.[41]
Further, the deposit exception creates an 'apparent inconsistency' in the
law:[42] it leads to the contradictory proposition that, in some cases,
a 'penal deposit' is valid.[43]

Another view exists, however. In *Comr of Taxation v Reliance Carpet
Co Pty Ltd*, the Australian High Court held that if a contract contains
a true deposit clause, the court has no *jurisdiction* to review the clause
under the penalty rule.[44] The court interpreted a passage from Lord
Browne-Wilkinson's judgment in *Workers Trust* as supporting the
proposition.[45] In short, it is not the case that the rule generally applies,
but deposit clauses are exceptional; rather, the rule does not apply at all.

17.2.3 *Why the Penalty Rule Does Not, and Cannot,*
Apply to Deposit Clauses

The Australian High Court's argument in *Reliance Carpet* was one from
authority, as courts are bound to make. But precedents bind judges, not
lawyers' understandings. The question, then, is whether this view provides the best understanding of English law. This is indeed the case, as it
is the only sound, principled view. Two reasons follow.

17.2.3.1   Where Detriment Exists, There is No Breach

As stated, traditionally viewed the court's review jurisdiction under the
penalty rule only arises as regards a clause whereby, upon an actual or

---

[39] *Workers Trust* (n 25) [1993] AC 573 (PC) 578.
[40] E.g. Chris Rossiter, *Penalties and Forfeiture* (Lawbook Company 1992) 116.
[41] Carter (n 29) 264.
[42] *Luong Dinh Luu v Sovereign Developments Pty Ltd* [2006] NSWCA 40, (2006) 12 BPR 23,
      629 [24].
[43] Peel (n 29) [20–149].
[44] [2008] HCA 22, (2008) 236 CLR 342 [26]. See also *Havyn Pty Ltd v Webster* [2005]
      NSWCA 182, (2005) 12 BPR 22, 837 [137].
[45] *Workers Trust* (n 25) 578–79. See also *NLS Pty Ltd v Hughes* [1966] HCA 63, (1966) 120
      CLR 583, 588–89.

a causal breach, B comes under an obligation to pay money to A; to transfer a right to A; or to extinguish a right held against A.

However, at the time when a purchaser comes under a duty to pay the deposit money to the vendor, or transfer the right to the deposit payment to the vendor, the purchaser will have committed no breach of contract. This is because a deposit payment is *'payable in performance of a contractual obligation* antecedent to any breach'.[46] In other words, a breach of contract does not trigger the obligation to pay a deposit payment: that duty precedes any breach, and is independent of it.[47] It follows that, at the relevant time, although the purchaser's obligation to pay or transfer satisfies the detriment requirement of the penalty rule's jurisdictional test, the breach requirement remains unsatisfied. No review is possible.

17.2.3.2 Where a Breach Exists, There is No Detriment

Recall that, on the traditional view of deposit clauses, the purchaser 'contracts out' of her prima facie unjust enrichment claim right. A 'contracting-out' is an extinguishment of a right by another name. It seemingly follows that the detriment requirement of the jurisdictional test is satisfied. Further, if such an extinguishment occurs, it takes place when the vendor terminates the contract for the purchaser's breach.[48] Thus, the purchaser's causal breach triggers the relevant detriment. The breach requirement is also satisfied.

In fact, at the time when the purchaser breaches the contract and the vendor terminates it, no right that the purchaser holds against the vendor will be extinguished. Where the facts truly involve a deposit clause, the purchaser does not maintain an unjust enrichment claim right that is capable of extinguishment. It necessarily follows that the detriment requirement is unsatisfied, and that the court has no jurisdiction to review a deposit clause under the penalty rule.

These statements need unpacking. To do so, one must undertake a detailed analysis of the true nature of deposit payments, and deposit clauses.

Beginning with deposit payments, three important points must be made.

First, deposit payments are an earnest.[49] An earnest is a token given to demonstrate one's sincere intention and genuine commitment to

---

[46] *Havyn* (n 44) [134] (original emphasis).   [47] *Amble Assets* (n 21) [75].
[48] *Union Eagle* (n 32) 518; *Reliance Carpet* (n 44) [26].
[49] *Howe* (n 21) 101. See also *Brien v Dwyer* [1978] HCA 50, (1978) 141 CLR 378, 386, 398, 401, 406.

perform the bargain. In the sale context, it is a 'guarantee that the purchaser means business'.[50] An earnest may be monetary or a benefit in kind,[51] but it is always given on or about the contract date. The fact a payment operates as an earnest of performance provides it with its character as a deposit payment,[52] and distinguishes it from a part payment.[53] In essence, the expression 'deposit' and 'earnest money' are 'two words for the same thing'.[54]

Secondly, where X makes a deposit (earnest) payment to Y, necessarily it means that X makes the payment out-and-out, as a sign of commitment to the deal.[55] As such, the basis of the deposit payment is that if X does not perform, then the earnest money is 'lost' and Y can keep it.[56] This is the 'commitment basis'. However, it follows that if X performs, then Y must repay the earnest money. The authorities make clear that Y is not entitled to retain the deposit payment because X has a right to restitution of it, based on either an unjust enrichment claim right (due to a failure of basis) or a consensual restitution clause (if the contract contains one). The restitutionary right is 'one of great antiquity and very general prevalence'.[57]

Finally, in the sale contract context, a payment may have a dual character: it may display *both* an earnest character and a part payment character. A part payment is a right to a money sum or a non-monetary subject matter[58] transferred partially to satisfy the contract price. Importantly, those two characters are discrete: for an earnest and part payment are 'two distinct things'; and an earnest does not lose that character merely 'because the same thing might also avail as part payment'.[59] This has been the case for a very long time.[60]

Critically, according to the leading case of *Howe*, earnest payments that are also part payments are transferred on two contingent bases.[61]

[50] *Soper v Arnold* [1889] 14 App Cas 429 (HL) 435.
[51] *Omar v El-Wakil* [2001] EWCA Civ 1090, [2002] 2 P & CR 3 [24]; *Ward v Ellerton* [1927] VLR 494 (VSCFC) 501.
[52] *Union Eagle* (n 32) 518.
[53] *Fiorelli Properties Pty Ltd v Professional Fencemakers Pty Ltd* [2011] VSC 661, (2011) 34 VR 257 [62].
[54] *Linggi Plantations Ltd v Jagatheesan* [1972] 1 MLJ 89 (PC) 93.
[55] Cf Peter Birks, *An Introduction to the Law of Restitution* (Clarendon Press 1985) 224, 235; *Gribbon v Lutton* [2001] EWCA Civ 1956, [2002] QB 902 [61]–[62].
[56] *Howe* (n 21) 102 (Fry LJ); *Reliance Carpet* (n 44) [27].
[57] *Howe* (n 21) 101 (Fry LJ); *Reliance Carpet* (n 44) [27].
[58] *Ward* (n 51) 501 (right to goods).
[59] *Howe* (n 21) 102 (Fry LJ). See also *Reliance Carpet* (n 44) [27].
[60] See Statute of Frauds 1677 (29 Car II c 3) s 17.   [61] *Howe* (n 21) 95, 101–02.

On the one hand, if the purchaser performs and the contract completes, the payment goes partially to satisfy the contract price.[62] As such, the payment is made on account of the contract price. This is the 'accounting basis'. To explain, if the contract completes, then given its earnest character the vendor must return the deposit payment to the purchaser: the purchaser is entitled to restitution based on an unjust enrichment claim due to a failure of the commitment basis (or possibly a consensual restitution clause). However, given its part payment character, the purchaser must repay the same amount to the vendor: the vendor has rendered counter-performance, such that a part payment in the relevant amount is properly due and payable, and the vendor is entitled to keep it once paid. To promote administrative convenience, the parties agree that the purchaser pays the money on account in the first place.

On the other hand, if the purchaser defaults and the contract does not complete, the vendor is entitled to retain the payment.[63] Accordingly, the payment is made out-and-out. In other words, the payment is made on the commitment basis. It follows that, if the contract does not complete, then given its part payment character the purchaser is entitled to recover the payment: she has a right to restitution for unjust enrichment due to a failure of basis, given that she has not received the counter-performance for which she bargained. However, given its earnest character, the vendor is entitled to retain the payment in order to satisfy the commitment basis. To uphold the principle of avoiding circuity of action, the vendor is not required to pay anything at all.

This analysis raises two essential points regarding construction.

For one, the first question in any analysis of putative deposit clauses in a sale contract context is one of characterisation. That is, where a purchaser transfers an initial payment to the vendor under a sale contract, one must ask whether the payment is properly a dual earnest payment *and* part payment, or whether it is a mere part payment. The answer to this question is not necessarily straightforward, as the label the parties give to the payment is not determinative.[64] As such, a payment contractually described as a 'deposit payment' in truth may be a simple part payment.[65] Conversely, in

---

[62] *Workers Trust* (n 25) 578–79; *Havyn* (n 44) [130].

[63] *McDonald v Dennys Lascelles Ltd* [1933] HCA 25, (1933) 48 CLR 457, 470; *Workers Trust* (n 25) 578–79.

[64] *Elson (Inspector of Taxes) v Prices Tailors Ltd* [1963] 1 WLR 287 (Ch) 291–92; *Iannello v Sharpe* [2007] NSWCA 61, (2007) 69 NSWLR 452 [31].

[65] E.g. *Palmer v Temple* (1839) 9 A & E 508, 112 ER 1304.

principle a court may hold that a payment not described as a 'deposit' is in fact one. However, if the contract does not identify the nature of the payment, courts are predisposed to interpreting the relevant clause as providing for a part payment.[66]

For another, to characterise the payment properly, one must consider various factors. Although it is not conclusive, the label that the parties have given to the payment in the relevant clause is an important factor in determining whether the payment is partially an earnest payment, or not. Another such factor is the timing of the payment. In addition, a significant factor is proportionality: that is, the proportion or percentage of the contract price that the payment constitutes. The last factor concerns reasonableness. Recall that, in *Workers Trust*, Lord Browne-Wilkinson articulated several principles regarding how a court should assess whether a payment is reasonable, including setting an ordinary benchmark of 10 per cent and introducing a 'special circumstances' qualifier. It is conventionally thought that English courts use these principles to evaluate whether a putative deposit clause is valid.[67] That is wrong. Properly understood, these are rules of construction that assist in determining whether a payment is, properly construed, objectively reasonable. If it is, then the payment is a deposit payment, and it is necessarily valid. No question of potential invalidity arises. It follows, then, that the *Workers Trust* principles regarding reasonableness relate to construction, not validity.

This analysis displays much explanatory power. For example, it explicates why, in *Workers Trust*, Lord Browne-Wilkinson held that if a 'deposit payment' is unreasonable, then the relevant clause is invalid. This is because if a putative deposit payment is unreasonable, three propositions must follow. First, the relevant payment is in truth a mere part payment. Secondly, the contract per hypothesis also contains a part payment forfeiture clause, which clause properly falls within the penalty rule jurisdiction.[68] Finally, a part payment forfeiture clause will likely fail the penal rule test of validity, if correctly applied.

---

[66] *Dies v British and International Mining and Finance Corp Ltd* [1939] 1 KB 724 (KB) 743.

[67] E.g. Peel (n 29) [20–148].

[68] Cf *Cavendish* (n 2) [16] but note [170]. In particular, a (reclassified) part payment forfeiture clause will satisfy the detriment requirement, as it will extinguish one party's unjust enrichment claim right: *Stockloser v Johnson* [1954] 1 QB 476 (CA) 489–90, 493. Note that in *Stockloser* Denning LJ held that, before the vendor terminates the contract, the purchaser cannot recover in unjust enrichment. This is because the orthodox view is that no failure of basis occurs until the contract is discharged for breach: Burrows (n 22) 327–28; cf *Roxborough v Rothmans of Pall Mall Australia Ltd* [2001] HCA 68, (2001) 208

Turning to deposit clauses, three points must be elucidated.

To start, in all cases, if a contract contains a deposit clause, then necessarily it will include a separate clause reflecting the commitments basis. For example, in a sale contract context, if a deposit clause properly requires the purchaser to transfer a dual earnest and part payment, then she will transfer that payment partially on a commitment basis. In many cases, the parties will include in their contract an express clause that effectively encapsulates that commitment basis. However, if the contract does *not* contain this express clause, the court will imply a clause that encapsulates the commitment basis: that is, a 'commitment clause'. As Mitchell, Mitchell and Watterson state, the implied clause simply articulates 'what the parties have agreed should be the basis of the payment'.[69] Crucially, the court *inevitably* will imply a commitment clause, unless an express contrary provision exists.[70] The reasoning here is that the earnest notion necessarily leads to a commitment basis, and that basis necessarily forms a term of the parties' contract. In short, the commitment basis and a commitment clause go hand in hand.

Next, deposit clauses do not involve a *failure* of basis, but a *satisfaction* of it. To explain, as stated, the commitment basis holds as follows: where X makes a deposit (earnest) payment to Y, as a sign of her commitment to the deal, X makes the payment on the basis that Y can keep the earnest money if X does not perform. By reason of the express or implied commitment clause, that basis is contractual in nature. It follows that, if X fails to perform, necessarily the contractual basis will not fail. Rather, that basis will be fulfilled.[71] As the basis does not fail, X obtains no unjust enrichment claim right at any stage. As no unjust enrichment claim right arises, no such right is capable of being extinguished.

CLR 516; *Barnes v Eastenders Cash and Carry plc* [2014] UKSC 26, [2015] AC 1. However, once the vendor terminates, a failure of basis occurs and the purchaser's unjust enrichment claim right arises. The Court of Appeal has confirmed this analysis in the sale of goods contract context: *Clough Mill Ltd v Martin* [1985] 1 WLR 111 (CA) 117–18. It follows that, in the part payment context, the extinguished right is a crystallised claim right, not a contingent one.

[69] Charles Mitchell, Paul Mitchell and Stephen Watterson, *Goff and Jones: The Law of Unjust Enrichment* (9th edn, Sweet & Maxwell 2016) [14–02].

[70] *Hall v Burnell* [1911] 2 Ch 551 (Ch) 554, 556; *Havyn* (n 44) [131]; *Reliance Carpet* (n 44) [26] fn 30.

[71] Cf Graham Virgo, *The Principles of the Law of Restitution* (3rd edn, Oxford University Press 2015) 338.

Lastly, if one correctly applies the counterfactual test, it confirms that no extinguishment exists. As stated, under this test one must ask whether, but for the relevant clause, a party would have held a right against another party (for instance, a right to be paid, or repaid, money). If the answer is 'yes', then an extinguishment has occurred. So, suppose that a contract between X and Y includes a deposit payment clause and an express commitment clause. If we remove the express commitment clause, does X hold an unjust enrichment claim right against Y for a return of the deposit payment? The answer is 'no'. If no express commitment clause exists, a court inevitably will imply a commitment clause, such that the basis of the payment will not fail. It follows that no extinguishment has taken place.

This analysis exhibits great explanatory force, as it clarifies judicial comments that are otherwise difficult to rationalise. Take the following two examples. On the one hand, in *NLS*, the Australian High Court held that if payment is properly an earnest, then it stands outside the dichotomy that exists between liquidated damages and penalties.[72] This is because a deposit payment is simply not in the nature of agreed damages. On the other hand, in *Union Eagle*, the Privy Council acknowledged that 'in the normal case of a reasonable deposit, no inquiry is made as to whether [the sum] is a pre-estimate of damage or not'.[73] Put differently, in the case of a deposit clause, an English court does not apply the usual penalty rule test of validity. Why? This is because a judge obtains no power to review the relevant clause at the antecedent, jurisdictional stage of the penalty rule enquiry.

The conclusion can be succinctly stated. Where a deposit clause exists, a party has not 'forfeited anything in respect of the payment of the deposit'.[74] She does not give up a pre-existing right that she held before the story began. Nothing is extinguished. The detriment requirement of the penalty rule's jurisdictional test remains unsatisfied. The penalty rule, then, is properly irrelevant.

17.3   Security Deposit Clauses

17.3.1   Conventional Analysis

One controversial issue remains. It has been argued that, in the early twentieth century, some courts applied the penalty rule to a particular

---

[72] *NLS* (n 45) 589.   [73] *Union Eagle* (n 32) 518.   [74] *Havyn* (n 44) [135].

type of deposit clause.[75] The classic example case is the Privy Council's decision in *Comr of Public Works v Hills*.[76]

The facts, slightly simplified, were these. Under a construction contract a contractor agreed to build three railways for the Government of the Cape of Good Hope. The contract provided that the Government was to retain 10 per cent from the payments falling due as the lines were constructed, and that these moneys were to form a guarantee fund which was to be primarily applied to making good any construction defects. The agreement contained a clause stating that the Government was obligated to hand over the retained monies to the contractor in instalments upon its completing particular milestones. It further stipulated that if the contractor failed to complete constructing the final line by the deadline, the retained monies would be 'forfeited to the . . . Government as and for liquidated damages sustained by the . . . Government for the non-completion of the said line'.[77] The contractor failed to complete in the time prescribed. It then sought to recover the retained monies. The Government resisted.

The Privy Council held that the clause was properly an agreed damages clause, and hence fell within the penalty rule jurisdiction. As to the issue of validity, the Board held that 'the mere form of expression "penalty" or "liquidated damages" does not conclude the matter'.[78] Ultimately, it decided that the clause did not pass the relevant test of validity: the amount of the retained monies did not represent a genuine pre-estimate of the Government's anticipated loss. As such, the clause was penal.

In *NLS*, the Australian High Court held that the Privy Council's judgment in *Comr of Public Works* supported the view that a 'sum lodged by way of guarantee of performance' may be penal.[79] Later, in *Workers Trust*, Lord Browne-Wilkinson held that the judgment provided 'clear authority' supporting the Board's decision that the putative deposit clause in that case was a penalty, and that the purchaser was entitled to consequential relief.[80]

The facts of *Comr of Public Works* involved a particular type of payment. It is usually referred to as a 'security deposit'.[81] The clause

[75] Hossein Abedian and Michael P Furmston, 'Relief against Forfeiture after Breach of an Essential Time Stipulation' (1998) 12 JCL 189, 191 fn 12.
[76] [1906] AC 368 (PC). See also *Pye v British Automobile Commercial Syndicate Ltd* [1906] 1 KB 425 (KB).
[77] *Comr of Public Works* (n 76) 373.   [78] Ibid 375.   [79] *NLS* (n 45) 588.
[80] *Workers Trust* (n 25) 582.   [81] E.g. Carter (n 29) 267.

under which it is paid is commonly known as a 'security deposit clause'. The proposition advanced, then, is seemingly that the penalty rule applies to a security deposit clause, which is merely a particular form of deposit clause. If that assertion is correct, then the argument that the chapter advances is wrong. That is not the case. The assertion is misconceived.

17.3.2 Compensation Fund and Extinguished Compensation Fund Clauses

To resolve this controversy, we must closely analyse the concept of a security deposit clause. Three points follow.

First, a security deposit clause is one that provides Y with a fund from which he can recoup compensation for any breach of contract by X. For example, in a residential tenancy agreement, the tenant is often required to pay a deposit, typically of one month's rent. The security deposit payment provides the landlord with 'a fund from which he can recoup compensation for any breach of contract by the tenant',[82] such as a breach of her duty to repair. Importantly, if X commits no breach, Y must refund the entire amount of the fund. Further, if X commits one or more breaches of the tenancy agreement causing Y loss, but a surplus remains after Y has deducted the amount necessary to compensate him, then Y must return the surplus to X.[83]

Secondly, the 'security deposit' label is a misnomer. The instant payment is indeed a 'security', in the sense that X makes the payment as a guarantee that she will perform her obligations, and Y must return to X any amount that he does not appropriate from the fund for a compensatory purpose. However, the 'deposit' label is inapt. The payment in play is not an earnest. An earnest is paid out-and-out, such that if X fails to perform, then the entire sum is 'lost' and Y can keep it. Put differently, X cannot recover the amount by which the earnest money exceeds Y's loss. Conversely, X transfers a 'security deposit' payment on the basis that, if she does not perform in some way, Y will deduct the sum necessary to repair his loss. He will then refund the surplus to X. In short, a 'security deposit' is not paid out-and-out. Given the preceding analysis, the instant concept is more faithfully labelled a 'compensation fund'.

Finally, in some contexts, a payment may have a dual character: it may exhibit *both* an earnest character and a compensation fund character. For example, a deposit paid upon booking a hotel room or hiring a car

---

[82] *Ng* (n 29) [23].   [83] Ibid.

displays both characters: the payment 'serves [the compensation fund] function as well as being an earnest of performance'.[84] These two characters, however, are completely separate.

In principle, earnest payments that are also payments in the nature of compensation funds are transferred on two contingent bases, as follows.

On the one hand, if X performs and takes possession, the payment forms the compensation fund. Thus, the payment is made on account of the fund, and on the accounting basis. Take, for instance, a hotel room booking. Assume a would-be guest books a hotel room in advance, and pays the deposit payment. If the guest later takes possession of the room, then given its earnest character the hotelier must return the payment to the guest: the guest has a claim to restitution based on unjust enrichment, as the commitment basis has failed. However, given its compensation fund character, the guest must repay the same amount to the hotelier: the hotelier will only provide the guest with the use of the room if the guest hands over the relevant fund, such that a payment in the same amount is properly due and payable. Here as elsewhere,[85] to foster administrative convenience the parties agree that the guest pays the money on account at the start of the story.

On the other hand, if X defaults and does not take possession, then Y is entitled to retain the payment. Hence, the payment is one made out-and-out, and on the commitment basis. Returning to the example proffered, if the would-be guest does not take possession of the room, then given its compensation fund character the guest is entitled to recover the payment: she holds an unjust enrichment claim right due to a failure of basis, given that she will not receive the relevant counter-performance of the use of the room. However, given its earnest character, the hotelier is entitled to retain the payment in order to satisfy the commitment basis. As in other cases,[86] the need to avoid circuity of action means the hotelier is not required to pay anything at all.

It is true that some of the early twentieth-century cases involved a compensation fund clause.[87] However, in each case that clause was unproblematic. A compensation fund clause clearly does not fall within the penalty rule jurisdiction, as there is no relevant payment, transfer or

---

[84] Ibid.   [85] Text following n 62.   [86] Text following n 63.
[87] Note that *Pye* (n 76) is best interpreted as involving an *implied* compensation fund clause.

extinguishment. However, in each case the pertinent contract also contained a clause requiring B to abrogate her right to recover from A any part of the compensation fund upon breach.[88] Such a clause is best labelled an 'extinguished compensation fund' clause. It follows that, if a contract includes an extinguished compensation fund clause and it is engaged, A will not return to B any surplus (or excess).

17.3.3   Does the Penalty Rule Apply to Extinguished Compensation Fund Clauses?

This examination brings to light the true question: does a clause that removes B's right to recover any part of the compensation fund from A fall within the penalty rule jurisdiction? In other words, does the penalty rule apply to extinguished compensation fund clauses? It must. The supporting reasoning is threefold.

To begin with, if a contract contains a compensation fund clause, B will obtain a recovery right arising from either consent or unjust enrichment.

As to the former, in many cases the contract itself will contain a clause expressly entitling B to recover from A any surplus that remains after A has made good his factual detriment resulting from B's breaches.[89] If so, the relevant claim right is restitutionary, but it is consensual in nature.

As to the latter, if the contract is silent as to what is to occur to any surplus, then one must interpret the terms of the contract to determine the basis of the payment. The fact the contract contains a compensation fund clause suggests that B has transferred to A the compensation fund on the following basis: A will use the monies to make good any losses that he suffers as a result of B's breach. If the fund that B pays over to A exceeds the amount of A's factual detriment, then the basis fails in respect of that surplus. Therefore, B obtains an unjust enrichment claim right against A to recover that excessive amount.

Next, if a contract contains an extinguished compensation fund clause, then upon B's breach a relevant extinguishment will occur sufficient to satisfy the detriment requirement of the penalty rule jurisdictional test. This is because such a clause effectively will require B to relinquish a pre-existing restitutionary claim right upon breach. Applying the counterfactual test, we must ask: if we remove an express extinguished compensation fund clause, does B hold a consensual or

---

[88] *Comr of Public Works* (n 76); *Pye* (n 76).   [89] E.g. *Comr of Public Works* (n 76) 373.

unjust enrichment claim right against A for a return of the surplus? The answer is 'yes'. In a counterfactual world, B would be entitled to restitution of the excess based on an express contractual right or the law of unjust enrichment (due to a failure of basis). In the real world, she is not so entitled. An extinguishment has occurred.

Lastly, the Privy Council's decision in *Comr of Public Works* is best understood in these terms. That is, properly analysed, the case involved an extinguished compensation fund clause. This explains why the Board applied the penalty rule. Consider each of the three clauses.

The first clause, relating to the 'guarantee fund', was properly a compensation fund clause: the express purpose of the fund was to compensate the Government for any losses arising from the contractor's defective construction works. Importantly, as the Government was only entitled to retain 10 per cent from the payments that had 'fallen due' to the contractor, the contractor's right to the retained payments was an *accrued* right. The Government's retaining of the monies to which the contractor had an accrued right was directly analogous to a situation where the contractor had paid over the same particular sums to the Government.

The second 'hand over' clause was correctly a consensual restitution clause: it created an express contractual right to the return of the retained monies that effectively formed a surplus in the fund.

The third clause, concerning the 'forfeiture' of the contractor's rights, was in fact an extinguished compensation fund clause. Properly understood, the clause basically stated that if the contractor defaulted, it would relinquish its contractual right to recover any of the retained monies comprising the compensation fund as at the time of its default. Such a clause clearly satisfied both the detriment and breach requirements of the jurisdictional test. It necessarily followed that the Board was able to review the clause.

A simple conclusion follows from this analysis. It is this. The following two situations are substantively the same. On the one hand, B agrees to and does pay over to A a compensation fund of £50,000, and she also agrees under an extinguished compensation fund clause to give up her right to recover any excess. On the other hand, B agrees to pay to A the sum of £50,000 as agreed compensatory damages, and then pays that sum over to A *before* she breaches her obligations under the contract and engages the agreed damages clause. The penalty rule properly applies in each case. It decides the fate of the relevant clause.

17.4 Conclusion

It has been said that deposit clauses are in a 'sui generis category' to which the penalty rule and the part payment forfeiture rule do not apply.[90] This chapter has illustrated that, as regards the penalty rule, that observation is correct.

As best understood, the penalty rule jurisdictional test contains two requirements: pursuant to the relevant clause, B's breach of contract must cause her to suffer a relevant detriment. B's breach of contract may include an actual or causal breach. Relevant detriments include B's payment of a sum to A, B's transfer of a right to A, and B's extinguishment of a right that B holds against A.

Deposit clauses deal with deposit payments. Sale contracts most commonly contain such clauses. The true nature of deposit payments is that they are an earnest – a token given to demonstrate one's sincere intention and genuine commitment to perform the bargain. As such, they are payments made out-and-out, as a sign of commitment to the deal. Whether the contracting parties expressly address the basis upon which X makes a deposit payment or not, such a payment is always made on the basis that, if X walks away from the deal, she is never to see the payment again. This is the commitment basis.

Currently the orthodox view is that the penalty rule, contextually applied, governs whether a putative deposit clause is valid or not. But this view is controversial. This chapter has shown that this view is controversial because it is incorrect. As correctly understood, the penalty rule does not, and cannot, apply to deposit clauses. For one, where a relevant detriment exists, there is no breach. So, when a purchaser comes under a duty to pay the deposit money to a vendor, or transfer the right to the deposit payment to a vendor, the purchaser will have committed no (actual) breach of contract at all. For another, where a relevant breach exists, there is no detriment. Thus, when a purchaser pays a deposit under a sale contract and a vendor later terminates it for the purchaser's (causal) breach, no right that the purchaser holds against the vendor will be extinguished. Given the commitment basis, the purchaser does not hold an unjust enrichment claim right that is capable of being given up.

This chapter also demonstrated that a 'security deposit' may indeed act as security, but it is not properly a deposit, for it is not an earnest. Rather,

---

[90] Havyn (n 44) [133].

the concept is more accurately labelled a 'compensation fund' – a clause that provides A with a fund from which he can recoup compensation for any breach of contract by B. The penalty rule does not apply to such clauses, as no relevant detriment exists. However, a related type of clause is an extinguished compensation fund clause – a clause obligating B to relinquish her right to recover from A any part of the compensation fund upon breach. These clauses are properly reviewable agreed damages clauses, for there exists a relevant detriment arising upon a breach.

The notion of a 'penal deposit', then, is a fallacy.

If the argument this chapter has advanced is correct, the need for an anomalous exception to the penalty rule for a 'true' deposit clause disappears. A deposit clause is not an exceptional form of agreed damages clause. Properly understood, it is not an agreed damages clause at all. The rule is therefore irrelevant. Cast in that light, English commercial law is more coherent, and more intelligibly explained. Above all else, it is a little less controversial.

18

Flawed Assets Clauses

LOUISE GULLIFER

18.1 Introduction

Flawed assets are not remedies. A flawed asset is a contractual obligation which only has to be performed if a contingency arises. Since it is an obligation, there is a correlative right, which is an asset in the hands of the obligee – hence the name. The asset is less valuable to the obligee than it would be without the flaw, and the flaw is, therefore, of benefit to the obligor. The nature of this benefit varies, but usually it is to protect the obligor from the failure of obligee (or another party to a different contract with the obligor) to perform its contractual obligations. Since there are usually other ways of obtaining the same protection which could, conceivably, be said to fall within the umbrella of 'contractual remedies', it does make some sense to consider flawed assets as part of a discussion of the wide scope of commercial remedies.

Many contractual obligations are only payable once (and if) a contingency occurs. For example, a term loan or deposit is not repayable until a certain period of time has elapsed and a lottery prize is only payable if the ticket-holder has the winning ticket. Sometimes the contingency (or condition) is within the control of the contractual counterparty, so that the price of goods or services may not be payable until the goods have been delivered or the services performed, and a subordinated debt is not payable until the senior creditors have been paid in full. As with many other contractual devices, such as the right to terminate a contract on breach or the occurrence of a contingency, the conditionality of a debt can be used to protect the debtor from having to perform himself if it is unlikely, or certain, that his counterparty is not going to perform. Usually there can be no objection to the creation of such an obligation. Parties to a contract are permitted to define the obligations they owe to each other in whatever terms they like.[1] If the obligor successfully bargains for its obligation to be conditional, the law should not interfere. In some commercial situations, the obligee will expect some benefit in return for the flaw; for example, a higher interest rate payable on a long-term loan or deposit. In other situations, the flaw may be standard market practice as a method of protecting the obligor, such as payment on satisfactory completion of a service.

Viewed in this way, there can be nothing objectionable in the creation of a flawed asset, or to its validity both against the contractual counter-party and any third party, either one to whom the (flawed) right is assigned or an insolvency officer (a liquidator, administrator or trustee in bankruptcy). However, there have recently been two potential lines of attack on the use of flawed assets, both of which are based on the idea of protecting creditors of the obligee (other than the obligor). This is partly at least because the flawed asset technique is sometimes used as an alternative to other methods of protection (such as a security interest or a right of set-off) which are subject to limitations designed to protect third-party creditors, and it is thought that, therefore, limitations should also apply to flawed assets.

The first line of attack is an argument that a flawed asset is a security interest, and should therefore be subject to any limitations placed on the creation and enforcement of security interests. This argument relates largely to the use of the flawed asset technique by banks to protect themselves against the failure of a depositor (or a party connected to a depositor) to repay a loan facility made available to it by the bank. The repayment of the deposit by the bank is made conditional upon the repayment to the bank. In a loose sense, this can be said to 'secure' the repayment of the loan. This has led to suggestions in certain jurisdictions (though not yet in England and Wales) that a flawed asset arrangement, particularly if it includes other rights such as a right of set-off, should be re-characterised as a security interest. This chapter will explore the arguments made in these jurisdictions, and consider whether they have any merit under English law, and, if so, what the consequences would be.

The second line of attack is that a flawed asset arrangement contra-venes the anti-deprivation principle. This argument has largely been made in the context of a particular clause in the ISDA Master

---

[1] Subject to the statutory controls on unfair terms now contained in Part 2 of the Consumer Rights Act 2015, some statutory controls in the Unfair Contract Terms Act 1977 (ss 3(2)(b) and 13) and the penalty clause jurisdiction.

Agreement which provides that the obligation of a party to perform is conditional upon the other party not being in default. Since a party may be in default by entering insolvency proceedings, the fact that the non-defaulting party's obligation to perform does not arise can be said to be attributable to the onset of insolvency. The obligee is thereby deprived of the benefit of the obligor's performance, and the transaction will fall foul of the principle unless it is commercially justifiable or otherwise falls within an exception to the principle.[2] This chapter will explore the effect of insolvency of the obligee on the flawed asset arrangement, and whether there are any reasons in English law why the flawed asset should not take effect according to its terms.

18.2   The Flawed Asset in Context

18.2.1   If Neither Party is Insolvent

If a bank that makes a loan of £500 to a borrower A wishes to protect itself against the risk of non-payment, it could insist that A deposit £500 with it on terms that the deposit is not repayable until the loan is repaid. This is a 'pure' flawed asset, and is very effective from the bank's point of view. The deposit is, of course, just a debt due from the bank to A.[3] If this debt is conditional upon the repayment of the loan, then if the loan is not repaid the bank does not need to do anything. It is protected automatically by the fact that it does not need to repay the deposit; there is no question of enforcing any right or remedy, and it does not need to sue A to recover the loan. Of course, if the loan is made at a rate of interest higher than that accruing on the deposit, then the bank is unprotected as to the balance, but this can be overcome by requiring a larger amount to be deposited in the first place. The protection, then, at least outside the insolvency of either party, is very simple and satisfactory. This arrangement is unlikely to arise where there is straight loan to A (since if A had £500 to deposit, why would it want to borrow that sum?), but is common where the 'loan' is in fact a line of credit which can be drawn on when necessary,[4] or the borrower's (contingent) obligation to indemnify a bank in respect of a bank guarantee or letter of credit.[5]

---

[2] *Belmont Park Investments Pty Ltd v BNY Corporate Trustee Services Ltd* [2011] UKSC 38, [2012] 1 AC 383.
[3] *Foley v Hill* (1848) 2 HLC 28, 9 ER 1002.   [4] As in the *Drummond* case discussed below.
[5] I am grateful to Toby Mann of Clifford Chance for this point.

Sometimes, where A and B are connected, either by relationship (such as companies in the same group) or conceivably by contract, the loan is made to borrower A and the deposit by depositor B.[6] The protection of the bank, again outside insolvency, is the same. The bank is under no obligation to repay the deposit unless and until the loan is repaid.[7]

In order to obtain the protection outlined above, there is no need for the agreement to provide for a right of set-off, although agreements often do so provide. In fact, careful drafting is required for a contractual right of set-off to be effective outside insolvency. Since the bank's debt to the depositor is not due until the loan is repaid, the two debts are never payable at the same time.[8] Of course, if either party actually wanted to be able to exercise a right of set-off, the contract could provide for this, by modifying the condition so that on notice by one or either party, the deposit becomes payable and is immediately set off against the loan.[9] The bank might wish to do this if the amount due on the loan was increasing by the accrual of interest so that it exceeded the amount of the deposit. Payment by set-off would prevent this.[10] The depositor might also wish the loan obligation to be extinguished by set-off if the amount of the deposit exceeded the amount due under the loan, since until the loan was repaid the depositor could not withdraw the excess.[11] The effect of these modifications, however, may be to make the

---

[6] It is likely, though not necessary for the efficacy of the flawed asset, that B has guaranteed A's liability under the loan. For an example of this structure, see *Fraser v Oystertec* [2004] EWHC 1582, [2006] 1 BCLC 491.

[7] See *Fraser* (n 6), where the court refused to make a third-party order in respect of the conditional debt on the grounds that it was not due or accruing due within CPR 72.2.

[8] See Robert Stevens, 'Contractual Aspects of Debt Financing' in Dan Prentice and Arad Reisberg (eds), *Corporate Finance Law in the UK and EU* (Oxford University Press 2011) 8.7.

[9] Even if this is not provided for in the contract, it is possible that the court will hold that this is the real intention of the parties, and imply a term to that effect. See Richard Calnan, 'Security over deposits after BCCI (No 8)' [1996] 3 JIBFL 111. Note that contractual set-off can operate in the two-party *and* the three-party cases.

[10] It would, of course, also be in the interests of the borrower to stop interest accruing by repaying the loan by the use of the deposit.

[11] This would, of course, depend on the terms of the condition: withdrawal of 'excess' cash deposited might be permitted, but it is likely that the bank would wish, if commercially possible, to be 'oversecured'. It could, however, be argued that, as a matter of the commercial construction of the agreement, the condition only applied to the amount outstanding, and the bank would therefore be liable to repay any balance, see Richard Calnan, *Taking Security: Law and Practice* (2nd edn, Jordan Publishing 2012) [12–31].

arrangement more susceptible to re-characterisation, or more vulnerable to being void in the insolvency of a party.

18.2.2   Two Party Arrangement: If A is Insolvent[12]

We will first take the simple case where the borrower and the depositor are the same person, A. If A goes into liquidation,[13] contractual set-off does not apply, and the only applicable set-off is insolvency set-off. On A's entry into liquidation, the conditional debt owed by the bank to A does not change its nature in the absence of express provision. It is not payable until A pays the loan to the bank. There is therefore no present debt due at the commencement of the liquidation, which is the date of account of insolvency set-off. However, insolvency set-off (which in theory applies automatically at the date of account, that is, when A enters liquidation) applies to all mutual debts, whether present, future, certain or contingent.[14] This applies to both sides of the set-off, that is, both the debt due by the insolvent company and the debt due to it.[15] In the scenario considered here, the loan is a future (or present) obligation[16] and the deposit a contingent one.[17] In due course, it will be the task of the liquidator to put a value on each debt and effect any set-off. The liquidator can take account of anything that has happened between the date of account and the date of valuation (the hindsight principle[18]). Thus, if the loan has become due, it will be valued at its full amount plus interest.[19] The deposit, though, is still not payable if the loan has not been paid.[20] Since the loan will not be paid (in full) by any method other than set-off, the deposit will never become payable, and so the liquidator will have to value it at zero. The operation of insolvency set-off would, therefore, leave the entire amount of the loan as a provable

---

[12]   Since this chapter is considering commercial remedies, it will be assumed that A (and B where relevant) is a company.

[13]   A similar analysis applies if A goes into administration, but the timing is different.

[14]   Insolvency Rules 1986 (SI 1986/1925) 4.90(4).

[15]   Insolvency Rules 4.90(3) and (4)(b). The position is otherwise if A is an individual.

[16]   It may, of course, have been accelerated before the onset of insolvency as a result of contractual provision.

[17]   For further discussion as to the status of the flawed asset owed to the insolvent party as a contingent debt, see section 18.4.1 below.

[18]   *MS Fashions Ltd v Bank of Credit and Commerce International SA (No 2)* [1993] Ch 425 (CA) 432–33 and Insolvency Rules 4.86 and 4.90(5).

[19]   If it has not, it will be discounted according to the formula set out in Insolvency Rule 11.13 (for liquidation) or Rule 2.105 (for administration).

[20]   In the absence of contractual stipulation.

debt. This will not be a problem for the bank: it can just not prove in the liquidation,[21] and it will never have to pay A. It might be a problem for the liquidator, especially if the deposit is of a greater amount than the outstanding loan. It may then be in the interest of the liquidator to pay the full amount of the loan in order to enable him to claim the full amount of the deposit from the bank.[22] The end position would then be the same as if there had been a set-off, or as if the bank had enforced a security interest by appropriating the deposit to the payment of the loan and accounted for the balance. An alternative analysis is that the loan obligation is contingent and should be valued at full value, because, if there were a set-off, the loan would be paid. The application of insolvency set-off would therefore result in the entire amount of the deposit being set off against the entire amount of the debt.[23] This analysis, though attractive and probably practical, is circular and does not take full account of the true nature of the flawed asset.[24]

Of course, the parties could try to manufacture an insolvency set-off by adjusting the contractual provisions: this is discussed in detail below.[25]

18.2.3 Two Party Arrangement: If the Bank is Insolvent

In this situation, the obligation to pay the loan is owed by a solvent party, and so will be paid. Therefore, one analysis is that the contingent debt (the bank's obligation to pay) should be valued in full, and insolvency set-off should apply.[26] Still, the problem with this analysis is that there are not mutual debts due at the same time: it is at the moment when the loan obligation is paid that the contingent debt arises.[27] As there are no mutual debts there can be no insolvency set-off. This time, the first analysis is more attractive but still has the technical problems identified. In the interests of certainty, it would therefore be in A's interest to bargain for the provision

---

[21] If the bank did prove, then (depending on the terms of the condition) it might become liable to pay the liquidator as payment of a dividend would amount to the discharge of the debt.

[22] This would depend on the wording and interpretation of the condition. See n 11 above.

[23] I am grateful to Tim Cleary, of Clifford Chance, for this alternative analysis.

[24] The first analysis given is also more consistent with that of Rose LJ in Re Bank of Credit and Commerce International SA (No 8) [1996] Ch 245 (CA) 262–63; the second has some support from MS Fashions (n 18).

[25] See section 18.4.1.

[26] This analysis has some support from MS Fashions, where, at least in one of the cases before the Court of Appeal, repayment of the deposit was conditional upon payment to the bank in full (at 445), yet insolvency set-off was held to apply (at 448).

[27] I am grateful to Robert Stevens for discussion of this point.

mentioned in the last paragraph, although there is the possibility of this being vulnerable under the anti-deprivation principle.[28]

18.2.4   Three Party Arrangement: If B is Insolvent

As discussed above, the borrower and the depositor may be different legal persons. Here, without more, insolvency set-off cannot apply as there is no mutuality.[29] Thus, where there is a 'pure' flawed asset, the bank can just refuse to pay B. The liquidator takes the debt as he finds it, including the flaw. So long as the arrangement is not re-characterised as a security interest (in which case it would also bind the liquidator, but only to the extent of the outstanding debt) or contravenes the anti-deprivation principle,[30] the bank is completely protected. If the liquidator wants to recover against the bank, he has various options. He can pay the debt on behalf of A, release the flaw and then proceed against A under a right of subrogation, or he can agree with the bank that the debt is paid out of the deposit, and proceed against A.[31]

B may, of course, itself be liable to the bank in relation to the loan, either as a guarantor or under a 'principal debtor' clause.[32] Here, insolvency set-off is potentially available, but, in the absence of the kind of contractual provisions discussed above, the contingent debt due from the bank will be valued at zero.

18.2.5   Three Party Arrangement: If the Bank is Insolvent

The analysis here is a combination of section 18.2.3 and section 18.2.4 above. There will be no insolvency set-off due to lack of mutuality, so the bank's liquidator can sue A and (once it has recovered and the flaw has been released) all B will get is a dividend. If B is itself liable as a guarantor, if the liquidator recovers in full from A, the flaw is released, but so is B's liability and so there can be no set-off: B will only receive a dividend. If the liquidator does not recover from A, the problem identified in 18.2.3 arises: since the bank's debt is contingent on payment by B, there is no time when they will be owed mutually and there is unlikely to be insolvency set-off.

---

[28] See section 18.4.2 below.

[29] *Re Bank of Credit and Commerce International SA (No 8)* [1998] AC 214 (HL).

[30] The principle would only potentially be contravened if the flaw is triggered by the onset of B's insolvency proceedings. See section 18.4.2.

[31] *BCCI* (CA) (n 24) 262–63.   [32] As in *MS Fashions* (n 18).

18.3 Is a Flawed Asset Arrangement a Security Interest?

This question can also arise the other way round, that is, 'is a (purported) security interest a flawed asset arrangement?' In English law cases, the relationship between a flawed asset arrangement and a security interest has largely been explored in answer to this formulation. Before the House of Lords' decision in *Re BCCI (No 8)*,[33] in which Lord Hoffmann recognised (albeit obiter) the validity of a charge-back,[34] a charge-back was not considered possible. Where an agreement purported to create one, courts generally took the view that, to respect the parties' intentions, the bundle of rights and obligations created by the agreement should take effect as a flawed asset arrangement,[35] or a right of set-off.[36] Even now that it is clear that a charge-back can be validly created, courts still opine that, if they are wrong that a charge-back has been validly created, the arrangement will take effect as a flawed asset.[37]

The first formulation of the question has not been considered as such by the English courts. Lenders here relying on cash collateral tend to rely on a charge, either on its own or as part of a 'triple cocktail' (a charge, a flawed asset and a right of set-off). While there will often be advantages in relying on a charge, particularly if it falls within the FCARs,[38] there may be disadvantages or uncertainties resulting from this route. Thus, a bank might wish to create a flawed asset arrangement and not a charge. Further, a bank with a triple cocktail arrangement might wish to rely on set-off rather than on the charge. The extent to which a bank with a triple cocktail can do this is unclear, as it depends on whether the existence of the charge breaks the necessary mutuality for solvent or insolvency

---

[33] *BCCI* (HL) (n 29). [34] A charge over a debt in favour of the debtor.

[35] See *BCCI* (CA) (n 24) 262–63. There was no mutuality in that case, so insolvency set-off could not apply and the arrangement was overtly described as a 'flawed asset'.

[36] *Re Charge Card Services Ltd (No 2)* [1987] Ch 150 (Ch); *MS Fashions* (n 18); *Broad v Commissioner of Stamp Duties (NSW)* [1980] 2 NSWLR 40. Cf *Jackson v Esanda Finance Corporation Ltd* [1993] 11 ACLC 138, where on holding a charge-back invalid the court expressed no opinion as to the effect of the parties' agreement. These decisions tend to ignore the problem identified earlier that a limitation on the bank's repayment obligation will prevent set-off arising, either outside or within insolvency (see above).

[37] *Fraser* (n 6) [12]. In *Re Lehman Brothers International (Europe) (In Administration)* [2012] EWHC 2997 (Ch), [2014] 2 BCLC 295 it was conceded that the flawed asset characterisation could only be pursued if it were held that the arrangement did not take effect as a charge. Since it did, the alternative characterisation was not pursued: [47]–[48].

[38] Financial Collateral Arrangements (No 2) Regulations 2003 ('FCARs'). If a charge fell within the FCARs it would not require registration, and restrictions on enforcement or priority on insolvency would be disapplied.

set-off.[39] At least outside insolvency, though, the bank can presumably disclaim its right to rely on the charge and rely on its other rights instead. It therefore could be of importance whether those rights themselves amount to a security interest.

Developments in two Commonwealth jurisdictions raise the possibility of re-characterisation of a flawed asset arrangement as a security interest. The Australian Personal Property Securities Act 2009 includes a 'flawed asset arrangement' within the definition of a security interest.[40] Commentators have struggled to see how a simple flawed asset (a conditional obligation) could amount to an interest in property, but have concluded that this is possible if the flawed asset is combined with other rights, such as a right of set-off.[41]

In *Caisse Populaire Desjardins de l'Est de Drummond v Canada*[42] ('*Drummond*'), the Canadian Supreme Court held that an arrangement including a contractual set-off and a flawed asset was a 'security interest' within the meaning of s 224(1.3) of the Income Tax Act 1985, which gave priority to the Revenue over such an interest. While this decision could be dismissed as based on the interpretation of a particular tax statute,[43] the reasoning of the majority that the arrangement conferred 'an interest on a creditor in the debtor's property to secure an obligation'[44] has led to it being treated in Canada and Australia as raising the question of whether such an arrangement is a security interest within their personal property security regimes.[45] The analysis in the case is particularly interesting because of the blurring of the lines between contract and property.

---

[39] This is a complicated issue which will not be discussed here.
[40] Section 12(2). See also Personal Property Securities Act 1999 (New Zealand), s 17(3).
[41] Diccon Loxton, 'One Flaw over the Cuckoo's Nest – Making Sense of the "Flawed Asset Arrangement" Example, Security Interest Definition and Set-off Exclusion in the PPSA' (2011) 34 UNSWLJ 472; Pip Giddins, 'Flawed Assets and the Australian Personal Property Securities Act 2009' [2011] JIBFL 539; Anthony Duggan and David Brown, *Australian Personal Property Securities Law* (2nd edn, LexisNexis Butterworths Australia, 2016) [3.14].
[42] [2009] SCC 29, [2009] 2 SCR 94.
[43] Rothstein J, giving the majority opinion, commented at [14] that: 'In this case, Parliament has chosen an expansive definition of "security interest" in s 224(1.3) ITA in order to enable maximum recovery by the Crown under its deemed trust.'
[44] *Drummond* (n 42).
[45] Loxton (n 41) 509–15; Roderick J Wood, 'Journey to the Outer Limits of Secured Transactions Law' (2010) 48 CBLJ 482; Duggan and Brown (n 41) [3.52]–[3.57]. The case is also discussed in books on English law. See Rory Derham, *The Law of Set-Off* (4th edn, Oxford University Press 2010) [16.93]–[16.110] and Louise Gullifer (ed), *Goode on Legal Problems of Credit and Security* (5th edn, Sweet & Maxwell 2013) [1–20], [1–21].

The arrangement in *Drummond* concerned a line of credit made available by the bank to the debtor. The debtor deposited a sum of money in a five-year term savings account 'to secure' the repayment of the loan. It was a term of the deposit agreement that the deposit could not be negotiated or transferred, or given as security to anyone but the bank ('negative pledge'). No principal or interest was repayable before the end of the five-year term ('fixed term limit'). The 'security through savings' agreement provided that the bank was permitted to withhold the deposit as long as the line of credit had not been cancelled ('flawed asset limit'), and that in the case of default there should be set-off between the credit line and deposit, regardless of whether it had matured or not[46] ('contractual set-off'). This agreement also included a hypothec (charge) of the deposit 'to further secure repayment of any sum owed' under the line of credit. It appears that this charge was not relied upon by the bank, which instead, on default, exercised the right of set-off.[47]

Thus, the arrangement which the Supreme Court was considering was a combination of four provisions: the fixed term limit, the flawed asset limit, the negative pledge and the right of set-off on default. The majority took the view that although these provisions individually created personal obligations, collectively they amounted to the creation of a security interest, that is, an interest in property.[48] The minority, however, took the view that the mere combination of a number of personal rights could not create a right *in rem*.[49]

Rothstein J, giving the judgment of the majority, differentiated between a 'bare' right of set-off and the current arrangement. A bare right of set-off is where one party has the right (on a particular trigger) to set off any monetary obligation which it happens to owe at the time against an outstanding obligation owed to it. In the *Drummond* situation, an obligation owed by the bank was earmarked from the start as the subject matter of the set-off. Moreover, it was protected from dissipation by the fixed term limit, the flawed asset limit and the negative pledge. These 'restrictions on the debtor's property' were 'to ensure that the creditor remains continuously liable to the debtor so that the set-off

---

[46] It should be noted that the set-off was not inconsistent with the extent of the flaw in the asset: the bank had a power to withhold which need not be exercised if it wished to rely on set-off, and set-off was available even if the deposit had not matured.

[47] Presumably, this was the choice of the bank to avoid being subject to the deemed trust in favour of the Revenue. See Duggan and Brown (n 41) [3.59] fn 129 where it is pointed out that 'the case proceeded on the basis that the bank was free to choose between the menu of remedy options set out in the agreement'. See also *Drummond* (n 42) [131].

[48] *Drummond* (n 42) [36], [39].   [49] Ibid [121]–[125].

remedy will be effective'.[50] What was not made particularly clear was how these protections turned two limits on the extent of the bank's obligation (the fixed term limit and the flawed asset limit), and a restriction on the creditor's right to assign the debt (the negative pledge) into an interest in property. What was the property in which the creditor had an interest? The only contender was the debt that the creditor itself owed. Now, we know that this is not a barrier to the creditor having a charge over that debt,[51] but that is expressly what the bank did not rely upon. The majority did refer to the functional approach under the Canadian personal property legislation,[52] and it may be that they were influenced by the fact that, under that regime, parties cannot attempt, by other means, to achieve the same economic purpose as security. As the strong dissenting judgment pointed out, however, this does not permit the court to discover an interest in property where one does not exist.[53] The functional approach merely allows an interest in property which is expressed to be absolute (such as is retained under a reservation-of-title clause) to be treated as a security interest if it has the function of securing on obligation.

Turning to English law, the characterisation of a flawed asset arrangement will depend on the precise contractual terms of the arrangement. This is true of all characterisation and is not limited to the present context. While the courts have repeatedly said that the characterisation of a transaction is a matter of determining the (legal) substance[54] rather than the form,[55] parties are usually permitted to structure their agreement as they wish, so long as it is internally consistent. In deciding whether an absolute or security interest has been created,[56] the courts have followed this approach. However, when deciding whether a charge is fixed or floating, the courts construe the agreement in order to determine what rights and obligations have been created, and then

---

[50] Ibid [39].   [51] *BCCI* (HL) (n 29).   [52] *Drummond* (n 42) [42].

[53] Ibid [109], [111], [121]–[122].

[54] It is quite clear that it is the legal substance which governs and not the economic substance. See *Welsh Development Agency v Export Finance Co Ltd* [1992] BCLC 148 (CA) 185 (Staughton LJ) relying on Lord Devlin in *Chow Yoong Hong v Choong Fah Rubber Manufactory* [1962] AC 209 (PC) 216.

[55] *McEntire v Crossley* [1895] AC 457 (HL) 462–63; *Helby v Matthews* [1895] AC 471 (HL) 475; *Re George Inglefield Ltd* [1933] Ch 1 (CA) 27. See also *Beconwood Securities Pty Ltd v ANZ Banking Group* [2008] FCA 594, [2008] 66 ACSR 116 (Fed Ct Aust) [40].

[56] *Welsh Development Agency* (n 54); *Orion Finance Ltd v Crown Financial Management Ltd* [1996] 2 BCLC 78.

characterise this objectively as a matter of law.[57] An approach somewhere in between these two has been adopted in the cases deciding whether a transaction creates a charge or merely personal rights. Two objective criteria are used: whether there is a contractual appropriation of the asset to the debt and whether the chargee has a specifically enforceable right to look to the asset for the discharge of the liability. The question is governed by the intention of the parties, but this includes both express and implied intention, so that express words may not be determinative if upon a proper understanding of the admissible evidence, the transaction has a different legal effect.[58]

The differences in approach in these three situations can be explained by the ease with which objective criteria can be applied to the bundle of rights and obligations created by the agreement independently of the labels put on those rights and obligations by the parties. In the fixed/floating charge cases, the criterion is whether the charged assets can be disposed of without consent of the chargee. It is (relatively) easy to determine this without reference to the parties' label. In the absolute interest/security cases, it is nearly impossible to determine whether a sale and leaseback arrangement (for example) is what it purports to be once all references to passing of property are stripped out: all one is left with is the economic substance. As this cannot be determinative, characterisation has to proceed on the basis of whether what it created is inconsistent with the parties' intention.[59] The cases concerning the line between property and contract sit somewhere in the middle. The criterion of specific enforceability can, to some extent, be objectively applied when the asset is completely separate from the liability, but is protected so as to provide a fund from which the liability could be met. The question is whether there is a specifically enforceable obligation to use the fund to meet the liability.[60] This criterion does not work so well when the 'asset' is a flawed asset, as the lender does not need to enforce by action. This leaves the other criterion: whether there is a contractual appropriation of the asset to the liability.

---

[57] *Agnew v Commissioner for Inland Revenue* [2001] UKPC 28, [2001] 2 AC 710 [31]–[32]; *Smith v Bridgend CBC* [2001] UKHL 58, [2002] 1 AC 336 [42]; *Re Spectrum Plus Ltd* [2005] UKHL 41, [2005] 2 AC 680 [119], [141].
[58] *Re TXU Europe Group plc* [2003] EWHC 3105 (Ch), [2004] Pens LR 175 [35]. See also *Swiss Bank Corporation v Lloyds Bank Ltd* [1982] AC 584 (HL) 595.
[59] Examples of this are the cases dealing with extended retention-of-title clauses.
[60] *Re TXU* (n 58); *Flightline Ltd v Edwards* [2003] EWCA Civ 63, [2003] 1 WLR 1200.

The bundle of rights and obligations created in the *Drummond* case are hard to describe without regard to the labels put on them. The label is that the rights are contractual and are qualified by the terms of the contract. The fixed term limit and the flawed asset limit merely qualify the bank's obligation, and the negative pledge creates a personal obligation not to encumber. These contractual provisions do, of course, have the economic effect of preserving the bank's ability to extinguish its obligation by set-off, and if they had not been there, that ability might have been lost by the depositor demanding payment of the deposit. This does not, however, amount to an appropriation of an asset to the payment of a debt.[61]

Does the addition of the right of set-off make any difference? A right merely to set off any mutual obligations that happen to be outstanding is clearly not a security interest, and it is difficult to see why the fact that the obligations are specified should make any difference. It could be said that this amounts to an appropriation of the asset (the right of the depositor to have the deposit paid back when the flaw is lifted) to payment of the debt (the liability of the depositor), and that this appropriation is made more evident by the restrictions on the asset. After all, it could be argued that, had the bank enforced its charge over the deposit, the enforcement would have taken exactly the same form as the set-off, that is, two account entries extinguishing the deposit obligation and leaving the balance of the credit line liability payable. Stripped of all labels, the rights and obligations are (it could be argued) indistinguishable from a charge. The only differences are the consequences: in Canadian law a charge would be subject to the deemed trust in favour of the revenue; in English law, the set-off would take place automatically on insolvency,[62] while a charge would require the chargee to take steps to enforce it. The characterising court, though, still has to decide whether a charge, on the one hand, or a flawed asset plus set-off arrangement, on the other hand, has been created. If the rights and obligations created by each are indistinguishable, but parties are allowed to create either, the determining factor must surely be the intention of the parties as to the structure of their arrangement, evidenced by the words they have used. Thus, if the parties intend

---

[61] In a different context, the right to restrain misapplication of assets has been held not to constitute a security interest as it is negative rather than a positive right to be paid out of those assets. See *Flightline* (n 60).

[62] This is on the basis that the bank had exercised its right to set-off or in some other way waived the flawed asset limitation.

to create a security interest (e.g. by using the word 'charge') the courts will give effect to this,[63] but if the rights and obligations they intend to create are purely personal in form, the courts are likely to give effect to this and not re-characterise the transaction as a security interest.[64] This approach is consistent with the general principle of freedom of contract under English law.

Under English law, a flawed asset arrangement re-characterised as a charge is unlikely to be registrable.[65] The presence of the flaw will mean that the collateral is 'in the possession or under the control' of the collateral taker (the bank) and so, if the flawed asset's obligor is a bank or other financial institution,[66] the FCARs will apply. There are also some advantages in the bank having a security interest rather than a flawed asset. The device will not fall foul of the anti-deprivation principle,[67] and, in a cross-border case, a security interest may be less vulnerable under foreign law than a contractual arrangement.[68] Thus, the actual consequences of re-characterisation may not be great in most cases, but any blurring of the line between contract and property is always potentially troublesome.

18.4 Invalidity on Insolvency[69]

This section discusses whether a flawed asset arrangement is vulnerable to being unenforceable on insolvency as contrary to the *pari passu* principle ('PPP') or the anti-deprivation principle ('ADP'). These principles give some limited protection to creditors of an insolvent party

---

[63] If there is an intention to create a security interest, the parties will not be permitted to avoid any registration requirements by labelling it something other than 'charge'. See *Re Lehman Brothers* (n 37) [48].

[64] See Derham (n 45) [16.93]–[16.107], who takes the view that some set-off agreements are charges, although many are not. Broadly speaking, he agrees with the majority reasoning in *Caisse Populaire* that when a right of set-off is combined with a flawed asset, this can create a security interest, commenting that there seems to be little, if any, difference between a provision for set-off and for appropriation or application of the credit balance to the payment of the debt.

[65] This is also the case in the United States (UCC 9–312(b)(1)) and Australia (Australian PPSA s 25), but not in Canada, where security interests over cash collateral are registrable, at least at the moment.

[66] This is because 'cash' is defined in the FCARs as money credited to an account.

[67] Discussed below in section 18.4.

[68] I am indebted to Tim Cleary of Clifford Chance for this point.

[69] To make the discussion more straightforward, the position on liquidation rather than administration is discussed here.

against the insolvent party having agreed contractual terms which detrimentally affect creditors on insolvency.[70] The clearest formulation of the two principles is given by David Richards J in the *Football Creditors* case:

> The first principle in issue is the pari passu principle, which requires the assets of an insolvent person to be distributed among the creditors on a pari passu basis, subject only to such exceptions as the general law may permit. The pari passu basis of distribution means that all creditors will receive the same percentage of their debts out of the available assets. Parties are not free to contract out of the operation of this principle, except by the creation and, when required, registration of security over the debtor's assets ... The second principle is what is now known as the anti-deprivation rule, but which used to be called fraud on the bankruptcy law. This principle renders void any provision by which a debtor is deprived of assets by reason of insolvency with the effect that they are not available in the insolvency proceeding. The purpose of the deprivation may, but need not, be to ensure priority payment to a particular creditor or creditors. This principle is subject to a number of specific exceptions and general qualifications which will need to be considered.[71]

Although the principles are aimed at different mischiefs,[72] there can be some overlap in application to particular facts. There are some specific differences between them. Of most relevance here is that the PPP applies regardless of the intention and motivation of the parties in entering into the contract, while a contractual arrangement will not contravene the ADP if it is a bona fide commercial transaction which does not have as a main purpose the deprivation of the property of the insolvent party.[73] If a contractual provision offends either principle it is void as against the insolvent party. Ironically, if a flawed asset arrangement is re-characterised as a security interest, it will not fall foul of either principle: the grant of a security interest has the effect of taking an asset outside the estate of the insolvent grantor, and, so long as it is properly created and, if necessary, registered, cannot be challenged as contrary to either principle.

---

[70] The principles supplement statutory provisions which enable certain transactions entered into by the insolvent party in the run-up to insolvency, and after the onset of insolvency, to be set aside (Insolvency Act 1986, ss 127, 238, 239, 245 and 423).

[71] *Revenue and Customs Commissioners v Football League Ltd* [2012] EWHC 1372 (Ch), [2012] Bus LR 1539 [4], [5].

[72] Roy Goode, 'Perpetual Trustee and Flip Clauses in Swap Transactions' (2011) 127 LQR 1, 3–4 cited in *Belmont* (n 2) [1].

[73] *Belmont* (n 2)[104] (Lord Collins).

18.4.1   The PPP

This principle only applies to the distribution of assets of the insolvent party at the commencement of insolvency proceedings.[74] The insolvent party's rights under a contract to which it is a party constitute an asset. The nature of that asset, however, is determined by the terms of that contract. It cannot contravene the PPP, for example, if the contract provides that the insolvent party is due £100 for goods when the market price is £150. The contract is just a bad bargain, and, as long as the £100 is distributed among unsecured creditors *pari passu*, the PPP has nothing to say about that contract. The same, therefore, must be true of a 'pure' flawed asset. If payment is conditional upon payment in full of a debt due from the insolvent party, then the PPP can have nothing to say about the nature of that asset.

This conclusion accords with the decision of the Court of Appeal in *Lomas v JFB Firth Rixson Inc*.[75] That case concerned clause 2(a)(iii) of the ISDA Master Agreement, which provided that each party's obligations under the agreement were conditional upon there not having been an event of default by the counterparty. In the *Lomas* case the non-insolvent party was 'out of the money' in relation to the derivatives transactions entered into with the insolvent counterparty, so the administrator wished to sue the non-insolvent party for the sums which would have been due to the insolvent party were it not for clause 2(a)(iii). The administrator argued that the clause contravened both the ADP and the PPP. In relation to the latter, Longmore LJ concluded that: 'Section 2(a)(iii) does not infringe the *pari passu* rule because it operates at most to prevent the relevant debt ever becoming payable. There is therefore no property which is capable of being distributed.'[76] Further, the intentions of the parties in agreeing to the flawed asset are irrelevant, so it does not matter if the bank included the clause specifically to protect itself on the insolvency of its counterparty. The PPP is not a general 'anti-avoidance' provision,[77] and an insolvency officer cannot complain if the insolvent estate is not as valuable as it might be had the parties agreed a different contract.

While this is reasonably straightforward, it is worth considering the position if the flawed asset clause is modified by the addition of a right of set-off. Set-off does affect the distribution of an asset, in the sense that the

---

[74] *Football Creditors* (n 71) [66].
[75] [2012] EWCA Civ 419, [2012] 2 All ER (Comm) 1076.   [76] Ibid [98].
[77] *Football Creditors* (n 71) [137].

debt due to the insolvency party is set off pound for pound against that due from the insolvent party, rather than the former being distributed *pari passu* among all the creditors. If a contractual right of set-off has the same effect as insolvency set-off (which itself is an exception to the PPP), the contractual right will not offend that principle, except to the extent that it falls outside insolvency set-off.[78]

With this in mind, let us consider the position if, in a two-party case, a flawed asset is combined with a right on the part of either party to make the deposit immediately payable and set off against the outstanding loan. If this right is exercised before the liquidation of the depositor, there is no issue, since the insolvent party's asset will no longer exist. What is the position if the right is exercised after liquidation?

Contingent debts due to an insolvent company can be the subject of insolvency set-off.[79] Would the flawed asset in our example count as a contingent debt? Contingent debts owed *to* the insolvent company are not defined in the Insolvency Rules and have been little considered in the case law. It is clear that a contingent provable debt owed *by* the company is one arising from an obligation that is entered into before the onset of insolvency,[80] and a contractual obligation is the archetypal example of this.[81] While there is no express provision in the Rules that the debt owed *to* the company must be a provable debt, it seems reasonably clear from the wording of Rule 4.90 that for a contingent liability to be included in insolvency set-off, the relevant obligation must have arisen before the date of account,[82] and that the same criteria as to what amounts to a contingent debt apply to those owed *by* and *to* the insolvent company.[83] The flawed asset here is clearly an obligation arising from a contract entered into before the onset of insolvency, giving rise to a potential liability if one of two contingencies occurs, namely that the loan obligation is repaid or the bank gives notice making the deposit immediately payable. Does it matter that these 'contingencies' are within the exclusive control of the parties? It does not seem to matter that the contingency is within the control of the insolvent company (i.e. the insolvency officer): a post-insolvency breach of a pre-insolvency contract by the company can give rise to a debt owed *by* the insolvent company

---

[78] *British Eagle International Airways Ltd v Cie National Air France* [1975] 1 WLR 758 (HL).
[79] Insolvency Rules 4.90(4)(b).   [80] Insolvency Rules 13.12(1)(b).
[81] *Re Nortel Companies* [2013] UKSC 52, [2014] AC 209 [75].
[82] See especially Rules 4.90(4) and the definition of 'debt' in Rule 13.12.
[83] *Revenue and Customs Commissioners v Millichap* [2011] BPIR 145, [2011] CLY 1876 (Ch).

which can be subject of insolvency set-off.[84] If the same criteria for a contingent debt are to be applied to a debt due *to* the company as those applicable to a debt due *by* the company, then it must be the case that a debt can be contingent if triggered by an action of the non-insolvent party. Therefore, the notice can be seen as triggering the contingency, and, by application of the hindsight principle, the set-off falls within insolvency set-off and cannot contravene the PPP. While this could be seen as permitting the solvent party to obtain an advantageous set-off to the detriment of other creditors, this is not the case, since the flaw in the asset meant that there was never an unlimited debt available for distribution to those creditors.

In relation to a three-party case, as mentioned above, there is no mutuality and therefore no insolvency set-off: any set-off provision will therefore fall foul of the PPP. Of course, this will not be the case if the bank is principally liable on the debt as guarantor or under a principal debtor clause. Such clauses cannot themselves fall foul of the principle, since they are either triggered before insolvency (in which case there is no issue) or after insolvency, in which case the debt is contingent at the onset of insolvency.

The same reasoning will apply to a provision that the deposit debt automatically becomes payable on the insolvency of the borrower. Such a provision, which would enable insolvency set-off to take place providing that there is mutuality, will not fall foul of the PPP for the reasons explained above, but could potentially fall foul of the ADP in the insolvency of the bank.

18.4.2 The ADP

This principle applies to a contractual provision which has the effect that an insolvent party is deprived of an asset at the onset of insolvency. It therefore only applies to provisions which are triggered by that onset.[85] The 'pure' flawed asset as described in this chapter will therefore not fall within the principle: the deposit debt is not payable unless the loan is paid in full, and non-payment of the loan (even if seen as a trigger for non-payment of the deposit) is a continuing event, not synonymous

---

[84] *Re Asphaltic Wood Pavement Co* (1885) 30 Ch D 216 (CA), referred to in *Re Charge Card Services Ltd* [1987] Ch 150 (Ch) 180 and *Secretary of State for Trade and Industry v Frid* [2004] UKHL 24, [2004] 2 AC 506 [9].

[85] *Belmont* (n 2) [14].

with the onset of insolvency.[86] The obligation to pay in the *Lomas* case, however, was only not payable because of the bankruptcy of the counter-party, bankruptcy being an event of default which prevented the obliga-tion becoming payable.[87]

As mentioned above, the ADP exists to prevent a 'fraud on the bank-ruptcy'. It applies to contractual provisions whereby an asset belonging to the insolvent party is removed from the estate on insolvency. It can, of course, be seen that such a provision could be included in a contract for 'good' reasons (such as the protection of a party who would otherwise be very adversely affected by the insolvency) or 'bad' reasons (such as a malicious desire to harm the other creditors or an attempt to gain a windfall by 'gambling' on the insolvency of the counterparty). The difficulty (for the ADP) is how to distinguish between the two. The Supreme Court, rather than saying that bad faith or fraudulent provisions are void, has introduced the opposite test: commercially justifiable provi-sions are valid.[88]

Another problem is that it is relatively easy to avoid the application of the ADP by drafting. One simple way to do this is to make the trigger for the deprivation something other than insolvency. The courts have not tackled this method of avoidance, and have, indeed, said that anti-avoidance in this regard is up to Parliament.[89] Another method of drafting around the ADP is to provide, when granting an asset to a company, that the grant is conditional upon the company not becoming insolvent. This has, in the cases, become known as a 'flawed asset'.[90] The Supreme Court is more equivocal about this drafting technique: while the distinction between a determinable and a defeasible interest is said to be 'too well established to be dislodged otherwise than by legislation',[91] it is clear that at least some flawed assets will fall within the ADP, as otherwise it would be so easy to avoid the principle that the ADP 'would be left with little value'.[92]

---

[86] A trigger, such as default, which occurred after the onset of insolvency could, however, engage the ADP. See *Football Creditors* (n 71) [156].

[87] Even this is not strictly true, since the bankruptcy of the counterparty's credit support provider had occurred first (see *Lehman Brothers* (n 37)) and also prevented the obliga-tion arising (see *Lomas* (n 75) [93]).

[88] The difficulty in applying this test is discussed below.

[89] See *Perpetual Trustee Co Ltd and Another v BNY Corporate Trustee Services Ltd* [2009] EWCA Civ 1160, [2010] Ch 347 [92] (Lord Neuberger). See also *Football Creditors* (n 71) [188].

[90] *Belmont* (n 2) [89].   [91] Ibid [88].

[92] Ibid [89]. See also Lord Mance's approach: while he says, at [163], that 'there is some scope for looking at the substance, rather than the form', he also says, at [165], that:

There is a distinction between a contractual provision dealing with a separate asset (e.g. a tangible asset) and where the contract itself constitutes the asset.[93] In the latter situation, so long as the contract is internally consistent,[94] all the 'flaw' is doing is to define the obligations and rights of the parties.[95] To re-characterise it as creating an obligation (an asset) and then taking it away (on insolvency) could be said to be a rewriting of the parties' contract, which can only be justified by legislation.[96] Despite this argument, the courts have, on occasion, applied a 'substance over form' approach to find a deprivation,[97] and then have had to consider whether the transaction was commercially justified. This criterion, though, is not easy to apply.

This can be illustrated by considering why a contract might contain a clause making a payment by X to Y conditional upon Y not becoming insolvent. A 'good' reason is likely to be that X, who is otherwise happy to perform its obligations, does not wish to perform them if Y is insolvent. This must be either because X is already owed a debt by Y or that, at the onset of insolvency, Y is still to perform part of the bargain. In the former situation, X will normally be able to rely on insolvency set-off and so will not need the flaw. In the latter situation, however, X will be concerned that Y will not perform, and so, it can be said, has a commercially justifiable reason for protecting itself against having to make payments for services which are unlikely to be rendered or goods with are unlikely to be delivered.[98] Here, the flawed asset which arises on insolvency is no different from the examples of a non-contentious flaw set out at the beginning of this chapter, where payment is made conditional on

---

'Courts cannot rewrite or review contractual arrangements to give them an effect contrary to the substance of what the parties have agreed, even though this means that the bankrupt has less property than would otherwise be the case before and when he becomes bankrupt.'

[93] See *Belmont* (n 2) [160] where Lord Mance says that, where the contractual rights are the asset, it is easier to suggest a commercial basis for the deprivation.

[94] See Richard Calnan, 'Anti-deprivation: A Missed Opportunity' (2011) 9 JIBFL 531, 532.

[95] See the approach of Lord Mance in *Belmont* (n 2) [168] (no deprivation because of inherent flaw).

[96] The same difficulty arises in another sphere in relation to the difference between duty-defining clauses and exclusion clauses (see Edwin Peel, *Treitel on the Law of Contract* (14th edn, Sweet & Maxwell 2015) [7–020]). Section 13 of the Unfair Contract Terms Act 1977 is a limited attempt to deal with this issue.

[97] See, for example, *Lomas* (n 75) [86].

[98] This is the 'quid pro quo' approach set out by Briggs J in *Lomas v JFB Firth Rixson Inc* [2010] EWHC 3372 (Ch), [2011] 2 BCLC 120 [108] and confirmed by the Supreme Court in *Belmont* (n 2) [100], [131]–[132].

performance of services or delivery of goods. It surely cannot be objectionable if a contract provides for payment before performance in most circumstances,[99] but that this is denied if the performing party is insolvent. If a paying party has to make a payment despite the insolvency of the performing party, it will only have a right to damages for breach.[100]

It could, of course, be said that X can rely on insolvency set-off: it will not have to make its payment gross but net of its claim against Y for breach. Therefore, it could be said, X is sufficiently protected and it does not need, commercially, to use a flawed asset to give it protection. The only effect of the flawed asset (as opposed to what would be achieved anyway by insolvency set-off) is to enable X to refuse to pay any amount due over and above the amount due from Y, and this is a deprivation to Y.

It could further be argued that the 'quid pro quo' approach favoured in the cases, is, at least in part, based on a series of cases whereby a lessor or a licensor is relieved of its obligation to perform if the lessee or licensee becomes insolvent.[101] This situation, however, is the reverse of that considered here: the lessor or licensor is the performing party, and there is every reason for the performing party not to have to perform if it is unlikely to be paid. In this situation performance will be rendered (in that the lease or licence will remain in effect on the insolvency of the counterparty in the absence of a termination or flawed asset clause) and once this has happened all the performing party has is a provable debt. Even if performance can be withheld, an obligation to perform cannot be set off against an obligation to pay. The analogy with the situation where a payment obligation is flawed is, therefore, not perfect. Thus, there is no necessary reason why the commercial justification in the lease/licence cases also applies in the payment/obligation cases.

These arguments, while theoretically attractive, ignore the desire by parties to protect themselves *ex ante* against the uncertainties of what might actually happen *ex post*. At the time when an agreement is made, it might be uncertain which party would become insolvent, and at what point in the cycle of the agreement. The agreement might be such that the

---

[99] Depending on the bargaining power of the parties, the price may reflect the element of financing included in this arrangement.

[100] There could, perhaps, be a personal claim for the return of the payment on the grounds of total failure of consideration, but this will depend on the exact terms of the contract and whether the payment is completely referable to the performance that was not rendered, as opposed to any performance that had been rendered.

[101] *Whitmore v Mason* (1861) 2 J & H 204, 70 ER 1031; *Ex parte Barter* (1884) 26 Ch D 510 (CA).

executory obligations of each party will vary throughout the cycle of the agreement (as with a derivative contract), so these uncertainties would be material. Added to this, it might be uncertain whether the assessment of damages by a liquidator, when calculating insolvency set-off, would fully compensate the non-insolvent party for its loss: a flawed asset would obviate the need to litigate on this point. It is, therefore, commercially justifiable for the parties to protect themselves against these uncertainties, and such protection should not be struck down just because, in some cases, the non-insolvent party may appear to obtain a windfall.[102]

These competing arguments, however, demonstrate the difficulties caused by the 'commercial justification' limit placed on the operation of the ADP by the Supreme Court in *Belmont*. Flawed asset provisions in simple contracts can usually be justified on the basis that making a payment conditional on a counterparty's performance (or lack of breach) is a standard means of protection, and almost any provision in a contract of any complexity can be justified on the uncertainty reasoning in the last paragraph. The ADP should really only apply to actual fraud.[103] A more robust approach to upholding the parties' agreement as to the extent of the asset (the rights and obligations) created by the contract itself (respecting the flawed asset) would reduce the need to apply the 'commercial justification' criterion, and would limit it to the most egregious cases of avoidance and fraud. These would be either where the flaw, properly interpreted, did not represent the true intention of the parties,[104] or where parties have clearly agreed for the non-insolvent party to obtain a windfall on insolvency with no countervailing benefit to the insolvent party.[105]

18.5 Conclusion

The thesis of this chapter is that, generally speaking, conditional obligations contained in a contract are part of the parties' bargain and should be respected by the courts both outside and within insolvency. This chapter has examined some of the more inventive uses of flawed assets, and the

---

[102] See *Lomas* (n 75) [87].

[103] See the description of 'bad reasons' given earlier in section 18.4.2.

[104] This could be determined, for example, by inconsistency with other terms of the agreement.

[105] Another possibility is for more use to be made of s 423 of the Insolvency Act 1986 (transaction defrauding creditors), which is not time-limited like other statutory transaction-avoidance provisions.

consequences of such arrangements. The question of whether flawed asset arrangements are likely to be re-characterised as security interests may have few practical consequences in many situations, but raises important issues about how the line between property and contract is drawn, and the correct approach of the courts to re-characterising a contractual transaction. On their face, flawed assets, even if combined with set-off, are purely contractual devices, and to re-characterise them as interests in property involves imputing to the parties different intentions in relation to the rights and obligations that they have created than those which they have evidenced by their agreement.

The treatment of flawed assets in insolvency again depends on whether the courts are prepared to give effect to the intention of the parties to only create a limited asset. There seems to be no reason why a flaw not triggered by insolvency should not bind an insolvency officer. The contingent debt created will potentially fall within insolvency set-off, but will be valued at zero if there is no prospect of the flaw being removed. An added provision for set-off will only operate once the flaw is removed, and will also only be effective on insolvency if it falls within insolvency set-off. Insolvency set-off, however, is now very wide and includes contingent debts in both directions, so provided that there is mutuality, it is possible (with skilful drafting) for set-off to be effective and not fall foul of the PPP. The anti-deprivation principle is itself of uncertain ambit, and should, it is argued, be seen as a bulwark against fraud. Where the 'asset' of which the insolvent party is arguably deprived is a contractual right and limited within that contract, the courts should respect this if, on the ordinary principles of contractual interpretation, it is the intention of the parties. There is therefore no need to investigate whether the transaction is commercially justifiable, and, instead, the investigation should focus on whether the flaw actually represents the intentions of the parties and whether there is an intention on the part of the parties to defraud creditors.

19

Subrogation

STEPHEN WATTERSON

19.1 Introduction

Where C-claimant is responsible for discharging D-debtor's liabilities to
X-creditor, the courts sometimes hold that C is entitled to be 'subrogated'
to X-creditor's rights. Such subrogation ('subrogation to another's *extinguished* rights')[1] offers a valuable remedial option for commercial parties – whether C is, for example, the victim of theft or fraud, a guarantor,
or a disappointed lender who discovers that its bargained-for security is
defective. This is particularly true where X was a *secured* creditor, and
C obtains the benefits of security by 'subrogation'. Why does this occur?
In its landmark decision in *Banque Financière de la Cité v Parc
(Battersea) Ltd*,[2] the House of Lords supplied a controversial new explanation, recently affirmed by the Supreme Court in *Menelaou v Bank of
Cyprus UK Ltd*:[3] such subrogation is a 'restitutionary' remedy, afforded
by equity to reverse 'unjust enrichment'.

Much might be written about the *Menelaou* decision. Detractors will say
that it shows that hard cases make bad law. Indeed, *Menelaou* arguably
represents the worst of all possible worlds. Four of five Supreme Court
Justices *seemed* to endorse the post-*Banque Financière* 'orthodoxy' that
subrogation may be awarded to remedy 'unjust enrichment'. But was that
endorsement clear and unqualified? The same opinions suggest some
judicial receptivity to an *alternative* explanation for the remedy, rooted
in 'orthodox proprietary' reasoning. Even more dramatically, Lord
Carnwath appeared to advocate wholesale re-thinking of whether, and in
what form, a proprietary remedy might be appropriate to reverse unjust
enrichment and, as part of that process, jettisoning the 'anomalous'

---

[1] This terminology derives from Charles Mitchell and Stephen Watterson, *Subrogation Law
and Practice* (Oxford University Press 2007).
[2] [1999] 1 AC 221 (HL) ('*Banque Financière*').
[3] [2015] UKSC 66, [2016] AC 176 ('*Menelaou*').

subrogation remedy altogether. All then seems far from well. The quest to identify a stable foundation for the subrogation remedy continues.

This short chapter cannot comprehensively examine the questions when, why and in what form the subrogation remedy should be available. Its modest aim is to clarify the parameters of future debate, by exposing two under-examined questions raised by *Menelaou*. First, if subrogation belongs within the law of unjust enrichment, what is its role? Secondly, might subrogation be better explained, not as a remedy for unjust enrichment, but via 'orthodox proprietary' reasoning, and what might turn on this?

19.2   The Remedy's Role Within the Law of Unjust Enrichment

In *Menelaou*, the Supreme Court conceded that the subrogation remedy was at least unusual. The standard restitutionary response to unjust enrichment is a 'monetary restitutionary award': an order to pay a money sum reflecting the monetary value of the defendant's enrichment.[4] It may only be a small step from the recognition of subrogation's exceptional nature, to the bolder conclusion that subrogation cannot be part of a coherent law of unjust enrichment. The High Court of Australia has denied that subrogation has anything to do with 'unjust enrichment' partly for this very reason.[5] Significantly, in *Menelaou* itself, Lord Carnwath also seemed to see no part for subrogation within the English law of unjust enrichment. He doubted Lord Clarke's assumption[6] that *Banque Financière* had 'rationalised the older [subrogation] cases through the prism of unjust enrichment',[7] and hinted that, whilst a proprietary remedy might be awarded to remedy unjust enrichment, it was needlessly obscuring to resort to the concept of 'subrogation' for this purpose. Thus, Lord Carnwath began with the provocative suggestion that:

> [I]t is surely time for the principles of restitution or unjust enrichment to be allowed to stand on their own feet. A proprietary remedy may arguably be justified because, ... such a remedy, rather than a personal remedy, is the most appropriate response to the unjust enrichment found in this case; but not because of some tenuous relationship with a vendor's lien which has no continuing existence or practical relevance.[8]

[4] *Menelaou* (n 3) [55] (Lord Clarke), [81] (Lord Neuberger) (Lords Wilson and Kerr concurring).
[5] *Bofinger v Kingsway Group* [2009] HCA 44, (2009) 239 CLR 269 [97] (*'Bofinger'*).
[6] *Menelaou* (n 3) [50].   [7] Ibid [108].   [8] Ibid [109].

He continued in a similar vein, when he took issue with Lord Hoffmann's
rationalisation of the subrogation remedy in *Banque Financière*:

> It is not clear to me, with respect, how describing the concept [of sub-
> rogation] as a 'metaphor' adds anything by way of explanatory force. . . .
> Professor Birks . . . observ[ed] that in the law of restitution, subrogation
> 'really adds nothing' to the techniques otherwise available: 'it is in the
> nature of a metaphor which can be done without' . . . I would respectfully
> agree. In the context of the law of unjust enrichment, the issue should be
> the nature of the appropriate remedy, not whether it conforms to an
> analogy derived from some other area of the law.[9]

These are important challenges. They suggest a pressing need to reconsider, and clarify, the subrogation remedy's role.

19.2.1 Two Models of Subrogation's Role

What then is subrogation's role? At present, two models are discernable.
Much turns upon which is preferred. The *discrete model* affords the
remedy a distinct and irreducible role within the law of unjust enrichment. The alternative, *reductionist model* suggests that subrogation is
a redundant concept, which should dissolve away.

19.2.1.1 The Reductionist Model

Two key premises underpin the reductionist model. First, where
C discharges D's liability to X, and D's release constitutes an unjust
enrichment obtained at C's expense, the law's primary response is to
afford C the standard monetary restitutionary remedy against D, reflecting the monetary value of the unjust enrichment resulting from D's
release. Secondly, in cases hitherto identified as 'subrogation' cases,
where D's liability to X was secured over D's assets, 'subrogation' is an
obscuring misnomer. C is not, or should not be, 'subrogated' to X's
position, either literally or metaphorically.[10] All that is or should be
happening is that the courts are *reinforcing* C's monetary claim against
D, by imposing a new equitable lien/charge as security for its satisfaction.

On this view, the newly imposed lien/charge has no independent
restitutionary rationale. It is merely a supplementary device, ancillary
to the 'real' or 'primary' unjust enrichment remedy: the standard monetary restitutionary remedy. No reference back to X's rights, as paid-off
creditor, is required: the charge is an independent, newly imposed

---

[9] Ibid [117].   [10] Cf *Banque Financière* (n 2) (Lord Hoffmann).

charge, with its own characteristics, whose only function is to afford C a secured monetary claim.

This account would seem particularly compelling if the law of unjust enrichment only recognised and reversed what Lodder labels 'factual' enrichments: the receipt of *value* by a defendant, in the form of money, or some non-money benefit susceptible to valuation in money.[11] *Monetary restitution* is the natural restitutionary response to such enrichments.[12] Indeed, any other response looks anomalous, with the possible exception of a lien/charge, imposed to better ensure the satisfaction of D's monetary restitutionary liability.[13]

There are nevertheless difficulties with this reductionist account. Above all, it is not a viable descriptive theory of English subrogation cases: it ignores much of what the courts have said and done, and continue to say and do.[14] Have the courts proceeded in error, blind to the 'truth'? Not necessarily: a better account may yet be available.

19.2.1.2   The Discrete Model

On examination, the best available defence of subrogation's 'discrete' role as a restitutionary remedy assumes that the law of unjust enrichment is not confined to the monetary reversal of 'factual' enrichments, but might also embrace, and respond differently to, a second species of 'enrichment'. Some years ago, Robert Chambers proposed a distinction between enrichment by the receipt of 'value' and enrichment by the receipt of 'rights'.[15] Andrew Lodder has since offered the alternative terminology of 'legal' enrichment to capture a wider category that comprises both the acquisition of rights and, of immediate relevance, the release of duties/liabilities.[16] On Lodder's account, either might be treated as 'factual' enrichments, and reversed by the standard monetary restitutionary remedy. However, viewing them as 'legal' enrichments, the law might respond differently, reversing the enrichment 'in law' via a 'specific' restitutionary mechanism. For example, the law might achieve specific restitution, when D is enriched by the 'acquisition of rights', via C's

---

[11]   Andrew Lodder, *Enrichment in the Law of Unjust Enrichment and Restitution* (Hart Publishing 2012) ch 3.

[12]   Cf ibid 64.   [13]   Cf ibid ch 5, contemplating a lien/charge having this role.

[14]   See section 19.2.2.1 below.

[15]   Robert Chambers, 'Two Kinds of Enrichment' in Robert Chambers, Charles Mitchell and James Penner (eds), *Philosophical Foundations of the Law of Unjust Enrichment* (Oxford University Press 2009) ch 9.

[16]   Lodder (n 11) ch 5.

entitlement to rescind a defective transfer of title, or the imposition of a trust in C's favour over the rights acquired by D.[17]

This important refinement suggests a distinctive and irreducible role for the remedy of subrogation to another's extinguished rights: it is a *specific restitutionary mechanism*, designed to reverse a *particular subset of legal enrichments*.[18] Contextually, the remedy is limited to circumstances that involve the *release of another's (X's) rights*, achieved *at a third party's (C's) expense*: what generally triggers such subrogation is the discharge of D's liabilities to X, by a payment for which C, a third party, was relevantly responsible. Such facts could certainly yield the standard monetary restitutionary remedy, addressed to D's 'factual' enrichment: a monetary award reflecting the monetary value of D's discharged liabilities to X. However, in some of the same circumstances, equity can apparently afford C a different remedy – the subrogation remedy – which operates as a specific restitutionary mechanism, addressed to the release of D's liabilities, *conceived as a 'legal' enrichment*. Equity reverses *in specie* the unjust enrichment that would otherwise accrue from the release, to D and relevant others, by substantially re-creating the released liabilities/rights in favour of C, a new party: C is afforded new rights, against D and others, which presumptively replicate those previously enjoyed by X.[19]

If this account is plausible, then Lord Carnwath may have spoken too hastily in *Menelaou*. When he criticised the invocation of 'metaphors' and insisted that 'the issue should be the nature of the appropriate remedy, not whether it conforms to an analogy derived from some other area of the law',[20] he may have missed the true nature of the subrogation remedy. If the release of another's liabilities is an unjust enrichment, which is appropriately reversed *in specie*, the subrogation remedy is *a peculiarly appropriate* remedial mechanism. Furthermore, far from an irrelevant distraction, any 'analogy' drawn with the rights of X, the paid-off creditor, is a practical and a legal necessity. Since it is the release of X's rights which requires 'reversal', those rights must be the

---

[17] Ibid 64–66.

[18] See Stephen Watterson, 'Modelling Subrogation as an "Equitable Remedy"' (2016) 2 CJCCL (609) (Watterson, 'Modelling Subrogation', especially Part II.).

[19] Ibid. A similar enrichment could arise in a bipartite setting (e.g. C-creditor mistakenly releases his security for D-debtor's liabilities) and C might be afforded specific relief, which restores C's released rights/equivalents. This would not be 'subrogation': C does not step into *another's* shoes, literally/metaphorically. He re-acquires his own previously released rights/equivalents. E.g. *NRAM plc v Evans* [2015] EWHC 1543 (Ch).

[20] *Menelaou* (n 3) [117].

primary reference point, when shaping the remedy required to 'reverse' that enrichment *in specie.*

One caveat is nevertheless required. Whilst the discrete model seems most faithful to what recent cases *say* about the remedy's basis and nature, it involves some contestable assumptions about the nature of 'restitutionary remedies' afforded by the law of unjust enrichment. In a bipartite setting,[21] restoration of C's previously released rights against D achieves 'specific restitution' in the narrowest/truest sense: restoring *to* C rights that *he* formerly held against D. In contrast, the subrogation remedy necessitates a broader understanding of 'specific restitution'. The remedy generates equivalents of D's released liabilities to X, in favour of a *new party, C.* This reverses D's enrichment *in specie,* but only via a 'restitutionary' mechanism *that affords C rights of a nature that he did not previously hold.* This broader understanding might require a corresponding commitment to a particular position in a more general controversy within unjust enrichment scholarship concerning the essential nature of 'restitutionary remedies'. Is the law's remedial focus on the reversal of D's unjust enrichment alone, or a more two-sided process, whereby the existence and extent of any restitutionary remedy is limited by reference to C's equivalent/corresponding loss?[22]

19.2.2   Potential Implications of the Two Models

How much turns on the choice between these models? Any choice will certainly reflect deeper assumptions about the law of unjust enrichment's legitimate scope and purpose.[23] However, it also has significant ground-level implications.

19.2.2.1   The Nature of C's Rights, Generated 'by Subrogation'

The discrete model's point of departure is the rights that X previously held, which were discharged at C's expense: equity responds to their

---

[21] See n 19.

[22] Lodder advocates the former, broader conception: Lodder (n 11) 7–8. Cf Peter Birks, *Unjust Enrichment* (2nd edn, Oxford University Press 2005) 78–86; Andrew Burrows, *The Law of Restitution* (3rd edn, Oxford University Press 2011) 64–69; Graham Virgo, *The Principles of the Law of Restitution* (3rd edn, Oxford University Press 2015) 116–18; Charles Mitchell, Paul Mitchell and Stephen Watterson, *Goff and Jones: The Law of Unjust Enrichment* (9th edn, Sweet & Maxwell 2016) [6.106]–[6.117]; Michael Rush, *The Defence of Passing On* (Hart Publishing 2006) Part II.

[23] See section 19.2.2.3 below.

discharge by affording C *new* rights against D and relevant others, which presumptively replicate X's extinguished rights. It is debatable whether the objective of specific restitution requires the perfect replication of X's rights in all respects, or only the replication of salient core characteristics.[24] However, subject to that caveat, where X held a security interest for D's liabilities, C might acquire an equivalent (new) security interest, by 'subrogation', which: (i) is equivalent in nature and priority to X's security; (ii) brings equivalent enforcement mechanisms; and (iii) secures a monetary liability similar in nature and quantum to that previously owed to X.

Adopting the alternative, reductionist model, 'subrogation' is not an independent restitutionary remedy, with a distinctive function: courts merely impose a new equitable lien/charge to reinforce C's standard monetary restitutionary remedy against the discharged debtor, D. Contextually, the fact that the discharged liability was secured by a charge over D's assets might help to explain why it might be acceptable to afford C the advantages of a new security interest over those assets. However, this would be the only reason for paying regard to X's rights: the content and characteristics of X's rights would not otherwise influence the nature of C's entitlement. Accordingly, where X held a security interest for D's liabilities, which C discharged: (i) C's charge would be a new, independent *and bare* equitable lien/charge, which would not replicate the nature and priority-ranking of X's security; (ii) C could employ enforcement mechanisms characteristic of a new bare equitable lien/charge, but could *not* invoke other mechanisms previously available under X's security (e.g. powers to sell or appoint a receiver, without court order); and (iii) the underlying monetary liability secured by C's lien/charge would be a standard monetary restitutionary liability, born of unjust enrichment, and would not be designed to replicate the nature and characteristics of D's released liability to X.

What of the cases? Cumulatively, the picture is compelling. Almost all features of the subrogation remedy, as assumed in later twentieth-century cases and beyond, *and* the language in which the remedy is discussed, much better align with the discrete model.

First, in several influential pre-*Banque Financière* cases, the courts' language implied that C acquires rights that are at least akin to those held by X, the paid-off creditor. X's rights were sometimes said to be 'kept

---

[24] This might bring the discrete model's practical implications closer to the reductionist model's; nevertheless, their underlying premises remain fundamentally different.

alive' in equity for C's benefit,[25] or C was said to be in a position akin to an 'equitable assignee' of X's rights.[26] The courts also occasionally explicitly invoked the metaphor of C 'stepping into X's shoes'.[27]

Secondly, post-*Banque Financière*, the courts typically express the nature of subrogation differently, yet still use language that draws a close comparison with the rights previously held by X, as the discrete model requires. In particular, it is said that C is not literally an assignee of X's rights,[28] but instead acquires new rights, arising in equity,[29] whose characteristics and content prima facie replicate, and can be no greater than, those rights which X previously held.[30]

Thirdly, this apparent replication of X's position is manifested in several ways. In particular, where X held security for D's liabilities, the security interest that C acquires 'by subrogation' presumptively inherits the priority-ranking that X's security had *vis-à-vis* pre-existing interests.[31] Some cases also assume that C has security which is of equivalent nature to X's security, such that C can rely upon enforcement mechanisms characteristic of that particular type of security (e.g. a right to possession, or powers to appoint a receiver, or to sell, conferred by the terms of X's security).[32] Other cases have gone further, in assuming that where X held a registered charge over D's registered title to land, C might be entitled to be registered as holder of that charge (or at least an equivalent) via subrogation.[33]

---

[25] E.g. *Chetwynd v Allen* [1899] 1 Ch 353 (Ch) 357; *Butler v Rice* [1910] 2 Ch 277 (Ch) 282 ('*Butler*'); *Ghana Commercial Bank v Chandiram* [1960] AC 732 (PC) 745 ('*Ghana Commercial Bank*'); *Western Trust & Savings Ltd v Rock* [1993] NPC 89 (CA) ('*Western Trust*').

[26] E.g. *Burston Finance Ltd v Speirway Ltd* [1974] 1 WLR 1648 (Ch) 1652 ('*Burston Finance*'); *Western Trust* (n 25).

[27] *Castle Phillips Finance Co Ltd v Piddington* (1995) 70 P&CR 592 (CA) 602 ('*Piddington*').

[28] Cf *Banque Financière* (n 2) 236–37 (Lord Hoffmann).

[29] Esp *Day v Tiuta International Ltd* [2014] EWCA Civ 1246 [43] ('*Day*').

[30] E.g. *Filby v Mortgage Express (No 2)* [2004] EWCA Civ 759 [63] ('*Filby*'). Cf also *Halifax plc v Omar* [2002] EWCA Civ 121 [84] ('*Omar*'); *Day* (n 29) [43]. Cf earlier *Halifax Mortgage Services Ltd v Muirhead* (1998) 78 P&CR 419 (CA) 426–28 ('*Muirhead*'). See further Mitchell and Watterson (n 1) [8.05] ff.

[31] E.g. *Eagle Star Insurance Ltd v Karasiewicz* [2002] EWCA Civ 940 ('*Karasiewicz*'); *Kali v Chawla* [2007] EWHC 2357 (Ch), [2008] BIPR 415 ('*Kali*'); *Barons Finance Ltd v Kensington Mortgage Co* [2011] EWCA Civ 1592. See Mitchell and Watterson (n 1) [4.09] ff, [8.61]–[8.62], [8.68]. Cf too *Banque Financière* (n 2).

[32] Esp *Day* (n 29) (equivalent powers to appoint a receiver). Cf *Thurstan v Nottingham Permanent Building Society* [1902] 1 Ch 1 (CA) 14 (no right to possession where C was subrogated to an unpaid vendor's lien).

[33] Esp *Piddington* (n 27); *Cheltenham & Gloucester plc v Appleyard* [2004] EWCA Civ 291 ('*Appleyard*'); *Primlake Ltd v Matthews Associates* [2009] EWHC 2774 (Ch) ('*Primlake*

SUBROGATION

Fourthly, this replication of X's position is also reflected in the personal liability secured by C's subrogation-based security. Numerous cases assume that C's subrogation entitlement *prima facie* encompasses personal rights equivalent to those previously held by X against D. That means, in particular, an equivalent right to interest, at an equivalent rate.[34] This is hard to square with the reductionist model, whereby the lien/charge simply secures a new monetary restitutionary liability, arising to reverse D's factual enrichment.

Fifthly, only the discrete model explains the more complex form of entitlement sometimes afforded by 'sub-subrogation': where C, having paid off liabilities owed to X, is entitled to acquire, by subrogation, a subrogation entitlement equivalent to that which X previously held, in respect of an *earlier* creditor's extinguished rights.[35]

Finally, only the discrete model explains both why C's security interest inherits the priority-ranking of X's security interest,[36] and the landmark decision in *Banque Financière*, where the House of Lords held that C (BFC) should be treated as holding a first-ranking charge, equivalent to the paid-off charge of X (RTB), but only *vis-à-vis* a second-ranking charge-holder (OOL), which would otherwise be unjustly enriched at C's expense.[37]

19.2.2.2 The Possibility/Impossibility of Subrogation to 'Personal Rights'

Allied to the question of what rights C might acquire by subrogation is whether subrogation might be available where C discharges D's *unsecured* liabilities to X. The reductionist model suggests not: the law's remedial objectives are sufficiently achieved by the standard monetary restitutionary remedy. The discrete model points in the opposite direction. Even the release of unsecured liabilities could qualify as a 'legal' enrichment, which the law could reverse *in specie* by recognising *new personal rights* for C against D, which presumptively replicate the

---

(2009)'); *Anfield (UK) v Bank of Scotland plc* [2010] EWHC 2374 (Ch), [2011] 1 WLR 2414 ('*Anfield*'). Cf Mitchell and Watterson (n 1) [8.113]–[8.123].

[34] E.g.*Western Trust* (n 25); *Piddington* (n 27) 602; *Muirhead* (n 30); *Filby* (n 30) [63]–[67]; *Kali* (n 31) [31] ff, [42]; *Primlake* (2009) (n 33) [26].

[35] See Mitchell and Watterson (n 1) [9.16]–[9.37]; *Piddington* (n 27) 600–01; *UCB Group Ltd v Hedworth (No 2)* [2003] EWCA Civ 1717, [2003] 3 FCR 739 [134]–[148]; *Kingsway Finance Co Ltd v Wang Qingyi* [2013] HKCFI 1178 [26]–[31], affd [2014] HKCA 578 [35]–[37].

[36] See n 31 above.

[37] *Banque Financière* (n 2), explained in Mitchell and Watterson (n 1) [8.48]–[8.60].

446 STEPHEN WATTERSON

characteristics and content of X's extinguished rights. That is consistent with how C's rights are sometimes conceptualised, where C is subrogated to X's security: it is sometimes assumed that C acquires an equivalent of X's security *and* the underlying personal rights, which X's security previously secured.[38] It is also something that courts have long tolerated where C discharged D's unsecured liabilities to X.[39] Can that be correct? *Ex hypothesi*, C could establish a cause of action in unjust enrichment, yielding the standard monetary restitutionary remedy against D, reflecting the monetary value of D's release from liability. Would subrogation to D's unsecured liabilities therefore be a needlessly duplicative remedy?

There are reasons to hesitate before reaching that conclusion. First, such subrogation is not invariably redundant for C: it may sometimes offer advantages over the standard monetary restitutionary remedy.[40] In particular, C might acquire a right with the same preferential status in the insolvency of D-debtor, as the debt previously owed to X.[41] Of course, it must not be unthinkingly assumed that it is invariably appropriate to afford C, via subrogation, all advantages that X enjoyed.[42] However, insofar as such replication is justified, the subrogation remedy has residual value.

Secondly, arguably, subrogation sometimes offers the *best tailored response*, given the nature of the 'enrichment' accruing to D from the release of X's rights; and the law might be justified in using such a specific restitutionary mechanism *in preference to*, and *to the exclusion of*, an ordinary monetary liability. In its conventional form, the standard monetary restitutionary remedy involves an immediate liability to pay the value in money of the released liabilities. That presents no difficulty in the typical case, where the liabilities discharged were presently due, crystallised liabilities. But what if the liabilities were, at the time of their discharge, deferred, or otherwise conditional, or unliquidated/uncrystallised? Might the standard monetary restitutionary remedy be unjustifiably burdensome, insofar as it transforms D's former liability into

---

[38] See esp the interest cases (n 34), and *Primlake* (2009) (n 33) (which recognised the appropriateness of a money judgment against the discharged debtors).
[39] E.g. *Baroness Wenlock v The River Dee Co* (1887) 19 QBD 155 (CA) 166; *Filby* (n 30); *Niru Battery Manufacturing Co v Milestone Trading (No 2)* [2004] EWCA Civ 487, [2004] 2 All ER (Comm) 289. See Mitchell and Watterson (n 1) [8.32] ff, [9.39]–[9.40].
[40] Cf Mitchell and Watterson (n 1) [8.33] ff.
[41] E.g. where the debts discharged constituted wages owed to an insolvent company's employees: e.g. *Cook v Italiano Family Fruit Co Pty Ltd* [2010] FCA 1355, (2010) 190 FCR 474 [63] ff.
[42] See section 19.2.2.1 above.

something more immediate, unconditional, and crystallised than was previously owed? No similar complaint could be made of the subrogation remedy, which would replicate the characteristics of D's former liability, and for that reason, might be justifiably preferred.[43]

19.2.2.3 Subrogation's Place within Unjust Enrichment's Remedial Armoury

The choice between models also brings important wider implications for the law of unjust enrichment, and for the subrogation remedy's place within it.

First, the discrete model requires a broader understanding of the scope of the law of unjust enrichment, and of the remedial mechanisms through which unjust enrichments may be addressed. Adopting this model, the subrogation cases provide important support for claims that the law of unjust enrichment is not categorically restricted to the monetary reversal of 'factual' enrichments, but may also encompass 'legal' enrichments – the acquisition of rights or release of duties/liabilities – which may be reversed via 'specific' mechanisms in a wider range of situations. The subrogation cases also suggest something about the nature of the law's 'restitutionary' response: that the focus is on the reversal of D's unjust enrichment.[44] In contrast, insofar as the reductionist model rejects any category of 'legal' enrichment, the law's remedial armoury looks far narrower. Its focus would be on the reversal of 'factual' enrichments, for which the standard monetary restitutionary remedy seems peculiarly apt. Other mechanisms sometimes said to be responses to unjust enrichment would look difficult to explain: e.g. the imposition of a trust; powers to rescind; the *in specie* reversal of a release of rights in two-party cases; the *in specie* reversal of a release of rights, via the subrogation remedy, in three-party cases.

Secondly, the reductionist model has dramatic implications for the remedy's existence. If its assumptions are valid, subrogation is not a distinctive

---

[43] Cf *Swynson Ltd v Lowick Rose LLP (in liq)* [2015] EWCA Civ 629, [2015] PNLR 28 [57]–[59] (Sales LJ) (subrogation to X's discharged tort claim?); *Re Walters' Deed of Guarantee* [1933] Ch 321 (Ch) (subrogation to X's 'entitlement' to preference share dividends?). Cf also the unsuccessful unjust enrichment argument before Cranston J in *Clark v In Focus Asset Management & Tax Solutions Ltd* [2012] EWHC 3669 (QB), [2013] PNLR 14 [37]–[44] (a *two*-party case, where C had arguably lost the right to bring an ordinary civil suit against D owing to C's mistaken acceptance of an ombudsman decision; if this *could* have been characterised as an unjust enrichment which required reversal, the appropriate remedy might be to 'restore' the lost right of action).

[44] See section 19.2.1.2 above.

remedy: the 'subrogation' label merely denotes a sub-category of cases where the courts recognise a new equitable lien/charge to secure a standard monetary restitutionary liability; the language of 'subrogation' reveals nothing about the content of the rights that C acquires; and the discharge of any earlier security is at best a contextual consideration that helps to explain why the advantage of a new lien/charge is not unjustified. Why then devote separate chapters of unjust enrichment texts to the subrogation remedy? The cases might seem better located in sections detailing when courts sometimes reinforce a personal claim in unjust enrichment via a newly imposed lien/charge.

Thirdly, in contrast, the discrete model allows a richer understanding of claimants' remedial options. It affords the subrogation remedy a fundamentally different function from the standard monetary restitutionary remedy, reflecting the insight that the same event (discharge of another's liability) may be perceived through two different lenses, and depending on the perspective, remedied via two different mechanisms. Whilst they may be concurrently available, neither mechanism can be collapsed into the other, nor are they precisely co-extensive in ambit. The subrogation remedy will not be appropriate in every case where a personal claim might lie; conversely, the subrogation remedy may exceptionally be more appropriate, and justifiable to the exclusion of any personal claim. Beyond this, the discrete model reveals a more complex reality, whereby: (i) a subrogation-based charge is distinguishable from any bare lien/charge newly imposed to secure C's personal claim; (ii) the same facts could support the recognition of either response; (iii) even where the fully replicative subrogation remedy is inappropriate, the law could still secure C's personal claim via a newly imposed bare lien/charge.

19.3 An Alternative 'Orthodox Proprietary Basis' for the Subrogation Remedy?

Menelaou offers a further challenge to prevailing accounts of the subrogation remedy. There are passing indications that there might be an alternative and more 'straightforward' route to justifying the remedy: an 'orthodox proprietary' rationale. This was not the basis on which four of five Supreme Court Justices, at least, decided the case. Nevertheless, Lord Neuberger's opinion, in particular, suggests strong receptivity to this alternative foundation for the remedy. Its nature and implications warrant close scrutiny.

19.3.1   Disambiguating the 'Orthodox Proprietary' Rationale

19.3.1.1   The Menelaou Statements

In *Menelaou*, the 'majority' unquestionably accepted that subrogation *can* be awarded as a remedy for unjust enrichment, and determined its availability on that basis.[45] In doing so, they denied that it was necessary for the Bank to establish that the money paid to the vendor (the paid-off creditor) was 'the Bank's' money;[46] and they appeared to recognise a distinction between 'unjust enrichment claims' (as the Bank's claim was understood to be) and 'proprietary claims'/'claims to vindicate property rights' (as discussed in *Foskett v McKeown*).[47] However, Lord Neuberger also indicated that *if* the money paid to the vendor was the 'Bank's' money, there might be an alternative 'proprietary' basis for subrogation. Early in his opinion, he explained that the Bank's primary case was that it had a 'claim based on unjust enrichment' against Miss Menelaou, which 'was or should be satisfied by subrogating the Bank to the [vendor's] lien'.[48] Both steps in the Bank's argument were made out. However, Lord Neuberger was also 'attracted to the view that the [B]ank's case on the first step could be justified on the alternative basis of an orthodox proprietary claim rather than on unjust enrichment'. On that assumption, it would be 'even clearer' that the Bank's claim should be satisfied by subrogation.[49] Lord Neuberger concluded with an elliptical passage, with which Lord Clarke also expressed agreement:

> My strong, if provisional, opinion that the [B]ank had a proprietary interest in the £875,000 which was used to purchase the freehold leads me to wonder whether the conclusion that the [B]ank's unjust enrichment claim is satisfied by subrogation could in fact be regarded as controversial, even before *Orakpo* and *Banque Financière* were decided. The reasons which persuade me that the unjust enrichment claim can properly be satisfied by subrogation to the lien ... are precious close to those which persuade me that there is a very strong case for saying that the [B]ank had a proprietary interest in the £875,000 ...[50]

Lord Carnwath's 'minority' opinion is harder to interpret. He was 'less convinced' of the case for 'rationalising' the older subrogation cases

---

[45] *Menelaou* (n 3) (Lords Clarke and Neuberger, Lords Kerr and Wilson agreeing).
[46] Ibid [53] (Lord Clarke), [84]–[98] (Lord Neuberger).
[47] Ibid [37] (Lord Clarke), [98] (Lord Neuberger).   [48] Ibid [58].   [49] Ibid [58]–[59].
[50] Ibid [106] (citations omitted). And see [54] (postscript) (Lord Clarke), endorsing Lord Neuberger's 'tentative conclusions and reasoning in paras 103, 104 and 106'.

through the 'prism of unjust enrichment',[51] and preferred to resolve the case through a 'strict application of the traditional rules of subrogation without any need to extend them beyond their established limits'.[52] He appeared content to adopt the conventional assumption that subrogation might be available where C's money was used to pay off the claims of X-secured creditor against D, particularly where C, a lender, had bargained for some form of security, which did not materialise.[53] Furthermore, relying heavily on *Boscawen v Bajwa*,[54] Lord Carnwath considered that, if C did not directly pay X,[55] then 'traditional principles' required a 'tracing link': C would need to 'trace' 'his' monies into the payment received by X.[56]

19.3.1.2 Three Possible Interpretations

What do these references to an 'orthodox proprietary' basis for subrogation mean?

One possibility is that they are *bare categorical statements*. They locate some recognised examples of subrogation 'within' 'traditional' property law doctrine, without suggesting anything about the particular reasons why the relevant subrogation entitlement is afforded, beyond a *negative*: it is not afforded as a response to 'unjust enrichment'. This interpretation must be discounted. There are traces of such an approach in some early post-*Banque Financière* decisions, which set up an opposition between 'traditional' principles and *Banque Financière*'s novel unjust enrichment analysis.[57] However, Lord Neuberger undoubtedly meant something more. He assumed that the Bank might have an alternative basis for its claim, if it could establish a proprietary entitlement to the monies paid to the vendor. The subrogation remedy was not merely afforded *by* the 'law of property': the claimant's pre-existing proprietary entitlement to the monies had an *essential part* in this alternative legal explanation for the remedy.

What other interpretations are available? One is that Lord Neuberger was merely identifying a circumstance that supported/reinforced C's claim to the subrogation remedy, *for the purpose of reversing unjust enrichment*. Another interpretation, which seems truest to his words, is that he was identifying an *independent juristic basis* for the subrogation

---

[51] Ibid [108].   [52] Ibid [107].   [53] Ibid [111] ff.

[54] [1996] 1 WLR 328 (CA) ('*Boscawen*').

[55] Cf *Menelaou* (n 3) [129], distinguishing *Banque Financière* (n 2).

[56] Ibid [121]–[132], rejecting the sufficiency of e.g. a mere causal connection.

[57] E.g. *Omar* (n 30); *Karasiewicz* (n 31).

remedy, grounded in C's pre-existing property rights. This last, and more radical interpretation, requires extended exploration.

19.3.2 An Independent Juristic Basis for the Subrogation Remedy?

19.3.2.1 Foundations

On what assumptions might C's property rights supply an independent basis for the subrogation remedy? Any 'proprietary' rationale must certainly require more than that C paid (his) money to D, or that C paid (his) money to X and discharged D's debt. C's prior title is not an independently sufficient explanation for C to acquire rights against D or X. C may well have intended to transfer the money, legally and beneficially, to the recipient; title then generally passes. Of course, the fact that the monies paid had previously belonged to C might be a necessary step in explaining why C might have a remedy against D or X; but C's prior title alone is not a sufficient foundation for a remedy, to reverse unjust enrichment or *a fortiori*, to 'vindicate'/'protect' C's property rights.

What else might references to a 'proprietary' rationale for subrogation mean? The only seriously plausible candidate is that the remedy is afforded to protect/vindicate some pre-existing entitlement of C from unauthorised interference/appropriation. This would chime with some accounts of English law, which maintain that the 'vindication of property rights' provides an independent foundation of rights/duties/liabilities (including restitutionary rights/duties/liabilities).[58] Where C's asset is misappropriated, English law is undoubtedly generous, in that, independently of any claim based on wrongdoing, it may: (i) subject the unwarranted recipient to a monetary restitutionary liability, reflecting the value of the property received or still held; (ii) afford C-owner a new entitlement to an unauthorised traceable product, in the original or later recipient's hands (subject to title-defeating rules); and (iii) afford C-owner further monetary claims consequent on (ii). According to these 'proprietary' accounts, such rights/liabilities, even when 'restitutionary', are not appropriately explained by the law of unjust enrichment. They are structurally different from standard unjust enrichment claims, and have independent normative foundations, perhaps rooted in a contingent choice made by English law regarding the nature/content of an 'owner's' rights, and the appropriate manner of their protection/vindication. Could the subrogation remedy be a natural

---

[58] See esp Virgo (n 22).

extension of the same premises? If D uses C's money to acquire a new asset, the law affords C new rights to that traceable exchange product in which the value derived from C's money survives. If D instead uses C's money to discharge a liability to X, the law correspondingly affords C new rights, replicating X's rights.

One response to such 'proprietary' explanations is that, contrary to the House of Lords' decision in *Foskett v McKeown*,[59] rights to unauthorised traceable substitutes are better analysed as rights born of the law of unjust enrichment;[60] and that *a fortiori*, the subrogation remedy, afforded where 'C's' money is traceably applied to discharge D's liabilities to X, can be similarly explained. However, even if the *Foskett* decision is correct about the basis of rights to traceable substitutes, that does not compel a corresponding 'proprietary' explanation for the subrogation remedy. For, even if the law affords C-owner's original title extended protection by affording C rights to an unauthorised exchange product, it is doing something rather different if it responds to the use of C's monies to discharge a debt, by re-creating equivalents of X's rights, which were extinguished, in favour of C. This is strikingly demonstrated by Millett LJ's own words in *Boscawen v Bajwa*.[61] Notwithstanding the position he later took in *Foskett*, the subrogation remedy, established in *Boscawen* via tracing, was described as a 'restitutionary remedy' for 'unjust enrichment'.

Putting these reservations to one side, the 'proprietary' rationale is both a possible interpretation, and the only seriously arguable interpretation of Lord Neuberger's *dicta* in *Menelaou*. Its implications deserve close examination.

19.3.2.2 Explanatory Potential and Implications

How much case law might be explained via the 'proprietary' rationale? Subrogation cases are diverse, but mostly span three key contextual categories, distinguished according to the capacity in which C pays X, or in which monies derived from C are paid to X. The 'proprietary' rationale's force varies considerably, depending on the category in view.

19.3.2.2.1 'Simple Misappropriation Cases' *Simple misappropriation* cases are most readily explained via the 'proprietary' rationale. They closely fit the model and its normative foundations: a debt owed to X is

---

[59] [2001] 1 AC 102 (HL).
[60] Cf Burrows (n 22) 118–19, 169–71; *Goff and Jones* (n 22) [8.152]–[8.165].
[61] *Boscawen* (n 54).

traceably discharged, without C's authority, using monies initially obtained from C via some unauthorised/non-consensual disposition.[62] The cases vary widely, encompassing trust monies misappropriated in breach of trust,[63] corporate funds misappropriated via unauthorised acts of directors,[64] funds forming part of a deceased's estate wrongly paid out under an invalid will or will provision,[65] partnership funds misappropriated by a partner,[66] and simple theft.[67]

19.3.2.2.2 'Common Liability Cases' In contrast, the proprietary rationale is wholly incapable of explaining *common liability cases*. Here, C has paid X in discharge of his own liability to X, in circumstances that entitle C to recoupment/contribution from D, on the basis that C and D owed common liabilities to X, and that this was a burden which, as between C and D, D should have borne, wholly or partially. It is well established that C is *prima facie* entitled to be subrogated to X's rights here, supplementing the monetary remedy available directly against D via a recoupment/contribution claim. Nevertheless, it is impossible to maintain that these rights are afforded to 'protect'/'vindicate' C's pre-existing rights in the monies paid. Given C's intentional payment to X, to discharge his own liability, C could not plausibly claim that he retains title to the money in X's hands: debtors unconditionally discharge their debts by affording their creditors beneficial enjoyment of monies paid.[68] Nor does the fact that the monies paid were previously C's mean that C's claim against D has a 'proprietary' basis. That would extend the 'vindication' idea to the point of rendering it meaningless and incoherent,[69] and obscure the only viable normative explanation for these cases. At root, they reflect the law's quest to ensure the just distribution of the burden of a common liability. What seems normatively salient is that, via C's payment, C immediately bears a burden that D should more justly have

---

[62] See *Goff and Jones* (n 22) [8.144]–[8.148]; Mitchell and Watterson (n 1) [6.38]–[6.50].

[63] E.g. *Scotlife Home Loans (No 2) Ltd v Melinek* (1999) 78 P&CR 389 (CA) ('*Melinek*'). Cf also *Trustees Executors Ltd v Steve G Ltd* [2013] NZHC 16 [107]–[118] ('*Steve G*').

[64] E.g. *Primlake Ltd v Matthews Associates Ltd* [2006] EWHC 1227 (Ch), [2007] 1 BCLC 666 ('*Primlake* (2006)').

[65] E.g. *Gertsch v Atsas* [1999] NSWSC 898 ('*Gertsch*'). Cf *Re Diplock* [1948] Ch 465 (CA), explained in *Boscawen* (n 54).

[66] E.g. *Raulfs v Fishy Bite Ltd* [2008] NSWSC 1195.

[67] E.g. *National Australia Bank Ltd v Rusu* [2001] NSWSC 32.

[68] E.g. David Fox, *Property Rights in Money* (Oxford University Press 2008) [1.97] ff.

[69] See section 19.3.2.1 above; a 'vindication' analysis also cannot differentiate cases where C is entitled to full recoupment or only partial contribution.

borne. Establishing that X was paid using monies 'belonging' to C merely serves to demonstrate that C immediately 'bore' the burden.

19.3.2.2.3 'Lending Cases'

'Lending Cases' The *lending cases* occupy difficult middle ground, and warrant deeper analysis. Here, C is a lender who intended to advance funds, typically to finance a property purchase or to re-finance existing borrowing. During the twentieth century, the English courts proved exceptionally generous in allowing such lenders to be subrogated to the rights of an existing secured creditor who was paid off using the monies loaned. Pre-*Banque Financière*, such subrogation was often afforded on the basis that when a third party pays off another's security interest, he is 'presumed, unless the contrary appears, to intend that the [security interest] shall be kept alive for his own benefit'.[70] Despite its apparent breadth, this presumption was generally invoked only where C-lender intended to loan on a *secured* basis,[71] and did not receive the bargained-for security: i.e. the subrogation remedy typically came to the rescue of *disappointed secured lenders*.[72] In such cases, the qualification might be added, that whilst C-lender bargained for new security, C-lender presumably intended to keep alive the previous security, 'save in so far as it was replaced'.[73]

The authorities reveal numerous reasons why the bargained-for security might prove deficient: e.g. the security was not actually granted; or more often, the security apparently granted was void/voidable *ab initio*, or valid but without the desired priority-ranking.[74] In *Banque Financière*,[75] Lord Hoffmann famously criticised the fictitious over-reference to parties' intentions in these cases: in truth, equity afforded subrogation as a restitutionary remedy to prevent/reverse unjust enrichment. This has become the new orthodoxy.[76] Outcomes have not significantly differed; the key change is in the language of judicial reasoning. If an 'unjust factor' is explicitly identified, the lender's disappointed expectations of security are typically thought to support relief because of some relevant 'mistake'/'failure of basis'.[77]

---

[70] E.g. *Ghana Commercial Bank* (n 25) 745.
[71] Cf *Boodle Hatfield & Co v British Films Ltd* (1986) 2 BCC 99221 (Ch).
[72] *Burston Finance* (n 26) 1652 (Walton J) ('one of [subrogation's] chief uses').
[73] E.g. *Ghana Commercial Bank* (n 25) 745.
[74] See generally Mitchell and Watterson (n 1) [6.57] ff, [6.80] ff.
[75] *Banque Financière* (n 2).
[76] E.g. *Menelaou* (n 3) [50] (Lord Clarke). Cf early scepticism in *Omar* (n 30).
[77] E.g. mistake: *Banque Financière* (n 2); *Filby* (n 30); failure of basis: *Appleyard* (n 33); *Anfield* (n 33); *Lehman Commercial Mortgage Conduit Ltd v Gatedale Ltd* [2012] EWHC

This summary highlights an immediate difficulty for any 'proprietary' rationale, as a theory of past subrogation cases. Remarkably few lending cases explicitly reason in proprietary terms.[78] Many may be susceptible to such explanation, but a significant number are not, without straining proprietary reasoning beyond breaking-point.

To understand why, imagine a simple scenario where C-lender intended to make a loan to D-borrower. The loan-monies discharge D-borrower's debts to X-creditor via *three alternative paths*:

Case 1.   The loan-monies are initially transferred to solicitors and held for C-lender pending completion. They are later disbursed by the solicitors, directly to X-creditor, or to D-borrower and then to X-creditor.

Case 2.   The loan-monies are disbursed directly by C-lender to D-borrower, who then uses them to pay X-creditor.

Case 3.   The loan-monies are disbursed directly by C-lender to X-creditor.

How might a 'proprietary' explanation yield a subrogation remedy here?

Four routes to a 'conventional' proprietary basis

Route 1 is peculiarly appropriate for *Case 1*, where loan-monies are received by C-lender's solicitors as trustees, to be disbursed only in accordance with C-lender's instructions. If the solicitors subsequently disburse the monies contrary to their instructions, they act beyond their authority and in breach of trust. That unauthorised disposition will not overreach C-lender's pre-existing beneficial title to the monies, and should allow C-lender, on conventional principles, to trace the monies into any recipient's hands. That should readily allow the conclusion that X-creditor, who was immediately paid by the solicitors, received what still qualifies as C-lender's money, in discharge of D-borrower's debts. So viewed, the case approximates to the simple misappropriation cases.

---

848 (Ch). See too *Menelaou* (n 3) [21] (Lord Clarke). See further Mitchell and Watterson (n 1) ch 6.

[78] Statements that the subrogation remedy 'gives effect to'/'enforces'/'vindicates' a 'pre-existing equity' (*Boscawen* (n 54) 335, 342; *Omar* (n 30) [81]; *Karasiewicz* (n 31) [20]; *Day* (n 29) [42]) are not assertions that subrogation 'vindicates' property rights. They affirm the 'institutional' nature of the remedy: where subrogation-justifying facts exist, C typically acquires an immediate equitable entitlement, effective *in rem*, which is confirmed/crystallised and enforced by a later court order. Without more, they reveal nothing about why the pre-existing 'equity' arises. See Watterson, 'Modelling Subrogation' (n 18).

Route 2 offers an equivalent solution for *Case 2*, where C-lender disbursed the loan-monies *to D-borrower*, who subsequently paid them to X-creditor. Loan-monies so paid ordinarily become the borrower's, legally *and beneficially*. Nevertheless, wider transactional circumstances will sometimes result in C-lender having a persisting entitlement to the monies in the borrower's hands. One option, *reflecting the parties' intentions*, is a *Quistclose*-style arrangement, such that D-borrower is initially a trustee for C-lender, pending application of the loan-monies in some specified manner. If D-borrower's use of the loan-monies to pay X-creditor is contrary to that authority, C-lender will be equivalently placed to a lender who is the victim of a solicitor's unauthorised disbursement. In other situations, C-lender would need to demonstrate some persisting entitlement to the monies in D-borrower's hands, *by imposition of law*, and *contrary to the intended transaction*. For example, C-lender might show that the loan was procured by D-borrower's fraud, in circumstances that would render D-borrower an immediate constructive trustee of the loan-monies received for C-lender, or that would afford C-lender an equity to rescind the loan transaction, triggering a similar trust upon rescission. Having established such a title, and that the monies were later used to pay X-creditor, C-lender might again appear equivalently placed to the victim of a simple misappropriation, or a lender who is the victim of a solicitor's unauthorised disbursement.

Routes 1 and *2* come closest to the normative core of accounts that view the protection/vindication of C's pre-existing rights as a source of legal entitlements: in both cases, C-lender can identify monies in a third party's hands to which it has 'title', which are subsequently used, without C's authority, to pay X-creditor. Neither explanation fits *Case 3*, where C-lender directly paid X-creditor. Here, there is no third-party misapplication of 'C's' monies: *C-lender itself intentionally paid X-creditor*. How can C-lender base its claim on its pre-existing property rights? Independently of any title-clearing argument available to X-creditor, legal and beneficial title will presumptively pass, reflecting C-lender's intention that this should occur. To explain why C-lender might have a remedy, consequent upon the payment to X-creditor in *Case 3*, two other 'proprietary' explanations are therefore required.

Route 3 asks whether, but for any title-clearing argument available to X-creditor, the law would afford C-lender some entitlement to the monies received by X-creditor (e.g. via rendering X-creditor a constructive trustee for C-lender)? If it would, then the discharge of D-borrower's debt might be deemed the immediate product of what remains, at the point of X's receipt, 'C-lender's' money: X-creditor would typically obtain a good title, clear of C's persisting title, simultaneously with D-borrower's discharge (that discharge constituting the giving of value that would support a *bona fide* purchase defence). Any subrogation remedy consequent on D-borrower's discharge might then appear to have a conventional 'proprietary' basis.

Route 4 involves a subtly different inquiry: had the loan-monies immediately been transferred to D-borrower, rather than directly to X-creditor for D-borrower's benefit, would the law have afforded C-lender an entitlement to the loan-monies in D-borrower's hands (e.g. via rendering D-borrower a constructive trustee for C-lender)? The basic premise is that *Case 3* is a compressed version of *Case 2*, and that the remedial consequences should align. In 'long-form'-*Case 2*, where C-lender initially transferred the monies to *D-borrower*, C-lender might establish an entitlement to the loan-monies in D-borrower's hands, which could be traced into the later payment to X-creditor, to supply a 'proprietary' basis for the subrogation remedy. *Ex hypothesi*, the positions of C-lender and D-borrower should be no different in 'short-form'-*Case 3*, where C-lender pays X-creditor *directly, for* D-borrower.

Explaining the authorities in 'proprietary' terms

What of the authorities? Analysis can usefully focus on *Case 1*, the scenario present in most reported decisions, where the loan-monies are disbursed *via solicitors* to X-creditor. There are two key modern examples of 'proprietary' reasoning being used to support subrogation in that situation.

Boscawen v Bajwa[79] is a leading authority for *Route 1*. Solicitors had released the loan-monies prematurely to X-creditor, the vendor's mortgagee, ahead of completion of the purchase transaction which ultimately fell through. Millett LJ reasoned that the solicitors' premature disbursement was a breach of trust, which enabled C-lender to trace the monies into the payment to X-creditor, and the discharge of D-vendor's debt. This in turn justified the availability of subrogation *vis-à-vis* D.

Filby v Mortgage Express (No 2)[80] is susceptible to multiple rationalisations. C-lender intended to loan money to Mr and Mrs Filby, secured by first mortgage over their jointly owned home. In fact, Mr Filby had forged the signatures of Mrs Filby, and the loan and mortgage documentation was substantially ineffective. One basis given for the conclusion that

---

[79] *Boscawen* (n 54).   [80] *Filby* (n 30).

C-lender was subrogated to the rights of creditors paid off using the loan-monies was a 'straight application of the orthodox analysis of the remedy' offered in *Boscawen*. C-lender had 'retained . . . beneficial ownership' of the monies that were used to discharge the Filbys' debts, because the solicitors acting for C-lender had held the loan-monies on an express trust and had disbursed the monies contrary to its terms: *Route 1*.[81] May LJ also appeared to offer an independent basis for the same conclusion, consistent with *Routes 3/4*. This relied upon the wider transactional context, that C-lender was fraudulently induced to advance the monies pursuant to what was substantially a void transaction.

These are obviously significant cases. However, they offer rather inconclusive support for suggestions that there is an 'orthodox proprietary' basis for the subrogation remedy, which is distinct from and exclusive of the 'unjust enrichment' basis. Despite their 'proprietary' reasoning, both decisions ultimately ground the subrogation remedy in 'unjust enrichment'. The unlawful use of C-lender's money, established *via tracing*, supplied the reason why the consequential release of D's liability was an 'unjust enrichment' that required reversal. Thus, in *Boscawen*, Millett LJ said that:

> Tracing was the process by which [C] sought to establish that its money was applied in the discharge of [X's] charge: subrogation was the remedy [which C] sought *in order to deprive Mr Bajwa . . . of the unjust enrichment which he would thereby otherwise obtain at the Abbey National's expense*.[82]

May LJ used similar language in *Filby*.[83]

Some may reject this language, claiming that it involves 'unjust enrichment' in a 'descriptive' rather than claim-justifying 'substantive' sense.[84] Nevertheless, there are reasons to take these statements at face value. First, subsequent decisions have treated *Boscawen* as a leading authority for the *general* characterisation of subrogation as a remedy for 'unjust enrichment'.[85] Secondly, Millett LJ's explanation for C-lender's remedy, which relied on the solicitors' unauthorised disbursement, makes it equivalent to the simple misappropriation cases.[86] Significantly, some key English

---

[81] Ibid [29], [31].   [82] *Boscawen* (n 54) 335 (emphasis added).   [83] *Filby* (n 30) [30].
[84] E.g. Virgo (n 22) 8–10.
[85] *Banque Financière* (n 2) esp 236 (Lord Hoffmann) (much quoted in later cases). Cf too e.g. *Muirhead* (n 30) 425–26; *Birmingham Midshires Mortgage Services Ltd v Sabherwal* (2000) 80 P&CR 256 [37]; *Appleyard* (n 33); *Day* (n 29) [79]; also *Steve G* (n 63) [107]–[118].
[86] See section 19.3.2.2.1 above.

cases of the latter type also explicitly characterise the remedy as an 'unjust enrichment' remedy, based on the 'unlawful' use of C's monies.[87] Thirdly, Millett LJ hinted in *Boscawen* that the subrogation remedy might be vulnerable to a change of position defence.[88] This defence is often said to be *peculiar* to unjust enrichment claims, and in *Foskett*,[89] Lord Millett himself implied that it had no relevance to a claim to 'vindicate ... property rights'. It is difficult to maintain, given Millett LJ's express language in *Boscawen*, and this clear opposition, that he was regarding the subrogation remedy as a claim to 'vindicate ... property rights'. Fourthly, the majority's emphatic insistence in *Foskett*[90] that rights to unauthorised traceable substitutes of misappropriated trust funds are afforded 'by the law of property', and are not unjust enrichment-generated, does not dictate that where such funds are traceably used to discharge another's security interest, any subrogation remedy must be explained by the same event. The law could consistently maintain that C's entitlement to an unauthorised traceable substitute is generated by the law, independently of unjust enrichment; but that if C can trace his monies into the discharge of another's debt, the subrogation remedy may be awarded as a restitutionary remedy for the unjust enrichment that would otherwise result.[91]

A bigger obstacle to any 'proprietary' rationale is ultimately that *Boscawen* and *Filby* are relatively isolated cases. Other lending cases *might* be explained using proprietary reasoning. Nevertheless, a 'proprietary' rationale does not capture the reasoning actually used by the courts, and past cases have granted subrogation remedies to lenders in circumstances that are not readily explained using the necessary 'proprietary' terms.

To understand why, recall that a 'proprietary' rationale requires these decisions to be supported in one of two ways. One must *either* (i) explain why, in the circumstances, the loan-monies were improperly disbursed by C-lender's solicitor (*Route 1*), or (ii) explain why, *in light of wider transactional circumstances*, the law would have afforded C-lender

---

[87] Esp *Primlake* (2006) (n 64) [337]–[340]. Cf also from Australia, pre-*Bofinger*: *Gertsch* (n 65); and from New Zealand: *Steve G* (n 63) [107]–[118].

[88] *Boscawen* (n 54) 341 (cf also 334). See Mitchell and Watterson (n 1) ch 7; *Gertsch* (n 65); *Anfield* (n 33) [31], [38].

[89] *Foskett* (n 59) 129.   [90] Ibid.

[91] Two of the *Foskett* majority were leading proponents of the unjust enrichment rationalisation of the subrogation remedy: Lord Millett (*Boscawen* (n 54)); Lord Hoffmann (*Banque Financière* (n 2)).

a persisting title, *on some other basis*, to the monies transferred (*Routes 2, 3 or 4*).

Route 1 demands close investigation into the exact limits on a conveyancing solicitor's disbursement authority. A solicitor's authority will certainly be routinely limited such that some transactional deficiencies will render any disbursement 'unauthorised': e.g. if the loan-monies are disbursed without the solicitor having ensured that the agreed security was duly executed. Nevertheless, *Route 1* cannot explain all past outcomes: the transactional deficiencies thought sufficient to warrant subrogation in practice are substantially broader than those one might place at the solicitor's door on the basis that, given the terms of the solicitor's disbursement authority, they entail an improper disbursement. This is clearly true where the subrogation-triggering deficiency only arises *after* the loan-monies were disbursed;[92] but it is also true of some problems that render the security deficient, in validity/extent/priority, that existed *at the time* the loan-monies were disbursed.

Additionally, *Route 1* attributes overriding significance to a *contingent* feature – the solicitor's limited disbursement authority – which past cases do not suggest is normatively decisive. These cases suggest that where C-lender loaned money, and the bargained-for security is deficient, the deficiency is a *sufficient explanation* for the subrogation remedy, *without further inquiry being required into whether the loan-monies were 'improperly' disbursed by solicitors*. This suggests that the real justification for the remedy stems from the wider transactional context, which sees C-lender agree to advance funds only on certain conditions, which are not satisfied. The limits on the conveyancing solicitor's disbursement authority are *corollaries* of that wider transactional context, and not themselves conclusive of the subrogation remedy's availability/unavailability. To test this, imagine that C-lender does not obtain the bargained-for security, and that: *either* (i) C-lender supplied the loan-monies via solicitors, *without* relevantly limiting the solicitors' disbursement authority; *or* (ii) C-lender supplied the loan-monies via solicitors, *limiting* the solicitors' disbursement authority in terms which mean it would be improper to disburse the funds in the circumstances; *or* (iii) C-lender released the loan-monies directly. If X-creditor is paid by C-lender's solicitor or C-lender, can C-lender be subrogated to X-creditor's rights? *Route 1* is only available in situation (ii): only in that instance is there an

---

[92] E.g. *Anfield* (n 33). See also the earlier cases noted in Mitchell and Watterson (n 1) [6.92]–[6.94].

intervening breach of trust which renders the solicitors' disbursement of the loan-monies an unauthorised disposition of C-lender's funds. However, that makes subrogation's availability turn on a fact which the cases' reasoning and outcomes suggest is not normatively salient/decisive: subrogation is available *in all three situations*. The salient circumstances, common *to all three situations*, are that C-lender supplied monies which were used to discharge X-creditor's debt, and that C's expectation of security for its advance was disappointed.

Do *Routes 2–4* offer any better explanation? Each makes subrogation's availability depend on wider property law's position regarding the circumstances in which C-lender, in paying money to another, might retain/regain title. They fare no better. The courts have almost never sought to explain why C-lender might have established a persisting title to the monies paid over.[93] Furthermore, had they done so, they would immediately have encountered difficult territory. Once outside simple cases involving an unauthorised disposal of C's monies, several highly contested questions would need to be confronted. These include: (i) whether a recipient of monies paid as a consequence of a mistake (induced/uninduced) or on a basis/subject to a condition which has failed to materialise (immediately/subsequently) is ever rendered a trustee for the payer; (ii) whether this does or should depend on establishing further facts to demonstrate that the relevant party's 'conscience' was sufficiently affected; (iii) whether any trust is or should be immediate, or crystallises only on exercise of a power held by C; (iv) the significance of the existence and status of any contract under which the monies were apparently paid (valid/void/voidable). Whatever the correct answers are to such questions, past cases have largely defined subrogation's boundaries without explicit reference to them. It would be wholly fortuitous if *Routes 2–4* provided a good, and *a fortiori* perfect, fit.

19.3.2.3 The Future of the 'Proprietary' Rationale

Imperfect fit with past cases should certainly not prevent courts invoking 'proprietary' reasoning in future, *if* such reasoning has independent normative force, and would be more conducive to the rational development and containment of the law. These important questions must be confronted in future work. Five observations can be offered here, to assist in framing that debate.

---

[93] Routine statements that C-lender 'paid' another's debts are inconclusive; read in context, they only disclose that C-lender was the *de facto* source of the relevant funds.

First, the *Menelaou* 'majority' did not say that the 'proprietary' rationale was the only route to a subrogation remedy. It was offered as an *alternative* basis, *alongside* 'unjust enrichment', on which the 'majority' actually based their decision. The key question is therefore: how much credence does the 'proprietary' rationale deserve as a *concurrent* basis for the subrogation remedy?

Secondly, the 'proprietary' rationale is not required to explain the availability of subrogation in 'core' cases, involving simple misappropriations or close equivalents, where a 'vindication of pre-existing property rights' theory is most persuasively engaged.[94] An unjust enrichment analysis can yield the same conclusions via the unjust factor variously described as 'want of authority', 'lack of consent', or 'ignorance'.[95]

Thirdly, to explain subrogation's availability *beyond* those 'core' cases, any proprietary rationale must be refined in a manner that subtly shifts the explanation's normative power. The most plausible extended analysis inquires whether X-creditor was immediately paid with C's money, in circumstances where the law would afford C a persisting (new/continuing) title to the money in the recipient's hands. Unfortunately, greater explanatory reach is purchased at the cost of equivocation. To see why, imagine that C is induced by D's fraud to pay X, in discharge of D's debt, and that (but for any title-clearing argument available to X) the law would have afforded C title to the monies paid, e.g. via a constructive trust, such that the subrogation remedy might be considered to have a 'proprietary' foundation. Would the subrogation remedy here have an 'orthodox proprietary' basis or 'vindicate C's pre-existing property rights', in the same sense as in 'core' misappropriation cases? Equivalence is achieved only by glossing the rather different circumstances that may cause the law to afford C a persisting title. In 'core' misappropriation cases, the law responds to a third party's unauthorised disposal of C's money. In the immediate example, the law responds to D's having induced C, via a fraudulently induced mistake, to pay his money to X, for D's benefit. An all-embracing analysis that maintains that '*since* the law would have afforded C a persisting title, *therefore* the subrogation

---

[94] See section 19.3.2.2.1 above.

[95] See esp *Goff and Jones* (n 22) ch 8. Cf the alternative view that most cases susceptible to this explanation are best understood as essentially 'title-based' claims, which are different in structure and rationale from unjust enrichment claims that serve to reverse 'defective transfers'. Notwithstanding the arguments of Virgo (n 22) and others, the courts have treated these situations as equally within the law of unjust enrichment: e.g. *Lipkin Gorman v Karpnale Ltd* [1991] 2 AC 548 (HL).

remedy's juristic basis is the "protection" of C's title' appears thin, in glossing the different and independently substantial reasons why the law might respond as it does.

Fourthly, a 'proprietary' rationale offers no obviously better answer to some basic justificatory questions. In particular, why does the use of what still qualifies as C's money, to pay X-creditor, require C to have new rights, presumptively equivalent to X-creditor's earlier rights? That response is not logically dictated. If the explanation is that it is inappropriate for D (and relevant others) to be fortuitously allowed the advantage of this release from liability, resulting from the use of C's monies, is this adequately captured by a 'proprietary' rationale? Or might it be more transparently articulated via concepts of 'unjust enrichment', as the language actually used by the courts implies?

Finally, a 'proprietary' rationale might perhaps be comprehensible as a *containment strategy*, if it was the exclusive basis for the subrogation remedy. The remedy's availability would then be parasitic on established positions adopted elsewhere within the wider law of property (e.g. regarding whether a recipient of money from C is rendered a trustee by operation of law), and would restrict the remedy's availability in a manner sensitive to transactional concerns (e.g. the wider law would be unlikely to afford C a persisting title to monies paid, if this would contradict a valid transaction under which the monies were paid).

There are nevertheless two key problems. First, an independent 'proprietary' rationale cannot achieve containment if recognised alongside unjust enrichment as an alternative basis for the remedy: the unjust enrichment rationale could still roam freely beyond its strictures. Secondly, if rational containment is desired, might this be better achieved *within* the newly 'orthodox' unjust enrichment rationale? There is no reason why the subrogation remedy should be available wherever C establishes that the discharge of another's liability is an 'unjust enrichment' that yields a standard monetary restitutionary remedy: the law could and should more tightly limit the availability of specific/proprietary restitutionary mechanisms. Past subrogation decisions are justifiably criticised for their failure to confront this crucial boundary issue. Nevertheless, it is not impossible, *within an unjust enrichment framework*, to develop a defensible account of the circumstances in which a specific/proprietary restitutionary mechanism is warranted. Furthermore, in developing any such account, courts should certainly look to wider property law for guidance: e.g. looking to circumstances in which a mistaken transfer, or a transfer on a basis/subject to a condition which fails, might be reversed via the imposition of a trust. Such cross-referencing with wider property law's commitments does not involve or require the adoption of any independent 'proprietary' explanation for the subrogation remedy. Legal coherence merely demands that the remedy should not, without good reasons that reflect its distinctive nature or contextual applications, extend too far beyond the circumstances in which the wider law is prepared in equivalent situations to afford a specific/proprietary mechanism that 'restores' rights to C.

19.4 Conclusions

Much ink will certainly be spilt unpicking *Menelaou* over the next few years. The peculiarities of the particular case must not, however, blind us to some fundamental issues at stake. Two broader points emerge from this chapter's selective foray into that difficult territory. First, the exercise of justifying the subrogation remedy vitally depends on the correct understanding of the remedy's role. What is the best sense that might be made of the modern orthodoxy that subrogation is a 'restitutionary remedy' for 'unjust enrichment'? Of the two available 'restitutionary' models, the 'discrete model' undoubtedly offers the best fit. This is important. A remedy that responds to the release of another's liabilities by affording a claimant rights equivalent to those discharged, is a distinctive remedy, which promises real benefits for a claimant over an unsecured monetary restitutionary claim. Its availability demands a further layer of justification, beyond that which suffices to support any monetary liability. Looking forwards, judges and scholars must therefore do rather more than they have done hitherto to identify and articulate the premises on which such relief is warranted. Secondly, when it comes to addressing that justificatory question, we must be wary of the simple temptations of taxonomy. The fundamental question 'why *should* a claimant be afforded rights equivalent to the rights of a paid-off creditor?' becomes no easier to answer merely by shifting one's justificatory perspective from an unjust enrichment framework, to an alternative framework. The 'proprietary' rationale, briefly floated in *Menelaou*, does not offer a viable descriptive theory for past subrogation decisions. Neither is it manifestly a more appropriate basis for future development of the law, either alongside, or in place of, an unjust enrichment-focused rationale.

20

Equitable Set-off

PG TURNER

20.1 Introduction

Set-offs are processes of high utility and, in some points, technical
delicacy. Used in a general sense, 'set-off' means any of several processes
by which a monetary demand held by party A against party B and
a monetary cross-demand held by party B against party A are set against
one another. Set-offs dispense with the need for both the demand and the
cross-demand to be fully performed. Only the party whose monetary
liability is not exhausted by the set-off remains liable, and then only to a
correspondingly reduced extent. The means of reaching those results
vary between the various species of set-off, each species having distinct
governing rules.

It should not be thought strange to speak of set-offs in a book on
commercial remedies. Writers refer to set-offs as remedies, following a
familiar manner:[1] when speaking of remedies, common lawyers often
mean those measures to which a person can have resort in a conflict with
another. Seldom is 'remedy' confined to mean relief ordered by a court.[2]
As measures to which persons commonly resort in disputes with others,
set-offs are a proper subject of enquiry in an investigation of commercial
remedies.

In English law, the species of set-off have come into being at different
times. The first in a series of enactments to establish so-called 'insolvency

The author is grateful for the comments and suggestions of those who attended the
conference at which this chapter was initially presented, as well as to the Hon JC
Campbell, Ms Jessica Hudson and the Hon Justice Leeming. The usual disclaimers apply.
[1] E.g. Phillip Wood, *English and International Set-off* (Sweet & Maxwell 1989) [4–49];
Sheelagh McCracken, *The Banker's Remedy of Set-off* (3rd edn, Bloomsbury Professional
2010); Louise Gullifer, *Goode on Legal Problems of Credit and Security* (5th edn, Sweet &
Maxwell 2013) [7–01], [7–05].
[2] Cf Peter Birks, 'Rights, Wrongs, and Remedies' (2000) 20 OJLS 1, 19–25.

set-off' was made in the reign of Queen Anne.[3] Extended from natural persons to registered companies, insolvency set-off is of great importance today. Two decades after the creation of insolvency set-off, a second species – so-called 'legal set-off' – was established by a statute of 1728; statute confirmed it in 1734.[4] Legal set-off permits unconnected liquidated demands that are due and payable to be set off at the conclusion of litigation. And by analogical extension, equity sometimes permits liquidated demands to be set off where the requirements of these Statutes of Set-off are not strictly satisfied. Thirdly, the common law and equity courts together developed a purely procedural species by which judgments, and orders for costs can be set off by order of the court.[5] Though discretionary and accurately enough described as 'equitable' on occasion, analytically this variety of set-off is not a creature of the equity jurisdiction as such.

Each species of set-off experiences controversy today. This chapter is concerned alone with a further kind of set-off, known as substantive or true equitable set-off.[6] This is wholly equitable in origin. Its origin remains fundamental to its workings and development, for while substantive equitable set-off is not new to the remedial scene, its nature has changed as the procedural setting in which it applies has altered. Working through the consequences has taken time.

Focusing on situations where the set-off is asserted against a common law demand, this chapter addresses five controversies. What is the test for substantive equitable set-offs? What is entailed by this type of set-off being substantive? To what extent is substantive equitable set-off a self-help doctrine or remedy? Can substantive equitable set-offs operate where one of the parties is insolvent, given that insolvency set-off exists? Finally, it will be asked in what way discretion attends substantive set-offs.

Answers are bound up with the most basic elements of equitable set-off. Attention will therefore be turned to the history of equitable set-off in order to explain the procedural changes that found the controversies of today. Once understood, those changes supply possible answers to the questions considered in this chapter.

---

[3] 4 & 5 Anne c 4, s 11 (1705).   [4] 2 Geo II c 22 (1728); 8 Geo II c 24 (1734).

[5] E.g. *State of New South Wales v Hamod* [2011] NSWCA 376, [36]; *Fearns v Anglo-Dutch Paint and Chemical Co Ltd* [2010] EWHC 2366 (Ch), [2011] 1 WLR 366 [36]–[39].

[6] 'Transaction set-off' can refer either to substantive equitable set-off or to common law abatement: Wood (n 1) [1–11]–[1–12], [1–23]. Abatement is not discussed here.

20.2 Procedure

Equitable set-offs derive their substantiveness from an important change in the procedure for their enforcement. Before the Judicature Acts of 1873 and 1875 commenced – in 1875, in England[7] – a party who successfully asserted an equitable set-off in Chancery was awarded an injunction to restrain the enforcement of the other party's legal demand or the execution of a judgment thereon. The cross-claimant thus needed an injunction to restrain proceedings or execution at law: a common injunction, that is. Once law and equity could be administered together in all superior courts, common injunctions were dispensable. Their abolition in the Judicature legislation[8] laid the way for a different formulation of doctrine, as Morris LJ explained in *Hanak v Green*[9] and as Derham has since explained so well.[10] Equitable set-offs could no longer be said to arise where a court of equity would restrain proceedings at law for the entirety of the demand (or execution of judgment therefor). The source of restraint – the common injunction – no longer existed.

However, the Judicature legislation did not as such change the doctrines of equitable set-off. The Judicature Acts and Rules contained three provisions relevant to equitable set-off. First, as a matter of mere procedure, the 1875 Rules provided that a defendant might 'set-off, or set up, by way of counter-claim against the claims of the plaintiff, any right or claim, whether such set-off or counter-claim sound in damages or not', but not when, in the opinion of the court, 'such set-off or counter-claim cannot be conveniently disposed of in the pending action, or ought not to be allowed'.[11] Secondly, the 1873 Act provided that the assignees of choses in action should take 'subject to all equities which would have been entitled to priority over the right of the assignee if this Act had not passed', including equities amounting to equitable set-offs.[12] The third provision is the most significant. By the 1873 Act, it was 'provided that matters that formerly gave rise to an equitable defence or to the right to an injunction to restrain proceedings' – i.e. a common injunction – 'should thenceforth give rise to a defence in a court possessing both common law and equitable jurisdiction'.[13]

---

[7] With exceptions too minor to warrant discussion here, the Judicature Act 1873 and the Judicature Act 1875 commenced on 1 November 1875. Regarding the London Bankruptcy Court, see the Bankruptcy Act 1883, ss 93, 102(3).
[8] Judicature Act 1873, s 24(5).   [9] [1958] 2 QB 9 (CA).
[10] Rory Derham, *Derham on the Law of Set-off* (4th edn, Oxford University Press 2010) ch 4.
[11] Judicature Act 1875, Sch 1 O XIX r 3.   [12] Judicature Act 1873, s 25(6).
[13] Ibid s 24(1)–(2).

Though these provisions did not change the occasions on which an equitable set-off would be found, they changed the procedure by which a set-off gained force. Before 1875, equitable set-offs gained force from the plaintiff's common injunction to restrain the enforcement of the defendant's common law demand or judgment. After 1875, that force came from the merely notional availability of a common injunction; it could not come from a common injunction because no such thing now existed. The substantive rationale of equitable set-off was unchanged – before and after 1875, a plaintiff needed an equity to inhibit the full enforcement of a cross-demand – but the procedural notion at the root of equitable set-offs was altered.

Steadily, legal reasoning changed too. Some courts after the Judicature system commenced tested for equitable set-offs by asking whether a court of equity before Judicature would have granted an injunction restraining the claimant from enforcing a demand in full.[14] Other courts omitted the reference to practice before 1875 and asked simply whether an injunction would issue to restrain the enforcement of the demand in full.[15] On either view, it became necessary to formulate the doctrine of equitable set-off in terms recognising that a set-off might exist where no kind of injunction had been sought or obtained. From these changes the controversies discussed in this chapter arise.

20.3   Tests

The most basic is that over when there will be a substantive equitable set-off. This controversy has been a staple of the past forty or so years.[16] With each pronouncement on set-off by a court, lawyers dare to hope that the law will, at last, settle. That the disturbance goes on is due to the courts' hesitance to acknowledge that each of the several available tests depends on a different combination or balancing of the competing values at stake. It is likely that the law will settle satisfactorily in England only once either the Court of Appeal or the Supreme Court openly evaluates the

---

[14] *E Pellas & Co v Neptune Marine Insurance Co* (1879) 5 CPD 34 (CA) 41; *Hanak* (n 9) 23–24, 26; *Bank of Boston Connecticut v European Grain and Shipping Ltd (The Dominique)* [1989] AC 1056 (HL) 1101; *Filross Securities Ltd v Midgeley* [1998] 3 EGLR 43 (CA) 45 (CA).

[15] *British Anzani (Felixstowe) Ltd v International Marine Management (UK) Ltd* [1980] QB 137 (QB) 155.

[16] For another treatment of the controversy, see Andrew Berriman, 'Classical Equitable Set-off' (2013) 25 Bond L Rev 89.

competing value judgments; identifies convincing reasons for favouring a particular value judgment over others; and formulates a test for equitable set-off embodying the chosen combination and balancing of values.

The controversy over the test for equitable set-offs has arisen from the changed procedure for enforcing equitable set-offs. However, the controversy has roots in three more particular sources which must be mentioned if the current state of English law is to be understood.

One root lies in the Privy Council's decision in *Government of Newfoundland v Newfoundland Railway Co*[17] on appeal from Newfoundland where, in effect, the Supreme Court possessed a Judicature system.[18] At the time, the leading English decision on equitable set-off was *Rawson v Samuel*,[19] in which Lord Cottenham LC said that the cross-demand must 'impeach' the opposing demand if an equitable set-off is to arise. However, in *Government of Newfoundland*, the Privy Council upheld a set-off against an assignee of a chose in action without speaking of impeachment, and without ritually restating that *Rawson v Samuel* was authoritative. Hence the (fragile) supposition that the Privy Council intended to formulate a test of equitable set-off wider than Lord Cottenham's.[20]

A second root lies in the Court of Appeal's decision in *Hanak v Green*.[21] There Morris LJ conducted a 'masterly',[22] 'authoritative'[23] and 'definitive'[24] survey of the decided cases and formulated a test without employing the word 'impeachment'. He did not purport to alter the law,[25] yet *Hanak v Green* has fuelled controversy. With the agreement of Hodson LJ and Sellers LJ, Morris LJ found an equitable set-off in circumstances where prior decisions suggested that no equitable set-off would exist.[26]

For now it suffices to mention a third root of controversy, which brings the survey to the beginning of the forty years just elapsed. This is the

---

[17] (1888) 13 App Cas 199.

[18] Mark R Gillen and Faye Woodman (eds), *The Law of Trusts: A Contextual Approach* (2nd edn, Emond Montgomery Publications 2008) 58.

[19] (1841) Cr & Ph 161, 41 ER 451.   [20] See Derham (n 10) [4.12], [4.27], [17.06]–[17.09].

[21] Above n 9.

[22] *Gilbert-Ash (Northern) Ltd v Modern Engineering (Bristol) Ltd* [1974] AC 689 (HL) 717 (Lord Diplock).

[23] *BICC plc v Burndy Corp* [1985] Ch 232 (CA) 247.   [24] *Fearns* (n 5) [19].

[25] *Hanak* (n 9) 20–21, 23–25. He referred to impeachment in his account of the development of equitable set-off, but did not make impeachment an element of his preferred formulation.

[26] Wood (n 1) [4–42]; Derham (n 10) [4.05].

judgment of Lord Denning MR in the *Federal Commerce and Navigation Co Ltd v Molena Alpha Inc (The Nanfri)*,[27] in which his Lordship said it was unnecessary and undesirable to look back to old cases, particularly those decided before the Judicature reforms took effect, in order to decide in what circumstances an equitable set-off will arise. While he looked to the future, Lord Denning also looked to the past. He said that equitable set-offs will properly occur where a cross-claim 'go[es] directly to impeach the plaintiff's demands'.[28] Expressed in more 'modern' language, he thought that that was the same as saying that the cross claim must be 'so closely connected with the [plaintiff's] demands that it would be manifestly unjust to allow [the plaintiff] to enforce payment without taking into account the cross-claim'.[29] From Lord Denning's treatment of the law, the points of controversy arising have included his putative refusal to use authorities, whatever their status, predating 1875 and whether he sought to alter the grounds on which equitable set-offs arise.

In the period since *The Nanfri*, these roots have sustained controversy in which the stems are so closely twined together that they are impossible to pull apart. As far as the test for equitable set-off is concerned, it is submitted that this controversy exists as a competition among rival formulations of the test for equitable set-off.

Between the formulations in several cases there are various differences in nuance of meaning. What they should do with those formulations is a difficulty felt by the courts. According to Potter LJ, the Court of Appeal has wisely refused to become bogged down in the analysis of differences of wording and meaning.[30] Rix LJ later remarked that Potter LJ was himself wise to notice that wisdom – and, he implied, to have heeded it.[31] However, no judge is known to have said that analysis of the differences of nuance of meaning in different formulations should never be undertaken – although few judges appear eager to undertake it.

To maintain that such analysis should never be done would be too absolute a position. When sophistry thwarts justice, it is wisely eschewed. But the persistence of rival tests suggests that more is at stake than a mere choice of words. Some analysis by a court of the differences in nuance of meaning among the rival formulations of the tests for equitable set-off is likely to prove necessary, for a survey shows that at least four approaches

---

[27] [1978] QB 927 (CA).   [28] Ibid 975   [29] Ibid 974–75.

[30] *Bim Kemi AB v Blackburn Chemicals Ltd* [2001] EWCA Civ 457, [2001] 2 Lloyd's Rep 93 [29].

[31] *Geldof Metaalconstructie NV v Simon Carves Ltd* [2010] EWCA Civ 667, (2010) 130 Con LR 37 [43](iii).

are available for courts to take. That indeterminacy affords judges a leeway to choose among formulations, and reach judgments, resting on inconsistent values.

First, there are cases adopting 'traditional' formulations of doctrine and applying them in a 'traditional' manner. Normally these cases formulate the test for equitable set-off in terms of impeachment and apply that test consistently with *Rawson v Samuel*.[32] Owing perhaps to a stricter adherence to *stare decisis*, courts in Australia, for example, acknowledge *Rawson v Samuel* – rather than *Hanak v Green* or subsequent English decisions – as the leading authority.[33] Certain decisions in England display the same intention to keep the basis and limits of equitable set-off the same as they were before Judicature. Hence the reasoning of Lord Wilberforce, for the House of Lords, in *Aries Tanker Corp v Total Transport Ltd*.[34]

Some decisions are awkward to categorise. In *Edlington Properties Ltd v JH Fenner & Co Ltd*,[35] Neuberger LJ applied an impeachment formulation. He saw this as the same, in substance, as the formulation of Morris LJ in *Hanak v Green* which, in fact, was applied more loosely than the impeachment test as traditionally understood. Did Neuberger LJ therefore see himself as applying the impeachment test in the way Lord Cottenham LC understood it, in which case *Edlington Properties* falls under this heading? Or did Neuberger LJ see himself as applying a formulation in language familiar to Lord Cottenham LC, while also allowing for looser application? If the latter, then his Lordship's pronouncements instead fall within the fourth category, below.

Secondly, some cases adopt new formulations of the test for equitable set-off without intending thereby to narrow or extend the doctrine's ambit. For example, although not all interpretations of his judgment agree, in *Bank of Boston Connecticut v European Grain and Shipping Ltd (The Dominique)*, Lord Brandon of Oakbrook arguably sought to 'dethrone' the impeachment formulation of the grounds on which equitable set-offs arise without affecting the substance of the law.[36] Whether Lord Denning, in contrast, intended to change the law *and* the language

---

[32] Subject, that is, to allowance for the consequences of procedural changes wrought by the Judicature legislation.

[33] JD Heydon, MJ Leeming and PG Turner, *Meagher, Gummow and Lehane's Equity: Doctrines and Remedies* (5th edn, LexisNexis 2015) [39–060](g), [39–080].

[34] [1977] 1 WLR 185 (HL) 193. See also *Leon Corp v Atlantic Lines and Navigation Co Inc (The Leon)* [1985] 2 Lloyd's Rep 470 (Ch) 473–75.

[35] [2006] EWCA Civ 403, [2006] 1 WLR 1583.

[36] *Bank of Boston* (n 14) 1101, 1106. See *Geldof Metaalconstructie* (n 31) [28]–[31].

of the test for equitable set-off is less clear. In *The Nanfri*, his Lordship posed an impeachment formulation alongside a formulation in terms of close connection and manifest injustice. He identified the two formulations as equivalents of each other.[37] Did either formulation correspond with the doctrine as understood in the *Rawson v Samuel* line of authority? Lord Denning's use of the impeachment formulation is one sign that both did. However, there are signs in the opposite direction. Lord Denning wished to free modern courts of the 'burden' of having to find, understand and read prior authorities on equitable set-off. Modern courts, he thought, ought to develop the law anew, case by case, unconstrained by *Rawson v Samuel*. His Lordship's reasoning displays contradictions. Nevertheless, in substance he seems to have wished to change both the law and the words by which equitable set-offs are tested.

A third kind of case expresses the test for equitable set-off both without referring to impeachment and in a novel manner. On the interpretation given above, Lord Denning's judgment in *The Nanfri* is an instance. The judgment of Simon Brown LJ in *Esso Petroleum Co Ltd v Milton*[38] is a second instance; it is joined by other cases in which the 'manifest injustice' element of Lord Denning's test is read as making equitable set-offs a function of judicial discretion.[39] A third instance may be Morris LJ's judgment in *Hanak v Green*. If Morris LJ was conscious that the set-off in that case would not have arisen on prior authority, then his Lordship not only reformulated the test for equitable set-off: he also sought to reform the principle. The true reading is obscure. A fourth instance may be the Privy Council's decision in the *Newfoundland Railway Co*, which some think reformulated and reformed the law of equitable set-off.[40] However, it is not clear that Derham's scepticism[41] can be gainsaid.

Fourthly, there may be cases in which the impeachment formulation continues to be maintained while also intending that formulation to apply more loosely. If the decision of Neuberger LJ in *Edlington Properties Ltd v JH Fenner & Co Ltd*[42] was made knowing that *Hanak v Green* loosened the application of the test for equitable set-off and in the

---

[37] See The Nanfri (n 27) 974–75. These formulations were used without expressed approval or disapproval in *International Energy Group Ltd v Zurich Insurance plc UK Branch* [2015] UKSC 33, [2016] AC 509 [90].

[38] [1997] 1 WLR 938 (CA) 951, 953.

[39] *Sankey v The Helping Hands Group plc* [2000] CP Rep 11 (CA).   [40] Ibid.

[41] Rory Derham, 'Recent Issues in Relation to Set-off' (1994) 68 ALJ 331, 334–37.

[42] See n 35.

belief that that is desirable, then his Lordship's pronouncements illustrate this category. *British Anzani (Felixstowe) Ltd v International Marine Management (UK) Ltd*[43] can be put in this category more confidently.

At least this many approaches are open to a judge. The differences between each suggest that the reason that a matter as basic as the test for equitable set-off remains confused is that rival formulations obscure a leeway for judges to choose between tests embodying conflicting value judgments. The choices essentially reduce to two questions.

First, should the test for equitable set-off be expressed with or without the word impeachment? So expressed, the question seems arid and trivial. But so many lawyers have held such firm views on the matter that the question is undoubtedly important. It is important because there is the sense that the proper formulation of the test for equitable set-off is being hampered by unexpressed concerns about what the advocacy of one test or another might entail. For instance, Lord Brandon and others have thought 'impeachment' an antiquated term.[44] It is conceivable that those who reject impeachment formulations suspect dogmatic adherence to impeachment formulations of masking antiquarianism, or a false assumption that legal innovation never occurred in the past, or inconsiderateness of people wishing to find their legal rights in today's everyday language. It is conceivable that those favouring impeachment formulations suspect dogmatic rejection of impeachment formulations of masking unthinking enthusiasm for legal change, as distinct from legal improvement. One can only speculate as to what unexpressed concerns there might actually be. Nevertheless, the preferences of different judges for one formulation over another often appear to have been weighted by what the judge fears or hopes a given formulation entails, rather than by considering the merits of different formulations on their own terms. In answering the question, whether the test for impeachment should be expressed with or without the word impeachment, frank recognition of the baggage weighing down the arguments either way will be needed. And that will require analysis of the nuances of different formulations of the 'test' applied in past decisions.

The other question to which the leeway for choice reduces is: should equitable set-offs arise on wider grounds than those articulated by Lord Cottenham LC in *Rawson v Samuel* and often applied thereafter? The answer depends on how the mischief that equitable set-offs seek to address is conceived, and on how far that mischief can sensibly be

---

[43] See n 15.   [44] *Bank of Boston* (n 14) 1102; *Bim Kemi* (n 30) [36].

addressed once allowance is made for competing interests, principles and concerns. Most would agree that the inequity addressed by equitable set-off is that of permitting a demand to be pressed and enforced in full when it is undermined by a cross-demand held by another. Judicial opinions then diverge. Some judges have thought that the threshold of inequity – whether expressed as impeachment or otherwise – a difficult threshold to cross. Other judges have crossed the threshold nimbly.

When considering how widely equitable set-offs should arise, appeals to rhetoric[45] ought to be declined. The question demands an objective, measured answer. For all that a widening of equitable set-off will on occasion benefit a commercial party, on occasion the same commercial party could well be inconvenienced or harmed by another's assertion of a widened doctrine of equitable set-off.

The basic character of the doctrine ought to be kept in mind. Every equitable set-off represents an incursion into the rights of the demand-holder. Equitable set-offs prevent a person from enjoying the entitlements which, as the holder of a legal demand, are formally conferred on the person by law. In the equity jurisdiction, restraining the inequitable exercise of a person's strict legal rights is a classical technique. It is also serious, and to be exercised carefully. As Lord Erskine LC once said: '[t]here is no branch of the jurisdiction of this Court [of Chancery] more delicate than that, which goes to restrain the exercise of a legal right'.[46] The types of demands and cross-demands that can be set off all arise as of right, or virtually as of right. Equitable set-off constrains the exercise of legally strong demands. The wider the domain of equitable set-off, the more equitable set-offs will be found where there is no inequity sufficient to justify restraining the demand-holder from enforcing a legally strong demand in full.

20.4   Substantive Nature

Since *Hanak v Green*, it has become understood that equitable set-off operates substantively, not as a pure matter of procedure. The implications continue to be worked out. Among other things, because equitable set-off is substantive it can operate outside of legal proceedings.[47] Court

---

[45] E.g. Wood (n 1) [4–9] ('What is really going on is a progressive liberalisation of transaction set-off under the guise of equitable set-off and a shaking off of the shackles which imprison independent set-off to judicial proceedings and to liquidated claims ... ').

[46] *Sanders v Pope* (1806) 12 Ves Jr 282, 289, 33 ER 108, 110.

[47] Cf *Muscat v Smith* [2003] EWCA Civ 962, [2003] 1 WLR 2853 [44].

processes need not be engaged, nor need any curial relief be obtained, before an equitable set-off can commence. However, where a set-off occurs, there has been controversy regarding whether the set-off immediately extinguishes the demand to the extent of the cross-demand.[48]

In *Aries Tanker*, the House of Lords decided that an equitable set-off does not extinguish the demand to the extent of the cross-demand when the set-off arises; extinguishment to the extent of the cross-demand only occurs upon the entry of judgment, at which point the entirety of both the demand and the cross-demand merge into the judgment.[49] Contrary opinions have been ventured, apparently without appreciating what *Aries Tanker* decided. However, in *Fearns v Anglo-Dutch Paint and Chemical Co Ltd*,[50] the High Court recently dismissed those opinions as contradicting the House of Lords' decision.[51]

Though the rudiments of equitable set-off in a Judicature system require this result, the treatment of principle in *Fearns* has been criticised on (with respect) invalid grounds.[52] The litigants in *Fearns* disagreed over whether substantive equitable set-off immediately extinguishes the impeached demand to the extent that it is impeached. Logically, the only two available answers were that the set-off extinguished the demand to the extent of the cross-demand at the moment the set-off arose, or it did not; if the latter, then the demand would be extinguished to the extent of the cross-demand only when judgment was entered. On the authority of *Aries Tanker*, the court held the latter. Starting with the principle that an equitable set-off 'prevent[s] each party from enforcing or relying on its claim to the extent of the other claim where the connection between the claims would make this manifestly unjust',[53] the judge explained that 'if, after such a set-off has been validly asserted, one of the claims is later satisfied from another source, or withdrawn, the other claim remains in existence and can thereafter be enforced (in full)'.[54] It followed that an

---

[48] Among writers, the view that equitable set-off operates to extinguish the claim has been supported by Wood (n 1) [1–43], [1–51]–[1–52], [4–1], [4–24], [4–48](a), [6–11], [24–41], McCracken (n 1) 141–42 and Louise Gullifer (ed), *Goode on Legal Problems of Credit and Security* (4th edn, Sweet & Maxwell 2008) [7–55] and criticised or rejected by Derham (n 10) [4.29]–[4.34] and Gullifer (n 1) [7–54].

[49] See n 34 188.   [50] See n 5.

[51] See also *Equitas Ltd v Walsham Bros & Co Ltd* [2013] EWHC 3264 (Comm), [2014] Lloyd's Rep IR 398, [173]–[185]; *Stemcor UK Ltd v Global Steel Holdings Ltd* [2015] EWHC 363 (Comm), [2015] 1 Lloyds Rep 580 [34].

[52] Pascal Pichonnaz and Louise Gullifer, *Set-off in Arbitration and Commercial Transactions* (Oxford University Press 2014) [5.43].

[53] *Fearns* (n 5) [26].   [54] Ibid.

equitable set-off does not extinguish the impeached demand, for 'if the injustice is later removed by payment of the cross-demand from another source, the main claim can be enforced'.[55] The criticism that this reasoning 'rather assume[s] its conclusion, since if the set-off had extinguished either demand, it could not be satisfied from another source' is not to the point.[56] Not only was the judge aware that his conclusion flowed whence he began; he wished to show as much. Holding that a demand is extinguished to the extent of the cross-demand at the time at which the set-off arises would presumably have immunised the judge's reasoning to criticism. However, that conclusion would have contradicted *Aries Tanker* and the basis of equitable set-offs in a Judicature system: that set-offs operate to restrain a person's freedom to enforce an impeached demand to its full extent, without allowing for the cross-demand. The conclusion that equitable set-offs do not automatically extinguish the impeached demand to the extent of the cross-demand was the only available answer that fitted within existing case law and principles.

Fearns shows that the substantive nature of equitable set-off is developing in a pattern familiar from the development of several equitable doctrines: developments by which the prospect of obtaining specific equitable relief founds substantive entitlements even where specific equitable relief has not been sought.[57] To say that a set-off exists only so long as a relevant cross-demand impeaches the claimant's demand – and not once the cross-demand has been otherwise satisfied or, say, discharged – is effectively to say that the defence of equitable set-off is commensurate with the availability of an injunction to restrain the enforcement of the demand to its full extent, even though such an injunction has not been obtained or sought. To say that the set-off continues once the cross-demand has been otherwise satisfied or discharged would be to make the defence exceed its rationale. It would overly favour the holder of the cross-demand, since the defence would exist when no cross-demand disparaging the claimant's demand any longer exists. Set-offs would exist in circumstances in which the claimant should be free to exercise a demand to its full extent. And set-offs could be abused where, in justice, the occasion for the set-off has passed.

---

[55] Pichonnaz and Gullifer (n 52) [5.43].   [56] Ibid [5.43].

[57] E.g. *Commissioner of Taxation v Bamford* [2010] HCA 10, (2010) 240 CLR 481 [39]; PG Turner, 'Understanding the Constructive Trust between Vendor and Purchaser' (2012) 128 LQR 582, 589–92.

20.5   Self-help

The recognition that equitable set-offs are not confined to operating in legal proceedings has led to consideration of equitable set-off as a 'self-help remedy', and thence to controversy. Learned writers have said that equitable set-off is, or ought to be, a self-help remedy.[58] Of course, whether that is so turns on how 'self-help remedy' is defined. If defined as a legally recognised measure to which parties may resort without obtaining a court order, then equitable set-off is a self-help remedy. What else the 'self-help' label imports is disputed.

Labelling set-off as a self-help remedy invites one to compare and contrast equitable set-off with measures more commonly referred to as self-help: measures including the forfeiture of interests and estates, the levying of distress, and the exercise of contractual rights to rescind a contract *ab initio* or to terminate it *in futuro*.[59] Like equitable set-offs, each of these operations has legal effect without the active party first having obtained a favourable court order, or even having commenced legal proceedings. Is equitable set-off any the less a self-help remedy because it is equitable? Does the force of self-help remedies differ according to whether they depend on doctrines of the common law or of equity? Both questions, it is suggested, are properly answered 'Yes'.

Rights to forfeit and to exercise contractual rights of rescission or termination are rights recognised and enforceable at common law. They typically involve bringing another party's common law rights to an end. Equitable set-offs do not operate in this fashion. When an equitable set-off affects a common law debt, for example, none of the creditor's common law entitlements is extinguished. All of the creditor's legal entitlements as regards the debtor remain. It is merely that in equity they are suspended: in equity, the creditor's attempts to exercise its common law rights are ineffective to the extent of the set-off.

The comparison with distress is different, but as straightforward in principle. A right of distress has a suspensory effect. While the creditor lawfully distrains against the debtor's goods, the debtor's entitlements to possess and use the relevant goods are trumped. A suspensory effect is therefore common to distress and equitable set-offs. But distress operates by conferring an additional common law right (on the creditor). Equitable set-off creates no new common law rights. It accordingly has

---

[58] Especially Wood (n 1) [1–20], [1–25], [4–1], [4–4], [4–24], [4–86] [6–12], [24–41]; Pichonnaz and Gullifer (n 52) [5.48].
[59] For other examples, see Gullifer (n 1) [7–36]–[7–38].

less force than the self-help remedy of distress. Indeed, at common law an equitable set-off has no force. By these measures, equitable set-off is less a self-help remedy than are self-help remedies at common law.

To date this difference has been overlooked. Indeed, beginning with Lord Denning's judgment in *The Nanfri*, a consensus has formed that equitable set-off can found a common law cause of action to recover damages for breach of contract. The Court of Appeal in that case held a ship owner liable to pay damages for wrongfully repudiating a charterparty in response to the hirers' refusal to pay the stipulated sum of hire in full where the hirers had the benefit of equitable set-offs. Lord Denning considered situations in which a contract 'gives a creditor a right to take the law into his own hands ... if a sum is not paid' and said of a ship owner's contractual right to withdraw a vessel for non-payment of hire:

> When the debtor has a true set-off it goes in reduction of the sums owing to the creditor. If the creditor does not allow it to be deducted, he is in peril. *He will be liable in damages if he exercises his contractual right of withdrawal wrongly.*[60]

Authors have repeated or adopted Lord Denning's analysis.[61] Hence the apparent consensus that the ship owner's liability in damages stems from a contractual cause of action based on the hirers' equitable set-off. Indeed, some writers go further, arguing that this set-off-based liability creates dangers for the charterer – dangers that ought to be cut down by depriving an equitable set-off of effect until it has been 'asserted' or 'declared' by the charterer.[62] That is, Lord Denning's treatment of set-offs as self-help remedies is generally accepted but, for some, only if qualified to weaken their self-help quality.

Ignoring for now the asserted dangers of equitable set-offs, it is very difficult to see that an equitable set-off alone can confer a common law cause of action for breach of contract on the party entitled to the set-off. Indeed, the suggestion can fairly be called a fusion fallacy.[63] It would produce a result that could not have obtained through the application of settled law before the Judicature system commenced. Before 1 November

---

[60] See The Nanfri (n 27) 974 (italics added).

[61] Wood (n 1) [2–57] (repeating); Derham (n 10) [4.46] (adopting); Gullifer (n 1) [7–56] (adopting).

[62] Wood (n 1), discussed in Derham (n 10) [4.37].

[63] RP Meagher, WMC Gummow and JRF Lehane, *Equity: Doctrines and Remedies* (Butterworths 1975) [220]–[222].

1875, in principle the charterer could have restrained the owner from withdrawing the ship, and could perhaps have obtained a declaration that a purported withdrawal was void in equity.[64] After 1858, it is doubtful that the charterer could have obtained damages under Lord Cairns' Act in lieu of, or in addition to, an injunction[65] if the owner had already withdrawn the ship since the framers of Lord Cairns' Act evidently intended it to apply only to claims for relief in respect of common law rights;[66] equitable set-offs operate only in equity.

Since Judicature, the result should be, and in principle is, the same – except that since common injunctions were abolished, the test for equitable set-offs depends on the *notional* availability of injunctive relief. So much was indicated in *Hanak v Green*[67] and by the House of Lords in *Bank of Boston*.[68] As a common injunction was a negative restraint, the enforcement of an equitable set-off was and is purely negative. The holder of a demand was restrained, and is now notionally restrained, from enforcing the demand to the extent of the cross-demand founding the set-off. That explains why substantive equitable set-offs operate as defences in a Judicature system. They can be relied upon to commence proceedings in equitable jurisdiction. Because of equitable set-offs, measures based on asserting the impeached legal rights are, in equity, invalid. However, equitable set-offs do not confer novel rights of action, especially rights to sue at common law.[69] In that sense, substantive equitable set-offs operate as shields, not as swords. It is true that, during the twentieth century, English courts assumed power to award damages under Lord Cairns' Act in claims to protect and fulfil purely equitable entitlements. However, that dubious change does not confer an action for breach of contract on a party who asserts an equitable set-off. Moreover, unlike an award of damages for breach of contract, damages under Lord Cairns' Act were – and, under its modern statutory successor, are – discretionary.[70]

---

[64] Heydon, Leeming and Turner (n 33) [19–005]–[19–025].   [65] 21 & 22 Vict c 27, s 2.

[66] Chancery Commissioners, *Third Report of Her Majesty's Commissioners Appointed to Inquire into the Process, Practice, and System of Pleading in the Court of Chancery* (Eyre and Spottiswoode 1856) 1–4.

[67] Above n 9.   [68] See Banks of Boston (n 14) 1101.

[69] *SL Sethia Liners Ltd v Naviagro Maritime Corp* [1981] 1 Lloyd's Rep 18 (QB) 26; *Roadshow Entertainment Pty Ltd v (ACN 053 006 269) Pty Ltd* (1997) 42 NSWLR 462 (CA) 481; Derham (n 10) [4.30] (equitable set-off operates 'in equity as a complete or partial defeasance of the plaintiff's claim'); Gullifer (n 1) [7–16] ('purely defensive'), [7–54]–[7–55].

[70] Heydon, Leeming and Turner (n 33) [24–125]–[25–140].

If Lord Denning's position and the one described here conflict, they conflict because the accounts of Lord Denning and others adopting or repeating his view make too little allowance for the fact that equitable set-offs operate merely as restraints on the exercise and enforcement of the entitlements making up a person's claim. Consider this development of Lord Denning's charter example:

> A charterer possessed of the right, and who pays less than the sum stipulated in the contract, is not considered to be in breach of contract. Therefore, when the time charter contains the usual provision whereby the owner can withdraw the vessel in the event of non-payment of hire . . . the charterer can tender a reduced amount in consequence of the cross-demand without bringing into existence the right of withdrawal. If the owner does not accept the tender, it acts at its peril. It will be liable in damages if it withdraws the vessel. If, on the other hand, the defence [of substantive equitable set-off] were procedural rather than substantive, the owner would have been entitled to withdraw the vessel because, until there had been a judgment for a set-off, the charterer would be regarded as having defaulted in payment.[71]

Unless it is appreciated that this describes the position only in equity, and not at common law, this account will mislead. At common law, the opposite of each point in the passage holds true. A charterer who pays less than the stipulated hire *is* considered to be in breach of contract. The charterer *cannot* tender a reduced amount in consequence of the cross-demand without bringing into existence a right of withdrawal. Without more, for withdrawing the vessel the owner faces *no* peril – and particularly no liability in damages. At common law, the charterer in those circumstances *would be* regarded as in default of payment, regardless of the fact that equitable set-off is substantive. The charterer's equitable set-off has a restraining effect *merely in equity*. By tendering less than the stipulated sum of hire, the charter will not be considered to be in breach of the contract *in equity*.[72] If necessary, equitable relief will issue to restrain the ship owner from relying on its strict legal right to treat the hirer as being in breach of contract.[73] Otherwise, the effect of equitable set-off would not be to affect the *exercise* of common law contractual rights: it would affect their very *existence*.

A further aspect of set-offs as self-help measures concerns whether equitable set-offs give rise to a peril that ought to be controlled as

---

[71] Derham (n 10) [4.46] (footnote omitted); see also [4.46]–[4.47].
[72] See *Roadshow Entertainment* (n 69) 481E.
[73] *Miwa Pty Ltd v Siantan Properties Pte Ltd* [2011] NSWCA 297, (2011) 15 BPR 29,545 [53].

foreshadowed above. Ought a set-off to gain force only once it has been asserted or declared by the party for whose benefit the set-off would operate?[74] The argument that the law already requires this has been said to be strong – as have the merits of the asserted requirement.

> This is because it would be very unfair on the claimant if, after he had [purported to exercise a contractual right of termination], a cross-claim were asserted which had the effect that the claimant's action was invalid or, even worse, held to be in breach of contract, rendering the claimant liable for damages for wrongful repudiation. Further, the uncertainty engendered would have a chilling effect on the exercise of self-help remedies, since a claimant would be unwilling to take the risk that a cross-claim might be asserted at a later date. A cross-claim does not have to be definitively quantified to be asserted, as long as the assertion is made reasonably and in good faith.[75]

The urgency of the argument weakens if the analysis so far is correct, for the worse of these perils – a potential liability for damages in contract arising from an equitable set-off – is not real. The only liability in 'damages' to which an equitable set-off can give rise in English law is an award of damages in lieu of or in addition to an injunction to enforce the set-off. In Australia, even that award is highly doubtful owing to the properly narrow local construction of Lord Cairns' Act.

Residual unfairness might nevertheless be thought to occur. The potential for this arises, again, from differences in the operation of set-offs before and since 1 November 1875. Before Judicature, a party had to assert the set-off before it could take effect. Equitable set-offs against common law demands took force through a common injunction restraining proceedings on, or execution of a judgment for, the entire demand at law. Asserting the set-off was necessary in that the party desiring the set-off had to obtain a common injunction, and to obtain a common injunction the plaintiff had to bring a bill asserting the plaintiff's entitlement to a set-off. The injunction restrained the defendant's future action, not past acts. No case has been found in which a court of equity declared a defendant's reliance on self-help measures invalid where the reliance predated the injunction. However, now that equitable set-offs can operate where injunctive relief has been neither sought nor obtained – the set-off operating because the party asserting it *could* obtain relief restraining the holder of the impeached demand from

---

[74] The origin of the suggestion appears to be Wood (n 1).
[75] Pichonnaz and Gullifer (n 52) [5.48]; see also [2.52] and Gullifer (n 1) [7–56].

asserting the demand in full[76] – an equitable set-off can operate earlier than it would have operated on the same facts before Judicature. The set-off can operate before the party asserting it has done any act asserting or declaring that its cross-demand impeaches the other party's demand. The holder of the impeached demand could rely on contractual provisions for self-help ignorant of the fact that an equitable set-off invalidates his or her actions not at law, but in equity.[77]

Against this party, the holder of the impeached demand may be protected in several ways. Where party B (who desires the set-off) has deceived party A (the holder of the impeached demand) into thinking that no set-off exists or will be relied on, the fraud will ground a complaint in fraud by party A. Where the party B represents to party A that there is no set-off, an estoppel by representation may protect the demand-holder. Similarly, a promise by party B not to enforce a set-off against party A in the future may found a promissory estoppel. Reliance of a relevant kind would need to be shown in order for each kind of estoppel to arise.[78]

For the holder of the impeached demand, the problems will be acute where the party desiring the set-off has taken no positive action amounting to fraud or founding an estoppel. However, remoulding the law to require a set-off to be declared or asserted before it can take effect would be problematic. Earlier in this chapter, it was seen that the test for an equitable set-off is indeterminate. Greater uncertainty would follow if the law were changed to require a set-off to be declared or asserted before it could take effect, for none of the tests for equitable set-off currently open to a court would be a test: any of them could be satisfied and yet the set-off would lack effect unless and until the set-off should be asserted against the holder of the demand.

Placing this degree of control over the operation of set-offs in the hands of the party holding the impeaching cross-demand could open the way to abuse. If a rule required party A to have notice of party B's intention to assert a cross-demand by way of set-off before the set-off could operate, then party A would nonetheless be vulnerable to the defendant's caprice. It would be party B's choice when to assert the cross-demand; whether and when party B might do so would be a matter of speculation. Although it is said that allowing set-offs to arise without first

[76] See n 57 and accompanying text.   [77] Gullifer (n 1) [7–56].
[78] See generally *Bibby Factors Northwest Ltd v HFD Ltd* [2015] EWCA Civ 1908, [2016] 1 Lloyd's Rep 517 [34]–[53].

being asserted will engender uncertainty that 'would have a chilling effect on the exercise of self-help remedies',[79] at least as much uncertainty could arise from the requirement that a set-off be asserted or declared.[80] The holder of the demand would not know whether to plan on the basis that the cross-demand will or will not be asserted or declared.

Requiring that the set-off be asserted in good faith, before it can operate, could salvage party A's position. Perhaps for this reason, it has been said a set-off can only be asserted in good faith.[81] As an equitable doctrine, good faith has some bearing on set-off. At the least it could engage a court's discretion not to give effect to a set-off where it would be contrary to recognised equitable principles to do so. Under that discretion, a Judicature court would be free to refuse to enforce a set-off if the party asserting it, say, had unclean hands. However, there is no requirement that a set-off be asserted reasonably and in good faith before it can take effect.[82] There is merely a requirement that, where the cross-demand is unliquidated, the party relying thereon to support a set-off must have *quantified* the cross-demand reasonably and in good faith.

On present indications, the law might develop to permit courts to refuse to enforce equitable set-offs in these situations either on the ground that (a) courts possess discretion – be it a general discretion or several narrower specific discretions; or (b) on specific non-discretionary grounds, such as that enforcing the set-off would give the party desiring the set-off the benefit of fraud, accident, mistake or surprise. The alternative ways of protecting party A's position would be less coherent with the substantive nature of the modern doctrine of equitable set-off, or would be unattractive in other ways. A good faith requirement could be imprecise: if it applied only to the assertion of the set-off, then any unconscientiousness in thereafter continuing to press the set-off would not be caught. And to require the party desiring the set-off to have behaved in good faith throughout would be more exacting of that party than the conventional equitable defence of unclean hands, and other equitable doctrines founded on conscience. Basing rules for the protection of party A, in these situations, on doctrines of retrospectivity[83] would introduce unneeded complexity. The difficulties of a rule requiring

[79] Pichonnaz and Gullifer (n 52) [5.48].
[80] This is implicitly recognised in Gullifer (n 1) [7–56].
[81] *Fearns* (n 5) [30], [50] (*obiter dicta*); Pichonnaz and Gullifer (n 52) [5.44], [5.46].
[82] *Santiren Shipping Ltd v Unimarine SA* [1981] 1 All ER 340 (QB) 346.
[83] Wood (n 1) [4–26], [6–12]; Gullifer (n 48) [7–54]–[7–55].

that the set-off be asserted or declared before it can take effect have already been stated.

On balance, it is submitted that the authorities support the following propositions. Substantive equitable set-off is a self-help defence in only a narrow sense. Other matters being equal, equity will recognise that a set-off operates whether or not the party asserting it asserts it in legal proceedings or otherwise. If equitable relief is later granted, it will be granted on the basis that the set-off took effect at the time at which the cross-demand first impeached the demand. In order for a substantive equitable set-off to arise, it is enough that the holder of a relevant cross-demand *can* assert that the cross-demand impeaches the demand so as to give rise to a set-off defence. It is not necessary that the holder of the cross demand should have made that assertion. This flows from the basic nature of substantive equitable set-off as a negative doctrine restraining the unconscientious exercise of the strict right conferred by the impeached demand.

20.6   Insolvency

The relationship between substantive equitable set-off and set-off under bankruptcy and insolvency legislation is unsettled. Where at least one of the parties is insolvent, legislation provides for a mandatory automatic set-off of mutual liabilities between the parties.[84] Insolvency set-off thus differs from equitable set-off. By stipulation, parties can exclude equitable set-offs but not set-offs under insolvency legislation. Further, whereas an equitable set-off extinguishes the relevant liabilities only upon the entry of judgment, insolvency set-offs extinguish the liabilities immediately upon a declaration of bankruptcy or the placing of a company into liquidation.

These, presumably, are the features of insolvency set-off beneath the submission[85] that equitable set-off does not operate in insolvency. However, they do not support it. The submission assumes that the provisions for insolvency set-off pre-empt equitable set-off by extending farther than the terms of the insolvency legislation. No doubt the provisions on insolvency set-off operate beyond their literal terms, even if only to fulfil the purpose of the provisions. Thus, in *Smith v Bridgend County Borough Council*,[86] Lord Hoffmann explained that the mere existence of

---

[84] Insolvency Act 1986, s 323; Insolvency Rules 1986, r 4.90: 'mutual credits, mutual debts or other mutual dealings between the company and any creditor'.

[85] *Re Bank of Credit and Commerce International SA (No 8)* [1996] Ch 245 (CA) 269; Roy Goode, *Principles of Corporate Insolvency Law* (4th edn, Sweet & Maxwell 2011) [9–13].

[86] [2001] UKHL 58, [2001] 1 AC 336.

mutual liabilities, within the literal meaning of the insolvency set-off provisions, does not allow a creditor who converted the debtor's goods by retaining possession thereof without permission to set off the creditor's liability in tort against the debt, under the insolvency set-off provisions.[87] The purpose of the provisions does not include allowing a creditor to improve its position in a debtor's insolvency by converting the debtor's property. But the submission that the insolvency set-off provisions pre-empt equitable set-offs goes beyond purposive construction. It assumes that the provisions have a wider purpose which somehow displaces equitable set-off altogether.

The arguments against this doctrine are more persuasive than the arguments in favour.[88] While the insolvency legislation clearly enough establishes a policy against a distribution of assets among creditors other than *pari passu*, even without directly saying so, it is untenable to read the insolvency legislation or the insolvency set-off provisions in particular as establishing a public policy or an implication against the operation of equitable set-offs. The types of demands subject to insolvency set-off and equitable set-off are different; equitable set-off does not have a strict requirement of mutuality; nor need the demands both be liquidated in equity, as they must be for insolvency set-off. And the fact that one obligor may be declared bankrupt or placed into liquidation is insufficient to effect or destroy the impeachment of one party's demand by the other party's cross-demand. Put simply, there is no inconsistency between the terms, purpose and policy of the insolvency set-off provisions and the factors upon which equitable set-offs depend and the manner in which they operate. In the absence of support for such a policy or implication, it ought not to be assumed that the entitlements of commercial (or other) parties have been abridged.

Indeed, the provisions of the insolvency legislation positively suggest that equitable set-offs ought to operate in insolvency, all else being equal. For instance, trustees in bankruptcy take their title to their debtors' assets subject to the claims, titles and interests of others, and to the flaws to which their debtors' assets may otherwise be subject. Equitable interests and estates are among these. So must be equitable set-offs: the title of a bankruptcy trustee to a demand must be subject to impeachment by a cross-demand – all else being equal – even if the cross-demand only begins impeaching the demand after the debtor enters bankruptcy. The clearest illustration is where a debtor enters bankruptcy after having

---

[87] Ibid [35]–[36]. See Gullifer (n 1) [7–84].   [88] Derham (n 10) [6.25]–[6.32].

assigned a chose in action, and the debtor later becomes entitled to enforce an equitable set-off against the assignee on the basis that the assignee took his or her assignment subject to the equities.[89] Similar points can be elaborated for corporate insolvency.

The simplicity of the proposition that equitable set-offs are precluded by the advent of insolvency does not answer these points, which support the contrary proposition.

20.7   Discretion

Once English courts began to entertain new formulations of the test for substantive equitable set-off, it was inevitable that they should consider how far equitable set-offs are discretionary. That enquiry would in any case have been pertinent since, apart from equitable discretionary considerations of universal application – such as the defence of unclean hands – narrower discretions peculiar to individual equitable doctrines often apply. For example, the scope of the discretion applicable to the grant and refusal of equitable relief from forfeiture differs from the scope of the discretion applicable to the grant and refusal of injunctive relief. The manner in which the discretion applies to each of those remedies also differs: general discretionary doctrines aside, peculiar discretionary considerations apply to relief from forfeiture and injunctive relief.

The same might be thought true of equitable set-offs. However, provoked by the language of some Court of Appeal decisions, the courts have entertained the idea that the very application of an equitable set-off is a matter of discretion. Focusing on Lord Denning's formulation that an equitable set-off arises where the demands are sufficiently closely connected that it would be unjust to permit the demand to be asserted without allowing for the cross-demand, they have occasionally supposed that a set-off only exists if a court, exercising a wide discretion, so decides.[90] A major difficulty for this theory is that many authoritative statements of the law contradict it. Whatever criticisms might be made of certain recent Court of Appeal decisions – especially *Muscat v Smith*[91] and *Bim Kemi*[92] – their rejection of a discretionary test for equitable set-off is, with respect, justified.[93]

---

[89] Ibid [6.26]; Look Chan Ho, 'Equity and Insolvency', in PG Turner (ed), *Equity and Administration* (Cambridge University Press 2016) ch 6.

[90] Above nn 38–39.   [91] Above n 47.   [92] See n 30.

[93] See also *Bibby Factors* (n 78) [47]–[48].

Once that role for discretion in the law of equitable set-off is rejected, what role for discretion remains? Because the substantive qualities of equitable set-off are still developing, the role of discretion in equitable set-offs remains debatable. Though there is scant authority, it should be accepted that general equitable defences including the defence of unclean hands apply to equitable set-offs as they apply to equitable doctrines and remedies generally.[94]

Similarly, a party relying on an equitable set-off should in appropriate cases be offered relief only upon terms that would do reciprocal justice to the other party to the set-off, or to relevant third parties. That, too, is a general requirement of those seeking equitable relief. Can the reliance on an equitable set-off be subject to conditions where no equitable relief is claimed consequent upon the set-off? Such a claim amounts to a claim for a bare declaration. Though conditional entitlements to relief can be declared, English courts have no power to impose conditions on the making of declarations.[95] And can relief be offered on terms if common law or statutory relief is claimed consequent on the set-off? Presumably not. Common law relief is not subject to a requirement that the party seeking it do equity; unless the relief available under a statute adopts equitable principles, the grant of statutory relief would presumably also be free of a requirement to do equity.

Relief on terms aside, it is unknown how far there is discretion peculiar to equitable set-off. There is support for the existence of equitable discretion to deny an equitable set-off where: one party's conduct is a substantial cause of the liability of the other party against which the first party seeks to set off its demand;[96] the quantum of the cross-claim is highly speculative; quantifying the cross-claim would require the taking of a long and complicated account; or quantifying the cross-claim would considerably delay matters, leading to prejudice unable to be undone by imposing conditions on relief.[97]

Given that substantive equitable set-offs deny a claimant's strict entitlement to enforce a demand to the extent of the cross-demand,

[94] Cf Pichonnaz and Gullifer (n 52) [8.46] (stating a wider doctrine). In principle, doctrines of estoppel and waiver may also defeat the operation of an equitable set-off: Derham (n 10) [4.49].

[95] Heydon, Leeming and Turner (n 33) [19–275], [19–315].

[96] See the explanation of *Bluestorm Ltd v Portvale Holdings Ltd* [2004] 2 EGLR 38 (CA) in Derham (n 10) [4.59].

[97] Derham, ibid [4.58]–[4.69], [4.61]. See also [2.102], [2.134], [4.03], [4.65], [4.68]; *Tomlinson v Cut Price Deli Pty Ltd* (1992) 38 FCR 490, 496–98 (Fed Ct); *Roadshow Entertainment* (n 69) 489.

principles on when a court may, in its discretion, refuse to enforce a set-off could be developed through analogies with the discretion applicable to other equitable doctrines that prevent a party from relying on its strict legal rights. As noted above, the courts may come to rely on the heads of fraud, accident, mistake and surprise to establish non-discretionary grounds on which to refuse to enforce an equitable set-off. Apart from that potential development, the notions of fraud, accident, mistake and surprise could be weighty considerations in the exercise of a discretion to refuse to enforce an equitable set-off. The words 'fraud, accident, mistake and surprise' may be antique. However, they capture varieties of conduct which still animate equitable doctrines and sustain claims for equitable relief, especially where one party wishes to assert a strict right against another. They could help to identify situations in which the assertion of an equitable entitlement to a set-off would be against conscience.

20.8 Conclusion

The controversies surrounding equitable set-off concern the basic attributes of the doctrine in its modern form. Concentration on the rudiments of the modern doctrine is required if the current controversies – and others that will inevitably arise – are to be solved to general satisfaction. Substantive or true equitable set-off today continues the features of equitable set-off prior to the introduction of Judicature courts, in operating purely as a negative restraint on the unconscientious assertion of all the rights comprised in the ownership or holding of a demand in circumstances where the demand is impeached by another's cross-demand. The proper formulation of a test for equitable set-off draws attention to the seriousness, in law of restraining a person who lawfully holds a demand from enforcing and enjoying all the elements of that demand. And yet it is the nature of equitable set-offs to do so. Widening the availability of equitable set-offs is not an unalloyed good. Though the procedural context in which equitable set-offs can be pressed in litigation changed upon the advent of Judicature, this chapter has suggested that the procedural idea at the root of equitable set-offs – that they operate as purely negative restraints – is the idea from which solutions to the controversies discussed can be derived.

PART V

Special Contexts

21

Commercial Remedies in International Cases

LOUISE MERRETT

21.1 Introduction

Businesses and transactions are increasingly global and commercial cases regularly have connections with a number of different countries. In the majority of cases in the English commercial court, at least one of the parties is foreign.[1] However, traditionally the granting of remedies remained a local matter. Regardless of the connections with different jurisdictions, or what law applied to other issues in the case (the *lex causae* or substantive applicable law), an English court awarded English remedies. This was because remedies were categorised as procedural and accordingly exclusively in the province of the *lex fori* (law of the forum). With the Europeanisation of choice of law rules on contract and tort in the Rome I Regulation (RIR)[2] and Rome II Regulation (RIIR),[3] this traditional approach may no longer survive. The purpose of this chapter is to consider the implications for the granting of commercial remedies in international cases. The focus will be on two areas of particular controversy:

(i) the assessment of damages; and
(ii) whether an English court can be required to grant a remedy which is not known in English law or where the rules or conditions for granting such a remedy differ under English law.

---

[1] Four out of five cases in the Commercial Court over the period 2011–14 involved a foreign party: 'Freedom of Information Request 88097' (HM Courts & Tribunals Service, January 2014) <www.gov.uk/government/publications/foi-releases-for-january-2014> accessed 2 January 2016.

[2] Regulation (EC) 593/2008 of 17 June 2008 on the law applicable to contractual obligations [2008] OJ L177/6.

[3] Regulation (EC) 864/2007 of 11 July 2007 on the law applicable to non-contractual obligations [2007] OJ L199/40.

At first sight, the RIR and RIIR require a radical reassessment of the substance *v* procedure distinction. In particular, the assessment of damages and the consequences of breach, both under English law traditionally matters for the *lex fori*, are now expressly made subject to the applicable law. However, the extent to which these Regulations will require a fundamental change of practice in the English courts is less clear. The evidence from recent cases suggests that it is unlikely that English judges will be required to assume the role of judges from other jurisdictions in relation to remedies. While matters of principle are now more likely to be governed by the *lex causae*, practicality and convenience suggests that there will still be a crucial role for local law. In the context of damages, mode of proof remains a matter of procedural law. Furthermore, questions of fact, provided they are relevant according to the *lex causae*, are always a matter for the local court to determine. It seems that the granting of pre-judgment statutory interest may also remain a matter for English law. In the context of other remedies, the Regulations support the view that the granting of remedies is an aspect of liability rather than procedure and accordingly ought, in principle, to be governed by the applicable law. However, the practical impact of the Regulations is limited in two significant respects. First, the English court is limited to remedies which are 'within its own armoury'.[4] Secondly, as the recent case of *Actavis UK Ltd v Eli Lilly & Co* illustrates,[5] English courts may well take a restrictive view of matters of principle which are to be determined by a foreign applicable law.

Before focusing on these two specific areas, the traditional position is explained (in section 21.2). An overview is then given of the approach adopted in the European Regulations (section 21.3). The areas of particular controversy are then discussed in sections 21.4 and 21.5.

21.2   The Traditional Approach

21.2.1   The Basic Rule

In a case involving international elements, private international law rules relating to choice of law determine what law applies to the substantive issues in the case. However, before those choice of law rules are applied, a prior distinction needs to be drawn between matters of substance and

---

[4] Richard Garnett, *Substance and Procedure in Private International Law* (Oxford University Press 2012) para 10.17.
[5] [2014] EWHC 1511 (Pat), [2014] 4 All ER 331.

matters of procedure. That is because while matters of substance are governed by the *lex causae*, matters of procedure are always governed by the *lex fori*.[6] Thus: 'in almost every national system of private international law, one rule is universally accepted and applied: matters of procedure are governed by the law of the forum'.[7] If a matter is characterised as procedural the choice of law process is effectively bypassed as the local law automatically applies.

The main justification for applying the *lex fori* to matters of procedure is one of practicality and convenience; there are matters which it only makes sense to be governed by local law.[8] However, while the basic rule is well established, distinguishing between questions of substance and questions of procedure has caused considerable difficulty. Furthermore, '[n]ational approaches differ: English private international law, like the rest of the common law world, traditionally treated a broader range of issues as procedural ... than most civilian systems',[9] guaranteeing a greater role for the *lex fori*.

21.2.2 Different Approaches to the Substance v Procedure Distinction

Traditionally, European civil law systems drew a distinction between the rules by which the judge conducted the proceedings and the rules by which the judge resolved the dispute before the court.[10] English law, by

---

[6] This classification may also be an important issue in *temporal* conflict of laws: if matters are procedural they are likely to be governed by the rules in force at the time of the trial whereas in relation to matters of substance, the rules at the time the offence was committed are likely to apply (Ofer Malcai and Ronit Levine-Schnur, 'Which Came First, the Procedure or the Substance? Justificational Priority and the Substance–Procedure Distinction' (2014) 34(1) OJLS 1, 1).

[7] Garnett (n 4) para 2.01; he traces the history of the rule at para 2.02 ff. 'One of the eternal truths of every system of private international law is that a distinction must be made between substance and procedure, between right and remedy.': James Fawcett and Janeen Carruthers, *Cheshire, North and Fawcett, Private International Law* (14th edn, Oxford University Press 2008) 75.

[8] See Garnett (n 4) para 2.09; and, explaining the position in Scotland, Janeen M Carruthers, 'Substance and Procedure in the Conflict of Laws: A Continuing Debate in Relation to Damages' [2004] ICLQ 691, 692: 'a legal system's rules of procedure are usually complex and interrelated and to isolate a particular foreign rule and apply it against the very different background of Scottish procedural rules would be absurd'.

[9] Martin Illmer, 'Neutrality Matters – Some Thoughts about the Rome Regulations and the So-called Dichotomy of Substance and Procedure in European Private International Law' [2009] CJQ 237, 238.

[10] Garnett (n 4) para 2.02.

contrast, drew a distinction between the 'right' and the 'remedy'. More recently, in common law countries, particularly Canada and Australia, new definitions of substance and/or procedure have been developed.[11] In *John Pfeiffer Pty Ltd v Rogerson*, the High Court of Australia said that:

> matters that affect the existence, extent or enforceability of the rights or duties of the parties to an action are matters that, on their face, appear to be concerned with issues of substance, not with issues of procedure. Or to adopt the formulation put forward by Mason CJ in *McKain*,[12] 'rules which are directed to governing or regulating the mode or conduct of court proceedings' are procedural and all other provisions or rules are to be classified as substantive.[13]

According to this test, matters of substance are defined as those which affect the 'existence, extent or enforceability of the rights or duties of the parties'. Conversely, rules of procedure govern or regulate the mode or conduct of court proceedings.

A similar approach was taken by the Supreme Court of Canada in *Tolofson v Jensen*:

> The forum's procedural rules exist for the convenience of the court … They aid the forum court to 'administer [its] machinery as distinguished from its product'[14] … the purpose of substantive/procedural classification is to determine which rules will make the machinery of the forum court run smoothly as distinguished from those determinative of the rights of *both* parties.[15]

However, these definitions cannot provide any bright-line distinction between substance and procedure.[16] Many rules which regulate the mode and conduct of proceedings, for example, rules relating to discovery, clearly have the potential to affect the substantive outcome of a case.

In English law, the traditional right *v* remedy distinction attempted to separate the right (which is substantive) from the remedy (which is procedural). Applying this distinction to the assessment of damages, heads of damage were substantive whereas the assessment of damages

---

[11] See further Richard Fentiman, *International Commercial Litigation* (2nd edn, Oxford University Press 2015) para 5.05.
[12] Citing *McKain v R W Miller & Co (SA) Pty Ltd* (1991) 174 CLR 1, 26–27.
[13] [2000] HCA 36, (2000) 203 CLR 503, 543–44. This passage was cited by Sir William Aldous in the Court of Appeal in *Harding v Wealands* [2004] EWCA Civ 1735, [2005] 1 WLR 1539 [90].
[14] *Poyser v Minors* (1881) 7 QBD 329, 333.   [15] [1994] 3 SCR 1022, 1067, 1071–72.
[16] In *Pfeiffer* (n 13), Kirby J noted that there was no bright line between 'substance' and 'procedure': [133].

was procedural. But again the distinction is not easy to draw in every case as the separation cannot be total. As Goulding J has observed, 'right and remedy are indissolubly connected and correlated ... it is as idle to ask whether the court vindicates the suitor's substantive right or gives a suitor a procedural remedy as to ask whether thought is a mental or a cerebral process'.[17]

The well-known case of *Harding v Wealands* illustrates the practical significance of the substance *v* procedure distinction as well as the impact of applying the different approaches outlined above.[18] The English claimant was severely injured in a car accident in New South Wales. The car was owned and being driven by the defendant, his Australian girlfriend. The claimant commenced proceedings in England and liability was conceded by the defendant's insurers. This left the issue of quantification of damages.

At the time of the tort, the choice of law rules were those set out in the Private International Law (Miscellaneous Provisions) Act 1995 ('the 1995 Act'). According to section 11 of the 1995 Act, New South Wales law applied, being the law of the place where the tort was committed.[19] The English rules on damages differed in a number of respects from the rules in New South Wales. In particular, New South Wales law (specifically the Motor Accidents Compensation Act 1999 ('MACA 1999')) included a number of provisions which limited the level of damages including: a cap on non-economic loss; limits on loss of earnings and gratuitous case; a discount rate of 5 per cent in respect of future economic loss and rules limiting payment of interest. The result was that damages would be approximately 30 per cent higher if assessed according to the English rules. The question of whether the rules of the MACA 1999 were substantive, and accordingly applied as part of the applicable law, or procedural in which case they would not apply, was accordingly crucial.

The basic distinction between substance and procedure was preserved by section 14(3)(b) of the 1995 Act which provided that nothing in the

---

[17] Andrew Scott, 'Substance and Procedure and Choice of Law in Torts' [2007] LMCLQ 44, 58 citing *Chase Manhattan Bank NA v Israel-British Bank (London) Ltd* [1981] Ch 105, 124.

[18] [2004] EWCA Civ 1735, [2005] 1 WLR 1539 [2006] UKHL 32, [2007] 2 AC 1.

[19] It was possible to displace the presumed applicable law in favour of a substantially more appropriate law under s 12 of the Act. The judge at first instance had held the law of England should apply to determine the issues relating to quantum pursuant to s 12. The Court of Appeal disagreed and refused to displace New South Wales law: *Harding v Wealands* [2004] EWCA Civ 1735, [2005] 1 WLR 1539 [20] (Waller LJ), [45] (Arden LJ), [76] (Sir William Aldous).

Act 'affects any rules of evidence, pleading or practice or authorises questions of procedure in any proceedings to be determined otherwise than in accordance with the law of the forum'. As described above, the traditional distinction drawn at common law was that matters relating to the existence of liability, including heads of damages, were substantive, whereas the assessment of damages was procedural. Waller LJ, dissenting in the Court of Appeal, concluded that on the basis of that traditional distinction all of the rules in the MACA 1999 went to the assessment of damages and were thus procedural. However, the majority of the Court of Appeal declined to apply the traditional common law approach. Drawing on the Canadian and Australian case law referred to above, the majority applied a narrower definition of procedure. Arden LJ referred to the definition of substance in *Pfeiffer*, that is laws that bear on the 'existence, extent or enforceability of remedies, rights and obligations', and held that on that basis all of the rules at issue were substantive.[20] Procedure, on the other hand, 'covers matters as to the mode and conduct of trial'.[21] Sir William Aldous's starting point was that the word 'procedure' in the 1995 Act should be given its natural meaning, namely, 'the mode or rules used to govern and regulate the conduct of the court's proceedings'.[22] On that basis, all of the rules were substantive rather than procedural.

The House of Lords unanimously overturned the decision of the majority of Court of Appeal and held that all of the provisions were procedural. Their Lordships concluded that the 1995 Act had codified the previous common law distinction between heads of damages and assessment of damages, and that (agreeing with Waller LJ in the Court of Appeal) according to that traditional distinction all of the rules were procedural.[23] Lord Hoffmann noted that '[e]ven if there appeared to be more logic in the principle in Pfeiffer's case ... the question is not what the law should be but what Parliament thought it was in 1995'.[24] Similarly, Lord Roger emphasised that the traditional common law policy may be criticised as being liable to encourage forum shopping or on some other ground, 'but it is the policy of the legislature'.[25] Whilst it was

---

[20] Ibid [54], citing *Pfeiffer* (n 13) [102].   [21] Ibid [61].   [22] Ibid [86].

[23] Cf the Supreme Court in *Cox v Ergo Versicherung AG* [2014] UKSC 22, [2014] AC 1379 commenting that, even on the basis of the traditional distinction, it seemed surprising that all of the provisions in *Harding v Wealands* [2006] UKHL 32, [2007] 2 AC 1, including, for example, the exclusion of economic loss, were said to fall within procedure: [15] (Lord Sumption) and [43] (Lord Mance).

[24] *Harding v Wealands* (n 23) [51].   [25] Ibid [64].

accepted that in its narrow and perhaps most usual sense, 'procedure' relates to rules 'which make the machinery of the forum court run smoothly', their Lordships concluded that 'procedure' had been defined in a special way for the purposes of private international law at common law and that that definition was codified by the 1995 Act.[26] For the purposes of this chapter, the important point to note is that the reasoning of the House of Lords in *Harding v Wealands* depended on the crystallising effect of the 1995 Act.[27] The decision cannot be binding in the completely different context of the RIR and RIIR.[28] The new Regulations accordingly necessitate a re-evaluation and, as explored in the remainder of this chapter, almost certainly a new approach.

21.3   The Approach to Substance *v* Procedure in RIR and RIIR

21.3.1   Introduction

The RIR and RIIR now provide choice of law rules for all cases of contract and tort before the English courts.[29] One of the key aims of the Regulations is to improve the predictability of outcome of litigation by ensuring that the conflict of law rules in the Member States designate the same national substantive law irrespective of the country in which an action is brought.[30]

The RIR applies to 'contractual obligations' (Art 1(1) RIR) while the RIIR applies to 'non-contractual obligations' (Art 1(1) RIIR); but 'evidence and procedure' are excluded from the scope of both Regulations.[31]

---

[26] Ibid [65] (Lord Rodger).

[27] See, criticising the decision, Pippa Rogerson 'Damages – Substance or Procedure? *Harding* v *Wealands*' [2006] CLJ 515, 516 concluding: 'never has Geoffrey Cheshire's epithet of the paralysing hand of the parliamentary draftsman been so true'; and Scott (n 17) 51.

[28] Lord Mance in *Cox* (n 23), a case decided under the 1995 Act, commented that '[t]he distinction has, for torts committed since 11 January 2009, been, happily, superseded by the RIIR': [407].

[29] The RIR rules apply to contracts entered into on or after 17 December 2009, and the RIIR applies to torts where the events occurred after 11 January 2009, in both cases irrespective of any connection with the European Union and regardless of whether the law specified is the law of a European country.

[30] RIR Recital (6) and RIIR Recital (6).

[31] Article 1(3) of the RIR provides that the Regulation 'shall not apply to evidence and procedure, without prejudice to Art 18'. Similarly, under Art 1(3) of the RIIR the Regulation 'shall not apply to evidence and procedure, without prejudice to Articles 21 and 22'. Article 18 RIR and Arts 21 and 22 RIIR lay down special rules concerning the burden of proof, mode of proof and formal validity.

Thus, the starting point seems to remain the traditional private international law distinction between substance and procedure. However, for two reasons, the traditional English law approach to this distinction can no longer be applied.

First, because these terms now form part of a European Regulation, an autonomous Community meaning must be given to 'evidence and procedure'. It is a key feature of the interpretation of European legislation that courts must adopt a purposive approach. Furthermore, in order to ensure that the Regulations are applied uniformly in the different Member States, usually an autonomous Community definition will apply to terms used in the Regulations.[32] Adopting different national law approaches to the classification of substance v procedure would undermine the uniform choice of law rules which European legislation has sought to introduce.[33] Furthermore, the special interpretation traditionally given to procedure in English law has the potential of undermining the choice of law process itself and encouraging forum shopping. Thus, the broad, non-vernacular, meaning given to procedure in English common law, identified and applied by the House of Lords in *Harding v Wealands*, is not appropriate in the context of the European legislation.[34]

Secondly, while not providing an overall definition of substance or procedure, both Regulations state that certain matters are to be governed by the applicable law. In the case of these issues, the express and direct attribution of the applicable law supersedes any question of whether the issue would otherwise be classified as substance or procedure according to any particular national law characterisation.[35]

---

[32] See, for example, the Court of Justice Case C–383/95 *Rutten v Cross Medical Ltd* [1997] ECR 5 [12]–[13].

[33] Illmer (n 9) 243; Elsabe Schoeman, 'Rome II and the Substance–Procedure Dichotomy: Crossing the Rubicon' [2010] LMCLQ 81, 82: 'the stated goal of improving the "foreseeability of solutions regarding the applicable law" [citing Commission, 'Proposal for a Regulation of the European Parliament and the Council on the Law Applicable to Non-contractual Obligations ("Rome II")' COM (2003) 427 final, 4; RIIR Recital (6)] will be seriously jeopardised should different Member Sates characterise crucial issues differently and, as a result, reach different conclusions as to the relative scope of the *lex causae* . . . and the *lex fori*'. See also Andrew Dickinson, *The Rome II Regulation: The Law Applicable to Non-contractual Obligations* (Oxford University Press 2008) para 14.54.

[34] See generally on evidence and procedure as European terms of art in European legislation: Adrian Briggs, *Private International Law in English Courts* (Oxford University Press 2014) para 2.110 ff.

[35] See, similarly, in relation to the provisions on assignment in the Rome Convention, *Raiffeisen Zentralbank Osterreich AG v Five Star General Trading LLC* [2001] EWCA Civ 68, [43] and [48].

The most significant of these provisions in the context of damages and remedies are discussed below. However, the attribution of the applicable law is non-exclusive. This means that, even if a matter is not expressly referred to the applicable law under one of these provisions, the issue will still be governed by the applicable law if it is a contractual or non-contractual obligation and it is not excluded by any provision of the Regulation.

21.3.1.1   Matters Expressly Governed by the Applicable Law in RIR and RIIR

Art 12 RIR provides that the law applicable to a contract by virtue of the Regulation shall govern, in particular:

> (c) within the limits of the powers conferred on the court by its procedural law, the consequences of a total or partial breach of obligations, including the assessment of damages in so far as it is governed by rules of law.

Art 15 RIIR provides that the law applicable to non-contractual obligations under the Regulation shall govern in particular:

> (c) the existence, the nature and the assessment of damage or the remedy claimed;
> (d) within the limits of powers conferred on the court by its procedural law, the measures which a court may take to prevent or terminate injury or damage or to ensure the provision of compensation.

The matters listed are governed by the applicable law without the need for any prior classification as being substantive. However, problems remain with the interpretation of these provisions. The rest of this chapter will focus on two areas which are particularly controversial in the context of commercial remedies:

(1) the quantification of damages; and
(2) foreign remedies.

21.4   The Quantification of Damages

Within the broad issue of the quantification of damages, a number of controversial questions arise including how to treat:

(1) the distinction between questions of fact and law;
(2) mode and method of proof or hearing; and
(3) interest.

21.4.1 Introduction

As has been described, both the RIR and the RIIR expressly provide that 'the assessment of damages' (or in the case of the RIIR 'damage') is to be determined by the applicable law (Arts 12(c) and 15(c) respectively). However, the full consequences of this apparently very significant change from the traditional English position are yet to be determined.

In the RIR, the allocation of the applicable law to determine questions relating to the assessment of damages is subject to two qualifications. First, the applicable law applies but 'within the limits of the powers conferred on the court by its procedural law'. Secondly, the applicable law applies only 'in so far as [the assessment of damages] is governed by rules of law'. The RIIR, on the other hand, refers to the assessment of damage (not damages) without either of these provisos. In the following discussion, consideration will be given to each of the three sub-issues outlined above, both on the basis of the specific wording of these provisions (and provisos) and also more generally as to whether the issue falls within the autonomous definition of evidence or procedure which is excluded from the scope of both Regulations.

21.4.2 The Distinction between Fact and Law

When it comes to quantifying the amount of damages to be awarded, a concern often raised is whether a *lex causae* approach is capable adequately of taking into account the local circumstances of the claimant. In a case like *Harding v Wealands*, for example, if the victim is injured in one country – whose law is likely to be the applicable law – but is now resident in another country, it is in his country of residence that the losses will actually be felt.[36] When damages were assessed according to the *lex fori*, this was often (although not necessarily) also the law of the place where the claimant was resident.[37]

The important starting point must be that regardless of whether the *lex fori*, *lex causae* or any other law applies to the assessment of damages,

---

[36] In *Harding v Wealands* (n 23), Lord Rodger noted that quantification should, where possible, correspond to the social environment of the place where the claimant resides: [70]. Garnett reads this as an admission that the procedural classification was being used to conceal a law of habitual residence being applied: (n 4) para 11.27.

[37] Others have suggested that the remedial consequences of a violated right should be governed by the law of the place where the order will have its effect. See Adrian Briggs, 'Conflict of Laws and Commercial Remedies' in Andrew Burrows and Edwin Peel (eds), *Commercial Remedies: Current Issues and Problems* (Oxford University Press 2003) ch 22.

questions of fact are different.[38] This is expressly acknowledged by the second proviso in Art 12(c) RIR which provides that the applicable law governs the assessment of damages 'in so far as it is governed by rules of law'.[39] Factual issues are not subject to any law, whether the *lex fori* or the substantive *lex causae*. This is crucial because the factors which tie a particular loss or injury to a country where that loss is actually being felt are likely to be factual. Thus, the real costs or losses suffered by the claimant in the country where he or she is resident will in any event be taken into account. For example, if the claimant can no longer work, the question of whether loss of earnings is recoverable is for the applicable law; but the quantum of loss of earnings depends essentially on questions of fact, what the claimant was earning or could have earned but for the injury. Damages for the cost of adapting a house or car, if available, will be determined on the basis of evidence of local costs of building equipment, labour etc.

A similar idea seems to lie behind Recital (33) RIIR which provides:

> According to the current national rules on compensation awarded to victims of road traffic accidents, when quantifying damages for personal injury in cases in which the accident takes place in a State other than that of the habitual residence of the victim, the court seised should take into account all the relevant actual circumstances of the specific victim, including the actual losses and costs of after-care and medical attention.

Although the precise effect of this Recital is uncertain, it certainly reflects the importance of looking at the actual costs and losses suffered by the victim.[40]

Although the express proviso 'in so far as governed by rules of law' does not appear in the RIIR,[41] the distinction between facts and law is

---

[38] In *Dicey, Morris and Collins* questions of fact are said to be 'obviously for the *lex fori*': Lord Collins of Mapesbury (gen ed), *Dicey, Morris and Collins on the Conflict of Laws* (15th edn, Sweet & Maxwell 2012) para 32–154.

[39] The Giuliano-Lagarde Report stated that this formulation (which also appeared in the Rome Convention) is intended to exclude assessment of damages which is only concerned with questions of fact (e.g. arithmetical calculation of loss where the formula for such calculation is not dictated by law); see further HG Beale (gen ed), *Chitty on Contracts* (31st edn, Sweet & Maxwell 2012) para 30–338.

[40] The Court of Appeal in *Wall v Mutuelle de Poitiers Assurances* [2014] EWCA Civ 138, [2014] 1 WLR 4263 [11] noted that this was no doubt partly because they were matters of fact. See also *Stylianou v Toyoshima* [2013] EWHC 2188 (QB) [78] (Sir Robert Nelson): 'The solution to the problem [of Recital (33)] lies ... not in the choice of any particular law ... but in the court looking at the actual costs, for example, of aftercare in the victim's place of residence, and taking those into account when assessing damages, but only insofar as the applicable law permits it to do so.'

[41] These textual differences are discussed in detail in Michael Wilderspin, *The European Private International Law of Obligations* (4th edn Sweet & Maxwell 2015) para 16–029.

inherent in the choice of law process. Most commentators consider that
the omission was 'inadvertent' and that the distinction between facts and
law should equally apply.[42] Furthermore, although Art 15(c) refers to the
assessment of damage not damages which may be thought to point to the
factual issue of the assessment of damage, ultimately the factual determination of loss must be a matter of evidence for the *lex fori*. This means
that the choice between *lex fori* and *lex causae* may not be as clear cut as it
appears: both can take into account local factual evidence which is likely
to be central to the quantification of damages.

Rules of law relating to the assessment of damages which exist in the
lex causae are likely to be of a different nature. For example, the rules in
the MACA 1999 at issue in *Harding v Wealands* were not based on the
cost of living in Australia; rather they reflected policy considerations in
relation to the level of insurance premiums. Similarly, a system with
generous liability rules may also couple those rules with caps or limits
on the recoverable damages.[43] These types of legal rules are really about
local policies or principles rather than local factual conditions. As such,
they go hand in hand with rules governing liability and it is right that they
should be applied as part of the applicable law irrespective of where the
victim is actually suffering loss.

Although most of the cases concern personal injury claims, a similar
distinction between rules of law and questions of fact will need to be
drawn in other areas. For example, in a sale of goods case where the
contract is governed by English law, the Sale of Goods Act 1979 measure
of damages will apply. The market price rule set out in that Act is
a reflection of rules on mitigation and remoteness and is clearly
a matter relating to the assessment of damages under Art 12(c) RIR.
But if the question is what the market price was at which the goods could

---

[42] See Garnett (n 4) para 11.58 and the references cited. See also *Wall* (n 40) [23] where the
Court of Appeal suggested that it was sensible to interpret Art 15(c) as being implicitly
limited to the assessment of damages 'in so far as prescribed by law'. Cf *Stylianou
v Toyoshima* [2013] EWHC 2188 [93] where Sir Robert Nelson refused to imply the
same proviso into Art 15(c). See also Adam Rushworth, 'Remedies and the Rome II
Regulation' in John Ahern and William Binchy (eds), *The Rome II Regulation on the Law
Applicable to Non-contractual Obligations: A New International Litigation Regime*
(Martinus Nijhoff 2009) 206, concluding that the same result is reached under the RIIR
since matters of evidence are for the *lex fori* and 'nothing can be more evidential than the
determination of the facts of the case'.

[43] The converse example is referred to by Rushworth (n 42) 217, whereby in the English tort
of deceit it is hard to establish liability but once liability is established more generous rules
on remoteness are applied.

have been bought, this is a question of fact determined according to evidence of the actual market price at the place where the goods were or should have been delivered. In *Excalibur Ventures LLC v Texas Keystone Inc* the court had to classify a rule concerning the date on which damages are to be assessed.[44] Lord Justice Christopher Clarke held that this was a rule of substance and was a matter for the applicable law of the contract. Thus the principle of New York law that contract damages are measured at the time of the breach applied as it was not a matter of procedure, quantification or determination of fact:

> The date by reference to which damages are to be assessed is, in my view, a matter for New York law ... 'Where ... a rule of law imposes a limit on compensation, or draws distinctions between penalties and liquidated damages, or provides a principle by which the measure of damages for, say, non-delivery of goods can be calculated, the applicability of the rule will depend on the governing law.'[45] ... It seems to me that the date at which damages are, or are, *prima facie*, to be calculated is a rule or principle of law.[46]

21.4.3   Mode of Assessment and Proof

The Court of Appeal in *Wall v Mutuelle De Poitiers Assurances* confirmed that mode of assessment and proof remains a matter for the *lex fori*.[47] The English claimant was injured in a motorcycle accident while on holiday in France. The defendant French insurers admitted negligence and accepted the jurisdiction of the English courts; the only issue was as to the quantum of damages. The applicable law under the RIIR was French law. The issue for the Court of Appeal was the extent to which French law governed the way in which expert evidence was to be adduced. The defendant argued that since the applicable law was French law, and under French law the court selects one or sometimes two court-appointed experts to assist the judge, expert evidence should be ordered on that basis. The judge at first instance disagreed and held that English law applied. Sir Richard Buxton, refusing permission to appeal on the papers observed: 'An English judge ... would need to be persuaded that a revolution had taken place before he countenanced the determination of procedures for the adduction of evidence by reference to any system of law other than the *lex fori*.' However, the defendant, relying on Art 15 RIIR, argued that just such a revolution had taken place. Since matters relating to 'the assessment of damage' were now

---

[44] [2013] EWHC 2767 (Comm).   [45] Citing Beale (n 39) 30–338.
[46] *Excalibur* (n 44) [1422]–[1424].   [47] [2014] EWCA Civ 138, [2014] 1 WLR 4263.

for the applicable law, French law should apply.[48] This argument was again rejected by the Court of Appeal. Nothing in the Regulation mandated a court, trying a case to which a foreign law applied, to award the same amount of damages as the foreign court would award. Furthermore, 'it cannot be the case that the Regulation envisages that the law of the place where the damage occurs should govern the way in which evidence of fact or opinion is to be given to the court which has to determine the case. An English court is ill-equipped to receive expert evidence given in the French manner.'[49] Longmore LJ also commented that he had little doubt that 'in the reverse situation, a French court would think it unhelpful (to put it mildly) to be presented with English-style expert evidence about the consequences of an English accident to a French driver or motorcyclist, in the form of reports from experts in (say) 10 disciplines presented by each party and having to choose between them without resort to its own method of dealing with expert evidence'.[50] Jackson LJ agreed, adding that the natural meaning of evidence and procedure in Art 1(3) RIIR included the giving of expert evidence. Furthermore, he added, it is unrealistic and inefficient to expect courts to adopt the evidential practices of a different jurisdiction when determining questions of fact.[51] Examples of other matters which on the same basis would still be for the *lex fori* might include rules about discovery and witness statements, as well as whether damages are to be assessed by a jury.[52]

21.4.4   Interest

The position in relation to granting interest on damages awards may well be different depending on the type of interest at issue. Interest awards are discussed in detail in chapter 11, in summary they may encompass:

---

[48] In renewing its application for permission to appeal, the defendant relied on Professor Briggs's view that RIIR had indeed brought about such a revolution through the termination of English private international law and its replacement by a European private international law: Adrian Briggs, 'When in Rome, Choose as the Romans Choose' (2009) 125 LQR 191; see *Wall* (n 40) [6] (Longmore LJ).

[49] *Wall* (n 40) [12].   [50] Ibid [14] (Longmore LJ).

[51] Ibid [41]–[43]. He also noted that the costs rules of each jurisdiction are linked to the particular evidential practices developed in that jurisdiction.

[52] The latter was an example given by Arden LJ in the Court of Appeal in *Harding v Wealands* [2004] EWCA Civ 1735, [2005] 1 WLR 1539 [57]. See also David Richards J in *Re T & N Ltd* [2005] EWHC 2990 (Ch), [2006] 1 WLR 1792 [83] noting '[t]here is no question of an English court empanelling a jury to assess the damages [in accordance with foreign law]' and see Wilderspin (n 41) para 16–050.

(a) contractually agreed interest;
(b) interest *as* damages – following the ruling in *Sempra Metals* that no special rules apply to deny or restrict the recovery of interest as damages, 'normal rules apply';[53]
(c) post-judgment interest under section 17(1) Judgments Act 1838; and
(d) pre-judgment statutory interest under section 35A Senior Courts Act 1981.[54]

In the first two cases, the award of interest is clearly a matter of substance to be governed by the relevant applicable law. Interest payable under an express contractual agreement is like any other contractually agreed sum and must be for the applicable law of the contract. A claim for interest *as* damages under *Sempra Metals* is also simply a further head of damages which may be able to be claimed, whether the claim is in contract, tort or unjust enrichment, and should accordingly be governed by the law applicable to the relevant claim. In other words *Sempra Metals* claims will apply only when English law governs the claim. Conversely, it is clear that post-judgment interest under section 17(1) is payable on *all* English judgments. This is clear from the wording of the statute itself which provides that '*every* judgment debt shall carry interest' (emphasis added).

The position in relation to pre-judgment interest under section 35A is much less clear. In particular, does it belong to the *Sempra Metals* or section 17 side of the line? It may be assumed that section 35A interest can be added to any judgment of the English court, regardless of whether the substantive claim was governed by a foreign law. It is not clear that this is right, or even if it is, why that should be so.

Courts have stressed that the purpose of section 35A is compensatory i.e. the award of damages reflects the cost to the plaintiff of being deprived of its money.[55] If an award under section 35A is simply another head of damage to be added to a claim, then, as in the case of a *Sempra Metals*

---

[53] *Sempra Metals Ltd v IRC* [2007] UKHL 34, [2008] 1 AC 561.
[54] Interest can also be awarded under the Late Payment of Commercial Debts (Interest) Act 1998 which deals expressly with this issue as it contains a non-avoidance provision in s 12(2) which means that the Act has effect in relation to a contract expressly governed by a foreign law if, but for that choice, the contract would have been governed by UK law. Section 12(1) also contains a self-denying provision which says that the Act will not apply because of an express choice of English law if there is no significant connection with the UK.
[55] See *Tate & Lyle Food and Distribution Ltd v Greater London Council* [1982] 1 WLR 149, 154.

claim for damages, one would expect the claim for interest to be governed by the relevant applicable law (under Art 12 RIR or Art 15 RIIR). That would mean that section 35A would only apply to claims governed by English law. However, a claim under section 35A is not a head of damages in the normal sense. This is clear from the fact that:

(i) A broad pragmatic approach is taken to assessment of loss – the losses are not those of the particular plaintiff itself.
(ii) Section 35A applies in cases where there is no obvious wrong e.g. interest on awards for pain and suffering or on certain restitutionary remedies. That is because it is the failure to pay a sum which is legally due which *is itself* being treated as a wrong for the purposes of the 1981 Act. This is further illustrated by the fact that section 35A interest is always due as a default measure; but the claimant may be able to claim more if it suffered further damages under *Sempra Metals*.[56]
(iii) A claim under section 35A does not need to be pleaded.
(iv) The claim arises only in connection with legal proceedings in that a claimant cannot claim under section 35A if the sum is paid before proceedings are commenced.

Thus, section 35A interest is not simply a further head of loss to be added to an existing claim, rather it is a *sui generis* independent claim based on the wrong of being kept out of money. This wrong is created by section 35A which also provides the measure of loss for that wrong. In terms of classification for private international law purposes, this distinguishes a claim under section 35A from a claim for interest *as* damages. It is accordingly arguable that the substantive applicable law need not apply, and that section 35A can be applied to all claims in England because:

(1) the claim is procedural on the basis that it is a presumed sum awarded as part of the court's machinery to reflect the delay between the sum being due and the judgment being given; and/or
(2) even if the claim is substantive, the claim for interest under section 35A is a *sui generis* claim which applies as an overriding rule of English law.

This approach is supported by the decision in *Maher v Groupama Grand Est*.[57] The Court of Appeal agreed that a distinction needed to be

---

[56] See Andrew Burrows, ch 11 above.
[57] [2009] EWCA Civ 1191, [2010] 1 WLR 1564, [25]–[37] following Hobhouse J in *Midland International Trade Service v Al Sudairy* (QB, 11 April 1990) *Financial Times*, 2 May 1990 and also consistent with *Abdel Hadi Abdallah Al Qahtani & Sons Beverage Industry Co*

drawn between the existence of a right to recover interest as a head of damages (i.e. a *Sempra Metals* claim) which is governed by the substantive law (in that case French law) and a claim under section 35A. The court held that whether or not a substantive right existed, the court had available to it the remedy created by section 35A of the 1981 Act.[58] Furthermore, although the court referred to section 35A providing a 'remedy' (which it could be argued under RIIR should be governed by the substantive law), it is clear from the reasoning that the court saw section 35A as a procedural remedy of a special kind not simply a head of loss. In particular, Moore-Bick LJ relied on authority which viewed section 35A as being 'more like an award of costs than anything else – not part of the debt or damages claimed itself but something apart on its own'.[59]

21.5   The Availability of Foreign Remedies in English Courts

The second controversial area is the extent to which English courts may be required to grant foreign remedies, or apply foreign rules relating to the granting of remedies.

As has been described, at common law the granting of remedies was treated as procedural and accordingly a matter for the *lex fori*; indeed this was the fundamental basis of the right *v* remedies distinction. Thus: 'Although the matter has received little discussion and is the subject of only scanty authority, it was generally stated that at common law the availability of the equitable remedies of specific performance or injunction was a matter for the lex *fori* ... The right to an interlocutory injunction would seem to be a matter of procedure for the *lex fori* as would other forms of interlocutory relief.'[60]

However, even before the Regulations, the application of the *lex fori* to remedies may well have been narrower than the traditional rights *v* remedy distinction appeared to suggest. In *Fiona Trust & Holding Corp v Privalov*, Andrew Smith J had to consider whether he could order an account in relation to a claim governed by Russian law.[61] The claimants argued that English law governed what remedies were available, including whether they were entitled to an account of profits if

---

v Antliff [2010] EWHC 1735 (Comm) [54]. Applied in *JSC BTA Bank v Ablyazov* [2013] EWHC 867 (Comm) [26].
[58]   *Maher* (n 57) [40] (Moore-Bick LJ).
[59]   Ibid [33] (Moore-Bick LJ) relying on *Jefford v Gee* [1970] 2 QB 130 (CA).
[60]   Beale (n 39) *Chitty* para 30–339.   [61]   [2010] EWHC 3199 (Comm).

the defendants were liable for what English law would regard as liability for dishonest assistance. Andrew Smith J disagreed. First, it was arguable that the availability of an account was equivalent to the availability of a head of damage and accordingly for the *lex causae*. Secondly, even if English law as the *lex fori* did apply, that did not mean that the court would determine what remedies would be available on the particular facts under English law. The questions were: what was the nature of the liability under the foreign law and what remedy or remedies would English law provide for English law liability similar or analogous to the kind of liability established under the foreign law?[62] On the facts of the case, liability arose under Art 1064 of the Russian Civil Code, which imposed a liability similar to or analogous to English tortious liability giving rise to a claim for compensatory damages. Andrew Smith J noted that it was nothing to the point that, on the particular facts that gave rise to a liability under Art 1064, English law would recognise a cause of action which afforded the remedy of an account. However, it will be argued below that even this does not go far enough. Under the Regulations, the question is now: what remedy most closely approximates the remedy which would be available under the foreign applicable law? Thus, if Russian law had given an account of profits for tortious liability, English law should do the same. That is because remedies are now, under the Regulations, a matter for the *lex causae*, subject only to two qualifications.

First, the court is limited by the machinery which it has available. The grant of a foreign remedy, even if available in principle, may be subject to practical limitations.

Secondly, in relation to interlocutory relief, a distinction may need to be drawn between measures which go to the substantive rights of the parties, such as an interlocutory injunction, and other measures such as search orders or freezing orders.

21.5.1 *Final Non-monetary Relief*

The wording of RIR and RIIR differs, but both support the view that the availability of final non-monetary relief should now be for the applicable law.

As has been described, Art 12(c) RIR allocates the applicable law to determine 'the consequences of a total or partial breach' of contract. This

---

[62] Ibid [158].

provision is clearly wide enough to include the availability of non-monetary final remedies, such as specific performance, injunction or declaration.[63]

The position under the RIIR is more complex. Article 15(c) allocates the applicable law to determine the 'existence, nature and assessment of damage *or the remedy claimed*' (emphasis added). However, this express reference to 'remedies' appears only in the English and Dutch versions of the Regulation.[64] Article 15(d) also allocates the applicable law to decide 'measures which the court may take to prevent or terminate injury or damage or to ensure the provision of compensation'. The availability of final specific remedies, such as an injunction or specific performance, seems to come within either the 'remedy' claimed in Art 15(c) or the measures which a court may take to prevent or terminate injury or damage in Art 15(d) of RIIR.

However, the application of the *lex causae* under Art 12(c) RIR and Art 15(d) RIIR is subject to the proviso 'within the limits of the powers conferred on the court by its procedural law'.[65] Because remedies are 'part of the court's machinery for resolving disputes' they are to that extent procedural.[66] In other words, English law cannot grant a foreign remedy where there is no practical way of putting it into effect. As Garnett puts it, the forum can only grant remedies 'within its own armoury'.[67] Save to that limited extent, it is for the *lex causae* to determine whether relief should be granted. Thus, the availability of specific performance and the conditions under which it is granted are now matters for the applicable law. If a contract is governed by Scots law, and Scots judges make orders for specific performance more readily than English judges, then *prima facie* the English judge must also make such an order. However, there may be practical limitations. The English law requirement that an order for specific performance does not require

---

[63] See Fentiman (n 11) para 5.23 and Wilderspin (n 41) para 14–036.

[64] See for a full analysis of the textual differences Wilderspin (n 41) paras 16-029–16-036. See also Dickinson (n 33) *Updating Supplement* (Oxford University Press 2010) para 14.25, which notes that other language versions use narrower terminology suggesting the restriction of Art 15(c) to monetary remedies.

[65] This is not the case under Art 15(c). However, Wilderspin (n 41) notes (paras 16-029–16-036) that this does not matter as no provision can require the English court to grant a remedy that it has no statutory or inherent jurisdiction to grant. See also Collins (n 38) para 34–059; and Janeen Carruthers, 'Has the Forum Lost its Grip?' in Ahern and Binchy (n 42) 42, noting that common sense requires that Art 15(c) RIIR should be interpreted as being implicitly procedurally limited in the same way.

[66] See Garnett (n 4) para 10.01.   [67] Ibid para 10.17.

supervision of the court, at least in part, reflects the fact that no machinery exists in England for supervising an order of specific performance.
Thus, that particular limitation may well apply even if the foreign *lex
causae* has no such rule because the English court simply has no practical
way of supervising an order that that foreign court would make.[68]

But even this practical proviso is not absolute: the court may well be
required to apply and perhaps even amend a remedy which is similar to
and achieves the same result as the foreign remedy. This idea has parallels
in other areas of law. In particular, Art 54 of the Brussels I Regulation
recast provides that if an enforceable judgment contains a measure or an
order which is not known in the law of the Member State addressed, that
measure or order shall, to the extent possible, be adapted to a measure or
order known in the law of that Member State which has equivalent effect
attached to it and which pursues similar aims or interests.[69] Although Art
54 is a new article in the BIR recast, it has been suggested that it is
probably intended to preserve and to generalise what was formerly an
implicit judicial obligation to give the fullest cross-border effect reasonably possible to judgments containing measures or orders unknown in
the legal system addressed.[70] Thus, as the Court of Justice of the European
Union has pointed out, whilst execution of a judgment is governed by the
domestic law of the court in which execution is sought, 'the application, for
the purposes of the execution of a judgment, of the procedural rules of the
state in which enforcement is sought may not impair the effectiveness of the
scheme of the convention as regards the enforcement of orders'.[71] Similarly,
the RIR and RIIR may require a Member State to give effect to the applicable
law as determined by those Regulations by making use of a remedy, measure
or order in the domestic law of that Member State which most closely
mirrors the remedy which would be awarded under the applicable law.[72]
Indeed, it has been suggested that the court will 'need to be resourceful in

---

[68] See Garnett (n 4) para 10.20, reaching a similar conclusion.
[69] Regulation (EU) No 1215/2012 of 12 December 2012 on jurisdiction and the recognition
      and enforcement of judgments in civil and commercial matters (recast) [2012] OJ L351/1.
[70] See Jonathan Fitchen, 'Enforcement of Civil and Commercial Judgments under the New
      Brussels Ia Regulation (Regulation 1215/2012)' [2015] ICCLR 145, 147.
[71] Case C 145/86 *Hoffmann v Krieg* [1988] ECR 645 [29].
[72] There is also a similarity with the principle of equivalence that applies when considering
      whether a domestic remedy meets the requirements of a case of breach of Community
      law. However, this doctrine requires that the remedy provided by the Member State must
      not make the Community right 'virtually impossible or extremely difficult to exercise':
      Matra Communications SA v Home Office [1999] 1 WLR 1646 [2]. The obligation to adapt
      a local remedy under the RIR and RIIR may well go further.

exercising its procedural powers in order to secure an outcome as close as possible to that available under the applicable law'.[73]

21.5.2   Interlocutory Relief

In the context of interlocutory relief the position may depend on the type of relief being sought. A claimant may seek a short-term injunction to preserve the position pending trial, for example, an injunction to stop an employee from working for a competitor or to stop disputed goods being sold pending final determination of the case. The availability of relief in such cases depends primarily on establishing potential liability against the defendant and mirrors the type of final relief that might be granted. Such relief is accordingly to be characterised in the same way as final non-monetary relief and again falls within the 'consequences of breach' (under Art 12(c)) or 'ways of preventing or halting the damages' (under Art 15(d)).[74] Furthermore, both Art 12 and Art 15 are a non-exhaustive list of matters to be governed by the applicable law. The grant of interim relief will be governed by the Regulations unless excluded as a matter of evidence or procedure. According to a broad common sense meaning of those words, the grant of these forms of interim relief does not seem to be procedural.

This seems to have been the view taken, albeit tentatively, by Sir Andrew Morritt in *OJSC TNK-BP Holding v Lazurenko*.[75] The underlying claim related to the alleged misuse of confidential material and the applicable law was Russian law. Both Russian law experts had made it clear that under Russian law there could be no *quia timet* injunction, interim or final, to restrain a threatened disclosure. The judge noted:

> Rome I Article [12] and Rome II Article 15 may have changed the common law position under which the availability of remedies was a matter for the lex fori. They appear to make the availability of remedies a matter for the lex causae. In this case that is Russian law. It would follow that TNK-BP has not demonstrated any cause of action or serious

---

[73] Wilderspin (n 41) para 16–058. See also Collins (n 38) para 7–015; the court must 'strive to invoke the most analogous remedy or procedure available in English law'. See also Dickinson (n 33) para 14.34, advocating a 'best fit' approach.

[74] Cf Garnett (n 4) who says that most commentators agree that the provision in the RIR referring to the consequences of breach does not embrace any forms of interlocutory relief: para 10.19. Cf Dickinson (n 33) para 14.35 concluding that Art 15(d) RIIR also includes interim measures, including injunctions, to prevent or halt damage.

[75] [2012] EWHC 2781 (Ch).

question to be tried in respect of its claim for an interim quia timet injunction.[76]

Thus, where interim relief is effectively a pre-trial version of a final remedy, there seems to be no reason why the availability of such a remedy should not be governed by the *lex causae*, subject again to the appropriate procedural machinery being available. However, other forms of provisional interim relief such as freezing injunctions or search orders may well be different. Although they could be said to fall within measures 'to ensure provision of compensation' under Art 15(d) RIIR, such orders seem more naturally to fall within the enforcement mechanisms of the court and accordingly more naturally matters of procedure rather than liability.[77]

The granting of foreign remedies was at issue in the recent case of *Actavis UK Ltd v Eli Lilly & Co*.[78] The case involved a complex patent dispute encompassing a number of different jurisdictions. It was common ground that the law applicable to the question of whether the acts would infringe each non-UK designation of the patent was the *lex loci protectionis*, that is, the substantive patent law of the relevant country. However, a dispute arose as to the law which was applicable to the other conditions to be satisfied by the claimant in order to obtain a negative declaration (in this context a declaration of non-infringement 'DNI'). The claimant contended that the rules for obtaining a DNI were matters of procedure within Art 1(3) RIIR and thus were for English law. The defendant contended that the rules fell within the scope of the *lex causae*.

Arnold J noted that each legal system had its own rules which specified the conditions which had to be satisfied in order to obtain a DNI in

---

[76] Ibid [20]. However, he also noted that there was no authority to that effect, the issue was not fully argued and that doubts have been expressed in Sir Lawrence Collins (gen ed) *Dicey, Morris and Collins on the Conflict of Laws* (14th edn, Sweet & Maxwell, 2006) para 32–203 and *Halsbury's Laws* (5th edn, 2011) vol 19, para 646, n 9. In the most recent supplement to the 15th edn of *Dicey, Morris and Collins*, the sentence previously found in the main work stating 'There can be no doubt that the availability of interlocutory relief remains essentially a matter of procedure governed by the *lex fori*' is deleted with reference to this passage in *OJSC TNK* (n 75): Lord Collins of Mapesbury and Jonathan Harris (gen eds), *Dicey, Morris and Collins on the Conflict of Laws: Second Cumulative Supplement to the Fifteenth Edition* (Sweet & Maxwell 2015) para 32–155. See also Wilderspin (n 41) para 16–059, concluding that interlocutory injunctions may be for the applicable law under RIIR.

[77] See Garnett (n 4) para 10.06 and Rushworth (n 42) 202.

[78] [2014] EWHC 1511 (Pat), [2014] 4 All ER 331.

addition to establishing that the product or process did not infringe the patent. They fell broadly into two different types:

(i) rules based on a fact-sensitive concept of interest or purpose e.g. the English law requirement of a 'useful purpose'; and
(ii) rules based on pre-action notification requirements.

The judge held that as all of the rules dealt with the same kind of issue, they should be characterised in the same way. The first kind of rule ensured that the claimant had a sufficient justification for seeking an adjudication by the court. The second kind of rule was aimed at avoiding unnecessary litigation and ensuring that the dispute was sufficiently well defined for the court to adjudicate on it. Thus, they were 'rules which are designed to ensure that the machinery of the court is only invoked to determine disputes which genuinely require adjudication by the court and to ensure that the dispute is sufficiently well defined for the court to adjudicate on it'.[79]

Arnold J accepted that it was well arguable that Art 15(c) RIIR extends beyond the assessment of damages and embraces the final remedy claimed. The applicable law would accordingly extend to whether a proprietary remedy, such as tracing, is available. On the other hand 'remedy' cannot extend to any remedy or any aspect of any remedy. Thus, while he accepted that the question of whether an injunction may be granted to restrain future infringement is clearly governed by *lex causae* under Art 15(d),[80] Art 15(d) contains the limitation 'within the limits of the powers conferred on the court by its procedural law'. According to Arnold J, the distinction is between the question of the principle of whether an injunction will be granted and the 'procedural conditions' which must be observed. Thus the question of principle of whether a DNI is available at all is a matter for the applicable law. But he concluded that the rules at issue were procedural conditions, so governed by English law.

It is right that some 'procedural conditions' have to be governed by the *lex fori*. For example, the English rule that three clear days' notice must be given save in cases of urgency seems to be a good example of a matter which it only makes sense to be governed by the *lex fori*.[81] Similarly, a rule requiring pre-action notification also seems to be part of the procedural mechanism for the grant of a remedy. Conversely, questions such as the burden of proof that needs to be satisfied and rules relating to the balance

---

[79] Ibid [220].   [80] He referred to *OJSC TNK* (n 75) [20], discussed above.
[81] *Actavis* (n 78) [228] (Arnold J).

of convenience seem to be matters of principle for the applicable law. Arnold J held that it was necessary to characterise all of the rules at issue in the same way, and on that basis held that they were all procedural. But it is not clear that that is the correct approach. The rules he identified in category (i), and in particular, the English law requirement that the declaration serves a useful purpose, does not seem to be part of the procedural machinery for granting an injunction, rather it seems to be a substantive requirement for the granting of relief and accordingly arguably should have been a matter for the *lex causae*.

21.6   Conclusion

One of the many consequences of the Europeanisation of choice of law rules in the RIR and RIIR is the need to reassess the traditional common law approach to the characterisation of substance *v* procedure. In particular, the assessment of damages and the consequences of breach, both under English law traditionally matters for the *lex fori*, are now expressly made subject to the applicable law. However, while matters of principle are now more likely to governed by the *lex causae*, practicality and convenience will dictate that there remains a crucial role for local law. Mode of proof remains a matter of procedural law. Furthermore, questions of fact are always a matter for the local court to determine according to evidence relating to the actual losses and expenses incurred. It is also likely that pre-judgment statutory interest under section 35A will continue to be added to all awards for damages. When it comes to granting foreign remedies, English courts will be limited by the procedural mechanisms available to them. Thus, whilst legally the Regulations are revolutionary in a number of ways, the practical implications for the granting of remedies in international cases may well be more limited.

22

Remedies of the Criminal Courts

MATTHEW DYSON AND PAUL JARVIS

22.1 Introduction

On 13 June 2014, Ketan Somaia was convicted by a jury at the Central Criminal Court in London of nine counts of obtaining a money transfer by deception.[1] The prosecution had not been brought by the Crown Prosecution Service (CPS) but by a private individual, Mr Murli Mirchandani. Mr Mirchandani did so on the basis that he had been fraudulently induced by Mr Somaia to pay US$19.5 million in short-term loans with high rates of interest. Mr Somaia was sentenced to eight years' imprisonment. The case made headlines in the national press[2] and highlighted the increasingly apparent willingness on the part of private parties to use the machinery of the criminal justice system to settle their commercial disputes. Other examples, often reported in the mainstream media, range from Championship football perjury and fraud[3] and commercial car sales[4] to contentious family disputes[5] and significant intellectual property litigation, such as advertising revenue from pirate movie websites.[6] This surge has led to the creation of boutique firms which

---

[1] Theft Act 1968, s 15A.

[2] Paul Peachey, 'Two-tier Justice: Private Prosecution Revolution' *The Independent* (London, 16 August 2014) <www.independent.co.uk/news/uk/crime/twotier-justice-private-prosecution-revolution-9672543.html>. All links were last accessed in January 2017 unless otherwise stated.

[3] Press Association and staff, 'Phil Gartside and Nine Others Sent to Crown Court over Perjury Claims' *The Guardian* (London, 25 February 2015) <www.theguardian.com/football/2015/feb/25/phil-gartside-bolton-wanderers-allegations-perjury-fraud-tony-mcgill>.

[4] *R (House of Cars Ltd) v Derby Car and Van Rental, Kevin Overton* [2012] CTLC 62.

[5] Andrzej Bojarski, Kate Tompkins and Cameron Crowe, 'Private Criminal Prosecutions in Financial Remedies Cases' (*Family Law Week*, 2013) <www.familylawweek.co.uk/site.aspx?i=ed111632>.

[6] Josh Halliday, 'Surfthechannel Owner Sentenced to Four Years over Piracy' *The Guardian* (London, 14 August 2012) <www.theguardian.com/technology/2012/aug/14/anton-vickerman-surfthechannel-sentenced>; David Northfield, 'Protecting IP through private

engage exclusively in private prosecution work,[7] as well as solicitors (both criminal and non-criminal specialists),[8] and even accountancy firms,[9] to offer their services; they clearly believe there is significant money to be made for their clients and for themselves.

How much should private parties be able to harness the criminal law for their commercial aims? Three sets of *analytical questions* will be used:

(a) What is the *utility* to commercial parties of the criminal proceedings?

(b) What is the *context* of the criminal law, its nature and purpose? Is the criminal law made up only of rules, or also skills, understanding and competence about whether to apply the rules?

(c) How can lawyers *advance commercial interests* through the criminal law? In practice, what skills and understanding are needed to succeed, with a particular focus on where the commercial party is not the defendant?

To address these questions, the chapter will be organised around three *stages* of criminal proceedings:

(1) *investigative*, including searches and seizures;

(2) *procedural*, in particular, private prosecutions; and

(3) *remedial*, including compensation, confiscation and restitution.

22.2   Investigation

22.2.1   Investigation Introduction

State agents and criminal courts have extensive investigative powers that are of great *utility to commercial parties*. Some of these are statutory, such as the powers under the Proceeds of Crime Act 2002 (POCA) to investigate financial affairs; some are professional, with extensive databases, skilled professional investigators and networks of information. These powers are exercised by public bodies for state purposes, for the prevention and

---

prosecutions' (Fieldfisher, 20 January 2015) <www.fieldfisher.com/publications/2015/01/protecting-ip-through-private-prosecutions#sthash.8cENbSP8.dpbs>.

[7] 'What is a Private Prosecution?' (Edmonds Marshall McMahon, undated) <www.emmlegal.com/what-is-a-private-prosecution/>.

[8] 'Private Prosecutions' (Russell-Cooke Solicitors, undated) <www.russell-cooke.co.uk/service-detail.cfm?id=213>; Melinka Berridge, 'Private Prosecutions' (Kingsley Napley, undated) <www.kingsleynapley.co.uk/client-services/criminal-litigation/private-prosecutions>.

[9] Jane Croft and Caroline Binham, 'EY to Offer Businesses Help with Private Prosecutions for Fraud' *Financial Times* (London, 20 November 2014), <www.ft.com/content/14317698-700a-11e4-bc6a-00144feabdc0>.

punishment of crime. They are part of the wider *criminal law context* of balancing the power of the state against the liberty of those within its jurisdiction. There are important values at work when these powers are exercised, such as autonomy, welfare, legal certainty and the rule of law, but there are also practically important constraints, particularly the cost to the public purse. At present, the law formally allows some *means for commercial parties to advance their interests* through or with the assistance of the investigative activities of the state, but appears unwilling to undermine convictions obtained with assistance beyond those means. What is more, scope for commercial interests has widened significantly in the last two decades under pressure from private parties, and may well continue to widen.

22.2.2 Deals with State Agencies

The phenomenon of deals between private parties and state investigators may not be recent, but it has certainly been more prominent in the last decade. One of the most important recent cases is *R v Hounsham*,[10] where the defendants were convicted of conspiracy to defraud insurance companies arising out a number of staged road traffic accidents. It emerged during the evidence of one of the insurance company representatives that three victims (the insurance companies) had, quite possibly at the investigating officer's request, funded the 'arrest' stage of the investigation by the Hampshire Police Force.[11] The defendants appealed, submitting that such deals were abusive and fatally compromised the impartiality of the investigation: 'He who pays the piper calls the tune', as the defence put it.[12] Gage LJ agreed, noting that soliciting funds from potential victims:

> [I]s fraught with danger. It may compromise the essential independence and objectivity of the police . . . [or lead them to be] selective as to which crimes to investigate and which not to investigate. It might lead to victims persuading a police investigating team to act partially. It might also lead to investigating officers carrying out a more thorough preparation of the evidence in a case of a 'paying' victim; or a less careful preparation of the evidence in the case of a non-contributing victim . . .[13]

He was also unsure whether any powers to make such deals existed, even under section 93 of the Police Act 1996 (the power to accept gifts and loans): 'Even assuming it does have such powers, we find it difficult to

---

[10] [2005] EWCA Crim 1366.   [11] Ibid [15]–[16].   [12] Ibid [29].
[13] Ibid [31]; see NW Taylor, 'Trial: Abuse of Process' [2005] Crim LR 991, 994.

conceive of a situation where it would be sensible to exercise those powers in connection with criminal investigations.'[14]

Nonetheless, these failings were not found to have been sufficiently serious that the trial judge should have stayed the proceedings, even though the trial judge had thought that the initial deal was lawful when the Court of Appeal said it was not. It could not be said that the defendants had been deprived of a fair trial or that it would have been unfair to try them on the basis of flagrant prosecutorial malpractice and so there was no abuse of process justifying a stay of the proceedings. Another mechanism will be needed for when such deals are discovered earlier in the process.

22.2.3 Deals and Commercial Remedies

Financial deals also raise important questions of commercial remedies, as the saga of *R v Zinga* in 2014 shows.[15] Virgin Media commenced a private prosecution against Mr Zinga for selling set-top boxes to decode Virgin Media material without paying a subscription. Three issues in the case will interest commercial parties: the search warrant, the aborted compensation deal and the confiscation order that ultimately resulted.

First, in *R v Zinga*[16] in 2012, the police applied for a search warrant at the behest of the private prosecutor but failed to disclose to the Magistrates' Court the identity of, and the fact of their relationship with, the private prosecutor; this was potentially an abuse of process. The Court of Appeal accepted that the duty of full and frank disclosure that persists in respect of any application for a search warrant had been breached by the inexplicable failure to mention the identity of the intended prosecutor, but the convictions were unaffected as the Magistrates' Court would have issued the warrant even if full disclosure had been made.[17] Earlier case law on Premier League decoder boxes had seen search warrants declared unlawful where they did not mention a relevant defence under EU law,[18] but even there the illegally obtained material was still given to the private prosecutor.[19]

Secondly, Virgin Media entered into an agreement with the Commercial Partnership Manager of the Metropolitan Police for the police's

---

[14] Ibid [32].   [15] [2014] EWCA Crim 52, [2014] 1 WLR 2228.

[16] [2012] EWCA Crim 2357, [2013] Lloyd's Rep FC 102.

[17] See *R (On the Application of Golfrate Property Management Ltd v Southwark Crown Court)* [2014] EWHC 840 (Admin), [2014] 2 Cr App R 12 [22]–[26] (Lord Thomas CJ) for the correct test.

[18] *R (On the Application of Vuciterni) v Brent Magistrates' Court* [2012] EWHC 2140 (Admin), [2012] CTLC 171.

[19] *R (On the Application of Vuciterni) v Brent Magistrates' Court* [2013] EWHC 910 (Admin).

investigatory services required for confiscation proceedings. For this, Virgin Media would pay a charge *and* make an unconditional cash donation of 25 per cent of any money received through a compensation order.[20] This gift was to be handled through section 93(1) of the Police Act 1996, in a deliberate attempt to use the avenue raised but not approved in *Hounsham*.[21] The Court of Appeal found that this deal, and perhaps the putative *Hounsham* exception, clearly created an incentive to the police to investigate a specific crime and lose their independence.

Thirdly, ultimately, the deal's corrosive effect was rendered moot as Virgin Media abandoned the claim for the compensation order. The company feared the continuing doubts about the propriety of the arrangement and because the alternative, confiscation, could still destroy this business model. Perhaps the Metropolitan Police were not even consulted about this change, since the gift had been conditional on receiving funds through a compensation order. More likely, under the current Asset Recovery Incentivisation Scheme, the estimated 18.75 per cent each to the police and the CPS was sufficient.[22]

Lord Thomas CJ urged[23] the Home Office and ACPO (now the NPCC – the National Police Chiefs' Council) to come up with new guidelines on how to regulate financial arrangements between the police and commercial organisations. It does not appear that such guidance has been developed or released,[24] other than as noted in the case, a review by the Mayor of London's Office for payments to the Metropolitan Police of over £50,000.[25] The guidance on the CPS website dealing with 'Intellectual Property Crime' simply notes that the CPS must be, and must be seen to be, independent of any third parties assisting it.[26]

---

[20] *Zinga 2014* (n 15) [43].

[21] Assumed to be correct also in *R v Smallman* [2010] EWCA Crim 548.

[22] These are understood to be the figures under Home Office Circular 27 of 2005 Revised National Best Practice on Confiscation Order Enforcement, though a response to a Freedom of Information Act request suggests that these are the current figures and different to the 2005 Circular: letter from J Fanshaw to M Dyson (4 September 2015) <www.whatdotheyknow.com/request/284667/response/702064/attach/3/attachment.pdf>.

[23] *Zinga 2014* (n 15) [54].

[24] The closest guidance is a general one on charges for policing, focused on events: NPCC, 'National Policing Guidelines on Charging for Police Services' (April 2005). (July 2013), <www.npcc.police.uk/documents/finance/2015/NPCC%20Guidelines%20on%20Charging%20for%20Police%20Services.pdf>. 'The Guidelines will be revised in April 2017.'

[25] *Zinga 2014* (n 15) [51].

[26] See www.cps.gov.uk/legal/h_to_k/intellectual_property_crime/.

22.2.4 *Post-investigation Materials*

The next logical question is how much any valuable investigative materials and evidence can be accessed once the police investigation has been completed. In what might be the earliest case, *R v DPP, ex p Hallas* in 1988,[27] the applicant sought, amongst other things, an order of *mandamus* to force the DPP to disclose to her statements, evidence and photographs from the police investigation, held by the CPS. The applicant's son had been killed by a car whilst riding his motor cycle and she thought the driver should have been charged with a homicide offence, not merely offences related to dangerous and intoxicated driving. The DPP refused to disclose the materials, arguing it would not be in the public interest to do so. The Court of Appeal held the applicant had no right to the information.[28] No such right was conferred by section 6 of the Prosecution of Offences Act 1985, enshrining the common law right to bring a private prosecution. Macpherson J pointed out that her solicitors could collect that evidence as they regularly do,[29] the CPS having offered the contact details of witnesses. In theory, the CPS could also have charged for the information if it had wished, though that might suggest that the investigation and charging stages could be affected by perceived future profitability.

If *Hallas* is right that there is no general right to the information, what can create such a right? The best argument[30] is that the interests of justice would grant a right, once a prosecution, which is always in the name of the Crown, has begun. It would be given effect through the Criminal Procedure (Attendance of Witnesses) Act 1965, section 1, whereby the Crown Court can compel an individual to attend and/or hand over all relevant evidence. This can be seen in *Redford/Pawsey* one year later.[31] The CPS had refused to disclose the statements of witnesses who had not given their consent to disclosure. The Court of Appeal ordered their release: prosecuting counsel has a responsibility not only to the family of the victim but also the ordinary general responsibilities of prosecution counsel, which includes disclosing all unused witness statements as normal.[32] Compared to *Hallas*, the prosecution was already begun, so the 1965 Act was engaged and the Crown was, at least nominally, the prosecutor. In addition, the CPS had not claimed public policy was against disclosure, perhaps because the application was to force the

---

[27] (1988) 87 Cr App R 340 (QB).   [28] Ibid 342–43.   [29] Ibid 343.
[30] Cf Freedom of Information Act 2000, ss 30–32 shielding criminal investigations from requests under that Act.
[31] [1989] Crim LR 152 (CA).   [32] (1982) 74 Cr App R 302 (CC).

investigating officer to disclose material, rather than directly for the CPS to disclose material which could be used indirectly to cast doubt on its charging decisions.

The argument that material is confidential can still be a stumbling block. This can be seen from *Taylor v DSFO* in 1999,[33] where unused and potentially defamatory material from an earlier Serious Fraud Office (SFO) investigation was disclosed by the SFO to a defendant when later charged. The defendant and another sued in defamation, but ultimately the House of Lords held that, while the material should be disclosed, it would be subject to obligations of confidentiality: it could be used for their criminal defence but that excluded their use for a defamation action, particularly now that the amount of such material being disclosed was increasing.[34]

One of the first cases to reconsider the role that private bodies can play in the exercise by police officers of their public powers was *Scopelight v Chief Constable of Northumbria*.[35] The Federation Against Copyright Theft (FACT), a private commercial organisation operating as a trade body to counter copyright piracy, complained to Northumbria police about the applicant's website. The police obtained a search warrant under section 8 of the Police and Criminal Evidence Act (PACE) 1984. FACT officers were present as the warrant expressly permitted them to be. They took immediate possession of some evidence and later received more after the CPS declined to prosecute. The claimants commenced civil proceedings against the police and FACT claiming damages and the delivery up of what they said was by then wrongfully retained property. FACT then instigated criminal proceedings against the claimants for offences under the Copyright, Designs and Patents Act 1988, conspiracy to defraud and money-laundering. The claimants were successful at first instance, but the Court of Appeal allowed an appeal. The CPS was not the exclusive determiner of what was in the public interest, nor of retention of material under PACE. The police had to consider each case on its merits, including, *inter alia*, the identity and motive of the prosecutor, the gravity of the allegations about this defendant and the role of the material retained as well as why the CPS declined to prosecute contrasted with any public interest.[36]

Scopelight permits the police to investigate criminal offences, retain and then hand over material from those investigations for the purpose

[33] [1999] 2 AC 177 (HL).   [34] Ibid 209.   [35] [2009] EWCA Civ 1156, [2010] QB 438.
[36] Ibid [52]–[53].

of private prosecutions. FACT clearly benefited. It had not paid for the investigation, but had made the initial complaint and obtained evidence from it. Scopelight's claim, for its property and for damages, could not prevent the property being used as evidence in a private prosecution.

22.2.5   Investigation Conclusion

In summary:

(1) payments supporting police investigations have been condemned but convictions thereby obtained nonetheless affirmed;
(2) search warrants have been obtained discretely for private prosecutors and their information shared even when the warrant was unlawfully obtained;
(3) deals for compensation orders have so far been rejected;
(4) commercial decisions about prosecution cannot benefit from investigative materials, but once commenced, prosecutions are public matters and must receive all relevant evidence;
(5) the police can, where appropriate, hand over to a private prosecutor evidence they had obtained before the CPS declined to prosecute.

It is clearly controversial that a private party, commercial or not, buys access to the state's investigative powers if that in any way leads to a different form of state-sanctioned justice. The state already benefits by fines and by confiscating the assets of convicted defendants, but there is no benefit to a private person. A private person should only benefit if by his actions the criminal justice system benefits significantly more, financially or otherwise.

22.3   Procedure

22.3.1   Procedure Introduction

There can be obvious *commercial utility* in a criminal prosecution as well as, or instead of, a civil claim. First, criminal prosecutions, even without convictions, will likely cause more reputational harm to the defendant through greater media attention than civil cases. Secondly, criminal justice is usually meted out faster than civil justice. Thirdly, under the Civil Evidence Act 1968, a conviction is admissible as evidence of the facts upon which it was founded in a later civil claim on the same matter.

Indeed, it is strong evidence normally, and conclusive in defamation;[37] conversely, a civil judgment is not even admissible in later criminal proceedings. The two routes in the *criminal law system* are to 'encourage' a public prosecution, or for the commercial party to bring its own private prosecution. To *advance their interests* effectively, commercial parties must choose their route carefully, particularly since starting on one route will likely seal off the other through the doctrine of *autrefois acquit*, otherwise known as double jeopardy.[38]

22.3.2 'Encourage' Public Prosecution

When the state prosecutes, a private party will not have to expend its own time and resources but it will not have any control over the proceedings, only a right to be informed and consulted at key stages.[39] Sometimes commercial complexities may be beyond the resources of the state to investigate or understand as a commercial party does. A commercial party will be more likely to understand the civil concepts underlying the wrong, rather than be trying to fit that wrong into a public prosecutor's criminal-centred map of the law. Three recent examples follow, showing that the Crown can get civil aspects of criminal prosecutions wrong, with terminal results.[40]

22.3.2.1 Evans

The saga of *Evans & Others*[41] concerned an attempt by Celtic Energy to shed its obligations to restore land which had been used to mine coal. Those obligations were to the Coal Authority and the mineral planning authorities (MPAs), who could perform and force reimbursement in

---

[37] Matthew Dyson, 'Civil Law Responses to Criminal Judgments in England and Spain' (2012) 3 *Journal of European Tort Law* 308; Matthew Dyson and John Randall QC, 'Criminal Convictions and the Civil Courts' [2015] CLJ 78.

[38] *Connelly v DPP* [1964] AC 1254 (HL); *DPP v Humphrys* [1977] AC 1 (HL); unless there is significant new evidence: Criminal Justice Act 2003, Part 10.

[39] Victims Code of December 2013; Directive 2012/29/EU of the European Parliament and of the Council of 25 October 2012 establishing minimum standards on the rights, support and protection of victims of crime, and replacing Council Framework Decision 2001/220/JHA [2012] OJ L315/57.

[40] See too *Vuciterni* [2013] (n 19) [33]–[34].

[41] See (1) *R v Evans & Others* [2014] 1 WLR 2817 (CC) ('the Dismissal Application'); (2) *Evans & Others v SFO* [2014] EWHC 3803 (QB), [2015] 1 WLR 3526 ('the Voluntary Bill of Indictment Refusal'); (3) *R v Evans & Others* [2015] EWHC 263 (QB), [2015] 1 WLR 3595 ('the Costs Preliminary Issues Ruling'); and (4) *Evans & Others v SFO* [2015] EWHC 1525 (QB), [2015] 3 Costs LR 557 ('Costs Assessment Ruling').

default; likely in the tens of millions of pounds. Celtic sought to divest itself of the restoration obligation by selling the freehold titles to the land, thinking the obligation would attach to the land. Shell corporations in the British Virgin Islands, effectively under Celtic personnel's control, bought the sites for £1 each. Ultimately, the officers of Celtic received a substantial windfall.

On these facts, the prosecution charged officers of Celtic, their solicitors and their counsel with being parties to a conspiracy to defraud. The defendants successfully had the charges dismissed, featuring complex planning, property and criminal law.[42] The Crown had failed to specify the wrong involved in the conspiracy to defraud and how the victims, the Coal Authority and MPAs would suffer loss by it. A second attempt, when the Crown sought a voluntary bill of indictment, was better argued, suggesting unlawfulness under section 418 of the Companies Act 2006,[43] a *criminal offence*, and/or section 423 of the Insolvency Act 1986,[44] a *civil wrong*. It is worthy of note that, in preparing for the application for a voluntary bill of indictment, the prosecution instructed *commercial* junior counsel, who may have been responsible for this re-imaging of the prosecution's case. This second attempt also failed because Fulford LJ saw no reason why those arguments could not have been mounted at the dismissal stage. If they had been, then the outcome of the dismissal application could have been very different.

22.3.2.2   Quillan

In *Quillan*,[45] like *Evans*, 'the facts are complex as are the issues of law'.[46] Nine defendants were charged with counts of conspiracy to cheat, conspiracy to defraud, conspiracy to launder money and false accounting. At the close of the prosecution's somewhat confusing case,[47] the defendants successfully pleaded that there was no case to answer. The main defendants were independent financial advisors who promoted pension schemes whereby a series of loans would be taken, and thus shares bought, from other defendants, ultimately receiving tax relief to be

---

[42] *Evans* (Costs Assessment Ruling) (n 41) [21(ii)].

[43] Section 418 requires directors to disclose certain information to auditors, including this sale.

[44] Section 423 concerns 'transactions defrauding creditors', here a sale at an undervalue.

[45] [2015] EWCA Crim 538, [2015] 2 Cr App R 3.

[46] David Ormerod, 'R. v Quillan (Gary): Appeal – Ruling of no Case to Answer' [2015] Crim LR 618, 622.

[47] *Quillan* (n 45) [47].

further invested. From the clients' perspective, it was risk-free as they never used their own money but did receive payments for lending their names; from the state's, it was a sham since the only new money in the scheme was from the tax relief.[48] The prosecution ultimately alleged two contradictory bases.

The first argument was that the tax relief had been *unlawfully* obtained by cheating Her Majesty's Revenue and Customs (HMRC). This did not succeed because the Crown merely called the transactions 'shams', without proving that word's 'well-established legal meaning':[49] that 'the contributions [from the clients] lacked any true legal substance'[50] because this would have required that the clients were conscious partners in the sham transactions. The court was particularly critical of the prosecution's lack of specificity in the sham:

> Yet the prosecution had throughout studiously refrained from alleging that the clients were necessarily implicated in the alleged fraud ... For this reason ... the sham allegation is in our judgment a hopeless one which could never have been permitted to go before the jury.[51]

The second argument was that if the tax relief has been lawfully obtained, the defendants had conspired to defraud either (i) HMRC, or (ii) the client, by *unlawfully* extracting the relief from the scheme. However, neither party suffered a proven loss.

If the public prosecutor had appreciated the requirements that needed to be met before a sham trust could be established he or she might have avoided these difficulties; the prosecutor might also have charged the *clients* with conspiracy to cheat.

22.3.2.3   GH

In *GH*,[52] the defendant was charged with entering into or becoming concerned in a money-laundering arrangement, contrary to section 328(1) of the POCA. The prosecution case was that B ran various websites offering cut-price but fraudulent motor insurance. At B's request, GH opened two bank accounts to channel the money from B's customers to B. The prosecution contended that whilst GH may not have known the details of B's fraud, he must have known or suspected that B had some criminal purpose in mind. Ultimately the Supreme Court overturned the trial judge's finding of no

---

[48] Ibid [57]–[72].   [49] Ibid [86].   [50] Ibid [88].   [51] Ibid [89].
[52] [2015] UKSC 24, [2015] 1 WLR 2126.

case to answer, but it did so despite the poor phrasing of the prosecution's case. The issue was the identification of the 'criminal property': the Crown argued that the property was criminal on being paid in, as it was a 'chose in action'. The Supreme Court found this bland assertion was underargued, as it would have required a bilateral contract, which the Crown had not attempted to prove. Lord Toulson noted that the prosecution had not only to present the case:

> [I]n a readily comprehensible way . . . but also to ensure that its tackle is properly in order. Abstract references to a chose in action, without the basis being clearly and properly identified and articulated, is a recipe for confusion.[53]

Thankfully for the prosecution, the court found that once the money was in GH's account, it was criminal property so the offence could still be made out.

22.3.2.4   Conclusions

In these three examples, the prosecution relied on abstract references to 'unlawfulness' (*Evans*), 'sham' (*Quillan*) and 'chose in action' (*GH*) to make out its case. It did not occur to the prosecution in *Evans* until it was too late that the unlawfulness it needed to find could have come from beyond the realm of the criminal law, as is the case with section 423 of the Insolvency Act 1986. It never occurred to the prosecution in *Quillan* and *GH* that the civil concepts it was seeking to invoke were more than just convenient labels but well-known doctrines that needed to be understood and proved. The failure in *Evans* and *Quillan* was fatal, but not so in *GH*. The lesson is that criminal lawyers are not always adept at understanding the circumstances in which the civil law can be helpful in a criminal case (*Evans*) and the circumstances in which it should be avoided (*GH*) or at least treated with real caution (*Quillan*). Commercial parties might have the resources and understanding to get it right first time.

22.3.3   Commence Private Prosecution

To retain control of proceedings, a commercial party will have to bring a private prosecution. However, a prosecutor is not akin to a claimant; there are certain responsibilities the prosecutor must assume that are entirely alien to the civil litigator. There are also different and perhaps

---

[53] Ibid [42].

surprising procedural and evidential rules.[54] One potentially attractive difference is a generous costs regime.

22.3.3.1 Definition of Private Prosecutor

Before 1880, most prosecutions were private; brought by the victim under various incentives and pressures from the state.[55] From the 1880s to the late 1970s, police forces were the predominant prosecutors, supplemented by the Director of Public Prosecutions (DPP).[56] From the 1970s, many police forces had their own department of solicitors to prosecute their cases and the modern system of prosecution has developed from there.[57] Under the Prosecution of Offences Act 1985, most prosecutions in England and Wales are brought by the CPS, under the guidance of the DPP, but the right to bring a private prosecution persists. In *Jones v Whalley*,[58] a private prosecution for assault occasioning actual bodily harm, Lord Mance reflected that: 'The right of the private prosecution operates and has been explained at the highest level as a safeguard against wrongful refusal or failure by public prosecuting authorities to institute proceedings.'[59]

The 'privateness' of the prosecutor has many implications.[60] Two important limitations are, first, that a private person cannot usually conduct the litigation itself, a lawyer is required;[61] and secondly, the private prosecutor has no special power to arrest and charge an

---

[54] For some examples of differences, in rules and in legal culture, see Matthew Dyson and John Randall QC, 'England's Splendid Isolation' in Matthew Dyson (ed), *Comparing Tort and Crime* (Cambridge University Press 2015).

[55] Matthew Dyson, 'The Timing of Tortious and Criminal Actions for the Same Wrong' [2012] CLJ 86, 106–07.

[56] Created by the Prosecution of Offences Act 1879, s 7; amended by Prosecution of Offences Act 1908, s 2(3), reaffirming the existing right to bring private prosecutions, but noting that the DPP may take over the proceedings at any time. The purpose of this provision was 'to ensure that cases which ought in the public interest to be pursued were not abandoned or inefficiently conducted, whether through lack of means, inertia or any other reason': *R (On the Application of Gujra) v CPS* [2012] UKSC 52; [2013] 1 AC 484 [93] (Lord Mance).

[57] Douglas Hay, 'Controlling the English Prosecutor' (1983) 21(1) Osgoode Hall LJ 165.

[58] [2006] UKHL 41, [2007] 1 AC 63.   [59] Ibid [43].

[60] *R (Barry) v Birmingham Magistrates' Court* [2009] EWHC 2571 (Admin), [2010] 1 Cr App R 13 [13].

[61] Many private prosecutions are initiated by the laying of an information before a justice of the peace in the Magistrates' Court. This is an activity reserved for authorised persons, under Legal Services Act 2007, s 14 and Sch 2, s 4(1)(a); cf the mistake by the private commercial party which voided the proceedings in *Media Protection Services Ltd v Crawford* [2012] EWHC 2373 (Admin), [2013] 1 WLR 1068.

individual with a criminal offence. Instead, a private prosecutor must lay an information before the Magistrates' Court,[62] thereby inviting the court to either issue a summons requiring the suspect to attend court on a particular day upon pain of arrest, or issue a warrant for the arrest of the suspect so that the police can use their statutory powers to arrest him and bring him before the court.[63]

22.3.3.2   Limits on the Right of Private Prosecution

The commercial party that becomes a private prosecutor will need to appreciate that the *right* to commence a private prosecution, whilst constitutionally important, is not unfettered.[64]

First, some offences can only be initiated by certain prosecutorial bodies. A key example is where a statute creating an offence also limits who can prosecute it.[65] The Supreme Court has recently resisted efforts to read one such provision as impliedly *excluding* all other offences, since of course such a designated prosecutor can, unless otherwise stated, act as a private prosecutor.[66]

Secondly, there are certain offences that private citizens can only prosecute with the consent of either the DPP or the Law Officers, meaning either the Attorney General (AG) or the Solicitor General.[67]

Thirdly, the DPP has a power under section 6(2) of the Prosecution of Offences Act 1985 to take over the conduct of any prosecution initiated by a private prosecutor and either prosecute the case herself or discontinue it. As of June 2009,[68] the same test has been applied to a CPS

---

[62] Section 1(1) of the Magistrates' Court Act 1980; see Part 7 of the Criminal Procedure Rules 2015.

[63] A public prosecutor might also use a written charge and a requisition, pursuant to s 29 of the Criminal Justice Act 2003.

[64] See generally, Law Commission, *Consents to Prosecution* (Law Com No 255, 1998), subject to some later reforms.

[65] See *R v Cubitt* [1889] 22 QBD 622, where a private prosecution under the Sea Fisheries Act 1883 was precluded by these words in s 11 of the statute: 'The provisions of this Act . . . shall be enforced by sea-fishery officers.' For cases where similar wording led to the opposite conclusion, see *R v Stewart* [1896] 1 QB 300 (QB) and *RSPCA v Woodhouse* [1984] CLY 693 (CC).

[66] *R v Rollins* [2010] 1 WLR 1922, regarding the Financial Services and Markets Act 2000, s 401(2) designating, *inter alia*, the Financial Services Authority (now the Financial Conduct Authority).

[67] 'Consents to Prosecute' (CPS, undated) <www.cps.gov.uk/legal/a_to_c/consent_to_prosecute>; see also Law Commission (n 64) Appendix A.

[68] 'Private Prosecutions' (CPS, undated) <www.cps.gov.uk/legal/p_to_r/private_prosecutions>. This followed a recommendation of the Auld Review of the Criminal Courts of England and Wales (September 2001) ch 10, para 50.

decision to prosecute as much as to the DPP's decision to take over a private prosecution.[69] This 'Full Code Test'[70] requires, first, a reasonable prospect the defendant will be convicted of the offence it is proposed to charge him with; and, secondly, that it is in the public interest to prosecute. If the Full Code Test is *not* met, the DPP can take over a private prosecution and discontinue it. If the Full Code Test is met, the DPP can take over a private prosecution and continue with it if there is a particular need for her to do so, which will generally be the case if the allegations are serious or there are issues with disclosure etc. While private prosecutors do not need to notify the DPP of their prosecution, they will still need to carefully phrase their case, to show the need for the prosecution to take place lest it be taken over and discontinued.

Fourthly, the AG can terminate a private prosecution by entering a *nolle prosequi* in relation to any indictable matter before the Crown Court. This will have the effect of staying the proceedings, but it does not amount to an acquittal.

Fifthly, vexatious prosecutors (whether against the same or different persons) can be barred from further prosecutions.[71]

Sixthly, the justice of the peace before whom an information is laid may refuse, in the exercise of her discretion, to issue a summons or a warrant. This might be on the grounds that the application is frivolous, vexatious or an abuse of process.[72] In addition, the magistrates or the court clerk should be satisfied that the information alleges an offence known to law; that it was served within any applicable time limit; and that the person laying the information has authority to prosecute that offence.[73] If a public prosecution has been discontinued and a private prosecutor lays an information for the justices to issue a summons in respect of the same offence, there is no rule which requires the justices to refuse to issue in the absence of special circumstances,[74] but special circumstances will need to exist before the justices should issue a summons on the application of the private prosecutor if the public prosecution is *still* ongoing.[75]

---

[69] *R v Director of Public Prosecutions, ex p Duckenfield* [2000] 1 WLR 55 (QB).

[70] Issued pursuant Prosecution of Offences Act 1985, s 10.

[71] Senior Courts Act 1981, s 42.

[72] *R v West London Metropolitan Stipendiary Magistrate, ex p Klahn* [1979] 1 WLR 933 (QB).

[73] *R v Gateshead Justices, ex p Tesco Stores Ltd* [1981] QB 470 (QB) 478; *R (Latham) v Northampton Magistrates' Court* [2008] EWHC 245 (Admin).

[74] *Duckenfield* (n 69).

[75] *R (Charlson) v Guildford Magistrates' Court* [2006] EWHC 2318 (Admin), [2006] 1 WLR 3494 [19].

Finally, and importantly, as with a public prosecution, a private prosecution can be stayed by the court as an abuse of the process of the court where the offender cannot receive a fair trial or where it would be unfair to try to him.[76]

In addition, there is a more general obligation on the private prosecutor to behave as a minister of justice, not as a party to litigation. This principle has been neatly expressed by the Supreme Court of Canada in *R v Boucher*:

> Counsel have a duty to see that all available legal proof of the facts is presented: it should be done firmly and pressed to its legitimate strength, but it must also be done fairly. The role of the prosecutor excludes any notion of winning or losing; his function is a matter of public duty that which in civil life there can be none charged with greater personal responsibility. It is to be efficiently performed with an ingrained sense of the dignity, the seriousness and the justness of judicial proceedings.[77]

The principle, and attendant, if potentially vague, obligations, apply in England and Wales to private prosecutors.[78] Private prosecutors must act with the same care and dispatch as the public prosecutor. They must have credible evidence of the offender's guilt and be motivated, in part at least, by selflessness rather than selfishness. As Latham LJ noted in *R (Dacre) v City of Westminster Magistrates' Court*:

> [I]t is inevitable that many private prosecutions will be brought with mixed motives ... The neighbour who sought to take out a private summons for assault would not merely have the public interest as his motive.[79]

It follows that mixed motives on the part of the private prospector will not risk the prosecution being stayed as an abuse of process so long as the 'improper' motive is not the primary motive.[80]

In practice, it will be lawyers who litigate and thus bear these responsibilities. Commercial clients cannot instruct their lawyers to ignore these responsibilities, such as by failing to disclose relevant information or call credible witnesses.

---

[76] *R v Horseferry Road Magistrates' Court, ex p Bennett* [1994] 1 AC 42 (HL). This also potentially raises the risk of a civil claim for malicious prosecution.

[77] [1955] SCR 16, 23–24; affirmed by the Supreme Court of Canada in *R v Cook* (1997) 114 CCC (3d) 481; see also Superior Court of Justice of Ontario in *R v Suarez-Noa*, 2015 ONSC 3823 [6].

[78] *R v Belmarsh Magistrates' Court, ex p Watts* [1999] 2 Cr App R 188, 200.

[79] [2008] EWHC 1667 (Admin), [2009] 1 WLR 2241 [30].

[80] *Re Serif Systems Ltd* [1997] CLY 1373 (QB) (Auld LJ); *Speed Seal Products Ltd v Paddington* [1985] 1 WLR 1327 (CA) 1335 (Fox LJ).

22.3.3.3 Costs

Private prosecutions must initially be privately funded,[81] but criminal judges have a discretion to award costs and the outcome can be quite generous.

First, the risk of paying for the defendant's costs is low. The prosecutor will only pay the defendant's costs in cases of demonstrably poor litigation practice. Under section 19 of the Prosecution of Offences Act 1985, the court can order that a party who has incurred costs as a result of an unnecessary or improper act or omission by, or on behalf of, another party to the proceedings, should be indemnified by that party. The error must be 'clear and stark',[82] but if so, reasonable expenses will be ordered, even before the case has been completed. Section 19 is reinforced by Regulations[83] and the Criminal Procedure Rules.[84] Of course, all these rules are in practice limited by the need for the defaulting party to have the means to indemnify. In one recent case, a swingeing costs order was made even against the SFO.[85]

Secondly, no matter the outcome of the prosecution, the state allows prosecutors to apply to central funds to be indemnified against reasonable costs, including for witnesses, concerned in bringing *indictable offences*. Under section 17 of the 1985 Act, the general rule is that the court must make an order, but in the case of a private prosecutor it may decline to do so if, for example, the prosecution was started or continued unreasonably.[86] The courts have confirmed that they will scrutinise the costs carefully, including testing the market and examining the Ministry of Justice's guidance on reasonable rates, as well as steps taken to involve the public prosecutor.[87] This includes the fact that all other things being equal, a private prosecution would be more expensive.[88]

Thirdly, if the defendant is found guilty, the private prosecutor can make an application under section 18 of the 1985 Act

---

[81] Legal Aid, Sentencing and Punishment of Offenders Act 2012, Sch 3.

[82] *R v Evans* (Costs Preliminary Issues Ruling) (n 41) [148(vi)].   [83] SI 1986/1335, reg 3.

[84] Part 45.

[85] *Evans* (Costs Assessment Ruling) (n 41), [148(vi)]). For an illustration of a case where a section 19 order was made against a private prosecutor, see *R (on the application of Aisling Hubert) v Manchester Crown Court* [2015] EWHC 3734 (Admin).

[86] Practice Direction (Costs in Criminal Proceedings) [2014] EWCA Crim 1570, para 2.6.4; *R v Esher and Walton Justices, ex p Victor Value & Co Ltd* [1967] 111 SJ 473 (QB).

[87] *R (On the Application of Virgin Media Ltd) v Zinga* [2014] EWCA Crim 1823, [2015] 1 Cr App R 2 [22(i)], [45] and [42].

[88] Ibid [42] and [45]. The Legal Aid Agency has directed the National Taxing Team to disallow any part of a claim for costs under section 17 that is referable to the costs of an investigation (as opposed to a prosecution) carried out by a private prosecutor where the proceedings were commenced after 1 September 2016: see <www.gov.uk/government/uploads/system/uploads/attachment_data/file/541880/investigative-expenses-guidance.pdf>. The Legal Aid Agency's position is that such costs should be recovered from the convicted defendant.

for just and reasonable costs against the offender, subject to his means.[89]

22.3.4   Procedure Conclusion

The commercial party who resolves to engage the mechanics of the criminal justice system faces a finely balanced choice between prompting the public prosecutor into action and taking that action for itself. There may be circumstances where a failed private prosecution could still lead to a successful public prosecution, and vice versa, but they are rare. The balance is in part a trade-off of control against effort and risk. The generous criminal regime appears to be a particularly weighty consideration.

22.4   Remedies

22.4.1   Remedies Introduction

The remedies of Magistrates' and Crown Courts can provide significant *commercial utility* in speed, simplicity and cost. For example, compensation and restitution orders provide quick and effective solutions to simple cases, avoiding the need to go to a civil court. They provide compensation for harm suffered even where there is no underlying civil wrong actionable. Confiscation is a powerful tool to remove the gain from wrongdoing, breaking illegal business models though without directly benefiting the commercial party. Criminal remedies are far wider[90] and more directly coercive than civil law remedies, since civil law largely looks to damages and injunctions. Yet *criminal law* principles require remedies to be proportional to the wrong and many are limited by the defendant's means. A criminal court would imprison a defendant, but would not seek their bankruptcy. However, criminal orders also cumulate so *a commercial party might cause* the defendant to lose even more than in a civil claim. For instance, if a defendant obtains £1 million by way of fraud but his assets are £4 million then he could lose most of that in the criminal courts – a fine of £1 million, say, confiscation order of £1 million (his benefit), compensation of £1 million (the loss) and prosecution costs on top.

22.4.2   Criminal Law Remedies

Commercial parties may also be interested in what the criminal courts can award as 'remedies'. 'Remedy' in this context means a disposition of

---

[89] Costs Practice Direction (n 86) para 3.4.
[90] Only the most important can be discussed here.

the criminal court in response to a criminal offence being established. Remedies in English criminal courts are in the control of the court, but certain orders are on application. The prosecutor cannot instruct the court, nor agree with the defence, on what the sentence will be.[91] The prosecutor cannot therefore 'settle' as if it were civil litigation, but can offer up negotiations with the defence to the court's scrutiny.[92]

22.4.2.1 Compensation Orders

The award of financial compensation for harm wrongfully inflicted is a classic domain not of criminal law but of private law. The focus here will be on tort, such as the economic torts, the tort of deceit, or negligence.

English law has historically been reluctant to involve criminal courts in awarding compensation.[93] It was not until 1972 that the first general power to order compensation was created. The power is now found in the Powers of Criminal Courts (Sentencing) Act 2000 (PCC(S)A 2000), sections 130–34. Under section 130, criminal courts are able to award a compensation order for 'any personal injury, loss or damage resulting from that offence or any other offence which is taken into consideration by the court in determining sentence'.[94] There are five key ways in which compensation orders differ from tort claims.

First, and most importantly, compensation orders for crime are in many ways narrower than compensation for civil claims. In particular, the means of the defendant will be taken into account in the criminal law,[95] while not in tort law.[96] Indeed, a criminal court must not make any financial order, including any compensation order, against a defendant, which he cannot reasonably afford to pay either immediately or by instalments over a reasonable and finite period.[97] Moreover, courts will not make compensation orders where the case before the criminal court is not 'clear' and would require time, effort and expertise to solve

---

[91] See, in particular, the views of Thomas LJ in *R v Innospec Ltd* [2010] Lloyd's Rep FC 462.
[92] A private prosecutor probably cannot enter into a deferred prosecution agreement either.
[93] See generally, Matthew Dyson, 'Connecting Tort and Crime: Comparative Legal History in England and Spain since 1850' [2008–2009] *Cambridge Yearbook of European Legal Studies* 247, 248–63.
[94] Exceptions exist for road traffic offences and homicide.
[95] PCC(S)A 2000 s 130(11); *R v Carrington* [2014] EWCA Crim 325, [2014] 2 Cr App R (S) 41 (loans cannot be required).
[96] For example *Rookes v Barnard* [1964] AC 1129 (HL) 1128.
[97] Generally orders are not made to run for more than twelve to eighteen months. For example *R v Yehou* [1997] 2 Cr App R (S) 48 (CA); cf *R v Ganyo* [2012] 1 Cr App R (S) 108 (CA).

uncertain facts or law.[98] While, 'clear' financial losses are recoverable,[99] in practice such claims will need to be very carefully considered, as *Zinga* shows.

Secondly, the victim no longer has to be directly involved in the claim: the order is available 'on application or otherwise', as victims had too often missed the opportunity to apply.[100] Judges must explain why they are not making an order if they do not.[101] Yet effective compensation will require clear evidence of a kind best supplied by the commercial party not a less interested public prosecutor.[102]

Thirdly, criminal compensation has recognised different heads of claim from those available in tort. In particular, criminal compensation might be available where no tortious liability exists. This was made clear by the case of *Chappell*, on fraudulent VAT payments, in 1985:

> It does not however follow that the criminal remedy is the mirror of an underlying civil remedy. Indeed it plainly is not so, for the Court has a discretion ... and will take into account factors such as the offender's means and the moral desirability or otherwise of making him pay.[103]

Fourthly, some component parts of the law are different, such as causation. A classic example is a conviction under the Trade Descriptions Act 1968, as in *R v Thomson Holidays*.[104] There the Court of Appeal (Criminal Division) held that civil rules of causation were not to be imported into the criminal law.[105]

Fifthly, enforcement differs from civil law.[106] English compensation orders are enforced in the Magistrates' Court, irrespective of the court in which they were made, by basically criminal procedures, to that extent making life much easier for the victim. However, all the sanctions are limited by the assets of the defendant. Distraint of goods is available, as are civil enforcement orders like a charging order. However, there must

---

[98] For example *R v Crown Court at Liverpool & Another, ex p Cooke* [1997] 1 WLR 700 (QB) 708–09.

[99] Cf *R v Berwick* [2007] EWCA Crim 3297, [2008] 2 Cr App R (S) 31 and *Hyde v Emery* (1984) 6 Cr App R (S) 206 (CA) with *R v Pola* [2009] EWCA Crim 655, [2010] 1 Cr App R (S) 6; they were originally excluded as too complex: Kenneth Younger, *Advisory Council on the Penal System Report on Reparation by the Offender* (HMSO 1970) [59].

[100] Matthew Dyson, 'Connecting Tort and Crime' (n 93) 259–60.

[101] PCC(S)A 2000 s 130(3).

[102] Such as the employee theft case of *R (Faithfull) v Crown Court at Ipswich* [2007] EWHC 2763 (Admin), [2008] 1 WLR 1636 [31]–[32].

[103] *R v Chappell* (1985) 80 Cr App R 31 (CA) 34–35.   [104] [1974] QB 592 (CA).

[105] Ibid 599.

[106] See generally *R v Jawad* [2013] EWCA Crim 644, [2013] 1 WLR 3861 [16]–[19].

first be a further means of enquiry before they are used. If imprisonment in default is ordered, then the obligation to pay the compensation order is extinguished.

22.4.2.2 Confiscation Orders

While compensation focuses on the victim's *loss*, confiscation seeks to deprive the defendant of his *gain* by forfeiting its value to the state.[107] In addition, a commercial party might seek to incentivise the state, as it shares out confiscation orders made within the criminal justice agencies. Yet can *private prosecutors* seek an order from which they cannot personally benefit? *Zinga* confirmed that they could: the Court of Appeal held that 'prosecutor' in section 6 of the POCA should be given its natural meaning and include a private prosecutor. In fact, there are good grounds to doubt that this was the intention of Parliament,[108] but it is a sensible enough rule.

Confiscation is both controversial and relatively new,[109] created by statute after a failed attempt to forfeit drug-related property.[110] Under the POCA, Part 2,[111] benefits from offending can be stripped and paid to the state, subject to the defendant still having sufficient assets to do so. A person benefits from an offence if they 'obtain property as a result of or in connection with' that offence according to section 76(4). This definition is itself very broad, going beyond simple net benefit[112] and, if multiple defendants obtain property together, they are each deemed to have obtained all of it.[113] A number of presumptions operate to make these powers even broader. For instance, with a number of serious offences, 'a criminal lifestyle' enables the court to assume that everything which has passed through the defendant's hands in the six years

---

[107] See generally Mark Sutherland Williams, Michael Hopmeier and Rupert Jones (eds), *The Proceeds of Crime* (4th edn, Oxford University Press 2013).

[108] Where a court orders confiscation of its own motion, a private prosecutor is statutorily unable to carry out any financial investigations required: Leonard Leigh, 'Private Prosecutors and Public Authorities: Co-operation in Law Enforcement' [2014] Crim LR 439, 441–43.

[109] Drug Trafficking Offences Act 1986, expanded by the Criminal Justice Act 1988 to any indictable offence and some summary offences.

[110] See *R v Cuthbertson* [1981] AC 470 (HL).

[111] Related powers also exist under the Misuse of Drugs Act 1971 and the Terrorism Act 2000.

[112] Peter Alldridge, 'The Limits of Confiscation' [2011] Crim LR 827, 835–42.

[113] *R v Jennings* [2008] UKHL 29, [2008] 1 AC 1046; though recovery will be not be enforced to the extent that a sum has been recovered from another in respect of the same benefit: *R v Ahmad and Ahmad* [2014] UKSC 36, [2015] AC 299.

preceding the institution of proceedings, together with everything he currently owns, was derived from criminal activity unless he can prove the contrary or show that 'there would be a serious risk of injustice' if that assumption were made.[114] There are extensive supporting powers, such as disclosure and restraint.[115] Somewhat surprisingly, where confiscation does not follow a conviction, there is no need for any offence ever to have been proven while the profits of crime are apparently being stripped from the defendant.[116]

While criminal in nature, confiscation proceedings have the civil standard of proof, more permissive rules of evidence (apparently those of a sentencing hearing) and are technically not penal,[117] so defendants do not benefit from the protection of Arts 6.2 and 6.3 of the European Convention on Human Rights (ECHR).[118] However, the ECHR has been used to require proportionality between the Act and the confiscation order: a 'sticking plaster' over this 'serious mess'[119] according to Peter Alldridge. The Supreme Court's decision in *R v Waya*[120] has been described as a seismic shift,[121] generally leading to lower awards but with somewhat uncertain principles.[122]

22.4.2.3   Restitution Orders

Of greater value to potential civil litigants have been criminal powers to restore specific property.[123] Civil courts have generally found it more convenient to order the value of the property to be paid. Criminal courts routinely order specific restoration, perhaps removing some of the pressure for a civil power to restore specific property by dealing with the most obvious and egregious instance of a lack of a civil right to recover the property (identifiable, movable property in the hands of a state agent). For commercial parties, restitution orders are perhaps most useful for

---

[114] POCA, s 10.   [115] Sutherland Williams et al (n 107) chs 2–4.

[116] A growing trend: Colin King, 'Civil Forfeiture and Article 6 of the ECHR: Due Process Implications for England & Wales and Ireland' (2014) 34(4) LS 371, 372–76 and see *Serious Organised Crime Agency v Gale* [2011] UKSC 49, [2011] 1 WLR 2760.

[117] In the sense that they do not affect the defendant's sentence: POCA, s 13(4).

[118] *HM Advocate v McIntosh (No 1)* [2001] 3 WLR 107 [14]–[28].

[119] Peter Alldridge, 'Proceeds of Crime Law since 2003 – Two Key Areas' [2014] Crim LR 171, 187.

[120] [2012] UKSC 51, [2013] 1 AC 294.

[121] *R v Harvey* [2013] EWCA Crim 1104, [2005] EWCA Crim 1366 [38].

[122] See generally, Alldridge, 'Proceeds of Crime Law since 2003' (n 119).

[123] See generally Matthew Dyson and Sarah Green, 'The Properties of the Law: Restoring Personal Property through Crime and Tort' in Matthew Dyson (ed), *Unravelling Tort and Crime* (Cambridge University Press 2014).

specific goods not easily obtainable in the market and are easier than distraint.

While technically not 'restitution orders' a related form of order is a disposition under the Police (Property) Act 1897. Where property comes into the possession of the police, such as from an investigation, but also where handed in as lost, a magistrate can order the disposition of the property to anyone appropriate, usually the apparent owner. That person becomes owner in law after six months' possession. Under POCA 2002 , ch 3, an application to a Magistrates' Court can be made for the seizure, detention, and forfeiture of cash.

22.4.2.4 The Hierarchy of Criminal Orders

If a defendant cannot satisfy all the orders that could be made against him, the criminal courts must prioritise in the following way.

(1) Compensation order.
  (a) It takes priority over a fine;[124] where compensation and confiscation are ordered 'back-to-back' the compensation order will first be paid out of the confiscation order, and any remaining assets go to satisfy the confiscation order.[125]
  (b) Someone who has received a compensation order can still bring a claim in tort or contract later, and be awarded damages in full, but they will not *recover* any sum already paid under the order.[126] *However*, if a confiscation order has already been given effect, there is no retroactive reallocation of those assets in order to satisfy a later compensation order or later civil claim,[127] the only hope would be a variation of the confiscation order before full enforcement. This is particularly the case since compensation orders are often not fully enforced. In *R v Jawad*,[128] a confiscation order for £174,000 was made against the defendant after conviction for frauds against Lloyds Bank. It included the loss caused to the bank. Lloyds then sought and was granted a compensation order for its loss of £64,000. The Court of Appeal ordered that if the defendant paid the compensation order in full within 28 days that amount would be deducted from the confiscation order.[129]

---

[124] PCC(S)A 2000, s 130(12).   [125] POCA, s 13(5)–(6).   [126] PCC(S)A 2000, s 134.
[127] See, for example, *R (Faithfull)* (n 102).
[128] *R v Jawad* [2013] EWCA Crim 644, [2013] 1 WLR 3861.   [129] Ibid [27].

(c) There is no double punishment from awarding exemplary damages and subsequently a confiscation order. This happened, for instance, in 2005 when the bookseller Borders obtained £280,000 in compensatory damages, £100,000 in punitive damages *and* a confiscation order was made against a street trader selling stock unlawfully obtained from Borders.[130] Though in such parallel actions confiscation was said to do better than punitive damages,[131] such a claim might be harder to make after *Waya* held that confiscation was not meant to punish.

(2) Between a fine and confiscation, the difference is rather in the mode of calculation (statutory versus the defendant's gain), the mode of application (sentencing versus the prosecutor's application) and the ultimate allocation within the criminal justice system (state versus state agencies).

(3) Compensation orders may be used instead of other punishments, as can fines, though they are typically additional to other dispositions save in minor cases. Confiscation is technically not a sentence,[132] so will not affect other personal sanctions, such as imprisonment.

22.4.3 Other Remedies

Commercial parties might be interested in at least two injunctive orders in the criminal courts.

22.4.3.1 Serious Crime Prevention Orders (SCPOs)

These orders[133] can be imposed by the Crown Court to protect the public by preventing, restricting, or disrupting an offender's involvement in serious crime. The orders can last for up to five years[134] and can be imposed on individuals, corporations, partnerships and unincorporated associations.[135] The DPP or Director of the SFO can apply after the conviction of a principal or facilitator of fraud, money laundering, public revenue offences, copyright offences, environmental offences and computer misuse offences, *or where conduct was likely to facilitate one of these offences.* SCPOs can prohibit or restrict financial dealings,

---

[130] *Borders (UK) Ltd v Commissioner of Police of the Metropolis and Another* [2005] EWCA Civ 197, [2005] Po LR 1; cf poor phrasing of cases in section 22.3.2.
[131] Ibid [41]. [132] Save in terms of appeal jurisdiction: *R (Faithfull)* (n 102).
[133] Part 1 of the Serious Crime Act 2007. [134] Ibid s 16. [135] Ibid s 5(3)–(4).

working arrangements, access to premises (including a dwelling) and travel arrangements as well as order the surrender of documents. Those documents can then be disclosed to others to check their accuracy and prevent crime.[136] As the Court of Appeal emphasised in *R v Seale*,[137] SCPOs: 'can only be made for the statutory purpose: they are designed to be preventative rather than punitive; they must be necessary and proportionate; and they must be enforceable'.

22.4.3.2 Disqualification as Company Director

Whenever an offender is convicted of an indictable offence in connection with the promotion, formation, management, liquidation or striking-off of any company, the court may make a disqualification order[138] against him that:

(1) he shall not be a director of a company, act as a receiver of a company's property or in any way, be concerned in the promotion, formation or management of a company unless (in each case) he has the leave of the court; and
(2) he shall not act as an insolvency practitioner.

The purpose of such an order is to protect the public from directors who abuse their positions 'for reasons of dishonesty, or naivety or incompetence'.[139] The Crown Court's order lasts up to fifteen years; breaching an order is a criminal offence which carries a maximum sentence of two years' imprisonment.[140]

22.4.4 *Remedies Conclusion*

There are a wide range of criminal and non-criminal powers which can achieve significant commercial goals, from restoration of property to disqualifying individuals from running companies. Even where a commercial party is not directly involved in the litigation, they must take care that their interests in compensation are being respected within the state's efforts to enforce the criminal law and deter criminal behaviour.

---

[136] Serious Crime Act 2015, s 50, which inserted s 5A into the Serious Crime Act 2007 with effect from 3 May 2015 (SI 2015/820).
[137] [2014] EWCA Crim 650 [12].
[138] Company Directors Disqualification Act 1986, s 1; per s 1(4) the court may consider matters other than criminal convictions.
[139] Potter LJ in *R v Edwards* [1998] 2 Cr App R (S) 213 (CA), 215.
[140] Company Directors Disqualification Act 1986, s 13.

22.5   Conclusion

A commercial party has much to gain from criminal law remedies. Indeed, commercial parties are already finding the criminal courts useful. They might seek compensation for realisable sums, a recent example being £8 million out of £11 million lost;[141] such parties have even decided that a confiscation order for the amount lost, as a trade-off for police investigative assistance, was still commercially advantageous even though that money would go to the state and not to them. There are significant benefits in the personal censuring and gain-deprivation powers of the criminal courts, the rough justice of confiscation particularly making restitution scholarship look somewhat arcane and complicated. Even without seeking specific immediate results, a commercial party might benefit from investigative work done by the police or other state agency.

However, there are significant questions about whether these kinds of proceedings should be brought at all, and if so, what the best way of bringing them is. The criminal law has purposes beyond those of commercial parties and has imposed some limitations on how its mechanisms are used by non-state actors. This is a simplification of a wider debate about whether something is public because of *who does it* or *why it is done*.[142]

For the commercial party, one key trade-off is in the control of the proceedings. The state is concerned that the decisions about prosecution live up to evidential and public interest tests. The body of criminal law does not simply exist to be selected from, as private law is.[143] It has its own strengths, and corresponding balances. The state must not disproportionately sanction those within its jurisdiction and it must uphold, and be seen to uphold, rule of law values in a way that a private litigant does not. A private person should not 'buy' justice and the state should not 'sell' it. Similarly, private prosecutions must not become a way to shift the risk and uncertainty of a prosecution to the private sector.

Commercial parties seeking the advantages that the criminal courts offer must understand the differences of rules, structure and culture. They must understand the formal test the CPS will apply to all prosecutions *but also* the culture and context in which it will apply it. Similarly,

---

[141] *Zinga 2014* (n 15) [8].

[142] For example, Malcolm Thorburn, 'Reinventing the Night Watchman State' (2010) 60 *University of Toronto Law Journal* 425, 442; cf Alon Harel, 'Why Only the State May Inflict Criminal Sanctions: The Case against Privately Inflicted Sanctions' (2008) 14 *Legal Theory* 113.

[143] *Photo Production Ltd v Securicor Transport Ltd* [1980] AC 827 (HL) 848.

too often private and public prosecutors are making what appear to be ham-fisted attempts to push civil law terminology into criminal courts and vice versa. Civil law makes far less fine divisions between wrongs than the criminal law; *but it also* typically requires less statutory interpretation, with its attendant principles like reading definitional doubt in favour of the defendant. Commercial parties also need to understand the mechanisms by which their involvement in the criminal courts might be challenged, particularly the somewhat nebulous concept of abuse of process.

We already know commercial parties are increasingly using the criminal courts to advance their interests. We think they can do so better, while still safeguarding the values of the criminal law.

PART VI

The Future

Codification of Remedies for Breach of Commercial Contracts: A Blueprint

NEIL ANDREWS

23.1 Abstract

Myriad cases encrust the remedies for breach of contract.[1] It will be shown, however, that the central parts of the remedial system are amenable to a restatement or synopsis. English law, although globally significant, is especially tough on outsiders. It is time to render its main features accessible. A good place to start is the system of remedies for breach of contract. Thirty-one rules are formulated in section 23.11.[2] Sections 23.2 to 23.10 contain brief reflections on this synoptic exercise. The main gains are: time is saved and clarity promoted; the difficult topic of remedies becomes less intimidating and easier both to apply and debate; a vital chapter of English commercial law is demystified, for the benefit of all, notably, busy lawyers and judges, non-lawyers, foreign parties and advisors.

23.2 Introduction

The main part of this chapter is a distillation of the law governing judicial responses to breach of contract. Those responses are known as 'remedies' (made on application by an aggrieved party). But the courts do not monopolise remedies. It is necessary to include self-help remedies, notably the forfeiting of deposits in response to contractual default.

---

[1] E.g. the topic of contractual remedies requires reference to c 1,600 cases: Adam Kramer, *The Law of Contract Damages* (Hart 2014), table of cases. And the topic of specific performance, c 2,000 cases: Gareth H Jones and William Goodhart, *Specific Performance* (2nd edn, Butterworths 1996), table of contents.

[2] Technically, the thirty-first rule might be jettisoned because the topic of Restitution or Unjust Enrichment lies almost wholly outside the compass of contractual breach (the exception is the remedy of account consequent on breach).

The aim has been to offer rules which are neither too detailed, otherwise this will reintroduce the present vice of excessive complication, nor too thin, for generalities are more likely to mislead than provide secure guidance.

The law concerning contractual remedies, and indeed English contract law in general, is mostly founded on precedents, sometimes single-judge decisions, other times multiple-judgment decisions by appellate panels in the Court of Appeal, House of Lords, or the Supreme Court (the Privy Council's tradition is to give a single majority opinion, although individual dissenting judgments occur). Many of these judgments are long and complicated.

The task of extracting the law from the primary source of judicial decision is beyond the skill of non-lawyers (even those, for example, regularly engaged as experts or arbitrators). This is so for three reasons: the length and complexity of these judgments, the disorderly presentation of the law, and technical (sometimes rather archaic) jargon.

Even the experienced lawyer will find it laborious and demanding to pinpoint the law on a particular topic. The result is that (even before the challenge of applying the law to the facts of a difficult case) the law of contract is expensive to find and hard to summarise.

In a fast-moving age, and because not all parties have adequate resources to afford expert professional assistance, law which can only be identified after a trawl through extensive authorities must be condemned as not fit for purpose.

Before presenting the rules, there are eight short sections providing reflections on the task of encapsulating English law in this field.

23.3   Is it Helpful to be Concise?

The topic of remedies for breach of contract is notoriously complex. Its main rival is the law concerning breach. But 'remedies' romps home each academic year as the subject which students find most fiddly. The two reasons for this difficulty are the welter of case law and the ramification of rules and qualifications across the established heads of remedy. Indeed specialist textbooks confine attention to particular remedies,[3] or even to sub-divisions of a remedy.[4] The subject cries out for a succinct and

---

[3] Kramer (n 1) ch 17; *McGregor on Damages* (19th edn, Sweet & Maxwell 2014) [10–112] ff; Gareth H Jones and William Goodhart (n 1); Katy Barnett, *Accounting for Profit for Breach of Contract* (Hart 2012).

[4] James Edelman, *Gain-Based Damages: Contract, Tort, Equity and Intellectual Property* (Hart 2002).

comprehensive overview. In a sense, we have no choice but to accept this challenge of rendering the law straightforward and comprehensible.

23.4   Loose Ends

A by-product of drafting a synopsis is that the areas of uncertainty are brought into focus. Because English law is mature and this area is frequently revisited by the courts, there is no shortage of material. English contract law is seldom, if ever, void for incompleteness. Instead it is occasionally void for uncertainty, or at least some points are not yet definitively established.

The main loose ends are: (i) the legitimate interest qualification upon the creditor's capacity to invoice for unwanted performance, under the *White & Carter* doctrine;[5] (ii) the scope of the exception to the breach date providing the date for assessment of damages;[6] (iii) whether the remoteness rule incorporates assumption of responsibility reasoning and, if so, how this is to be encapsulated and, if not, how the dualism of separate remoteness and scope of duty rules would operate.[7] The penalty

---

[5] See the author's discussion in Neil Andrews, *Contract Law* (2nd edn, Cambridge University Press 2015) [18.03]–[18.06] and literature there cited concerning *White & Carter (Councils) Ltd v McGregor* [1962] AC 413 (HL), 431. Notable cases include *Clea Shipping Corporation v Bulk Oil International ('The Alaskan Trader')* [1984] 1 All ER 129 (QB) 136–37 (Lloyd J); *Reichman v Beveridge* [2006] EWCA Civ 1659, [2007] 1 P & CR 20; *Isabella Shipowner SA v Shagang Shipping Co Ltd ('The Aquafaith')* [2012] EWHC 1077 (Comm), [2012] 2 All ER (Comm) 461, [44] (Cooke J).

[6] Andrews (n 5) [18.21], concerning *Golden Strait Corporation v Nippon Yusen Kubishika Kaisha ('The Golden Victory')* [2007] UKHL 12, [2007] 2 AC 353; Jonathan Morgan, 'A Victory for "Justice" over Commercial Certainty' (2007) 66 CLJ 263, 264–65; Brian Coote 'Breach, Anticipatory Breach, or the Breach Anticipated?' (2007) 123 LQR 503, 510; FMB Reynolds, '"The Golden Victory" – A Misguided Decision' (2008) HKLJ 333; Michael Mustill, 'The Golden Victory – Some Reflections' (2008) 124 LQR 569; Andrew S Burrows, in Mads Andenas and Duncan Fairgrieve (eds), *Tom Bingham and the Transformation of the Law: A Liber Amicorum* (Oxford University Press 2009) 598–601. For earlier references, see AS Burrows, *Remedies for Torts and Breach of Contract* (3rd edn, Oxford University Press 2004) 188ff; cf Stephen Waddams; 'The Date for the Assessment of Damages' (1981) 97 LQR 445.

[7] Andrews (n 5) [18.20], concerning *Transfield Shipping Inc v Mercator ('The Achilleas')* [2008] UKHL 48, [2009] 1 AC 61; David Foxton, 'Damages for Early Redelivery under Time Charterparties' [2009] LMCLQ 461–87; Janet O'Sullivan, 'Damages for Lost Profits for Late Redelivery: Too Remote?' (2009) 68 CLJ 34–37; Edwin Peel, 'Remoteness Revisited' (2009) 125 LQR 6–12; Adam Kramer, 'The New Test of Remoteness in Contract' (2009) 125 LQR 408–15; Greg Gordon, 'Hadley v Baxendale Revisited' (2009) 13 *Edinburgh Law Review* 125–30; David McLaughlan, 'Remoteness Re-invented?' (2009) 9 *Oxford University Commonwealth Law Journal* 109–39; Brian Coote 'Contract as Assumption and Remoteness of Damage' (2010) 26 JCL 211; Lord Hoffmann,

548 NEIL ANDREWS

doctrine is no longer a loose end because the Supreme Court in the *El Makdessi* case (2015) made clear that it has retained the common law penalty doctrine, which is soundly based, although it has been slightly reformulated (see Rule 26 below).[8]

23.5 The Scope of Remedies for Breach of Contract

A restatement of remedies must embrace the obvious judicial remedies ('the big four'): debt, damages, specific performance, injunctions. This list must be extended to cover the minor judicial remedies of declarations and the grant of a stay in response to certain types of breach (notably breach of arbitration or mediation agreements).

'The Achilleas: Custom and Practice or Foreseeability?' (2010) 14 *Edinburgh Law Review* 47–61; Paul CK Lee, 'Contractual Interpretation and Remoteness' [2010] LMCLQ 150–76; Shantanu S Naravane, 'The Implications of Transfield for Concurrent Liability in Tort and Contract' [2012] JBL 404–18; Victor P Goldberg, 'The Achilleas: Forsaking Foreseeability' (2013) 66 CLP 107–30; Mark Stiggelbout, 'Contractual Remoteness, "Scope of Duty" and Intention' [2012] LMCLQ 97–121; Howard Hunter, 'Has the Achilleas Sunk?' (2014) 31 JCL 120–30; *Supershield Ltd v Siemens Building Technologies FE Ltd* [2010] EWCA Civ 7, [2010] 2 All ER (Comm) 1185 [37] (Toulson LJ); *Sylvia Shipping Co Ltd v Progress Bulk Carriers Ltd* [2010] EWHC 542 (Comm), [2010] 2 Lloyd's Rep 81 [40]–[41] (Hamblen J); *ASM Shipping Ltd of India v TTMI Ltd of England ('The Amer Energy')* [2009] 1 Lloyd's Rep 293 (QB) [17]–[19] (Flaux J); *Ispat Industries Ltd v Western Bulk Pte Ltd* [2011] EWHC 93 (Comm) [52] (Teare J); *Shah v HSBC Private Bank (UK) Ltd* [2012] EWHC 1283 (QB) [227], [232] (Supperstone J); *James Grimes Partnership Ltd v Gubbins* [2013] EWCA Civ 37, [2013] BLR 126; [20], [24] (Keane LJ) (noted by James Goodwin, 'A Remotely Interesting Case' (2013) 129 LQR 486–88).
8 *Cavendish Square Holdings BV v El Makdessi* [2015] UKSC 67; [2016] AC 1172; the background literature is extensive: Andrews (n 5) [19.22]–[19.24]; GH Treitel, *Remedies for Breach of Contract: A Comparative Account* (Oxford University Press 1988) 208–34; Mindy Chen-Wishart, 'Controlling the Power to Agree Damages' in Peter BH Birks (ed), *Wrongs and Remedies in the Twenty-First Century* (Oxford University Press 1996); Tony Downes, 'Rethinking Penalty Clauses' in Peter BH Birks (ed), *Wrongs and Remedies in the Twenty-First Century* (Oxford University Press 1996); Scottish Law Commission, *Penalty Clauses* (Scot Law Com No 171, 1999); Louise Gullifer, 'Agreed Remedies' in Andrew Burrows and Edwin Peel (eds), *Commercial Remedies: Current Issues and Problems* (Oxford University Press 2003) 191; Burrows, *Remedies for Torts and Breach of Contract* (n 6), 440–55, especially 449–51; Solène Rowan, 'For the Recognition of Remedial Terms Agreed Inter Partes' (2010) 126 LQR 448, 460 ff; Roger Halson, *Contract Law* (2nd edn, Pearson 2013) 504–17; Roger Halson, 'Neglected Insights into Agreed Remedies' in David Campbell, Linda Mulcahy and Sally Wheeler (eds), *Changing Concepts of Contract: Essays in Honour of Ian Macneil* (Palgrave 2013) ch 5; *McGregor* (n 3) ch 15. On the nineteenth-century history of this topic, see Michael Lobban, 'Contractual Remedies' in William Cornish and others, *The Oxford History of the Laws of England*, vol XII, *1820–1914: Private Law* (Oxford University Press 2010) 523 ff.

The order in which these will be treated here is both traditional and scientific: debt takes the lead because it is the most significant; damages follow because they concern money and this is also (predominantly)[9] a common law remedy; and the sibling coercive remedies of specific performance and injunctions then enter.

Discussion of debt necessitates discussion of the entire obligation rule (Rule 2) because that determines whether the duty to pay has arisen. The potential creditor's capacity to postpone payment until the other party's obligations have been completed is a valuable source of self-help protection.

As the UNIDROIT *Principles of International Commercial Contracts* project reveals, breach of contract cannot be practically separated from the topics of set-off and limitation of actions (Rules 29 and 30).[10]

But not all pertinent procedure can be examined. And so there is no reference to the law concerning interim injunctions,[11] freezing relief,[12] or the system of enforcing judgments,[13] or to the *minutiae* of contempt of court.[14]

23.6 Minor Judicial Remedies

Undoubtedly the big four are debt, damages, specific performance, and injunctions. The tiddlers are declarations, accounts awarded on the exceptional basis of the criteria established in *Attorney-General v Blake*,[15] and

---

[9] See Rule 8(iii) below concerning damages in equity under the Senior Courts Act 1981, s 50.

[10] International Institute for the Unification of Private Law (UNIDROIT) *Principles of International Commercial Contracts* (3rd edn, 2010) chs 8 and 10, concerning set-off and limitation of actions; included in the 2004 and 2010 editions, but not included in the first edition, 1994: <http://www.unidroit.org/english/principles/contracts/principles2010/integralversionprinciples2010-e.pdf> accessed 5 February 2016.

[11] Neil Andrews, *Andrews on Civil Processes* (Intersentia 2013) vol 1 (*Court Proceedings*), [10.14] ff; Steven Gee, *Commercial Injunctions* (6th edn, Lexis Nexis 2016) (forthcoming); Iain S Goldrein and KHP Wilkinson (eds), *Commercial Litigation: Pre-emptive Remedies* (Thomsons, updated service) Part A, section 1; Adrian Zuckerman, *Zuckerman on Civil Procedure* (3rd edn, Thomsons 2013) ch 10.

[12] *Andrews on Civil Processes* (n 11) vol 1 (*Court Proceedings*) ch 21; Gee (n 11).

[13] *Andrews on Civil Processes* (n 11) vol 1 (*Court Proceedings*) ch 17.

[14] Ibid [17.27] ff; David Eady and ATH Smith, *Arlidge, Eady and Smith on Contempt* (4th edn, Sweet & Maxwell 2013).

[15] [2001] 1 AC 268 (HL); Edelman (n 4) ch 5; Ewan McKendrick, 'Breach of Contract, Restitution for Wrongs and Punishment' in Andrew Burrows and Edwin Peel (eds), *Commercial Remedies: Current Issues and Problems* (Oxford University Press 2003) 93–119; Burrows, *Remedies for Torts and Breach of Contract* (n 6) 395–407.

'stays'. 'Interest' on judgments and claims for interest following late payment of debts tend to fall between the cracks in courses on contract law
(Rule 18).

23.7   Constraints on Self-Help

Procedural realism favours self-help. The courts cannot be expected to be
the exclusive guardians of contractual compliance. The law of deposits
cannot, however, be too severely weighted in favour of the depositee.
English law seems to strike the right balance (Rules 27 and 28). Similarly,
it is pleasing that the law favours the aggrieved party who has not received
effective performance and so withholds payment pending completion of
the relevant job (Rule 2).

23.8   Are There Any Non-Commercial Remedies?

There is very little within this subject matter which is distinctly non-
commercial. General principles and rules abound. But consumer disappointment must be confined to consumers, and aggravation and vexation
cannot be convincingly claimed by claimants who are not flesh-and-
blood natural persons (Rule 10).

23.9   Are There Any Obvious Gaps or Necessary Changes?

Stone-wall refusal to grant punitive damages for breach of contract is a
remarkable example of consistency on the part of the English courts
(Rule 8(iv)). But one wonders when the *cause célèbre* will reach the
Supreme Court, at which point perhaps this dyke might begin to develop
a trickle.

The *White & Carter* point concerning 'legitimate interest' (Rule 1(iv))
might be usefully re-examined by the Supreme Court.[16] This author
doubts whether the minority view in that case will be preferred.
It seems more likely that the majority will be affirmed, but the bounds
of 'legitimate interest' might be clarified.

The dust is still settling following the minor judicial earthquakes of the
Transfield case (remoteness and scope of duty reasoning, Rule 15),[17] '*The*

---

[16] Andrews, *Contract Law* (n 5) [18.03]–[18.06] and literature there cited; concerning *White
& Carter v McGregor* (n 5).
[17] *The Achilleas* (n 7); Andrews, *Contract Law* (n 5) [18.20].

Golden Victory' (assessment date for damages, Rule 4),[18] and *Attorney-General v Blake* (Rule 23).[19]

No significant change seems likely within the law governing specific performance and injunctions (Rules 19 to 21).

23.10   Is the Law Still Too Detailed?

The thirty-one Rules listed here have been formulated with the aim that they should be neither too detailed – otherwise this will reintroduce the present vice of excessive complication – nor too thin – for generalities are more likely to mislead than provide secure guidance. A series of 'headline' statements would not be helpful. As the law of misrepresentation reminds us, the reader is to be protected against half-truths. The challenge is to encapsulate the law's conceptual structure, broad propositions being suitably qualified, but avoiding entanglement in the fine-mesh of case law discussion.

23.11   The Draft Codification of Remedies for Breach of Commercial Contracts

23.11.1   *Contractual Judicial Remedies*

23.11.1.1   Rule 1. Debt Claims[20]

(i) *Action for an agreed sum: common law remedy.* A contracting party's failure to pay a debt (a sum fixed by agreement or ascertainable in amount) will entitle the creditor to bring a common law claim for payment of that sum (also known as the action for an agreed sum) (and for supplementary claims for interest, Rule 18). The remedy is not discretionary and is instead available as of right.

(ii) *Debt obligations enforced by specific performance.* Exceptionally, payment of a debt is enforced by an injunctive order, sanctioned by contempt of court. This might be appropriate if the debt comprises a series of periodic payments. Specific performance is an equitable and discretionary remedy. It is only available if the

---

[18] *The Golden Victory* (n 6); Andrews, *Contract Law* (n 5) [18.21].

[19] See n 15; Edelman, *Gain-Based Damages* (n 4) ch 5; McKendrick (n 15) 93–119; Burrows, *Remedies for Torts and Breach of Contract* (n 6) 395–407.

[20] *Chitty on Contracts* (32nd edn, Sweet & Maxwell 2015) [24–10], [26–92], [26–103]–[26–106]; Andrews and others, *Contractual Duties* (Sweet & Maxwell 2012) ch 19 (2nd edn appearing 2017).

common law pecuniary remedies (debt and damages) are inadequate in the relevant context.

(iii) *Penal sums.* The 'penalty doctrine' (Rule 26) renders unenforceable an agreement requiring the debtor to pay a sum exceeding the principal and interest owed.

(iv) *Rejection of a party's attempt to cancel a contract.* Here the situation is that one party (the eventual debtor) attempts to call off the job, but this suggested cancellation is rejected by the other party (an unaccepted renunciation, also known as an attempted anticipatory breach). The latter might be in a position to complete performance. If so, he will acquire the right to claim in debt (the so-called 'agreed sum'). But there are two restrictions upon this possibility of completing performance and suing in debt:

    (a) performance by the claimant does not require the other party's co-operation (as where property is made available for the other's use under a contract of hire or under a lease, or the performance takes the form of advertising or manufacture without the other needing to collaborate or assist); and

    (b) the claimant had no good reason to ignore the attempted cancellation (the case law presents this from the perspective of the performing party lacking a 'legitimate interest' in maintaining the contract in play). Consistent with the principle of *pacta sunt servanda*, requirement (b) will be applied generously in favour of the claimant who has performed in these circumstances.

23.11.2   Incomplete Performance

23.11.2.1   Rule 2. No Duty to Pay for Incomplete Performance[21]

(i) In contracts for services, or for goods and services, payment might be postponed until performance is completed. The 'entire obligation' rule will then prevent the contractor from becoming entitled to payment until conclusion of the job.

(ii) The 'substantial performance' doctrine might render the performing party entitled to claim the agreed sum (debt, Rule 1) even if that party's performance has not been perfect.

---

[21] *Chitty* (n 20) [21–028] ff; Andrews and others, *Contractual Duties* (n 20) ch 15.

Then the innocent party's protection in respect of the imperfect element is confined to a cross-claim or deduction in respect of defective performance.

(iii) Substantial performance will not arise if the failure to perform is significant: this depends on questions of proportionality, reasonableness and fairness.

23.11.3   Damages

23.11.3.1   Rule 3. Damages 'Once and for All': No Second Claim[22]

Damages will be awarded on a one-off basis in respect of the whole of the relevant loss and not determined in instalments or reviewed from time to time.

23.11.3.2   Rule 4. Date for Assessing Damages[23]

(i) Damages are assessed with regard to the facts as they subsisted at the time of breach, unless post-breach facts reveal that the supposed loss has been reduced or eliminated.

(ii) The breach date rule is unlikely to be applied in respect of land transactions.

23.11.3.3   Rule 5. Defendant's Least Onerous Mode of Performance[24]

(i) Damages will only be awarded if the claimant is entitled to recover compensation in respect of benefits which the defendant was legally obliged to confer. However, where it is clear that the claimant has suffered loss in respect of a legally protected right, but the defendant

---

[22] Chitty (n 20) [25–008]; Kramer (n 1) s 1.2 C; *McGregor on Damages* (n 3) ch 11.

[23] *Chitty* (n 20) [26–014], [26–088]–[26–092]; Kramer (n 1) ch 17; *McGregor* (n 3) [10–112] ff; as for the qualification in (i) ('unless post-breach facts reveal that the supposed loss has been reduced or eliminated'), the Supreme Court in *Bunge SA v Nidera BV* [2015] UKSC 43; [2015] 3 All ER 1082 (at [21] to [23], *per* Lord Sumption, and [83], *per* Lord Toulson) endorsed the majority analysis in *The Golden Victory* (n 6) (noted Morgan (n 6); Coote (n 6); Mustill (n 6); Rix (n 6) 679) held that damages for anticipatory breach should reflect post-breach events if those events have in fact reduced or eliminated the claimant's loss; see also *Flame SA v Glory Wealth Shipping Pte Ltd* ('*The Glory Wealth*') [2013] EWHC 3153 (Comm); [2014] QB 1080 (Teare J) (noted Edwin Peel 'Desideratum or Principle: The "Compensatory Principle" Revisited' (2015) 131 LQR 29).

[24] *Chitty* (n 20) [26–075]; Kramer (n 1) s 13.3 B; *McGregor* (n 3) [10–104] ff; Andrews and others, *Contractual Duties* (n 20) [21.76]–[21.84]; Kim Lewison, *Interpretation of Contracts* (6th edn, Sweet & Maxwell 2015) [8.09].

had a choice between two or more ways to perform, the claimant will be awarded damages on the less or least onerous basis, tilting matters in favour of the defendant.

(ii) Where, however, the defendant's performance involves a single obligation, within which he enjoys elements of discretion, compensation will be based on the level of performance which that party would have adopted acting (a) in his own commercial self-interest but (b) consistently with the contract and (c) in good faith.

23.11.3.4   Rule 6. Claimant's Poverty Irrelevant[25]

A claimant cannot be prevented from recovering loss merely because that loss stems from, or is exacerbated by, his lack of funds.

23.11.3.5   Rule 7. Litigation Costs and Damages[26]

Costs incurred in bringing or defending a claim against the other party are recoverable only under the costs regime of the procedural rules, unless (a) party B's breach led to party A incurring litigation expenses *vis-à-vis* a third party; or (b) B's breach led A to incur litigation costs in a *foreign jurisdiction*.

23.11.3.6   Rule 8. Expectation Loss and Reliance Loss[27]

 (i) The main aim of compensatory damages for breach of contract is to place the innocent party in the position he would have been in if the contract had been properly performed. This is the so-called 'expectation' or 'loss of bargain' measure.

 (ii) Another type of damages for breach of contract is to restore the claimant monetarily to the position he enjoyed before the contract was breached. This is the so-called 'reliance loss' measure.

(iii) Compensatory damages for breach of contract are awarded normally on common law principles, but the court has a statutory power (section 50, Senior Courts Act 1981) to award damages instead of, or in addition to, specific performance (Rule 19) or an injunction (Rule 20).[28] Such damages are the same as those at

---

[25] *Chitty* (n 20) [26–083] ff; Kramer (n 1) s 16.7 B.

[26] *Chitty* (n 20) [26–150]; *McGregor* (n 3) ch 20; Louise Merrett, 'Costs as Damages' (2009) 125 LQR 468; Kramer (n 1) ss 20.2–20.4.

[27] *Chitty* (n 20) [26–019] ff; Kramer (n 1) s 1.3; *McGregor* (n 3) [4–02] ff; Andrews and others, *Contractual Duties* (n 20) [21.034] ff.

[28] Senior Courts Act 1981, s 50; *Chitty* (n 20) [26–005], [26–047], [27–083]–[27–090]; Jones and Goodhart (n 1) 275 ff; Kramer (n 1) s 1.2 B(iii); *McGregor* (n 3) [11–29]; JA Jolowicz,

common law, except that damages can be awarded under this provision even before breach has occurred.[29]

(iv) Contractual damages are intended to compensate the claimant, rather than to punish the defendant.[30]

23.11.3.7 Rule 9. Cost of Cure or Reinstatement Damages[31]

Such damages are designed to fund substitute performance and thus rectify breach (where the innocent party has already paid for substitute performance such damages provide reimbursement of that party's expenses in financing such substitute performance). However, such damages might exceed the diminution in value of the relevant subject matter. And so courts will not award cost of cure damages if they appear pointless, disproportionate, or the claim is unacceptably vindictive.

23.11.3.8 Rule 10. Injured Feelings and Distress[32]

In general, a defendant is not liable for psychological distress caused by breach of contract, even though the distress is not too remote a consequence of the breach. However, damages are available under these heads:

'Damages in Equity – A Study of Lord Cairns' Act' (1975) 34 CLJ 224. The leading cases are: *Johnson v Agnew* [1980] AC 367 (HL); *Oakacre Ltd v Claire Cleaners (Holdings) Ltd* [1982] Ch 197 (Ch); *Jaggard v Sawyer* [1995] 1 WLR 269 (CA) (injunction refused, discussing the circumstances in which injunctions will be withheld; damages in lieu awarded under the Senior Courts Act 1981, s 50).

[29] *Oakacre Ltd v Claire Cleaners (Holdings) Ltd* (n 29) (damages awarded instead of specific performance; latter sought in good faith before breach had occurred).

[30] *Ruxley Electronics and Construction Ltd v Forsyth* [1996] AC 344 (HL) 365; *Addis v Gramophone Co Ltd* [1909] AC 488 (HL) (considered in *Edwards v Chesterfield Royal Hospital NHS Foundation Trust* [2011] UKSC 58, [2012] 2 AC 22; on which see Catherine Barnard and Louise Merrett, 'Winners and Losers: Edwards and the Unfair Law of Dismissal' (2013) 72 CLJ 313); Kramer (n 1) s 23.3; Ralph Cunnington, 'Should Punitive Damages be Part of the Judicial Arsenal in Contract Cases?' (2006) 26 LS 369; Solène Rowan, 'Reflections on the Introduction of Punitive Damages for Breach of Contract' (2010) 30 OJLS 495; otherwise in Canada, *Royal Bank of Canada v W Got & Associates Electric Ltd* (2000) 17 DLR (4th) 385 (Supreme Court of Canada), noted by James Edelman, 'Exemplary Damages for Breach of Contract' (2001) 117 LQR 539; *Whiten v Pilot Insurance Co* [2002] SCC 18, [2002] 1 SCR 595 (SCC); *Honda Canada Inc v Keays* [2008] SCC 39, (2008) 294 DLR (4th) 371, noted by Mitchell McInnes, 'Contractual Damages for Mental Distress – Again' (2009) 125 LQR 16, at 19–20; as for punitive damages in English tort law, see *Kuddus v Chief Constable of Leicestershire* [2001] UKHL 29, [2002] 2 AC 122; *A v Bottrill* [2002] UKPC 44, [2003] 1 AC 449.

[31] Chitty (n 20) [26–036] ff; Kramer (n 1) ss 4.3, 4.4; McGregor (n 3) [25–044], [26–052]; Andrews and others, *Contractual Duties* (n 20) [21.65]–[21.75].

[32] Chitty (n 20) [26–140] ff; Kramer (n 1) ch 19; McGregor (n 3) [5–015] ff; Andrews and others, *Contractual Duties* (n 20) ch 22.

(i) 'physical' discomfort (including noise), which engenders such nega-
    tive feelings; or

(ii) consumer disappointment ('consumer surplus' compensation):
     such a claim is for 'loss' which, although palpable to consumers, is
     not reflected concretely in the 'market'; or

(iii) the contract has as one of its main purposes:

    (a) the avoidance of aggravation (e.g. a surveyor fails properly to
    inspect property and the claimant's purchase of that defective
    or problematic property causes him 'heart-ache'; or a lawyer
    was paid by his client to obtain injunctive relief against violent
    or threatening persons, but negligently failed to obtain the
    remedy and the client was exposed to violence or threats,
    etc); or

    (b) the contract is intrinsically aimed at conferring pleasure (nota-
    bly, holiday companies, or photographers at 'one-off' special
    occasions).

23.11.3.9   Rule 11. Award for Failure to Negotiate Release Fee ('Hypothetical Bargain Damages')[33]

This award is made after the event: to simulate a notional fee which might
have been exacted from the defendant if he had sought permission to 'buy
out', wholly or partially, the claimant's contractual rights as against the
defendant (such as a restriction on the capacity of the defendant to build
on land subject to a restrictive covenant in favour of the claimant). Such
an award is available where there is no other identifiable financial loss, the
main criterion being that 'it would be manifestly unjust to leave the
claimants with an award for no or nominal damages'.

23.11.3.10   Rule 12. Restrictions upon Damages[34]

The following restrictions upon recovery of damages for breach of contract apply to any claim for substantial damages (damages which are not
nominal):

(i) *certainty of loss* (*loss not too* speculative): the loss must be proved
    sufficiently ('loss of chance' damages are available only if the relevant
    chance was 'real' or 'substantial') (Rule 13);

---

[33] *Chitty* (n 20) [26–051]–[26–054]; Kramer (n 1) chs 10, 22; *McGregor* (n 3) [25–052] ff;
Andrews and others, *Contractual Duties* (n 20) [26–016] ff.

[34] *Chitty* (n 20) [26–058]–[26–138] ff; Kramer (n 1) chs 14–16; *McGregor* (n 3) chs 6–10;
Andrews and others, *Contractual Duties* (n 20) chs 23–24.

(ii) *causation*: the loss should be causally connected to the breach (Rule 14);

(iii) *remoteness*: the loss must not be too remote (Rule 15);

(iv) *mitigation*: the claimant must not have failed to mitigate loss (Rule 16).

(Contributory negligence, allowing damages to be reduced on a percentage basis, is not a general defence: Rule 17.)

23.11.3.11 Rule 13. Loss of a Chance[35]

Loss of chance damages are available only if the relevant chance was 'real' or 'substantial', otherwise the claim will fail because the chance is too speculative.

23.11.3.12 Rule 14. Causation[36]

The defendant's breach must have been the 'effective cause' of the claimant's loss. It is not enough in contract law that the connection between breach and loss satisfies a 'but for' inquiry.

23.11.3.13 Rule 15. Remoteness[37]

(i) The party in breach of contract is not liable to compensate for a type of loss if it was not reasonably envisaged at the time of formation as a serious possibility, taking into account the ordinary course of things and any special risks of which the guilty party was aware or to which he was alerted.

(ii) There is no need to have contemplated the scale of the loss, unless the claim is for unusually high levels of lost profit.

(iii) Exceptionally, the test formulated in (i) might need to be supplemented, and the guilty party's liability adjusted, by reference to objective market expectations concerning the scope of a person's liability in that particular context.

---

[35] *Chitty* (n 20) [26–071]–[26–073]; Kramer (n 1) s 13.5; *McGregor* (n 3) ch 10; Andrews and others, *Contractual Duties* (n 20) [24–028] ff.

[36] *Chitty* (n 20) [26–058] ff; Kramer (n 1) chs 15–16; *McGregor* (n 3) [8–137] ff; Andrews and others, *Contractual Duties* (n 20) [24.02]–[24.26].

[37] *Chitty* (n 20) [26–107] ff, esp at [26–111]; Andrews, *Contract Law* (n 5) [18.16] ff; Kramer (n 1) ch 14; *McGregor* (n 3) [8–155] ff; Andrews and others, *Contractual Duties* (n 20) ch 23; where contractual and tortious duties of care overlap on the facts of the case, the relevant remoteness test governing a claim for economic loss is the contractual test: *Wellesley Partners LLP v Withers LLP* [2015] EWCA Civ 1146, [2016] Ch 529 [80], [157], [186].

23.11.3.14   Rule 16. Mitigation[38]

(i)   An innocent party must take reasonable steps to reduce or eliminate the loss resulting from the other party's breach of contract (and the same requirement applies to loss arising from tortious misconduct). To the extent that this party fails to take such steps, the claim for compensation will fail.

(ii) The innocent party must adjust his compensatory claim to reflect losses avoided and any benefits which in fact accrue to him as a result of steps taken by him in response to the relevant breach. It will be different if the claimant's gain or saving has no sufficient connection with the defendant's breach other than an 'historical connection'.

(iii) The innocent party is entitled to recover from the defendant any expense or additional loss incurred when taking reasonable steps to mitigate the loss, even if the attempt at mitigation was unsuccessful, provided this attempt was reasonable.

23.11.3.15   Rule 17. Contributory Negligence[39]

The defence of contributory negligence applies only where the relevant contractual obligation is (a) to exercise reasonable care and (b) the breach of contract occurs within a relationship where the defendant *is also liable to the claimant in the tort of negligence for the same default.*

23.11.4   *Interest on Money Awards and the Currency of the Award*

23.11.4.1   Rule 18. Interest and Currency

(i)   The court can award interest as follows:[40]
  (a) when giving judgment on the principal sum (for damages or debt), the court has a statutory power to award *simple* interest;
  (b) *simple* interest can also be awarded under statute if the principal sum was (fully) paid only after commencement of formal proceedings but before judgment was obtained;

---

[38] *Chitty* (n 20) [26–079] ff; Kramer (n 1) s 15.3; *McGregor* (n 3) ch 9; Andrews and others, *Contractual Duties* (n 20) [24–038] ff. The decision cited at [26–099] in *Chitty* has been reversed by the Court of Appeal: *Fulton Shipping Inc of Panama v Globalia Business Travel SAU* [2015] EWCA Civ 1299 [2016] 1 WLR 2450 (proceeding to final appeal).

[39] *Chitty* (n 20) [26–077]; Kramer (n 1) s 15.5; *McGregor* (n 3) [7–009] ff; Andrews and others, *Contractual Duties* (n 20) [24.70]–[24.76].

[40] On Proposition (i): *Chitty* (n 20) [26–175], [26–227] ff; Kramer (n 1) ch 7 (and related issues); *McGregor* (n 3) ch 18.

(c) *simple and compound* interest can be awarded at common law for breaches of contract, provided the contractual remoteness test (Rule 15) is satisfied.

(ii) The currency of the judgment or award for payment of money (whether damages, liquidated damages, debt, or other types of payment) will often be, but need not invariably be, that of the forum (in England and Wales, pounds sterling).[41]

23.11.5   Specific Performance and Injunctions

23.11.5.1   Rule 19. Specific Performance[42]

(i) Specific performance is a final and mandatory order to compel performance of a positive obligation.

(ii) The party who fails to comply with such an order will be in contempt of court.

(iii) Specific performance is available only if the contractual promise is supported by consideration, and provided also that common law remedies, of debt (Rule 1) or damages (Rules 3 to 17), are inadequate in the relevant case.

(iv) Specific performance is an equitable remedy: the common law does not award specific performance, and instead the principles governing this remedy remain the product of the parallel system of Equity. Because the remedy is founded on equitable principles, it is technically not available as of right (unlike common law claims for debt or damages). Accordingly, specific performance is discretionary. However, there is a considerable uniformity of treatment in the award or denial of this remedy in particular contexts (see (v) to (vi) below) or by reference to established factors (see the list of such factors at (vii) below).

This remedy is narrow in scope in England and Wales. It is mainly used to compel performance of the seller and buyer's obligations in contracts for the sale or exchange of interests in land.

---

[41] *Chitty* (n 20) [30–371] ff; Kramer (n 1) s 1.5; *McGregor* (n 3) [19–025] ff.

[42] *Chitty* (n 20) [27–001]–[27–064]; Jones and Goodhart (n 1); Burrows (n 6) ch 20; Andrews and others, *Contractual Duties* (n 20) ch 27; ICF Spry, *The Principles of Equitable Remedies: Specific Performance, Injunctions, Rectification and Equitable Damages* (9th edn, Thomson Reuters Australia 2013).

(v) There can be no specific performance of contracts for personal services (statute specifically renders the remedy unavailable to compel an individual to work for an employer).

(vi) Specific performance is not awarded to compel transfers of chattels unless they are special or even 'unique'.

(vii) Even if the relevant context is *prima facie* amenable to this remedy, various subsidiary factors regulate the court's 'discretion' to order specific performance:

    (a) whether the claimant's conduct has been unmeritorious ('lack of clean hands'); (b) delay and acquiescence; (c) 'mutuality' (when the claimant, who is seeking specific performance, has yet to satisfy his side of the bargain, the court must consider whether the defendant is protected against the risk of default by the claimant); (d) vagueness; (e) problems of continuing supervision; and (f) hardship.

23.11.5.2   Rule 20. Injunctions[43]

(i) Injunctions can be awarded to prevent a defendant breaching a 'negative' promise, that is, an undertaking not to do something.

(ii) An injunction can be awarded either to prevent the anticipated breach ('prohibitory', that is, preventing prohibited performance which would be contrary to a negative undertaking) or to reverse the relevant wrong (a 'mandatory' injunction, compelling performance of a positive obligation). When a final injunction is mandatory, English law labels the order as one for 'specific performance' (Rule 19).

(iii) The party who fails to comply with an injunction will be in contempt of court. Contempt also arises if a party breaches a formal 'undertaking' given by that party in court in substitution for a formal injunctive order.

(iv) There is a discretion to award damages 'in lieu' of an injunction.

23.11.5.3   Rule 21. Danger of Excessive Coercion[44]

Injunctions will not be awarded if the indirect effect will be to apply such compulsion to require a person to perform personal relations or remain in a close relationship of mutual trust and confidence.

---

[43] *Chitty* (n 20) [27–065] ff; Andrews and others, *Contractual Duties* (n 20) ch 28; Spry (n 42).

[44] *Chitty* (n 20) [27–070] ff; Andrews and others, *Contractual Duties* (n 20) [28–027] ff; Spry (n 42).

23.11.6 Minor Remedies

23.11.6.1 Rule 22. Declarations[45]

In making a declaration, the tribunal states definitively the facts and legal result in the proceedings. A declaration might be the only relief sought or granted.

23.11.6.2 Rule 23. Targeting the Gain Made by Breach ('Account')[46]

(i) *Gain-based relief.* The remedy requires the defendant to 'disgorge' ('account for') a gain made as a result of the bare breach of contract. The defendant's gain forms the basis of the claim. The remedy is granted regardless of whether the claimant has suffered substantial loss.

(ii) *Exceptional power to award in respect of a bare breach of contract.* Exceptionally, the court might grant the equitable remedy of an account of profits for a bare breach of contract, that is, even though the contractual breach has involved neither a breach of fiduciary duty (e.g. breaches of contract by agents or solicitors), nor infringement of a proprietary right.

(iii) *Constraining factors.* The remedy of account for a bare breach of contract, as summarised at (ii), is granted only in exceptional situations (and the pattern of the English decisions has been to refuse such relief). The remedy is equitable and hence discretionary. An account in respect of a bare breach of contract will be granted only if all four of the following criteria are satisfied: first, the claimant can show a legitimate interest in seeking this remedy; secondly, all other remedies are inadequate; thirdly, the tribunal, in its discretion, regards this as an appropriate response to the breach; and, fourthly, the gain is attributable to that breach.

(iv) *Supplementing the main order.* Where an account would be available, applying the preceding propositions, but the party in breach has yet to acquire or receive the relevant gain (or the full extent of the gain), a supplementary remedy might be available, such as an injunction to prevent such enrichment from occurring or at least from recurring.

---

[45] Jeremy Woolf, *Zamir and Woolf: The Declaratory Judgment* (4th edn, Sweet & Maxwell 2011); Lord Collins of Mapesbury and others (gen eds), *Dicey, Morris and Collins on the Conflicts of Laws* (15th edn, Sweet & Maxwell 2012) [12–048] ff.

[46] *Chitty* (n 20) [26–046] ff; Barnett (n 3); Edelman (n 4) ch 5; McKendrick (n 15) 93–119; Burrows (n 6) 395–407; Andrews and others, *Contractual Duties* (n 20) ch 26.

23.11.6.3   Rule 24. Staying Proceedings to Prevent Breach[47]

This is a procedural decision by the court to place proceedings in suspense until the 'stay' is lifted. A 'stay' is sometimes a contractual remedy in the sense that it can be a judicial response to a breach of contract. The main context has been the staying of civil proceedings commenced prematurely in breach of a mediation or arbitration agreement.

23.11.7   Liquidated Damages

23.11.7.1   Rule 25. Agreed Compensation

A liquidated damages clause can fix in advance of breach the measure of damages which the innocent party will receive in the event of breach (the clause will be upheld unless the sum is punitive: see next Rule).

23.11.7.2   Rule 26. Penalties[48]

A clause will impose a penalty, and so be invalid and unenforceable (and also incapable of being enforced partially or on terms), if:

---

[47] Andrews, *Andrews on Civil Processes* (n 11) vol 2 (*'Arbitration and Mediation'*) [10.03] ff.

[48] Rule 26 encapsulates the Supreme Court's decision in *Cavendish Square Holdings BV v El Makdessi* [2015] UKSC 67; [2016] AC 1172 in which Lords Neuberger and Sumption said, in their joint judgment, at [32]: 'The true test is whether the impugned provision is a secondary obligation which imposes a detriment on the contract-breaker out of all proportion to any legitimate interest of the innocent party in the enforcement of the primary obligation. The innocent party can have no proper interest in simply punishing the defaulter. His interest is in performance or in some appropriate alternative to performance. In the case of a straightforward damages clause, that interest will rarely extend beyond compensation for the breach ... But compensation is not necessarily the only legitimate interest that the innocent party may have in the performance of the defaulter's primary obligations.' Lord Mance said at [152]: ' ... the dichotomy between the compensatory and the penal is not exclusive. There may be interests beyond the compensatory which justify the imposition on a party in breach of an additional financial burden ... What is necessary in each case is to consider, first, whether any (and if so what) legitimate business interest is served and protected by the clause, and, second, whether, assuming such an interest to exist, the provision made for the interest is nevertheless in the circumstances extravagant, exorbitant or unconscionable. In judging what is extravagant, exorbitant or unconscionable, I consider (despite contrary expressions of view) that the extent to which the parties were negotiating at arm's length on the basis of legal advice and had every opportunity to appreciate what they were agreeing must at least be a relevant factor.' Lord Hodge said at [249]: 'When the court makes a value judgment on whether a provision is exorbitant or unconscionable, it has regard to the legitimate interests, commercial or otherwise, which the innocent party has sought to protect.'

(i) it requires the guilty party to pay an extravagant and unconscionable sum to the innocent party (or suffer a similar detriment) which is disproportionate to the innocent party's legitimate interest in gaining protection against either:

(a) loss (i.e. the greatest loss that could be contemplated, at the time the contract was formed, as likely to flow from breach of the relevant term); or

(b) harm to some wider legitimate interest (commercial or otherwise).

(ii) But the anti-penalty rule applies only to sums payable, or other detriment suffered, upon breach and not in other circumstances, and a tribunal will be reluctant to upset clauses agreed between commercial parties.

23.11.8   Self-help: Deposits

23.11.8.1   Rule 27. Nature of Deposits[49]

(i) A deposit is a sum paid (or payable) to secure performance by the payor. That sum is validly forfeited if the payor has contractually defaulted and the transaction has been justifiably terminated for this reason.

(ii) The innocent party is entitled to seek compensation in excess of the deposit, if such additional loss can be shown (and provided the claimant can satisfy the various rules governing the recovery of compensation).

(iii) The 'penalty jurisdiction' (Rule 26) does not govern deposits. And so the entire deposit can be validly forfeited even though the innocent party's actual loss is less than the amount of the deposit (see Rule 28 for controls on excessive deposits).

23.11.8.2   Rule 28. Deposits Which are Excessive or Unjustifiably Forfeited[50]

(i) There is a common law power to regulate excessive deposits.

(ii) In the case of contracts for the sale or exchange of land in England and Wales, there is a statutory discretion to relieve against forfeiture of deposits in such contracts.

---

[49] *Chitty* (n 20) [26–205] ff; *Goff and Jones on the Law of Unjust Enrichment* (9th edn, Sweet & Maxwell 2016) ch 14; Lewison (n 24) [17.13].

[50] *Chitty* (n 20) [26–205] ff; *Goff and Jones* (n 49) ch 14.

(iii) *Deposits and Consumer Contracts for the Supply of Goods, Digital Content, or Services.* In some circumstances the Consumer Rights Act 2015 (Sch 2, Part 1, para 4) provides that a trader cannot validly forfeit a deposit in a contract concerning such matters.

23.11.9 Set-off

23.11.9.1 Rule 29. Types of Set-off[51]

(i) *Mutual debts.* When party A brings proceedings against party B, there can be set-off of mutual debts or ascertained sums. There is no need for any factual connection between the obligations owed by the parties to the relevant litigation. Set-off in this context occurs at judgment. This form of set-off is not discretionary.

(ii) *Abatement.* A claim for the price in respect of goods or services is subject to set-off in respect of the claimant's defective supply or performance. This form of set-off is not discretionary.

(iii) *Transactional or equitable set-off.* Where A sues B (normally, but not necessarily, for an ascertained sum), B can raise a set-off if B's cross-claim is so closely connected with the main demand that it would be manifestly unjust to allow the claimant to enforce payment without taking into account the cross-claim. This form of set-off is discretionary.

(iv) *Insolvency set-off.* Where A, a creditor, is insolvent, and A's trustee in bankruptcy or liquidator sues B, who is solvent, B can set-off in full the sum owed by A to B. Insolvency set-off cannot be excluded by agreement.

(v) In the case of categories (i) to (iii), but not (iv), the parties can agree to exclude a prospective right of set-off from their dealings.

(vi) Categories (ii) and (iii) of set-off do not apply to the claim for freight under a voyage charterparty.

(vii) Categories (ii) and (iii) of set-off do not apply to claims based on the following special modes of payment: letters of credit, bills of exchange (including cheques), direct debit agreements.

---

[51] Andrews, *Andrews on Civil Processes* (n 11) vol 1, [7.05]–[7.45]; *Derham on the Law of Set-off* (4th edn, Oxford University Press 2010); Gerard McMeel, *The Construction of Contracts: Interpretation, Implication and Rectification* (2nd edn, Oxford University Press 2011) [23.57] ff. JD Heydon, MJ Leeming and PG Turner (eds), *Meagher, Gummow and Lehane's Equity: Doctrines and Remedies* (5th edn, LexisNexis Butterworths 2014) Part 7(4); Pascal Pichonnaz and Louise Gullifer, *Set-off in Arbitration and Commercial Transactions* (Oxford University Press 2014).

(viii) A taxpayer cannot raise set-off in response to a claim by the Crown for any taxes, duties or penalties.

23.11.10   Limitation of Actions

23.11.10.1   Rule 30. Statutory and Equitable Limitation of Actions[52]

(i) *General regime.*

    (a) In general (see below for qualifications) the period of limitation governing debt (including recovery of rent) or damages claims for breach of contract is six years from the date when the cause of action (ground of claim) arises, but twelve years if the claim is based on a deed.

    (b) The Contracts (Rights of Third Parties) Act 1999 applies the six-year and twelve-year periods mentioned at (a) to third-party claims upon simple contracts and contracts founded upon deeds.

(ii) The parties can agree to extend or reduce the limitation period.[53]

(iii) In very clear circumstances a party might be estopped from relying on the limitation period, provided A has made a representation to B, on which the latter has relied detrimentally, that A will not rely on the limitation period.

(iv) The periods mentioned at (i) do not apply to the following:

    (a) a claim in respect of personal injury or death (the period is instead three years);

    (b) recovery of the proceeds of sale of land (the period is twelve years);

    (c) mortgagee's recovery of the principal sum (the period is twelve years);

    (d) contribution claims under the Civil Liability (Contribution) Act 1978 (the period is two years); contribution claims falling outside the statute are subject to the ordinary six-year period mentioned at (i)(a).

(v) A six-year period of limitation applies to restitutionary claims for recovery of money paid by the claimant under mistake of fact or law, or for total failure of consideration.

---

[52] Andrews, *Andrews on Civil Processes* (n 11) vol 1, ch 8; *Chitty* (n 20) ch 28; Andrew McGee, *Limitation Periods* (7th edn, Sweet & Maxwell 2014); Lewison (n 24) [12.17]; JD Heydon, MJ Leeming and PG Turner (eds), *Meagher, Gummow and Lehane's Equity: Doctrines and Remedies* (n 51).

[53] Lewison (n 24) [12.17].

  (vi) The limitation periods mentioned at (i), (iv) and (v) above are subject to statutory exceptions based on fraud, or deliberate concealment, or mistake.

 (vii) Provided the right of action has not already become time-barred, the limitation period recommences if the defendant acknowledges, in written and signed form, the claimant's claim or title, or if he makes a payment in respect of it.

(viii) Claims for injunctions or specific performance are subject to the principles of 'laches' and 'acquiescence', rather than the periods mentioned above. The tribunal will have regard to the claimant's conduct or acquiescence and any detriment or unfairness to the defendant.

  (ix) The court has a statutory discretion to disapply a foreign limitation period if it will lead to undue hardship.

23.11.11   Restitution and Unjust Enrichment

23.11.11.1   Rule 31. Types of Restitutionary Claim[54]

  (i) Restitutionary claims are based on the defendant's unjust enrichment. The claim is not for the claimant's loss, but for the defendant's enrichment at the claimant's expense.

 (ii) There are three main forms of restitutionary relief relevant to contract law: (a) money recovered for a total failure of consideration; (b) recovery in respect of goods or services; and (c) disgorgement of gains made in breach of contract.[55]

(iii) The relevant enrichment can be money or services or goods. This cause of action can take various forms: it might be that the benefit was conferred as a result of the claimant's mistake of fact or law; or that there was a (total) failure of consideration, or duress, or undue influence, or abuse of fiduciary relationship, or an unjustified tax demand.

23.12   Concluding Remarks

Although this text is designed to reflect the law, some points might require close examination. Then it might be necessary, reasonable, and

---

[54] *Chitty* (n 20) ch 29; Andrew Burrows, *The Law of Restitution* (3rd edn, Oxford University Press 2011); *Goff and Jones* (n 49).

[55] With the exception of category (c), Rule 31 might be jettisoned: Restitution or Unjust Enrichment is not dependent on contractual breach (the exception is the remedy of account consequent on breach).

proportionate, for parties' advisors to 'drill down' into complex law which underlies these leading propositions.

The authority of the state is useful in giving legal texts binding force. But even this is unnecessary if the work is done well and the marketplace of users is attracted to adopt or use it, for example, within arbitration proceedings.

Nor should one overlook the possibility that courts can smile on certain passages or phrases (formulations of individual rules) and declare that they are helpful, or even canonical.

INDEX